A CONTEMPORARY UNDERSTANDING

THE
QUR'AN
WITH REFERENCES TO THE BIBLE

BIBLICAL REFERENCES
New Revised Standard Version (NRSV)

ISBN: 978-0-9965924-4-4

PUBLISHED IN THE UNITED STATES OF AMERICA

BOOK DESIGN
www.timmyroland.com

COVER IMAGE
www.shutterstock.com

To our grandchildren...

This translation of the Qur'an is dedicated to our grandchildren, half of them Muslim, half of them Christian. If we, as their adults, do not learn how to live, love and respect each other, and to pass this on to them and their parents, we will have allowed them to learn all the hate and fear that is so dominant in the world today.

It is said that people fear what they don't understand.

We pray that this translation of the Qur'an with references to the Bible will enable our grandchildren to share our understanding of the peaceful and inclusive Holy books of the religions claimed by more than half the people on the planet, both of which promote God's love and mercy to all human beings.

Safi Kaskas & David Hungerford

CONTENTS

CONTENTS

CONTENTS

A CONTEMPORARY UNDERSTANDING

THE
QUR'AN
WITH REFERENCES TO THE BIBLE

Safi Kaskas
David Hungerford

Bridges of Reconciliation
FAIRFAX, VIRGINA

Acknowledgement

I like to thank and acknowledge all those who contributed to make this modern translation of the Qur'an a reality. I don't know how this team came together, but I like to believe that God picked and chose whoever He thought will best serve this purpose.

Notably among the contributors are the following people:

Mrs. Eman Kaskas

Ms. Maha Kaskas

Dr. Charles Cohen

Dr. Sadig Malki

Mr. Samuel Shropshire

Mr. Mohammad Jawhar Mahaba

Mr. Tim Gilman

Mrs. Mary Wills Perry

Mr. Daniel DeSmit

FOREWORD
NUMBER **ONE**

The clarion call of our most sacred holy books share one common cause; the tantamount task of reconciling the world to God, and men and women to each other. These scriptures serve to remind of us of man's fallen nature throughout history, and our unquenchable necessity of a merciful and gracious God. Unfortunate to humankind, both past and present, is the obfuscation of the poetic power and reconciling work of the Qur'an. Current geopolitical events and radical extremists mar the Qur'an, giving rise to further misunderstandings and bloodshed. The path of peace, portrayed by the Prophet; further lost in translation.

It gives me pleasure, as I continue working in the struggle for peace, to write the forward to this new and vastly improved English translation of the Qur'an. I believe that as the world cries out for peace; we who promote faith, are obligated to provide the most accurate and understandable text possible. The time has come for Christians to read the Qur'an. And equally, the time has come for Muslims to understand their holy book through the lens of peace and it's power for good in this tragic violent world.

The first English translation of the Qur'an emerged in the 17th century, and present translations number in the dozens. "So," you may ask, "Why the need for another translation?" English like all translations, is a living language, changing and evolving. English translations of the Qur'an are stiff, archaic and fail to communicate common current verbiage. Interpretations complicate simple renderings and mystify meanings of the original text. And some translations emerged for specific purposes, not altogether "pure and holy", but with intentional bias for political or religious influence.

The Qur'an was one of the first major books compiled using 7th century classical Arabic. Its unique poetic style is highly praised and admired and the focal point of essays and elaborate study. Most of the estimated 1.5 billion Muslims live outside the Arabic-speaking Middle East and at least 90 percent cannot read and/or understand this ancient Semitic writing. The original text might be likened to Shakespeare's old English, recognizable, yet barely understood in the 21st century. In contrast, 700 million Muslims have a working knowledge of English, with estimates of 2 billion English speakers worldwide. The significance of this translation is intentional: provide a 21st century Qur'an for a predominately English-speaking world.

In addition, meanings of ancient words and idioms are often lost or change over time. The Western linguistic mindset limits the meanings of words, while Semitic words relish their diverse and variable meanings. For example, salaam, commonly known as "peace." also means "to turn, submit, surrender, complete, and security." This challenge demands scrupulous translation techniques and scholarly review.

This translation is the culmination of years of laborious effort on the part of two accomplished professionals: Dr. Safi Kaskas, PhD, a Muslim from the Middle East, and Dr. David Hungerford, an orthopedic surgeon and Christian from the United States. Each contributed an amazing blend of culture, experience and faith traditions; while passionately pouring their lives and fortunes into an incomparable translation.

Moreover, the translation contains a critical element that makes it a standout publication. Years of painstaking scholarly research are presented in over 3,000 footnotes that stunningly reference hundreds of similar Bible verses. These footnotes explain commonly misunderstood and abused verses of the Qur'an, and awakens Christians and Muslims to vast areas of common ground existent within the Qur'an and Bible.

Drs. Kaskas' and Hungerford's underlying motivation for the translation and inclusion of the extensive footnotes are not intended to promote a particular school of Islam or Christian apologetics. These exist in abundance. Their goal is to build bridges of better understanding, undermine radicalism and enlighten ignorance. This powerful instrument offers Muslims and Christians a fresh insight on the "straight path" to reconciling with God and man; sorely needed and missing from other translations.

Having sojourned with them during this exciting process, I can attest that this publication offers an excellent and overdue tool for study and reflection for the academic and the curious, regardless of education, background, age, or faith tradition. It is time the world had an accurate and understandable rendition of Islam's Holy Book for the modern English reader, accomplished by both a Christian and Muslims that incorporates thousands of heretofore missing links to the Bible.

A word of caution! Do not skip the Biblical footnotes that coincide with the Qur'an! You will appreciate the scriptural overlap, and their usefulness for reconciling peace!

Mark Siljander

FOREWORD
NUMBER **TWO**

نسألك اللهم، برحمتك و قدرتك،	We ask you, O God, by your mercy and your power,
أن تجعلنا ممن يعرف حقك،	to put us among those who know your truth,
و يتبع رضاك، و يتجنب سخطك،	and follow your will and avoid your wrath,
و يسبع بأسمائك الحسنى،	and praise your beautiful names,
و يتكلم بأمثالك العليا.	and proclaim your sublime examples.
أنت الراحم الرحمان الرحيم.	You are the Compassionate, the Merciful.

- an anonymous second / eighth century Arab Christian1

They are not all alike. Among the People of the Book are upright people, reading God's verses day and night as they bow down. They believe in God and the last day, order what is obviously right, forbid what is obviously wrong, and they are quick to do good deeds. They are righteous. The good they do will not be forgotten. God knows those who are mindful of Him. Q3:113-115

The Qur'an is first and foremost an ecumenical book. In fact, the word Muslim was not originally meant as a delineator of a new religion, but rather an adjective to describe those who had submitted to the straight way of the Judeo-Christian tradition as clarified by the Qur'an. Christian commentators on the early Islamic movement also did not think of Muslims as other-than-Christian for more than a hundred years. Muslims, according to the majority of early Christian commentators, were a kind of Christian, not unlike the Nestorians, Jacobites, and Chalcedonians were kinds of Christians. Subsequent land wars between Chalcedonians, Jacobites, Nestorians, and Muslims encouraged the development of Qur'anic interpretations that justified young men on one side to murder young men on the other. Thus the polemical narratives appeared as the result of political ambition. However, the Qur'an, in its context, did not intend its later political hijacking.

The primary concern of the Qur'an is to correct those who wasted their worship on gods that did not exist, and to draw together those who worship the one true God of Abraham. It is a warner, a reminder, a reflective testament

• • •

1 - This quote is from the author of the first Arabic Christian apology, which elsewhere I have given the title On the Unified Trinity. This particular text can be found in (Samir & Nielsen, 1994, pp. 67-68).

to those volumes of the book of God which came before it: including the *Torah,* the *Zabur,* and the *Injeel* (Q3:84). The Qur'an rallies its readers to recognize the latest and final messenger in a long tradition of earlier messengers, whose lives were similarly purposed to calling the faithful to submission to God's will.

A few years ago I completed an extensive study of the Qur'an in history. In the book, *The Qur'an in Christian-Muslim Dialogue,* I surveyed the major themes of the dialogue, including the corruption of scripture, the nature of Jesus, the crucifixion, the incarnation, and the nature of God. The first three centuries of Islam were compared to the most recent century now to find out if any gains had been made in the conversation. What I found was that very often, the Qur'an in its original context disagreed heavily with both the dominant Christian and Islamic polemical interpretations of the text. The Qur'an, in its context, intends to draw faithful Muslims and Christians together. It is decidedly ecumenical in this intent.

Typically divisive revelations in the Qur'an are more likely than not corrections of historically extant heresies of its milieu. Though many potential candidates for Christian heresies as targets of Qur'anic rejection have been researched and dismissed over the years. Still, what is concretely known of Arabian Christianity at the time of the Qur'anic revelation was that it was neither Catholic nor Orthodox, strictly speaking. Nestorians, Jacobites, Chalcedonians, Arians, and Philoponians all vied for prestige as the dominant Christology of Arabian Christians. Yet the Qur'an carves away at the excesses in all of these. For example:

1. The Qur'an accuses the People of the Book of corrupting their interpretation of their scriptures, but not the texts (Q2:116-117), even though historical proof exists that the 4 Ezra text included in the Syriac Bible at the time was most certainly corrupted by Christians.
2. The historicity of the crucifixion of Christ is not a major issue in the Qur'an. Yet, while addressing Jews specifically, the Qur'an makes perfectly clear that they are not permitted to take any credit for having slain the Messiah (Q4:155-158). It is Jewish arrogance in their claim of having killed the Messiah that is under scrutiny, not the historicity of the event.
3. The Qur'an corrects the eating restrictions and Mariolatry of the Nazoraeans and adoptionism of the Nestorians (Q5:5, 116).
4. The Qur'an corrects the Jewish equation of Ezra with the Christian view of Jesus (Q9:30).
5. The polytheists of the time believed that gods had sons and daughters. Some Christians in Southern Arabia too believed that Jesus was literally the biological offspring of God and Mary, that

there were three separate Christian gods. Thus the Qur'an strictly forbids the genetic implications of the Son of God metaphor (Q112).

6. Perhaps most wisely, the Qur'an parses between the unacceptable tritheism of Abū Hāritha of Najrān while confirming and defending the Christian theology of Waraqa ibn Nawfal of Mecca (Q4:171, 5:73).

The Qur'an responds to a number of kinds of Christians, and in this endeavour, though there is no single "Qur'anic Christian" to speak of, there is still a kind of Qur'anic Christianity to which this book calls its audience. The Qur'an extends its ecumenical voice with surgical precision. Yet unfortunately that voice is too often lost in the momentum of exclusivity festering in the wake of a millennium of wars between Christians and Muslims.

The Qur'an is a strong enough bridge to mend the Christian-Muslim divide, when it is read according to its own view of itself, and its historical context is valued (Q2:62; 5:69). Yet there are some ambiguities that remain in its presentation. Those who believe the Qur'an to be the Word of God must accept those ambiguities as an intentional quality of revelation. Indeed, the Qur'an says of itself that the unclear *(mutashābihāt)* verses are intentionally so (Q3:7). And if ambiguity is an intentional quality of revelation, then humble orthodoxy is the appropriate response. A humble orthodoxy allows for the intentional ambiguity of scripture to cover disputes on issues that lack clarity.

Where Christians and Muslims are divided, and cannot resolve their differences, the Qur'an prescribes an appropriate arena for combat. We are to compete with each other in good deeds:

> To every community there is a direction to turn to, so compete to do good deeds wherever you may be. God will bring you all. God has power over all things. Q2:148
> We have assigned to each of you a law and a way of life. If God had wanted, He could have made all of you a single community, but instead He is testing you by means of what He has revealed to you. So compete in doing what is good. You will all return to God, and He will clarify these matter about which You have differed. Q5:48

Social justice is a wonderful arena for competition, as Micah 6:8 encourages us, "O people, the LORD has told you what is good, and this is what he requires of you: to do what is right, to love mercy, and to walk humbly with your God." It is an appropriate response from the people of the book to accept this Qur'anic challenge. Very well then. Let us compete with one another in the care for the poor, the widow, the orphan, and the marginalized (Q2:177; 4:35, 75, 135).

The World Council of Churches supports the, "common pursuit of justice, peace and constructive action on behalf of the common good of all people."[2] Prince al-Hasan bin Talal of Jordan laments that, "In both communities, such negative feelings or attitudes towards the 'other' have been basically atavistic rather than rational in nature."[3] Yet historically, social justice tends to bring the communities together. When we look at the end result of social justice, sincere Muslims and Christians tend to produce similar fruit. Yet, "does a spring of water bubble out with both fresh water and bitter water? Does a fig tree produce olives, or a grapevine produce figs? No, and you can't draw fresh water from a salty spring" (James 3:11-12). Perhaps like fruit shares a common source.

When we speak of a common source, we must begin with a common God. In this endeavour, there is a lot of shared ground in the Christian challenge to describe One God in Three Persons with the Islamic challenge to describe One God in the Divine Names. As I noted elsewhere and could not summarize better here:

> Theologically, there may be decreasing distinction between the concepts of unity in plurality in God described as Trinity, or God described in his Most Beautiful Names. The manner in which these concepts are described by representatives of the two religious traditions has tremendous overlap. The mutual challenge of Nasr and Rahner, for example, is the explanation of plurality within God while maintaining monotheism. They agree that one God is all that is outside of creation, and that all of creation comes from one God, and yet as soon as theologians open their mouths to add any description to God whether in terms of Person or Attribute, the description appears to be immediately deficient. Muslim and Christian theologians thus face a similar limitation that only silence from both can truly honour, what Rahner calls, "the ultimately forbidden goal," of rendering logically and intelligently the mystery of God.[4] Thus in silence under the recognition of the ultimate truth of monotheism, Muslims and Christians stand with a single perichoretic theology, for whatever else might be spoken about God out loud by either, betrays the transcendence of God in the theology of both. (Block, 2014)

Acknowledging the ambiguity inherent in our scriptures leaves room for ecumenical possibilities in relationship. Without syncretising, or transgressing either book, affirmation of the tremendous overlap in content is appropriate.

• • •

2 - World Council of Churches Office on Interreligious Relations, 2001, p. 486
3 - Talal, 2000, p. 165
4 - Rahner, 2010, p. 81

This affirmation is finding its way into popular discourse. A well-known American Evangelical minister once prayed publically:

> Almighty God, our Father, everything we see and everything we can't see exists because of you alone. It all comes from you. It all belongs to you. It all exists for your glory! History is your story. The Scripture tells us, "Hear O Israel, the Lord is our God, the Lord is One!" And you are the compassionate and merciful one toward everyone you have made.[5]

Based on Dr. Kaskas translation: The Qur'an, A Contemporary Understanding, this present book by Dr. Kaskas and Dr. Hungerford represents an ecumenical undertaking in line with the Qur'an's own heart. The Qur'an speaks of itself as a single volume in a multi-volume work. Thus the extant previous books are appropriate providers of context for the Qur'an to confirm, remind, and clarify. It cannot confirm, clarify, or remind of what is not available. Yet in the 1400 years since the Qur'an was revealed to us, never before has a Qur'anic translation into English been attempted along with cross-references to the previous books that it speaks so highly of. This work attempts to highlight the ecumenical nature of the Qur'an, and honour its view of itself as a reminder and confirmer of what came before it. But what is available of the previous books?

The *Torah* (five books of Moses) are the revelatory pillar of the Jewish community. The text referred to in the Qur'an is likely that which existed at the time of Muhammad and was available already in a number of languages. The Jews of Arabia would have held the *Torah* in Hebrew, and Christians held the same in Syriac.

There were multiple non-canonical gospels still in circulation during the Christological controversies of the 6th Century CE. Yet the *Injeel* mentioned in the Qur'an is not clearly defined, and thus the term was generally understood by its audience. It must therefore refer to whatever compendium of gospels that were common to the Christians of the Arabian Peninsula at the time of Muhammad. Christians from Muhammad's home town of Mecca were likely Nestorian, while those of the Northern Ghassanids were Monophysite. The Southern Arabian Christians, based in Najrān and Żafar, with at least two bishops and six churches between them, were very likely caught up in the Philoponian Tritheist heresy.

• • •

5 - Rick Warren in (Volf, 2011, p. 5). The first Biblical quote is from Deuteronomy 6:4, "Listen, O Israel! The Lord is our God, the Lord alone." The sentence following contains an allusion to Pslam 145:8-9, "The Lord is merciful and compassionate, slow to get angry and filled with unfailing love. The Lord is good to everyone. He showers compassion on all his creation." The phraseology of the last sentence quoted of Christian minister Rick Warren is an unmistakable employment of 'al-rahmān al-rahīm', a most common phrase of Islamic thought.

THE QUR'AN

Historians generally agree that although Arabic was commonly spoken, the liturgical language of Arabian Christians was most likely Syriac. In the pluralistic milieu of Arabia during the time of Muhammad, colloquial references to the *evangel* (Arabic: *Injeel*) would have therefore referred most likely to whatever collection of gospels appeared in the popular Peshitta Syriac Bible. These were not the whole collection of disputed gospels, but only the four gospels of Matthew, Mark, Luke, and John. Alternatively, the use of a singular term, *Injeel,* as a reference to the *evangel* in the Qur'an may indicate the Diatessaron, a Syriac synopsis of the four standard gospels that appeared in the second century CE. In either case, it is well agreed that the Diatessaron shares its content with the Peshitta.

The Qur'an confirms and reminds its audience of what came before it in the form of the previous books. The previous books, including the *Torah, Zabur,* and *Injeel,* form the liturgical context into which the Qur'an is intended to be read. The only glaring weakness in these authors' study is language. Language is a principle concern of the Qur'an, and thus the Hebrew and Greek originals of the *Torah* and *Injeel* should be taken as the authoritative texts, along with the Arabic of the Qur'an. It is a weakness of our age that the common tongue is English, and a study of this kind is better offered in a common tongue.

The audience's knowledge of the content of the previous books is assumed by the Qur'an, which reminds its people that as the Word of God, these previous books are protected and cannot be changed (Q6:34). The idea that humans are capable of corrupting the message of the *Torah, Zabur*, and *Injeel,* despite God's own declaration of His protection over them, is as grievous and misguided as the Jewish claim that they had somehow usurped God's plan by killing His Messiah.

These authors have done an excellent job of employing the Qur'an in its original intent, as an ecumenical work. As this is the first known cross-referencing Qur'an of its kind, and it is presented in a language foreign to all of the original texts which it employs, certainly some margin of error will serve to entice further generations of Qur'anic scholars to sharpen these findings. In the meantime, this work should stand as an initial roadmap, highlighting the routes between the Qur'an and its self-delineated literary context. May the intrepid theologian and historian be equally blessed by this monumental work.

Personally, I freely embrace the intentional ambiguity of scripture as a buffer into which any of my concerns with this work would fit. I thank Dr. Kaskas and Dr. Hungerford for doing what was right to do over what was most comfortable, and I hope that as both a Christian theologian and a Qur'anic scholar, I learn as well as they have, to handle with care the sacraments of others. I am blessed by their scholarship, as well as their friendship.

Dr. C. Jonn Block

INTRODUCTION
NUMBER **ONE**

The year was 1967. I was still living in Beirut, Lebanon and a close friend had given me the first English translation of the Qur'an that I had ever read. It was by Abdullah Yusuf Ali. I was very impressed with that translation and Ali's attempt to convey the musical rhythm and richness of the Arabic with poetic English versification. His translation opened my mind to a new understanding of the Qur'an within multiple linguistic and cultural dimensions. Later, I moved to the United States where I learned that the best way to communicate my ideas is to use the simplest and most direct language possible.

In the States, a journey started, where I had wide exposure to the religious pluralism that exists there. I visited Baptist churches, Methodists, Unitarian and Catholics among others. However, after 9/11, I found myself engaged with a national group of Evangelicals and a journey toward reconciliation started.

This project is a result of this journey. I started it with three goals in mind:

1 - To have a simple, easy to read and understand English translation of the meanings of the Qur'an.
2 - To have a translation that represents a fresh understanding of the original Arabic based on the presently available tools of knowledge.
3 - To have a translation that will be a tool of reconciliation. So it will not strive to emphasize the differences between Islam and the other Abrahamic religions (wall-building), rather it will emphasize the commonalities (bridge-building).

The Team

A modern, easy to read and understand translation of the Qur'an was the initial part of the project. The second part was to find equivalent meaning in the Bible to relevant Qur'anic verses. While we were organizing to undertake this major endeavor, it did not escape us that this work had never been done before. A large team with expertise was needed, but the previous experience that I and other senior team members had in the organization and implementation of large projects helped tremendously.

xi

While I have been the main translator, I was not working alone. A group of Evangelical Americans who share the same goals were working with me led by Dr. David Hungerford. Another group of Muslims were in Jeddah and were also working hard on a daily basis to see this idea become a reality.

Many times during the last few years of working on this project, I felt the hand of God directing me and bringing people along the way to specifically assist and help in needed tasks. The internet helped in many ways. I used the internet extensively and engaged volunteer programmers to help compare the Arabic original with the meaning of verses by various commentators as well as several translations by specific translators. I also used it to create a virtual office, where the team's members met and discussed problems and moved forward. Team management was essential for the completion of this project in the limited time span we had. Many team members were working full time on the project, while others donated time as they were able.

Once the basic translation draft was completed, the team effort that was invested in finishing the work was truly international. People were in different places in the world working on the same document and striving to produce a good translation that will make a difference in the lives of their fellow human beings.

Simplicity is not as simple as you think

Muslims, who grew up reading the Qur'an, always appreciated its flowing words, like a stream in the spring, when it's talking about the believers and its harshness when talking about the idolaters and those who opposed God's messengers. I grew up listening to its rhythmic verses and always felt safe knowing God was there for me. I talked to Him while praying and He spoke back through the Qur'an. But as I started reading about westerners' reaction to the Qur'an, I learned that they have a problem with my favorite book.

They complained about the Qur'an. They had a problem with its origin, its organization, its structure and many had problems accepting any concept of post biblical revelation. Others, who wanted to work with it, had problems understanding why it is not biographical or historical and most of all, why it is not linear.

So for me to claim that I want to present the Qur'an's meaning in a simple, easy to read and understand English translation sounded straight forward only in theory. In practice, it was not. The Qur'an is not a book like any other book with a beginning and an end. Its inner logic is different from what we've come to expect.

Muslims believe it is the Words of God revealed to Prophet Mohammad﷽ over a period of 23 years. Its internal organization is a mystery to the western mind, especially when one realizes that the first verses received by Prophet Mohammad in 610 CE were:

> *Recite in the name of your Lord who created -(01) Created the human being from a clinging substance. (02) Recite, and your Lord is the most generous (03) Who taught by the pen (04) taught human being that*

which he knew not. (05)

Yet they are placed at the beginning of chapter 96 Al-Alaq (The Clinging Form), while the last verse revealed to him shortly before his death in 632 CE, was verse 281 of the second chapter:

Beware of a Day when you are returned to God and every soul will be paid in full for what it has earned, and none will be wronged. (281)

Muslim traditions hold that when the angel Gabriel brought down these revelations to Prophet Mohammad▨, he also told him where to place them, in a type of large puzzle, which was assembled over twenty-three years into the present form of a book which became the Qur'an.

However, to understand the Qur'an, one must realize that it was compiled not in the historic order the revelations were received but as God desired the message to be conveyed. These were only some of the issues we had to keep in mind before the translation started.

Another issue has to do with the identity of the principal speaker in the Qur'an. By the time an average Western reader realizes that it is, in fact, God speaking to His Prophet and not Mohammadﷺ talking to us, another issue presents itself as one wonders why God is referring to Himself in so many different pronouns, often in the same sentence, such as "He", "We" or "I", with the corresponding changes of the pronoun from "His" to "Our" or "My", or from "Him" to "Us" or "Me" or "God". In the mind of a Western reader, who is accustomed to reading the Bible, this lack of uniformity presents difficulties.

As Mohammad Asad says in his Forward to The Message of The Qur'an, "They seem to be unaware of the fact that these changes are not accidental, but are obviously deliberate, a linguistic device meant to stress the idea that God is not a "person" and cannot, therefore, be really circumscribed by the pronouns applicable to finite beings."

Then Western readers may ask why "We", "Our" and "Us"? Is there more than one person within One God? The answer is a definite "No". The "We" is the royal plural required in Arabic, and Hebrew as a sign of respect.

Another issue is that in the original Arabic manuscripts from the seventh and the early eighth century there were no comas or periods indicating when a particular sentence begins and where it ends within a particular chapter. Other translations usually translate the verses in a continuous manner. This we decided, is part of the difficulty experienced by Westerners that does not exist when an Arab is reading the original Qur'an in Arabic. Reciting the Qur'an in Arabic on a regular basis for over 1450 years, the recitation was always subject to rules that are well set and known. Fathers taught their children to recite and then to read the Qur'an, using these same rules from the Prophet onward. So, we transformed what we do while reading the Arabic to the English translation. We grouped the verses dealing with the same subject together in a paragraph.

Then the problem of grammar and using the same tense in the same sentence came to mind. One of our American proof readers brought to my attention that I am not using the same tense within a sentence and I should, as this is good grammar. I of course agreed and started to correct the sentence, then suddenly stopped. I usually either recall the verse in Arabic before changing anything within the translation or go back to the text if needed. Upon reflecting on what the Qur'an is saying, I realized that God is using past and future in the same sentence, which led me to think that either God does not understand grammar or He is communicating something that I need to understand. At that moment it simultaneously occurred to me that time for God is not the same concept that we have. We have past, present and future because we live on a planet. However, for God, time is very different. I realized at that moment that I need to stick to the original Arabic in translating the verses which reflect that time is relative rather than using English grammar rules. This, I can understand will bring criticism and will drive some people crazy.

After considering all of this, we had to consider the geopolitical tension around the world in the post 9/11 era. Trying to present the Qur'an in a positive way is evidently a threat to a lot of people, including some Muslims, who are so fearful about Western intentions to the degree they are weary of any attempt to change the status quo. Hearing about an attempt to compare the Qur'an and the Bible in order to emphasize commonalities will make some Muslims very suspicious. The same suspicion I experienced from some religiously fervent Americans and Europeans groups, who would see it as an insult to the Bible when you compare it to the Qur'an. To many Western Christians in the U.S. and Europe, the Qur'an is the "book of the devil." They see nothing good that can come out of it. They either want to burn it or ban its reading all together. Some even warn of a "Chrislam" movement when they hear of Muslims speaking positively about Jesus.

I can now look back at my several years of hard work and smile. I will never be fully satisfied with the results because we're dealing with the translation of the words of God, the Qur'an, but I am convinced that there is a humble contribution here toward simplifying the language and making the meaning more accessible to average readers.

Seeing the Qur'an with fresh eyes

The second purpose of this translation is to convey a modern understanding of the Qur'an rather than a traditional, historic understanding. This translation is a translation of the meaning based on the translator's understanding. In fact, all translations represent the translator's personal reading and understanding and should be considered very personal and must be read as a subjective interpretation.

During the last fifty years human knowledge has expanded further than the entire knowledge accumulated throughout human history. It is only logical to read the Qur'an with fresh eyes and to understand it in view of all this new knowledge[1] that has become available to us.

When the Qur'an was revealed, it represented a new level of lin¬guistic evolution. It was arranged in a composition that is different from all other texts that existed in Arabic. Early Muslims focused on its uniqueness and its linguistic miracle. However, we are suggesting that the authenticity of the Qur'an is confirmed today by modern scientific discoveries and not by its aesthetic impact only.

The Qur'an according to Prophet Mohammed ﷺ, is a continuous miracle. Its meaning will continue to unfold as our tools of knowledge expand and advance allowing us to understand it more widely and with further depth.

A tool of reconciliation

It is said that people fear what they don't understand. Most of the tension that exists in the West in the post 9/11 era is because Christians fear Muslims and their book, the Qur'an. This is because some translations by Westerners mislead rather than clarify what the Qur'an says. Let's take the one by N. J. Dawood's 1956, Penguin Classic. In that translation, "often Dawood mistranslates one single word to give it totally the (Is it appropriate here to mention the word, its mistranslation compared to its correct translation?) opposite meaning. Dawood's translation is the one that most non-Muslims site when they accuse the Qur'an, Islam or Muslims, often with great convictions, of having no option but to be fanatical, violent and depraved."[2] Having said this, I should point out that some translations by Muslims, do more harm to Muslims than any Western translator was ever able to do. Take for example "The Noble Qur'an in the English Language by Muhammad Taqi al-Din al-Hilali and Muhammad Muhsin Khan." This translation reads more like a supremacist Muslim, anti-Semitic, anti-Christian polemic than a translation of the Qur'an. It was at one time the most freely distributed translation throughout the English-speaking world. People assumed that it had credibility, because it had the seal of approval from both the University of Medina and the Saudi Dar al-Ifta. However, as American Muslims grew more aware of its biased contents and supremacist attitude towards the People of the Book, they started rejecting it and they refuse to place it in many mosques.

I meant for this new translation to be a tool of reconciliation between Muslims and the followers of the other Abrahamic religions. In an environment of tension, working for reconciliation and peace is long overdue. If we are to prevent a much larger disaster from happening, we must work for a better understanding. My Islamic faith has taught me that it is my duty, and I hope the duty of every person of goodwill, to try to work towards peace and true reconciliation.

•   •   •

1 - Hence we came to understand At-Tarig in chapter 86 not as the late night visitor, but the Pulsar. I even have its knocking sound on tape from NASA http://vimeo.com/44284337. And Sijjeen not as a place in Hell but as a locked in data base. Not like our data but like God's data that He, all praise be to Him, hinted its existence to us, but was impossible for my father to even imagine existing.

2 - Reading the Qur'an: The Contemporary Relevance of the Sacred Text of Islam Hardcover by Ziauddin Sardar

This same desire to work for peace led me to meet a group of Evangelicals working on a translation of the Qur'an for the purpose of using it as a tool of reconciliation and to bring both Muslims and Christians closer together.

We joined hands to become a team of believers, dedicated to mutual respect and peace among the followers of Christianity and Islam, devoted to create a new, simple translation of the Qur'an to accomplish the following objectives:

To promote reconciliation.
To be a bridge between believers in the God of Abraham.
To promote mutual values.

Later, we were joined by Jewish scholars who were as dedicated to our vision as we. This translation emphasizes the common ground between the Qur'an and the previous books using references to the Bible passages[3] every time the Qur'an mentions prophets, people, events or subjects referred to in the Bible. To our knowledge, this is the first time such a comparison has been done since the birth of Islam and the revelation of the Qur'an. We believe in the goodness of what we are doing, in serving God's purpose through serving other believers.

This, we are certain, will lead to a better understanding between believers as Christians and Jews will have a chance to see the Qur'an as a continuation of the same message. While Muslims, who have not been willing to examine the Bible for themselves, will have a chance to see the connection that historically exists in the progression of God's message to human beings. Moreover, the references to common prophets, people and events will help the reader to reflect on both as books of revelation. If this translation succeeds in bringing the followers of the various Abrahamic religions closer together, it will accomplish its third major objective. A task that we think is long overdue.

Safi Kaskas
October, 2015

• • •

3 - We used mainly the New Revised Standard Version Bible NSRV

INTRODUCTION
NUMBER **TWO**

The authors have worked together to produce a translation of the Qur'an into contemporary, easy to understand English. There are many English translations of the Qur'an from which to choose. However, there are none to our knowledge that are a collaboration of a native Arabic speaking devout Muslim and a native English speaking devout Christian. Dr. Kaskas is a Lebanese Muslim and Dr. Hungerford is an American Christian. Dr. Kaskas, who is a naturalized American, did the initial translation from Arabic to English. The two authors then sat side by side and optimized each verse, line by line, into contemporary easy to understand English. This was no simple task. Many words in any language have more than one meaning. Also there are some words in one language that simply do not have a corresponding single word in the target language, and which have to be translated by a phrase. A great deal of effort has been made to ensure that the meaning of the Arabic has been clearly translated into that same meaning in contemporary English.

The second phase of the project has been to choose verses from the Bible that correspond to the meaning of selected verses of the Qur'an. Many of the Biblical stories from the lives of the Prophets, from the life of Jesus, from the Creation of the Universe and the beginning of mankind, from the historical events recorded in the Bible and from the attributes of God as expressed in the Bible are repeated in the Qur'an. In our experience many Christians and many Muslims are completely unaware of the rich trove of common themes in these books which are considered Holy to more than half the people on the planet. Although some have a vague awareness of the 'common ground', few are aware of the extent of the similarities. The selection of the verses has also been a combined effort of the two authors and have been chosen for relevance within the context of the verse. No attempt was made to be all inclusive for to do so, the number of similar verses would have unnecessarily overwhelmed the text.

This work has taken several years and has been done with several purposes in mind. We have a deep respect and love for each other and also respect for each other's faith communities. We also both have long and extensive histories of working to reflect our understanding of God's love and forgiveness both within and outside our faith communities. We are distressed at the current level of misunderstanding, distrust and outright hostility today between those who claim Abraham as their Patriarch, Jews, Christians and Muslims. We believe that part of the solution to those problems is to dispel the ignorance about the common ground between our respective Holy Books. We encourage English speaking Jews, Christians and Muslims to read this translation to develop a deeper understanding of the common heritage that we share and to reach out to the 'other', in a spirit of friendship and cooperation that our Holy Books command and which the current situation requires.

David Hungerford
October, 2015

From Revelations to a Book
THE HISTORY OF THE QUR'AN[1]

The Town of Mecca

According to Arabian traditions, and later confirmed by the Qur'an, the town of Mecca was established by the Patriarch Abraham and his son Ishmael. The location is not very far from the west coast of the Red Sea in a rocky valley with few agricultural resources.

There were at least two possible reasons for Abraham to have chosen that location to settle his son Ishmael in that arid valley. He was directed by God according to the Qur'an to rebuild the small square building called the Ka'ba, the ancient house that was built there by Adam for the sole purpose of worshipping God. Later the well of Zamzam would appear.

As Mecca happened to be on the caravan route from the Indian Ocean to the Mediterranean and with fresh water, it naturally became a trading post where people could hear about the faith of Abraham and carry it with them to wherever they were going. With the Ka'ba, the House of God, located in the center of town, Mecca became Arabia's most important place of pilgrimage for all Arab tribes.

As time went by, tribalism influenced the way Arabs worshiped God. The Meccans claimed descent from Abraham through Ishmael, and their place of worship, the Ka'ba, was still called the House of God, but in time the chief objects of worship became a number of idols placed inside. These were used as intercessors. Each tribe adopted an idol that was viewed as the protector of that individual tribe, and by the 4th century, large numbers of pilgrims from all over the Arabian Peninsula and beyond visited Mecca on an annual pilgrimage. But this was not only for religious reason. People visited Mecca to celebrate, trade, recite poetry in poetry competitions, commit immoral acts, and worship the many idols inside and around the Ka'ba.

•   •   •

1 - The Qur'an. The early biographies; Ibn Hisham and Al-Tabari. Modern biographies; Mohammad Hussein Heikal.

The birth of Mohammad

It was in the year 570 CE that Mohammad was born in Mecca. His father, Abdullah, belonged to the Hashemite family of Quraish. His mother, Aaminah, was a descendant from the same tribe. Returning with a caravan from Syria and Palestine, Abdullah stopped in Yathrib, an oasis to the north of Mecca, to visit relatives. There, he fell ill and died several months before his son's birth.

It was customary to send the sons of Quraish into the desert to spend their early childhood with Bedouin tribes. Apart from considerations of health, this represented a return to their roots, an opportunity to experience the freedom that accompanied the vastness of the desert.

Mohammad was taken by Halima of the Banu Sa'd tribe, and spent four or five years with her family, tending the sheep and learning the Arabic language from the Bedouins, whose speech was proper Arabic.

When he was six, not long after he had rejoined his mother, she took him on a visit to town of Yathrib, where his father had died, and she herself fell ill with one of the fevers prevalent in that area, dying on the journey home. Mohammad now came under the guardianship of his grandfather, Abdul-Muttalib, chief of the Hashemite clan. When the boy was eight years old, Abdul-Muttalib died, and thus he entered the care of the new Hashemite chieftain, his uncle Abu Talib. During this time, the young Mohammad was still tending sheep. When he reached the age of nine, he was taken by his uncle on the caravan journey to Syria so that he could learn to lead a caravan and the art of trade.

He continued working as a merchant, making a reputation for himself. Among the wealthy merchants of Mecca was a wealthy widow named Khadeeja. Impressed by what she heard of Mohammad, who was now commonly known as *Al-Ameen* (the trustworthy). She employed him to be in charge of her trade to Syria. Being impressed by his confidence and success in the way he handled her trade, his atypical competence and his personal charm, she asked him to marry her. By this time Mohammad was twenty-five, and Khadeeja was forty. Khadija bore Mohammad six children. All of their children, but Fatema died during his lifetime.

For the next fifteen years or so Mohammad lived the life of a prosperous merchant. He was now a man of substance, respected in the community, admired both for his generosity and his wisdom. Yet he was spiritually troubled, and became increasingly so, as he approached middle age. He then developed one habit uncommon to merchants; from time to time he withdrew into the mountains surrounding Mecca to meditate and pray.

Mohammad was among the few who rejected the prevailing idol worship and longed for the faith of Abraham. Such seekers of the truth were known as Hunafa', a word originally meaning "those who turn away" from idolatry. These people did not form a community, but rather each sought the truth by the light of their own inner consciousness. But with his continuous search for the truth, Mohammad increasingly felt the need to contemplate, and this lead him to seek seclusion in a cave on Mount Hira near Mecca. There, he would retreat for days to think, reflect and meditate. It was there that he was undergoing preparation for the enormous task which would be placed upon his shoulders, the task of prophethood and to convey the last revelations of God to his people and the rest of humanity.

The first revelation

The 7th day in the month of Ramadan that year (610 CE) was like any other day Mohammad spent in solitude in a cave high above Mecca. But that night changed his life. He had fallen asleep in the cave when he suddenly was awakened with an overwhelming feeling of a divine presence. An angel was there. Mohammad must have been terrified, especially when the angel enveloped him in a terrifying embrace so that it felt as though his very breath was being squeezed from his body. The angel gave him one command:

"Iqra'!" ("Read!") Mohammad protested in vain that he could not read. But the command was issued twice more, and each time he would feel he was reaching the end of his endurance, and he uttered the same response. Finally, the angel released him, and Mohammad found divinely inspired words pouring out of his mouth:

> *"Recite in the name of your Lord who created; created the human being from a clinging substance. Recite! Your Lord is the Most Generous, who taught by the pen, taught the human being that which he knew not."* (Qur'an 96:1-5)

So the angel was not asking him to read but to recite the words God puts in his mouth.[2] Thus began the magnificent story of God's last testament to humanity.

The encounter of an Arab, fourteen centuries ago, with a being from the realm of the unseen was an event of such momentous significance[3] that it would affect the lives of hundreds of millions of men and women, building a great civilization and raising from the dust beauty and splendor previously unknown. The word *Iqra'*, echoing around the valleys of the Hejaz, broke the mold in which the known world was cast; and this man, alone among the rocks, took upon his shoulders a burden which would have crushed the mountains had it descended upon them.

Mohammad had reached an age of maturity. The impact of this tremendous encounter may be said to have cleansed his soul. The man who descended from the mountain was like gold refined by the fire and was not the same man who had ascended it.

For the moment, however, he was terrified as a man pursued. As he tumbled down the mountain, he heard a great voice crying, "Mohammad! You are the Messenger of God, and I am Gabriel!" He looked upwards, and the

• • •

2 - This might be what Deuteronomy 18:18 refers to "I will raise them up a Prophet from among their brethren, like unto thee, and will put my words in his mouth; and he shall speak unto them all that I shall command him" (Deuteronomy 18:18 - KJV). However Christians do not believe it refers to Muhammad.
3 - This experience is mentioned in the Quran 53:4-9.

angel filled the horizon. Wherever he turned, the figure was there, inescapably present. He rushed home, running, falling, crawling and shaking, he cried to Khadeeja: "Cover me! Cover me!" She laid him down, placing a cloak over him, held him in her arms, soothing him and trying to calm him. As soon as he had recovered a little, he told her what had happened and shared his fears that he might be now possessed by a spirit. Mohammad was terrified. She held him close and comforted him:

> "Never! By God! God will never disgrace you. You keep good relations with your relatives, help the poor, serve your guests generously, and assist those affected by calamities." (Saheeh Al-Bukhari)

She saw in her husband a virtuous man—who's honest and just, given to helping the poor. The first person on the face of the earth to believe in the Message entrusted to Mohammad was his own wife, Khadeeja. At once, she went to see an older male cousin, Waraqa, a *Haneef*, who had become a follower of Jesus and had studied the Scriptures. After hearing from her about Mohammad's experience, Waraqa recognized him from the prophecies of the Bible to be the awaited prophet, and he confirmed that what had appeared to him in the cave was indeed the angel Gabriel:

> "This is the Keeper of Secrets (Gabriel) who came to Moses" (Saheeh Al-Bukhari).

The Prophet continued to receive revelations for the remainder of his life, memorized and written down by his companions on pieces of sheepskin and whatever else was available.

The scribes
The revelation of the Qur'an was not an isolated event in the Prophet's life. It was a constant stream of verses descending to him throughout the 23 years of his apostolic mission in Mecca and Medina. The Prophet appointed numerous companions of his to serve as scribes, writing down the latest verses as soon as they were revealed. The most notable among them were Zaid bin Thabit, Ubayy ibn Ka'b, Abdullah Ibn Mas'ud, Mu'awiyah ibn Abi Sufyan, Khalid ibn Al Waleed and Az Zubayr ibn Al Awwam.[4] For the most part, new verses would be written on bones, hide or parchment.

The scribes did not just write the new revelations, adding them next to the previous ones in chronological order, but they followed the Prophet's instructions. The organization of the revelations into verses and chapters and their order was revealed by God to His Prophet through the Archangel Gabriel known to Muslims to be the Holy Spirit. Gabriel himself told the Prophet where to place each verse and in which chapter. It was a process much like putting together a huge puzzle that took 23 years to complete.

• • •

4 - Ibn Hajar al-'Asqalani, Al-Isabah fee Tamyeez as-Sahabah, Beirut: Dar al-Fikr, 1978; Bayard Dodge, Mohammad M. Azami, in Kuttab al-Nabi, Beirut: Al-Maktab al-Islami, 1974, in fact mentions 48 persons who were used to write for the Prophet (p).

The final result is the book we know as the Qur'an. The logic followed in the structure and composition of the Qur'an is believed by Muslims to be God's logic.

How the Qur'an is organized

With the death of the Prophet the revelations stopped. The last revelation[5] shortly before his death, was verse 281[6] of the second surah:

> "Beware of a day when you are returned to God and every soul will be paid in full for what it has earned, and none will be wronged."

Muslims found themselves alone without the Prophet to guide them, a new faith based on the Qur'an and the way the Prophet used to manage Muslims' affairs and daily events called (in Arabic) the Sunna.

The Qur'an is composed of 114 parts or chapters of unequal length. Each chapter is called a *surah* in Arabic, divided into units, referred to as *ayas*, literally 'signs' or verses in English. These verses are not standard in length, but Muslims believe Mohammad was directed by God as to where each begins and ends. The shortest of the chapters *(surahs)* has ten words, and the longest, which is placed second in the Qur'anic text, has 6,100 words. The first chapter, the *Al Fatihah* ("The Opening"), is relatively short having just twenty-five words. From the second chapter onward, the chapters gradually decrease in length, although this is not a hard and fast rule. The last sixty chapters take up about as much space as the second. Some of the longer verses are much longer than the shortest chapters. All chapters, except one, begin with *Bsimillah hir-Rahman nir-Rahim*, ("In the Name of God, the Merciful to All, the Mercy Giver"). Each chapter has a name that usually refers to a key word within it. For example, the longest chapter, *Al-Baqara,* or "The Cow", is named after the story of God commanding the Jews to offer a sacrifice of a cow, which begins by God saying:

> When Moses told his people, "God commands you to sacrifice a cow," they said, "Are you making fun of us?" Moses answered, "God forbid that I should be so foolish." (Qur'an 2:67)

Since the various chapters are of various lengths, the Qur'an was theoretically divided by scholars of the first century (Islamic Calendar) into thirty roughly equal parts, each part is called a *juz'* in Arabic.

This organization of the revelations into chapters and verses was well-known to the companions.[7] Each Ramadan, the Prophet would repeat after Gabriel and or recite from memory the entire Qur'an in its exact order as instructed, in the presence of a number of his companions.[8] In the year of his

• • •

5 - Sahih Al Boukhari, Al Manakib, Hadith Ibn Abbas about the compilation of the Qur'an.
6 - Ibid
7 - Ahmad von Denffer, Ulum al-Quran, The Islamic Foundation, UK, 1983, p.41-42;
   Arthur Jeffery, Materials for the History of the Text of the Quran, Leiden: Brill, 1937, p.31.
8 - Saheeh Al-Bukhari Vol.6, Hadith No.519
9 - Saheeh Al-Bukhari Vol.6, Hadith Nos.518 & 520

death, he recited it twice.[9] Thereby, the order of verses in each chapter and the order of the chapters became reinforced in the memories of each of the companions present.

It is important to note that Mohammad would have the scribes read back the verses to him after writing them down so he could proofread them, making certain there were no errors.

To further ensure that there were no errors, Mohammad ordered that no one record anything else, not even his words, *hadith*, on the same sheet as the Qur'an. Regarding the sheets that the Qur'an was written down on, he stated "And whoever has written anything from me other than the Qur'an should erase it". This was done to ensure that no other words were accidentally added to the text of the Qur'an.

As the companions spread out to various provinces with different populations, they took their recitations with them in order to instruct others.[10] In this way, the same Qur'an became widely retained in the memories of many people across vast and diverse areas of land.

It is important to know, however, that the Qur'an was not primarily preserved by writing it down. Arabia in the 600s was an oral society. Very few people could read and write, thus huge emphasis was placed on the ability to memorize long poems. Before Islam, Mecca was a center of Arabic poetry. Annual festivals were held that brought together the best poets from all over the Arabian Peninsula. Exuberant attendees would memorize the exact words recited by their favorite poets and quote them years and decades later.

Thus, in this type of oral society, the vast majority of the companions learned and retained the Qur'an by memorizing it.[11] Its rhythmic nature made it easy to memorize.

The recitation of the Qur'an was not heard by just a few select companions. It was heard and memorized by hundreds of people, many of them travelers to Medina. Thus, chapters and verses of the Qur'an quickly spread during the life of the Prophet to all corners of the Arabian Peninsula. Those who had heard verses from the Prophet would go and spread them to tribes far away, who would also memorize them. In this way, the Qur'an achieved a literary status known among the Arabs as *tawator*, or reaching a consensus on authenticity when various recitations confirm one another. This meant it was so vastly disseminated to so many different groups of people, who all had the same exact wording, that it is inconceivable that that any one person or group could have changed it. The entire Qur'an's authenticity is confirmed through correlated recitation *(mutawatir)*, because it was widespread during the life of the Prophet through oral tradition. Ibn Hisham, in his famous biography of the Prophet, *Seerah Al-Nabi*, stated that the *Qur'an* we have with us today has been handed down orally by a large number of the Prophet's companions, with a consensus that this was the actual *Qur'an* that had been revealed to

• • •

10 - Ibn Hisham, Seerah al-Nabi, Cairo, n.d., Vol.1, p.199.
11 - Narrated *Qatadah:* I asked *Anas Ibn Malik:* 'Who collected the Qur'an at the time of Prophet?' He replied: 'Four, all of whom were from the *Ansar: Ubay Ibn Ka'ab, Mu'adh Ibn Jabal, Zayd Ibn Thabit and Abu Zayd.'(Bukhari, Kitab Fada'ilu'l-Qur'an)

Mohammad.

Collection after the death of the Prophet

As reading the Qur'an became widespread across the Islamic world, it was impossible for verses to be changed without Muslims in other parts of the world noticing and correcting them. Furthermore, after the Qur'an was completed near the end of the Prophet's life, Mohammad made sure that numerous companions knew the entire Qur'an by heart.

Shortly after the death of the Prophet, the first caliph, however, felt a need to have a central copy of the entire Qur'an for safe keeping. Abu Bakr, who ruled from 632 to 634 C.E., feared that if the number of people who had the Qur'an memorized dwindled, the community would be in danger of losing the Qur'an.[12] As a result, he ordered a committee be organized, under the leadership of Zaid bin Thabit,[13] to collect all the written pieces of Qur'an that were spread throughout the community. The plan was to collect them all into one central place that could be preserved and protected long after those who had memorized the Qur'an had died.

Zaid accepted verses only from people he knew to be trustworthy. He only accepted verses written on pieces of parchment that had been written down in the presence of the Prophet. As well, there had to be witnesses who could attest to that fact. These fragments of Qur'an that he collected were each compared with the memorized Qur'an itself, ensuring that there was no discrepancy between the written and oral versions.[14]

When the task was completed, a finalized collection of all the verses was assembled and presented to Abu Bakr, who secured it in the archives of the young Muslim state in Medina. Because of the numerous memorizers of Qur'an present in Medina at the time, it can be assumed with certainty that this copy that Abu Bakr had, matched exactly the revelations that Mohammad had received. Had there been any discrepancies, the people of Medina would have raised the issue. There is, however, no record of any opposition to Abu Bakr's project or its outcome.

Later this collection representing the entire Qur'an went to Omar Ibn Al Khattab the second caliph (ruled from 23 August 634 to November 644 C.E.), who gave it to his daughter Hafsa, the Prophet's widow, for safe keeping.

The Mushaf of Uthman

During the caliphate of Uthman (644 to 656 C.E.), a new issue regarding the Qur'an arose in the Muslim community: pronunciation. During the life of the Prophet , the Qur'an was revealed in seven different dialects - *qira'as*. The

• • •

12 - The main source of all accounts related to the collection of the Qur'an originate in Sahih Al Bukhari, Fadae'l Al Qur'an, section 6 named Jame'a Al Qur'an.

13 - Zayd ibn Thabit (ثَابِت زيد بن) was the personal scribe of Muhammad and was from the Medina converts known as Ansar (Supporters). When Zayd was 15 years old, he was among those chosen by Muhammad to write down the verses of the Quran. http://en.wikipedia.org/wiki/Zayd_ibn_Thabit

dialects differed slightly in their pronunciation of certain letters and words. These seven dialects were not an innovation resulting from corruption of the Qur'an in later years, as their authenticity was mentioned by the Prophet and recorded in the *Hadith* compilations of Bukhari and Muslim[15] and recognized by his companions. The reason for the different dialects was to make it easier for different tribes around the Arabian Peninsula to learn and understand the Qur'an.

During Uthman's reign, people coming into the Muslim world at its periphery, in places like Persia, Azerbaijan, Armenia, and North Africa were beginning to learn the Qur'an. An issue arose for them when it came to pronunciation of words, as they would hear different Arabs pronouncing the same verses differently. Although the different pronunciations were sanctioned by the Prophet and there was no inherent harm in people reciting and teaching them, it led to confusion among new non-Arab Muslims.

Uthman responded by commissioning a group to come together, organize the Qur'an according to the dialect of the tribe of Quraysh (the Prophet's tribe), and spread that authorized copy throughout the world. Uthman's team (which again included Zaid bin Thabit) compiled a complete written codex of the Qur'an with sheets of vellum (known as a *mus'haf* – from the word for page, sahifa) based on first hand manuscripts along with the memories of the best Qur'an reciters of Medina. This *mus'haf* was then compared with the copy that Abu Bakr commissioned, to make sure there were no discrepancies. Uthman then ordered numerous copies of the *mus'haf* to be made, which were sent to far off provinces throughout the world, along with reciters who would teach people to properly recite the Qur'an.

Because the Qur'an was now compiled and being reproduced on regular basis, there was no need for the numerous fragments of verses that people had in their possession. He thus ordered that those fragments be destroyed so they could not be used in the future to cause confusion among the masses. Although some Orientalists use this incident to try to claim that there were some discrepancies that Uthman wanted to eliminate, that claim lacks any supporting evidence. The entire community in Medina, including numerous eminent companions such as Ali ibn Abi Talib, willingly went along with this plan. Had he been eliminating legitimate differences, the people of Medina would have surely objected or even revolted against Uthman, neither of which happened. Instead, the *Mus'haf of Uthman* was accepted by the entire community as authentic and correct.

The script of the Qur'an

The *Mus'haf of Uthman* lacked any diacritical marks (dots that differentiated

• • •

15 - In Islamic terminology, the term *hadith* refers to reports of statements or actions of Muhammad, or of his tacit approval or criticism of something said or done in his presence. The two most accepted books on hadith are the two written by Imam Abū 'Abd Allāh Mu'ammad al-Bukhari known as Sahih al-Bukhari considered as one of the most *sahih* (authentic) of all *hadith* compilations. The other compilation of *hadith* known as Sahil Muslim is a collection of hadīth compiled by *Imām Muslim ibn al-Hajjāj al-Naysāburi*. His collection is considered to be one of the most authentic collections of the Sunnah of the Prophet.

the letters and vowel markings). The letters seen in his *mus'haf* are thus merely the basic Arabic letters.

Uthman sent reciters with his copies of the mus'haf, to teach the people, especially non-Arabs, the proper pronunciation and recitation of the Qur'an. However, we must remember that the main way the Qur'an was preserved was orally, and the written copies were only meant to be a supplement to oral recitation. If someone already has a verse memorized, the basic letters in a copy of Uthman's mus'haf serves only as a visual aid when reciting.

Over time, during the mid-700s, the Muslim world became an empire. Cities flourished, and written documents became a necessity for the young empire's business. This is when diacritical marks began to be added to the mus'hafs throughout the world. This was done as the Muslim world shifted from an oral to a written society, to further facilitate reading from a copy of the Qur'an, and to eliminate errors.

According to tradition, it was for this reason that Muawiyah (602 – 680) of the Umayyad dynasty, ordered Ziad Ibn Abih, his *wālī* in Basra (governed 664–673), to find someone who would devise a method to transcribe correct reading. Ziad Ibn Abih, in turn, appointed Abu Al Aswad Al Du'ali (ca. 603CE – 688CE/69AH) for the task. Abu Al Aswad was a close companion of Imam Ali and according to some traditions he might have learned his system of dots to signal the three short vowels (along with their respective allophones) of Arabic from the Imam himself. This system of dots predates the *i'jām*, dots used to distinguish between different consonants.

Fragments from a large number of Qur'an codices from the 8th and 9th century C.E. that we have today were written originally with the Kufic script and dots were added later.

Later, on the orders of the Umayyad Caliph 'Abd al-Malik a Qura'nic text with diacritical marks was produced. This, to a certain extent, removed the difficulty of reading the Kufic script. Several difficulties however, remained. The diacritical marks for vowels, for example, were for a time only dots. Instead of a *fathah*, a dot was placed at the beginning of the letter and, instead of *kasrah*, a dot below and, for a *dammah*, a dot above at the end of a letter. This led to ambiguity. It was not until Khalil ibn Ahmad al-Farahidi (718 – 786 CE) set about explaining the *maddah*, i.e. the lengthening of certain words, the doubling of letters, the diacritical marks of vowelling and the pause, that the difficulty of reading script was finally removed.

The Qur'an text most widely used today is based on the *Rasm Uthmani* (Uthmanic way of writing the Qur'an) and in the *Hafs* tradition of recitation, as approved by Al-Azhar University in Cairo in 1922. This is in fact the Arabic text that we translated.

Today, all modern *mus'hafs* include diacritical marks on the basic letters along with vowel markings to make reading easier.

Finally, as part of my passion to verify the authenticity of the currently printed copies of the Qur'an, I spent years searching the early original scripts thought to be from the late 1st century / early 2nd century (AH).

Fragments from a large number of Qur'an codices were discovered in Yemen in 1972. They are now lodged in the House of Manuscript in Sana'a. I presently own a copy of this manuscript thought to be the oldest copy of the Qur'an in existence.

One of the most famous of the Qur'an's manuscripts is the one kept in the Topkapi Palace Museum, Istanbul, Turkey. It is an early manuscript of the Quran dated to the late 1st century / early 2nd century (AH). A number of copies were produced faithful to the original in every way in 2009, and I own one of them.

The third copy of an original manuscript that I own, is the one called the "Qur'ān Of 'Uthmān" that was displayed for some time at Al-Hussein Mosque, Cairo, Egypt, and thought by some people to be from 1st / 2nd Century (AH). However, paleographer 'alā'al-Dīn al-Munajjid did not consider this manuscript to be from the time of caliph 'Uthmān. He said that, in all probability, it was a copy made on the order of the Governor of Egypt 'Abd al-'Azīz ibn Marwān, brother of Umayyad caliph 'Abd al-Malik ibn Marwān (646-705). Therefore, it can be one of the oldest copies of the Qur'an written in Egypt in the second half of 1st century (AH).

A Koran fragment from the University of Tübingen Library has been dated to the 7th century - the earliest phase of Islam - making it at least a century older than previously thought. Expert analysis of three samples of the manuscript parchment concluded that it was more than 95 percent likely to have originated in the period 649-675 AD - 20 to 40 years after the death of the Prophet Mohammed. Such scientific dating of early Koran manuscripts is rare.

Perhaps the oldest certified manuscript of the Qur'an at this time is the one owned by the University of Tübingen in Gemany. On10.11.2014, it was announced that a Tübingen fragment was tested by the Coranica project, a collaboration between the Académie des Inscriptions et Belles-Lettres Paris and the Berlin-Brandenburgischen Academy of the Sciences and Humanities, sponsored by the German Research Foundation (DFG) and France's Agence Nationale de la Recherche (ANR). The project investigates the Qur'an in the context of its historical background using documents such as manuscripts and information derived from archaeological excavations.

The fragment in question is one of more than 20 in the University Library Collection written in Kufic script, one of the oldest forms of Arabic writing. The manuscript came to the University in 1864 as part of the collection of the Prussian consul Johann Gottfried Wetzstein.

Analysis showed that the Tübingen University fragment was written 20-40 years after the death of the Prophet Mohammad.

It can be viewed online at:

http://idb.ub.uni-tuebingen.de/diglit/MaVI165

METHODOLOGY
THE TRANSLATION STRATEGIES

The translation strategies, methods and procedures

One of the troublesome problems of translation is the disparity among languages. The bigger the gap between the source language and the translation language, the more difficult is the transfer of the message from the former to the latter. Nowhere is this more obvious than in the translation of the Qur'an from the original Arabic into English.

The difference between Arabic and English and the variation in cultures make the process of translating a real challenge. Among the problematic factors involved in such a translation is form, meaning, style, proverbs, idioms, etc. I am going to concentrate mainly on the strategies and procedures I used for understanding the Qur'an, translating its meaning and later finding equivalent meaning for its verses within the Old and the New Testaments.

Typically, a translation is a simple process of transferring a written text from its source language to an equivalent written text in the target language. However, in order to do this successfully, the translator has to first understand the text in its source language. In our case this task is not easy. The Qur'an as an Arabic text has gone through more than two hundred attempts to translate it into English, and none of them claims or was later credited with capturing the meaning sufficiently.

Without going into an analysis of the other translations and their positive and/or negative contributions, I would like to move directly to the strategies, methodology and procedures used to produce this translation.

Here are some basic assumptions we made in order to develop our methodology.

1 - The Qur'an is a text written in the classical Arabic language, so the only way we can effectively understand its meaning is through a proficient knowledge of classical Arabic.
We based our understanding of Qur'anic Arabic on the following assumptions:

THE QUR'AN

a) - The Qur'anic Arabic as a language is the root of today's Arabic but far superior to it. In the Qur'anic Arabic the words used are fixed and will not change. But to understand a word, we did not go to dictionaries or to classical commentators only, but we went through the process of comparing the word in a verse to the same word in other verses. If a traditional commentator explained a certain word in a certain way, and we found that this contradicted the way the Qur'an used this word in other verses we opted to use the Qur'anic understanding.

b) - Arabic grammar; the set of rules that explain how words are used in Arabic, was created after the revelation of the Qur'an. The rules had to conform to the Qur'an and not the other way around. However, while translating the Qur'anic Arabic we had to observe English grammar rules to the best of our ability in order to make the translation as communicative as possible.

c) - The same goes for the tense of verbs used in the Qur'an. In some verses God uses the present tense and then switches to future or present continuous tense. We understand that using the same tense is proper English, but tense has to do with time, and time is relative to living on the planet Earth which is limited to human beings but not God. However, we tried to use English grammar rules to the best of our ability as stated above.

d) - The Qur'anic Arabic does not have synonyms. Every word used has a specific meaning. So while we attempted to render the exact contextual meaning of the original, we also endeavored to be as faithful to the original by using specific terms/words translation such as *zalemeen* translated to "unjust" or "criminals" and not "evildoers" or "sinners" on some occasions and as "wrongdoers" on others.

e) - The words and the verses carry important meanings. If we understand the meaning of a verse to be inconsequential, then we should conclude that we have misunderstood the meaning.

2 - The Qur'anic Arabic, did not historically or stylistically reflect the language of the 7th century CE. The revealed verses represented a new level of linguistic evolution. They displayed textual qualities that Arabs had not known before. They contained vocabulary of non-Arabic origin that their pre-Islamic poetry had not used. They were composed in a way that is different from the entire Arabic textual body of that period. So while we refer to the Arabs' understanding of a word at the time of the Qur'an's revelation, we need to keep in mind that our own contemporary understanding of that word's meaning is evolving as our understanding of our environment is expanding. For example, when the 7th century Arabs heard for the first time Surat At Tariq (86 The Knocker) the word "knocker" for them used to mean

the late night visitor as reflected by the early Qur'anic commentators. But since the verse refers to the knocker as a piercing star, so they concluded the knocker to be the planet Jupiter as it shows up late at night and disappears during the day. Today, we understand it to be a pulsating star.[1] In adding new discoveries to our knowledge, humans take part in constructing the new meaning of the Qur'anic language in as much as they find in the text the discoveries they have just made. To limit our understanding of the Qur'anic verses to the historical Arabic of the 7th century would mean a regression in our ability to understand our modern world and a return to a pre-modern understanding of the divine text.

3 - Before translating the text, we found it necessary to read and understand a number of classical commentaries to acquire a better historic understanding of the text and to re-examine differences in interpretations.

Many people assume that there is one authentic interpretation of the Qur'an. This is far from true. Even the closest companions of the Prophet differed early on in understanding various verses. In fact, no one interpretation can command the following of a majority of Muslims. Islam, in fact, does not have an institution in charge of such interpretation, and there is hardly any major issue on which Muslim scholars do not differ. These differences, more often than not, are due to traditional interpretations of the Qur'anic text based on various stories told by the Prophet's companions. They, also, may represent a later understanding by scholars when striving to find and represent new understanding. This practice was no longer allowed after the 12 th C.E. Today, traditional scholars still base their understanding of the Qur'an on the same traditional interpretations, except when they are forced to catch up with obvious scientific discoveries.

4 - Historically, Arabs were astonished by the text's aesthetic and rhetorical beauty. We are too. However, we propose that the Qur'an should not be considered simply as a historic, culturally-specific text, but as an entity that exists in and by itself. Its text is fixed and does not change. Yet, we are changing. We gain more understanding of the same text through our gradual growth and our expanding knowledge. Hence, we conclude that the Qur'an has a fixed text and a dynamic meaning. It always allows its intelligent reader to understand it in a contemporary manner, especially if a dialectical relationship is established between the text and its reader. This relationship is usually more obvious when the Qur'an is read by an Arab in Arabic. I kept this principle in mind while translating, but only the reader can judge whether the translation is good enough to produce such results.

•   •   •

1 - A celestial object, thought to be a rapidly rotating neutron star, that emits regular pulses of radio waves and other electromagnetic radiation at rates of up to one thousand pulses per second.

5 - The Qur'an explains the purpose of our existence on earth and the values needed to make that purpose meaningful. While doing this, it celebrates our unique human consciousness. It urges us repeatedly to think, to reflect, to observe and to learn. Its basic message directs us to consider the existence of a Creator who is the primary cause beyond all existence through His innovative and intelligent creation. The purpose of our short life on earth, it tells us, is to exercise our freedom of choice. Freedom is essential for our existence on earth if we are to be responsible for our choices. The two basic choices we are urged to make are: to recognize God as our Creator, to worship him and to serve others. If we are free to choose and we opt to reject God as our creator and reject the resurrection after death and the eternal life that will follow and egotistically choose to put our own interest ahead of everyone else, we will go away from God. But if we chose to serve Him through serving others, we will draw nearer and nearer to Him. At the end, we are judged based on our choices and His mercy. An eternal life will await the God-conscious people in Heaven. While those who have rejected God and spend their lives serving themselves instead of Him will end in an eternal Hell.

6 - The Quran does not contradict itself, and is not dependent on outside sources to explain its meaning. It is, in a sense, self-sufficient. One part of the Qur'an helps to explain another. Hence, when we translate a verse in a certain way, we should make sure that other verses affirm our understanding of that verse. If such evidence is lacking, or if, in fact, our translation is clearly contradicted by other verses, then we should understand that we have a false understanding. Considering its claim for its divine origin, it is impossible to have contradictions amongst the various verses of the Qur'an. The distinguishing feature of a good interpretation is that the Qur'an contains an abundance of evidence to support it. However, the Prophetﷺ expanded and explained further certain verses with general meaning regarding, for instance, acts of worship.

7 - The Qur'an teaches that Muhammadﷺ was both a prophet and a messenger of God. So the Qur'an contains both the verses given to the Prophet, addressing the creation around us and the universal laws, as well as the verses of the Message given to him as a messenger addressing how to best worship God and how to live successfully alongside others on this planet. The Messenger Muhammadﷺ explained these verses in detail, especially those related to worshipping God. Hence, the way Muslims perform their ritual prayers, the way they fast and all other acts of worship are practiced according to the example and teachings of the Messenger. They can't be changed. Other verses the Prophet very wisely did not explain because he did not want us to be committed to a seventh century understanding of the world around

us. For this reason, we look today to NASA to better understand the universe around us and not to a historic interpretation given by a companion or an early scholar.

8 - The translator believes that the Qur'an is the indirect speech of God, verbally revealed to Prophet Muhammad ﷺ through the Archangel Gabriel (Holy Spirit). We regard it as the miracle given to Muhammad ﷺ to prove his prophethood. It is also a book of guidance to humanity. As such, we assume it corresponds and parallels the universe which is also the words of God materializing all around us. In order to understand our world, we need to grasp the meaning of both, the words of God as the universe and His revealed words. The more we understand one, the better we understand the other. As such, we are called by the Qur'an to reflect on the basic universal laws as we can observe them in the world around us. The Qur'an as a book of revelations should not contradict the reality around us and should not contradict reason. Therefore, we assume that the best way to understand the Qur'an is through sound rational analysis. Hence, a new reading of the Qur'an based on the tools of knowledge available to us today should provide a better and deeper understanding beyond the existing traditional exegetical commentaries. On the surface, this seems to contradict the fact that the Qur'an itself calls on us to believe in its divine origin based on faith and not reason. We are also called to believe in resurrection after death, the Day of Judgment, Heaven and Hell and Eternity. All this is in what the Qur'an calls "Ghaib" translated as: what is beyond our senses and/or human perception. A believer is required to accept these doctrines based on faith, defined as "the substance of things hoped for, the evidence of things not seen" (Hebrew 11:1).

9 - The Qur'an does not discriminate or generalize in its condemnation of any people. God describes Himself in the Qur'an as "the Just". The principle of "no soul will bear the burden of another" (17:15) was mentioned in the Qur'an 5 times. Most classical commentators mentioned specific Jews or specific Christians addressed by a specific verse. We are taught to ask whether the pronoun Al (the) before the name is specific or general. As such, I understand most of what is mentioned in the Qur'an about "the Jews" or "the Christians" to concern only those who were involved with a particular event—not all Jews or all Christians.

10 - The original text had no punctuations and was not divided into paragraphs. Early Muslims learned to recite the Qur'an from memory, the way they originally learned it from the Prophet. Punctuation marks were added later, but Muslims knew instinctively where to stop. However, westerners who are newly introduced to the Qur'an find it very hard to make sense of a text that is not organized the way they are used to. Most translators, did a continuous translation of the text

of each chapter without paying attention to the difficulties non-Muslims face when they read it. We found it necessary to divide the text of each chapter into paragraphs following the meaning and the subject matter. In addition, the Qur'an is not that easy to understand by the average Arab, let alone the average westerner. While it has an inner logic in the way it tackles various issues, it will help to facilitate showing this inner logic by organizing references to the subject matter to help the reader understand.

Based on these assumptions we developed the following general principles for the methodology used for this translation:

1 - The translation will be done with the goal of accuracy, naturalness, and clarity.

    a. The meaning of the original text is to be translated accurately, exactly.

    b. We will translate the meaning of ideas. This is not word-for-word translation.

    c. Meaning will have priority over form.

    d. Naturalness of expression will have priority over form.

    e. Translated materials should sound natural and be readily understood by the target audience. This includes word order, grammar, sentence length, idiomatic phrases and figurative expressions.

    f. Vocabulary will be carefully chosen, with common words preferred over outdated and with the goal of producing a translation that is clearly and correctly understood by all English speakers, especially the younger generation.

2 - We determined after careful sociolinguistic research, that our primary target audience is an average American with a high school education. The language used should reflect this choice. We used common English, used in everyday life, where the reader will not usually have to use a dictionary to understand the words. Other fringe audiences outside the U.S. are also considered, such as English-speaking people in Southeast Asia.

3 - When reviewing the Arabic text of the Qur'an, we tried to define the culture-bound terms and allusions usually taken for granted by Muslims familiar with the Qur'anic terminology and the use of names of people and places and opted to use the Anglicized version, in order to better communicate the meaning.

4 - To give the closest approximation of the source language, it was necessary to opt for creating a glossary of words and concepts and to use some explanatory footnotes.

5 - Grammatical and syntactic structures do not often correspond between Arabic and English. We, therefore, found it often misleading to maintain the same form as the Qur'anic source text. So, changes of form were often necessary. We, therefore, employed as many or as few terms as are required to communicate the original meaning as accurately as possible.

6 - We recognized early on that the transfer into English should be done by mother-tongue speakers. Therefore, we recruited and worked with a team of native- speaking Americans.

7 - We also realized the need to test the translation as extensively as possible in the United States and among other English-speaking communities in other parts of the world, in order to ensure that it communicates the meaning clearly and naturally, keeping in mind the sensitivities and experience of our targeted audience.

8 - We left the monitoring for qualitative and stylistic errors in the text to the revision stage where we did several re-evaluation attempts. Several qualified volunteers proofread and contrasted the translation with other existing translations of the same text done by other translators. They looked into the differences and identified them. I, as the main translator, had to make sure that what we have is closest to the original meaning.

A CONTEMPORARY UNDERSTANDING

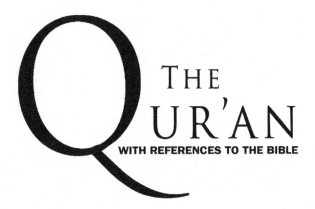

THE
QUR'AN
WITH REFERENCES TO THE BIBLE

Safi Kaskas
David Hungerford

Bridges of Reconciliation
FAIRFAX, VIRGINA

CHAPTER **ONE**

AL-FATIHA[1]

THE OPENING

In the name of God,[2] the Merciful-to-all,[3] the Mercy Giver:[4] (01)
Praise be to God[5], the Lord of the Worlds[6], (02)
The Merciful-to-all, the Mercy Giver, (03)
Master of the Day of Judgment.[7] (04)
It is You we worship, and it is You we seek for help. (05)
Guide us to the straight path[8], (06)
The path of those whom You have blessed[9], with whom You are not angry
and who have not gone astray. (07) [10]

· · ·

[1] Al-Fatiha, is the first chapter of the Qur'an. It is also known as Fatihat al-Kitab (The Opening of the Book)
Recitation of this Chapter is an obligatory part of *Salat* (daily prayer). Muslims memorize this chapter and recite
it at the beginning of each of the five daily prayers and all other voluntary prayers they perform.
[2] The invocation "In the name of God, the Merciful to All, the Mercy Giver," which occurs at the beginning
of every chapter except chapter 9, At-Tawbah (Repentance), constitutes an integral part of chapter 1,
and is therefore numbered as the first verse of this chapter, but it is not counted in other chapters.
[3] Both the divine epithets *rahman* and *rahim* derive from the noun *rahmah*, which signifies "mercy,"
"compassion," "loving tenderness," and "grace." *Rahman* exemplifies the quality of abounding grace inherent
in, and inseparable from, the concept of God's Being. Psalm 103:8, 145:8: "The Lord is gracious and merciful,
slow to anger and abounding in steadfast love." The Qur'an mentioned at least 99 attributes or beautiful
names of God.
[4] *Rahim* is an intensive form (of the verb) which emphasizes that the quality of giving mercy is inherent
in God's nature. *Rahim* expresses the manifestation of that grace (attribute) in, and its effect upon, His creation.
[5] Psalm 25:4-6 Make me to know your ways, O Lord; teach me your paths.[5] Lead me in your truth, and teach me,
for you are the God of my salvation; for you I wait all day long.[6] Be mindful of your mercy, O Lord, and of your
steadfast love, for they have been from of old. Deuteronomy 6:4 The Lord our God is one Lord.
[6] Luke 4:8 Jesus answered him, "It is written, 'Worship the Lord your God, and serve only him.'" Deuteronomy
10:14 "Behold, to the Lord your God belong heaven and the highest heavens, the earth and all that is in it.
[7] Matthew 12:36 "I tell you, on the day of judgment you will have to give an account for every careless word
you utter.
[8] Deuteronomy 6:25 If we diligently observe this entire commandment before the Lord our God,
as he has commanded us, we will be in the right."
[9] Deuteronomy 7:12 If you heed these ordinances, by diligently observing them, the Lord your God will maintain
with you the covenant loyalty that he swore to your ancestors; [13] he will love you, bless you, and multiply you;
[10] Matthew 6:9-14 Pray then this way: Our Father in heaven, hallowed be your name. Your kingdom come. Your
will be done, on earth as it is in heaen. Give us our daily bread. And forgive us our debts, as we also have forgiven
our debtors. And do not bring us to the time of trial, but rescue us from the evil one.

CHAPTER TWO

AL-BAQARAH[12]

THE COW

THE **MEDINA** PERIOD

In the name of God, the Merciful-to-all, the Mercy Giver:
Alef Lam Meem[12] (01)

This is the Book that, without doubt, has guidance for those who are mindful of God; (02) who believe in the existence of what is beyond human perception, perform prayers, and contribute some of what We[13] have provided to them, (03) those who believe in what We revealed to you and what We revealed before you; they are certain of the hereafter. (04) Such people are guided by their Lord and are successful.(05) As for the unbelievers, it is all the same whether you warn them or not, they will not believe. (06) God has sealed their hearts and their hearing and covered their sight. They will have a terrible punishment.[14] (07)

Some people say, "We believe in God and in the last day," but they are not believers. (08) They try to fool God and the Believers, but they fool only

. . .

---

[11] The title of this chapter, the longest in the Quran, derives from the story narrated in verses 67-73. It is the first chapter revealed in its entirety after the Prophet's migration to Medina. Most of it dates to his first two years there, but verses 275-281 were revealed during the last months before the Prophet's death. Verse 281 is considered to be the very last revelation that he received.

[12] Here and at the beginning of many chapters there are letters of unknown meaning called Al Muquatta'at. Numerous theories have been proposed, but there is no agreement on what they signify yet.

[13] "We" is employed throughout the Qur'an when God speaks. This usage is the "royal we." It does not imply that God is not one.

[14] Matthew 25:41, 46, "Then he will say to those at his left hand, 'You that are accursed, depart from me into the eternal fire prepared for the devil and his angels'. . . [46] And these will go away into eternal punishment, but the righteous into eternal life"; and Revelation 20:10, "And the devil who had deceived them was thrown into the lake of fire and sulphur, where the beast and the false prophet were, and they will be tormented day and night for ever and ever."

themselves and do not even realize it. [09] They have a sickness in their hearts,[15] and God has made them even sicker. They will have painful punishment[16] because of their lies. [10] When they are told, "Do not cause corruption in the land," they say, "But we are reformers!" [11] They are truly corrupters and do not realize it. [12] when they are told, "Believe just like other people have believed," they say, "Will we believe like fools?" They are the fools, but they do not know it. [13] If they meet believers, they say, "We have believed." But when they are alone with their devils, they tell them, "We are with you. We were only mocking them." [14] God will mock them, and will increase their arrogance as they stray. [15] They have sold guidance for error, what an unprofitable trade; they have not been guided. [16] They are like one who lights a fire, and when it shines around him, God takes away their light and leaves them in darkness, where they are unable to see. [17] Deaf, dumb, and blind, they will not return (to the path).[17] [18] Or, they are like a cloudburst in the sky that has darkness, thunder, and lightning. They put their fingers in their ears because of the lightning bolts, afraid of death. God surrounds those who deny (the truth). [19] The lightning almost blinds them. Whenever it shines, they walk by its light. When it is dark, they stand still. If God had willed, he would have taken away their hearing and their sight. God has power over all things. [20]

People, worship your Lord who created you and those before you, that you may be mindful of God, [21] He, who spread out the earth for you and built the sky. He sent rain from the sky, and through it, brought forth fruits as provision for you.[18] So do not knowingly set up rivals for God. [22] And If you are in doubt concerning our revelation to our servant, bring a chapter like it and call your witnesses other than God, if you are telling the truth. [23] If you do not do that— and you never will—beware of Hell, whose fuel is people and rocks. It was prepared for the unbelievers. [24]

Give good news to the believers who do virtuous deeds; they will have Heavenly Gardens with flowing rivers.[19] Every time they are provided fruit from it, they will say, "This is similar to what we were provided before." It appears to them that they are given the same thing. There they will have perfectly pure spouses, (and there) they will be eternally. [25]

God is not reluctant to present a proverb about a mosquito or something bigger. Believers know that it is truth from their Lord, but the unbelievers say, "What does God mean by this?" It is a proverb that misguides many and guides

· · ·

[15] Isaiah 1:4,5 4 Ah, sinful nation, people laden with iniquity, offspring who do evil, children who deal corruptly, who have forsaken the Lord, who have despised the Holy One of Israel, who are utterly estranged! 5 Why do you seek further beatings? Why do you continue to rebel? The whole head is sick, and the whole heart faint.

[16] Jeremiah 23:12 Therefore their way shall be to them like slippery paths in the darkness, into which they shall be driven and fall; for I will bring disaster upon them in the year of their punishment, says the Lord.

[17] Revelation 3:17, "For you say, 'I am rich, I have prospered, and I need nothing.' You do not realize that you are wretched, pitiable, poor, blind, and naked."

[18] Matthew 5:45, "so that you may be children of your Father in heaven; for he makes his sun rise on the evil and on the good, and sends rain on the righteous and on the unrighteous."

[19] Revelation 22:1-2, "Then the angel showed me the river of the water of life, bright as crystal, flowing from the throne of God and of the Lamb through the middle of the street of the city. 2 On either side of the river is the tree of life with its twelve kinds of fruit, producing its fruit each month; and the leaves of the tree are for the healing of the nations."

many.[20] It misguides only the defiantly disobedient. (26) Those who break God's covenant after it is confirmed and sever what God commanded to be joined and corrupt the earth—they are the doomed. (27) How can you deny the truth in God when you were dead, and He made you alive? Then He will make you die, then make you alive, and then you will return to Him. (28) It is He who created everything on the earth for you, and then turned toward heaven, and He made them seven Heavens.[21] He has knowledge of all things.[22] (29)

When your Lord told the angels, "I will place a steward [23] on earth," they said, "Will you put someone there who will corrupt it and shed blood, while we glorify, praise, and sanctify You?" He said, "I know things you do not know." (30) He taught Adam the names of everything and then showed them to the angels. He said, "Tell me the names of these if you are so sure of yourselves." (31) They said, "May You be exalted in your glory! We know nothing except what You have taught us. You are the All-Knowing, the Wise."[24] (32) He said, "Adam, tell them their names." When he told them their names, He said, "Did I not tell you that I know the hidden reality of the heavens and the earth, and I know what you show and what you hide." (33)

When we told the angels, "Bow down to Adam," they all bowed down, except for Iblīs,[25] who refused out of arrogance. He was one who denied the truth. (34) We said, "Adam, live with your spouse in the Heavenly Garden, and eat freely whatever you want, but do not come near this tree, or you will be unjust." (35) But Satan made them slip and caused them to be expelled from where they were, and We said, "Go down, you will be enemies to one another, and on earth you will have a temporary abode and livelihood." (36) Then Adam received word from his Lord, and He accepted his repentance. He alone is the Accepter of Repentance, the Mercy Giver.[26] (37) We said, "All of you go down[27] from it (the Garden). When my guidance comes to you, whoever follows my guidance will not have fear or grieve." (38) Those who deny the truth and reject our revelations are headed for Hell, where they will be eternally. (39)

Children of Israel, remember my grace which I gave you. Fulfill your promise, and I will fulfill My promise, as I am the One you should revere. (40) Believe in my

• • •

[20] Matthew 13:10,11 "Then the disciples came and asked him, "Why do you speak to them in parables?" [11] He answered, "To you it has been given to know the secrets of the kingdom of heaven, but to them it has not been given."
[21] The Arabic word *sama* means both "Heaven" or "sky." The number "seven" should be understood figuratively rather than literally, i.e., God has created many heavens, He has accomplished many acts of creation. As in Hebrew or Persian, Arabic often uses numbers to convey the sense of "multiplicity" rather than a specific number.
[22] 1 John 3:20. whenever our hearts condemn us; for God is greater than our hearts, and he knows everything.
[23] The word in Arabic is *khalifah*, sometimes translated "vicegerent." In Islamic political discourse, the term has taken on a number of meanings to refer to rulers who succeeded Prophet Muhammad's political authority. Here it denotes man's rightful supremacy on earth.
[24] Isaiah 40 This entire Chapter declares the greatness of God, including His omniscience (all-knowing) and wisdom
[25] Iblis is the proper name given in the Qur'an to the heavenly being who rebelled and refused to obey God's order to bow down to Adam. He is later referred to as Satan
[26] Ephesians 2:4, "But God, who is rich in mercy, out of the great love with which he loved us."
[27] The Arabic word *Ihbita* means "to go down from a higher place or state of being to a lower place or state of being."

revelation,[28] confirming the revelations that you already have.[29] Do not be the first to deny it, and do not barter away my verses for trivial gain, but be mindful of Me. [41] And do not mix truth with error or knowingly hide the truth. [42] Perform prayers, and pay the purifying alms, and kneel together with those who are kneeling. [43] As you read the Book, do you command others to be virtuous and yet forget yourselves? Don't you comprehend? [30(44)] Seek help in endurance and prayers. (Doing this) is a burden, except for the humble, [45] who assume they will meet their Lord, and they will return to Him.[31 (46)]

Children of Israel, remember my grace which I gave you. I preferred[32] you above all mankind.[33 (47)] And beware of a day when no soul can benefit another soul, nor will any intercession be accepted on its behalf, nor will any ransom be accepted from it; nor will they be helped. [48] When We rescued you from Pharaoh's people, who subjected you to malicious punishment, slaughtering your sons and sparing only your women, it was a great trial from your Lord.[34 (49)] When We divided the sea for you, and rescued you and drowned Pharaoh's people as you watched, [50] when We appointed for Moses (Musa) forty nights, then you chose to worship the calf in his absence, and were unjust.[35 (51)] Afterwards, We pardoned you so that you might give thanks.[36 (52)]

We gave Moses the Book and (the *furqaan*) a standard[37] by which We judge right from wrong, so that you might be guided. [53] Then Moses told his people, "My people, you have sinned against yourselves by worshipping the calf, so repent[38] to your Creator and then kill yourself.[39] That would be better for you in

• • •

28 The Qur'an.

29 The Torah

30 Romans 2:3 Do you imagine, whoever you are, that when you judge those who do such things and yet do them yourself, you will escape the judgment of God?

31 Romans 14:12, "So then, each of us will be accountable to God."

32 God preferred them by sending them prophets and revelation, but they often disobeyed. See Qur'an 3:112

33Or, "the worlds."

34 Exodus 14:31 Israel saw the great work that the Lord did against the Egyptians. So the people feared the Lord and believed in the Lord and in his servant Moses.

35 Exodus 31-33, So Moses returned to the Lord and said, "Alas, this people has sinned a great sin; they have made for themselves gods of gold. 32 But now, if you will only forgive their sin—but if not, blot me out of the book that you have written." 33 But the Lord said to Moses, "Whoever has sinned against me I will blot out of my book."

36 Revelation 11:17 We give you thanks, Lord God Almighty, who are and who were, for you have taken your great power and begun to reign. Psalm 136:26 O give thanks to the God of heaven, for his steadfast love endures forever.

37 The Arabic word *furqaan*, here translated as "standard," comes from the root faraqa, "to differ," "to distinguish," and may refer to the Ten Commandments. In any case, it is something given to Moses and then to Muhammad.

38 Ezekiel 14:6, "Therefore say to the house of Israel, Thus says the Lord God: Repent and turn away from your idols; and turn away your faces from all your abominations."

39 Exodus 32:27-29 "27He said to them, "Thus says the Lord, the God of Israel, 'Put your sword on your side, each of you! Go back and forth from gate to gate throughout the camp, and each of you kill your bother, your friend, and your neighbor.'" 28 The sons of Levi did as Moses commanded, and about three thousand of the people fell that day. 29 Moses said, "Today you have ordained yourselves for the service of the Lord, each one at the cost of a son or a brother, and so have brought a blessing on yourselves this day."

your Creator's sight. Then He turned to you, accepting your repentance. He is always forgiving,[40] the Mercy Giver. (54) Then you said, "Moses, we will not believe you until we see God clearly." Thunderbolts overtook you as you watched. (55) Then We resurrected you after your death, so that you might give thanks.[41] (56) and We provided shade for you with clouds and sent manna and quail down to you (saying,) "Eat of the good things We have provided you."[42] They did not cheat us, but they cheated themselves. (57) And when We said, "Enter this village and eat freely whatever you want. But enter the door humbly, and say, 'Relieve[43] us from the burden of our sins.' We will forgive your sins and increase the rewards of those who do good."[44] (58) Those who were unjust substituted words other than those given to them, so We sent down a plague from heaven on the unjust for their disobedience.[45] (59)

When Moses prayed for water for his people, We said, "Strike the rock with your staff," and twelve springs broke forth from it.[46] All people knew their drinking place. Eat and drink from God's provision, and do not act unjustly on earth by spreading corruption. (60) When you said, "Moses, we will not put up with just one kind of food. Pray to your Lord for us. Let Him bring us herbs, cucumbers, garlic, lentils, and onions that grow from the earth for us."[47] He said, "Will you trade what is good for what is less? Go down to Egypt.[48] You can have all that you ask." Humiliation and misery struck them, and they incurred the wrath of God because they persistently rejected His messages and killed prophets[49] contrary to all that is right. They were transgressors. (61) Truly those Believers in this message, as well as the Jews,[50] the Christians,[51] and the

· · ·

---

[40] Daniel 9:9, "To the Lord our God belong mercy and forgiveness, for we have rebelled against him."

[41] "After your death" This is a sign from God to the people of Israel that He is the only one who gives or takes life even if some of them refuse to kill themselves, God already made them to Die.

[42] Psalm 105:40 They asked, and He brought quail, and gave them food from heaven in abundance."

[43] Or, humiliation or abasement or alleviation

[44] Isaiah 1:18 Come now, let us argue it out, says the Lord: though your sins are like scarlet, they shall be like snow; though they are red like crimson, they shall become like wool.

[45] Or, "immorality," "transgression."

[46] Exodus 17:6. I will be standing there in front of you on the rock at Horeb. Strike the rock, and water will come out of it, so that the people may drink.' Moses did so, in the sight of the elders of Israel.

[47] Numbers 11:1, 5, 6 Now when the people complained in the hearing of the Lord about their misfortunes, [5] We remember the fish we used to eat in Egypt for nothing, the cucumbers, the melons, the leeks, the onions, and the garlic; [6] but now our strength is dried up, and there is nothing at all but this manna to look at."

[48] Numbers 14:3 "Why is the Lord bringing us into this land, to fall by the sword? Our wives and our little ones will become booty; would it not be better for us to go back to Egypt?"

[49] Matthew 23:37 "Jerusalem, Jerusalem, the city that kills the prophets and stones those who are sent to it! How often have I desired to gather your children together as a hen gathers her brood under her wings, and you were not willing!"

[50] Or those who repented and turned back to the truth. This refers to the Jews, probably when they repented after worshiping the golden calf Idol (Surahs 2:54, 92, 7:138, 148-150,).

[51] The word Christians (in Arabic *Maseheein*) is never mentioned in the Qur'an. Instead, the Qur'an mentions the word /Nasara/ and it is historically equated by Muslim commentators to Christians but its origins are not clear. Some have suggested that the word is derived from Nazareth, the town where Jesus was brought up, as it is implied in the Gospel, Matthew 2:23, Acts 24:5. Others believe that it is because the Arabic word /ansaar/ (helpers/supporters) (root: nasr) refers to the followers of Jesus who are called supporters of God in Qur'an (Surah 61:14, 3:52).

Sabeans,[52] whoever believes in God and in the Last Day and does righteous deeds will have their reward from their Lord, and will not have fear, nor will they grieve.[53 (62)]

When We made a covenant with you and raised the mountain over you, (We said), "Hold fast to what We give you, and remember what is in it, so that you may be mindful of God. [(63)] Even after that you turned away. If not for the grace and mercy of God towards you, you would have ended up being lost. [(64)] You know those of you who profane the Sabbath,[54] so We told them, "Be despicable apes." [(65)] We made them a warning for their time and for all times to come and a sermon for those that are mindful of God. [(66)]

When Moses told his people, "God commands you to sacrifice a cow,"[55] they said, "Are you making fun of us?" Moses answered, "God forbid that I should be so foolish." [(67)] They said, "Pray to your Lord for us that He would clarify for us which kind." He said, "He says that it is a heifer,[56] neither old, nor virgin, but middle-aged, so do as you are told. [(68)] They said, "Pray to your Lord for us to clarify to us what color she should be." Moses said, "He says it is a yellow heifer, bright yellow-colored, pleasing to look at." [(69)] They said, "Pray to your Lord for us, to clarify which one she is. The heifers look alike to us. If God wills, we will be guided." [(70)]. Moses said, "He says it is a cow never yoked[57] to plow the ground, or to water the furrows, whole and without blemish." They said, "Now you have spoken the truth." They almost missed the opportunity to sacrifice it. [(71)] When you (Israelites) killed a person and fought about it, God brought to light what you hid. [(72)] So We said, "Strike the body with parts of the cow; in this way, God brings life from death and shows you his signs, so you might comprehend." [(73)] Then, after that, your hearts were hardened. They were as hard as stone or harder. For there are rocks from which streams gush forth, and some from which water flows when they split open, and others which fall down in awe of God. He is not unaware of what you do. [(74)]

Do you really hope that they will be true to you when some of them heard God's words, comprehended it and then knowingly altered it? [(75)] When they meet believers, they say, "We believe," and when they are alone by themselves, they say, "Do you tell them what God has disclosed to you so they dispute with you about it with your Lord?" Have you no sense? [(76)] Do they not know that God knows what they conceal and what they reveal? [(77)]

Some of them are illiterate, and know only a little of the Book. They are guessing. [(78)] How terrible it is to those who write the Book with their hands and

• • •

[52] Sabeans are mentioned only three times in the Qur'an (here, 5:69 and 22:17,). They may have been followers of John the Baptizer, as some by that name still exist in Iraq today, a tribe of Christians in northern Arabia who were known for praying seven times a day, or the Mandeans. Whoever they are, they seem to have been monotheists.

[53] This verse promises all monotheists—Jews, Christians and Sabeans as well as Muslims—eternal comfort if they believe in God and the Last Day, and do good deeds.

[54] Ezekiel 20:21 "But the children rebelled against Me; they did not follow my statutes, and were not careful to observe my ordinances, by whose observances everyone shall live; they profaned my Sabbaths. Then I thought I would pour out my wrath and spend my anger against them in the wilderness."

[55] Numbers 19:2, "This is a statute of the law that the Lord has commanded: Tell the Israelites to bring you a red heifer without defect, in which there is no blemish and on which no yoke has been laid."

[56] Numbers 19:2. (Note that Numb. 19:2 does not specify an age.)

[57] Deuteronomy 21:3 "The elders of the town nearest the body shall take a heifer that has never been worked, one that has not pulled in the yoke;"

then say, "This is from God," to sell it for a little money.[58] How terrible it is for them for what their hands have written, and how terrible for them what they have earned. [79] They said, "we will spend only a few days in Hell."[59] Have you made a covenant with God that He will not break? Or do you say what you do not know about God? [80] Truly, those who do evil and are caught in their sins will be in Hell eternally. [81] Those who believe and do good deeds will go to Heaven, where they will remain eternally. [82]

We made a covenant with the Children of Israel[60]: worship God alone, be good to parents, relatives, orphans and the poor. Speak nicely to people, perform prayers and pay the purifying alms.[61] Then, all but a few of you turned away as you weren't interested. [83] We took your pledge; you do not shed one another's blood or drive one another from your homelands. Then you acknowledged it and witnessed it. [84] (Nevertheless), here you are, you kill one another and expel some of your own people from their homeland. You assist each other against your own in sin and hostility. But when they come to you as captives, you ransom them, though it is forbidden for you to expel them. Do you believe in part of the Book but not in the rest? What is the repayment for those of you who do that but humiliation in this world? and on the day of resurrection they will be sent to the severest punishment.[62] God is aware of what you do.[63] [85] The punishment of those who trade this life for the hereafter will not be lightened, and they will not be saved. [86]

We gave Moses the Book and he was followed by other messengers and (We) gave Jesus (Isa), the son of Mary, all evidence of the truth, and strengthened him with the Holy Spirit. Whenever a messenger comes to you with a message you do not like, you become arrogant calling some of them liars, and murdering some of them. [87] They said, "Our hearts are hardened." God has rejected them in their unbelief. How little they believe! [88] And when a Book came to them from God confirming what they have,[64] while they were themselves asking for help against the unbelievers, they did not believe the Book. Although they recognized (the truth), they denied it. God rejects the unbelievers. [89] They sell their souls for nothing of value, denying what God has revealed, out of resentment that God reveals his grace to whom he will of his worshipers. They angered God more and more. The unbelievers will have disgraceful punishment.[65] [90] If they are told, "Believe in what God has revealed," they say, "We believe in what was revealed to us." They do not believe in what came afterward, though It is the truth confirming what they have already received. Say, "Why then do you murder

• • •

[58] God's warning against those scholars who are responsible for corrupting the text of the Bible and misleading their followers to make money.

[59] This reference is particularly for Jews who believe that the Children of Israel will suffer only very limited punishment for their sins in the Day of Judgment and will be quickly reprieved by virtue of their belonging to "the chosen people," a belief which the Qur'an rejects.

[60] Deuteronomy 6:25 If we diligently observe this entire commandment before the Lord our God, as he has commanded us, we will be in the right."

[61] The word zakat before Islam meant charity.

[62] Matthew 25:46 "And these will go away into eternal punishment, but the righteous into eternal life."

[63] Romans 11:33 O the depth of the riches and wisdom and knowledge of God! How unsearchable are his judgments and how inscrutable his ways!

[64] The Qur'an confirms the truth in the book that existed in the days of Muhammad.

[65] Matthew 25:41 "Then He will also say to those at his left hand, 'You that are accursed, depart from me into the eternal fire prepared for the devil and his angels;"

God's prophets beforehand, if you are believers?"[66] [(91)] Moses came to you with clear signs, but then when he was away you chose to worship the calf[67] and were unjust. [(92)]

And when We made a covenant with you and raised the mountain[68] above you, saying, "Cling firmly to what we bring you and listen," they said, "We listened and disobeyed." Then, in their unbelief, their hearts were filled with the (worship of the) calf. Say, "It is dreadful what your faith commands you to do, if you are in fact believers." [(93)] Say, "If you have a clear and exclusive title to Heaven, you should long for death, if you are telling the truth." [(94)] They will not wish for it at all because of what their hands have done. God knows the unjust. [(95)] You will discover that they cling to life even more than the idol-worshippers. Any of them would desire to live a thousand years, but none will avoid punishment by living a long time. God sees what they do. [(96)]

Say, "Those that are enemies to Gabriel should know that he has brought it (the Qur'an) down to your heart by God's permission, confirming what is already revealed and a guidance and good news to believers. [(97)] For anyone who is an enemy of God, His angels, His Messengers, Gabriel and Michael, God is the enemy of the unbelievers.[69] [(98)]

We have revealed clear verses and miracles to you. Only those who defy God would not believe them. [(99)] Whenever they make a covenant, some of them violate it. Most of them do not believe. [(100)]

And when a messenger from God comes to them confirming what they have, some recipients of the Book throw God's Book behind their backs as if they knew nothing of it.[70] [(101)] Instead they followed what the evil ones used to practice during Solomon's reign. Not that Solomon himself was one who denied the truth; it was the evil ones who denied the truth. They taught people witchcraft and what was revealed in Babylon to the two angels Harut and Marut. Although these two never taught it to anyone without first declaring, "We are but a temptation

• • •

[66] Luke 11:48-50 "So you are witnesses and approve the deeds of your ancestors; for they killed them, and you build their tombs. [49]"Therefore also the wisdom of God said, 'I will send to them prophets and apostles, some of whom they will kill and persecute,' [50] so that this generation may be charged with the blood of all the prophets shed since the foundation of the world,"

[67] Exodus 32:1-4 , "When the people saw that Moses delayed to come down from the mountain, the people gathered around Aaron and said to him, 'Come, make gods for us, who shall go before us; as for this Moses, the man who brought us up out of the land of Egypt, we do not know what has become of him.' [2]Aaron said to them, 'Take off the gold rings that are on the ears of your wives, your sons, and your daughters, and bring them to me.' [3]So all the people took off the gold rings from their ears, and brought them to Aaron. [4]He took the gold from them, formed it in a mold, and cast an image of a calf; and they said, 'These are your gods, O Israel, who brought you up out of the land of Egypt!'

[68] Mount Sinai

[69] According to several authentic Traditions, some of the learned men from among the Jews of Medina described Gabriel as "the enemy of the Jews", and this for three reasons: firstly, all the prophecies of the misfortune which was to befall the Jews in the course of their early history were said to have been transmitted to them by Gabriel, who thus became in their eyes a "harbinger of evil" (in contrast to the angel Michael, whom they regarded as a bearer of happy predictions and, therefore, as their "friend"); secondly, because the Qur'an states repeatedly that it was Gabriel who conveyed its message to Muhammad, whereas the Jews were of the opinion that only a descendant of Israel could legitimately claim divine revelation; and, thirdly, because the Qur'an - revealed through Gabriel - abounds in criticism of certain Jewish beliefs and attitudes and describes them as opposed to the genuine message of Moses.

[70] The Qur'an is probably referring here to Deuteronomy 18:15-18, the prophecies relating to the coming of the Arabian Prophet, a prophet from among their brethren, but the Jews rejected them.

to evil: do not deny (God's) truth." From these two, they learned what can separate a man from his wife, although they harm no one with it except by God's permission. They learned what harmed them, not what benefited them, knowing full well that whoever acquired (this knowledge) would have no share in the Hereafter. Surely, evil is the (price) for which they sold their souls, if only they realized that. [102] If they had believed and been God conscious, God would have rewarded them well, if they only knew it. [103]

Believers, do not say, "Listen to us" but rather say "Have patience and listen to us." Those who reject the truth will have painful punishment.[71] [104] Neither those people of the Book who deny the truth, nor the idol worshippers would like anything good to come down to you from your Lord. But God assigns his mercy to whom he wills.[72] God has boundless grace. [105] Any verse (from the previous Book) We cause to be abrogated or forgotten We will replace with one like it or better. Do you not know that God has power over all things[73]? [106] Do you not know that God owns the Kingdom of the heavens and the earth? Besides God, you have no helper or protector.[74] [107] Or do you want to ask your Messenger as Moses was asked previously? Whoever exchanges faith for unbelief has strayed from the straight path. [108] Even after truth became clear to them, many of the people of the Book, out of their selfish envy, wish they could turn you back to unbelief after you became believers. So forgive and forbear until God makes His will clear. God has power over all things.[75] [109]

Perform the prayers and give the purifying alms.[76] Whatever good you do here you will find later with God. God discerns what you do. [110]

They said, "Only Jews and Christians[77] will enter heaven." That is their wishful thinking. Say, "Present your proof if you are telling the truth." [111] Rather, whoever turns his face in submission towards God [78] while acting generously have their reward from their Lord, and will neither fear nor grieve.[79] [112] The Jews

• • •

[71] Matthew 25:41 Then he will say to those at his left hand, "You that are accursed, depart from me into the eternal fire prepared for the devil and his angels;

[72] Romans 9:15,18 "For he says to Moses, 'I will have mercy on whom I have mercy, and I will have compassion on whom I have compassion.' [18] So then he has mercy on whomsoever he chooses, and he hardens the heart of whomsoever he chooses".

[73] Mark 10:27 "Jesus looked at them and said, "For mortals it is impossible, but not for God; for God all things are possible."

[74] Hosea 13:4 "Yet I have been the Lord your God ever since the land of Egypt; you know no God but me, and besides me there is no savior".

[75] Job 42:2 "'I know that you can do all things, and that no purpose of yours can be thwarted."

[76] the word zakat here probably means charity.

[77] The word Christians (in Arabic *Maseheein)* is never mentioned in the Qur'an. Instead the Qur'an mentions the word /nasara/ and it is historically equated by Muslim commentators to Christians but its origins are not clear. Some have suggested that the word is derived from Nazareth, the town where Jesus was brought up, as it is implied in the Gospel, (Matthew 2:23, Acts 24:5). Others believe that it is because the Arabic word /ansaar/ (helpers/supporters) (root: nasr) refers to the followers of Jesus who are called supporters of God in the Qur'an (61:14, 3:52).

[78] Lit., "who submit his face to God". Since the face of a person is the most expressive part of his body, it is used in classical Arabic to denote one's whole personality, or whole being. This expression, repeated in the Qur'an several times, provides a perfect definition of Islam, which derived from the root-verb aslama, "he submit himself" - means "self-submit (to God)"; and it is in this sense that the terms islam and muslim are used throughout the Qur'an.

[79] According to the Qur'an, salvation is not reserved for any particular "religion", but is open to everyone who consciously realizes the oneness of God, surrenders himself to His will and, by living righteously, gives practical evidence to this spiritual attitude.

said, "Christians are without valid grounds," and the Christians said, "The Jews are without valid grounds," while they chant the Book. The ignorant speak similarly. God will judge between them on the day of resurrection concerning their differences. [80] [(113)]

Who could be more unjust than the one who forbids God's name to be mentioned in his places of worship and then tries to get them destroyed? They should be afraid to enter them. They will have shame in this world and terrible punishment[81] in the Hereafter. [(114)] To God belong the East and the West, and His face is wherever you turn. God is Infinite, All-knowing.[82] [(115)]

They said, "God has taken a son." May He be exalted in His glory. All things in the heavens and on the earth belong to Him.[83] All things devoutly obey His will, [(116)] the Originator of the heavens and the earth[84]. If He decrees something, he simply says to it, "Be,"[85] and It is. [(117)] and the ignorant said, "If only God would speak to us or give us a sign." Those before them spoke similarly.[86] Their hearts are similar. We have made signs clear to people who are certain. [(118)] We have sent you with the Truth as a bearer of good news and a warner. You will not be held accountable for those who are going to Hell. [(119)] The Jews and Christians will not be pleased with you until you follow their ways. Say, "God's guidance is the guidance." If you follow their whims, after having received knowledge, you will not have anyone to protect you from God or to help you. [(120)] Those to whom We gave the Book and read it the way it should be read, believe in it, and whoever denies It is a doomed. [(121)]

O Children of Israel, remember my grace which I gave you and that I preferred you above all People. [(122)] And beware of a day when no soul stands in for another. Ransom will not be accepted, nor will intercession benefit any of them, nor will any be helped. [(123)]

. . .

---

[80] In other words, "God will confirm the truth of what was true (in their respective beliefs) and show the falseness of what was false (therein)" (Muhammad 'Abduh in Manar I, 428). The Qur'an maintains throughout that there is a substantial element of truth in all faiths based on divine revelation, and that their subsequent divergences are the result of "wishful beliefs" [(111)] and of a gradual corruption of the original teachings. (See also Surah 22: 67-69.)

[81] Matthew 25:41 Then he will say to those at his left hand, "You that are accursed, depart from me into the eternal fire prepared for the devil and his angels;

[82] Psalm 139:4-6 Even before there is a word on my tongue, O Lord, You know it completely. [5]You hem me in, behind and before, and lay your hand upon me. [6]Such knowledge is too wonderful for me; It is so high, I cannot attain to it."

[83] Psalm 89:11, The heavens are Yours, the earth also is Yours; The world and all that is in it—you have founded them." Deuteronomy 10:14, "Although heaven and the heaven of heavens belong to the Lord your God, the earth with all that is in it,"

[84] Genesis 1:1, "In the beginning when God created the heavens and the earth," Isaiah 42:5, "Thus says God, the Lord, who created the heavens and stretched them out, who spread out the earth and what comes from it, who gives breath to the people upon it and spirit to those who walk in it: Isaiah 45:18, "For thus says the Lord, who created the heavens (he is God!), who formed the earth and made it (he established it; he did not create it a chaos; he formed it to be inhabited!): I am the Lord, and there is no other."

[85] Psalm 33: 9 For he spoke, and it came to be; he commanded, and it stood firm.

[86] Luke 11:16 "Others, to test him, kept demanding from him a sign from heaven."

When God tested Abram with certain words and he fulfilled them, God said, "I will make you a leader of men." He said, "And (what about) my seed?"[87] He said, "My covenant does not extend to the unjust." [124]

We made the House[88] a destination and a sanctuary for people, and made the place where Abram stood a place of prayer. We commanded Abram[89] and Ishmael to purify My House for those who walk around it, the devout and those who kneel and bow down.[90] [125] When Abram said, "Lord, make this town safe.[91] Provide fruit for its inhabitants who believe in God and the last day." He said, "I will let them who deny the truth have pleasure for a short time, then I will force them into the punishment of Hell,[92] a dreadful destiny." [126]

When Abram and Ishmael constructed the foundations of the sanctuary,[93] (they prayed), "May Our Lord, accept this work from us. You hear all and know all. [127] Our Lord make us submit ourselves to you, and make from of our descendants a nation submissive to You. Show us how to properly worship You and accept our repentance, for You are the one who always accept our repentance and are the Merciful-to-all[94] [128] May Our Lord send them a messenger from among them who recites your revelations, teaching them the Book and Wisdom, and purify them. You are the Almighty,[95] the Wise.[96] [129]

Who but a fool would abandon Abram's faith? We have chosen him in this world, and in the hereafter; he is righteous.[130] When his Lord told him, "Submit," he said, "I have submitted to the Lord of the worlds."[97] [131] Abram commanded his sons to do the same as did Jacob, "Sons, your God is One, He has chosen this faith for you, so do not die unless you have submitted to Him."[132]

Or were you witnesses when Jacob was on his deathbed,[98] when he asked his sons, "What will you worship after I die?" They said, "We will worship your God

• • •

[87] Genesis 15:2 "But Abram said, 'O Lord GOD, what will you give me, for I continue childless, and the heir of my house is Eliezer of Damascus?"

[88] "al bayt" lit. "the House (of Worship)"'- mentioned here is the Ka'ba in Mecca, its foundation goes back by Arab tradition to Adam. The Qur'an teaches that it has been built by Abraham and his son Ishmael as the first temple ever dedicated to the One God. Psalm 84:7 As they pass through the Valley of Baca, they make it a place of springs; the autumn rains also cover it with pools.

[89] Ibid

[90] Four rites are here enumerated 1. who walk around the Ka'bah is the seven-fold circumambulation (tawaf) of the Ka'bah 2. The Devout retiring to the place as a spiritual retreat, for contemplation & prayer (I'tikaf) 3. those who kneel the posture of bending the back in prayer (Ruku') 4. bow down prostrating oneself to the ground in prayer (sujud). The cleanliness & purity is required for the sake of the devotes who undertake these rites.

[91] Hebrews 11:10 "For he looked forward to the city that has foundations, whose architect and builder is God."

[92] 2 Thessalonians 1:9 These will suffer the punishment of eternal destruction, separated from the presence of the Lord and from the glory of his might,

[93] The Ka'ba and the Holy Sanctuary around it.

[94] Psalm 116:5 "Gracious is the Lord, and righteous; our God is merciful.", Psalm 103:8, "The Lord is merciful and gracious, slow to anger and abounding in steadfast love."

[95] Job 9:4, "He is wise in heart, and mighty in strength—who has resisted him, and succeeded? —"

[96] Proverbs 2:6 "For the Lord gives wisdom; from his mouth come knowledge and understanding;"

[97] Psalm 47:2 "For the Lord, the Most High, is awesome, a great King over all the earth."

[98] The death –bed scene is described in the Jewish tradition in Genesis 49, Hebrews 11:21 By faith Jacob, when dying, blessed each of the sons of Joseph, "bowing in worship over the top of his staff."

and the God of your fathers Abram[99] and Ishmael and Isaac. (He is) one God and We have submitted to Him." [133] That nation has passed away. They have what they deserve, and you have what you deserve. You will not be questioned about what they did. [134]

They said, "Become Jews or Christians, and you will be guided." Say, rather, " We will follow the faith of Abram, who turned away from all that is false,[100] and was not one who ascribed divinity to anything other than God." [135] Say,[101] (Prophet) "We believe in God and what was revealed to us and what was revealed to Abram, Ishmael, Isaac, Jacob, and the tribes, what was given to Moses and Jesus, and what was given to the prophets from their Lord. We do not distinguish between any of them, and we are submitted to Him." [136] If they believe as you believe, they are guided, but if they turn away, they are in dispute. God will protect you from them, and He hears all and knows all.[102] [137] This is God's identifying color, and who is better than God at giving us a color of identity? And it is He Whom we worship. [138]

Say, "Do you argue with us about God, when He is our Lord and your Lord? We have our works and you have your works, and we are sincere towards him. [139] Or do you say that Abram, Ishmael, Isaac, Jacob, and the tribes were Jews or Christians?" Say, "Do you know more than God does?" And who is more wicked than the one who conceals a testimony with him from God? God is never unaware of what you do." [140] That nation has passed away. It has received what it deserves, and you will receive what you deserve. You are not accountable for what they did.[103] [141]

Foolish people will say, "What turned them away from their former prayer direction?"[104] Say, "East and West belong to God. He guides whoever wants to be guided to a straight path."[105] [142] We have made you a moderate nation,[106] so you may bear witness to humanity and the messenger may bear witness to you.[107] We made your former prayer direction only so that we could know who

• • •

[99] In classical Arabic, as in ancient Hebrew usage, the term ab ("father who raises") was applied not only to the direct male parent but also to grandfathers, uncles as even more distant ancestors, as well as direct ascendants

[100] Hanif is derived from the verb "Hanafa", lit. "he inclined towards a right state or tendency". in pre-Islamic times, this term had a definitely monotheistic connotation, and was used to describe a man who turned away from sin and worldliness and from all dubious beliefs, especially idol-worship.

[101] The command "say" in Arabic can be either singular or plural. When at the beginning of the sentence as a singular command, is usually a command to Prophet Muhammad from God. It is clear in Arabic but we opted to add Prophet in brackets to make it clear.

[102] 1 John 3:20 "whenever our hearts condemn us; for God is greater than our hearts, and he knows everything"

[103] The Qur'an stresses that each person is responsible for his/her own deeds. In that sense a child is not responsible for his father's sins.

[104] The change of the prayer direction for Muslims from Jerusalem to the Ka'bah in Mecca the first temple historically dedicated to the One God. It was built around a 1000 years before the Temple in Jerusalem. See http://bethelbooks.com/times/3/

[105] Proverbs 3:6, In all your ways acknowledge him, and he will make straight your paths.

[106] moderate community a community that avoids extremes in either sides & keeps an equitable balance. It should be realistic in its appreciation of man's nature and capabilities, rejecting both over indulgence and exaggerated asceticism.

[107] "your way of life is to be an example to all mankind, just as the messenger is an example to you" (Safi Kaskas) Hebrews 13:7 "Remember your leaders, those who spoke the word of God to you; consider the outcome of their way of life, and imitate their faith."

would follow the messenger and who would turn away from him. This change was too much to bear except for those whom God has guided. God will surely not lose sight of your faith. God is Compassionate and Merciful-to-all people. [143]
We have seen you turning your face toward the heavens so We will certainly turn a prayer direction for you that will please you. So turn your face toward the Sacred Sanctuary in Mecca, and wherever you are, turn your faces toward it. Those who were given the Book know that it is the truth from their Lord. God is aware of what they do. [144] If you brought every revelation to those who were given the Book, they would not follow your prayer direction, and you will not follow their prayer direction, and some of them do not follow each other's' prayer direction. If you follow their desires after knowledge has come to you, you will be unjust. [145] Those to whom we gave the Book know it as they know their children,[108] but a group of them knowingly hide the truth. [146] This is the truth from your Lord, so do not doubt. [147] To every community there is a direction to turn to, so compete to do good deeds wherever you may be. God will bring you all. God has power over all things.[109] [148]

Wherever you go, turn your face toward the Sacred Sanctuary. This is the truth from your Lord. God is aware of what you do. [149] Wherever you go, turn your face toward the Sacred Sanctuary, and wherever you all are, turn your faces toward it, so that people should have no argument against you. Except for the unjust among them, do not fear them, but fear Me,[110] and I will complete my grace to you, so that you might be guided.[111] [150] For this We sent one of your own people as a messenger reciting our revelations to you, purifying you, teaching you the Book and Wisdom, and teaching you what you didn't know. [151] So remember Me, and I will remember you. Thank Me and do not be ungrateful to Me.[112] [152]

Believers, seek help through patience and prayers. God helps those who endure in hard times."[113] [153] Do not say that those killed in God's path are dead; they are alive, though you do not realize it. [154] We will certainly send you trials of fear, hunger, and the loss of wealth, people and crops, so give good news to the steadfast, [155] who say when disaster strikes them, "We belong to God and will return to Him."[114] [156] It is they who have their Lord's grace and mercy, and they are guided. [157]

· · ·

---

[108] Or sons

[109] 2 Chronicles 20:6 "and said: "O Lord, God of our ancestors, are you not the God in heaven? Do you not rule over all the kingdoms of the nations.? In your hand are power and might, so that no one is able to withstand you."

[110] Matthew 10:28 "Do not fear those who kill the body but cannot kill the soul. Rather fear him who can destroy both soul and body in hell."

[111] Psalm 27:1 "The Lord is my light and my salvation; whom shall I fear? The Lord is the stronghold of my life; of whom shall I be afraid?"

[112] Psalm 50:23 "Those who bring thanksgiving as their sacrifice honor me; to those who go the right way I will show the salvation of God."

[113] Romans 12:12 "Rejoice in hope, be patient in suffering, preserve in prayer."

[114] Romans 14:12, "So then, each of us will be accountable to God."

Safa and Marwa[115] are among the rites of God. Whoever makes the Pilgrimage to the House, or performs the Umrah must stride between them[116]. Regarding those who voluntarily do good, God is grateful and All-knowing. [158] Those who hide evidence of the truth and the guidance revealed after We made it clear to the people in the Book, those God will reject, and they will be rejected by others, [159] except for those who repent and make amends and declare the truth. I will accept their repentance. I am the Ever-Forgiving, the Merciful-to-all. [160] God will reject from His mercy those who denied the truth, who died in their unbelief, and they will be cursed by God, angels and all people. [161] They will be there (in Hell) forever, and their punishment will not be lightened, nor will they be relieved. [162] Your God is one God.[117] There is no God but Him,[118] the Merciful-to-all, the Mercy Giver.[119] [163] The creation of the heavens and the earth,[120] the difference of night and day, the ships that sail the seas to benefit people, the rain God sends down to give life to a lifeless earth and all kinds of creatures that He scattered over it, the directing of the winds and clouds that run a course between heaven and earth, are all signs to people who comprehend[121]. [164] Still some people equate others to God, and they love them as only God should be loved. Believers, love God more than anything. If the unjust could only see, and they will see when suffering becomes their destiny that all power is God's[122] and that God is severe in punishment. [165] When those who were followed disown their followers and all see punishment and are at their wit's end, [166] the followers will say, "If only we had another chance, we would disown them just as they have disowned us." Thus God will make them bitterly regret their works. They will not leave Hell. [167]

People, eat of what is permitted and delicious on earth. Do not follow Satan's steps; he is clearly your enemy. [168] He commands you to do evil and to behave shamelessly, and to say things about God you do not know. [169] If they are told, "Follow what God has revealed," they say, "Rather We will follow what we found our fathers doing." even though their fathers did not understand anything and were not guided. [170] Unbelievers are like ones who call out to that which hears nothing more than a scream and a cry. They are deaf, dumb, and blind; they do not comprehend. [171] Believers, eat the good things we provided you, and thank

• • •

[115] Ishmael was thirsty and crying. His mother Hagar was runing between Safa and Marwa looking for water. "God heard the boy crying, and the angel of God called to Hagar from heaven and said to her, "What is the matter, Hagar? Do not be afraid; God has heard the boy crying as he lies there." (Genesis 21:17-19)

[116] In celebration of God's mercy on Hagar and her son Ishmael, when he made water flow from the well of Zamzam few yards east of the Qua'ba. Millions of pilgrims visit the well each year while performing the Hajj or Umrah pilgrimages, in order to drink its water.

[117] Mark 12:29, Jesus answered, 'The first is, "Hear, O Israel: the Lord our God, the Lord is one;

[118] Exodus 20:3 "you shall have no other gods before me."

[119] Isaiah 63:9 "in all their distress. It was no messenger or angel but his presence that saved them; in his love and his pity he redeemed them; he lifted them up and carried them all the days of old."

[120] Genesis 1:1, "In the beginning when God created the heavens and the earth." Isaiah 42:5, "Thus says God, the Lord, who created the heavens and stretched them out, who spread out the earth and what comes from it, who gives breath to the people upon it and spirit to those who walk in it." Isaiah 45:18 "For thus says the Lord, who created the heavens (he is God!), who formed the earth and made it (he established it; he did not create it a chaos, he formed it to be inhabited!): I am the Lord, and there is no other."

[121] John 11:40 "Jesus said to her, "Did I not tell you that if you believed, you would see the glory of God?"

[122] Psalm 29:4, "The voice of the Lord is powerful, The voice of the Lord is full of majesty."

God, if you truly worship Him. [172] He has forbidden you to eat dead animals, blood, pork, and meat offered in any name other than God.[123] If someone is forced to do so unwillingly and unintentionally, he does not sin. God is forgiving and Merciful-to-all.[124] [173]

Those who hide part of what God has revealed in the Book and barter it away for a small price will consume nothing in their bellies except fire, and God will neither speak to them on the Day of Resurrection nor purify them. They will have painful punishment.[125] [174] It is they who accept misguidance in exchange for guidance, and punishment in exchange for forgiveness. Yet they have no tolerance for the Fire! [175] That is because God revealed the Book in truth, and those who differed about the Book are deeply divided. [176]

Righteousness is not a matter of turning your faces eastward or westward. Rather, righteousness is believing in God and the Last Day and the angels and the Book and the prophets; giving money for the love of Him to relatives, orphans, the poor, stranded travelers, beggars, and to free slaves[126]; performing prayers, paying the purifying alms; keeping promises, and enduring misery and hard times in time of threat. It is they who have proved themselves true, and it is they who are mindful of God. [177]

Believers, just retribution is prescribed in the case of those killed: a free person for a free person, a slave for a slave, a female for a female. But If the aggrieved brother pardons the guilty person, then grant any reasonable demand and pay with kindness. This is a relief and mercy from your Lord. However, if anyone then goes beyond these limits he will have painful punishment.[127] [178] You who have understanding, there is life for you (by practicing) just retribution, so that you may continue to be mindful of God. [179] If any of you is close to death and leaves possessions, it is an obligation that he includes fairly his parents and relatives in a will. This is a duty for those who are mindful of God. [180] But whoever changes the terms after hearing it is a sin on the one who changes it. God hears all [128] and knows all.[129] [181] He who is concerned that the person leaving a will is deviating from fairness or sinning and then reconciles them, he does not sin. God is forgiving [130] and Merciful-to-all.[131] [182]

• • •

[123] Acts 15:29, "that you abstain from what has been sacrificed to idols and from blood and from what is strangled and from fornication. If you keep yourselves from these, you will do well. Farewell.", Leviticus 11:7,39, "The pig, for even though it has divided hoofs and is cloven-footed, it does not chew the cud; it is unclean for you. [39]"If an animal of which you may eat dies, anyone who touches its carcass shall be unclean until the evening."

[124] Psalm 57:1-2 Be merciful to me, O God, be merciful to me, for in you my soul takes refuge; in the shadow of your wings I will take refuge, until the destroying storms pass by. 2 I cry to God Most High, to God who fulfills his purpose for me.

[125] Matthew 25:41 Then he will say to those at his left hand, "You that are accursed, depart from me into the eternal fire prepared for the devil and his angels;

[126] Mark 10:21 Looking at the man, Jesus felt genuine love for him. "There is still one thing you haven't done," he told him. "Go and sell all your possessions and give the money to the poor, and you will have treasure in heaven. Then come, follow me."

[127] Proverbs 15:10 grievous punishment is for him who forsakes the way; he who hates reproof will die.

[128] Psalm 116:1 I love the Lord, because he has heard my voice and my supplications. see also 1 John 5:14 And this is the boldness we have in him, that if we ask anything according to his will, he will hear us.'

[129] Psalm 44:21 "would not God discover this? For he knows the secrets of the heart."

[130] Daniel 9:9. To the Lord our God belong mercy and forgiveness, for we have rebelled against him,

[131] Psalm 145:8 The Lord is gracious and merciful; Slow to anger and abounding in steadfast love.

Believers, God commanded fasting for you just as he commanded it for those who came before you so that you might be mindful of God. [(183)] Fast for a specific number of days, and if someone is sick or traveling, then alternate days. For those who can afford a redemption should feed a poor person. If someone voluntarily does good, it is goodness for him. Fasting is good for you, if you only knew. [(184)] The month of Ramadan is when the Qur'an was revealed, giving guidance to humanity, and clear messages of guidance and a standard for distinguishing right from wrong. Whoever lives to see this month should fast. Whoever is sick or traveling should fast on alternate days. God wants it to be easy for you, not hard, so you can complete the days you missed. So praise God for his guidance to you, and give thanks.[132] [(185)] If My worshipers ask you about Me, I am near, answering the prayer of the one who prays to Me. [133] They should respond to Me and believe in Me in order to be guided.[134] [(186)]

Sex with your wives is permitted on the night of a fast. They are clothing to you and you to them.[135] God knows that you used to betray yourselves, so He turned to you and forgave you. So now, have sex with them, and seek what God has ordained for you. (You may) eat and drink until you can distinguish a white thread from a black one in the dawn, then complete the fast until night. Do not have sex with them while you are secluded in the places of worship.[136] These are God's boundaries. So don't go near them. This is how God shows people His messages so that they would be mindful of Him. [(187)] Do not abuse other people's wealth using wrong means, and do not bribe authorities in order to take possession of other people's wealth knowingly and sinfully. [(188)]

They ask you about new moons. Say, "They show times for people and for the Hajj." It is not right to enter houses from the back. Rather, righteousness is to be mindful of God and to enter houses through their front doors. Always be mindful of God,[137] so that you may succeed. [(189)] Fight in God's path[138] against those who fight you, but do not be aggressors,[139] for God does not love

• • •

[132] Psalm 34:1-3 I will bless the Lord at all times; his praise shall continually be in my mouth. [2] My soul makes its boast in the Lord; let the humble hear and be glad. 3 O magnify the Lord with me, and let us exalt his name together.

[133] Psalm 34:4-5, I sought the Lord, and he answered me, and delivered me from all my fears. [5] Look to him, and be radiant; so your faces shall never be ashamed. 50:15, "Call on me in the day of trouble; I will deliver you, and you shall glorify me.", 120:1 In my distress I cry to the Lord, that he may answer me." Matthew 7:7, "Ask, and it will be given to you; search, and you will find; knock, and the door will be opened for you."

[134] Hebrews 11:6 And without faith it is impossible to please God, for whoever would approach him must believe that he exists and that he rewards those who seek him.

[135] 1 Corinthians 7:1-4 Now concerning the matters about which you wrote: 'It is well for a man not to touch a woman.' [2]But because of cases of sexual immorality, each man should have his own wife and each woman her own husband. [3]The husband should give to his wife her conjugal rights, and likewise the wife to her husband. [4]For the wife does not have authority over her own body, but the husband does; likewise, the husband does not have authority over his own body, but the wife does.

[136] 1 Corinthian 7:5 Do not deprive one another except perhaps by agreement for a set time, to devote yourselves to prayer, and then come together again, so that Satan may not tempt you because of your lack of self-control.

[137] Psalm 7:17 I will give to the Lord the thanks due to his righteousness, and sing praise to the name of the Lord, the Most High.

[138] https://constantlyreforming.wordpress.com/every-battle-in-the-bible/

[139] The Qur'an allows self-defense but doesn't allow aggression.

aggressors. (190) (If they start a fight) kill them wherever you find them,[140] and expel them from wherever they expelled you. For oppression[141] is worse than murder. Do not fight them at the Holy Sanctuary unless they fight you in it. If they fight you, kill them. That is the reward of the unbelievers. (191) If they stop, God is forgiving [142] and Merciful-to-all. (192) Fight them until there is no more persecution and until all worship is devoted only to God. If they stop, there should be no aggression[143] except toward the unjust. (193) Fight back during the sacred month: violation of sanctity (calls for) just retribution. Whoever attacks you, attack them as you were attacked. Be mindful of God, and know that God is with those who are mindful of Him. (194) Spend your money in the path of God, and do not contribute to your own destruction, but do good. God loves those who do good. (195)

Do your Hajj[144] and the Umrah [145] for God. If you are prevented, then send what offerings for sacrifice are possible, and do not shave your heads until the offerings arrive. If one of you is sick or has a head injury, then one can be redeemed by fasting, giving the purifying alms or offering a sacrifice. When you are secure, whoever breaks one's purification between the Umrah[146] until the Hajj should offer whatever sacrifice one can; or, if one cannot, one should fast three days during the Hajj, and then seven when one returns, ten days in all. This (observance) is for those whose families are not present at the Sacred Sanctuary. Be mindful of God, and know that God is severe in punishment. (196)

The Hajj is in the prescribed months; for him who decides to perform the Hajj, there should be no vulgarity, bad behavior, or argument during the Hajj. God knows the good deeds you do, so do lots of them. And take provision for yourself. The best of all provision is being mindful of God. So be mindful of Me, you who have insights. (197) It is not wrong to seek your Lord's blessing. So when you flow down from (Mount) Arafat,[147] remember God at the sacred place. Remember Him as He guided you after you had gone astray. (198) Then surge onward with all

• • •

[140] To understand the verses 2:190-3 and those it is referring to, it is important to understand its context. Ibn Abbas, the famous companion of the Prophet and Qur'anic exegete, says that this passage was revealed in reference to the Quraysh. The Quraysh tribe had persecuted the Muslims and tortured them for thirteen years in Makkah. They had driven Muslims out of their homes, seized their properties and wealth, and fought battles against them after the Muslims sought refuge in Madinah. The Muslims were apprehensive about another attack occurring during their sacred pilgrimage when fighting was prohibited for Muslims. This is why these verses were revealed to reassure the Muslims that they would be able to defend themselves against a Qurayshi attack during pilgrimage. Such fighting never actually took place between them and Quraysh, for a peace agreement was upheld and the pilgrimage was permitted.

[141] The Arabic term used here is (Fitna) which can mean enticement, inducement etc. meaning that this situation was a reaction to oppression.

[142] Ephesians 2:4 But God, who is rich in mercy, out of the great love with which he loved us

[143] The phrase "there should be no aggression" was explained by Ibn Abbas to mean, "Do not attack women, children, elderly, or anyone who is not fighting against you," and thus harming any non-combatants is deemed a transgression against God Almighty.

[144] The Mecca pilgrimage Hajj takes place once a year, in the month of Dhu'l-Hijjah. For more details, see http://www.slideshare.net/tanveerpadder5/complete-step-by-step-guide-to-hajj-2013

[145] Umrah can be performed at any time of the year the pilgrims are required to walk seven times around the Ka'bah and seven times between As-Safa and Al-Marwah.

[146] Umrah means to perform tawaf round the Kaaba and sa'i between the hills of Al Safa and Al Marwah. See Glossary.

[147] Or "come down from (Mount) Arafat like a flood" here and in the following two usages.

the others, and ask God's forgiveness. He is forgiving and Merciful-to-all.[148] [(199)] When you have completed your rituals,[149] remember God at least as much as you remember your fathers, or even more. Some people say, "Our Lord, bless us in this world."[150] ." They have no share in the Hereafter. [(200)] Others say, "Our Lord, give us goodness in this world and goodness in the Hereafter. Protect us from the punishment of Hell." [(201)] Those have the portion of blessings they deserve. God is swift in reckoning judgment. [(202)] Remember God on certain appointed days. Whoever completes the process in two days is not guilty, and whoever stays longer out of minding God will not be guilty. Know that you will be gathered to Him.[151] [(203)]

Among the people there is a kind of person whose view of this life pleases you. He even calls God as witness to what is in his heart, yet he is the fiercest of (your) opponents. [(204)] When he leaves you, he goes throughout the land, spreading corruption, destroying crops and animals. God does not like corruption. [(205)] If he is told, "Be mindful of God," arrogance leads him to sin. He is headed to Hell, a dreadful destination. [(206)] Some people give their life away, desiring God's pleasure. God is compassionate [152] to His worshipers. [(207)] Believers, enter wholeheartedly into submission to God, and do not follow the steps of Satan; he is clearly your enemy. [(208)]If you should stumble after clear signs have come to you, be aware that God is Powerful[153] and Wise.[154] [(209)]

Are these people waiting to see God and the angels coming to them in a formation of clouds? At that point, the matter would already be over. All matters are referred to God. [155] [(210)] Ask the Children of Israel how many times We brought them clear signs. If anyone alters God's grace after having received it, God is stern in punishment. [(211)] This life has been made attractive to the unbelievers, and they ridicule the believers, but those who are mindful of God will be above them on the Day of Resurrection. God provides bountifully for all He wills. [(212)] Human beings were (once) all one nation. God sent prophets carrying good news and warnings, and with them He sent the Book in Truth to judge between people in matters on which they differ. Yet rivalry between those who received it led them to disagreement, even after having received clear signs. God willingly guided believers to the truth about which they differed. God guides whoever wants to be guided into a straight path [156] [(213)]

• • •

---

[148] Psalm 145:8, The Lord is gracious and merciful; Slow to anger and great in loving kindness

[149] Or "your sacrifices."

[150] Matthew 6:24 "No one can serve two masters; for a slave will either hate the one and love the other, or be devoted to the one and despite the other. You cannot serve God and wealth."

[151] Isaiah 34:16 Seek from the book of the Lord, and read: Not one of these will be missing; None will lack its mate. For His mouth has commanded, And His Spirit has gathered them.

[152] James 5:11 "Indeed we call blessed those who showed endurance. You have heard of the endurance of Job, and you have seen the purpose of the Lord, how the Lord is compassionate and merciful".

[153] Job 11:7 "Can you find out the deep things of God? Can you find out the limit of the Almighty?"

[154] Job 9:4, He is wise in heart, and mighty in strength —who has resisted him, and succeeded? —

[155] Psalm 95:7-9 For he is our God and we are the people of his pasture, and the sheep of his hand. O that today you would listen to his voice! [8] Do not harden your hearts, as at Meribah, as on the day at Massah in the wilderness, [9] when your ancestors tested me, and put me to the proof, though they had seen my work.

[156] Psalm 25:4-6 Make me to know your ways, O Lord; teach me your paths. [5] Lead me in your truth, and teach me, for you are the God of my salvation; for you I wait all day long. [6] Be mindful of your mercy, O Lord, and of your steadfast love, for they have been from of old.

Or do you think you will enter Heaven without experiencing the trials of those who were before you. They experienced misery, hard times, and they were so shaken that even their messenger and the believers with him cried, "When will God's help arrive?" Truly, God's help is near.[157] (214) They ask you (Prophet) what they should contribute. Say, "The possessions you contribute should be for parents, relatives, orphans, the poor, and the stranded traveler." God is fully aware of all the good you do. (215)

Fighting[158] is ordained for you, even though it repulses you. You may hate something that is good for you, or love something that is evil for you. God knows, but you do not. (216) They ask you about fighting during the sacred month. Say, "Fighting in it is a big offense. But turning people away from the path of God, denying Him, preventing access to the Sacred Sanctuary, and expelling its residents is a bigger offense to God because sedition is a bigger offense than murder. They will not stop fighting you as long as there is the possibility of turning you away from your faith. But if any of you denies the faith and dies in a state of unbelief, their deeds will come to nothing in this world and the Hereafter. They will be in Hell, where they will remain forever. (217) Those who have believed and journeyed and struggled in God's path, they may hope for God's mercy.[159] God is forgiving and Merciful-to-all. (218)

They ask you about intoxicants[160] and gambling.[161] Say, "There is great sin in them, and also some benefit for people. The sin is greater than the benefit." They ask you what they should contribute. Say, "Whatever you can possibly give." Thus God makes signs clear to you so that you might think about (219) this world and the Hereafter. They ask you about orphans, say, "Improving their lot in life is good.[162] If you mingle your affairs with them, (they are) your brethren." God knows the difference between one who corrupts and one who improves things. If God had wanted, He would have made things difficult for you. God is strong and wise. (220)

• • •

---

[157] 2 Corinthians 6:2 For he says, 'At an acceptable time I have listened to you, and on a day of salvation I have helped you.' See, now is the acceptable time; see, now is the day of salvation!

[158] The word "Qital", which refers to physical fighting. Fighting is ordained for Muslims in order to defend themselves and their rights, as well as the rights of others. The obligation to physically defend one's rights, and to establish justice is elaborated in this verse from the Quran: "How could you refuse to fight in God's cause for the helpless men, women and children who are screaming, "Lord! Lead us towards freedom, out of this land of oppressors! Through your grace, give us a protector and a helper!" (Surah 4:75)

[159] Psalm 42: Why are you cast down, O my soul, and why are you disquieted within me? Hope in God; for I shall again praise him, my help

[160] Leviticus 10:8-10 "And the Lord spoke to Aaron: [8] Drink no wine or strong drink, neither you nor your sons, when you enter the tent of meeting, that you may not die; it is a statute forever throughout your generations. [9] You are to distinguish between the holy and the common, and between the unclean and the clean."

[161] Proverbs 13:11, "Wealth hastily gained will dwindle, but those who gather little by little will increase it."

[162] James 1:27, "Religion that is pure and undefiled before God, the Father, is this: to care for orphans and widows in their distress, and to keep oneself unstained by the world."

Do not marry idolatrous women until they believe;[163] a believing slave woman is better than an idolatrous woman even if she pleases you. And do not give your women in marriage to idolaters until they believe. A believing slave is better than an idolater, even if he pleases you. They (idolaters) invite (you) to Hell, whereas God calls for Heaven and forgiveness by His permission. He makes his signs clear to people so that they may remember. [(221)]

They ask you about menstruation. Say, "It is painful, so keep away from women during their menstruation, and do not approach them until they are purified. When they are purified,[164] you may approach them the way God has ordained you." God loves the repentant and the purified. [(222)] Your wives are a field for you, so go into your fields however you want and do beforehand all that is necessary, being fully mindful of God and knowing that you will meet Him. Give good news to the believers. [(223)]

Do not use your oaths to God as an excuse for not doing good, being mindful of God, and making peace between people. God hears all [165] and knows all. [(224)] God does not blame you for foolishness in your oaths, but only as your hearts deserve. God is forgiving and gentle. [(225)] To those who swear not to have sexual relations with their wives, there is a waiting period of four months; if they change their minds, God is forgiving [166] and Merciful-to-all .[167] [(226)] If they insist on divorce, God hears all and knows all. [(227)] Divorced women will wait three menstruation periods (before re-marrying), for they are not allowed to hide what God has created in their wombs if they believe in God and the Last Day. Their husbands are entitled to take them back if they want to be reconciled. But, in accordance with justice, the rights of the wives (with regard to their husbands) are equal to the (husbands') rights with regard to them,[168] although husbands have a degree (of right) over them[169] God is almighty and wise.[170] [(228)]

Divorce is allowed twice, after which keep (your wives) kindly, or dismiss them generously. You (husbands) may not take back anything you have given them unless both of you fear that they may not be able to keep within the limits set by God. It is not then wrong for them if she buys her way out. These are God's limits, do not exceed them. Anyone who exceeds them is unjust. [(229)] If he divorces her (for the third time), she is no longer allowed to remarry him until she marries another husband. Then, if (the latter) divorces her, it is not wrong

• • •

---

[163] Deuteronomy 7:3, "Do not intermarry with them, giving your daughters to their sons or taking their daughters for your sons . . ." 2 Corinthians 6:14, "Do not be mismatched with unbelievers. For what partnership is there between righteousness and lawlessness? Or what fellowship is there between light and darkness?"

[164] Leviticus 15:19, "When a woman has a discharge of blood that is her regular discharge from her body, she shall be in her impurity for seven days, and whoever touches her shall be unclean until the evening.

[165] 1 John 5:14 And this is the boldness we have in him, that if we ask anything according to his will, he hears us.

[166] Psalm 86:5, For you, O Lord, are good and forgiving, abounding in steadfast love to all who call on you.

[167] James 5:11 We count those blessed who endured. You have heard of the endurance of Job and have seen the outcome of the Lord's dealings, that the Lord is full of compassion and *is* merciful.

[168] 1 Corinthians 7:4 The wife does not have authority over her own body but yields it to her husband. n the same way, the husband does not have authority over his own body but yields it to his wife

[169] 1 Corinthians 11:3, "But I want you to understand that Christ is the head of every man, and the husband is the head of his wife, and God is the head of Christ."

[170] Job 9:4, He is wise in heart, and mighty in strength —who has resisted him, and succeeded?

for them to return (to each other) if they think that they can observe God's limits.[(230)]

If you divorce (your) women, and their waiting term is complete, either take them back kindly or let then go kindly. Do not take them back in order to harm them or to treat them belligerently. Anyone who does that sins against himself. Do not mock God's revelations, but remember God's grace to you and what He revealed to you from the Book and the wisdom through which He exhorts you. Be mindful of God, and know that God knows everything. [(231)] If you divorce women and their waiting term is complete do not prevent them from marrying their new husbands if they come to a fair agreement. This instruction is to all who believe in God and the Last Day. This (way) is the most virtuous and purest for you. God knows, and you do not. [(232)]

Mothers should nurse their children for two complete years if they wish to complete the nursing period. Their provision and clothing are, in fairness, the father's responsibility. [171] No soul should be burdened with more than it can possibly bear; neither should a mother be made to suffer because of her child, nor a father because of his child. An heir has similar duties. If both (parents) decide to separate, they will incur no sin. Nor will there be any blame if you decide to employ a wet nurse, provided you ensure the child's safety in a fair manner. But remain mindful of God, and know that God sees all that you do. [(233)]

Widows of those who die among you must wait four months and ten days (prior to remarrying). When they complete their waiting period, you are not to be blamed for what they may choose to do lawfully with themselves. God is aware of what you do. [(234)] You will not be blamed whether you publicly announce that you want to marry these women or decide to keep your proposal to yourself; God knows your intentions to propose to them. Do not make a secret arrangement with them, but speak decently to them, and do not confirm the marriage contract until the prescribed period is finished. And you should know that God knows what is in your soul, so be mindful of Him. Remember that God is most forgiving, most forbearing. [(235)]

There is nothing wrong with divorcing your wives before you have touched them or paid them their dowry, but make fair provision for them, the rich according to his means and the poor according to his. This is a duty for those who behave righteously. [(236)] If you divorce them before you touch them, but after you have given them their dowry, then let them have half of it, unless they renounce (their claim), or unless the one making the marriage-tie renounces it. Renouncing (the portion) is closer to being mindful of God. Do not forget the grace that is between you. God sees what you do. [(237)] Always be mindful of prayers [172] and perform the intermediate prayer and stand devoutly before God. [(238)] But If you fear danger, pray (whether you are) walking or riding, and remember God when you are safe again, because it is He Who has taught you what you did not know. [(239)]

Those of you who die and leave wives should have a will with a provision giving their widows a year without being driven from their homes. If they leave (on their own), you will not be blamed for what they may reasonably choose to

• • •

[171] i.e. the mother's food and clothing is the baby's father's responsibility.

[172] 1 Thessalonians 5:16, "Rejoice always, pray without ceasing, give thanks in all circumstances; for this is the will of God in Christ Jesus for you."

do with their lives. God is strong and wise. [240] Divorced women should be provided for adequately. This is an obligation on those who are mindful of God. [241] God thus makes his revelations clear to you, so that you might understand.[242]

Did you not see the thousands who left their homes to avoid death? God told them, "Die." Then he made them alive again. God is gracious to people, but most people do not give thanks.[173] [243] Fight in God's path, and know that God hears all [174] and knows all. [244] Who will make a good loan to God which will be repaid by him many times over?[175] It is God who withholds, and it is He Who gives abundantly, and it is to Him you will return.[176] [245]

Did you not see how, after Moses' time, the leaders of the Children of Israel told one of their prophets,[177] "Raise up a king for us,[178] and we will fight in God's cause?" He said, "If it is God's will for you to fight, would you refuse? They answered, "Why should we not fight in God's cause when we and our children have been driven from our homelands?" Yet, when they were commanded to fight, all but a few of them turned away. God had full knowledge of the unjust. [246] Their prophet[179] told them[180], "God has chosen Saul as your king." They said, "How can he be our king? We are more deserving of being king than he. He does not have a lot of money." He said, "God has chosen him over you, and has endowed him with knowledge and physical strength.[181] God gives his kingdom to whomever he wills."[182] God is Infinite, all-knowing [247] Their prophet told

• • •

---

[173] 2 Timothy 3:2 People will be lovers of themselves, lovers of money, boastful, proud, abusive, disobedient to their parents, ungrateful, unholy

[174] 1 John 5:14 And this is the boldness we have in him, that if we ask anything according to his will, he hears us.

[175] Proverbs 19:17, "Whoever is kind to the poor lends to the Lord, and will be repaid in full."

[176] Romans 14:12, "So then, each of us will be accountable to God."

[177] 1 Samuel 8:5," . . . and said to him, 'You are old and your sons do not follow in your ways; appoint for us, then, a king to govern us, like other nations.'"

[178] 1 Samuel 8:19-20, "But the people refused to listen to the voice of Samuel; they said, 'No! but we are determined to have a king over us, 20 so that we also may be like other nations, and that our king may govern us and go out before us and fight our battles.'"

[179] Samuel

[180] 1 Samuel 10:24 Samuel said to all the people, "Do you see the man the Lord has chosen? There is no one like him among all the people." Then the people shouted, "Long live the king!"

[181] 1 Samuel 10:23-24, "Then they ran and brought him from there. When he took his stand among the people, he was head and shoulders taller than any of them. Samuel said to all the people, 'Do you see the one whom the Lord has chosen? There is no one like him among all the people.' And all the people shouted, 'Long live the king!'"

[182] Daniel 2:37, "You, O king, the king of kings—to whom the God of heaven has given the kingdom, the power, the might, and the glory."

them, "The sign of his royal authority is that the Ark of the Covenant[183] will come to you, carried by angels, bearing inner peace from your Lord as well as reminders of the family of Moses and Aaron. [184] If you believe, that is a sign for you." (248)

When Saul divided the troops,[185] he said, "God will test you at a river. Whoever drinks from it is not with me, and whoever does not taste it is with me, except for those who scoop up a handful." All but a few drank from it. When he and the believers crossed it together, they said, "We do not have any strength against Goliath and his troops today."[186] Those who thought they were about to meet God said, "How often small groups have defeated large groups by God's authority. God is with those who endure." (249) When they met Goliath and his troops, they said, "Lord, give us endurance and make our feet firm and save us from the unbelievers." (250) So, with God's approval, they defeated them. David killed Goliath, [187] and God gave him the kingdom and wisdom, and taught him what He willed. If God had not driven some back by means of others, the earth would have been corrupted, but God shows grace to people. (251)

These are God's revelations, which We recite to you (Prophet) in Truth. You are one of the messengers. (252) We preferred some of those messengers over others. God spoke to some, and he raised some in degree;[188] We gave Jesus son of Mary clear signs, and strengthened him with the Holy Spirit. If God had willed, those after them would not have fought each other after clear evidence of the truth had come to them, but they fought. Some of them believed, and others denied the truth. If God had willed, they would not have fought. But God does whatever He wants. (253)

Believers, contribute some of what We have provided you before a day comes when there is no bargaining,[189] nor friends, nor intercession. Those who have denied the truth are unjust. (254) God is the only god, the Eternal and Self-Sustaining. He neither slumbers nor sleeps. He owns what is in the heavens and the earth. Who is he who intercedes with Him except with His permission? He knows what is before them and what is behind them. They know nothing of His

• • •

[183] The Islamic scholar Al Baidawi mentioned that the sakina could be Tawrat, the Books of Moses. According to Al-Jalalan, the relics in the Ark were the fragments of the two tablets, rods, robes, shoes, mitres of Moses and the vase of manna. (31) Al-Tha'alibi, in Qisas Al-Anbiya (The Stories of the Prophets), has given an earlier and later history of the Ark. See http://en.wikipedia.org/wiki/Ark_of_the_Covenant

[184] Hebrews 9:4, "In it stood the golden altar of incense and the ark of the covenant overlaid on all sides with gold, in which there were a golden urn holding the manna, and Aaron's rod that budded, and the tablets of the covenant" --specifies what this is: Aaron (Harun)'s rod, a pot of manna, and the stone tablets of the covenant.

[185] 1 Samuel 13:2, "Saul chose three thousand out of Israel; two thousand were with Saul in Michmash and the hill country of Bethel, and a thousand were with Jonathan in Gibeah of Benjamin; the rest of the people he sent home to their tents."

[186] 1 Samuel 17 the story of David and Goliath

[187] 1 Samuel 17:49-51 'David put his hand in his bag, took out a stone, slung it, and struck the Philistine on his forehead; the stone sank into his forehead, and he fell face down on the ground. [50] So David prevailed over the Philistine with a sling and a stone, striking down the Philistine and killing him; there was no sword in David's hand. [51] Then David ran and stood over the Philistine; he grasped his sword, drew it out of its sheath, and killed him; then he cut off his head with it. When the Philistines saw that their champion was dead, they fled.

[188] Or "honor" or "rank."

[189] Revelation 13:17, "so that no one can buy or sell who does not have the mark, that is, the name of the beast or the number of its name."

knowledge except what He wills. The throne of His majesty covers the heavens and the earth, and protecting them does not tire Him. He is Most high and Tremendous. (255)

There is no compulsion in religion.[190] The difference between guidance and error has been made clear. Whoever rejects false gods and believes in God has grasped a firm, unshakable support. God hears all and knows all (256) God protects believers and brings them out of the darkness of ignorance into enlightenment.[191] False gods are the protectors of the unbelievers, bringing them out of enlightenment into the darkness of ignorance. They will be eternally in Hell. (257)

Have you not considered the one who was given a kingship by God (and) then disputed with Abram about his Lord? Abram said, "My Lord gives life and causes death."[192] He said, "I also give life and death." Abram said, "God brings the sun from the East. So bring it from the West." The disbeliever was dumfounded. God does not guide unjust people. (258)

Or, (consider) the one who passed by a town which had fallen into ruin. He said, "How can God bring back those who were once alive here after their death?" God made him die for a hundred years, and then resurrected him. He said, "How long have you stayed?" He said, "A day or part of a day." He said, "You stayed for a hundred years. Look at your food and your drink. They have not gone bad. Look at your dead donkey. We will make you a sign for people. Look how We raise the bones, and then cover them with flesh."[193] When he saw it, he said, "I know that God has power over all things."[194] (259)

Abram said, "My Lord, show me how you give life to the dead." God said, "Have you not believed?" He said, "Yes I have, but assure my heart." God said, "Take four birds, kill them and cut them into pieces. Then put pieces of each on a mountain and call them.[195] They will come quickly to you. Know that God is Strong and Wise."[196] (260)

•   •   •

[190] Following Ibn Kathir commentary, traditionally most Muslim scholars interpret this verse to prohibit forced conversion to Islam but exclude apostasy from Islam, because punishment for apostasy, they say, is prescribed in hadith. There is a recent movement among Muslim scholars to accept this verse to be general and unlimited to any situation regardless of time and place. The essence of Islam is freedom to choose. This verse guarantees this fundamental value forever.

[191] 1 Peter 2:9 But you are a chosen race, a royal priesthood, a holy nation, God's own people, in order that you may proclaim the mighty acts of him who called you out of darkness into his marvelous light.

[192] 1 Samuel 2:6, "The Lord kills and brings to life; he brings down to Sheol and raises up." Deuteronomy 32:39, "See now that I, even I, am He; there is no god besides Me. I kill and I make alive; I wound and I heal; and no one can deliver from My hand."

[193] Ezekiel 37:1-6 The hand of the Lord came upon me, and he brought me out by the spirit of the Lord and set me down in the middle of a valley; it was full of bones. 2 He led me all around them; there were very many lying in the valley, and they were very dry. 3 He said to me, "Mortal, can these bones live?" I answered, "O Lord God, you know." 4 Then he said to me, "Prophesy to these bones, and say to them: O dry bones, hear the word of the Lord. 5 Thus says the Lord God to these bones: I will cause breath to enter you, and you shall live. 6 I will lay sinews on you, and will cause flesh to come upon you, and cover you with skin, and put breath in you, and you shall live; and you shall know that I am the Lord."

[194] 1 Chronicles 29:11 Yours, O Lord, are the greatness, the power, the glory, the victory, and the majesty; for all that is in the heavens and on the earth is yours; yours is the kingdom, O Lord, and you are exalted as head above all.,

[195] The word "them" that refers to the birds here is usually used for thinking/reasoning beings, so possibly the meaning is that God makes them obey his will as thinking/reasoning creatures can (and should).

[196] Psalm 24:8 Who is the King of glory? The Lord, strong and mighty, the Lord, mighty in battle.

Those who contribute their money in God's way are like a seed that sprouts seven heads, in each of which are a hundred grains.[197] God grants such multiple increase to whom He wills. God is Infinite and All-Knowing. (261) Those who spend their money in God's way and then do not follow what they spend with reproach or harm will have a reward from their Lord.[198] They will neither fear nor grieve. (262) A kind word and forgiveness are better than charity followed by hurt. God is Rich beyond need and Forbearing. (263) Believers do not ruin your charitable deeds with reproach and harm like one who does not believe in God or the Last Day and contributes his money so people will see him.[199] He is like a rock with dirt on it that was rained upon heavily and became hard and bare. Such people can do nothing with what they earned. God does not guide disbelieving people.[200] (264) Those who spend their money seeking God's pleasure and as an affirmation of their own faith are like a garden on a hill when heavy rain falls on it—it doubles its produce—and if heavy rain does not fall, there is dew. God sees what you do. (265) Do any of you want to have a garden with date palms and vineyards, with flowing rivers, having every kind of fruit, to then be overtaken by old age, with only weak children, and then a fiery whirlwind strikes it and burns it up? Thus God shows you signs so that you may contemplate.[201] (266)

Believers, contribute some of the good things You have earned, and of what We have produced for you from the earth. Do not choose the worst of it to give in charity that you yourself would be reluctant to accept. Know that God is Rich beyond need and Praiseworthy.[202] (267) Satan promises you poverty and orders you to commit immoral acts. God promises you His forgiveness and esteem. God is Infinite, All-Knowing. (268) He gives wisdom to whom He chooses, and whoever is given wisdom is blessed abundantly.[203] But only insightful people bear this in mind. (269) God knows what you contribute or what you vow. The unjust have no one to save them. (270) If you give charity visibly, it is good. But if you hide it while giving to the poor, it is better for you,[204] and He will atone[205] for some of your

• • •

[197] Matthew 13:8, "Other seeds fell on good soil and brought forth grain, some a hundredfold, some sixty, some thirty." Matthew 13:23, "But as for what was sown on good soil, this is the one who hears the word and understands it, who indeed bears fruit and yields, in one case a hundredfold, in another sixty, and in another thirty."

[198] Proverbs 19:17 "Whoever is kind to the poor lends to the Lord, and will be repaid in full."

[199] Matthew 6:1, "Beware of practicing your piety before others in order to be seen by them; for then you have no reward from your Father in heaven."

[200] 2 Thessalonians 2:11, "For this reason God sends them a powerful delusion, leading them to believe what is false . . ."

[201] Exodus 10:2 and that you may tell your children and grandchildren how I have made fools of the Egyptians and what signs I have done among them—so that you may know that I am the Lord.'

[202] Deuteronomy 10:21, He is your praise; he is your God, who has done for you these great and awesome things that your own eyes have seen.

[203] Matthew 13:45-46 The kingdom of heaven is like a merchant seeking fine pearls, [46] and upon finding one pearl of great value, he went and sold all that he had and bought it. Ecclesiastes 7:11," Wisdom is as good as an inheritance, an advantage to those who see the sun."

[204] Matthew 6:1-4, "Beware of practicing your piety before others in order to be seen by them; for then you have no reward from your Father in heaven. [2] So whenever you give alms, do not sound a trumpet before you, as the hypocrites do in the synagogues and in the streets, so that they may be praised by others. Truly I tell you, they have received their reward. [3] But when you give alms, do not let your left hand know what your right hand is doing, [4] so that your alms may be done in secret; and your Father who sees in secret will reward you."

[205] Or "expiate."

sins. God is well aware of what you do. [271] It is not for you to guide them. God guides whomever He wills. What charity you give benefits you when you contribute only to please God.[206] Your contributions will be paid back to you, and you will not be cheated.[207] [272] Give to the poor who are wholly committed to the path of God and who are unable to travel in the land. The unaware considers them rich because of their self-restraint. You will recognize them by their character traits. They are not always asking people to help them. God knows what you contribute. [273]

All those who contribute their money at night or during the day, both secretly and publicly, will receive a reward from their Lord. They will not be afraid, nor will they grieve. [274] Those who profit from usury[208] will rise up on the Day of Resurrection like someone tormented by Satan's touch because they say, "Selling is like usury,[209] but God allowed selling and forbade usury." So whoever stops when receiving his Lord's good advice may keep what was previously his, and his matter is with God. Those who return to (usury) will eternally be in Hell. [275] God condemns usury, while He blesses and multiplies charitable transactions. God does not love any sinful person who denies the truth.[210][276] Those who believe and do righteous deeds and perform their prayers and give the purifying alms have their reward from their Lord, and they will not fear or grieve. [277] Believers, always be aware of God, and quit what remains of usury, if you are believers. [278] If you do not, then be warned of a war from God and his Messenger; and if you repent, you may have your original capital. Wrong not, and you will not be wronged[211]. [279] However, if the borrower has financial difficulties, then defer payment until circumstances are better, and it would be for your own good, if you fully understood, to forgive the entire loan. [280] Beware of a day when you are returned to God and every soul will be paid in full for what it has earned, and none will be wronged. [281]

Believers, if you become indebted to each other for a stated term, put it in writing. Let a legal clerk draw it up between you. The clerk should not refuse to write as God has taught him. The one who owes should dictate and always be mindful of God, his Lord. No amount should be withheld from him. If the one who owes is foolish,[212] weak, or unable to dictate himself, let his legal guardian dictate and have it witnessed by two men, or, if there are not two, by one man and two women whom you approve as witnesses. If one of (the women) forgets, the other will remind her. Witnesses[213] should not refuse when they are called upon. Do not think it unimportant to write it down, whether a small or large

• • •

[206] Or "seek the face of."
[207] Proverbs 19:17 Whoever is kind to the poor lends to the Lord, and will be repaid in full.
[208] Very high or abusive rate of interest.
[209] Exodus 22:25, "If thou lend money to any of my people that is poor by thee, thou shalt not be to him as a usurer, neither shalt thou lay upon him usury." KJB
[210] Revelation 21:8 But as for the cowardly, the faithless, the polluted, the murderers, the fornicators, the sorcerers, the idolaters, and all liars, their place will be in the lake that burns with fire and sulphur, which is the second death.'
[211] Luke 6:37 "Do not judge, and you will not be judged. Do not condemn, and you will not be condemned.
[212] Or "ignorant."
[213] Deuteronomy 17:6, "On the evidence of two or three witnesses the death sentence shall be executed; a person must not be put to death on the evidence of only one witness." 19:15, "A single witness shall not suffice to convict a person of any crime or wrongdoing in connection with any offense that may be committed. Only on the evidence of two or three witnesses shall a charge be sustained."

amount, along with its specified terms. That is more equitable to God, more reliable for testimony, and more likely to preclude doubt, except when it is a current business (that) you manage among yourselves. (In that case), not writing it down is not wrong. Always have witnesses present whenever you trade with one another, and do not let any harm be done to either the legal clerk or witnesses. If you do, you will be sinning.[214] Be mindful of God, and God will teach you.[215] God knows everything.[216] (282) If you are on a trip and do not find a scribe, then an earnest payment should be paid. If you entrust things to each other, the one to whom it was entrusted should fulfill his pledge. He should be mindful of God, his Lord. Do not hide the testimony. Whoever hides it has a guilty heart. God knows what you do.[217] (283) To God belongs what is in the heavens and the earth.[218] Whether you reveal what is in your hearts or if you hide it, God will call you to account for it. He forgives whom He wills and punishes whom He wills. God has power over all things.[219] (284)

The Messenger believes in what was revealed to him by his Lord, as do the believers; they all believe in God, His angels, His Books and His Messengers. We do not distinguish between any of His Messengers. They said, "We have heard and obeyed. Our Lord, (we seek) Your forgiveness. To You is (our) destiny." (285) God does not burden a soul more than it can bear[220]. It has (the good) it has earned, and (the evil) it has incurred. Our Lord, do not blame us if we forget or err. Our Lord, do not make us bear a burden like those before us. Our Lord, do not make us bear what We have no strength to bear[221]. Pardon us, forgive us, and have mercy on us. You are our Master, so help us against the people who deny the truth. (286)

• • •

---

[214] Or "committing immorality."

[215] Isaiah 48:17 Thus says the Lord, your Redeemer, the Holy One of Israel: I am the Lord your God, who teaches you for your own good, who leads you in the way you should go.

[216] 1 Samuel 2:3 Talk no more so very proudly, let not arrogance come from your mouth; for the Lord is a God of knowledge, and by him actions are weighed.

[217] Romans 11:33 O the depth of the riches and wisdom and knowledge of God! How unsearchable are his judgments and how inscrutable his ways!

[218] Psalm 89:11 The heavens are yours, the earth also is yours; the world and all that is in it—you have founded them.

[219] 2 Chronicles 20:6 and said, 'O Lord, God of our ancestors, are you not God in heaven? Do you not rule over all the kingdoms of the nations? In your hand are power and might, so that no one is able to withstand you.

[220] 1 Corinthians 10:13 "No testing has overtaken you that is not common to everyone. God is faithful, and he will not let you be tested beyond your strength, but with the testing he will also provide the way out so that you may be able to endure it".

[221] Psalm 55:22 Cast your burden on the Lord, and he will sustain you; he will never permit the righteous to be moved.

CHAPTER THREE

AL-IMRAN
THE FAMILY OF IMRAN[222]

THE **MEDINA** PERIOD

In the name of God, the Merciful-to-all, the Mercy Giver:
Alef Lam Meem[223] (01)

God! There is no God but Him.[224] The Eternal, the Self-Sustainer. (02) He has sent down the Book [225] to you with the Truth to confirm what is available of other revelations, as it is He who sent down the Torah[226] and the Gospel (03) beforehand as guidance to people, and He revealed the Standard[227] by which we judge right from wrong. Those who do not believe God's signs will have severe punishment. God is Almighty[228] and capable of revenge.[229] (04) Nothing on earth or in heaven

. . .

---

[222] The title "The Family of 'Imran" has been derived from verses 33 and 35, in this chapter. The chapter had been revealed in Medinah at the third year of the Hijra, but some of its verses (61) were revealed much later, during the 10th year of Hijra. The Chapter relates the story of Mary and Jesus, as well as of Zachariah, the father of John the Baptist. They are all members of "The Family of 'Imran".

[223] Here and at the beginning of many chapters there are letters of unknown meaning called Al Muquatta'at. Numerous theories have been proposed, but there is no agreement on what they signify yet.

[224] Exodus 20:3 you shall have no other gods before me. The following verses also declare the oneness of God Mark 12:29, Deuteronomy 6:4, 2 Kings 19:15, Nehemiah 9:6, Isaiah 37:20, Isaiah 46:9, Zechariah 14:9, John 5:44

[225] See Tanzil in the Glossary

[226] The Law

[227] Or, "criterion." This word is only mentioned in seven verses (2:53, 185, 3:4, 8:29, 41, 21:48, 25:1), and not all of these verses refer to a book. It is not clear in this verse to whom it was revealed, but in 2:53 it is said to be revealed to Moses and in 21:48 to Moses and Aaron (Harun). 25:1 says "to his servant" and it is assumed to refer to Muhammad. Most probably it refers to the same Ten Commandments given to Moses.

[228] Job 9:4, "He is wise in heart, and mighty in strength."

[229] Hebrews 10:30, "For we know the one who said, 'Vengeance is mine, I will repay.' And again, 'The Lord will judge his people.'

is hidden from God.[230] [(05)] He forms you in the womb[231] as He wills. There is no God but Him, the Almighty,[232] the Wise.[233] [(06)] It is He who revealed this Book to you. Some of its verses are clear and definite in meaning; they are the Book's core. Others are ambiguous. Those with stubborn hearts follow the ambiguous verses[234], desiring to create confusion and their own interpretation, while absolutely no one but God knows their (exact) interpretation. Those who are grounded in knowledge say, "We believe it. It is all from our Lord." No one will take this to heart except those endowed with insight. [(07)] "Our Lord, do not let our hearts deviate after you have guided us. Give us your mercy. You are the Ever Giving. [(08)] Our Lord, You are gathering the people for a definite day.[235] God does not break His promise.[236] [(09)]

Neither the possessions nor the children of the unbelievers will help them at all with God.[237] They are fuel for Hell. [(10)] As in the case of Pharaoh's people and those before them, they have denied our signs, so God punished them for their sins. God is severe in punishment.[238] [(11)] Say to the unbelievers, "You will be defeated and gathered into Hell – a dreadful suffering place. [(12)] You already have a sign: Two groups met (in battle), one fighting in God's cause and the other denying Him; with their own eyes the unbelievers saw the believers as double in numbers." God provides help to whomever He wills. That is a lesson for those who have eyes to see. [(13)]

• • •

---

[230] Jeremiah 23:24, "Who can hide in secret places so that I cannot see them? says the Lord. Do I not fill heaven and earth? says the Lord." Hebrews 4:12, "Indeed, the word of God is living and active, sharper than any two-edged sword, piercing until it divides soul from spirit, joints from marrow; it is able to judge the thoughts and intentions of the heart." Mark 4:22, "For there is nothing hidden, except to be disclosed; nor is anything secret, except to come to light."

[231] Psalm 139:13-16, "For it was you who formed my inward parts; you knit me together in my mother's womb. I praise you, for I am fearfully and wonderfully made. Wonderful are your works; that I know very well. My frame was not hidden from you, when I was being made in secret, intricately woven in the depths of the earth. Your eyes beheld my unformed substance. In your book were written all the days that were formed for me, when none of them as yet existed."

[232] Revelation 21:22, I saw no temple in the city, for its temple is the Lord God the Almighty and the Lamb.

[233] Job 9:4, "He is wise in heart, and mighty in strength

[234] Mark 4:11-12 And He (Jesus) was saying to them, "To you has been given the mystery of the kingdom of God, but those who are outside get everything in parables, [12] so that while seeing, they may see and not perceive, and while hearing, they may hear and not understand, otherwise they might return and be forgiven."

[235] Isaiah 66:18 I will gather all nations and all people. Everyone will be gathered together to see my Glory. Zephaniah 3:8 Therefore wait for me," declares the Lord, "for the day I will stand up to testify. I have decided to assemble the nations, to gather the kingdoms and to pour out my wrath on them . . . Matthew 25:32, "All the nations will be gathered before him, and he will separate people one from another as a shepherd separates the sheep from the goats."

[236] Numbers 23:19, "God is not a human being, that he should lie, or a mortal, that he should change his mind. Has he promised, and will he not do it? Has he spoken, and will he not fulfill it?" Hebrews 6:18, "so that through two unchangeable things, in which it is impossible that God would prove false, we who have taken refuge might be strongly encouraged to seize the hope set before us."

[237] Psalm 49:7-9, "Truly, no ransom avails for one's life, there is no price one can give to God for it. [8] For the ransom of life is costly, and can never suffice, [9] that one should live on forever and never see the grave."

[238] Ezekiel 25:17, "I will execute great vengeance on them with wrathful punishments. Then they shall know that I am the Lord, when I lay my vengeance on them."

The love of worldly pleasures[239] is alluring to people: women, children, vast hoards of gold and silver, branded horses, cattle, and farmland. These are matters of this world. God has the best of destinations. [14] Say, "Will I tell you of better things than that? Those that were mindful of God will have Heavenly Gardens with their Lord, with flowing rivers. They will live there forever, with purified mates and God's grace." God is fully aware of His worshipers [15] who say, "Our Lord, We have believed, so forgive us our sins[240] and protect us from the punishment of Hell."[241] [16] They are the ones who are patient in hard times, true to their word, devout, generous and who pray before dawn for forgiveness.[17]

God bears witness that there is no God but Him, as do the angels, and those who are endowed with knowledge. He is the Upholder of Justice.[242] There is no God but Him, the Almighty,[243] the Wise. [18] To God true faith is submission,[244] (Islam), and those who received the Book differed only after receiving knowledge out of contention. God will be swift in reckoning with those who deny His revelations. [19] If they dispute with you, say, "My followers and I have totally submitted to God." Say to those who were given the Book and to the Gentiles, "Have you submitted?" If they submit, they have been guided. If they turn away, your responsibility is to only convey the message. God is well aware of His worshipers. [20]

Tell[245] those who deny God's revelations, who wrongfully kill prophets and kill those who call for justice, that they will have painful punishment.[246] [21] Their works have failed both in this world and in the Hereafter, and they have no one to rescue them. [22] Have you thought about those who were given a portion of the Book? They were asked to accept judgment according to God's Book, some of them being unreasonably stubborn, turned away [23] just because they declared, "We will only be in Hell for a few days." The lies they had fabricated caused them to betray their faith. [24] How then will they feel if we gather them for a definite day, when every soul is repaid as it deserves, and they will not be wronged? [25]

· · ·

[239] 1 Timothy 6:10, "For the love of money is a root of all kinds of evil, and in their eagerness to be rich some have wandered away from the faith and pierced themselves with many pains."
[240] Luke 11:4 And forgive us our sins, for we ourselves forgive everyone indebted to us. And do not bring us to the time of trial.'
[241] Luke 12:5 But I will warn you whom to fear: fear him who, after he has killed, has authority to cast into hell. Yes, I tell you, fear him!
[242] Isaiah 30:18, "Therefore the Lord waits to be gracious to you; therefore, he will rise up to show mercy to you. For the Lord is a God of justice; blessed are all those who wait for him."
[243] Job 9:4, "He is wise in heart, and mighty in strength"
[244] Submission is the translation we chose to use for the word Islam which is an action oriented verb and not a noun. Nowadays, Islam is used as a noun refering to a particular faith. Originally, when the word was revealed for the first time, people understood it to mean an act of submission to God, that one strives to achieve every moment of the day. As such, the Qur'an calls the followers of all God's prophets, Muslims. However, once the word Islam started being used as a noun, it became a tool to divide the followers of Prophet Muhammad from other people who submit but follow other prophets. See Glossary.
[245] Literally "Give good news."
[246] Psalm 39:11 You chastise mortals in punishment for sin, consuming like a moth what is dear to them; surely everyone is a mere breath.

Say, "God, Owner of all Sovereignty, You give sovereignty to whom You will and You take away sovereignty from whom You will;[247] You exalt whom You will, and You bring low whom You will.[248] Goodness is in Your hand. You can do anything.[249] (26) You make night flow into day, and day flow into night; You bring out the living from the dead, the dead from the living, and You provide bountifully, without measure, for those You will." (27)

The believers should not take unbelievers as allies[250] in preference to believers. Anyone who does that will completely isolate himself from God, unless you are seeking to protect your own selves from them. God warns you to beware of Him. God is our ultimate destination. (28) Say, "God knows what is in your hearts,[251] whether you hide or reveal it. He knows what is in the heavens and the earth. God has power over all things.[252] (29) On that day, every soul will find the good that it has done present before it. But it will wish that there were a great distance between it and the evil it has done. God cautions you about Himself. God is compassionate with His worshipers." (30) Say, "If you love God, follow me, God will surely love you[253] and forgive your sins. God is forgiving[254] and merciful."[255] (31) Say, "Obey God and the Messenger. But if they turn away, God does not love those who deny the truth." (32)

God chose Adam, Noah (Nuh), Abraham's family, and Imran's family[256] over all people--(33) a common line of descent, one following the other. God hears all and knows all. (34) Imran's wife[257] said, "Lord, I have vowed to you what is in my womb to be wholly dedicated to you; accept it from me. You hear all[258] and know

• • •

[247] Daniel 4:17, "The sentence is rendered by decree of the watchers, the decision is given by order of the holy ones, in order that all who live may know that the Most High is sovereign over the kingdom of mortals; he gives it to whom he will and sets over it the lowliest of human beings."
[248] 1 Chronicles 29:12 "Both riches and honor come from You, and You rule over all, and in Your hand is power and might; and it lies in Your hand to make great and to strengthen everyone.
[249] Job 42:2, "I know that you can do all things, and that no purpose of yours can be thwarted."
[250] 1 Corinthians 15:33, "Do not be deceived: 'Bad company ruins good morals.'"
[251] Luke 6:8,16:15 "Even though he knew what they were thinking, he said to the man who had the withered hand, 'Come and stand here.' He got up and stood there. 16:5 So he said to them, 'You are those who justify yourselves in the sight of others; but God knows your hearts; for what is prized by human beings is an abomination in the sight of God."
[252] Psalm 62:11, Once God has spoken; twice have I heard this: that power belongs to God,
[253] John 15:9-10 "I have loved you even as the Father has loved me. Remain in my love. 10 When you obey my commandments, you remain in my love, just as I obey my Father's commandments and remain in his love.
[254] Daniel 9:9. To the Lord our God belong mercy and forgiveness, for we have rebelled against him,
[255] Ephesians 2:4 But God, who is rich in mercy, out of the great love with which he loved us
[256] The Family of 'Imran comprises Moses and Aaron, whose father was 'Imran (the Amram of the Bible), and Aaron's descendants, the priestly caste among the Israelites - thus including John the Baptist, both of whose parents were of the same descent (Luke 1:5, "In the days of King Herod of Judea, there was a priest named Zechariah, who belonged to the priestly order of Abijah. His wife was a descendant of Aaron, and her name was Elizabeth."), as well as Jesus, whose mother Mary - a close relation of John - is spoken of elsewhere in the Qur'an (19:28) as a "sister of Aaron" and also a relatives of Elizabeth (the mother of John) in Luke 1:36 in the bible. in both cases embodying the ancient Semitic custom of linking a person's or a people's name with that of an illustrious forebear. The reference to the Family of 'Imran serves as an introduction to the stories of Zachariah, John, Mary, and Jesus.
[257] "Imran, father of Mary", who is Joachim.
[258] Psalm 5:3 O Lord, in the morning you hear my voice; in the morning I plead my case to you, and watch.

all."[259] [35] When she gave birth, she said, "Lord, I have delivered a female." God knows well what she delivered--that a male is not like a female. "I have named her Mary.[260] I seek your protection for her and her children, from the accursed Satan." [36] Her Lord accepted the female baby favorably and caused her to have a good upbringing and placed her in Zechariah's care. As often as Zechariah visited her in the inner sanctuary, he found she had food. He said, "Mary, how did you get this?" She said, "It is from God. God provides bountifully for whomever he wills." [37] There Zechariah prayed to his Lord. He said, "Lord, be gracious to me and give me such a blessed child. You certainly hear prayer. [38] The angels called to him as he stood praying in the inner sanctuary, "God gives you good news of John, who will confirm a Word from God,[261] He will be noble and chaste, a prophet and one of the righteous." [39] He said, "Lord, how can I have a boy when I am an old man, and my wife is barren The angel said, "It will be so. God does whatever He wills." [40] He said, "Lord, give me a sign." He said, "Your sign will be that you will not speak to people for three days[262] except by gestures. Remember your Lord frequently and glorify Him in the evening and the morning." [41]

The angels said, "Mary, God has chosen you, purified you, and chosen you above all women in the worlds.[263] [42] Mary, be dedicated to your Lord; bow down and kneel with those who are kneeling in prayer." [43] This is hidden knowledge that We reveal to you (Muhammad). You were not with them when they cast lots for which of them would take care of Mary, or when they quarreled. [44]

(When) the angels said, "Mary, God gives you good news of a word from Him, whose name will be the Messiah[264], Jesus (Esa) son of Mary, he will be highly distinguished[265] in this world and the Hereafter, and brought near to God.[266] [45] He will speak to people from the cradle[267] and when he's an old man. He's from among the righteous." [268][46] She said, "Lord, how can I have a boy when no man has ever touched me?"[269] He said, "God creates what He wills, when He decides

• • •

[259] Matthew 6:32 For it is the Gentiles who strive for all these things; and indeed your heavenly Father knows that you need all these things.
[260] Mary (Mariam in Arabic) is in this passage and in 66:12 presented as the daughter of Imran meaning she is a descendant from Imran the head of that clan. In the Torah, Miriam (also Mariam in Arabic), Moses, and Aaron (Harun) are presented as the children of Amram (see Exodus 6:20, Numbers 26:59). Mary's father is not specifically named in the New Testament. However, Mary is called a relative of Elizabeth (Luke 1:36) and Elizabeth was descended from Aaron (Harun), son of Amram (Luke 1:5). The reason the Qur'an calls her the daughter of Imran may be to designate her priestly line
[261] Luke 1:13-15 But the angel said to him, 'Do not be afraid, Zechariah, for your prayer has been heard. Your wife Elizabeth will bear you a son, and you will name him John. 14 You will have joy and gladness, and many will rejoice at his birth, 15 for he will be great in the sight of the Lord. He must never drink wine or strong drink; even before his birth he will be filled with the Holy Spirit.
[262] Luke 1:20, "But now, because you did not believe my words, which will be fulfilled in their time, you will become mute, unable to speak, until the day these things occur.' "
[263] Luke 1:30 The angel said to her, 'Do not be afraid, Mary, for you have found favor with God.
[264] Or "Christ." Arabic "Al-Masih." See Glossary.
[265] Or "illustrious", or "highly-regarded"
[266] Here the Qur'an tells us that Jesus will be brought in the Hereafter near to God.
[267] Here in the Qur'an Jesus is mentioned as a miraculous infant who speaks in the cradle. For what he says, see 19:30-33.
[268] http://www.youtube.com/watch?v=MxV9ueRjVXQ&html5=1
[269] Luke 1:34 Mary said to the angel, 'How can this be, since I am a virgin?'

a matter, He simply says to it: "Be!",[270] and then it is." [47] And He will teach him the Book,[271] the Wisdom,[272] the Torah, and the Gospel, [48] and he will be a messenger to the people of Israel[273], saying, "I have come to you with a sign from your Lord: I will create[274] a bird like for you from clay and breathe into it and by God's permission[275] it will be a bird. I, by God's permission, heal[276] men born blind[277] and lepers[278] and give life[279] to the dead. I will tell you what you may eat and what you should store in your homes.[280] There is a sign in this for you, if you will believe. [49] I will confirm what is available of the Torah, and I will make permissible for you some of the things that were forbidden to you. I have

• • •

[270] Psalm 33:9 For he spoke, and it came to be; he commanded, and it stood firm.

[271] The Book is in several places mentioned as what God revealed to Moses, which would be the Pentateuch, the first five books of the Old Testament.

[272] The "wisdom" probably refers to what the Jews called "ketubim" or "writings," which include the Psalm, Proverbs, Job, Ecclesiastes, and the Song of Solomon. The Arabic word "hikmah" means both "proverb" and "wisdom. "The Law. See Glossary. This three-part division of the Old Testament/Tanakh (Book, Wisdom and Law) parallels the Jewish division of it: law of Moses, the Prophets, and the Psalm (Luke 24:44 Then he said to them, "These are my words that I spoke to you while I was still with you written about me in the law of Moses, the prophets, and everything in the palms must be fulfilled.").

[273] Matthew 15:24 "He answered, "I was sent only to the lost sheep of the house of Israel."

[274] Here in the Qur'an Jesus creates by the will of God

[275] John 5:30 'I (Jesus) by myself can do nothing – as I hear I judge, and my judgment is just, because I seek not my will, but the will of him who has sent me'.

[276] Jesus's healing powers reached outside the curing of persons with bodily imperfections to include "all manner of disease among the people" (Matthew 4:23; emphasis added). Jesus, in His endless charity, cured not just individuals with bodily imperfections but in addition such whose illnesses were mental or emotional.

[277] John 9:1-7 As he walked along, he saw a man blind from birth. [2] His disciples asked him, 'Rabbi, who sinned, this man or his parents, that he was born blind?' [3] Jesus answered, 'Neither this man nor his parents sinned; he was born blind so that God's works might be revealed in him. [4] We must work the works of him who sent me while it is day; night is coming when no one can work. [5] As long as I am in the world, I am the light of the world.' [6] When he had said this, he spat on the ground and made mud with the saliva and spread the mud on the man's eyes, [7] saying to him,
'Go, wash in the pool of Siloam' (which means Sent). Then he went and washed and came back able to see.

[278] Matthew 8:2-4 and there was a leper who came to him and knelt before him, saying, 'Lord, if you choose, you can make me clean.' [3] He stretched out his hand and touched him, saying, 'I do choose. Be made clean!' Immediately his leprosy was cleansed. [4] Then Jesus said to him, 'See that you say nothing to anyone; but go, show yourself to the priest, and offer the gift that Moses commanded, as a testimony to them.'

[279] Mark 12:35-43, "While Jesus was still speaking, some people came from the house of Jairus, the synagogue leader. 'Your daughter is dead,' they said. 'Why bother the teacher anymore?' Overhearing what they said, Jesus told him, 'Don't be afraid; just believe.' He did not let anyone follow him except Peter, James and John the brother of James. When they came to the home of the synagogue leader, Jesus saw a commotion, with people crying and wailing loudly. He went in and said to them, 'Why all this commotion and wailing? The child is not dead but asleep.' But they laughed at him. After he put them all out, he took the child's father and mother and the disciples who were with him, and went in where the child was. He took her by the hand and said to her, 'Talitha koum!' (which means 'Little girl, I say to you, get up!'). Immediately the girl stood up and began to walk around (she was twelve years old). At this they were completely astonished. He gave strict orders not to let anyone know about this, and told them to give her something to eat."

[280] The Qur'an lists some other miracles in 3:52, 5: 110,112, 19:19,20,24,30-33. Miracles Jesus did are mentioned in Matthew 8-11, 14-15,17,21, Mark 1-9,11, Luke 2,4-9,22, John 2,4-6,9,11.

brought you a sign from your Lord, so be mindful of God and obey me.[281] [50] God is my Lord and your Lord,[282] so worship Him. This is the straight path."[283] [51]

When Jesus sensed their refusal to acknowledge the truth, he asked, "Who are my supporters in God's cause?" The disciples said, "We are God's supporters.[284] We have believed in God, so bear witness that we have submitted. [52] Our Lord, we believe in what You revealed, and we follow the Messenger, so record us as witnesses." [53] And they (the unbelievers) plotted (against Jesus) but God caused their schemes to fail, for God is the best of all plotters. [54]

God said, "Jesus, I will cause you to die and raise you up to me, and purify you from those who denied the truth, and I will exalt your followers over those who deny you until the Resurrection Day. Then you all will return to me, and I will judge between you in matters about which you disagree. [55] "But I will severely punish the unbelievers both in this world and the Hereafter, and they will have no one to help them." [56] As for the believers who do righteous deeds, God will pay them in full. God does not love the unjust. [57]

What we are relating to you (Muhammad) are verses and the Wise Reminder (the Qur'an). [58] To God, Jesus is like Adam, whom He created from dust, then He told him, "Be!"[285] and he was.[286] [59] This is the Truth from your Lord, so do not doubt. [60] If someone continues to argue with you about it after knowledge has come to you, say, "Come let us call your children and ours and your wives and ours and you and us, then let us praise God and call down His curse on the liars." [61] This is the truth of the matter, and there is no deity but God.[287] God is the Almighty,[288] the Wise.[289] [62] If they turn away, God is well aware of the corrupters. [63] People of the Book, "Come to a common word between us that we will not worship any but God, and we will not ascribe partners to Him, nor will we take each other as lords in addition to God." If they turn away, say, "Bear witness that we have submitted to God." [64]

•   •   •

---

[281] Matthew 7:21-27. Several prophets tell the people specifically, "obey me." (Nuh 26:108,110, 71:3, Hud 26: 126,131, Salih 26: 144,150, Lut 26:163, Shuaib 26:179, Aaron (Harun) 20:90, and Jesus 3:50, 43:63) Jesus is the only one who commands obedience in the context of the straight path. Several verses command people to obey "the Messenger" (3:32,132, 4:59, 5:92, 8:1,19,46, 24:54,56, 47:33, 58:13, 64:12), most of which refer to Muhammad.

[282] Mark 12:29-30 "Jesus answered, 'The first is, "Hear, O Israel: the Lord our God, the Lord is one; [30] you shall love the Lord your God with all your heart, and with all your soul, and with all your mind, and with all your strength."

[283] Proverbs 3:6, In all your ways acknowledge him, and he will make straight your paths.

[284] The word "ansaar" here is from the root nasr or victory. As if Jesus is asking who will support me toward victory. It is possible that the word "nasara" used in the Qur'an to describe Jesus followers is derived from the same root. However, it is always interpreted and translated as Christians.

[285] Psalm 33: 9 For he spoke, and it came to be; he commanded, and it stood firm.

[286] The phrase "whom He created from dust" is in the singular, not the dual, and refers only to Adam. The account of Jesus's conception through God's spirit and birth through the virgin Mary is told in 19:16, 66:12, and 21:91, whereas Adam's creation is told in 32:9 among other places. Adam was created first, and then God breathed of his spirit into him, whereas God breathed his spirit into Mariam, and then Jesus was conceived in her womb and later born.

[287] Exodus 20:3 you shall have no other gods before me.

[288] Psalm 93:4, More majestic than the thunders of mighty waters, more majestic than the waves of the sea, majestic on high is the Lord!

[289] Proverbs 2:6 For the Lord gives wisdom; from his mouth come knowledge and understanding;

People of the Book, "Why do you argue about Abraham, when the Torah and the Gospel were not revealed until after him? Do you not understand? [65] Here you are arguing about some things you know, so why do you argue about things which you do not know? God knows and you do not." [66] Abraham was neither a Jew nor a Christian, but he was one who turned away from all that is false, a monotheist who submitted to God; never an idolater. [67] The people who are most deserving of Abraham are surely those who followed him – as does this Prophet and all who believed. God is the guardian of the believers. [68]

Some People of the Book want to mislead you. They mislead only themselves, while not realizing it. [69] People of the Book, "Why do you deny God's revelations when you yourselves are witnesses?" [70] People of the Book, "Why do you clothe the Truth with falsehood, and knowingly hide the Truth?" [71] Some People of the Book said, "Believe in what was revealed to the believers at daybreak, and deny it at sunset, so they may return (to their ignorance). [72] Only trust those who follow your faith." Say, "True guidance is God's guidance. But you think it is impossible for anyone to be given the same revelation as you were given, or that they could use it to argue against you before your Lord." Say, "Grace is in God's hand, and He gives it to those He wills. God is infinite, All-knowing."[290] [73] He singles out for His mercy whomever He wills, and God has boundless grace." [74]

Some of the People of the Book you can trust with a lot of gold, and they will return it to you. If you give others of them merely one coin, they will not return it to you unless you constantly remind them. That is because they say, "We are under no obligation to the Gentiles." They knowingly say lies about God. [75] Indeed, God loves those who keep His covenant and are always mindful of Him. [76] Those who barter God's covenant and their oaths for a small price have no portion in the Hereafter, and God will not speak to them or look at them on the Resurrection Day, nor will He cleanse them of their sins. They will a have painful punishment. [77] Some of them distort the Book with their tongues, so that you would think that it is from the Book, when it is not. They say, it is from God, when it is not, and they knowingly tell lies about God. [78]

It is inconceivable that a man could have been given the Book, Wisdom and Prophecy by God and then have told people, "Worship me instead of God," rather than, "Be godly teachers[291] because of what you were taught from the Book and because of what you have studied." [79] He will not command you to take angels and prophets as lords. Would he command you to deny God after you have submitted? [80]

When God made a covenant with the prophets, (He said), "If after I give you the Book and the Wisdom, I then send a messenger confirming what is with you, you should believe in him and help him. Do you accept and make it binding on you?" They said, "We accept." He said, "Then bear witness, and I, too, will be your witness." [81] From now on, those who turn away are disobedient. [82] Do they seek to have faith in something other than God, when all that is in heaven and earth submit to Him willingly or unwillingly? And unto Him all must return.[292] [83]

• • •

[290] Romans 8:27 And God, who searches the heart, knows what is the mind of the Spirit, because the Spirit intercedes for the saints according to the will of God.

[291] 2 Timothy 2:2 And what you have heard from me in the presence of many witnesses entrust to faithful men who will be able to teach others also.

[292] Romans 14:12 So then each one of us must give and account to God

Say, "We believe in God and what He revealed to us and to Abraham, Ishmael, Isaac, Jacob, the tribes, and in what was given to Moses (Musa), Jesus and the prophets from their Lord. We do not distinguish between any of them, and we have submitted to Him." [84] If one seeks a faith other than submission to God[293] (Islam), it will never be accepted from him, and in the Hereafter he will be among the losers. [85] How can God guide those who deny Him after having believed and witnessed that the messenger is true and after having seen miracles? God does not guide unjust people. [86] Their reward is the curse of God, angels, and all such men. [87] They will remain in that state forever, and their punishment will not be lightened nor will they be given relief. [88] As for those who repent and do good beforehand, God is forgiving and Merciful-to-all.[294] [89] The unbelievers, if after they have believed they then became stubborn in their unbelief, their repentance will never be accepted. They are truly lost. [90] An earth full of gold will not be accepted as a ransom from anyone who dies in a state of unbelief denying God. They will have a painful punishment [295] and will not have anyone to help them. [91] You (believers) will not attain righteousness until you give from what you hold dearest to your heart. God knows well what you give away. [92]

Before the Torah was revealed, all food was lawful for the children of Israel except what Israel (Jacob) made unlawful for himself. If you are telling the truth, bring the Torah and read it. [93] Those who persist in inventing lies about God after that are truly unjust. [94]

Say, "God has spoken the Truth; therefore, follow the creed of Abraham, a monotheist. He was not an idolater. [95] The first house of worship established for humanity was the one in Bakka[296]. It is blessed and a source of guidance to humanity. [96] In it are signs and miracles. It was the place where Abraham stood. Whoever entered it was safe. Pilgrimage to the House[297] is a duty owed to God by all people who can find a way to do it. But if anyone decides to reject the truth, (they should know that) God is rich beyond need of the worlds. [97]

Say, "People of the Book, why do you reject God's revelations? God is witness to what you do." [98] Say, "People of the Book, why do you turn the believers away from God's path? Seeking to make it (seem) deviant, while you are witnesses (to the truth)? God is not oblivious to what you do. [99]

Believers, if you obey some of those who were given the Book, they will turn you back to unbelief. [100] How can you not believe when God's message is recited to you and His Messenger is among you? Whoever clings [298] to God has been guided to a straight path.[299] [101] Believers, be mindful of God as is due Him and

• • •

---

[293] Islam means total submission to God. James 4:7. Submit yourselves therefore to God. Resist the devil, and he will flee from you.

[294] James 5:11 Indeed we call blessed those who showed endurance. You have heard of the endurance of Job, and you have seen the purpose of the Lord, how the Lord is compassionate and merciful.

[295] 2 Thessalonians 1:9 These will suffer the punishment of eternal destruction, separated from the presence of the Lord and from the glory of his might,

[296] Psalm 84:4-6 Blessed are those who dwell in your house; they are ever praising you. [5] Blessed are those whose strength is in you, whose hearts are set on pilgrimage. [6] As they pass through the Valley of Baka, they make it a place of springs;

[297] It refers to the House of God, the Holy Sanctuary in Mekkah.

[298] Or "takes refuge in God."

[299] Proverbs 3:6 In all your ways acknowledge Him, And He will make your paths straight.

be sure you have submitted to Him before you die. [102] Cling all together to God's rope, and do not separate. Remember God's grace to you: when you were enemies He united your hearts and you became brothers through His grace. You were at the edge of a pit of Hell, and He rescued you from it. God makes His signs clear to you, so that you may be guided. [103] May there be a group among you that calls for all that is good, promotes what is right and prevents what is wrong. It is they who are successful. [104] Do not be like those, who after having received clear signs, disputed and were divided among themselves[300]. They will have a great punishment [301] waiting for them. [105] On the Day (of Judgment) when some faces are bright (with hope) while others are dark (with despair). Those whose faces are darkened will be asked "Have you denied God's Truth after believing? Then experience the punishment for your unbelief." [106] As for those whose faces were bright, they will live eternally in God's mercy. [107] These are God's revelations which we recite to you in Truth. God does not desire injustice for people. [108] Everything in the heavens and on earth belongs to God,[302] and all things will return to Him.[303] [109]

You are the best community brought forth for the good of mankind, promoting what is right, forbidding what is wrong, and believing in God. If the People of the Book had believed, it would have been better for them. Some of them are believers, but most are defiantly disobedient. [110] They will not do you much harm, and if they fight you, they will flee and not be helped. [111] They are disgraced wherever they are, except for a lifeline from God and from people, and they brought God's anger upon themselves. They are branded with humiliation because they, in their transgression and disobedience, persisted in denying God's signs and wrongly killed the prophets.[304] [112] They are not all alike. Among the People of the Book are upright people, reading God's verses all night as they bow down. [113] They believe in God and the Last Day, order what is right, forbid what is wrong, and they are quick to do good deeds. They are righteous. [114] The good they do will not be forgotten. God knows those who are mindful of Him.[115]

As for the unbelievers, neither their wealth nor their children will be of benefit to them before God. They are destined to Hell, where they will remain eternally. [116] The parable of what they spend in this worldly life is like a freezing wind that blew on a field belonging to people who wronged themselves, and it destroyed it. God did not cheat them, but they cheated themselves. [117]

Believers do not be close friends to outsiders who spare no effort to ruin you and want to see you suffer. Their hatred is apparent in what they say, and what their hearts hide is even worse. We have made Our revelations clear to you, if you would only use your reason. [118] Here you are loving them, but they do not

• • •

[300] Matthew 12:25 Jesus knew their thoughts and said to them, "Every kingdom divided against itself will be ruined, and every city or household divided against itself will not stand.

[301] Matthew 25:41 Then he will say to those at his left hand, "You that are accursed, depart from me into the eternal fire prepared for the devil and his angels;

[302] Psalm 89:11 The heavens are yours, the earth also is yours; the world and all that is in it—you have founded them.

[303] Ecclesiastes 12:7 and the dust returns to the earth as it was, and the breath returns to God who gave it.

[304] Nehemiah 9:26"But they became disobedient and rebelled against You, And cast Your law behind their backs and killed Your prophets who had admonished them So that they might return to You, And they committed great blasphemies.

love you. You believe in the entire Book, and when they meet you, they say, "We believe." When they depart, they bite their fingers in rage against you. Say, "Perish in you rage. God knows what is in your hearts." [119] If goodness befalls you, they are displeased, and if evil, then they rejoice. If you endure and are godly, their plots will not harm you at all. God surrounds all they do. [120]

Remember, Prophet, when you left your family at dawn to post the believers at their battle stations, knowing that God hears all[305] and knows all,[306] [121] when two of your groups were about to give up, God protected them. Let the believers put their trust in God. [122] You were very weak, and God gave you the victory at Badr[307]. So, remain mindful of God and be grateful. [123] When you said to the believers, "Will it not be enough that your Lord supplies you with three thousand angels?" [124] Yes! If you endure and are mindful of God, and the enemy suddenly attacks you, your Lord will provide five thousand swooping angels. [125] God makes it all good news for you so that your hearts will be at peace in Him. Victory is only from God, the Almighty,[308] the Wise.[309] [126] He destroyed a flank of the unbelievers and suppressed them, so they would retreat frustrated in failure. [127] You have nothing to do with the matter. Either He will accept their repentance or punish them because they are unjust. [128] To God belongs everything in the heavens and the earth.[310] He forgives whomever He wants and punishments whomever he wants. God is forgiving[311] and Merciful-to-all.[312] [129]

Believers, do not collect exorbitantly compounded interests from usury, and be mindful of God so that you will succeed. [130] Be aware that Hell was prepared for the unbelievers, [131] and obey God and his Messenger, that you may receive mercy[313]. [132] Rush toward forgiveness from your Lord and a Heavenly Garden as wide as the heavens and the earth, prepared for those who are mindful of God. [133] Those who give in good times and in bad, suppress their rage and pardon other people. God loves those who do good [134] and those who when they are promiscuous or wrong themselves, remember [314] God and ask forgiveness for

• • •

[305] 1 John 5:14 And this is the boldness we have in him, that if we ask anything according to his will, he hears us.

[306] Joshua 22:22 "The Mighty One, God, the Lord, the Mighty One, God, the Lord! He knows, and may Israel itself know. If *it was* in rebellion, or if in an unfaithful act against the Lord do not save us this day!

[307] The Battle of Badr, took place outside Medina and was fought on Saturday, 13 March 624 CE (17 Ramadan, 2 AH in the Islamic calendar) in the Hejaz region of western Arabia. It was a key battle in the early days of Islam and a turning point in the Prophet's struggle with his opponents among the Quraish of Mecca who came out to attack him and finish him.

[308] Genesis 17:1 Now when Abram was ninety-nine years old, the Lord appeared to Abram and said to him, "I am God Almighty; Walk before Me, and be blameless. Revelation 16:7 And i heard the altar saying, "Yes, O Lord God, the Almighty, true and righteous are Your judgments."

[309] Proverbs 2:6 For the Lord gives wisdom; From His mouth *come* knowledge and understanding.

[310] Acts 4:24 When they heard it, they raised their voices together to God and said, 'Sovereign Lord, who made the heaven and the earth, the sea, and everything in them,

[311] Daniel 9:9. To the Lord our God belong mercy and forgiveness, for we have rebelled against him,

[312] Psalms 86:5 For you, Lord, are good, and ready to forgive; and plenteous in mercy to all them that call on you. James 5:11 Indeed we call blessed those who showed endurance. You have heard of the endurance of Job, and you have seen the purpose of the Lord, how the Lord is compassionate and merciful.

[313] Hebrews 4:16 Let us therefore come boldly to the throne of grace, that we may obtain mercy, and find grace to help in time of need.

[314] Or "mention."

their sins. Who but God forgives sins? And they do not knowingly persist in the sins they commit. (135) Their reward is forgiveness from their Lord and Heavenly Gardens with flowing rivers. They will live there eternally. What an incredible reward for their works! (136)

Historic events guided by God's laws happened down through the ages. As you walk throughout the land consider the consequences of those who denied the truth. (137) This is a clear statement to Mankind. It is guidance, and instruction to those who are mindful of God. (138) Do not lose heart or despair. You will overcome if you are believers. (139)

If you have been wounded, know that the other side has been similarly wounded. We alternate such days between people, so God may know those who believe and to choose from among them some who (with their lives) will bear witness to the Truth. God does not love the unjust. (140) So God can test the believers and annihilate the unbelievers. (141) Or do you suppose that you will enter the Heavenly Garden while God has not yet made evident those among you who struggled and made evident those who endure? (142) You desired death (in God's cause) before you encountered it. Now you have seen it with your own eyes! (143)

Muhammad is only³¹⁵ a messenger. Other messengers have passed away before him. If he dies or is killed, will you turn back? Whoever turns back will not hurt God at all. God will reward those who give thanks.³¹⁶ (144) No soul can die without God's permission at a predetermined time. We will give rewards in this world to whoever wants them, and rewards in the Hereafter to whoever wants them. We will reward those who give thanks. (145) Many prophets have fought with godly people by their side. They did not lose heart or weaken or surrender when suffering for God's cause. God loves those who endure. (146) What they said was, "Lord, forgive us our sins and our over indulgences and make our feet firm, and save us from the unbelieving people." (147) So God gave them rewards in this world and best rewards in the life to come. God loves those who do good. (148)

Believers, if you obey the unbelievers, they will cause you to turn back (from faith), and you will become losers. (149) God is your protector and He is the best of all victors. (150) We will strike panic into the hearts of the unbelievers. They attributed partners to God, for which He has never sent down any authority. Their dwelling is Hell. What an awful dwelling for the unjust! (151) God has fulfilled His promise to you when you, with His permission, were about to destroy your enemy. He showed you what you love, and then you failed, disputed and disobeyed. Some of you long for this world, and others long for the life to come. Then, in order that He might put you to a test, He kept you from winning. Then, later He pardoned you. God is gracious towards the believers.³¹⁷ (152) As you fled up (the mountain), not listening to anyone, even as the Messenger was calling

• • •

³¹⁵ The word "only" should be taken in context with the rest of the Qur'an, where he is called, among other things, a prophet (81), a warner and bringer of good news (11:2), etc. The Qur'an also uses the word "only" about Jesus, who in 5:75 is also called "only" a messenger, but he is also called "the Messiah" "His Word, and a spirit from Him" (171), "highly exalted in this world and the hereafter, and brought near to God" (45).

³¹⁶ Psalm 57:9-11 I will give thanks to you, O Lord, among the peoples; I will sing praises to you among the nations ¹⁰ for your steadfast love is as high as the heavens; your faithfulness extends to the clouds. ¹¹ Be exalted, O God, above the heavens. Let your glory be over all the earth.

³¹⁷ Psalm 41:4 As for me, I said, "O Lord, be gracious to me; heal me, for I have sinned against you."

out to you from behind, God afflicted you with sorrow upon sorrow. (God has now forgiven you) so that you would not grieve over what you missed or what happened to you. God is well aware of what you do. [153] Then after the sorrow, He surrounded you with a sense of calm and drowsiness covered some of you, while others were feeling sorry for themselves, entertaining wrong and ignorant thoughts about God. They said, "Do we have a say about this matter?" Say, "The whole matter is God's." They hide their true feeling from you (Prophet). They say, "If we had a say about this we would not have been killed here." Say, "If you were in your houses, those destined to be killed would have gone out to meet their death. God wants to test what is within you and purify what is in your hearts. God knows what is in the hearts[318]." [154] As for those of you who ran away on the day the two groups met, Satan humiliated them by their own actions. However, God has pardoned them. God is forgiving and forbearing. [155]

Believers, do not be like the unbelievers and say about their brothers who went on a journey or a raid, "If they were with us, they would not have died or been killed[319]." God will make these thoughts turn into bitter regret in their hearts. It is God who gives life and causes death. God sees well what you do. [156] If you die or are killed in God's path, there is forgiveness and mercy from God[320] better than all the wealth one might accumulate.[321] [157] When you die or are killed, you will be assembled before God. [158]

By God's mercy, you (Prophet) were gentle[322] toward them. If you had been rude[323] and hard-hearted, they would have turned away from you. Pardon them, ask forgiveness for them, and consult them about the matter, but once you decide on a course of action, put your trust in God. God loves those who trust Him[324]. [159] If God supports you, no one can defeat you. But if He fails you, who then can help you? Let the believers put their trust in God. [160]

No prophet should deceive, and whoever deceives will be faced with his deceit on the Resurrection Day. Then every soul will be rewarded according to what it earned, and they will not be wronged. [161] Is someone who pursues God's acceptance, like the one who earns God's wrath? His dwelling is Hell, a dreadful destiny. [162] They are on different levels in the sight of God. God sees what they do. [163]

God was gracious to the believers by sending them a messenger from among them reciting to them His verses, purifying them and teaching them the Book and Wisdom, though they were previously in clear error. [164] And when you are stricken with a disaster even after you have inflicted twice as much damage (on

• • •

[318] Luke 16:15 God knows your hearts.

[319] Matthew 10:28 And do not fear those who kill the body but cannot kill the soul. Rather fear him who can destroy both soul and body in hell.

[320] Psalm 116:15 Precious in the sight of the Lord is the death of his faithful servants.

[321] Psalm 130:1-4 Out of the depths I cry to you, O Lord. ² Lord, hear my voice! Let your ears be attentive to the voice of my supplications! ³ If you, O Lord, should mark iniquities, Lord, who could stand? But there is forgiveness with you, so that you may be revered.

[322] Or "flexible," "pliant," "lenient" or "yielding."

[323] Or "coarse." 2 Timothy 2:25-26 correcting opponents with gentleness. God may perhaps grant that they will repent and come to know the truth, 26 and that they may escape from the snare of the devil, having been held captive by him to do his will. Titus 3:2, " . . . to speak evil of no one, to avoid quarreling, to be gentle, and to show every courtesy to everyone."

[324] Proverbs 3:5-6 Trust in the Lord with all your heart, and do not lean on your own understanding. 6 In all your ways acknowledge him, and he will make straight your paths.

the enemy), you say, "How can this be?" Say, "You brought this upon yourselves. God has power over all things."[325] (165) What happened to you on the day when the two groups met was according to God's will, in order to give believers a chance to prove their faith, (166) and to let the hypocrites be known. When they were told "Come fight in God's path or at least defend yourselves." They said, "If we had known how to fight, we would have followed you. "They were closer on that day to unbelief than they were to faith. They say with their mouths what is not in their hearts. God knows what they hide. (167)

As for those who remained behind, and said of their brothers, "If they obeyed us, they would not have been killed." Say, "Prevent death from reaching you, if you are telling the truth." (168) Never think of those who are killed in God's path as dead, but alive and provided for with their Lord, (169) rejoicing in what God has bestowed upon them of His favor, and they receive good news about those who remained behind who have not yet joined them - that there will be no fear for them, nor will they grieve. (170) They are rejoicing in God's blessings and favor from God, and that God does not allow the believers' rewards to be lost. (171) Those who responded to God and his Messenger after suffering defeat, who do good and are mindful of God, will have a great reward. (172) Those who were told by others, "People have gathered (an army) to fight you so fear them." This instead increased their faith, and they said, "It is sufficient for us to be on God's side. He is the best of protectors.[326] (173) So they returned with grace and favor from God; no harm had touched them. And they worked hard at pleasing God, for truly God's favor is great. (174) It is Satan who is trying to get you to fear his allies, so do not be afraid, but fear Me, if you are believers. (175)

Do not let those who rush to unbelief grieve you. They will not harm God at all. It is God's will that they will have no part in the life to come. They will have great punishment.[327] (176) Those who chose to deny God over faith will not harm God at all. They will have painful punishment. (177) Those who are adamantly denying God shouldn't think that granting them more time, is necessarily better for them. We give them more time, but they only increase their guilt. They will have shameful punishment. (178) God would not leave the believers in the state they are in, until He identifies the wicked from the sincere. Nor would God reveal to you His unseen plan, but God chooses messengers according to His will. So believe in God and his Messengers. If you believe and are mindful of God, you will have a great reward. (179) Those who are tightfisted with what God has given them out of His abundance must not think that it is good for them; in fact, it is terrible for them. Whatever they cruelly withhold will be hung around their necks on Resurrection Day. It is God who will inherit the heavens and the earth: God is well aware of all you do. (180)

God has heard those who said, "God is poor, and we are rich." We will write down what they said and their wrongful killing of the prophets[328] in defiance of

• • •

[325] Psalm 147:5 Great is our Lord, and abundant in power; his understanding is beyond measure.

[326] Romans 8:31 What then are we to say about these things? If God is for us, who is against us?

[327] 2 Thessalonians 1:9 These will suffer the punishment of eternal destruction, separated from the presence of the Lord and from the glory of his might,

[328] Luke 11:50-51, " . . . so that this generation may be charged with the blood of all the prophets shed since the foundation of the world, 51 from the blood of Abel to the blood of Zechariah, who perished between the altar and the sanctuary. Yes, I tell you, it will be charged against this generation."

all that is right. We tell them, "Experience the fire's punishment!"[329] [181] That is for what your hands have committed, because God is never unjust to his servants. [182] They are those who said that God has made a covenant with us not to believe in a messenger unless he brings us an offering[330] that fire consumes. Say, "Messengers before me have come to you with miracles including the one you mentioned, so why did you kill them [331] if you are telling the truth?" [183] And if they reject you,[332] so also were messengers rejected who came before you, who brought miracles, written texts [333] and the enlightening Book. [184] Every soul will experience death, and your true compensation will come on the Resurrection Day. The victor is he who is drawn away from Hell to enter the Heavenly Garden, for the life of this world is merely an illusion.[334] [185] You will certainly be tested in your wealth and yourselves and will certainly hear hurtful things from those previously given the Book and the idolaters. But if you endure [335] and are mindful of God, this proves the strength of your resolve. [186]

God made a covenant with those who were given the Book, to clearly show it to humanity and not hide it,[336] but they turned their backs on the covenant and bartered it for a small price. What an evil bargain they made. [187] Do not think that those who rejoice over what they were given and who love to be praised for what they did not do – do not think that they will escape from punishment. They will have agonizing punishment.[337] [188]

To God belongs the kingdom of the heavens and the earth.[338] God has power over all things.[339] [189] The creation of the heavens and the earth and the sequence of night and day are signs to those who are endowed with insight.[340] [190] They are those who remember God while standing and sitting and lying on their sides,

• • •

[329] Ezekiel 25:17 I will execute great vengeance on them with wrathful punishments. Then they shall know that I am the Lord, when I lay my vengeance on them.

[330] "an offering that fire consumes" In other words, unless he confirms to Mosaic Law, which prescribes burnt offerings as an essential part of divine services.
Although this aspect of the Law had been left in abeyance ever since the destruction of the Second Temple in Jerusalem, the Jews of post-Talmudic times were convinced that the Messiah promised to them would restore the Mosaic rites in their entirety; and so they refused to accept as a prophet anyone who did not conform to the Law of the Torah in every detail

[331] Matthew 23:30, "and you say, 'If we had lived in the days of our ancestors, we would not have taken part with them in shedding the blood of the prophets.'"

[332] Or "call (you) a liar" or "deny."

[333] Or "psalms."

[334] Psalm 90:5-6 You sweep them away; they are like a dream, like grass that is renewed in the morning;
6 in the morning it flourishes and is renewed; in the evening it fades and withers.

[335] James 5:11 Indeed we call blessed those who showed endurance. You have heard of the endurance of Job, and you have seen the purpose of the Lord, how the Lord is compassionate
and merciful.

[336] 1 Chronicles 16:24 Declare his glory among the nations, his marvelous works among
all the peoples.

[337] Matthew 25:41 Then he will say to those at his left hand, "You that are accursed, depart from me into the eternal fire prepared for the devil and his angels;

[338] Psalm 89:11 The heavens are yours, the earth also is yours; the world and all that is in it—you have founded them.

[339] Jeremiah 10:12 It is he who made the earth by his power, who established the world by his wisdom, and by his understanding stretched out the heavens.

[340] Or "having minds" or "having hearts"

and consider the creation of the heavens and the earth,[341] saying "Our Lord, you have not created this aimlessly[342]. May You be exalted in your glory[343]! So protect us from the punishment of Hell. [191] Our Lord, You humiliate those You condemn to Hell. There is no help for the unjust. [192] Our Lord, We have heard one calling us to faith, 'Believe in your Lord.' So we believed. Our Lord, forgive us our sins and wipe out our bad deeds, and let us die with the righteous. [193] Our Lord, bring us what You promised us through Your messengers, and do not shame us on the Day of Resurrection. You do not break Your promises." [194] So their Lord answered their prayer, "I will not allow any of your deeds to be lost, male or female, each one of you is like the other. I will wipe away the sins of those who emigrated and were expelled from their homes and were harmed for My sake, and who fought and were killed, and make them enter Heavenly Gardens graced with flowing rivers as a reward from God. God has great rewards." [195]

Do not be deceived by the (uninhibited) movement of the unbelievers throughout the land. [196] They have a short time of enjoyment, and then their dwelling is Hell, a dreadful dwelling place. [197] But those who are mindful of their Lord have Heavenly Gardens with flowing rivers, lodging there forever in dwellings from God. God has the best in store for the righteous. [198]

Among the people of the Book are those who believe in God and what was revealed to you and what was revealed to them. They stand in awe of God; they do not barter God's messages for trivial gain. They have their reward from their Lord: God is quick in settling accounts. [199] Believers, be patient in hard times, and encourage each other to endure[344], and always be ready. Remain mindful of God, so you may prosper. [200]

• • •

---

[341] Psalm 8:3-4, "When I look at your heavens, the work of your fingers, the moon and the stars that you have established; 4 what are human beings that you are mindful of them, mortals that you care for them?"

[342] Jeremiah 29:11 For I know the plans I have for you, declares the Lord, plans for welfare and not for evil, to give you a future and a hope.

[343] Psalm 19:1The heavens declare the glory of God, and the sky above proclaims his handiwork. Revelation: 4:11 "Worthy are you, our Lord and God, to receive glory and honor and power, for you created all things, and by your will they existed and were created."

[344] Matthew 24:13 But the one who endures to the end will be saved. Hebrews 10:36 For you have need of endurance, so that when you have done the will of God you may receive what is promised. Romans 12:12 Rejoice in hope, be patient in tribulation, be constant in prayer.

CHAPTER **FOUR**

AN-NISA
THE WOMEN

THE **MEDINA** PERIOD

In the name of God, the Merciful-to-all, the Mercy Giver:

People, be mindful of your Lord, who created you out of a single soul, and out of it created its mate,[345] and out of the two spread countless men and women.[346] Remain mindful of God, in whose name you make requests of one another and beware of severing ties of kinship. God is always watching over you. [01] Give orphans their property, so do not replace (their) good things with bad, and do not intentionally mix their property into your own to consume it (for yourself).[347] This is a great sin. [02] If you fear that you will not be fair to orphan girls, then you may marry whichever women seem good to you- two, or three, or four[348]. However, if you fear that you may not be able to treat them with equal fairness, then marry only one or from those whom your right hands held in trust. This will make it more likely that you do not deviate from the right course. [03] Give women their bridal gift upon marriage, but if they decide to give you back a portion, then you may enjoy it with a good conscience. [04]

Do not entrust to the incompetent any property of theirs for which God has made you responsible. Make provision for them from it, clothe them and speak to them in a kind way. [05] Mentor and train orphans until they reach marriageable age; then, if you find they are mature, hand over their possessions to them. Do not consume it wastefully or spend it before they come of age. If the guardian is rich, let him abstain (from charging fees). But if he's poor, he should

• • •

---

[345] Genesis 2:7, 21, 22, "Then the Lord God formed man from the dust of the ground, and breathed into his nostrils the breath of life; and the man became a living being. [21] So the Lord God caused a deep sleep to fall upon the man, and he slept; then he took one of his ribs and closed up its place with flesh. [22] And the rib that the Lord God had taken from the man he made into a woman and brought her to the man."
[346] Genesis 1:28 God blessed them, and God said to them, "Be fruitful and multiply, and fill the earth and subdue it; and have dominion over the fish of the sea and over the birds of the air and over every living thing that moves upon the earth."
[347] Psalm 82:3 Give justice to the weak and the orphan; maintain the right of the lowly and the destitute.
[348] 1 Chronicles 14:3 'And while he was living in Jerusalem, David took more wives and became the father of more sons and daughters.'

45

charge a fair fee. When you give them their property, call in witnesses, although God takes full account of everything you do. (06)

Men will have a share in what their parents and close relatives leave behind, and women will have a share in what their parents and close relatives leave behind, whether it is a little or a lot: this is ordained by God. (07) If other relatives, orphans and poor people are present at the distribution (of inheritance), give them something as well, and speak to them in a kind way. (08) Let those who fear for the future of their own helpless children, if they were to die, show the same concern (for orphans). Let them be mindful of God and speak justly. (09) Those who unjustly consume the possessions of orphans are filling their bellies with fire, and they will fuel a blazing flame! (10)

Concerning (the inheritance of) your children, God commands you that a son should receive the equivalent share of two daughters. If there are more than two daughters, they should have two-thirds of what (their parents) leave behind. If there is only one daughter, she will have half. As for the parents (of the deceased), each of them will have one-sixth of what he leaves behind if the deceased leaves children. If the deceased has left no children and his parents are his (only) heirs, then his mother will have one-third; and if he has brothers and sisters, then his mother will have one-sixth. (This should take place) after the payment of any will or debts. As for your parents and your children, you do not know which of them most deserves to benefit from you. This is a law from God, and He is all-knowing,[349] all wise.[350] (11)

You will inherit one-half of what your wives leave, provided they have no children. If they had a child, then you will have one-quarter of what they leave behind, (this should take place) after payment of any will is carried through or debts. Your widows will have one-quarter of what you leave behind, provided you have no child. If there is a child, the widow will receive one-eighth of what you leave behind. (This should take place) after payment of any will is carried through or debts.

If a man or a woman has no direct heir, but has a brother or sister, then each of these two will inherit one-sixth; but if there are more than two, then they will share in one-third (of the inheritance). (This should take place) after payment of any will or debts, with no harm done to anyone. This is a commandment from God. He is All-knowing and compassionate.[351] (12) These are the bounds set by God. God will admit those who obey Him and His messenger into Gardens (Jannah) with flowing rivers[352], and there they will stay. This is the ultimate victory.[353] (13) But whoever rebels against God and His Messenger and transgresses His bounds, He will admit him into the fire, and there they will stay where shameful suffering awaits them.[354] (14)

• • •

[349] Psalm 44:21 would not God discover this? For he knows the secrets of the heart.

[350] Job 9:4, He is wise in heart, and mighty in strength —who has resisted him, and succeeded?

[351] Psalm 145:17 The Lord is just in all his ways, and kind in all his doings.

[352] Revelation 22:1 Then the angel showed me the river of the water of life, bright as crystal, flowing from the throne of God and of the Lamb

[353] 1 John 5:4 for whatever is born of God conquers the world. And this is the victory that conquers the world, our faith.

[354] Isaiah 50:11 But all of you are kindlers of fire, lighters of firebrands. Walk in the flame of your fire, and among the brands that you have kindled! This is what you shall have from my hand: you shall lie down in torment.

As for those of your women[355] who are accused of committing unlawful sexual conduct,[356] call four witnesses from among you, and if they testify to their guilt, keep the women at home until death comes to them or until God shows them another way. [(15)] Punish both of the guilty parties, but if they both repent and mend their ways, leave them alone. God is always ready to accept repentance. He's the Mercy Giver.[357] [(16)] But God only accepts repentance[358] from those that do evil out of ignorance[359] and then repent soon after: It is they whom God will forgive; He is all-knowing,[360] all wise.[361] [(17)] Whereas repentance will not be accepted from those who continue to do evil deeds until their dying hour and then say, "I now repent," nor from those who die denying God. For those We have prepared a painful punishment.[362] [(18)]

Believers, it is not lawful for you to inherit women against their will, nor should you treat them harshly in the hopes of re-gaining some of the bridal-gift you gave them, unless they are obviously guilty of promiscuity. Live with your wives in a way that is fair and kind. If you dislike them, it may well be that you dislike something which God has made a source of abundant grace. [(19)] If you wish to replace one wife with another, do not take away what you have given to the first one, regardless of how much it is. [(20)] How could you take it away after you have been intimate with one another, and she has received a solemn pledge from you? [(21)]

Do not marry women that your fathers married- with the exception of what previously took place: this is a shameful deed and a hateful thing and leads to evil. [(22)] You are forbidden to take as wives your mothers,[363] your daughters,[364] your sisters, your paternal and maternal aunts,[365] a brother's daughters, a sister's daughters, your wet nurse, your milk-sisters, mothers-in law,[366] and your step-daughters- who are your foster children that are born of your wives with

• • •

[355] Or "wives."

[356] Or "lewdness", "adultery" or "abomination."

[357] Ephesians 2:4 But God, who is rich in mercy, out of the great love with which he loved us

[358] Ezekiel 14:6 "Therefore say to the house of Israel, 'This is what the Sovereign Lord says: Repent! Turn from your idols and renounce all your detestable practices!" Isaiah 55:6-7 "Seek the Lord while he may be found; call on him while he is near. Let the wicked forsake his way and the evil man his thoughts. Let him turn to the Lord, and he will have mercy on him, and to our God, for he will freely pardon."
James 4:8 "Come near to God and he will come near to you. Wash your hands, you sinners, and purify your hearts, you double-minded."

[359] Acts 17:30 The times of ignorance God overlooked, but now he commands all people everywhere to repent,

[360] 1 John 3:20 whenever our hearts condemn us; for God is greater than our hearts, and he knows everything

[361] Proverbs 2:6 For the Lord gives wisdom; from his mouth come knowledge and understanding;

[362] Matthew 25:46 And this will go away into eternal punishment, but the righteous into eternal life

[363] Leviticus 18:7 "You shall not uncover the nakedness of your father, which is the nakedness of your mother; she is your mother, you shall not uncover her nakedness."

[364] Leviticus 18:9, 11, "You shall not uncover the nakedness of your sister, your father's daughter or your mother's daughter, whether born at home or born abroad. [11] You shall not uncover the nakedness of your father's wife's daughter, begotten by your father, since she is your sister."

[365] The Arabic specifies both paternal and maternal aunts. Leviticus 18:12, 13, "You shall not uncover the nakedness of your father's sister; she is your father's flesh. You shall not uncover the nakedness of your mother's sister, for she is your mother's flesh."

[366] Leviticus 18:17, "You shall not uncover the nakedness of a woman and her daughter, and you shall not take her son's daughter or her daughter's daughter to uncover her nakedness; they are your flesh; it is depravity."

whom you have consummated your marriage. However, if you have not consummated your marriage, you will incur no sin (by marrying their daughters). You are forbidden to marry the wives of your begotten sons,[367] two sisters simultaneously,[368] with the exception of what previously took place. God is most forgiving[369] and Merciful-to-all. (23) (You are forbidden to marry) women who are already married,[370] except from those whom your right hands held in trust[371]. God has ordained all of this for you[372]. Other women are lawful to you as long as you seek to marry them and not for unlawful intimacy. If you wish to enjoy women through marriage, you will give them their bridal-gift. If you should mutually choose, after fulfilling this obligation, to do something else with the bridal-gift, you will not be blamed. God is All-Knowing and All-Wise. (24)

If any of you does not have the means to marry free believing women, then marry a believer from those whom your right hands held in trust. God knows all about your faith; each one of you is part of the same human family. Marry them with their guardian's consent, and give them their rightful bridal-gifts. Make them married women, not adulterous fornicators or lovers. If they commit adultery when they are married, their punishment should be half that of free women. This permission is for those of you who fear they will sin.[373] It is better for you to practice self-control[374]. God is most forgiving[375] and Merciful-to-all.[376] (25) God wishes to make His laws clear to you, and to guide you towards the righteous ways of those who preceded you. He wishes to redeem you.[377] He is all-knowing and all wise. (26) God wants to redeem you in mercy, but those who

• • •

[367] Leviticus 18:15, "you shall not uncover the nakedness of your daughter-in-law: she is your son's wife; you shall not uncover her nakedness."

[368] Leviticus 18:18, "And you shall not take a woman as a rival to her sister, uncovering her nakedness while her sister is still alive."

[369] Psalm 86:5 For you, O Lord, are good and forgiving, abounding in steadfast love to all who call upon you. Isaiah 43:25 I, I am He who blots out your transgression from my own sake, and I will not remember your sins.

[370] Leviticus 18:20, "You shall not have sexual relations with your kinsman's wife, and defile yourself with her."

[371] Most commentators speculate that this verse is talking about a married women captured at war and they speculate that a female war captive's previous marriage is considered dissolved. However, a new owner was not permitted to touch a slave woman whose husband was with her (Abu Hanifa, in Razi). All the comentators that I reviewed, failed however to bring one single example from the time of the Prophet backing their interpretation. Hence our disagreement with the traditional interpretation based on the saying of the Prophet that "these are your brothers and sisters whom God placed in your trust." Boukhari 2407.

[372] Deut 21:10-12 When you go to war against your enemies and the Lord your God delivers them into your hands and you take captives, [11] if you notice among the captives a beautiful woman and are attracted to her, you may take her as your wife. [12] Bring her into your home and have her shave her head, trim her nails.

[373] i.e. in controlling your passions. 1 Corinthians 7:9, "But if they are not practicing self-control, they should marry. For it is better to marry than to be aflame with passion."

[374] 1 Corinthians 7:6, "This I say by way of concession, not of command."

[375] Psalm 103:3 who forgives all your iniquity, who heals all your diseases

[376] Psalm 116:5, Gracious is the Lord, and righteous; our God is merciful to all.

[377] 2 Peter 3:9 The Lord is not slow about his promise, as some think of slowness, but is patient with you, not wanting any to perish, but all to come to repentance.

only follow their lusts want you to drift astray from the right path. [27] God wants to lighten your burden as human beings were created weak[378]. [28]

Believers, do not consume one another's possessions wrongfully, not even if It is a trade with mutual consent. Do not kill each other, for God is Merciful-to-all of you. [29] Whoever does these things with malicious intent, We will make them burn in Hell: for this is easy for God. [30] If you avoid the great sins which you have been forbidden, We will wipe away your minor bad deeds and will cause you to enter through an honorable gate. [31] Do not desire that which God has given more abundantly to some of you in preference to others.[379] Men will profit from what they earned, and women will profit from what they earned. Ask God to give to you out of His favor. God has full knowledge of everything. [32] We have appointed heirs to everything that parents and close relatives leave behind, including those to whom you have pledged to marry: give them their share. God is witness to everything. [33]

Husbands have charge of their wives with the wealth God has given to some over others, and with what they spend out of their wealth. Righteous wives are truly devout, and they guard what God has ordained them to guard in their husbands' absence. If you have reason to fear ill-will from your wives, remind them of the teachings of God, then ignore them when you go to bed, then strike[380] them. If they obey you, do not seek to harm them. God is most high and great. [34] If you have reason to fear that a problem might occur between married couples, appoint one arbiter from among his family and one arbiter from among her family. If they both want to set things right, God may bring about their reconciliation. God is all-knowing, fully aware. [35]

Worship God alone; do not attribute divinity to others. Be good to your parents,[381] close relatives, orphans, the needy,[382] to close and far neighbors, close friends, stranded travelers and those whom your right hands held in trust.[383] God does not love those who are conceited and full of pride;[384] [36] who are stingy and demand that others be the same, concealing God's blessings to them. We have prepared a humiliating punishment for all the unbelievers. [37]

• • •

[378] Matthew 11:28-30 "Come to Me, all who are weary and heavy-laden, and I will give you rest. [29] "Take My yoke upon you and learn from Me, for I am gentle and humble in heart, and you will find rest for your souls. [30] "For My yoke is easy and My burden is light."

[379] Exodus 20:17, "You shall not covet your neighbor's house; you shall not covet your neighbor's wife, or male or female slave, or ox, or donkey, or anything that belongs to your neighbor."

[380] Modern commentators understand this verse in a cultural context. In today's world, using force against women is a crime and it is not advisable. The verse was meant to limit punishing women at a time when men use to consider women without any rights. For this reason the Prophet said: "The best among you (men) will not strike (women)." For verification of this saying, see Sunan Al Beikahi Al Kubra 304/7 and Musanaf Ibn Shaiba 368/8. The Prophet also also said: "The best among you is the best toward his wife and I am the best among you." See Al Albani 156/1. It was reported in the biography and the Hadith that Prophet Muhammad never laid a hand on any woman.

[381] Exodus 20:12, "Honor your father and your mother, so that your days may be long in the land that the Lord your God is giving you."

[382] Psalm 82:3 Give justice to the weak and the orphan; maintain the right of the lowly and the destitute.

[383] Mark 12:29-31 Jesus answered, "The first is, 'Hear, O Israel: the Lord our God, the Lord is one; [30] you shall love the Lord your God with all your heart, and with all your soul, and with all your mind, and with all your strength.' [31] The second is this, 'You shall love your neighbor as yourself.' There is no other commandment greater than these."

[384] Psalm 5:4-5 For you are not a God who delights in wickedness; evil will not sojourn with you. [5] The boastful will not stand before your eyes; you hate all evildoers.

God does not love those who spend their possessions on others only to be publicly praised,[385] while they do not actually believe in God or the Last Day. Whoever has Satan as his companion has an evil companion. [38] What harm would it be to them to believe in God and the Last Day, and give charitably from what God has given to them? God knows them well. [39] God does not wrong anyone by so much as an atom's weight. If there is a good deed done, He will multiply it, and will bestow out of His grace a mighty reward. [40] What will the sinners do on Judgment Day when We bring forward witnesses from within every community, with you (Muhammad) as a witness against these people? [41] Those who denied the truth and disobeyed the Prophet will wish that the earth would swallow them. They will not be able to conceal from God anything that has happened. [42]

Believers, do not attempt to pray while you are in a state of drunkenness, but wait until you know what you are saying; nor if you are in a state of major ritual impurity, until you have bathed, unless you are travelling and are unable to do so. If you are ill, are travelling, have relieved yourselves,[386] or had intercourse, and cannot find any water, then find some pure dust and wipe your faces and your hands with it. God is always ready to pardon and forgive. [43]

(Prophet), have you not considered how those who have been granted their portion of the Book barter it away for error? They wish you, too, would lose the right path. [44] God knows your enemies best. No one can befriend and protect you as God does.[387] [45] Among those of the Jewish faith, some distort the meaning of the (revealed) words, taking them out of their context and saying, "We have heard, but we disobey," and, "Listen," (adding the insult) 'May you not hear,' – thus speaking abusively and implying that the (true) Faith is false. If they had said, "We have heard, and we obey," and "Hear us, and have patience with us," it would have been better and more appropriate for them. God has rejected them because of their refusal to acknowledge the truth. They have little faith. [46]

People of the Book, believe in what We have sent down to confirm what you already have before We wipe out (your sense of) direction, turning you back, or rejecting you, as We rejected those who broke the Sabbath. God's will is always done. [47] God does not forgive the attribution of partners to Him, although He forgives any lesser sin unto whomever He wills. He who attributes a partner to God has invented a terrible sin.[388] [48] (Prophet), have you considered those who claim purity for themselves? No! God purifies whomever He wills. No one will be wronged by as much as a hair's breadth. [49] See how they invent lies about God. This in itself is an obvious sin. [50] Do you not see how those given a portion of the Book, now believe in idols and the powers of evil and maintain that those who are bent on denying the truth are more surely guided than those who are

• • •

[385]Matthew 6:1-4, "Beware of practicing your piety before others in order to be seen by them; for then you have no reward from your Father in heaven. ² 'So whenever you give alms, do not sound a trumpet before you, as the hypocrites do in the synagogues and in the streets, so that they may be praised by others. Truly I tell you, they have received their reward. ³ But when you give alms, do not let your left hand know what your right hand is doing, ⁴ so that your alms may be done in secret; and your Father who sees in secret will reward you."

[386] i.e. have defecated

[387] Psalm 41:2 The Lord protects them and keeps them alive; they are called happy in the land. You do not give them up to the will of their enemies.

[388] Isaiah 43:11 I am the Lord, and besides me there is no savior.

believers? [51] Those are the ones God has rejected. You (Prophet) will not find anyone to help those God has rejected. [52]

Do they have a share in (God's) dominion? If they had this, they would not give away so much as the groove of a date seed. [53] Do they envy the favor God has granted to other people? We gave the descendants of Abraham the Book and Wisdom and we gave them a great kingdom,[389] [54] and some of them believed in him yet some of them turned away from him. Nothing could be as blazing as Hell. [55] Those who are bent on denying Our messages will endure fire: (and) every time their skin burns off We will replace it with new skin so that they may perpetually suffer. God is mighty and wise. [56] As for those who believe and do righteous deeds, We will bring them into Gardens with flowing rivers and they will live there eternally[390] They will have pure spouses there, and We will give them abundant shade [57]

God commands you to return things entrusted to you to their rightful owners,[391] and if you judge between people, do so with justice. God's instructions to you are excellent for He is All-hearing[392] and All-seeing.[393] [58] Believers, obey God and the messenger and those among you who have been entrusted with authority.[394] If you have a dispute about anything, refer it to God and the Messenger, if you truly believe in God and the Last Day. This is best to do and in turn gives the best results. [59] Do you (Prophet) not see those who claim they believe in what has been revealed to you and revealed before you, yet they still want to turn to unjust tyrants for judgment, even though they have been ordered to reject them? Satan wants to lead them astray. [60] When they are told, "Turn to God's revelation and the Messenger," you see the hypocrites turn away from you in disgust. [61] How will they fare when disaster strikes them because of what they themselves have done? They will come to you swearing by God, "We desired nothing but good and to achieve reconciliation." [62] God

• • •

---

[389] 1 Kings 2:12 So Solomon sat on the throne of his father David; and his kingdom was firmly established.

[390] Revelation 22:1-3 Then the angel showed me the river of the water of life, bright as crystal, flowing from the throne of God and of the Lamb [2] through the middle of the street of the city.
On either side of the river is the tree of life with its twelve kinds of fruit, producing its fruit each month; and the leaves of the tree are for the healing of the nations. [3] Nothing accursed will be found there any more. But the throne of God and of the Lamb will be in it, and his servants will worship him;

[391] Exodus 22:26, "If you take your neighbor's cloak in pawn, you shall restore it before the sun goes down . . . "

[392] Psalm 145:19 He fulfills the desire of all who fear him; he also hears their cry, and saves them their steps

[393] Job 34:21 all for his eyes are upon the ways of mortals, and sees

[394] Romans 13:1-5, "Let every person be subject to the governing authorities; for there is no authority except from God, and those authorities that exist have been instituted by God. [2] Therefore, whoever resists authority resists what God has appointed, and those who resist will incur judgment. [3] For rulers are not a terror to good conduct, but to bad. Do you wish to have no fear of the authority? Then do what is good, and you will receive its approval; [4] for it is God's servant for your good. But if you do what is wrong, you should be afraid, for the authority does not bear the sword in vain! It is the servant of God to execute wrath on the wrongdoer. [5] Therefore, one must be subject, not only because of wrath but also because of conscience."

knows well what is in these people's hearts,[395] so ignore what they say, instruct them, and admonish them. [63] It is God's will that all messengers He sent be obeyed. If they (hypocrites) had come to you (Prophet), after having wronged themselves, and asked God to forgive them, while you, too, were asking for their forgiveness, they would have found that God accepts repentance and is Merciful-to-all. [64]

By your Lord, they do not really believe unless they make you (prophet) judge their disputes, and then find no resentment to accept your decision, fully submitting. [65] If we had ordered them, "Lay down your lives!" or, "Leave your homes," they would not have done so, except for a few. However, if they had done what they were ordered to do, it would have been better for them and a stronger confirmation of their faith, [66] and We would have granted them, out of Our grace, a mighty reward, [67] and guided them to a straight path. [68] All the people who obey God and the Messenger will be among those God has blessed including the prophets, those that never strayed from the truth, those who bore witness to the truth and the righteous. What excellent companions [396] are these! [69] That is how God favors you, and no one knows better than God. [70]

Believers, be on your guard, then mobilize for war in small groups or together. [71] Among you there is the type of person that would lag behind, and then if calamity would strike you, he would say, "God has been gracious to me that I was not there with them." [72] Yet, if good fortune comes to you from God, such a person would say, as if there had been no question of love between you and him, "If I had only been with them, I would have profited a lot." [73] Let only those who are willing to trade life in this world for the Hereafter fight in God's cause. We will grant a mighty reward to all who fight in God's cause, whether they are killed or are victors. [74] How could you refuse to fight in God's cause for the helpless men, women and children who are screaming, "Lord! Lead us towards freedom, out of this land of oppressors! Through your grace, give us a protector and a helper!" [75] The believers fight for God's cause, whereas those who are bent on denying the truth fight for the cause of evil. Fight the allies of Satan. Satan's tactics are truly weak. [76]

(Prophet), are you not aware of those who have been told, "Refrain from fighting, perform prayer, and pay the purifying alms?" However, as soon as the fighting is ordained for them, some of them feared men even more than they feared God, saying, "Lord, why have You ordained fighting for us? If only You would give us just a little more time?" Say to them, "The enjoyment of this world is brief, whereas the life to come is far better for those who are mindful of God. You will not be wronged, not even a little bit. [77] Wherever you may be, death will overtake you, even if you are in high protected towers. When good fortune happens to them, some (people) say, "This is from God," whereas when harm comes to them, they say, "This is from you (Prophet)." Tell them, "Both come from God." What is the matter with these people? They hardly understand what

• • •

[395] Luke 6:8,16:15, "Even though he knew what they were thinking, he said to the man who had the withered hand, 'Come and stand here.' He got up and stood there. 16:15 So he said to them, 'You are those who justify yourselves in the sight of others; but God knows your hearts; for what is prized by human beings is an abomination in the sight of God."

[396] Psalm 119:62-64 At midnight I rise to praise you, because of your righteous ordinances. [63] I am a companion of all who fear you, of those who keep your precepts. [64] The earth, O Lord, is full of your steadfast love; teach me your statutes.

they are told. ⁽⁷⁸⁾ Anything good that happens to you is from God, and whatever evil happens to you is from yourself. We have sent you as a Prophet to all people, and it is enough that God is your witness. ⁽⁷⁹⁾ Whoever obeys the Messenger obeys God. We have not sent you to be the keeper for those who turn away. ⁽⁸⁰⁾ They say, "We obey you (Prophet)," but when they leave your presence, some of them plot during the night to disobey you. God records what they plot. Ignore them, and place your trust in God, for none is as worthy of trust as God. ⁽⁸¹⁾

Will they not, at least, try to understand this Qur'an? If it had been from anyone but God, they would have found many inconsistencies in it. ⁽⁸²⁾ Whenever a rumor pertaining to peace or war comes to them, they broadcast it. But had they referred it to the Messenger and to the believers who were in charge, they would have understood it and made sense of it. If it were not for God's favor and mercy on you, most of you would have followed Satan. ⁽⁸³⁾

So, (Messenger) fight in the cause of God. You are responsible only for yourself. Rally the believers, because God may well curb the strength of the unbelievers. God is stronger in might and in His ability to destroy.^{397 (84)} Whoever rallies for a good cause will share in its benefits; and whoever rallies for an evil cause will answer for his part in it. God watches everything. ⁽⁸⁵⁾ When you are greeted with a greeting, answer with an even better greeting, or (at least) respond with the same greeting. God keeps account of everything. ⁽⁸⁶⁾ He is God. There is no god but Him. He will gather all of you on the Resurrection Day.³⁹⁸ There is no doubt about it. Whose word could be truer than God's?^{399 (87)}

How is it that you are double-minded and divided over the hypocrites, seeing that God Himself has disowned them because of their disobedience? Do you, perhaps, want to guide those whom God has let go astray? Whomever God leads astray, you (Messenger) will never find a way for them.^{400 (88)} They would love to see you deny the truth just as they have denied it, so you will all be the same. Do not take them as allies until they migrate for God's cause. But if they turn on you with open hostility, then seize them and kill them wherever you may find them. Do not take any of them as your allies or supporters.^{401 (89)} Some seek refuge with people with whom you are bound by a treaty, or they come over to you because their consciences forbid them to go to war against you or against their own people. Had God willed, He would have given them power over you, and they would have fought you. So if they withdraw and do not fight you, and offer you peace, God does not allow you to harm them. ⁽⁹⁰⁾ You will find others who wish to

• • •

³⁹⁷ Hebrews 12:29, " . . . for indeed our God is a consuming fire." Romans 12:19, "Beloved, never avenge yourselves, but leave room for the wrath of God; for it is written, 'Vengeance is mine, I will repay, says the Lord.'"
³⁹⁸ Matthew 25:32 All the nations will be gathered before him, and he will separate people one from another as a shepherd separates the sheep from the goats,
³⁹⁹ Titus 1:2 in the hope of eternal life that God, who never lies, promised before the ages began—
⁴⁰⁰ 2 Thessalonians 2:11-12 "For this reason God sends them a powerful delusion, leading them to believe what is false."12 so that all who have not believed the truth but took pleasure in unrighteousness will be condemned."
⁴⁰¹ The Qur'an has four verses that command killing people who start a war to eliminate the new state or to threaten its stability (2:191, 4:89, 91, and 9:5), but none of these apply today. Similarly, the Torah has many verses that refer to killing others (Exodus 23:23-24, 28-30, 32:27, Numbers 21:35, 31:2,7-8, 17, Deuteronomy 7:2, 16, 9:3-4, Joshua 6:17-21, 8:2, Judges 21:11, 1 Samuel 15:3, 27:9, 11, 2 Chronicles 15:13) and none of them apply today either.)

be safe from you, and from their own people, but whenever they are back in a situation where they are tempted (to fight you), they succumb to it. So if they do not withdraw, offer peace, or restrain themselves from hostility, seize and kill them wherever you encounter them. We give you clear authority against such people. [91]

A believer should never kill another believer, but mistakes happen. If someone kills a believer by mistake, he must free one believing slave and pay compensation to the victim's relatives, unless they willingly forgo compensation. If the victim is a believer, but belonged to a community with which you are at war, then the compensation is only to free a believing slave; whereas, if the person killed belonged to a community with whom you have a treaty, then the compensation should be paid to his relatives in addition to freeing a believing slave. Anyone who does not have the means to do this must fast for two consecutive months. God ordains this atonement. God is All-Knowing, All-Wise.[402] [92] But whoever deliberately slays another believer, his punishment will be Hell. There, he will remain and God will condemn him, and will reject him, and will prepare horrible suffering for him. [93] So, believers, be careful when you fight in God's path, and use your discernment. Do not say to someone who offers you a greeting of peace, "You are not a believer, aspiring for worldly goods. God has plenty of gains for you. You were once in the same position, but God has been gracious to you. Therefore, use your discernment. God is always aware of what you do. [94]

Unequal are the passive believers who stay behind, to those who commit themselves, their possessions and their lives to struggling in God's cause. God has raised those who struggle to a rank far above those who stay behind. Even though God has promised the ultimate good unto all believers, those who struggle are favored with a tremendous reward, [95] high ranks conferred by Him, as well as forgiveness, and mercy. God is most Forgiving[403] and Merciful-to-all.[96]

When the angels gather the souls of those who wronged themselves,[404] they will wonder, "What was the matter with you?" They will say, "We were oppressed in our land." (The angels) will ask, "Was not God's earth vast enough for you to run away?" These people will have Hell as their refuge, a horrible destination.[97] The truly helpless, including men, women or children, who do not have the means to leave may be exempt. [98] God might just pardon them. God is forever pardoning and forgiving. [99] He who migrates for God's cause will find many safe places and abundant resources on earth. If anyone leaves his home as an emigrant for God and His Messenger, and then he dies, his reward is certain with God[405]. God is forever forgiving and Merciful-to-all. [100]

When you believers are travelling, you will not be blamed for shortening your prayers if you fear that the unbelievers may harm you. They are your sworn enemies. [101] (Prophet) When you are among believers and about to lead them in prayer, let a group of them stand up in prayer with you, taking their weapons

• • •

[402] Job 9:4 He is wise in heart, and mighty in strength – who has resisted him, and succeeded?
[403] Psalm 65:3 when we were overwhelmed by sins, you forgave our transgressions.
[404] The text refers to those who could have migrated with the Prophet from Mecca but did not.
[405] Matthew 19:29 And everyone who has left houses or brothers or sisters or father or mother or wife or children or fields for my sake will receive a hundred times as much and will inherit eternal life.

with them. When they have finished their prayer, let them take up their positions at the back while another group, who has not yet prayed, come forward to pray with you, also on their guard and armed with their weapons. The unbelievers would love to see you unarmed, so that they might take you in a surprise attack. You will not be blamed for laying down your weapons, while you pray if you encounter heavy rain or are ill; But be fully prepared against danger. God has prepared a shameful and humiliating punishment for the unbelievers. (102) When you have finished your prayer, continue to remember God- standing, sitting and lying down; and when you are safe again, observe your complete prayers. For all believers, prayer is a sacred duty to be performed at prescribed times. (103) Do not be hesitant when pursuing the enemy. If you are feeling pain, so are they. But you expect from God what they cannot expect. God is All-Knowing,[406] All-Wise.[407] (104)

We have sent down the Book to you (Prophet), with the Truth, so that you can judge between people according to what God has taught you. Do not be an advocate for those who are traitors, (105) but pray for God's forgiveness. God is most Forgiving [408] and Merciful-to-all. (106) Do not argue on behalf of those who betray their own souls. God does not love anyone given to treason and sin.[409] (107) They try to hide their actions from men, but from God they cannot hide them. God is with them while they are plotting during the night, saying things that are displeasing to Him. God is fully aware of everything they do. (108) Here you are pleading their cause in this world, but on the Resurrection Day who will plead with God on their behalf? Who will then be their advocate? (109) He who does evil or sins against himself and later prays asking for God to forgive him, will find God very forgiving and merciful. (110) He who commits sin does so against his own soul. God is All-knowing, All-Wise. (111) He who commits an offence or sin and then blames an innocent person has burdened himself with deceit and flagrant sin. (112)

If it were not for God's favor and mercy to you (Prophet), some of them would have led you astray. They only lead themselves astray. They cannot harm you in any way, and God has given you the Book and the Wisdom, and taught you what you did not know. God's favor on you is indeed tremendous. (113)

Nothing good comes from their secretive discussion, except for when they are encouraging charity, or good or reconciliation between people. To anyone who does this out of a longing for God's pleasure, We will give a great reward. (114) Whoever deviates, after guidance has been clearly given to him, contentiously opposes the Messenger and follows a path other than that of the believers, We will leave him on his chosen path and let him burn in Hell, an evil destination. (115)

God does not forgive the association of partners with Him, although He forgives any lesser sin of whomever He wills. Those people who worship deities besides Him have gone far, far astray. (116) In His place the idolaters invoke only

• • •

---

[406] 1 John 3:20 whenever our hearts condemn us; for God is greater than our hearts, and he knows everything.
[407] Job 9:4 He is wise in heart, and mighty in strength —who has resisted him, and succeeded? —
[408] Daniel 9:9. To the Lord our God belong mercy and forgiveness, for we have rebelled against him,
[409] Psalm 5:4-5 For you are not a God who delights in wickedness; evil will not sojourn with you.
5 The boastful will not stand before your eyes; you hate all evildoers.

idols with female names, thus invoking the rebellious Satan [117] whom God has rejected for having said, "I will certainly claim my due share of your servants, [118] and will lead them astray and fill them with vain desires. I will command them, and they will slit the ears of cattle. I will command them to corrupt God's creation." Whoever chooses Satan as their master, as opposed to God, is utterly ruined. [119] He makes them promises and fills them with vain desires; yet, whatever Satan promises them is nothing but an illusion. [120] Such people will have Hell as their home, and they will have no way out. [121] As for those who believe and do righteous deeds, [410] We will admit them into Gardens graced with flowing rivers, to remain eternally. This is a true promise from God. Who speaks more truthfully than God? [122] You will not be judged according to your wishes or according to the wishes of the People of the Book. Anyone who does evil will be judged for it and will not find anyone to protect him or help him. [123] Whereas, anyone, be it man or woman, who does good deeds and is a believer will enter Heaven, and will not be wronged by as much as a tiny bit. [124] Who could be better in faith than those who submit themselves to God, and do good, and follow the faith of Abraham, who turned away from all that is false? God took Abraham as a friend. [411][125] Everything in heaven and on earth belongs to God. [412] God is fully aware of everything. [126]

They ask you (Prophet) for a ruling about women. Say, "God gives you a ruling about them, along with what has been recited to you through the Book about orphan women (in your charge), from whom you withhold the prescribed shares (of their inheritance) and whom you wish to marry; and about helpless children; and about your duty to treat orphans with fairness. God has full knowledge of whatever good you do." [127]

If a woman has reason to fear ill-treatment or even a lack of interest from her husband, neither of them will be blamed if they come to a peaceful settlement, for peace is best. Selfishness is always present in human souls. If you do good and are mindful of God, He is well aware of all that you do. [128] You will never be able to treat your wives with equal fairness, regardless of how much you desire to do so. Do not allow yourself to incline more towards one and exclude the other, potentially leaving her dangling (between marriage and divorce). If you make amends and remain mindful of God, He's most forgiving and Merciful-to-all. [413][129]

If a husband and wife do separate, God will provide for each of them out of His plenty. God is limitless in His provision and wise. [130] All that is in heaven and on earth belongs to God. We have commanded those who were given the Book before your time, as well as you, to remain mindful [414] of God. Even if you ignore Him, everything in the heavens and on earth belong to Him, and God is rich

• • •

[410] Psalm 11:7 For the Lord is righteous; he loves righteous deeds; the upright shall behold his face.

[411] Isaiah 41:8, "But you, Israel, my servant, Jacob, whom I have chosen, the offspring of Abraham, my friend . . . "

[412] Psalm 89:11 The heavens are yours, the earth also is yours; the world and all that is in it—you have founded them.

[413] Isaiah 63:9 In all their affliction He was afflicted, And the angel of His presence saved them; In His love and in His mercy He redeemed them, And He lifted them and carried them all the days of old.

[414] Ecclesiastes 12:13, "The end of the matter; all has been heard. Fear God, and keep his commandments; for that is the whole duty of everyone."

beyond need and worthy of all praise. (131) Everything in the heavens and on earth belongs to God,[415] and He is sufficient for those who trust in Him.[416] (132) If He's willing, He can cause all of you to disappear and replace you with new people:[417] God is fully capable of doing this. (133) If someone desires the rewards of this world, the rewards of this world and the next are both God's to give. God hears[418] and sees everything.[419] (134)

Believers, uphold justice and bear witness to God, even if that witness is against yourself, your parents or your close relatives. Whether a person is rich or poor, God can best take care of both. Refrain from following your own desires, so that you do not act unjustly. If you distort the truth, God is fully aware of what you do. (135) Believers, hold on to your faith in God and His Messenger, as well as the Book that He has gradually sent down to His Messenger, as well as the Book that He sent down before. He who denies God, His angels, His Books, His Messengers, and the Last Day has gone far astray. (136) As for those who believe and then deny the truth, then believe again, and again deny the truth and become increasingly defiant, God will not forgive them, nor will He guide them. (137) (Prophet) tell these hypocrites that an agonizing punishment awaits them. (138)

Are those who ally themselves with the unbelievers rather than the believers doing so because they seek power through them? Power is only God's to give.[420] (139) He has already revealed to you in the Book that whenever you hear people denying and mocking God's message, you should avoid their company until they start talking about other things, or else you will become like them.[421] God will gather the hypocrites[422] in Hell, together with the unbelievers. (140) They wait to see what happens to you and, if God brings you success. They say, "Were we not on your side?" If the unbelievers have some success, they say to them, "Have we not earned your affection by defending you against those believers?" God will judge between everyone on the Resurrection Day, and God will never allow the unbelievers to harm the believers. (141)

The hypocrites try to deceive God, but it is He who causes them to be deceived. They rise to pray, they rise reluctantly, only to be seen and praised by men,[423] seldom remembering God, (142) wavering between this and that,

• • •

[415] Psalm 24:1, "The earth is the Lord's and all that is in it, the world, and those who live in it . . ."
[416] Proverbs 3:5-6 Trust in the Lord with all your heart, and do not rely on your own insight. [6] In all your ways acknowledge him, and he will make straight your paths.
[417] Matthew 21:43, "Therefore I tell you, the kingdom of God will be taken away from you and given to a people that produces the fruits of the kingdom."
[418] Deuteronomy 26:7 we cried to the Lord, the God of our ancestors; the Lord heard our voice and saw our affliction, our toil, and our oppression.
[419] Proverbs 15:3 The eyes of the Lord are in every place, keeping watch on the evil and the good.
[420] 2 Corinthians 4:7 But we have this treasure in clay jars, so that it may be made clear that this extraordinary power belongs to God and does not come from us.
[421] 1 Corinthians 15:33 Do not be deceived: Bad company ruins good morals."
[422] Revelation 21:8, "But as for the cowardly, the faithless, the polluted, the murderers, the fornicators, the sorcerers, the idolaters, and all liars, their place will be in the lake that burns with fire and sulphur, which is the second death."
[423] Matthew 6:5-8 "And whenever you pray, do not be like the hypocrites; for they love to stand and pray in the synagogues and at the street corners, so that they may be seen by others. Truly I tell you, they have received their reward. [6] But whenever you pray, go into your room and shut the door and pray to your Father who is in secret; and your Father who sees in secret will reward you.)

belonging neither to one side nor the other.[424] If God let someone stray, (Prophet) you will never find a way for him. [143] Believers, do not take the unbelievers as allies and protectors instead of the believers. Do you want to offer God clear evidence of your guilt? [144] The hypocrites will be in the lowest depths of Hell, and you will find no one to help them,[425] [145] except for those who repent, make amends, hold fast to God and are devoted in their faith to Him alone. They are one with the believers. God will grant a mighty reward to the believers. [146]

Why should God punish you (for your past sins) if you become thankful and believe in Him? God is always responsive to gratitude and is All-Knowing.[426] [147] God does not like any evil to be mentioned openly unless someone has been wronged. God is All-Hearing[427] and All-Knowing. [148] If you do good openly or in secret, or pardon others for something bad done to you, then God is most forgiving[428] and powerful.[429] [149]

As for those who ignore God and His Messenger by trying to make a distinction between them, saying, "We believe in the one, but we deny the other," and want to pursue a path in-between, [150] it is they who are truly unbelievers. We have prepared a humiliating punishment for the unbelievers. [151] As for those who believe in God and His Messengers and did not make any distinction between His Messengers, God will grant them their rewards. God is most forgiving and Merciful-to-all. [152]

The People of the Book demand that you (Prophet) make a Book physically come down to them from heaven. They demanded even more than this from Moses (Musa) when they said, "Let us see God face to face," and were then struck by a thunderbolt of punishment for their presumption. Even after clear revelations had come down to them, they started worshipping the calf. [430] We pardoned this and gave Moses clear authority [153] to raise the mountain above them in witness of their solemn pledge. We said to them, "Enter the gate humbly," and, "Do not break the Sabbath law."[431] We accepted from them a solemn pledge. [154] (We punished them) for breaking their pledge, for their refusal to acknowledge God's messages, for unjustly killing their prophets,[432] and for saying, "Our hearts are sealed." No, God has sealed their hearts as a result of

• • •

[424] James 1:7-8 for the doubter, being double-minded and unstable in every way, [8] must not expect to receive anything from the Lord.

[425] Hebrews 10:26 For if we willfully persist in sin after having received the knowledge of the truth, there no longer remains a sacrifice for sins,

[426] Romans 11:33 O the depth of the riches and wisdom and knowledge of God! How unsearchable are his judgments and how inscrutable his ways!

[427] Deuteronomy 26:7 we cried to the Lord, the God of our ancestors; the Lord heard our voice and saw our affliction, our toil, and our oppression

[428] But God, who is rich in mercy, out of the great love with which he loved us Ephesians 2:4

[429] Psalm 62:11 once God has spoken; twice have I heard this: that power belongs to God.

[430] Exodus 32:7-8 The Lord said to Moses, "Go down at once! Your people, whom you brought up out of the land of Egypt, have acted perversely; [8] they have been quick to turn aside from the way that I commanded them; they have cast for themselves an image of a calf, and have worshiped it and sacrificed to it.

[431] Ezekiel 20:20 and hallow my Sabbaths that they may be a sign between me and you, so that you may know that I the Lord am your God.

[432] Nehemiah 9:26 "Nevertheless they were disobedient and rebelled against you and cast your law behind their backs and killed your prophets, who had warned them in order to turn them back to you, and they committed great blasphemies.

their unbelief, and (now) they only believe in a few things, [155] and because they denied the truth and uttered a terrible slander against Mary, [156] and said, "We have killed the Messiah Jesus (Esa), son of Mary, the Messenger of God." However, they did not kill him, nor did they crucify him, though it was made to appear as if it had been so. Those who disagree are confused, having no (real) knowledge to follow, only supposition. They certainly did not kill him. [157] Rather, God raised him up to Himself. (see 3:58) God is Almighty and Wise.[433] [158] Yet, there is not one of the People of the Book but will believe in him before his death, and on the Resurrection Day Jesus will bear witness against them.[434] [159] Due to the wrongdoings done by the Jews, We denied them certain good things that had been permitted to them previously; and (We did this) because they frequently turned away from God;[435] [160] taking usury even though it had been forbidden them, and for wrongfully consuming other people's possessions. For those of them who continuously reject the truth, We have prepared painful punishment. [161] As for those among them who are deeply rooted in knowledge and the believers who believe in what has been revealed to you, and in what was revealed before you, and those who are (especially) constant in prayer, and give the purifying alms, and all who believe in God and the Last Day-- to them We will give a great reward. [162]

We have sent a revelation to you (Prophet), just as We inspired Noah and all the prophets after him -- as We inspired Abraham, and Ishmael, and Isaac, and Jacob, and their descendants, including Jesus and Job, and Jonah, and Aaron, and Solomon; and to David We gave the Psalms [163] and other messengers that We have already mentioned to you, as well as messengers that We have not mentioned to you. And God spoke directly to Moses.[436] [164] All of these were messengers bearing good news and warning, so that people would not have any excuse[437] before God after these messengers were sent. God is almighty and wise. [165] God (Himself) bears witness to what He has sent down to you: He sent it down from on high with His knowledge and with the angels bearing witness- although God is a sufficient witness. [166] Those who have denied the truth and turned others away from God's path[438] have gone far astray. [167] God will not forgive those who reject the truth and are unjust, nor will He guide them onto any path [168] except the path that leads to Hell, where they will live eternally. This is easy for God. [169]

People, the Messenger has come to you with the Truth from your Lord, so believe it for your own wellbeing. If you deny the truth, remember that to God belongs everything that is in the heavens and on earth. God is All-Knowing and

• • •

[433] Job 9:4, "He is wise in heart, and mighty in strength"

[434] 2 Timothy 4:1 In the presence of God and of Christ Jesus, who is to judge the living and the dead,

[435] 2 Chronicles 29:6 For our ancestors have been unfaithful and have done what was evil in the sight of the Lord our God; they have forsaken him, and have turned away their faces from the dwelling of the Lord, and turned their backs.

[436] Numbers 12:8, "With him I speak face to face—clearly, not in riddles; and he beholds the form of the Lord. Why then were you not afraid to speak against my servant Moses?"

[437] Romans 1:20 Ever since the creation of the world his eternal power and divine nature, invisible though they are, have been understood and seen through the things he has made. So they are without excuse;

[438] Matthew 23:13, "But woe to you, scribes and Pharisees, hypocrites! For you lock people out of the kingdom of heaven. For you do not go in yourselves, and when others are going in, you stop them."

All-Wise.[439] (170) People of the Book, do not be excessive in your beliefs, and do not say about God except the Truth. The Messiah, Jesus son of Mary, is the Messenger of God and His Word conveyed to Mary and a Spirit from Him. So believe in God and His Messengers and do not say "Three." Stop this for your own good. God is one God. So exalted is He, in His glory, from having a son. Everything belongs to Him that is in the heavens and on earth. None is as worthy to trust as He. (171)

The Messiah was never too proud to be God's servant, nor were the angels [440] who are near to Him (GOD). He will gather before Him (GOD) the arrogant and all those who are too proud to worship Him. (172) To those who believe and do good deeds, He will give them their just rewards, and give them even more out of His favor. Whereas, to those who felt too proud and arrogant, He will punish them with a painful punishment. They will find no one to protect them from God. (173)

People, convincing truth has now come to you from your Lord, and We have sent down to you clear enlightenment. (174) As for those who believe in Him, and hold fast to Him, God will admit them into His mercy and grace, and will guide them to Himself on a straight path.[441] (175)

They will ask you (Prophet) for a ruling. Say, "God gives you a ruling concerning those who die childless and who have no surviving parents. If a man dies childless and has a sister, she will inherit one-half of what he has left, just as he will inherit from her if she dies childless. But if there are two sisters, then they are entitled to two-thirds of the inheritance between them, but if there are brothers and sisters, then the male is entitled to twice the share of the female.

God makes this clear to you so that you do not go astray. God knows everything. (176)

• • •

---

[439] Proverbs 2:6 for the Lord gives wisdom; from his mouth come knowledge and understanding;

[440] Hebrews 1:14, "Are not all angels' spirits in the divine service, sent to serve for the sake of those who are to inherit salvation?"

[441] Proverbs 3:6 In all your ways acknowledge him, and he will make straight your paths.

CHAPTER FIVE

AL-MA'IDA
THE FEAST

THE **MEDINA** PERIOD

In the name of God, the Merciful-to-all, the Mercy Giver:

Believers, fulfill your obligations. Livestock animals are lawful for you to eat, except for what We will describe to you. You are not allowed to hunt while you are in a state of pilgrimage. God commands what He wills. [01] Believers, do not violate the laws pertaining to God's sacraments, the sacred month of pilgrimage, or the offerings, and do not prevent those who are going to the Sacred House from seeking favor, pleasure and acceptance from their Lord. Once your pilgrimage is over, then you are free to hunt. Never let your hatred for the people who barred you from the Sacred Sanctuary lead you to break the law. Help one another to do what is right-- to always be mindful of God, and do not encourage one another in sin and hostility. Always be mindful of God, because His punishment is severe.[442] [02]

You are forbidden to eat animals that you find already dead, blood, pork's meat[443], any animal over which any name other than God's has been invoked, any animal that has been strangled or beaten to death or killed by a fall or gored to death or mauled by a wild animal, unless you can still properly slaughter it. You are also forbidden to eat anything that has been sacrificed to idols.[444] You are forbidden to draw lots, since this is sinful conduct.[445] The unbelievers have lost all hope of you ever forsaking your faith. Do not be afraid of them, but stand in awe of Me. Today I have perfected your faith for you and have shed My grace

· · ·

---

[442] Ezekiel 25:17 I will execute great vengeance on them with wrathful punishments. Then they shall know that I am the Lord, when I lay my vengeance on them.

[443] Deuteronomy 14:8 'And the pig is unclean to you, because though it has a division in the horn of its foot, its food does not come back; their flesh may not be used for food or their dead bodies touched by you.'

[444] Acts 15:29 that you abstain from what has been sacrificed to idols and from blood and from what is strangled and from fornication. If you keep yourselves from these, you will do well.

[445] 2 Kings 17:17 They made their sons and their daughters pass through fire; they used divination and augury; and they sold themselves to do evil in the sight of the Lord, provoking him to anger.

upon you and have chosen submission[446] (Islam) to be your faith. As for him who is driven to what is forbidden by dire necessity, and not by an inclination to sin, God is All-Forgiving [447] and Merciful-to-all.[448] (03)

They will ask you (Prophet) what is lawful for them. Say, "All good things are lawful to you, including what you have taught your birds and beasts of prey to catch, teaching them as God has taught you. You may eat what they catch for you, but invoke God's name over it, and always be mindful of God". He is quick to take account.[449] (04) Today, all the good things of life have been made lawful for you. The food of the people of the Book is lawful to you just as your food is lawful to them. Virtuous, believing women are lawful to you as well as virtuous women from the People of the Book; provided that you give them their bridal gifts and marry them-- not taking them as lovers or secret mistresses. As for anyone who rejects faith in God, all of their works will come to nothing, and in the Hereafter they will be with the doomed. (05)

Believers, when you are about to pray, wash your face, your hands and arms up to the elbows, and pass your wet hands lightly over your head and wash your feet up to the ankles. After sexual intercourse, purify yourselves. If you are ill, or are travelling, or have just relieved yourself, or have had intimate contact with a woman and cannot find water, then take some dust and use it to wipe your face and hands. God does not wish to place any burden on you, but wants to make you pure and to perfect His grace on you, so that you may be thankful[450] (06).

Always remember God's grace on you and your pledge that binds you to Him when you said, "We hear, and we obey." Always be mindful of God.[451] God is fully aware of what is in your hearts.[452](07)

Believers, always be steadfast in your devotion to God, equitably bearing witness to truth. Never let hatred for any people lead you to deviate from being just to them. Be just, for that is closer to being mindful of God. Always be mindful of God. God is well aware of what you do. (08) God has promised forgiveness and rich rewards to those who have faith and do good works,[453] (5: 09) whereas; those who deny Our revelations and lie are destined for the blazing fire. (10)

. . .

---

[446] See Glossary

[447] Psalm 130:4 but there is a forgiveness with you, so that you may be revered.

[448] Psalm 145:8 The Lord is gracious and merciful, slow to anger and abounding in steadfast love

[449] Revelation 22:12 "See, I am coming soon; my reward is with me, to repay according to everyone's work."

[450] Psalm 119:1-5 Blessed are those whose way is blameless, who walk in the law of the Lord! [2] Blessed are those who keep his testimonies, who seek him with their whole heart, [3] who also do no wrong, but walk in his ways! [4] You have commanded your precepts to be kept diligently. [5] Oh that my ways may be steadfast in keeping your statutes! . . . 1 Thessalonians 5:18 Give thanks in all circumstances; for this is the will of God in Christ Jesus for you.

[451] Revelation 14:7 He said in a loud voice, "Fear God and give him glory, for the hour of his judgment has come; and worship him who made heaven and earth, the sea and the springs of water."

[452] Luke 16:15 So he said to them, "You are those who justify yourselves in the sight of others; but God knows your hearts; for what is prized by human beings is an abomination in the sight of God.

[453] Matthew 5:16 In the same way, let your light shine before others, so that they may see your good works and give glory to your Father in heaven. 1 Timothy 6:18 They are to do good, to be rich in good works, generous and ready to share

Believers, remember how God favored you when certain people were about to attack you, and He protected you from them. Be always mindful of God. Let the believers put their trust in Him. [11]

God took a pledge from the Children of Israel. We appointed twelve of them as leaders. And God said, "I am with you. If you are regular in prayer, give the purifying alms, and believe in My Messengers and support them, and lend God a good loan, I will cleanse you of your bad deeds and admit you into Gardens (Jannah) with flowing rivers. After this, any of you who deny the truth will be far from the right path."[454][12] But, because they broke their pledge, We rejected them and hardened their hearts. They distorted the meaning of the revealed words, and they have forgotten a lot of what they have been told to remember. You will always find deceit in all but a few of them. Forgive them and forget. God loves those who honor Him by forgiving. [13] And We also took the pledge from those who say "We are Christians[455]," but they have forgotten part of what they were told to keep in mind. That caused resentment and hatred among them, which We have permitted until the Resurrection Day, when God will explain to them what they have done. [14]

People of the Book, Our Messenger has come to you to clarify much of what you used to conceal of the Book and to overlook much. An enlightenment has now come to you from God and a clear Book. [15] Through it God guides those who follow what pleases Him to ways of peace and by His permission, He will bring them out from the darkness of ignorance into enlightenment, and will guide them to a straight path. [456] [16] Those who say, "God is the Messiah, the son of Mary," are defying the truth. Say, "If it had been God's will, could anyone have prevented Him from destroying the Messiah, son of Mary, together with his mother and everyone else on earth?" For God has control over the heavens and the earth and everything in between. He creates whatever He wants and has power over all things. [17]

The Jews and the Christians say, "We are God's children and His loved ones." Say to them, "Why does He punish you for your sins? No, you are only human beings of His creation. He forgives whomever He wills, and He punishes whomever He wills, for God has control over the heavens and the earth and everything in between. All journeys lead to Him." [18]

People of the Book, after a long time during which no messengers have appeared, Our Messenger comes to you now to make the truth clear to you so you should not say, "No one has come to give us good news or to warn us."

• • •

[454] Isaiah 59:13 transgressing, and denying the Lord, and turning away from following our God, talking oppression and revolt, conceiving lying words and uttering them from the heart
[455] The word Christians (in Arabic Maseheein) is never mentioned in the Qur'an. Instead the Qur'an mentions the word /nasara/ and it is historically equated by Muslim commentators to Christians but its origin is not clear. Some have suggested that the word is derived from Nazareth, the town where Jesus was brought up, as it is implied in the Gospel, (Matthew 2:23, Acts 24:5). Others believe that it is from the Arabic word /ansaar/ (helpers/supporters) (root: nasr) refers to the followers of Jesus who are called supporters of God in the Qur'an (61:14, 3:52).
[456] Proverbs 4:23-27 Keep your heart with all vigilance, for from it flow the springs of life. [24] Put away from you crooked speech, and put devious talk far from you. [25] Let your eyes look directly forward, and your gaze be straight before you. [26] Keep straight the path of your feet and all your ways will be sure. [27] Do not swerve to the right or to the left; turn your foot away from evil.

Someone did come to you to give you good news and to warn you. God has the power to do all things[457] (19)

Moses (Musa) said to his people, "My people, remember God's blessing on you when He raised up prophets among you, and appointed kings for you and gave you what He had not given anyone else in the world.[458] (20) My people, enter the holy land, which God has promised you; but do not turn back, or then you will be doomed."[459] (21)

They answered, "Moses, there are ferocious people in this land. We will not enter it until they leave.[460] If they leave, then we will enter." (22) Two men from among those who feared God, and whom God had blessed, said, "Enter through the gate, for as soon as you enter, you will be victorious. If you are truly believers, you must place your trust in God."[461] (23)

They said, "Moses, we will never enter while they are still there. Go forward with your Lord and fight, and we will stay here." (24) Moses said, "Lord, I do not have control over anyone except my brother and myself. Judge between us and those defiantly disobedient people." (25) God said, "The land is forbidden to them. They will wander aimlessly for forty years, on the earth.[462] Do not grieve over those who disobey." (26)

•   •   •

---

[457] Matthew 19:26 But Jesus looked at them and said, "For mortals it is impossible, but for God all things are possible."

[458] Deuteronomy 4:33 Has any people ever heard the voice of a god speaking out of a fire, as you have heard, and lived?

[459] Deuteronomy 27:3 You shall write on them all the words of this law when you have crossed over, to enter the land that the Lord your God is giving you, a land flowing with milk and honey, as the Lord, the God of your ancestors, promised you

[460] Numbers 13:32, 33 So they brought to the Israelites an unfavorable report of the land that they had spied out, saying, "The land that we have gone through as spies is a land that devours its inhabitants; and all the people that we saw in it are of great size. [33] There we saw the Nephilim (the Anakites come from the Nephilim); and to ourselves we seemed like grasshoppers, and so we seemed to them.")

[461] Numbers 14:6-9 And Joshua son of Nun and Caleb son of Jephunneh, who were among those who had spied out the land, tore their clothes [7] and said to all the congregation of the Israelites, "The land that we went through as spies is an exceedingly good land. [8] If the Lord is pleased with us, he will bring us into this land and give it to us, a land that flows with milk and honey. [9] Only, do not rebel against the Lord; and do not fear the people of the land, for they are no more than bread for us; their protection is removed from them, and the Lord is with us; do not fear them."

[462] Numbers 14:34-35 According to the number of the days in which you spied out the land, forty days, for every day a year, you shall bear your iniquity, forty years, and you shall know my displeasure." [35] I the Lord have spoken; surely I will do thus to all this wicked congregation gathered together against me: in this wilderness they shall come to a full end, and there they shall die.

(Prophet) tell them the truth about the story of Adams' two sons⁴⁶³ -- how each of them offered a sacrifice, one sacrifice being accepted and the other being rejected. One said, "I will kill you!" The other replied, "God only accepts the sacrifice of those who are mindful of Him. [27] Even if you try to kill me, I will not try to kill you. I fear God, the Lord of all the worlds.⁴⁶⁴ [28] I would rather you bear the burden of my sins as well as yours. Then you will be destined for the fire. That is the destiny of the unjust." [29]

His selfishness caused him to murder his brother. He killed him and became doomed. [30] God sent a raven to scratch the ground to show him how to cover his brother's body. He cried out, "How awful! Am I so helpless that I cannot do what this raven has done?" He then buried his brother and was filled with sorrow. [31] Because of this, We decreed to the Children of Israel that if anyone kills a human being, unless it is in punishment for murder or for spreading corruption on earth, it will be as though he killed all of human beings. And, if anyone saves a life, it will be as though he had saved the lives of all human beings. Our Messengers came to them with evidence of the truth. Yet, many of them continued to corrupt earth by their over indulgence. [32]

Those who wage war against God and His Messenger and strive to spread corruption on earth should be punished by death, crucifixion, the amputation of their hands and their feet, or should be entirely banished from (the face of) the earth. Such is their disgrace in this world. In the Hereafter, a terrible punishment awaits them-- [33] except for those who repent before you overpower them. You must bear in mind that God is forgiving ⁴⁶⁵ and Merciful-to-all.⁴⁶⁶ [34]

Believers, remain mindful of God, seek ways to come closer to Him, and strive for His cause so that you may prosper. [35] If the unbelievers possess all that is on earth, and twice as much, and offer it to ransom themselves from suffering on the Resurrection Day, it will not be accepted from them: they will have a painful punishment.⁴⁶⁷ [36] They will wish to come out of the fire, but they will not come out of it. It will be an everlasting punishment. [37]

• • •

⁴⁶³ Genesis 4:1-13, "Now the man knew his wife Eve, and she conceived and bore Cain, saying, 'I have produced a man with the help of the Lord.' ² Next she bore his brother Abel. Now Abel was a keeper of sheep, and Cain a tiller of the ground. ³ In the course of time Cain brought to the Lord an offering of the fruit of the ground, ⁴ and Abel for his part brought of the firstlings of his flock, their fat portions. And the Lord had regard for Abel and his offering, ⁵ but for Cain and his offering he had no regard. So Cain was very angry, and his countenance fell. ⁶ The Lord said to Cain, 'Why are you angry, and why has your countenance fallen? If you do well, will you not be accepted? ⁷ And if you do not do well, sin is lurking at the door; its desire is for you, but you must master it.' ⁸ Cain said to his brother Abel, 'Let us go out to the field.' And when they were in the field, Cain rose up against his brother Abel and killed him. ⁹ Then the Lord said to Cain, 'Where is your brother Abel?' He said, 'I do not know; am I my brother's keeper?' ¹⁰ And the Lord said, 'What have you done? Listen; your brother's blood is crying out to me from the ground! ¹¹ And now you are cursed from the ground, which has opened its mouth to receive your brother's blood from your hand. ¹² When you till the ground, it will no longer yield to you its strength; you will be a fugitive and a wanderer on the earth.' ¹³ Cain said to the Lord, 'My punishment is greater than I can bear!"

⁴⁶⁴ Deuteronomy 6:13-15 the Lord your God you shall fear, him you shall serve, ad by his name alone you shall swear. ¹⁴ do not follow others gods of the people who are all around you ¹⁵ because the Lord your God, who is present with you, is a jealous God.

⁴⁶⁵ Daniel 9:9. To the Lord our God belong mercy and forgiveness, for we have rebelled against him,

⁴⁶⁶ Psalm 116:5 Gracious is the Lord, and righteous; our God is merciful.

⁴⁶⁷ Matthew 25:41 Then he will say to those at his left hand, "You that are accursed, depart from me into the eternal fire prepared for the devil and his angels;

As for the men and women who steal[468], cut off their hands as punishment for what they have done. It is a deterrent ordered by God. God is almighty[469] and wise.[470] (38) As for him who repents after having done wrong, and makes amends, God will accept his repentance. God is most forgiving and most Merciful-to-all. (39)Do you not know that control of the heavens and the earth belongs to God? He punishes whomever He wills, and He forgives whomever He wills. God has the power to do anything. (40)

Messenger, do not be saddened by those who hurry to deny the truth; such as those who say, "We believe," and do not have any faith in their hearts and the Jews who eagerly listen to any lies and to those who have never met you. They distort the meaning of the words, taking them out of their context, saying, "If you have already been given this (in your Scriptures), accept it, but if you have not, then be on your guard!"

Do not be saddened by them, for if God wills someone to be tempted by evil, you will not be able to do anything for them.

These are the ones whose hearts God is not willing to cleanse. They will be disgraced in this world, and will have terrible suffering in the Hereafter. (41) They eagerly listen to lies and greedily profit from all that is evil. If they come to you (Prophet) for judgment, you can either judge between them or decline, for if you decline, they cannot harm you in any way. If you do judge, judge them fairly: God loves the just. (42)

Why do they come to you for judgment, seeing that they have the Torah with God's Law? Even then they will turn away from your judgment. These are not true believers. (43)

We revealed the Torah with guidance and enlightenment.[471] The prophets, who had submitted themselves to God, as well as the rabbis and the scholars, all judged according to that part of God's Book they were entrusted to preserve and to which they were witnesses.[472] So do not fear people. Only fear Me. Do not barter my verses for a small profit. Those who do not judge according to what God has revealed are unbelievers. (44)

In the Torah we prescribed for them a life for a life, an eye for an eye, a nose for a nose, an ear for an ear, a tooth for a tooth, and a similar retribution for wounds.[473] However, If anyone forgoes this out of charity, it will serve as an atonement for them. Those who do not judge in accordance with what God has revealed are unjust. (45)

We sent Jesus (Esa), the son of Mary, to follow in the footsteps of those earlier prophets, confirming what was available of the Torah. We gave him the Gospel. It has guidance and enlightenment[474], confirming what was available of

• • •

---

[468] Exodus 20:15 You shall not steal

[469] Job 9:4 "He is wise in heart, and mighty in strength"

[470] Proverbs 2:6 for the Lord gives wisdom; from his mouth come knowledge and understanding

[471] Psalm 119:130, "The unfolding of your words gives light; it imparts understanding to the simple."

[472] Romans 3:1, 2 Then what advantage has the Jew? Or what is the value of circumcision? ² Much, in every way. In the first place the Jews were entrusted with the oracles of God.)

[473] Exodus 21:23-25 If any harm follows, then you shall give life for life, ²⁴ eye for eye, tooth for tooth, hand for hand, foot for foot, ²⁵ burn for burn, wound for wound, stripe for stripe.

[474] John 1:9 The true light, which enlightens everyone, was coming into the world. James 1:17 Every good gift and every perfect gift is from above, coming down from the Father of lights with whom there is no variation or shadow due to change.

the Torah. It has guidance and an admonition for those who are mindful of God. [46] Let the followers of the Gospel judge according to what God has revealed in it. Those who do not judge in light of what God has revealed are deviators. [47]

(Prophet) We sent you the Book, setting forth the Truth, confirming what is available of earlier revelations and with final authority over them. Judge between them in accordance with what God has sent down. Do not follow their whims, which deviate from the Truth revealed to you.

We have assigned to each of you a law and a way of life. If God had wanted, He could have made all of you a single community, but instead He is testing you by means of what He has revealed to you. So compete in doing what is good. You will all return to God, and He will clarify these matters about which you have differed. [48]

(Prophet) Judge between them according to what God has revealed to them, and do not follow their whims. Be cautious. Do not let them tempt you away from what God has revealed to you. If they turn away, remember it is God's will to repay them for some of the sins they have committed. A great many people are deviators. [49] Do they want judgment according to the age of ignorance?[475] Is there any better judge than God for those who are firm in faith? [50]

Believers, do not take the Jews and Christians as allies.[476] They are only allies with one another, and whoever allies himself with them becomes one of them. God does not guide such unjust people. [51] You (Prophet) will see those with perverse hearts rushing to them and saying, "We are afraid that fortune may turn against us." God may bring about good fortune for the believers, or He may not. Then they will be overcome with remorse for the thoughts that they secretly harbored. [52] The believers will say to one another, "Are these the same men who swore by God with their most solemn oath that they were with you? All they did was in vain, and they lost everything." [53]

Believers, if you ever abandon your faith, God will replace you with people He loves and who love Him,[477] people who are meek toward the believers,

• • •

[475] An Islamic concept of "the state of ignorance of the guidance from God" or "Days of Ignorance" referring to the condition in which Arabs found themselves in pre-Islamic Arabia, i.e. prior to the revelation of the Quran to Muhammad.

[476] In his commentary, Al-Tabari explains that this verse is about two of the Prophet's companions; Obada Bin Al-Samet of Bani Hareth of the Khazraj and Abdullah Bin Ubay Bin Saloul. When the Jewish tribes broke their covenant with the Prophet and betrayed the Muslims, both of these companions came to the Prophet, Obada Bin Al-Samet decided to forsake his relationships and interests with the Jews while Abdullah Bin Ubay Bin Saloul refused and he put his own personal interest ahead of the Muslims 'best interest. Although this verse makes a general statement, the ruling is specific and is to be applied in a context similar to the historical context. In response to a similar question, Shaykh Yusuf Al-Qaradawi wrote about this topic extensively: "The answer is that these verses are not unconditional, to be applied to every Jew, Christian, or non-Muslim. Interpreting them in this manner contradicts the injunctions of the Qur'an which enjoin affection and kindness to the good and peace-loving peoples of every religion. The Qur'an says concerning the Christians: "you will find that the nearest in affection towards the believers are those who say, "We are Christians," because there are priests and monks among them, and because these people are not given to arrogance. [82].

The verses cited above (verse 5:51) were revealed in connection with those people who were hostile to Islam and made war upon the Muslims. Accordingly, it is not permissible for the Muslims to support or assist them - that is, to be their ally- nor to entrust them with secrets at the expense of his own religion and community. This point is explained in other verses.

[477] Matthew 21:43, "Therefore I tell you, the kingdom of God will be taken away from you and given to a people that produces the fruits of the kingdom.

uncompromising to the unbelievers; people who strive hard in God's cause, and do not fear being blamed by anyone. Such is God's grace, which He grants to whomever He wills. God has boundless grace and knowledge. [478] (54)

Your true allies are God, and His messenger, and the believers—those who are constant in prayer, pay the prescribed purifying alms, and bow down in worship. (55) All who ally themselves with God and His messenger and the believers will be victorious. (56)

Believers, do not befriend people who mock your faith and make fun of it, whether they are people who were given the Book before you or who are unbelievers. Remain mindful of God if you are truly believers. (57) When you make a call to prayer, they mock it and make fun of it because they are people who do not use reason. (58)

Say, "People of the Book, do you resent us for any reason other than that we believe in God and what He has revealed to us and what He revealed before us, or is it only because most of you are deviators?" (59)

Say, "Will I tell you, in the sight of God, who deserves a worse punishment than these? They whom God has rejected and whom He condemned and turned into apes and pigs [479] because they worshipped the powers of evil. They are worse in rank and farther astray from the right path." (60)

When they come to you, they say, "We believe." However, they come denying the truth and leave in the same state. God is fully aware of all they conceal. (61) You (Prophet) can see many of them outdoing one another in sin and hostility and making illegal profits. (62) If only their rabbis and scholars would stop them from speaking sinfully and making illegal profits. Their deeds are so evil! (63) Those Jews[480] said, "God hands are tied!" It is they whose hands are tied! They are cursed by God for what they have said. God's hands are open wide; He gives as He pleases. What has been sent down to you (Prophet) from your Lord is sure to make many of them even more stubborn in their arrogance and in their denial of the truth.

We have incited enmity and hatred among the People of the Book until the Resurrection Day. Whenever they kindle the fires of war, God extinguishes them

· · ·

[478] Psalm 27:1 The Lord is my light and my salvation; whom shall I fear? The Lord is the stronghold of my life; of whom shall I be afraid?

[479] This could be considered metaphorical, like the use of "blind, deaf and dumb" in 2:18, 5:71, 8:22, 43:40

[480] The Arabic says: Wa kaalat al Yahoud, or The Jews said. However, there is a rule to understand Qur'anic Arabic that requires to investigate the Al or the "The" and whether it is general or specific, referring to known people. In this case the verse refers to specific Jews. Most commentators mention that this verse would appear to be in response to a specific incident with some Jews of Medina. The Prophet's companion Abu Bakr, was sent with a message from the Prophet to Babu Kaynakaa' inviting them to accept Islam. He went to the Midrash where many of them were gathered around a Rabbi called Finhas Ben Azoura and another Rabbi called Ashia'. An argument took place when Rabbi Finhas sarcastically said to Abu Bakr: "you claim that our Lord is asking us to lend Him our wealth. Yet, it is only the poor who borrow from the rich. And if what you say is true, it follows that God is poor and we are rich, for if He were rich He would not ask us to lend Him our wealth". He said this apparently in response to verse 2:245 "Who will make a good loan to God, which He will repay many times over?" A fist fight pursued and the Rabbi went to the Prophet to complain to him about Abu Bakr aggressiveness while denying that he blasphemed against God. This story is also related in Asbab Al-Nuzul by Al-Wahidi.

and they work hard at spreading corruption on earth. God does not love the corrupters.[481] [64]

If the People of the Book would only truly believe and be mindful of God! We would wipe away their former evil deeds and bring them into Gardens of delight; [65] and if they would truly observe the Torah and the Gospel and all that has been revealed to them by their Lord, they would have been given an abundance of grace from heaven and earth. Some of them are on the right course, but most of them do what is evil. [66]

Prophet, proclaim everything that has been sent down to you from your Lord, for unless you do it fully, you will not have delivered His message. God will protect you from men. God does not guide people who refuse to acknowledge the truth. [67] Say, "People of the Book, You have no valid ground for your beliefs, unless you (truly) observe the Torah and the Gospel, and all that has been sent down to you from your Lord." Yet all that has been sent down to you (Prophet) by your Lord is bound to make many of them more stubborn in their arrogance and in their denial of the truth. Do not worry about unbelievers. [68] The believers, as well as the Jews, the Sabeans and the Christians: all who believe in God[482] and the Last Day and do righteous deeds, will have nothing to fear and they will not grieve. [69]

We made a covenant with the Children of Israel, and We sent messengers to them. Every time a messenger came to them with anything that was not to their liking, they rebelled. They accused some of them of lying and killed others.[483] [70] Thinking that they themselves would not be harmed, they became blind and deaf. God turned to them in mercy, yet many of them again became blind and deaf. God sees everything that they do. [71]

Those who say, "God is the Messiah, son of Mary," have defied God. The Messiah himself said, "Children of Israel, worship God. He is my Lord as well as your Lord." [484] If anyone associated others with God, He will not permit them to enter heaven. Their destiny will be Hell. No one can help such unjust people. [72]

Those who say, "God is the third of three" are denying the truth because there is only One God[485]. Unless they stop saying this, a painful punishment will happen to those of them who are determined to deny the truth. [73] Why do they

• • •

[481] Psalm 5:4-5 For you are not a God who delights in wickedness; evil will not sojourn with you. 5 The boastful will not stand before your eyes; you hate all evildoers.

[482] John 10:16 I have other sheep that are not of this sheep pen. I must bring them also. They too will listen to my voice, and there shall be one flock and one shepherd.

[483] Luke 11:47-49 Woe to you! For you build the tombs of the prophets whom your ancestors killed.48 So you are witnesses and approve of the deeds of your ancestors; for they killed them, and you build their tombs. 49 Therefore also the Wisdom of God said, 'I will send them prophets and apostles, some of whom they will kill and persecute,' Matthew 23:37 "Jerusalem, Jerusalem, who kills the prophets and stones those who are sent to her!

[484] John 20:17, "Jesus said to her, 'Do not hold on to me, because I have not yet ascended to the Father. But go to my brothers and say to them, 'I am ascending to my Father and your Father, to my God and your God.'", Mark 12:29, "Jesus answered, 'The first is, "Hear, O Israel: the Lord our God, the Lord is one…"

[485] Luke 4:8 And Jesus answered and said to him, Get you behind me, Satan: for it is written, You shall worship the Lord your God, and him only shall you serve. Mark 12:29, "Jesus answered, 'The first is, "Hear, O Israel: the Lord our God, the Lord is one…

not turn towards God in repentance and ask for His forgiveness? God is most forgiving[486] and Merciful-to-all.[487] (74)

The Messiah, son of Mary, was only a messenger. All (other) messengers had passed away before him, and his mother was one who never deviated from the truth. They both ate food. See how clear We make these messages for them and how deluded their minds are. (75)

Say, "How can you worship something other than God [488] that has no power to harm or to benefit you when God alone is All-Hearing,[489] All-Knowing?"[490] (76)

Say, "People of the Book, do not overstep the bounds of Truth in your religious beliefs. Do not follow the whims of the people who went astray before you. They have led many others astray, and they continue to stray from the right path." (77)

Those of the Children of Israel who defied God and denied the truth, have been cursed and rejected by the words of David and Jesus, the son of Mary, because they rebelled and persistently overstepped the limits.[491] (78) They did not prevent each other from doing hateful things. Their deeds were so evil! (79)

You (Prophet) see many of them allying themselves with the unbelievers. How evil is what their souls make them do! God has condemned them, and they will remain in punishment forever. (80) If they (truly) believed in God and their Prophet and all that was sent down to them, they would not take the unbelievers for their allies: but most of them are defiant (81)

You (Prophet) are sure to find that the most hostile to the believers are those Jews[492] as well as those who are bent on ascribing partners to God. While, you will find that the nearest in affection towards the believers are those who say, "We are Christians," because there are priests and monks among them, and because these people are not given to arrogance. (82) For, when they understand what has come down to this messenger, you can see their eyes tear up because they recognize the Truth in it, and they say, "Lord, we do believe. Make us one with all who bear witness to the Truth. (83) How could we fail to believe in God and in the Truth that has come to us when we long that our Lord include us in the company of the righteous?" (84) For saying this, God will reward them with

• • •

[486] Psalm 86:5 For you, O Lord, are good and forgiving, abounding in steadfast love to all who call on you
[487] Psalm 145:8, The Lord is gracious and merciful, slow to anger and abounding in steadfast love.
[488] Psalm 115:4-7, "Their idols are silver and gold, the work of human hands. [5] They have mouths, but do not speak; eyes, but do not see. [6] They have ears, but do not hear; noses, but do not smell. [7] They have hands, but do not feel; feet, but do not walk; they make no sound in their throats."
[489] 1 John 5:14 And this is the boldness we have in him, that if we ask anything according to his will, he hears us.
[490] 1 John 3:20 whenever our hearts condemn us; for God is greater than our hearts, and he knows everything
[491] All of Matthew 23 is a Jesus's rebuke of those of the Jews who 'persistently overstepped the limits' Matthew 23:29 - 33 "Woe to you, scribes and Pharisees, hypocrites! For you build the tombs of the prophets and decorate the graves of the righteous, [30] and you say, 'If we had lived in the days of our ancestors, we would not have taken part with them in shedding the blood of the prophets.' [31] Thus you testify against yourselves that you are descendants of those who murdered the prophets. [32] Fill up, then, the measure of your ancestors. [33] You snakes, you brood of vipers! How can you escape being sentenced to hell?
[492] Most commentators agree that this is specifically talking about the Jews that the Prophet called to Islam and it is not general.The same is true about the Christians mentioned in this verse. As a rule the Qur'an does not generalize its condemnation of any followers of any religion. It condemns the deeds of certain people only.

Heavenly Gardens with flowing rivers where they will permanently abide, for this is the reward for those who do good. [(85)] Whereas, those who reject the truth and deny Our messages are destined for the blazing fire. [(86)]

Believers, do not deprive yourselves of good things in life which God has made lawful to you,[493] but do not exceed the limits of what is right. God does not love those who exceed the limits of what is right. [(87)] Partake of the lawful and good things which God has provided for you and be mindful of God in Whom you believe. [(88)] God does not hold you accountable for oaths thoughtlessly sworn, but He will take you to task for earnestly sworn oaths. So, the breaking of an oath must be atoned by feeding ten needy persons with the same food as you would want for your own family, or by clothing them, or by freeing a slave, and if a person cannot find the means to do this, he will fast for three days. This will be the atonement for your oaths whenever you have sworn (and broken them). Be careful with your oaths. God makes His messages clear to you, so that you may be grateful. [(89)]

Believers, intoxicants, gambling, idolatry, and fortunetelling are repugnant and evil acts. They are evil acts of Satan. Avoid them so that you may prosper. [(90)] With intoxicants and gambling, Satan only seeks to incite hostility and hatred among you, and to turn you away from remembering God and from prayer. Will you not give them up?[494] [(91)] Obey God and obey the Messenger, and always be careful! If you pay no attention, know that Our Messenger's only duty is to clearly transmit the message. [(92)] Those who believe and do righteous deeds incur no sin for what they may have participated in, so long as they are mindful of God and believe and do righteous deeds, and continue to be mindful of God and to believe and grow ever more mindful of God and persevere in doing good: God loves those who do good deeds. [(93)]

Believers, God is sure to tempt you with wild game that come, within reach of your hands and weapons, so He can identify those who fear Him, even though they think He is not watching. Whoever oversteps the limits, will have a painful punishment.[495] [(94)]

Believers, do not hunt while you are in the state for sanctity. Whoever kills an animal intentionally must make amends by offering an equivalent domestic animal comparable to what was killed as defined by two just men—an offering to be delivered to the Ka'bah. Or, he may atone for his sin by feeding the needy, or by fasting an equivalent number of days, so that he may understand the seriousness of what he has done. God forgives what is past, but if anyone does it again, God will punish him severely. God is mighty,[496] and capable of exacting the penalty.[497] [(95)] It is permitted for you to catch and eat seafood. This is an enjoyment for you as well as for travelers, although you are forbidden to hunt on land while you are in the state of sanctity. Be mindful of God to whom you will be gathered. [(96)]

• • •

---

[493] Colossians 2:21-22, "'Do not handle, Do not taste, Do not touch'? All these regulations refer to things that perish with use; 22 they are simply human commands and teachings."

[494] Ephesians 5:18 Do not get drunk with wine, for that is debauchery; but be filled with the Spirit,

[495] Matthew 25:46 And these will go away into eternal punishment, but the righteous into eternal life.

[496] Psalm 24:8 Who is the King of glory? The Lord, strong and mighty, the Lord, mighty in battle.

[497] Ezekiel 25:17 I will execute great vengeance on them with wrathful punishments. Then they shall know that I am the Lord, when I lay my vengeance on them.)

God has made the Ka'bah, the Sacred House, a sanctuary for human beings, and the Sacred Months, the animals for sacrifice and their garlands, so that you will be aware that God has knowledge about all that is in the heavens and the earth. God knows about everything. [97] Know that God is severe in His punishment, and yet He is most forgiving and Merciful-to-all. [98] The Messenger only has a duty to deliver the message, as God knows what you reveal and what you hide. [99]

Say (Prophet), "The bad and the good are not equal, even though many of the bad things may greatly please you. People of understanding, be mindful of God so that you may prosper." [100] Believers, do not ask about matters that would trouble you if disclosed to you. But, if you ask about them while the Qur'an is being revealed, they will be made known to you. God has absolved (you from any obligation) in this respect. God is most forgiving and longsuffering. [101] People before your time have asked such questions, then later they rejected the answers. [102]

God has not ordained that certain kinds of cattle should be designated Bahirah, Saibah, Wasilah, or of Hami,[498] and set aside from the use of man, yet the unbelievers invent lies about God. Most of them do not use reason. [103] When they are told, "Accept what God has sent down and the Messenger," they answer, "What we inherited from our forefathers is enough for us."[499] Their forefathers knew nothing and were not guided. [104] Believers, you are responsible for your own souls; those who go astray cannot harm you if you are on the right path. All of you will return to God, and He will tell you what you used to do.[500] [105]

Believers, when death approaches you, let two just men from among you act as witnesses to the writing of your will. If death approaches you while you are travelling far from home, let two just men from among another people act as witnesses. Take hold of the two men after having prayed and, if you have any doubt in your mind, let each of them swear to God, "We will not sell our word for any price, even if it were for the sake of a near relative. We will not hide God's testimony, or else We will be counted among the sinful." [106]

If It is discovered that these two are guilty of this sin, then two of those whose rights have been usurped have a better right to bear witness. Let them swear to God, "Our testimony is truer than the testimony of those two, and we have not committed perjury, because that would make us unjust." [107] It will be more likely that people will offer the truth in their testimony because they will be afraid that others might refute their oaths. Remain mindful of God and listen. God does not guide those who are defiantly disobedient [108]

On the Day when God assembles all the messengers and asks, "What response did you receive?" They will answer, "We have no knowledge. You alone know these things that cannot be seen." [109]

· · ·

---

[498] Categories of animals pre-Islamic Arabs dedicated to the worship of their deities.

[499] Jeremiah 11:10 They have turned back to the iniquities of their ancestors of old, who refused to heed my words; they have gone after other gods to serve them; the house of Israel and the house of Judah have broken the covenant that I made with their ancestors.

[500] Matthew 25:32 All the nations will be gathered before him, and he will separate people one from another as a shepherd separates the sheep from the goats,

God will say, "Jesus, son of Mary, remember the grace which I bestowed upon you and your mother? How I strengthened you with the Holy Spirit [501] so you could speak from your cradle, and as a grown man? (Remember) when I taught you the Book, the Wisdom, the Torah and the Gospel? (Remember) when, with My permission, you fashioned the shape of a bird out of clay, breathed into it, and it became, with My permission, a bird? (Remember) when, with My permission, you healed the blind person and the leper;[502] when, by My permission, you brought the dead back to life?[503] (Remember) when I kept the Children of Israel from harming you when you came to them with all the evidence of the truth, and when those of them who were bent on denying the truth said, "This is clearly nothing but deception"? [110] And (mention) when I inspired the disciples to believe in Me and My messenger? They answered, "We believe and bear witness that we submit ourselves to You. [111]

And (mention) when the disciples said, "Jesus, son of Mary, can your Lord send us a feast from heaven?" (Jesus) answered, "Remain mindful of God, if you are (truly) believers." [112] They said, "We wish to eat from it so that our hearts might be reassured and that we might know that you have told us the truth and be among those who witness it." [113] Jesus, the son of Mary, said, "God, our Lord, send us a meal from heaven so that we can have a recurring celebration for the first and the last of us, and a sign from You. Provide for us because You are the best of providers." [114]

God answered, "I will send it down to you, but anyone who denies the truth after this will be punished with a punishment that I will not inflict on anyone else in the world." [115]

God said, "Jesus, son of Mary, did you say to people, 'Worship me and my mother as gods instead of God'?"[504] (Jesus) answered, "May You be exalted in Your limitless glory. It is not for me to say what I have no right to say[505]. Had I said this, You would have known it. You know all that is within me, whereas I do

• • •

[501] Matthew 3:16 And when Jesus had been baptized, just as he came up from the water, suddenly the heavens were opened to him and he saw the Spirit of God descending like a dove and alighting on him.
[502] Matthew 8:1-4 When Jesus had come down from the mountain, great crowds followed him; 2 and there was a leper who came to him and knelt before him, saying, 'Lord, if you choose, you can make me clean.' 3 He stretched out his hand and touched him, saying, 'I do choose. Be made clean!' Immediately his leprosy was cleansed. 4 Then Jesus said to him, 'See that you say nothing to anyone; but go, show yourself to the priest, and offer the gift that Moses commanded, as a testimony to them.
[503] Luke 7:12-17 As he approached the gate of the town, a man who had died was being carried out. He was his mother's only son, and she was a widow; and with her was a large crowd from the town. 13 When the Lord saw her, he had compassion for her and said to her, "Do not weep." 14 Then he came forward and touched the bier, and the bearers stood still. And he said, "Young man, I say to you, rise!" 15 The dead man sat up and began to speak, and Jesus gave him to his mother. 16 Fear seized all of them; and they glorified God, saying, "A great prophet has risen among us!" and "God has looked favorably on his people!" 17 This word about him spread throughout Judea and all the surrounding country.
[504] Luke 4:8 Jesus answered, "It is written: 'Worship the Lord your God and serve him only.'" Mathew 19:16-17 'One of the persons approaches Jesus, and says 'Good Master, what good things shall I do, that I shall attain eternal life.' And Jesus said unto him, 'Why do you call me good? For there is none good, except One, that is God – And if you want to enter life, keep the commandments'.
[505] John 17:3 'This is eternal life, so that you may know there is one true God, and Jesus Christ, who Thou has sent.' John 5:30 'I (Jesus) by myself can do nothing – as I hear I judge, and my judgment is just, because I seek not my will, but the will of thy who has sent me'.

not know what is in You.[506] It is You alone who has full knowledge of unknown things. [116] I told them only what You commanded me to say, "Worship God, who is my Lord as well as your Lord."[507] I was a witness to them during my time with them. But after you made me die, You were the One watching over them. You witness everything. [117] If you punish them, they are Your worshipers, and if You forgive them, You alone are the Almighty,[508] the Wise."[509] [118]

(On Judgment Day) God will say, "Today, the truthful will benefit from their truthfulness. They will have Gardens with flowing rivers, where they will abide forever. God is pleased with them, and they are pleased with Him. That is the supreme triumph!" [119]

The kingdom of the heavens and the earth and everything in them belongs to God.[510] He has power over all things.[511] [120]

• • •

---

[506] 1 Corinthians 2:11, "For what human being knows what is truly human except the human spirit that is within? So also no one comprehends what is truly God's except the Spirit of God."

[507] Luke 4:8 Jesus answered him, "It is written,'Worship the Lord your God, and serve only him

[508] Psalm 93:4 More majestic than the thunders of mighty waters, more majestic than the waves of the sea, majestic on high is the Lord!

[509] Proverbs 2:6 For the Lord gives wisdom; From His mouth *come* knowledge and understanding.

[510] Psalm 89:11 The heavens are yours, the earth also is yours; the world and all that is in it—you have founded them.

[511] 1 Chronicles 29:11 Yours, O Lord, are the greatness, the power, the glory, the victory, and the majesty; for all that is in the heavens and on the earth is yours; yours is the kingdom, O Lord, and you are exalted as head above all.

CHAPTER SIX

AL-ANA'M

LIVESTOCK

THE **MECCA** PERIOD

In the name of God, the Merciful to-all, the Mercy Giver:

Praise be to God, who created the heavens and the earth [512] and made darkness and light;[513] but, the unbelievers regard others as equal to their Lord.[514] [01] He created you out of clay[515] and specified a span of time[516] for you; a span, known only to him; however you still doubt. [02] He is God in the heavens and on earth; He knows all your secrets and what you reveal, and He knows what you earn. [03] Yet every time one of their Lord's messages came to them they ignored it. [04] They denied the Truth when it came to them; however, in time, they will come to understand the very thing they ridiculed. [05]

Do they not realize how many generations We destroyed before them--to whom We gave a (bountiful) place on earth, more so than you, and to whom We sent abundant rain,[517] and at whose feet We made running rivers flow? We destroyed them because of their sins, and We raised up other generations after them. [06] Even if We had sent down to you (Prophet) a written scripture that they could have touched with their own hands, the unbelievers would have said,

· · ·

---

[512] 1 Chronicles 29:11 Yours, O Lord, are the greatness, the power, the glory, the victory, and the majesty; for all that is in the heavens and on the earth is yours; yours is the kingdom, O Lord, and you are exalted as head above all.

[513] Genesis 1:3-5 "Then God said, 'Let there be light'; and there was light. [4] And God saw that the light was good; and God separated the light from the darkness. [5] God called the light Day, and the darkness he called Night. And there was evening and there was morning, the first day".

[514] Isaiah 46:5 "To whom will you liken me and make me equal, and compare me, as though we were alike?

[515] Genesis 2:7 "then the Lord God formed man from the dust of the ground, and breathed into his nostrils the breath of life; and the man became a living being".

[516] Psalm 139:16 "Your eyes beheld my unformed substance. In your book were written all the days that were formed for me, when none of them as yet existed".

[517] Deuteronomy 28:12 The Lord will open for you his rich storehouse, the heavens, to give the rain of your land in its season and to bless all your undertakings. You will lend to many nations, but you will not borrow.

"This is clearly nothing but a trick." [07] They say, "Why was no angel sent down to him?" But had We sent down an angel, it would have been over, with no further time given to them [08] and, If We had sent an angel, We would have certainly made him appear as a man, and thus We would have only confused them in the same way as they are now confusing themselves. [09]

Messengers have been ridiculed before you, but those who mocked them were overwhelmed by the very punishment they mocked. [10] Say, "Travel throughout the land and see what finally happened to those who rejected the truth." [11] Say, "To whom belongs everything that is in the heavens and on earth?" Say, "God! He decreed Himself to be Merciful-to-all." However, He will summon all of you to a definite Day of Resurrection.[518] Those who have lost their soul will not believe. [12] All that rests during the night and the day belong To Him and He alone, is All-Hearing[519] and All-Knowing.[520] [13] Say, "Why should I take a master for myself other than God, the Originator of the heavens and the earth, when it is He who feeds[521] and needs not to be fed?"[522] Say, "I am commanded to be the first (among you) to submit myself to Him, and not be among the idolaters." [14] Say, "If I disobey my Lord, I fear the punishment of the Great Day."[523] [15] God will be truly merciful to whoever is spared on that Day. This is the greatest victory![524] [16]

If God touches you with hardship, only He can remove it; and if He blesses you, it is His choice. He can do anything He wills.[525] [17] He alone is the Supreme Master over His creatures and He alone is All-Wise, the All-Aware. [18] Say, "What counts most as a witness to the truth?" Say, "God is witness between you and me. This Qur'an has been revealed to me to warn you and everyone it reaches." Could you in truth bear witness that there are other gods besides God? Say, "I bear no (such) witness." Say, "He is only One God,[526] and I have nothing to do with whatever you associate with Him." [19] Those to whom We have previously given the Book before, know this as well as they know their own children; yet those who deceive themselves refuse to believe. [20] Who does greater wrong than someone who fabricates lies against God or denies His revelations? Those who do such wrong will not prosper. [21] One Day We will gather them all together

• • •

---

[518] Acts 24:15 I have a hope in God—a hope that they themselves also accept—that there will be a resurrection of both the righteous and the unrighteous.

2 Chronicles 36:16 but they kept mocking the messengers of God, despising his words, and scoffing at his prophets, until the wrath of the Lord against his people became so great that there was no remedy.

[519] Psalm 4:3 But know that the Lord has set apart the faithful for himself; the Lord hears when I call to him.

[520] Psalm 44:21 Would not God find this out? For He knows the secrets of the heart

[521] Psalm 145:16 You open your hand, satisfying the desire of every living thing.

[522] Psalm 50:13 Do I eat the flesh of bulls, or drink the blood of goats?

[523] Matthew 25:46 And these will go away into eternal punishment, but the righteous into eternal life.'

[524] 1 John 5:4 for whatever is born of God conquers the world. And this is the victory that conquers the world, our faith.

[525] Job 42:2 I know that you can do all things, and that no purpose of yours can be thwarted.

[526] Deuteronomy 6:4 Hear, O Israel: The Lord is our God, the Lord is one.

and say to the idolaters, "Where are those beings you imagined to be partners with God?" [22] In their utter confusion, they will only say, "By God, our Lord, we did not mean to associate partners with Him." [23] See how they have lied to themselves and how the gods they invented have abandoned them. [24]

Among them are some who (appear) to listen to your (message, Prophet), but We have laid covers over their hearts [527] and deafness in their ears which prevent them from grasping the truth. Even if they saw every sign, [528] they would still not believe it. When they come to you, they argue with you. The unbelievers say, "These are nothing but fairy tales." [25] They tell others not to listen, while they stay away. They destroy no one but themselves, though they fail to realize this. [26] If you could only see them when they will have to stand before the fire and say, "If only we were brought back, we would not reject the revelations of our Lord, but would be among the believers." [27] The truth they used to conceal will become obvious to them, and if they were brought back, they would return to the very thing that was forbidden to them. [529] They are such liars! [28] Others used to say, "There is nothing beyond our life in this world. We will not be raised from the dead." [29] If you could only see when they are made to stand before their Lord, (and) He will say, "Is not this the Truth?" They will answer, "Yes, by our Lord." He will say, "Then taste the miseries that come from your having denied the truth." [30] Those who deny the encounter with their Lord, until, when the Last Hour [530] suddenly comes upon them, are lost. They cry, "How sorry we are for ignoring this!" They will bear the burdens of their sins on their backs. How dreadful those burdens will be! [31] The life of this world is nothing but play and amusement; and the life in the Hereafter is best for those who are mindful of God. Do you not understand? [32]

We know that you are saddened by what these people say (Prophet). It is not you they disbelieve; these unjust people are denying God's revelations. [33] There were other messengers before you who were disbelieved and who patiently endured all the lying accusations and persecution until We gave them victory. No one can alter God's words! You have already learned some of what happened to these messengers. [34] If you find rejection by the unbelievers so unbearable, then seek a tunnel into the ground or a ladder into the sky in order to bring them a sign, but (remember that), had God willed it, He would have guided all of them. Do not be among the ignorant. [35] Only those who can hear will respond; and as for the dead, God (alone) will raise them from the dead, and to Him they will return. [36]

They also say, "Why has no miraculous sign been sent down to him from his Lord" Say, "God has the power to send down a sign," though most people do not know this. [37] Every beast that crawls on the earth and every birds that flies with its two wings have formed communities like you. We have left nothing out of the

•   •   •

[527] 2 Corinthians 3:14 "But their minds were hardened. Indeed, to this very day, when they hear the reading of the old covenant, that same veil is still there, since only in Christ is it set aside".

[528] Acts 28:27 For this people's heart has grown dull, and their ears are hard of hearing, and they have shut their eyes; so that they might not look with their eyes, and listen with their ears, and understand with their heart and turn— and I would heal them."

[529] 2 Peter 2:22 It has happened to them according to the true proverb, "The dog turns back to its own vomit, and, The sow is washed only to wallow in the mud."

[530] Revelation 14:7 "He said in a loud voice, 'Fear God and give him glory, for the hour of his judgment has come; and worship him who made heaven and earth, the sea and the springs of water.'

Book. Later, they will be gathered to their Lord. [38] Those who reject Our messages are deaf, dumb and deep in darkness. Whomever God wills, He lets go astray,[531] and whomever He wills, He places upon a straight path. [39] Say, "Can you see yourselves invoking any but God when God's punishment falls on you (in this world), or when the Last Hour comes upon you, if you are truthful? [40] No! It is to Him alone that you would call. If it were His will, He may remove whatever harm that caused you to call on Him; and you will have forgotten all that you now associate with Him. [41]

We sent Our messengers unto people before your time (Prophet) and afflicted their people with misfortune and hardship [532] so that they might humble themselves. [42] When the misfortune fell on them, they did not humble themselves, but instead their hearts became hardened,[533] and Satan made their bad deeds alluring to them. [43] When they had forgotten all that they have been told to take to heart, we opened the gates to everything they wanted. Then, as they rejoiced in what had been granted, We struck them suddenly and they were in despair.[534] [44] The evildoers were wiped out. All praise is due to God, the Lord of the Worlds![535] [45]

Say, "Considered this—what if God should take away your hearing and your sight and seal your hearts? What god other than God is there that could bring it all back to you?" See how We explain Our revelations in many ways, and yet still they turn away in disdain. [46] Say, "Consider this, what if the punishment of God should come to you suddenly or gradually? Would anyone but the evildoers be destroyed?" [47] We send Our Messengers only to give good news and to warn. All who believe and live righteously do not need to fear, nor will they grieve. [48] As for those who rejected Our messages, suffering will afflict them as a result of all their sinful actions. [49] (Prophet) Say, "I do not say to you, 'God's treasures are with me,' nor (do I say), 'I know the things that are beyond human perception,' nor do I say to you, ' Behold, I am an angel'; I only follow what is revealed to me[536]. Say, "Can the blind and seeing be considered equal? Why will you not think?" [50]

Use the Qur'an to warn those who fear being gathered before their Lord with no one to protect them from Him or to intercede with Him, so that they might become (fully) aware of Him. [51] Don't drive away (any of) those who call upon

• • •

---

[531] 2 Thessalonians 2:11 "For this reason God sends them a powerful delusion, leading them to believe what is false"

[532] Job 36:15 He delivers the afflicted by their affliction, and opens their ear by adversity

[533] Exodus 8:19 And the magicians said to Pharaoh, "This is the finger of God!" But Pharaoh's heart was hardened, and he would not listen to them, just as the Lord had said.

[534] Luke 12:16 -21 "Then he told them a parable: 'The land of a rich man produced abundantly. [17] And he thought to himself, "What should I do, for I have no place to store my crops?" [18] Then he said, "I will do this: I will pull down my barns and build larger ones, and there I will store all my grain and my goods. [19] And I will say to my soul, Soul, you have ample goods laid up for many years; relax, eat, drink, be merry." [20] But God said to him, "You fool! This very night your life is being demanded of you. And the things you have prepared, whose will they be?" [21] So it is with those who store up treasures for themselves but are not rich towards God.'

[535] Psalm 47:7 for God is the king of all the earth; sing praises with a psalm.

[536] John 7:16-18 Then Jesus answered them, "My teaching is not mine but his who sent me. [17] Anyone who resolves to do the will of God will know whether the teaching is from God or whether I am speaking on my own. [18] Those who speak on their own seek their own glory; but the one who seeks the glory of him who sent him is true, and there is nothing false in him.

their Lord morning or evening, seeking His face. You are in no way accountable for them, just as they are in no way accountable for you. You have no right to drive them away, for then you would be among the unjust. [52] We have made some of them a test for others, to make the unbelievers say, "Is it these men that God has favored among us?" Does God not know best who is grateful (to Him)?[53]

When those who believe in Our messages come to you, say, "Peace be upon you. Your Lord has willed upon Himself to be Merciful-to-all. If any of you sins out of ignorance and then repents and lives righteously, God is most forgiving, a purveyor of mercy."[537] [54] We clearly spell out Our messages and (We do it) so that the path of those who force others to reject God's messages may be made clear. [55] Say, "I am forbidden to worship those you call on instead of God." Say, "I do not follow your vain desires, for if I did, I would stray from among those who have found the right path." [56] Say, "Behold, I take my stand based on clear evidence from my Lord, but still you deny it. I don't have in my power what you want me to hasten: judgment rests with none but God. He will declare the Truth, since it is He who is the best judge between Truth and falsehood." [57] Say, "If what you seek to rush were in my power, everything would have been decided between you and me, but God knows best who does wrong." [58] He holds the keys to the unknown. No one knows those keys but Him. He knows all that is on land and in the sea, and not a leaf falls[538] without Him knowing about it. There is not a grain in the earth's deep darkness, or anything living or dead that is not written in a clear record. [59] It is He who calls your souls back by night and knows what you have done by day and He brings you back to life each day until your fixed term is fulfilled. In the end, you must return to Him, and then He will make you understand all that you were doing (in life).[539] [60] He is the Supreme Master over His worshipers. He sends out heavenly forces to watch over you until, when death approaches any of you, those sent by Us take his soul. They don't overlook (anyone). [61] Then they will be brought before God, their true Lord. Judgment is truly His alone. He is the swiftest in taking accounts. [62]

Say, "Who saves you from the dark dangers of the land and the sea when you humbly and secretly call upon Him, and say, 'If He will save us from this (distress), we will be among the grateful'?" [63] Say, "God (alone) can save you from this and from every distress and still you attribute divinity to others besides Him." [64] Say, "It is He alone who has the power to afflict you with suffering from above or from beneath your feet, or to divide you into divisive factions and let you taste the fear of one another." See how We explain these messages so that they might understand; [65] yet your people still reject it even though it is the Truth. Say, "I am not your keeper. [66] Every news (from God) has a fixed time to be fulfilled, and in time you will come to realize (the truth)." [67]

Whenever you encounter those who speak with disrespect about Our revelations, turn away from them until they move on to another topic, and if Satan should ever cause you to forget, then, do not remain with those unjust people after realizing what they are doing. [68] Those who are mindful of God are

• • •

---

[537] Psalm 103:3 Who forgives all your iniquity, who heals all your diseases,

[538] Matthew 10:29-30 "Are not two sparrows sold for a penny? Yet not one of them will fall to the ground unperceived by your Father. [30] And even the hairs of your head are all counted".

[539] Romans 14:12 So then, each of us will be accountable to God.

not accountable for the wrongdoers[540] However, this is a reminder to them so that they may become mindful of God. [69] Leave behind those who turn their religion into amusement and a diversion and are mesmerized by the life of this world. Remind them with it, lest a soul be damned for what it has earned. It will have no one to protect it from God, and no one to intercede besides Him. Whatever ransom[541] he may offer will not be accepted. Such people will be held accountable for their actions. For them will be a drink of boiling water, and painful punishment [542] awaits them because of their persistence in denying the truth. [70]

Say, "Instead of God, will we call on something that can neither benefit nor harm us, [543] and turn back after God has guided us. (This would be) like someone seduced, having been tempted by Satan's earthly lusts, though his companions are calling him to guidance (saying), 'Come to us!'" Say, "God's guidance is the only guidance, and we are commanded to surrender ourselves to the Lord of the Worlds, [544] [71] and to keep up prayers and be mindful of Him. It is to Him that you all will be gathered. [72] It is He Who has created the heavens and the earth in Truth, and whenever He says, "Be!"[545] it will be. His word is the Truth. All control on the Day the Trumpet is blown belongs to Him. He knows all that is beyond human perception[546], as well as all that can be witnessed by human senses, for He alone is The-Wise, All-Aware. [73]

Remember when Abraham spoke to his father Azar, and said, "How can you take idols as gods? I see that you and your people are clearly lost." [74] In this way We made Abraham to understand God's mighty dominion over the heavens and the earth, so that he might become a firm believer. [75] When the night overshadowed him, he saw a star and said, "This is my Lord!" But when it went down he said, "I do not like things that disappear." [76] Then, when he saw the moon rising he said, "This is my Lord" but when it set, he said, "If my Lord does not guide me, I will definitely become one of those lost people." [77] Then, when he saw the sun rising he said, "This is my Lord! This is greater!" But when it (too) set, he said, "My people, I disown all that you worship other than God. [78] I have

• • •

[540] Acts 20:26 Therefore I declare to you this day that I am not responsible for the blood of any of you
[541] Psalm 49:7-8 Truly, no ransom avails for one's life, there is no price one can give to God for it. [8] For the ransom of life is costly, and can never suffice,
[542] Matthew 25:41,46, Then he will say to those at his left hand, 'You that are accursed, depart from me into the eternal fire prepared for the devil and his angels [46] And these will go away into eternal punishment, but the righteous into eternal life.
[543] Isaiah 44:9-11 All who make idols are nothing, and the things they delight in do not profit; their witnesses neither see nor know. And so they will be put to shame. [10] Who would fashion a god or cast an image that can do no good? [11] Look, all its devotees shall be put to shame; the artisans too are merely human. Let them all assemble, let them stand up; they shall be terrified, they shall all be put to shame.
[544] 2 Kings 19:15 And Hezekiah prayed before the Lord, and said: 'O Lord the God of Israel, who are enthroned above the cherubim, you are God, you alone, of all the kingdoms of the earth; you have made heaven and earth.
[545] Psalm 33: 9 For he spoke, and it came to be; he commanded, and it stood firm.
[546] Ghaib is a concept that had historically had a metaphysical connotation. It refers to that which is absent, hidden, or concealed, such is the date of someone's death, who he/she would marry. In the Islamic context, al-Ghaib refers to what is only known to God. It is mentioned in sixty different places in the Qu'ran, in six different forms to cover basically three meanings: The Unknown or Hidden, something that took place in the absence of someone and the future. Various translators translated Ghaib in different ways, the most common is the unseen.

turned my face to Him who brought into existence the heavens and the earth, and I have turned away from all that is false. I am not one of the idolaters." (79)

His people argued with him, and he said, "How can you argue with me about God when it is He who has guided me? I do not fear anything you associate with Him (for no evil can affect me) unless my Lord so wills. My Lord embraces everything within His knowledge. How can you not notice? (80) Why should I fear anything that you worship besides Him? Why are you not afraid to associate partners with Him when He never sent you authority to do so? Tell me, if you know the answer, which side is more entitled to feel secure? (81) It is those who have faith, and who have not mixed their faith with injustice. 547 It is they who will be secure, since it is they who have found the right path!" (82)

Such was the argument We gave to Abraham against his people. We raise in rank whoever We will. Your Lord is All-Wise548 All-Knowing.549 (83)

We gave him Isaac and Jacob. We guided each just as We had guided Noah (Nuh) before. Among his descendants were David, Solomon, Job, Joseph, Moses (Musa), and Aaron. In this way We reward those who do good; (84) Zachariah, John, Jesus and Elijah-- every one of them was righteous. (85) Ishmael, Elisha, Jonah, and Lot--We favored every one of them above other people, (86) and also some of their forefathers, their offspring and their brothers. We chose them and guided them on a straight path. (87) Such is God's guidance. He guides whomever He wills of his worshipers. Had they ascribed divinity to others besides Him, all their good works would have been in vain. (88) Those are the ones to whom We gave the Book, wisdom and prophethood. Even if these people now chose to deny the truth, We will entrust it to others who will never deny the truth.550 (89) These were the people God guided. Follow their guidance and say, "I ask no reward for it from you. It is a reminder to all people." (90)

They had not truly appreciated God when they said; God has never revealed anything to a mortal." Say, "Who was it then that sent down the Book which Moses brought as an enlightenment and guidance to men--Yet, you treat it as (mere) leaves of paper, showing some but hiding many. You were taught things that neither you nor your forefathers had ever known. Say, "God!" (has revealed the Book) Then leave them engrossed in their vain talk. (91) This is a blessed Book that We sent down to confirm what is available (of earlier revelations) in order that you may warn the foremost of cities 551 and its surroundings. Those who believe in the Hereafter believe it (this Book) and keep their prayers. (92)

Who could be more wicked than someone who invents lies about God or says, "This has been revealed to me," when no revelations have been sent to him, or says, "I can also reveal something equal to God's revelation?" If you could only see (how it will be) when these evildoers find themselves in the agonies of death, and the angels stretch out their hands to them (and call), "Give

•   •   •

---

547 The Qur'an uses the term injustice here, Zulm ظلم in Arabic. However, injustice here means polytheism. The prophet, explained this verse comparing it to 31:13 'Luqman said to his son while he was instructing him, "O my son, do not attribute any partners to God. Associating others with him is a great wrong."

548 Job 9:4 He is wise in the heart, and mighty in the strength – who has resisted him, and succeeded?

549 Psalm 44:21 would not discover this? For he knows the secrets of the heart.

550 Matthew 21:43 Therefore I tell you, the kingdom of God will be taken away from you and given to a people that produces the fruits of the kingdom.

551 Mecca

up your souls. Today you will be repaid with humiliating suffering for attributing something to God that is not true and for arrogantly resisting His Message." [93]

God will say, "Now you returned to Us alone, just as We first created you, and you have left behind all that We gave you (in your lifetime). We don't see those intercessors of yours that you claimed were partners with God. All the bonds between you (and your earthly life) are now severed, and all those you formerly fancied have deserted you." [94]

God is the One who splits the grain, and the seeds open. He brings out the living from the dead and the dead from the living. This is God, so how can you turn away from the truth? [95] He causes dawns to break, and He makes the night for rest, and He made the sun and the moon run precise courses. That is the design of the Almighty,[552] the All-Knowing. [96] It is He who set up the stars for you so that you might be guided by them in the midst of the deep darkness of the land and the sea. We have spelled out these messages for those who have knowledge. [97] It is He who brought you (all) into existence from a single soul and (has appoint each of you) a time-limit (on earth) and a resting place (after death). We have made Our revelations clear to those who comprehend. [98] It is He who sends down water from the sky.[553] With it, We sustain all living growth, then bring greenery from it, and from that We bring out grains, one riding on the other in close-packed rows.

From the palm tree comes dates in thick clusters, and there are gardens of vines and olive trees, and pomegranates, all so alike and yet so different. Watch their fruit while it ripens. In all this there are signs for the people who would believe[554]. [99] Some (people) have come to think of jinn as partners with God, although it is He who has created them, and in their ignorance they attribute sons and daughters to Him. May he be exalted in His glory and far higher than anything that men may ascribe to Him,[555] [100] the Originator of the heavens and earth. How could He have had a child without ever having a mate, since It is He who created everything, and He alone knows everything? [101] This is God, your Lord, and there is no God but Him[556], the Creator of everything. Worship Him alone. He is in charge of everything. [102] No human vision perceives[557] Him, whereas He perceives all they see. He is the All-Subtle, the All-Aware. [103]

Insights have come to you from your Lord. Whoever chooses to see does so for his own good, and whoever chooses to remain blind, does so to his own loss. "I am not your keeper." [104] We have explained Our revelations in various ways, so they will say, "You have received instructions" and to clarify it to people who have knowledge. [105] Follow what has been revealed to you by your Lord. There

• • •

[552] Psalm 94:4 More majestic than the thunders of mighty waters, More majestic than the waves of the sea, majestic on high is the Lord!

[553] Deuteronomy 28:12 The Lord will open for you his rich storehouse, the heavens, to give the rain of your land in its season and to bless all your undertakings. You will lend to many nations, but you will not borrow

[554] Matthew 6:28-29 Observe how the lilies of the field grow; they do not toil nor do they spin, [29] yet I say to you that not even Solomon in all his glory clothed himself like one of these.

[555] Exodus 15:11 "Who is like you, O Lord, among the gods? Who is like you, majestic in holiness, awesome in splendor, doing wonders?

[556] Exodus 20:3 Thou shalt have no other gods before me.

[557] John 3:8 The wind blows wherever it pleases. You hear its sound, but you cannot tell where it comes from or where it is going. So it is with everyone born of the Spirit."

is no God but Him, and turn away from those who associate others with God. [106] If God had so willed, they would not have ascribed divinity to anyone but Him. We have not made you their keeper, and neither are you responsible for their conduct. [107]

Don't insult those they worship other than God, lest in their hostility and ignorance, (they) insult God. Thus We made their deeds seem pleasing to each community, but in the end, they must return to their Lord and then He will make them (truly) understand all that they were doing. [108] They swear by God with their most solemn oaths that if a miracle were to be shown to them, they would believe in this Book. Say, "Miracles are up to God alone." And, for all you know, even if a miracle were shown to them, they would not believe.[558] [109] We will keep their hearts and their eyes turning. Just as they did not believe in the first place, We will leave them in their overwhelming arrogance, stumbling blindly. [110] Even if We send angels to them, and if the dead were to speak to them and We were to assemble before them, face to face, all the things that were ever created, they would still not believe in God unless God so willed, but most of them are ignorant. [111] Thus, We assigned evil humans and evil jinn as enemies to every prophet. They   whisper enticing words to one another in order to deceive. But they cannot do this unless your Lord had so willed. Therefore, desert them and their invented lies, [112] so that the hearts of those who do not believe in the Hereafter may incline towards their deceit, being content to continue doing whatever they are doing.[559] [113]

(Say), "Will I seek any judge other than God, when It is He who has sent down the Book, clearly spelling out the truth?" Those to whom We gave the Book before know that this is revealed by your Lord with the Truth. Don't be one of those who doubt. [114] Your Lord's word[560] has been fulfilled in Truth and justice. There is no power that could change His words. He is the All-Hearing, the All-Knowing. [115] If you obeyed the majority of those on earth, they will lead you away from the path of God. They follow nothing but speculation, and they are merely guessing. [116] Your Lord knows best who strays from his path and who is rightly-guided. [117]

(Believers) eat any (meat) over which God's name has been pronounced, if you truly believe in His messages. [118] Why not eat that over which God's name has been pronounced, knowing that He has clearly spelled out to you what He has forbidden you to eat, and even that you may eat if you are compelled[561] to do so? But many mislead others through their whims, even though they do not really know. Your Lord, however, is fully aware of these transgressors. [119]

• • •

---

[558] Mark 8:11-12 The Pharisees came out and began to argue with Him, seeking from Him a sign from heaven, to test Him. [12] Sighing deeply in His spirit, He (Jesus) said, "Why does this generation seek for a sign? Truly I say to you, no sign will be given to this generation." Luke 16: 29-31 Abraham replied, 'They have Moses and the prophets; they should listen to them.' [30] He said, 'No, father Abraham; but if someone goes to them from the dead, they will repent.' [31] He said to him, 'If they do not listen to Moses and the prophets, neither will they be convinced even if someone rises from the dead."

[559] Revelation 22:11 Let the evildoer still do evil, and the filthy still be filthy, and the righteous still do right, and the holy still be holy.'

[560] Word here is a reference to the Qur'an but it is equal to another word of God which is Jesus see 3:45.

[561] The foods that are forbidden are permitted if starvation is the only other option.

Abstain from sins[562] openly or in secret. Those who commit sins will be punished for all they have committed. [120] Do not eat that over which God's name has not been pronounced, for this would be sinful conduct.

The devils incite their followers to argue with you and if you listen to them, you, too, will become one of those idolaters. [121] Is a dead person whom We brought back to life and given enlightenment so that he might see his way among men, comparable to someone who is lost in deep darkness from which he cannot emerge? This is how it is. The evil deeds of the unbelievers are made to seem enticing to them, [122] so We placed the greatest opponents in every town to execute their schemes, but they only scheme against themselves without realizing it. [123] Whenever a revelation comes to them, they say, "We will not believe unless we are given the same revelation as God's Messengers were given." God knows best where to place His messages. Humiliation before God and severe punishment will befall those who are guilty of opposition through their schemes. [124] When God wishes to guide someone, He opens his heart to surrender to Him (Islam). And whomever He wills to let go astray, He tightens and constricts his chest, as if he were ascending up to the sky. This is how God inflicts horror upon those who will not believe. [125] (Prophet), this is your Lord's path. We have clearly explained Our revelations to those who take them to heart. [126] They will have the Home of Peace with their Lord, and as a result of their deeds He will be their Protector. [127]

On the Day when He will gather them together (and say), "Company of jinn, you have seduced many humans." And their allies among the people will say, "Our Lord, some of us made use of others, and we have (now) reached the appointed time that You have decreed for us." He will say, "The Fire is your residence, and there you will remain eternally, unless God wills it otherwise. your Lord is All-Wise and All-Knowing." [128]

In this way, We cause the unjust to seduce each other by means of their own doing. [129] "You who have lived in close company with jinn and like-minded humans, did not messengers not come from among you to recite My message and warn you of the coming of this Day (of Judgment)?" They will answer, "We bear witness against ourselves." The life of this world has seduced them, and so they will bear witness against themselves that they had rejected the truth. [130] This is because Your Lord would never destroy a community for its wrongdoing while its people are unaware. [131] Everyone will be judged according to their deeds. Your Lord is well aware of all they do. [132] Your Lord alone is rich beyond need, limitless in His grace. If He wills, He may put an end to all of you and put others in your place, just as He produced you from the offspring of other people. [133] What you are promised is bound to come and you cannot escape it. [134] Say, "My people, continue to do what you are doing, and so will I, and in time you will come to know to whom the future belongs." The unjust will never prosper.[563]
[135]

They allocate to God a share of the fruits of the field and the cattle, saying, "This belongs to God," they claim, "and this is for our idols that, we are

• • •

[562] Psalm 19:12-13 But who can detect their errors? Clear me from hidden faults. [13] Keep back your servant also from the insolent; do not let them have dominion over me. Then I shall be blameless, and innocent of great transgression.

[563] Galatians 6:7 Do not be deceived; God is not mocked, for you reap whatever you sow.

convinced, have a share in God's divinity." Their idols' share does not reach God, but God's share does reach their idols. How badly they judge! [136] In the same way, their belief in idols has seduced the pagans to kill their children, thus bringing them to ruin and confusing them in their faith. If God had so willed, they would not be doing all of this. So abandon them and all their lies. [137] They also falsely claim, "These cattle and fruits are sacred, and only those we allow may eat them." They also (declare that) certain cattle are exempt from labor, and there are some cattle over which they do not pronounce God's name, falsely attributing this to Him. He will repay them for all their lies. [138] They also say, "What is in the womb of such and such cattle is reserved for our men and forbidden to our women, but if the offspring is stillborn, then they may have a share of it." (God) will punish them for all that they (falsely) attribute (to Him): He is All-Wise, All- Knowing. [139] Those who kill their children out of ignorance and declare as forbidden what God has provided for them as sustenance, falsely ascribing (such prohibitions) to God, are lost. They have gone astray and have not found the right path. [140]

He has brought gardens into existence, both the cultivated ones and those that grow wild, as well as the palm-tree, fields with diverse produce, the olives, and pomegranate: all similar to one another and yet so different. Eat from their fruit when it becomes ripe and give what is due on harvest day. Do not be wasteful; He does not love the wasteful. [141] He gave you livestock for work and for meat, so eat whatever God has provided you. Do not follow in Satan's footsteps: he is your sworn enemy. [142] There are eight animals, in (four) pairs: a pair of sheep and a pair of goats. Ask (them, Prophet), "Has He forbidden the two males, or the two females, or that which is in the wombs of the two females? Tell me what you know in this respect." [143] And a pair of camels and a pair of cattle. Ask, "Has He forbidden the two males, or the two females, or that which is in the wombs of the two females? Were you present when God gave you these commands?" Who then is more wicked than a person who, in his ignorance, attributes his own invented lies to God, and thus misleads people? God does not guide such wicked people.[564] [144]

Say, "In all that has been revealed to me, I do not find anything forbidden to eat, except for a dead animal, flowing blood, and pork- It is impure, or a sinful offering dedicated to idols. However, if one is driven by necessity and neither desire nor excess, your Lord is very forgiving [565] and most Merciful-to-all."[566] [145] We forbade the Jews all animals that have claws and We forbade them the fat of both cattle and sheep, except what is on their backs and in their intestines or what sticks to their bones: thus, We punish them for their injustice. We are true to Our word. [146] If they accuse you of lying, say, "Your Lord is limitless in His mercy, but His punishment cannot be averted from those who force others to reject His messages." [147] Those who are bent on ascribing divinity to other than God will say, "If God had willed it, we would not have ascribed divinity to anyone beside Him, nor would our forefathers (have done so), and we also would not

• • •

---

[564] Psalm 5:4-5 For you are not a God who delights in wickedness; evil will not sojourn with you.
[5] The boastful will not stand before your eyes; you hate all evildoers. Luke 6:39 Can a blind man lead a blind man? Will they not both fell into a pit?
[565] Psalm 65:3 When deeds of iniquity overwhelm us, you forgive our transgressions.
[566] Psalm 103:8 The Lord is merciful and gracious, slow to anger and abounding in steadfast love.

have declared anything He has allowed as forbidden." In the same way, those who came before them continued to deny the truth until they came to taste Our punishment. Say, "Do you have any knowledge that you can offer us? You follow suppositions, and you only guess." [148] Say, "The final evidence rests with God alone. Had He so willed, He would have guided you all." [149] Say, "Bring forward your witnesses who can testify that God has forbidden all this," and if they (falsely) testify, do not testify with them. Do not follow the sinful views of those who have rejected Our messages, nor of those who do not believe in the Hereafter while they equate others with their Lord. [150]

Say, "Come; let me tell you what God has forbidden you[567]. Do not ascribe divinity to any one besides Him, [568] relate to your parents[569] in the best possible way, do not kill your children out of fear of poverty, since it is We who will provide sustenance for you and them. Do not commit any shameful deeds, [570] whether they are in open or in secret, and do not take any human life[571] which God has declared as sacred, other than in the pursuit of justice. This is what He commands you to do so that you may remember. [151] Stay away from the property of orphans, except to improve it, until he or she comes of age." Give full measure and weight in accordance with equity.[572]We do not burden any soul with more than it is able to bear.[573] When you voice an opinion, be just, even if it concerns a relative[574]. Fulfill your pledge to God. This is what He has commanded you to do so that you will remember. [152] This is My Straight Path; Follow it, and do not follow any other way, because it will cause you to deviate from it. This is what He commands you, so that you will be mindful of Him. [153]

Then, We gave Moses the Book, complete and perfect or those who do good, clearly explaining everything, a guidance and mercy, so that they may have faith in their encounter with their Lord. [154] This, too, is a blessed Book which We have sent down: follow it and be mindful of God, so that you might be graced with His mercy,[575] [155] so that you do not say, "a Book was only sent down to two groups before our time and we're unaware of their teachings," [156] or, so that you do not say, "If a Book had been sent down to us, we would have followed its guidance better than they did." Clear evidence, guidance and mercy has come to you from your Lord. Who could be more unjust than someone who rejects God's messages and turns away in contempt? We will recompense those who turn away from Our verses with the worst of punishment for their having turned

• • •

[567] These verses are thought to be the equivelant of the ten commendments. They are also defining the term "straight path".

[568] Exodus 20:3 "you shall have no other gods before me".

[569] Exodus 20:12 Honor your father and your mother, so that your days may be long in the land that the Lord your God is giving you.

[570] Or lewdness, adultery or abomination, Exodus 20:14 "You shall not commit adultery".

[571] Exodus 20:13 "'You shall not murder.

[572] Leviticus 19:36 You shall have honest balances, honest weights, an honest ephah, and an honest hin: I am the Lord your God, who brought you out of the land of Egypt.

[573] 1 Corinthians 10:13 "No testing has overtaken you that is not common to everyone. God is faithful, and he will not let you be tested beyond your strength, but with the testing he will also provide the way out so that you may be able to endure it".

[574] Exodus 20:16 "You shall not bear false witness against your neighbor.

[575] Joshua 1:8 This book of the law shall not depart out of your mouth; you shall meditate on it day and night, so that you may be careful to act in accordance with all that is written in it. For then you shall make your way prosperous, and then you shall be successful.

away. [157] Are they waiting for the angels to appear to them, or for your Lord to appear or for some of your Lord's signs to appear? On the Day when your Lord's signs appear, believing will be of no help to any human being who did not believe before, or who, while believing, did not do good deeds. Say, "Wait. We are also waiting." [158]

As for those who have broken the unity of their faith and have divided into different sects, you (Prophet) should have nothing to do with them. Their case rests with God, and in time He will make them understand what they were doing wrong. [159] Whoever comes (before God) with a good deed will gain ten times its credit, but whoever comes with an evil deed will be punished with no more than its equivalent. They will not be treated unfairly. [160] Say, "My Lord has guided me on to a straight path through an ever--true faith-- the way of Abraham, who turned away from all that is false and was not one of the idolaters." [161] Say, "My prayer and my acts of worship and my living and my dying belong to God,[576] the Lord of the Worlds, [162] in whose divinity no one has a share. I have been commanded and I will be the first to surrender myself to Him." [163] Say, "Why would I look for a Lord other than God when He is the Lord of all things?" Each soul is responsible for its own actions, and no bearer of burdens will bear the burdens of another.[577] In time you must all return to your Lord, and He will make you understand the truth about your differences. [164] It is He who has made you inherit the earth and has raised some of you in rank above others so that He might test you by means of what He has given to you. Your Lord is swift in punishment, but He is also forgiving and Merciful-to-all. [165]

•   •   •

---

[576] Romans 14:8 If we live, we live to the Lord, and if we die, we die to the Lord; so then, whether we live or whether we die, we are the Lord's.
[577] Galatians 6:5 "For every one shall bear his own burden."

CHAPTER SEVEN

AL-A'RAF
THE HEIGHTS

THE **MEDINA** PERIOD

In the name of God, the Merciful-to-all, the Mercy Giver:
Alif Lam Mim Sad [01]

A Book has been revealed to you. Let it cause no anxiety in your heart, as you will use it to warn and remind the believers. [02] Follow what has been sent down to you by your Lord, and follow no masters other than Him. How seldom do you remember! [03]

So many (rebellious) towns have We destroyed. Our punishment came to them at night or while they were resting in the afternoon. [04] Their only cry when Our punishment came to them was "How unjust we were!" [05] We will certainly question those to whom a message was sent, and We will certainly question the messengers. [06] We know and will tell them in detail and knowledge, as We were never absent. [07] On that Day, everyone's deeds will be weighed in the balance of Truth. Those whose good deeds weigh on the heavier side will be successful [08] whereas; those whose good deeds are on the lighter side will suffer loss because of their willful rejection of Our messages. [09]

We have given you a place on earth and appointed a means of livelihood for you, (yet) you are seldom grateful. [10] We have created you and formed you, and then We said to the angels, "Bow down before Adam," at which point, they all bowed down except for Iblīs:[578] he was not among those who bowed down. [11] (God) said, "What has stopped you from bowing down when I commanded you?" He answered, "I am better than him. You created me out of fire, but you only created him out of clay." [12] (God) said, "Get down from here, you are not allowed to be arrogant in this place.[579] Get out, you are disgraced." [13] Iblīs said, "Give me until the day they will be resurrected." [14] (God) replied, "You will have

• • •

[578] Iblīs is a name given in the Qur'an to Satan. We use Iblīs where the Qur'an uses it and we use Satan where the Qur'an uses it.

[579] Revelation 12:9 The great dragon was thrown down, that ancient serpent, who is called the Devil and Satan, the deceiver of the whole world—he was thrown down to the earth, and his angels were thrown down with him.

the time you want. [15] Iblīs said, "Now that You have caused me to fall into this, I will sit for them on Your straight path. [16] I will come at them openly as well as secretly, from their right and from their left and You will find that most of them are ungrateful." [17] (God) said, "Get out of here, you disgraced and disowned! As for those who will follow you, I will definitely fill Hell with all of you. [18] And Adam, you and your wife will live in this garden, and both of you eat whatever you may wish,[580] but do not approach this one tree or you will become unjust."[581] [19]

Then, Satan whispered[582] to them[583] to expose their nakedness, which had been hidden from them,[584] and he said, "Your Lord has forbidden you this tree so that you do not become angels or immortal."[585] [20] He swore to them, "I am a sincere advisor," [21] and he succeeded in deceiving them. As soon as the two had tasted (the fruit) of the tree,[586] their nakedness became obvious to them, and they started covering themselves with leaves from the Garden.[587] Their Lord called to them, "Did I not forbid that tree to you and tell you, 'Satan is your clear enemy?" [22] The two replied, "Lord, We have sinned against ourselves and unless You forgive us and have mercy on us, we will definitely be lost." [23] God said, "You get down to earth, as enemies to one another.[588] You will live and have your home there for a while. [24] There you will live," He added, "and there you will die, and from it you will be brought forth (on Resurrection Day)"[589] [25]

Children of Adam, We have sent down clothes to you to cover your nakedness and as a thing of beauty,[590] but the garment of awareness of God is the best of all.[591] These are blessings from God, so that you may remember. [26] Children of Adam, do not allow Satan to seduce you in the same way he caused

· · ·

[580] Genesis 2:16 And the Lord God commanded the man, "You may freely eat of every tree of the garden;
[581] Genesis 2:17 but of the tree of the knowledge of good and evil you shall not eat, for in the day that you eat of it you shall die."
[582] Genesis 3:1 Now the serpent was more crafty than any other wild animal that the Lord God had made. He said to the woman, "Did God say, 'You shall not eat from any tree in the garden'?"
[583] In the Qur'an, the blame of disobedience is placed upon both and not solely on Eve. Both Adam and Eve are held equally responsible. Additionally the Qur'an does not teach that mankind inherited an "original sin" from Adam or Eve. The Qur'an tells us that after they had sinned, God simply taught Adam how to repent and that was the end of that. God is indeed merciful and forgiving.
[584] Genesis 3:10 He said, "I heard the sound of you in the garden, and I was afraid, because I was naked; and I hid myself."
[585] Genesis 3:4,5 4 But the serpent said to the woman, "You will not die; 5 for God knows that when you eat of it your eyes will be opened, and you will be like God, knowing good and evil."
[586] Genesis 3:6 So when the woman saw that the tree was good for food, and that it was a delight to the eyes, and that the tree was to be desired to make one wise, she took of its fruit and ate; and she also gave some to her husband, who was with her, and he ate.
[587] Genesis 3:7 Then the eyes of both were opened, and they knew that they were naked; and they sewed fig leaves together and made loincloths for themselves.
[588] Genesis 3:14,15 The Lord God said to the serpent, "Because you have done this, cursed are you among all animals and among all wild creatures; upon your belly you shall go, and dust you shall eat all the days of your life. 15 I will put enmity between you and the woman, and between your offspring and hers; he will strike your head, and you will strike his heel."
[589] Genesis 3:19 By the sweat of your face you shall eat bread until you return to the ground, for out of it you were taken; you are dust, and to dust you shall return."
[590] Genesis 3:21 And the Lord God made garments of skins for the man and for his wife, and clothed them.
[591] Isaiah 61:10 I will greatly rejoice in the Lord, my whole being shall exult in my God; for he has clothed me with the garments of salvation, he has covered me with the robe of righteousness, as a bridegroom decks himself with a garland, and as a bride adorns herself with her jewels.

your ancestors to be driven out of the Garden. He deprived them of their garment (of God-consciousness) in order to make them aware of their nakedness. He and his tribe watch you from where you cannot see them. We have made satanic forces allies to those who do not believe; [27]

Whenever they commit a shameful deed, they say, "We found our forefathers doing it," and, "God has commanded us to do this." Say, "God does not command disgraceful deeds. How could you attribute something to God about which you have no knowledge?" [28] Say, "My Lord has commanded righteousness[592]." Face Him, and direct your worship straight to Him. Call on Him, devoting yourself only to Him[593]. Just as He first created you, so you will return. [29] Some (of you) He graced with guidance, while, others are doomed to stray. They have taken devils for their masters instead of God, thinking all the while that they have found the right path. [30] Children of Adam, dress well for every act of worship. Eat and drink, but do not waste. He does not love the wasteful. [31] Say, "Who is there to forbid the adornment and nourishment that God has provided for His worshipers?" Say, "They are given to those who believe during the life of this world, to be theirs alone on Resurrection Day." We clearly spell out these messages to people who understand. [32]

Say, "My Lord has forbidden immoral acts-- openly or in secret-- sinning and unjustified aggression, and ascribing divinity to others besides Him, and saying things about Him that you do not know." [33] A term has been set for every nation, and when the end of their term approaches, they can neither delay it nor hasten it by a single moment.[594] [34]

Children of Adam, when messengers come to you from among yourselves, conveying My messages to you, then all who are mindful of Me and live righteously don't need to fear nor will they grieve, [35] but those who reject Our messages and arrogantly disrespect them are destined for the fire, and there they will remain.[595] [36] Who could be more unjust than those who attribute their own lies to God or who reject His messages? Such people will have whatever has been allotted for them. Then when Our angels arrive to take them to die, they will ask, "Where are those beings that you invoked besides God?" (Those sinners) will reply, "They have deserted us," and (thus) they will bear witness against themselves that they had been denying the truth. [37] (God) says, "Join the crowds of jinn[596] and humans who have gone before you into the fire." Every time a crowd enters, it will curse its fellow beings, so that when they have all gathered inside, the last of them will say about the first, "Lord, It is they who have led us astray. Give them double suffering through fire." He will reply, "Every one of you deserves double suffering, though you don't know it." [38] The first of them will say to the last of them, "You were in no way better than us. Taste the punishment for all that you have earned."[597] [39]

• • •

---

[592] Genesis 15:6 And he believed the Lord, and he counted it to him as righteousness.

[593] Luke 4:8 Jesus answered, "It is written: 'Worship the Lord your God and serve him only.'"

[594] Luke 12:25 "And can any of you by worrying add a single hour to your span of life?"

[595] Jeremiah 6:19 Hear, O earth; I am going to bring disaster on this people, the fruit of their schemes, because they have not given heed to my words; and as for my teaching, they have rejected it.

[596] See Glossary

[597] Isaiah 50:11 But all of you are kindlers of fire, lighters of firebrands. Walk in the flame of your fire, and among the brands that you have kindled! This is what you shall have from my hand: you shall lie down in torment.

The gates of Heaven will not be opened for those who rejected Our messages and arrogantly scorned them. They will not enter Paradise any more than a thick, twisted thread can pass through a needle's eye[598]. This is how We pay those who force others to reject Our messages.[599] (40) Hell will be their resting place and covering as well. This is how We punish the unjust. (41)

We do not burden any soul with more than it is able to bear.[600] Those who believe and do righteous deeds are destined for Paradise, where they will live. (42) We will have removed all ill feeling from their hearts. Streams will flow at their feet, and they will say, "All praise is due to God, who has guided us to this, for we would certainly not have found the right path unless God had guided us. Our Lord's Messengers brought the Truth. A voice will call out to them, "This is the Paradise which you have inherited because of your past deeds."[601](43) The people of Paradise will call out to the people of the Fire, "Now We have found that what our Lord promised us has come true. Have you found that what your Lord promised you has come true?" They will answer, "Yes." A voice will proclaim from their midst, "God's rejection hangs over the unjust (44) who turn away from God's path[602] and try to make it crooked,[603] and who refuse to acknowledge the truth of the life to come." (45)

Between the two there will be a barrier[604] and on the heights are people who can recognize each by their features. They will call out to the people of paradise, "Peace be upon you," not having entered it themselves, but hoping to do so. (46) Whenever their eyes are turned towards the people of the fire, they will cry, "Lord, do not place us among the unjust people." (47) Those who had possessed this ability of discernment will call out to those they recognize by their marks (as sinners), saying, "How has your collection (of wealth) and all your false pride benefitted you? (48) Are these the people you swore God would never bless? (For now they have been told,) 'Enter paradise. There is no need to fear or grieve.'"(49)

The people of the fire will call out to the people of paradise, "Pour some water on us, or some of the sustenance which God has provided for you."[605] They

• • •

[598] Mark 10:23-25 And Jesus, looking around, said to His disciples, "How hard it will be for those who are wealthy to enter the kingdom of God!" 24 The disciples were amazed at His words. But Jesus answered again and said to them, "Children, how hard it is to enter the kingdom of God! 25 "It is easier for a *thick twisted thread* to go through the eye of a needle than for a rich man to enter the kingdom of God." Translation is mine (SK).

[599] Jeremiah 15:6 You have rejected me, says the Lord, you are going backwards; so I have stretched out my hand against you and destroyed you—I am weary of relenting.

[600] 1 Corinthians 10:13 No testing has overtaken you that is not common to everyone. God is faithful, and he will not let you be tested beyond your strength, but with the testing he will also provide the way out so that you may be able to endure it.

[601] Isaiah 25:1 O Lord, you are my God; I will exalt you, I will praise your name; for you have done wonderful things, plans formed of old, faithful and sure.

[602] Matthew 23:13 'But woe to you, scribes and Pharisees, hypocrites! For you lock people out of the kingdom of heaven. For you do not go in yourselves, and when others are going in, you stop them.

[603] Acts 13:10 and said, 'You son of the devil, you enemy of all righteousness, full of all deceit and villainy, will you not stop making crooked the straight paths of the Lord?

[604] Luke 16:26 Besides all this, between you and us a great chasm has been fixed, so that those who might want to pass from here to you cannot do so, and no one can cross from there to us."

[605] Luke 16:23-24 In Hades, where he was being tormented, he looked up and saw Abraham far away with Lazarus by his side. 24 He called out, "Father Abraham, have mercy on me, and send Lazarus to dip the tip of his finger in water and cool my tongue; for I am in agony in these flames."

said, "God has denied both to the unbelievers." ⁶⁰⁶⁽⁵⁰⁾ They are those who, enticed by the life of this world, took their religion lightly, like a mere game, and were deluded by worldly living. (God will say), "We will be ignoring them today as they ignored the coming of this Day, just as they denied Our messages." ⁽⁵¹⁾

We conveyed to them a Book in which We clearly and wisely spelled out guidance and grace to people who believe. ⁽⁵²⁾ Are they (the unbelievers) waiting for the final prophecy to unfold? On the Day when its final meaning will have unfolded, those who ignored it before will say, "Our Lord's Messengers spoke the Truth. Is there anyone to intercede for us now? Or, could we be brought back (to life) so that we might behave differently than how we behaved before?" They will have lost their souls and all the lies they had invented will have forsaken them. ⁽⁵³⁾

Your Lord is God, who has created the heavens and the earth in six days⁶⁰⁷ and is established on the throne of His majesty. He covers the day with the night in swift pursuit, with the sun⁶⁰⁸ and the moon and the stars subservient to His command.⁶⁰⁹ All creation is His and He commends all. Blessed is God, the Lord of all the worlds!⁶¹⁰ ⁽⁵⁴⁾ Call unto your Lord humbly, and in the secrecy of your hearts⁶¹¹. He does not love those who transgress the limits of what is right.⁶¹² ⁽⁵⁵⁾ Do not spread corruption on earth after it has been so well ordered. Call unto Him with fear and longing. The mercy of God is close to those who do good. ⁽⁵⁶⁾ It is God who sends the winds, bearing good news of His coming mercy, and when they have gathered the heavy clouds, We drive them to a dead land where We cause rain to fall,⁶¹³ bringing out all kinds of fruit, just as We will bring out the dead. Will you not remember? ⁽⁵⁷⁾ As for the good land, vegetation comes out by its Lord's will, but poor land produces in agony. We explain Our messages in various ways to those people who are grateful. ⁽⁵⁸⁾

We sent Noah to his people and he said, "My people, worship God alone. You have no god other than Him.⁶¹⁴ I am concerned that you will have the punishment on that Awesome Day." ⁽⁵⁹⁾ The notable ones among his people replied, "We see that you are obviously lost in error." ⁽⁶⁰⁾ (Noah) said, "My people, there is no error in me. I am a Messenger from the Lord of all the worlds. ⁽⁶¹⁾ I am delivering to you my Lord's messages and giving you good advice. I know (through revelation) from God what you do not know. ⁽⁶²⁾ Why do you think it is strange that a message from your Lord would come to you through a man from

• • •

⁶⁰⁶ Luke 16:25 But Abraham said, "Child, remember that during your lifetime you received your good things, and Lazarus in like manner evil things; but now he is comforted here, and you are in agony.
⁶⁰⁷ Revelation 4:11 'You are worthy, our Lord and God, to receive glory and honor and power, for you created all things, and by your will they existed and were created.'
⁶⁰⁸ Psalm 136:8 "the sun to rule over the day, for his steadfast love endures forever;
⁶⁰⁹ Psalm 136:9 the moon and stars to rule over the night, for his steadfast love endures forever
⁶¹⁰ 2 Kings 19:15 And Hezekiah prayed before the Lord, and said: 'O Lord the God of Israel, who are enthroned above the cherubim, you are God, you alone, of all the kingdoms of the earth; you have made heaven and earth.
⁶¹¹ Matthew 6:6 But when you pray, go into your room, close the door and pray to your Father, who is unseen.
⁶¹² Psalm 5:4-5 ᶠᵒʳ you are not a God who delights in wickedness; evil will not sojourn with you.
⁵ The boastful will not stand before your eyes; you hate all evildoers.
⁶¹³ Leviticus 26:4 I will give you your rains in their season, and the land shall yield its produce, and the trees of the field shall yield their fruit.
⁶¹⁴ Exodus 20:3 you shall have no other gods before me.

among yourselves, so that he might warn you and so that you might become mindful of God and so that you might be graced with His mercy?" [63] Yet, they called him a liar. We saved him and those who stood by him, in the ark, while We caused those who rejected Our messages to drown. They were blind. [64]

To the people of 'Aad[615] (We sent) their brother, Hud.[616] He said, "My people, worship God alone. You have no god other than Him. Will you not be mindful of Him?" [65] The notables among his people who refused to acknowledge the truth said, "We see that you are weak-minded, and we think you are a liar." [66] (Hud) said, "My people, there is no weak-mindedness in me. I am a Messenger from the Lord of the worlds. [67] I am delivering my Lord's messages to you and advising you truly and well. [68] Why are you surprised that your Lord would send you a reminder and a warning through one of your own? Remember how He made you heirs to Noah's people and increased your stature. Remember God's grace so that you might prosper." [69] They answered, "Have you come to us asking that we worship God alone and give up all that our forefathers worshiped? Then bring the (punishment) with which you have threatened us, if you are a man of truth." [70] (Hud) said, "You are already set to receive your Lord's condemnation and wrath. Do you argue with me about the names which you and your forefathers have invented, names for which God has given no authority? Wait, then, (for what will happen,) I will wait with you." [71] By Our grace, We saved him and those who stood by him, while We wiped out the last remnant of those who rejected Our messages and would not believe. [72]

To the people of Thamud[617] (We sent) their brother Salih[618] who said, "My people, Worship God alone. You have no god other than Him. Clear evidence has now come to you from your Lord. The she-camel belonging to God is to be a sign for you. Let her graze on God's earth, and do not do her harm in any way or you will be struck by a painful punishment. [73] Remember how He made you heirs to

• • •

[615] The people of Ad, to whom the prophet Hud has been sent, lived in area of curved sand hills in the southern part of the Arabian Peninsula, possibly in an area between eastern Yemen and western Oman. They were physically well built and renowned for their craftsmanship especially in the construction of tall buildings with lofty towers. They were outstanding among all the nations in power and wealth, which, unfortunately, made them arrogant and boastful. Their political power was held in the hand of unjust rulers, against whom no one dared to raise a voice. They were not ignorant of the existence of God, nor did they refuse to worship Him. What they did refuse was to worship God alone. They worshipped other gods, also, including idols. This is one sin God does not forgive.

[616] Prophet Hud, Ibn Jarir reported that he was Hud Ibn Shalikh, Ibn Arfakhshand, Ibn Sam, Ibn Noah. He also reported that Prophet Hud was from a tribe called Ad Ibn Us Ibn Sam Ibn Noah, who were Arabs living in Al Ahqaf in Yemen between Oman and Hadramaut, on a land called Ashar stretching out into the sea. The name of their valley was Mughiith. Some traditions claimed that Hud was the first person who spoke Arabic while others claimed that Noah was the first. It was also said that Adam was the first. Hud is prophet sent to Ad people

[617] After the destruction of the Ad, the tribe of Thamud succeeded them in power and glory. They also fell to idol-worshipping. As their material wealth increased so, too, did their evil ways while their virtue decreased. Like the people of Ad, they erected huge buildings on the plains and hewed beautiful homes out of the hills. Tyranny and oppression became prevalent as evil men ruled the land. The dwelling places of Salih's people, Thamud are situated somewhere between Al-Hijaz west of present-day Saudi Arabia and Ash-Sham (Syria and Surrounding regions), in the southeastern part of Midan (Madyan), which is situated east of the Gulf of Al-Aqabah. Chiseled out of the stone, their dwellings are still preserved.

[618] Prophet Salih, a man from the tribe of Thamud. His name was Salih Ibn Ubeid, Ibn Maseh, Ibn Ubeid, Ibn Hader, Ibn Thamud, Ibn Ather, Ibn Eram, Ibn Noah. Mostly known the Miracle story of a unique she camel. Salih was known for his wisdom, purity and goodness and had been greatly respected by his people before God's revelation came to him. Prophet Salih is prophet sent to Thamud people.

(the tribe of) 'Aad and settled you in the land, so that you were able to build castles for yourselves on its plains and carve houses out of the mountains. Remember God's grace, and do not spread corruption on earth. [74] The notables from among his people, who reveled in their arrogance towards all who were deemed weak, said to the believers among them, "Do you (really) know that Salih has been sent by his Lord?" They answered, "We believe in the message which he brought to us." [75] The arrogant ones said, "We refuse to regard as true what you have come to believe in." [76] They, then, cruelly slaughtered the she-camel and turned with disdain from their Lord's commandment and said, "Salih, bring about that (punishment) that you had threatened us with, if you are truly one of God's Messengers." [77] An earthquake seized them, and they lay lifeless in their homes. [78] (Salih) turned away from them and said, "My people, I delivered to you my Lord's message and gave you good advice but you did not love those who gave (you) good advice." [79]

And Lot, when he said to his people, "How can you practice this outrage? No one in the world has outdone you in this. [80] You lust[619] after men instead of women. You transgress all bounds." [81] His people's only answer was, "Expel them from your land. These people want to make themselves out to be pure. [82] We saved him and his household,[620] except his wife[621] who was among those that stayed behind. [83] We showered upon the others a rain (of destruction).[622] Consider the fate of those who force others to reject God's message. [84]

To (the people of) Midian[623], (We sent) their brother Shu'ayb.[624] He said, "My people, worship God alone. You have no god other than Him. Clear evidence of the truth has now come to you from your Lord. Give full measure and weight,[625] and do not deprive people of what is rightfully theirs, and do not spread corruption on earth after it has been well ordered. (All) of this is for your own good if you would only believe. [85] Do not lurk on every trail, threatening and trying to turn away all who believe in God from His path and trying to make it appear crooked.[626] Remember when you were few and He made you many. Look at what happened in the end to those who spread corruption. [86] "If there are some among you who have come to believe in the message which I bear, while

• • •

[619] Genesis 19:5 and they called to Lot, 'Where are the men who came to you tonight? Bring them out to us, so that we may know them.'

[620] Genesis 19:29 So it was that, when God destroyed the cities of the Plain, God remembered Abraham, and sent Lot out of the midst of the overthrow, when he overthrew the cities in which Lot had settled.

[621] Genesis 19:26 But Lot's wife, behind him, looked back, and she became a pillar of salt.

[622] Genesis 19:24 Then the Lord rained on Sodom and Gomorrah sulphur and fire from the Lord out of heaven;

[623] The people of Madyan were Arabs who lived in a territory stretching along the lands of Al-Hijaz (Western Saudi Arabia) to the part of which today is greater Syria & surrounding regions, and east of the Gulf of Al-Aqaba They were a greedy people who did not believe that God existed and who led wicked lives. They gave short measure, praised their goods beyond their worth, and hid their defects. They lied to their customers, thereby cheating them.

[624] Prophet Shu'ayb armed with many miracles. Shu'ayb preached to them, begging them to be mindful of God's favors and warning them of the consequences of their evil ways, but they only mocked him. Shu'aib remained calm as he reminded them of his kinship to them and that what he was doing was not for his personal gain. Shu'ayb is a prophet sent to Madyan people.

[625] Leviticus 19:36 You shall have honest balances, honest weights, an honest ephah, and an honest hin: I am the Lord your God, who brought you out of the land of Egypt.

[626] Acts 13:10 and said, 'You son of the devil, you enemy of all righteousness, full of all deceit and villainy, will you not stop making crooked the straight paths of the Lord?

others do not believe, then have patience in hard times till God judges between us. He is the best of all judges." [87]

The notables among his people who gloried in their arrogance said, "Shu'ayb, We will most certainly expel you and your fellow-believers from our land unless you return to our ways." (Shu'ayb said, "Why, even if we find it detestable? [88] If we were to return to your ways after God has saved us from them we would be guilty of blaspheming against God. It is inconceivable to return to them, unless God, our Lord, so wills." Our Lord comprehends everything within His knowledge. We place our trust in God. Lord, expose the Truth and judge between us and our people, for You are the best judge. [89] The notables among his people who were bent on denying the truth, said (to his followers), "If you follow Shu'ayb, you will be the losers." [90] An earthquake overtook them and they lay lifeless in their homes." [91] It was as if those who had rejected Shu'ayb never lived there. They were the losers. [92] He turned away from them and said, "My people, I delivered to you my Lord's message and gave you good advice. How could I mourn for the people who have denied the truth?" [93]

We have never sent a prophet to any community without first sending misfortune and hardship to its people so that they might humble themselves.[627] [94] We then transformed their hardship into prosperity, so that they were able to thrive but then they said (to themselves), "Misfortune and hardship befell our forefathers as well." Then We seized them suddenly when they were not expecting it. [95] If the people of those communities had believed and been mindful of Us, We would have showered them with grace out of heaven and earth, but they rejected the truth, and so We punished them for their misdeeds.[96]

Can the people of any community ever feel secure that Our punishment will not come upon them by night while they are asleep?[628] [97] Can the people of any community ever feel secure that Our punishment will not come upon them in broad daylight, while they are at play? [98] Can they ever feel secure from God's plan? Only the people who are lost feel secure from God's plan.[629] [99] Has it not become obvious to those who inherited the earth from former generations that if We willed, We could punish them (as well) for their sins, sealing their hearts so that they cannot hear? [100] To those (earlier) communities, some of whose stories We relate to you, messengers from among them came with evidence of the truth, but they would not believe in anything which they had already rejected. God seals the hearts of the unbelievers, [101] and in most of them We found that they did not honor their commitments. We found that most of them were defiant. [102]

· · ·

[627] Isaiah 66:2 All these things my hand has made, and so all these things are mine, says the Lord. But this is the one to whom I will look, to the humble and contrite in spirit, who trembles at my word.

[628] 1 Thessalonians 5.2-6 For you yourselves know very well that the day of the Lord will come like a thief in the night. When they say, 'There is peace and security', then sudden destruction will come upon them, as labor pains come upon a pregnant woman, and there will be no escape! But you, beloved, are not in darkness, for that day to surprise you like a thief; for you are all children of light and children of the day; we are not of the night or of darkness. So then, let us not fall asleep as others do, but let us keep awake and be sober.

[629] 2 Thessalonians 2:11 For this reason God sends them a powerful delusion, leading them to believe what is false.

Later, We sent Moses (Musa) with Our messages to Pharaoh[630] and his inner circle, and they rejected them. Consider what happened to those who used to spread corruption. [103] Moses said, "Pharaoh, I am a messenger from the Lord of the worlds.[631] [104] I cannot say anything about God but the Truth. I have now come to you with clear evidence from your Lord. send the children of Israel with me[632]." [105] (Pharaoh) said, "If you have come with a sign, produce it, if you are a man of truth." [106] (Moses) threw down his staff and it was clearly a snake.[633] [107] He pulled out his hand and it was white for all to see[634]. [108] The notables among Pharaoh's people said, "This is definitely a sorcerer with great knowledge [109] who wants to drive you out of your land. (Pharaoh said,) "What do you advise?" [110] They answered, "Let him and his brother wait a while, and send messengers to all cities [111] who will bring you every sorcerer of great knowledge."[635] [112]

The sorcerers came to Pharaoh (and) said, "We should be rewarded if we win." [113] (Pharaoh) answered, "Yes, and you will be among those who are near to me." [114] They said, "Moses, either you will throw (your staff first), or We will throw (first)." [115] He answered, "You throw (first)." When they threw down (their staffs), they cast a spell upon the people's eyes, and struck them with fear, producing mighty sorcery. [116] (Then) We inspired Moses, "Throw down your staff," and it swallowed up all their deceptions.[636] [117] Truth was confirmed and what they had produced came to nothing. [118] They were vanquished there and then, and they became utterly humiliated. [119] The sorcerers fell down bowing themselves [120] (and) said, "We have come to believe in the Lord of the worlds, [637] [121] the Lord of Moses and Aaron." [122] Pharaoh said, "How dare you believe in him before I give you permission. This is a plot which you have cunningly devised in (my) town in order to drive out its people. In time you will come to know (my revenge). [123] I will cut off your hands and feet in great numbers because of (your) perverseness, and then I will certainly crucify you together in great numbers." [124] They answered, "We return to Our Lord. [125] You take revenge against us only because we have come to believe in our Lord's messages as soon as they came to us. Lord, shower us with patience in hard times and make us die as men who have surrendered themselves to You." [126]

The notables among Pharaoh's people said, "Will you allow Moses and his people to spread corruption on earth and to (cause your people to) abandon you and your gods?" (Pharaoh) replied, "We will kill their sons in great numbers and

• • •

---

[630] Exodus 3:10 So come, I will send you to Pharaoh to bring my people, the Israelites, out of Egypt.

[631] Psalm 47:2,7 For the Lord, the Most High, is awesome, a great king over all the earth. For God is the king of all the earth; sing praises with a psalm.

[632] Exodus 5:1 Afterwards Moses and Aaron went to Pharaoh and said, 'Thus says the Lord, the God of Israel, "Let my people go, so that they may celebrate a festival to me in the wilderness."'

[633] Exodus 7:10 So Moses and Aaron went to Pharaoh and did as the Lord had commanded; Aaron threw down his staff before Pharaoh and his officials, and it became a snake

[634] Exodus 7:11 Again, the Lord said to him, 'Put your hand inside your cloak.' He put his hand into his cloak; and when he took it out, his hand was leprous, as white as snow.

[635] Exodus 7:11 Then Pharaoh summoned the wise men and the sorcerers; and they also, the magicians of Egypt, did the same by their secret arts.

[636] Exodus 7:12 Each one threw down his staff, and they became snakes; but Aaron's staff swallowed up theirs.

[637] Exodus 8:19 And the magicians said to Pharaoh, 'This is the finger of God!' But Pharaoh's heart was hardened, and he would not listen to them, just as the Lord had said.

will spare (only) their women.[638] We have complete power over them." (127) Moses said to his people, "Turn to God for help, and have patience in hard times. All of the earth belongs to God.[639] He gives it as a heritage to whomever He wills of His worshipers. The future belongs to those who are mindful of Him"[640] (128) (The children of Israel) said, "We were being persecuted long before you came to us, and since then too." (Moses) replied, "Your Lord may well destroy your enemy and make you successors to the land to see how you behave." (129)

We inflicted Pharaoh's people with drought and crop failure,[641] so that they might take heed. (130) Whenever good fortune came to them, they would say, "This is our due." Whenever affliction befell them, they would blame their bad fortune on Moses and those who followed him. Their (evil) fortune had been decreed by God, but most of them did not know it. (131) They said (to Moses), "We will not believe you, no matter what sign you produce to cast a spell on us." (132) We let loose on them floods, (plagues of) locusts,[642] lice,[643] frogs,[644] and (water turning into) blood[645]- all distinct signs, but they reveled in their arrogance for they were people lost in sin. (133) Whenever a plague struck them, they would cry, "Moses, pray for us to your Lord by virtue of the promise He has made with you. If you remove this plague from us, We will truly believe in you and will let the children of Israel go with you."[646] (134) When We removed the plague from them, giving them time to fulfill their promise, they would break their word[647]. (135) We exacted vengeance on them and caused them to drown in

• • •

---

[638] Exodus 1:17 But the midwives feared God; they did not do as the king of Egypt commanded them, but they let the boys live.

[639] Psalm 24:1 Of David. A Psalm. The earth is the Lord's and all that is in it, the world, and those who live in it;

[640] Psalm 5:12 For you bless the righteous, O Lord; you cover them with favor as with a shield.

[641] Genesis 47:13 Now there was no food in all the land, for the famine was very severe. The land of Egypt and the land of Canaan languished because of the famine., Exodus 9:13-10:20.

[642] Exodus 10:12-13 Then the Lord said to Moses, 'Stretch out your hand over the land of Egypt, so that the locusts may come upon it and eat every plant in the land, all that the hail has left.' [13] So Moses stretched out his staff over the land of Egypt, and the Lord brought an east wind upon the land all that day and all that night; when morning came, the east wind had brought the locusts.

[643] Exodus 8:16 Then the Lord said to Moses, 'Say to Aaron, "Stretch out your staff and strike the dust of the earth, so that it may become gnats throughout the whole land of Egypt."'

[644] Exodus 8:2-3 If you refuse to let them go, I will plague your whole country with frogs. [3] The river shall swarm with frogs; they shall come up into your palace, into your bedchamber and your bed, and into the houses of your officials and of your people, and into your ovens and your kneading bowls.

[645] Exodus 7:15-18 Go to Pharaoh in the morning as he is going out to the water, and station yourself to meet him on the bank of the Nile; and you shall take in your hand the staff that was turned into a serpent. [16] You shall say to him, 'The Lord, the God of the Hebrews, sent me to you, saying, "Let My people go, that they may serve Me in the wilderness. But behold, you have not listened until now." [17] Thus says the Lord, "By this you shall know that I am the Lord: behold, I will strike the water that is in the Nile with the staff that is in my hand, and it will be turned to blood. [18] The fish that are in the Nile will die, and the Nile will become foul, and the Egyptians will ʽfind difficulty in drinking water from the Nile."'"

[646] Exodus 10:28, 12:31 Then Pharaoh said to him, 'Get away from me! Take care that you do not see my face again, for on the day you see my face you shall die. 12:31 'Then he summoned Moses and Aaron in the night, and said, 'Rise up, go away from my people, both you and the Israelites! Go, worship the Lord, as you said.

[647] Exodus 8:30-32 So Moses went out from Pharaoh and made supplication to the Lord. [31] The Lord did as Moses asked, and removed the swarms of flies from Pharaoh, from his servants and from his people; not one remained. [32] But Pharaoh hardened his heart this time also, and he did not let the people go.

the sea,648 because they had rejected Our messages and paid no heed to them.
(136) For the people who had been deemed utterly low (in the past), We gave them the eastern and western parts of the land that We had blessed,649 as their heritage. Your Lord's good promise to the children of Israel was fulfilled as a result of their patience in hard times.650 Whereas We destroyed everything that the Pharaoh and his people had created and built. (137)

We brought the children of Israel across the sea651, where they came across people who were devoted to worshipping idols.652 (The children of Israel) said, "Moses, give us a god like the gods they have."653 He replied, "You are ignorant people!" (138) As for these here, what they are doing is doomed to destruction; and all that they have ever done is falsehood." (139) He said, "Why should I seek for you a god other than God, since it is He who has favored you above all other people?" (140) (He reminded them of the word of God), "We saved you from Pharaoh's people who caused you cruel suffering,, 654 killing your sons 655 in great numbers and sparing (only) your women, which was an awesome test from your Lord." (141)

We made an appointment for thirty nights (on Mount Sinai) for Moses, and We then added ten to them. The term set by his Lord was fulfilled in forty nights. 656 Moses said to his brother Aaron, "Take my place among my people and act righteously,657 and do not follow the path of those that spread corruption." (142) When Moses came at the appointed time and his Lord spoke to him, he said, "My

• • •

648 Exodus 14:27-28, So Moses stretched out his hand over the sea, and at dawn the sea returned to its normal depth. As the Egyptians fled before it, the Lord tossed the Egyptians into the sea. 28 The waters returned and covered the chariots and the chariot drivers, the entire army of Pharaoh that had followed them into the sea; not one of them remained.

649 Exodus 6:8 I will bring you into the land that I swore to give to Abraham, Isaac, and Jacob; I will give it to you for a possession. I am the Lord."'

650 Psalm 16:5-6 The Lord is my chosen portion and my cup; you hold my lot. 6 The boundary lines have fallen for me in pleasant places; I have a goodly heritage.

651 Exodus 14:15-16 Then the Lord said to Moses, 'Why do you cry out to me? 16 Tell the Israelites to go forward. But you lift up your staff, and stretch out your hand over the sea and divide it, that the Israelites may go into the sea on dry ground.

652 Exodus 34:12-16 Take care not to make a covenant with the inhabitants of the land to which you are going, or it will become a snare among you. 13 You shall tear down their altars, break their pillars, and cut down their sacred poles 14 (for you shall worship no other god, because the Lord, whose name is Jealous, is a jealous God). 15 You shall not make a covenant with the inhabitants of the land, for when they prostitute themselves to their gods and sacrifice to their gods, someone among them will invite you, and you will eat of the sacrifice. 16 And you will take wives from among their daughters for your sons, and their daughters who prostitute themselves to their gods will make your sons also prostitute themselves to their gods

653 See Exodus 32

654 Exodus 5:6-9 That same day Pharaoh commanded the taskmasters of the people, as well as their supervisors, 7 "You shall no longer give the people straw to make bricks, as before; let them go and gather straw for themselves. 8 But you shall require of them the same quantity of bricks as they have made previously; do not diminish it, for they are lazy; that is why they cry, 'Let us go and offer sacrifice to our God.' 9 Let heavier work be laid on them; then they will labor at it and pay no attention to deceptive words."

655 Exodus 1:16 'When you act as midwives to the Hebrew women, and see them on the birth stool, if it is a boy, kill him; but if it is a girl, she shall live.'

656 Exodus 24:18 Moses entered the cloud, and went up on the mountain. Moses was on the mountain for forty days and forty nights.

657 Exodus 24:14 To the elders he had said, 'Wait here for us, until we come to you again; for Aaron and Hur are with you; whoever has a dispute may go to them.'

Lord, show (Yourself) to me, so that I might see You."[658] (God) said, "You can never see Me. However, behold this mountain.[659] If it remains firm in its place, then you will see Me." As soon as his Lord revealed His limitless glory to the mountain, He caused it to crumble to dust and Moses fell down unconscious. After he recovered, he said, "May You be exalted in Your glory! I repent! I will be the first of the believers!" [143] (God) said, "Moses, I have chosen you above all people by virtue of the messages which I have entrusted to you and by virtue of My speaking (to you). Hold on to what I have given you, and be among the grateful." [144]

We inscribed everything for him in the Tablets[660] which taught and clearly explained everything. (We said,) "Hold on to them with (all your) strength, and tell your people to hold fast to those most excellent teachings." I will show you the fate of the disobedient people. [145] All those on earth who have behaved arrogantly for no reason, I will turn away from My signs. Even if they see every sign, they will not believe in them. And if they see the path of righteousness they will not take it. Whereas, if they see a path of error, they will take it because they have rejected Our messages and have paid no attention to them. [146] All of the deeds of those who reject Our messages, and thus the Truth of the life to come, will be in vain. Why should they be repaid for anything other than what they have done? [147]

In his absence, Moses' people started worshipping a calf, [661] making lowing sounds. It was made from their jewelry. Did they not see that it could neither speak to them nor guide them in any way? (Yet), they worshipped it because they were unjust. [148] (Later,) wringing their hands in remorse, having realized that they had gone astray, they would say, "Unless our Lord has mercy on us and grants us forgiveness, we will be lost."[662] [149]

When Moses returned to his people, full of wrath and sorrow, he exclaimed, "You have followed a foul and evil course in my absence![663] Have you abandoned your Lord's commandments? "He threw down the tablets[664] and seized his brother by the head, dragging him. Aaron cried, "Son of my mother! these

· · ·

[658] Exodus 33:18 Moses said, 'Show me your glory, I pray.'

[659] Exodus 33:21-22 And the Lord continued, 'See, there is a place by me where you shall stand on the rock; 22 and while my glory passes by I will put you in a cleft of the rock, and I will cover you with my hand until I have passed by;

[660] Exodus 24:12, 31:18 The Lord said to Moses, 'Come up to me on the mountain, and wait there; and I will give you the tablets of stone, with the law and the commandment, which I have written for their instruction. 31:18 When God finished speaking with Moses on Mount Sinai, he gave him the two tablets of the covenant, tablets of stone, written with the finger of God.

[661] Exodus 32:4 He took the gold from them, formed it in a mold, and cast an image of a calf; and they said, 'These are your gods, O Israel, who brought you up out of the land of Egypt!'

[662] Matthew 18:12-14 What do you think? If a shepherd has a hundred sheep, and one of them has gone astray, does he not leave the ninety-nine on the mountains and go in search of the one that went astray? 13 And if he finds it, truly I tell you, he rejoices over it more than over the ninety-nine that never went astray. 14 So it is not the will of your Father in heaven that one of these little ones should be lost.

[663] Exodus 32:1 When the people saw that Moses delayed to come down from the mountain, the people gathered around Aaron and said to him, 'Come, make gods for us, who shall go before us; as for this Moses, the man who brought us up out of the land of Egypt, we do not know what has become of him.'

[664] Exodus 32:19 as soon as he came near the camp and saw the calf and the dancing, Moses anger burned hot, and he threw the tablets from his hand and broke them at the foot of the mountain.

people overpowered me and almost killed me![665] Do not let my enemies rejoice at my suffering, and do not include me with those unjust people." [150] (Moses) said, "Lord, grant my brother and me forgiveness, and cover us with Your mercy. You are the most merciful of those who show mercy." [151] (To Aaron, he said,) "As for those who worshiped the calf, they will experience their Lord's anger and be disgraced in this world." This is the way we repay all who instigate trouble. [152] As for those who do bad deeds and afterwards repent and (truly) believe, your Lord is Forgiving [666] and Merciful. [667] [153]

When Moses' anger subsided, he picked up the tablets, on which were guidance and mercy for those who stood in awe of their Lord. [154] Moses chose seventy men[668] for our appointment. When they were seized with trembling,[669] he prayed, "Lord, had You willed, You would have destroyed them, and me as well. Will You destroy us for what the fools among us did? This is a trial from you, whereby You allow whomever You will to go astray and guide whomever You will.[670] You are near to us. Grant us forgiveness, and have mercy on us for You are the most forgiving of all. [155] Grant us good things in this world and in the life to come. We have turned to You in repentance." (God) answered, "I punish whomever I will, but My mercy encompasses everything. I grant it to those who are mindful of Me,[671] give the purifying alms and who believe in Our messages; [156] those who will follow the messenger, the gentile[672] Prophet they find described in the Torah [673] and in the Gospel[674], the Prophet who will command them to do what is obviously[675] right and forbid what is obviously wrong and allow them the good things in life and forbid them the bad things. He will release them from their burdens and shackles that bound them before. Those who will believe in him and honor him and support him and follow the enlightenment that has been sent down with him who will succeed." [157] Say (Muhammad), "People, I am the messenger of God to all, from Him who has control over the heavens

• • •

[665] Exodus 32:22-23 And Aaron said, 'Do not let the anger of my Lord burn hot; you know the people, that they are bent on evil. 23 They said to me, "Make us gods, who shall go before us; as for this Moses, the man who brought us up out of the land of Egypt, we do not know what has become of him."

[666] Daniel 9:9. To the Lord our God belong mercy and forgiveness, for we have rebelled against him,

[667] Psalm 116:5, Gracious is the Lord, and righteous; our God is merciful.

[668] Exodus 24:1 Then he said to Moses, 'Come up to the Lord, you and Aaron, Nadab, and Abihu, and seventy of the elders of Israel, and worship at a distance.

[669] Exodus 20:18 When all the people witnessed the thunder and lightning, the sound of the trumpet, and the mountain smoking, they were afraid and trembled and stood at a distance,

[670] Exodus 33:19 And he said, "I will make all my goodness pass before you, and will proclaim before you the name, 'The Lord'; and I will be gracious to whom I will be gracious, and will show mercy on whom I will show mercy.

[671] Romans 9:18 So then he has mercy on whomsoever he chooses, and he hardens the heart of whomsoever he chooses.

[672] Most translators and interpreters of the Qur'an understand the word Ummi to mean illiterate. Recently some modern commentators understood it to mean Gentile.

[673] According to this verse, followers of the Prophet see things in the former books that refer to him such as Deuteronomy 18:18 the KJB I will raise them up a Prophet from among their brethren, like unto thee, and will put my words in his mouth; and he shall speak unto them all that I shall command him.

[674] John 16:13 When the Spirit of truth comes, he will guide you into all the truth, for he will not speak on his own authority, but whatever he hears he will speak, and he will declare to you the things that are to come.

[675] What is obviously right or wrong is time, place and culture sensative.

and the earth. There is no god but Him. He (alone) gives life and causes death."[676] Believe in God and His Messenger, the gentile[677] Prophet who believed in God and His words. Follow Him, so that you may find guidance. (158)

Among the people of Moses, there is a group of people who would guide with the Truth and who act justly according to it. (159) We divided them into twelve tribes.[678] When his people asked Moses for water,[679] We inspired him, "Strike the rock with your staff"[680] and twelve springs gushed out so that all the people knew where to drink. We caused the clouds[681] to comfort them with their shade, and We sent down to them manna[682] and quail.[683] We said, "Eat the good things We have provided for you." They did no wrong to Us; they only wronged themselves. (160) When you were told, "Take this village as your home, and eat anywhere you like. But say, 'Remove the burden of our sins from us', and enter the gate humbly. Then We will forgive you of your sins and will abundantly reward those who do good." (161) Those among them who were bent on doing wrong substituted another saying for that which they had been given, so We released from heaven a plague against them as a punishment for all their injustices. (162)

(Prophet) Ask them about the town that stood by the sea and how its people would disregard the Sabbath[684] whenever their fish surfaced for them only on that day, and they would never come on other days. We tested them by means of their (own) disobedience. (163) Whenever people among them asked (those who tried to restrain the people who broke the Sabbath), "Why do you preach to people whom God is about to destroy or (at least) to punish with severe suffering?" The pious ones would answer, "In order to be free from blame before your Lord and so that these (transgressors) might also become mindful of Him." (164) When those (sinners) forgot all that they had been told to take to heart, We saved those that tried to prevent them doing evil, and severely punished the wrongdoers with dreadful suffering. (165) When they scornfully persisted in doing what they had been forbidden to do, We said to them, "Be as despicable as apes." (166) Your Lord made it known that until the Day of Resurrection, He would

• • •

[676] Deuteronomy 32:39 See now that I, even I, am he; there is no god besides me. I kill and I make alive; I wound and I heal; and no one can deliver from my hand.
[677] see 669 above
[678] Genesis 49:28 All these are the twelve tribes of Israel, and this is what their father said to them when he blessed them, blessing each one of them with a suitable blessing.
[679] Exodus 15:24, 17:2 And the people complained against Moses, saying, 'What shall we drink?' 17:2 The people quarreled with Moses, and said, 'Give us water to drink.' Moses said to them, 'Why do you quarrel with me? Why do you test the Lord?'
[680] Exodus 17:6 I will be standing there in front of you on the rock at Horeb. Strike the rock, and water will come out of it, so that the people may drink.' Moses did so, in the sight of the elders of Israel.
[681] Exodus 13:21 The Lord went in front of them in a pillar of cloud by day, to lead them along the way, and in a pillar of fire by night, to give them light, so that they might travel by day and by night.
[682] Exodus 16:4,8, 4 Then the Lord said to Moses, "I am going to rain bread from heaven for you, and each day the people shall go out and gather enough for that day. In that way I will test them, whether they will follow my instruction or not. 8 And Moses said, "When the Lord gives you meat to eat in the evening and your fill of bread in the morning, because the Lord has heard the complaining that you utter against him—what are we? Your complaining is not against us but against the Lord."
[683] Exodus 16:13 In the evening quails came up and covered the camp; and in the morning there was a layer of dew around the camp.
[684] Ezekiel 20:20 and hallow my Sabbaths that they may be a sign between me and you, so that you may know that I the Lord am your God.

send people to punish them with cruel suffering. Your Lord is swift in punishment but He is most Forgiving[685] and most Merciful-to-all.[686] (167)

We dispersed them as (separate) communities all over earth; some of them were righteous and some of them less so. We tried them with blessings and/or misfortune so that they might return (to the right path). (168) They have been succeeded by generations who, (in spite of) having inherited the Book, hold onto the momentary treasures of this world (in preference to the Hereafter) and say, "We will be forgiven". Yet if the same opportunity comes around again they will take it. Didn't they make a commitment based on the Book, not to say anything about God that was not the Truth and (haven't they) studied its contents well? Since the life in the Hereafter is the better (of the two) for all who are mindful of God, will you not use your common sense? (169) As for those who hold fast to the Book and are constant in prayer, We will not fail to reward those who do what is right. (170) When We caused Mount Sinai to shake above the children of Israel as if it were a (mere) shadow, and they thought it would fall on to them, did we not say, "Hold fast with (all your) strength onto what We have given to you and remember all that is within so that you might remain mindful of God"? (171)

When your Lord took out from the loins of the children of Adam all their descendants, He called upon them to bear witness about themselves, "Am I not your Lord?" To which they answer, "Yes, we bear witness of this." (We remind you of this) so that on the Day of Resurrection, you do not say, "We were unaware of this," (172) or so that you do not say, "It was our forefathers who began to ascribe divinity to other beings beside God and we were only their children. Will You destroy us because of the falsehoods they invented?" (173) We clearly spell out these messages and (We do it) so that they (those who have sinned) might return (to Us). (174)

Tell them the story of the man to whom We gave Our messages and who then cast them aside: Satan catches up with him and he strays, into error. (175) Had We so willed, We could have used those (messages) to raise him high but he always clung to the earth and followed his own desires. He was like a dog-who pants with his tongue hanging out whether you drive him away or leave him alone. That's the image of those who reject Our messages. Tell this story so that they might reflect on it. (176) The people who reject Our messages are an example of evil, for It is against themselves that they are sinning. (177) Only He whom God guides is truly guided, whereas those whom He lets go astray[687] are the losers. (178) There are many jinn and men who have hearts that fail to grasp the truth.[688] We have destined for Hell, those whose eyes fail to see and whose ears fail to

• • •

---

[685] 1 John 1:9 If we confess our sins, he who is faithful and just will forgive us our sins and cleanse us from all unrighteousness.

[686] Exodus 34:6, The Lord passed before him, and proclaimed, 'The Lord, the Lord, a God merciful and gracious, slow to anger, and abounding in steadfast love and faithfulness.

[687] 2 Thessalonians 2:11 For this reason God sends them a powerful delusion, leading them to believe what is false

[688] Psalm 32:9 Do not be like a horse or a mule, without understanding, whose temper must be curbed with bit and bridle, else it will not stay near you.

hear.[689] They are like cattle. No, they are even less mindful of the right path. It is they who are (truly) oblivious. (179)

The Most Beautiful Names belong to God: use them to call on Him and avoid those who take His name in vain. They will be punished for all that they do. (180) Among those whom We created, there are people who guide (others) in the way of the Truth and act justly in its light. (181) As for those who are bent on denying Our messages, We will bring them low, step by step, without their perceiving how it happened, (182) even if I give them more time. My subtle plan is unshakeable. (183) Has it never occurred to them that their companion (referring to the Prophet) is not mad but is giving them clear warning? (184) Have they never considered (God's) mighty dominion over the heavens and the earth and all that God has created and (asked themselves) whether the end of their own term might be near? What (other revelation) will they believe in if they do not believe in this? (185) For those whom God lets go astray, there is no guide and He will leave them in their presumptuous arrogance, blindly stumbling to and fro. (186)

They will ask you (Prophet) about the Last Hour[690]: "When will it come?" Say, "Knowledge of this rests with my Lord along. Only He will reveal it in its time. It will weigh heavily on the heavens and the earth (and) it will fall upon you suddenly." [691] They will continually ask you, as if you could gain insight into this (mystery). Say, "Knowledge of this rests with my Lord alone but most people are unaware (of this)." (187) Say (Prophet), "It is not with my power to bring benefit to, or avert harm from myself except as God may please. If I had knowledge of what is hidden, I would have abundant good things and no evil would ever touch me. I am only one who sounds a warning and a messenger of good news to people who will believe." (188)

He has created (all) of you out of one living entity[692] and out of it brought into being its mate,[693] so that man might incline towards women (with love). When he has embraced her, she conceives[694] (what begins as) a light burden, and continues to bear it. Then, when she grows heavy (with child), they both call onto God, their Lord, "If You grant us a healthy (child), We will be among the grateful." (189) Yet, as soon as He has granted them an upright child; they begin to give credit to associates alongside Him, giving them a share in bringing about what He has

• • •

[689] Matthew 13:13-15 while seeing they do not see, and while hearing they do not hear, nor do they understand. 14 "In their case the prophecy of Isaiah is being fulfilled, which says, 'you will keep on hearing, but will not understand; you will keep on seeing, but will not perceive; 15 For this people's heart has grown dull, and their ears are hard of hearing, and they have shut their eyes; so that they might not look with their eyes, and listen with their ears, and understand with their heart and turn—and I would heal them.'

[690] Revelation 14:7 He said in a loud voice, 'Fear God and give him glory, for the hour of his judgment has come; and worship him who made heaven and earth, the sea and the springs of water.'

[691] 1 Thessalonians 5:2-3 For you yourselves know very well that the day of the Lord will come like a thief in the night. 3 When they say, 'There is peace and security', then sudden destruction will come upon them, as labor pains come upon a pregnant woman, and there will be no escape!

[692] Genesis 2:7 then the Lord God formed man from the dust of the ground, and breathed into his nostrils the breath of life; and the man became a living being.

[693] Genesis 2:21-22 So the Lord God caused a deep sleep to fall upon the man, and he slept; then he took one of his ribs and closed up its place with flesh. And the rib that the Lord God had taken from the man he made into a woman and brought her to the man.

[694] Genesis 4:1Now the man knew his wife Eve, and she conceived and bore Cain, saying, "I have produced a man with the help of the Lord."

granted them. However, God is far above the partners they ascribe alongside Him. (190) Will they ascribe divinity alongside Him to beings that cannot create anything since they are created, (191) and are unable to give them help nor can they help themselves. (192)

If you (Believers) offer guidance to such people, they won't follow you: it makes no difference whether you offer it to them or remain silent. (193) All those that you call (idolaters) on beside God are only created beings like yourselves. Call on them and let them answer your prayers if what you claim is true. (194) Do They have feet to walk on? Do They have hands with which they can grasp? Do They have eyes with which they can see? Do They have ears with which they can hear? Say (Prophet), "Call to your aid all those to whom you ascribe a share in God's divinity," and then scheme (anything you may wish) against me. Do not spare me. (195) My protector is God, who has given me this Book from on high, for It is He who protects the righteous. (196) All those whom you call on instead of Him are neither able to give you help nor can they help themselves (197) and if you pray to them for guidance, they do not hear and although you may imagine that they see you, they do not see. (198) Be tolerant of man's nature and command the doing of what is right and leave alone all those who choose to remain ignorant. (199) If it should happen that a prompting from Satan stirs you up (to blind anger), seek refuge with God. He is All-Hearing,695 All-Knowing.696 (200) Those who are mindful of God think (of Him) when Satan prompts them to do something and immediately they begin to see (things) clearly, (201) even though their (godless) brethren would like to draw them into error. (202)

When you (Prophet) do not produce a miracle for them, some (people) will say, "Why do not you seek to obtain one?" Say, "I only follow whatever is being revealed to me from my Lord. This (revelation) is a means of insight from your Lord and a guidance and grace onto people who will believe. 697(203) Hence, when the Qur'an is recited, pay attention and listen to it in silence, so that you might be graced with (God's) mercy." (204) (Prophet) remember your Lord humbly and with awe and without raising your voice in the morning and in the evening. Do not allow yourself to be inattentive (205) Those who are in the presence of your Lord are never too proud to worship Him. They praise His limitless glory and bow down before Him.698 (206)

• • •

---

695 Psalm 5:3, O Lord, in the morning you hear my voice; in the morning I plead my case to you, and watch.
696 Job 37:16 Do You know the balancing of the clouds, the wondrous works of the one whose knowledge is perfect.
697 Isaiah 58:11 The Lord will guide you continually, and satisfy your needs in parched places, and make your bones strong; and you shall be like a watered garden, like a spring of water, whose waters never fail.
698 Exodus 15:11 "Who is like you, O Lord, among the gods?   Who is like you, majestic in holiness, awesome in splendor, doing wonders?

CHAPTER EIGHT

AL-ANFAL
SPOILS OF WAR

THE **MEDINA** PERIOD

In the name of God, the Merciful-to-all, the Mercy Giver:

They will ask you (Prophet) about the spoils of war. Say, "This is a matter that will be dealt with by God and His Messenger." So, remain mindful of God and settle your differences[699], and obey God and His Messenger if you are Believers. [01] Believers are those whose hearts tremble with awe whenever God is mentioned, and whose faith is strengthened whenever His revelations are recited and who place their trust in their Lord; [700][02] who keep up their prayer and spend out of what We provide them [03] Those are truly Believers. They have a high standing with their Lord, forgiveness of sins, and a generous provision. [04]

It is your Lord who took you out of your home to fight for the Truth, while some of the believers disliked it [05] arguing with you about the Truth after it was made clear to them, as if they were being driven towards death while staring it in the face. [06] God promised you that one of the two enemy groups would fall to you, and you wanted to fight the weaker one. God willed the Truth to prevail in accordance with His words and to wipe out the unbelievers [07] so He might prove the Truth to be true and falsehood to be false ,no matter how much resistance came from those who force others to reject God's messages. [701] [08] When you prayed to your Lord for help He responded favorably; "I will help you with a thousand angels in formation."[702] [09] God meant this as a message of hope

• • •

---

[699]Matthew 16:26 For what will it profit a man if he gains the whole world and forfeits his soul? Or what shall a man give in return for his soul?

[700] 1 Chronicles 16:28-30 Ascribe to the Lord, O families of the peoples, ascribe to the Lord glory and strength. [29] Ascribe to the Lord the glory due his name; bring an offering, and come before him. [30] Worship the Lord in holy splendor; Tremble before him, all the earth. The world is firmly established; it shall never be moved.

[701] Mujrimoun in modern Arabic has come to mean criminals. However, in the Qur'anic context it meant political dissent. Specifically, it means knowing that one is wrong rejecting the faith, but never the less forcing others to reject it.

[702] Psalm 68:17 With mighty chariots, twice ten thousand, thousands upon thousands, the Lord came from Sinai into the holy place.

and assurance for your hearts, so you would know that victory is only from God.[703] God is Almighty [704] and Wise.[705] (10) Then He made drowsiness overcome you as a blessing from Him to calm you down and sent rain[706] so that He may cleanse you from Satan's whispers; to strengthen your hearts and make your steadfast.[707] (11) Your Lord revealed to the angels, "I am with you. Make the Believers stand firm; I will put terror into the hearts of the unbelievers. So strike above their necks and cut off their fingers." (12) This is because they opposed God and His Messenger, and if anyone opposes God and His Messenger, God's punishment is severe.[708] (13) "This is it. Taste it." The punishment of fire awaits the unbelievers.[709] (14)

Believers, when you meet the unbelievers in battle, do not turn your backs on them, (15) for whoever turns his back on them, unless it is a battle tactic or an attempt to join another group, will earn the wrath of God and his home will be Hell, a terrible destination. (16) Believers, it was not you who killed the enemy, but God who killed them, and it was not you (Prophet) who threw terror into them but it was God who threw it, and He did all of this in order to test the believers. God is All-Hearing,[710] All-Knowing[711] (17) This is your reward. God will weaken the unbelievers' plots. (18) Believers, if you have been praying for victory, it has now come to you. If you abstain from sin, it will be for your own good, but if you return to sin, We will withdraw Our promise of help and your community will be of no use to you, regardless of their numbers. God is only with those who believe. (19)

Believers obey God and His Messenger and now that you hear His message, do not turn away from Him. (20) Do not be like those who say, "We have heard," when they were not listening. (21) The worst of all creatures in God's sight are those deaf and dumb ones who do not think.[712] (22) If God had seen any good in them, He would have made them hear, but even if He had, they would still have turned away and paid no attention. (23) Believers, respond to God and His Messenger whenever he calls you to that which will give you life.[713] Know that

• • •

[703] Psalm 39:7 "And now, O Lord, what do I wait for? My hope is in you.

[704] Job 9:4, "He is wise in heart, and mighty in strength"

[705] Proverbs 2:6 For the Lord gives wisdom; from his mouth come knowledge and understanding

[706] Psalm 68:9 Rain in abundance, O God, you showered abroad; you restored your heritage when it languished;

[707] Psalm 40:2 He drew me up from the desolate pit, out of the miry bog, and set my feet upon a rock, making my steps secure.

[708] Ezekiel 25:1I will execute great vengeance on them with wrathful punishments. Then they shall know that I am the Lord, when I lay my vengeance on them.

[709] Matthew 13:42 and they will throw them into the furnace of fire, where there will be weeping and gnashing of teeth.

[710] 1 John 5:14 And this is the boldness we have in him, that if we ask anything according to his will, he hear us

[711] 1 John 3:20 whenever our hearts condemn us; for God is greater than our hearts, and he knows everything.

[712] Matthew 13:15 For this people's heart has grown dull, and their ears are hard of hearing, and they have shut their eyes; so that they might not look with their eyes, and listen with their ears, and understand with their heart and turn—and I would heal them."

[713] Deuteronomy 30:19-20 I call heaven and earth to witness against you today that I have set before you life and death, blessings and curses. Choose life so that you and your descendants may live, [20] loving the Lord your God, obeying him, and holding fast to him; for that means life to you and length of days, so that you may live in the land that the Lord swore to give to your ancestors, to Abraham, to Isaac, and to Jacob.

God intervenes between a man and the desires of his heart and that you will be gathered to Him.[714] (24) Beware of discord that will not only afflict those who are unjust among you; and know that God is severe in punishment.[715] (25) Remember when you were just a few and helpless, afraid that people might snatch you away but He sheltered you and strengthened you with His help and provided you with good things so that you might be grateful[716]. (26) Believers, do not betray God and His Messenger, or knowingly betray (other people's) trust in you, (27) and know that your worldly possessions and your children are only a test and a temptation and that there is a tremendous reward with God.[717] (28) Believers, if you remain mindful of God, He will give you a standard by which to determine right from wrong, will wipe away your misdeeds and will forgive your sins. God's grace is limitless. (29)

As the unbelievers w ere plotting against you (Prophet) in order to prevent you (from delivering the message), or to kill you, or to drive you away. They plotted and so did God. He is the best of plotters. (8: 30) Whenever Our messages were conveyed to them, they would say, "We have heard this before and if we want, we can say things like this- these are nothing but ancient tales." (31) They would also say, "God, if this is the Truth from You, then rain down on us stones from the heavens or inflict some painful suffering on us." (32) God did not choose to punish them when you (Prophet) were still among them, nor would God punish them when they (might still) ask for forgiveness. (33) Why would God not punish them, when they are preventing people from reaching the Holy Sanctuary, even though they are not its guardians? Only those mindful of God can be its guardians but most of the unbelievers do not understand. (34) Their prayers before the House are nothing but whistling and clapping. 'So taste the punishment for your persistent denial of the truth'. (35) The unbelievers spend their wealth to turn people away from God's path. They will continue to spend it until it becomes a source of sorrow for them: in the end they will be overcome and will be gathered in Hell, (36) as God might separate the good from the bad and stack the bad together, herding them all to Hell; these are the truly lost. (37) Tell the unbelievers that if they stop, all their past will be forgiven, but if they persist they have an example in the fate of those who went before. (38) Fight them until there is no more persecution and all worship is devoted to God alone. If they stop, then God sees all that they do (39) but if they refuse, know that God is your protector, the best protector and the best helper.[718](40)

You should know that whatever spoils you acquire, one-fifth belongs to God and the Messenger, to close relatives and orphans, to the needy, and to the stranded travelers. (This you must observe) if you believe in God and what We

• • •

[714] Ecclesiastes 12:7 and the dust returns to the earth as it was, and the breath returns to God who gave it.

[715] Matthew 25:41 then he will say to those at his left hand, 'you that are accursed, depart from me into the eternal fire prepared for the devil and his angels

[716] Numbers 6:24-26 The Lord bless you and keep you; [25] the Lord make his face to shine upon you and be gracious to you; [26] the Lord lift up his countenance upon you and give you peace.

[717] Hebrews 11:6 And without faith it is impossible to please God, for whoever would approach him must believe that he exists and that he rewards those who seek him.

[718] Hosea 13:4 Yet I have been the Lord your God ever since the land of Egypt; you know no God but me, and besides me there is no savior

revealed to Our servant on the day of distinction (when Truth was distinguished from falsehood)- the day when two forces met in battle. God has power over all things.[719] (41) You were near the end of the valley (of Badr) and they were at the far end, and the caravan was below you. Even if you had made a prior arrangement to meet there, you would have missed it, but (You have met) so that God might bring about a matter already decided. This was so that those who would die might die in clear sight of the Truth and that he who would remain alive might live in clear sight of the Truth. God is All-Hearing,[720] All-Knowing. (42)

God made them to appear as few in your dream: had He made them appear as many, you would have lost heart and would have disagreed with one another about what to do. It is God who saved you from this. He fully knows the secrets of the hearts.[721] (43) When you met in battle, He made them appear as few in your eyes, just as He made you appear as few in their eyes, so that God might bring about a matter already decided. These matters are decided by God. (44)

Believers, when you come against an enemy in battle, be steadfast and remember to call on God without ceasing so that you may prosper[722]. (45) Obey God and His Messenger, and do not quarrel with one another[723] so that you do not lose momentum. Be patient; God is with those who are patient in hard times. (46) Do not be like those who came from their homeland full of arrogance and a desire to be seen and praised by men while they were turning others away from the path of God. God is fully aware of everything they do. (47) Satan made them think they were doing the right thing. He told you, "No one can overcome you today because I am with you," but as soon as the two forces came within sight of one another, he turned around and said, "I am not responsible for you. I see something that you do not see. I am afraid of God. God is severe in punishment."[724] (48)

The hypocrites and those who have sick hearts[725] say: "The Believers' faith has surely misled them," While he who trusts God will find that God is Almighty,[726] Wise. (49) If you could only see how it will be when the angels retrieve the unbelievers' souls, they will beat them on their faces and backs and (will say), "Experience the pain of burning (50) in return for what your own hands have done. God is never unjust to his worshipers." (51) They are like Pharaoh's people and those who lived before them: they rejected God's signs so God punished them

• • •

---

[719] Job 42:2 "I know that you can do all things, and that no purpose of yours can be thwarted

[720] 1 John 5:14 And this is the boldness we have in him, that if we ask anything according to his will, he hear us

[721] Psalm 44:21 would not God discover this? For he knows the secrets of the heart.

[722] 2 Chronicles 20:17 This battle is not for you to fight; take your position, stand still, and see the victory of the Lord on your behalf, O Judah and Jerusalem." Do not fear or be dismayed; tomorrow go out against them, and the Lord will be with you.'

[723] 2 Timothy 2:24-26 And the Lord's servant must not be quarrelsome but kindly to everyone, an apt teacher, patient, 25 correcting opponents with gentleness. God may perhaps grant that they will repent and come to know the truth, 26 and that they may escape from the snare of the devil, having been held captive by him to do his will.

[724] 2 Thessalonians 1:9 These will suffer the punishment of eternal destruction, separated from the presence of the Lord and from the glory of his might,

[725] Jeremiah 17:9-10 The heart is devious above all else; it is perverse—who can understand it? 10 I the Lord test the mind and search the heart, to give to all according to their ways, according to the fruit of their doings.

[726] Job 9:4 He is wise in heart, and mighty in strength —who has resisted him, and succeeded? —

for their sins. God is powerful [51] and severe in his punishment. [52] God never stops dispensing His grace to people[728] unless their souls' rebel. God is All-Hearing,[729] All-Seeing.[730] [53] They are like Pharaoh's people[731] and those who lived before them. They denied the Lord's signs. So We destroyed them because of their sins and caused Pharaoh's people to drown.[732] They were all unjust. [54]

In God's sight, the worst beasts are the unbelievers who refuse to believe. [55] Those You have made a covenant with who break this covenant on every occasion, not being mindful of God's presence. [56] If you face them at war, make a fearsome example of them for those who follow them, so that they may remember the Truth. [57] If you have reason to fear treachery from people (with whom you made a treaty), let them know that you intend to cancel the treaty so you will be on even terms. God does not love the treacherous.[733] [58] The unbelievers shouldn't think that they will escape God. This they can never do. [59] Prepare whatever forces you can so that you might frighten God's enemies and yours, and to frighten others unknown to you but known to God. Whatever you may do in God's cause, will be repaid to you in full and you will not be wronged.[734] [60] But if they incline towards peace, you incline to it as well and place your trust in God. He alone is All-Hearing, All-Knowing. [61] If they intend to deceive you, God will suffice as your protector. It is He who has strengthened you with His help by giving you followers [62] whose hearts He has brought together. Even if you had given away everything on earth, you could not have brought their hearts together. God brought them together. He is Almighty,[735] Wise.[736] [63] Prophet, God is a sufficient protector for you and for the believers who follow you. [64] Urge the believers to fight, if there are twenty of you who are patient in hard times, they will overcome two hundred, and if there are one hundred of you, they will overcome one thousand unbelievers,[737] for the unbelievers are people who do not comprehend. [65] God has lightened your burden for now. He knows that there is a weakness in you. If there are one hundred of you who are patient in hard times, you will overcome two hundred,

* * *

[727] Psalm 93:4 More majestic than the thunders of mighty waters, more majestic than the waves of the sea, majestic on high is the Lord!

[728] James 1:17 Every generous act of giving, with every perfect gift, is from above, coming down from the Father of lights, with whom there is no variation or shadow due to change.

[729] 1 John 5:14 And this is the boldness we have in him, that if we ask anything according to his will, he hear us

[730] Proverbs 15:3, The eyes of the Lord are in every place, keeping watch on the evil and the good.

[731] Exodus 11:9-10 The Lord said to Moses, 'Pharaoh will not listen to you, in order that my wonders may be multiplied in the land of Egypt.' [10] Moses and Aaron performed all these wonders before Pharaoh; but the Lord hardened Pharaoh's heart, and he did not let the people of Israel go out of his land.

[732] Exodus 14:27-28 So Moses stretched out his hand over the sea, and at dawn the sea returned to its normal depth. As the Egyptians fled before it, the Lord tossed the Egyptians into the sea. [28] The waters returned and covered the chariots and the chariot drivers, the entire army of Pharaoh that had followed them into the sea; not one of them remained.

[733] Psalm 5:4-5 For you are not a God who delights in wickedness; evil will not sojourn with you. [5] The boastful will not stand before your eyes; you hate all evildoers.

[734] Luke 6:38 give, and it will be given to you. A good measure, pressed down, shaken together, running over, will be put into your lap; for the measure you give will be the measure you get back."

[735] Psalm 24:8 Who is the King of glory? The Lord, strong and mighty, the Lord, mighty in battle

[736] Job 9:4 "He is wise in heart, and mighty in strength"

[737] Leviticus 26:8 Five of you shall give chase to a hundred, and a hundred of you shall give chase to ten thousand; your enemies shall fall before you by the sword.

and if there are one thousand of you, you will overcome two thousand by God's permission. God is with those who are patient in hard times. [66]

It is not right for a prophet to take prisoners of war before he has conquered the land. You (people) desire the temporary gains of this world, but God desires for you the good of the life to come. God is Almighty and Wise. [67] Had it not been for a predetermined decree from God, a severe punishment would have come upon you for what you took[738]. [68] Enjoy all the good and lawful spoils of war that you acquired, and remain mindful of God. God is the Forgiver[739] and the Merciful-to-all.[740] [69]

Prophet, tell the prisoners you have taken, "If God finds good in your hearts, He will give you something better than all that has been taken from you and He will forgive you. God is the Forgiver and the Merciful-to-all." [70] If they try to betray you, they have betrayed God before, and He gave you power over them. God is All-Knowing [741] and All-Wise.[742] [71]

Those who believed and who emigrated (to Medina) and struggled for God's cause with their possessions and lives, and those who have given refuge and help, are all allies of one another. As far as those who believed but did not emigrate, you do not owe them any protection until they have emigrated. If they are prevented from freely practicing their faith and ask you for help, you must help them, except against people with whom you have a treaty. God sees all that you do [72]

Unbelievers support each other. Unless you do likewise, there will be turmoil, and much corruption on earth. [73] Those who believed and emigrated, and struggled for God's cause, as well as those who gave them refuge and help, are true believers.[743] Forgiveness awaits them as well as excellent sustenance. [74] As for those who came to believe afterwards and emigrated and struggled alongside you, they are one with you. But in the Book of God, family members are nearer to one another. God knows everything. [75]

• • •

---

[738] They took prisoners for ransom.

[739] Isaiah 43:25 I am He who blots out your transgressions for my own sake, and I will not remember your sins.

[740] James 5:11 We count those blessed who endured. You have heard of the endurance of Job and have seen the outcome of the Lord's dealings, that the Lord is full of compassion and is merciful."

[741] Romans 11:33 O the depth of the riches and wisdom and knowledge of God! How unsearchable are his judgments and how inscrutable his ways!

[742] Job 9:4 "He is wise in heart, and mighty in strength"

[743] James 1:27 Religion that is pure and undefiled before God, the Father, is this: to care for orphans and widows in their distress, and to keep oneself unstained by the world.

CHAPTER **NINE**

AT-TAWBAH
REPENTANCE

THE **MEDINA** PERIOD

God and His Messenger repudiate the treaty made with the idolaters. [01]
"You are free to move around for four months, but you can never escape God, and God will disgrace all who deny the truth." [02] On the day of the great pilgrimage, there will be a proclamation from God and His Messenger to all people: "God and His Messenger are released from all treaty obligations with the idolaters. If you repent, it will be for your own good, but if you persist, know that you can never escape God." Warn the unbelievers that they will have a painful punishment.[744][03] As for those who have honored their treaty obligations, and have not assisted anyone against you, fulfill your agreement with them to the end of its term. God loves those who are mindful of Him. [04]

But once the sacred months are over, kill those idolaters wherever you find them,[745] besiege them, ambush them and imprison them. However, If they repent and pray, and pay the prescribed purifying alms, let them go on their way, for God is the Forgiver and the Mercy-Giver.[746] [05] If any of those idolaters seek your protection, protect him so that he will be able to hear the words of God. Take him to a place where he is safe, because they are people who do not know the truth. [06] How can there be a treaty between God and His Messenger with the idolaters,[747] except for those with whom you made a treaty at the Sacred House? As long as they remain true to you, be true to them. God loves those who are mindful of Him. [07] What sort of a treaty is this, since, if they gain the upper

• • •

---

[744] Revelation 20:15 and anyone whose name was not found written in the book of life was thrown into the lake of fire.
[745] Qur'anic exegetes al-Baydawi (d.685H) and al-Alusi (d.1270H) explain that this verse refers to those idol worshipers' Arabs who violated their peace treaties by waging war against the Muslims (nakitheen) and thus Abu Bakr al-Jassas (d.370H) notes that these verses are particular to the Arab idolaters who were in a state of war with the Muslims, and do not apply to anyone else.
[746] Ephesians 2:4 But God, who is rich in mercy, out of the great love with which he loved us Daniel 9:9 To the Lord our God belong mercy and forgiveness, for we have rebelled against him
[747] 2 Corinthians 6:14 Do not be mismatched with unbelievers. For what partnership is there between righteousness and lawlessness? Or what fellowship is there between light and darkness?

111

hand, they would not respect any agreement or obligation to protect (you). They please you with what they say, while their hearts remain averse (to you). Most of them are disobedient. [08] They have sold God's messages for small change and have turned others away from His path.[748] What they have done is truly evil. [09] They respect neither kinship nor treaty with believers, and it is they who are offenders. [10] If they repent, and pray, and pay the prescribed purifying alms, they become your brothers in faith; We spell out these messages clearly for people who understand. [11] If they violate their oaths after having made a treaty with you and condemn your faith, then fight against these leaders of ungodliness, who have no regard for their own oaths, so that they will stop their aggression. [12] Won't you fight against people who have broken their solemn oaths, and done all they can to drive the Messenger out, and attacked you first? Are you afraid of them? It is God whom you should fear if you are (truly) believers.[749] [13] Fight them. God will use your hands to punish them, and will disgrace them, and will give you victory over them. He will heal the believers' hearts [14] and will remove the fury from their hearts. God redeems whomever He wills. God knows[750] and is wise.[751] [15] Believers, do you think you will be spared without God testing your loyalty to the struggle in His cause, your loyalty to Him, His Messenger and the believers? God is totally aware of everything you do [16]

It is not for the idolaters to visit or tend God's places of worship while they testify that they deny the truth. Their deeds will come to nothing, and they will be eternally in the fire. [17] Only those who believe in God and the Last Day, who perform their prayers, give the purifying alms, and who are in awe of God[752] and no one else, shall visit and tend God's places of worship. Only such people can expect to be included among those who are guided by God. [18] Do you think that providing water to pilgrims and tending to the Sacred House is the same thing as believing in God and the Last Day, and persevering in God's path? They are not the same in God's sight. God does not grace unjust people with guidance. [19] Those who have believed, migrated and persevered in God's cause with their possessions and their lives have the highest rank with God. They are the ones who are victorious. [20] Their Lord brings them the good news of the grace that flows from Him and His approval, and of Gardens that await them, full of everlasting pleasure, [21] where they will live forever. God has a tremendous reward (for them). [22]

Believers, do not take your fathers and brothers for allies if unbelief is dearer to them than faith; those of you who do so are unjust. [23] Say, "If your fathers, your sons, your brothers, your spouses, your kin, the worldly goods you have

· · ·

[748] Matthew 23:13 "But woe to you, scribes and Pharisees, hypocrites! For you lock people out of the kingdom of heaven. For you do not go in yourselves, and when others are going in, you stop them.

[749] Proverbs 29:25 The fear of others lays a snare, but one who trusts in the Lord is secure

[750] Psalm 33:13-15 The Lord looks down from heaven; he sees all humankind. [14] From where he sits enthroned he watches all the inhabitants of the earth— [15] he who fashions the hearts of them all, and observes all their deeds.

[751] Proverbs 2:6 For the Lord gives wisdom; from his mouth come knowledge and understanding;

[752] Deuteronomy 10:12 So now, O Israel, what does the Lord your God require of you? Only to fear the Lord your God, to walk in all his ways, to love him, to serve the Lord your God with all your heart and with all your soul,

acquired, the trade you fear will decline, and the dwellings you love are dearer to you than God [753] and His Messenger and the struggle in His cause, then just wait until God brings about His punishment. God does not guide defiantly disobedient people. (24) God has helped you on many battlefields and on the day of the Battle of Hunayn[754], when you were so pleased with your great numbers— which proved to be of no use to you. The earth, despite its vastness, seemed so narrow to you that day. You turned around and ran. (25) Then God sent down His serenity on His Messenger and the believers, and He sent down invisible forces to punish those who reject the truth. This is what they deserve. (26) Then, after this, God in His mercy is free to forgive whomever He will. God is most forgiving [755] and Merciful-to-all. [756] (27)

Believers: idolaters are impure. From this year on, do not let them come near the Sacred House. If you fear poverty, then God, if He wills, will enrich you out of His favor. God knows everything and is wise. (28) Fight those People of the Book[757] who do not believe in God and the Last Day, those who do not forbid that which has been forbidden by God and His Messenger, and do not follow the religion of Truth, until they pay the exemption tax after having been subdued. (29) Some[758] Jews say, "Ezra is God's son," while some Christians[759] say, "The Messiah is God's son." This is what they say with their own mouths. They repeat the assertions made before by unbelievers. "May God destroy them". How perverted are their minds. (30)

They have taken their rabbis and their monks, and even Christ, the son of Mary, for their lords[760] instead of God,[761] when they were commanded to worship only one God. There is no god but Him. May He be exalted in His glory above all the partners they may ascribe to Him. (31) They want to suppress God's enlightenment with their words, but God will not allow it, for He wants to spread His enlightenment in all its fullness, no matter how much the unbelievers hate

• • •

[753] Matthew 10:37 Whoever loves father or mother more than me is not worthy of me; and whoever loves son or daughter more than me is not worthy of me;

[754] The battle of Hunayn took place in 630 between Mohammad and his follows and the Bedouin tribes of Hawazin. It resulted in a decisive victory with recovery of huge spoils of war for the Muslims.

[755] Psalm 65:3 When deeds of iniquity overwhelm us, you forgive our transgressions.

[756] Psalm 116:5 Gracious is the Lord, and righteous; our God is merciful.

[757] This verse was revealed in regards to a self-defense war against namely the Byzantine Empire and their Ghassanid allies. The hostility of the group in question is mentioned in this very Qur'anic passage, which goes on to state (32) that this instruction refers to those "who attempt to extinguish the light of Islam with their mouths ". Al-Dahhak (d.105H) explained that this meant "they wish to destroy Islam and Muslims."

[758] The Arabic says: Wa kaalat al Yahoud, or The Jews said. However there is a rule to understand Qur'anic Arabic that requires to investigate the Al or the "The" and whether it is general or specific, referring to known people. Here it means some Jews and not all Jews.

[759] The word Christians (in Arabic Maseheein) is never mentioned in the Qur'an. Instead the Qur'an mentions the word /nasara/ and it is historically equated by Muslim commentators to Christians but its origins are not clear. Some have suggested that the word is derived from Nazareth, the town where Jesus was brought up, as it is implied in the Gospel, (Matthew 2:23, Acts 24:5). Others believe that it is because the Arabic word /ansaar/ (helpers/supporters) (root: nasr) refers to the followers of Jesus who are called supporters of God in the Qur'an (61:14, 3:52).

[760] Or gods. The understanding of this word means a separate deity, not just a master.

[761] Apparently the people referred to here left the clear teaching of God and the Messiah, of both the Torah and the Gospel, "Hear, O Israel: the Lord our God is one Lord" (Deuteronomy 6:4, quoted in Mark 12:29 by Isa); "There is no God but One" (1 Corinthians 8:4, 1 Timothy 2:5). Nowhere in the Torah or Gospel does it say that there is more than one God.

it. [32] He has sent His Messenger with the guidance and the true faith, that he may exalt it above all religions, no matter how much the idolaters hate it. [33] Believers, many of the rabbis and monks wrongfully take men's wealth and turn people away from the path of God. Tell those who hoard gold and silver, and do not spend it in the path of God, tell them that they will have a very painful punishment. [34] On the day when their gold and silver will be heated in the fire of Hell and used to brand their foreheads, sides and backs, (they will be told:) "These are the treasures which you have hoarded. Now you will taste what you have hoarded."[762(35)]

According to God on the day when He created heavens and earth,[763] the number of months is twelve. Of these, four are sacred; this is the correct way. So, do not wrong one another during them. However, fight against the unbelievers collectively as they fight against you collectively. You should know that God is with those who are mindful of Him. [36] Postponing sacred months is an increase in the rejection of the truth, a means by which those rejecters are further mislead. They declare it lawful one year and unlawful the next, in order to correspond to the number of month made unlawful by God. They allow what God has forbidden. They are enticed by their own sins. God does not guide people who refuse to acknowledge the truth. [37]

Believers, what is the matter with you? When you are told to march forth to war in God's cause, you continue to cling to the earth. Are you content with this present life to the point that you prefer it to the life to come? The enjoyment of the present life is practically nothing in comparison to the life to come. [38] If you do not go forth (to fight), He will punish you severely and will replace you with others[764] (although) you will not bother Him at all. God is able to do all things.[765] [39] (It does not matter) if you do not support the Messenger, (since) God already supported him when the unbelievers expelled him. He was one of two men hiding in a cave, and he said to his companion, "Do not be panic, God is with us." Then God sent His peace down on him and supported him with forces that were invisible to you. He made the unbelievers' word the lowest and God's word supreme. God is Almighty [766] and All-Wise.[767] [40] March forth, whether young or old, and commit your possessions and your lives to God's cause; if only you knew how much this is for your own good. [768(41)] Had there been immediate profit and an easy journey, they would have followed you. But the distance was too far for them. Later, they will swear by God, "Had we been able, we would surely have marched with you." They will be damning their own souls. God knows they are liars. [42]

• • •

---

[762] James 5:1-6 Come now, you rich people, weep and wail for the miseries that are coming to you. Your riches have rotted, and your clothes are moth-eaten. Your gold and silver have rusted, and their rust will be evidence against you, and it will eat your flesh like fire.
[763] Genesis 1: In the beginning when God created the heavens and the earth,
[764] Matthew 21:43 Therefore I tell you, the kingdom of God will be taken away from you and given to a people that produces the fruits of the kingdom.
[765] Mark 10:27 Jesus looked at them and said, "For mortals it is impossible, but not for God; for God all things are possible."
[766] Psalm 24:8 Who is the King of glory? The Lord, strong and mighty, the Lord, mighty in battle.
[767] Job 9:4, "He is wise in heart, and mighty in strength"
[768] Exodus 33:7 Consecrate yourselves therefore, and be holy; for I am the Lord your God.

God forgives you (Prophet) for permitting them to stay behind before it was obvious which of them were truthful and which were liars. [43] Those who believe in God and the Last Day do not ask you for exemption from committing their possessions and their lives to the struggle. God knows who is mindful of Him. [44] Only those who do not believe in God and the Last Day ask you for exemption. Their hearts are full of doubts, and they are hesitant. [45] If they had truly wanted to march with you, they would have prepared. (But, knowing what was in their hearts,) God hated for them to join, so He held them back, and they were told, "Stay behind with those who remain." [46] Had they gone with you, they would have only made things more difficult. They would have spread rumors, causing divisions, because some of you are avid listeners to them. God knows exactly who the transgressors are. [47] They tried before to create conflict and hatch plots against you, until the Truth was revealed and God's command became evident, even though they despised it. [48] Some of them said, "Grant me leave and do not cause me to doubt." They were already doubting. Hell will always be ready to embrace those who refuse to believe. [49] If anything good happens to you, it will grieve them, and, should you have misfortune, they will say: "We knew it, and that is why we took precaution." They will turn away in delight. [50] Say, "Only what God has decreed will happen to us. He is our Supreme Lord. Let the believers place their trust in God." [51] Say, "Do you expect something other than one of the two glorious rewards (victory or death in God's cause) to be ours? We, too, are waiting to see whether your punishment will come directly from God or at our hands. Wait, then; we wait with you." [52] Say, "You may give (your contribution) willingly or unwillingly, but it will never be accepted from you. You are disobedient people." [53] The only thing that prevents their giving from being accepted is their refusal to acknowledge God and His Messenger. They never pray without reluctance, and they never spend without resentment. [54] Do not let their worldly goods or their children impress you. God intends to punish them with it in this world, and for their souls to depart while they are still unbelievers. [55]

They swear to God that they are part of you, but they are not. They are petrified, [56] and, if they could find a place of refuge, or a cave, or something to crawl into, they would run towards it quickly. [57] Some of them criticize you concerning the distribution of charitable gifts. They are content if they are given something, and they are very angry if they are given nothing. [58] If only they had been satisfied with what God and His Messenger gave them and said, "God is enough for us. We trust that God will give us out of His bounty, and so will His Messenger. We turn to God alone, with hope." [769] [59] The purifying alms funds are meant only for the poor and the needy, for those who administer the fund, for reconciling hearts, for freeing slaves, for helping those in debt to spend in God's cause, and for travelers in need. This is ordered by God. [770] God is All-Knowing [771] and All-Wise. [772] [60]

• • •

---

[769] Psalm 39:7 "And now, O Lord, what do I wait for? My hope is in you.

[770] James 1:27 Religion that is pure and undefiled before God, the Father, is this: to care for orphans and widows in their distress, and to keep oneself unstained by the world.

[771] 1 John 3:20 whenever our hearts condemn us; for God is greater than our hearts, and he knows everything.

[772] Proverbs 2:6, For the Lord gives wisdom; from his mouth come knowledge and understanding;

There are others who insult the Prophet by saying, "He will listen to anything." Say, "He listens for your own good. He believes in God and trusts the Believers, and he is a mercy to those of you who believe." And those who abuse the Messenger of God, will have a painful punishment.[773] [61] They swear by God, hoping to please you, but it is proper for them to please God and His Messenger, if they are Believers. [62] Did they not know that whoever opposes God and His Messenger will go to the fire of Hell (and) remain there forever? This is the greatest disgrace. [63]

The hypocrites fear lest a chapter be revealed that will expose what is in their hearts. Say, "Mock all you want. God will bring about what you fear." [64] If you were to question them, they would surely answer, "We were just joking and having fun." [774] Say, "Is it God, His messages and His Messenger that you were joking about? [65] Do not offer excuses. You have denied the truth after believing." Even though We may forgive some of you, We will punish others because they were guilty. [66] The hypocrites, both men and women, are all the same: they ordain what is wrong and forbid what is right.[775] They are tight fisted. They have forgotten God, and so He has forgotten them. They are defiantly disobedient.[776] [67] God has promised both the hypocrites—men and women—(and) the unbelievers the fire of Hell, where they will stay forever. This is sufficient for them. God has rejected them, and ever-lasting suffering awaits them. [68] (Unbelievers) you are just like your predecessors. They were more powerful than you and had more wealth and children. They enjoyed their share of worldly pleasures, just as you have been enjoying yours. You are as indulgent as they were. It is those people whose works became worthless in this world and in the Hereafter, and it is they who are the losers. [69] Have they not heard the stories of those who came before them? Noah's people, Ad's and Thamud's, Abraham's people, Midian's inhabitants, and the people of the destroyed towns.[777] Their messengers came to them with clear evidence of the truth, and so it was not God Who was unfair to them but they were unfair to themselves.[70]

The believers, both men and women, support each other; they order what is obviously[778] right and forbid what is obviously wrong, and they perform prayers, pay the prescribed purifying alms, and obey God and His Messenger. God will have mercy on them. He is Almighty[779] and All-Wise.[780] [71] God has promised the believers, men and women, Gardens with flowing rivers and nice homes in

• • •

---

[773] Matthew 25:46 And these will go away into eternal punishment, but the righteous into eternal life.'

[774] Proverbs 26:18-19 Like a maniac who shoots deadly firebrands and arrows, [19] so is one who deceives a neighbor and says, "I am only joking!"

[775] Matthew 23:13 "But woe to you, scribes and Pharisees, hypocrites! For you lock people out of the kingdom of heaven. For you do not go in yourselves, and when others are going in, you stop them.

[776] Romans 1:21 for though they knew God, they did not honor him as God or give thanks to him, but they became futile in their thinking, and their senseless minds were darkened.

[777] Or, the cities that were overthrown. Genesis 19:24-25. Then the Lord rained on Sodom and Gomorrah sulphur and fire from the Lord out of heaven; [25] and he overthrew those cities, and all the Plain, and all the inhabitants of the cities, and what grew on the ground.

[778] What is obviously right or wrong is time, place and culture sensitive.

[779] Psalm 93:4 More majestic than the thunders of mighty waters, more majestic than the waves of the sea, majestic on high is the Lord!

[780] Proverbs 2:6 For the Lord gives wisdom; from his mouth come knowledge and understanding;

Gardens of Eden. But the greatest pleasure[781] is God's continuous approval of them. That is the ultimate victory. [72]

Prophet, struggle hard against the unbelievers and the hypocrites, and be tough with them. If they do not repent[782], their final home will be Hell, a miserable destination. [73] The hypocrites swear by God that they have said nothing wrong, but they have definitely uttered words of blasphemy and become unbelievers after having submitted[783]. They plotted that which was beyond their ability. They resented that God and His Messenger had enriched them out of His favor. If they repent, it would be for their own good, but if they turn away, God will cause them to suffer painfully in this world and in the life to come, and no one on earth will be able to help or protect them. [74]

Some among them pledged to God, "If He give us out of His bounty, We will definitely spend on charity and will be among the righteous," [75] but when He gave them out of His bounty, they were stingy with it and defiantly turned away. [76] Because of their failure to fulfill their pledge to Him, and because of the lies they told, He caused hypocrisy to overtake their hearts until the Day they will meet Him.[784] [77] Do they not know that God knows all their secrets and their private conversations and that God is most knowing of everything that is beyond their perception? [78] They criticize the believers who voluntarily contribute, and ridicule the ones who had nothing to give except their own efforts. Instead, God ridicules them, and a painful punishment awaits them. [79] Praying or not praying for their forgiveness will make no difference. Even if you were to pray seventy times for their forgiveness, God will not forgive them because they reject God and His Messenger. God does not guide those who are defiantly disobedient people. [80]

After God's Messenger had left, those who remained behind were glad, because they hated to strive in God's way with their possessions and their lives. They had even said, "Do not go to war in this heat." Say, "The fire of Hell is a lot hotter!" If they could only understand. [81] Let them laugh a little because they will weep a lot in return for what they have earned. [82] So, (Prophet,) if God brings you face to face with them again, and they should ask you for permission to go to war with you, say, "You will never come with me, nor will you fight an enemy with me. You were happy to stay at home the first time, so, stay at home now with those who remain behind." [83]

Do not ever pray over any of them who died, and do not stand at their graves; they rejected God and His Messenger, and they died defiantly disobedient. [84] Do not let their worldly possessions and their children impress you. God wants to use such things to punish them in this world, and for their souls to depart in anguish while they are still denying the truth. [85] When a new revelation is given asking them to believe in God and to strive hard alongside His Messenger, even those of them with means ask your permission to stay, saying "Allow us to stay with those who remain at home." [86] They were happy to remain with those who

• • •

[781] Psalm 16:11 You show me the path of life. In your presence there is fullness of joy; in your right hand are pleasures for evermore.
[782] James 4:8 "Come near to God and he will come near to you. Wash your hands, you sinners, and purify your hearts, you double-minded."
[783] See Glossary, Submission or Islam.
[784] Proverbs 11:24 Some give freely, yet grow all the richer; others withhold what is due, and only suffer want.

were left behind, because their hearts have been sealed, and they do not understand! [87] However, the Messenger and all who share his faith strive hard in God's cause with their possessions and their lives, and great things await them in the life to come. It is they who will prosper.[785] [88] God has prepared Gardens with rivers flowing[786] through them. There, they will remain eternally. This is the ultimate victory! [89]

Some of the Bedouins, too, came (to the Messenger) to make excuses, asking to be granted exemption. Those who lied to God and His Messenger stayed behind at home. A painful punishment will fall on those who rejected faith. [90] No blame will be placed on the weak, or the sick, or those who have no means to equip themselves, provided that they are sincere towards God and His Messenger. In no way the righteous should be blamed. God is most forgiving [787] and Merciful-to-all.[788] [91] Blame will not be placed on those who come to you (Prophet, with the request) that you provide them with riding animals, and to whom you say, "I do not have rides for you." They turned away with their eyes overflowing with tears out of sorrow that they had nothing they could contribute. [92] The ones to be blamed are those wealthy (persons) who asked you for an exemption. They are happy to remain with those who are left behind. God has sealed their hearts and they don't realize it. [93]

They will offer you excuses when you return. Say, "Do not give us any excuses, we will not believe you. God has already told us about you. God will be watching your deeds, and so will His Messenger, and, in the end, you will be brought before Him the Knower of the unknown[789] and the known. He will make you truly understand (the negative impact of) what you were doing." [94] (Believers), when you return to them, they will swear by God in order to make you leave them alone. Leave them alone. They are despicable, and their destiny is Hell, fit payment for their actions. [95] They will swear to you to in order to make you accept them. God will never accept those who are defiantly disobedient. [96]

The Bedouins are the most hypocritical and stubborn in (their) rejection of faith and the least likely to comprehend the limits (of laws) that God has sent down to His Messenger. God knows everything, and He is Wise.[790] [97] Among the Bedouins, there are some who consider what they spend (in God's cause) to be

• • •

[785] 1 Samuel 12:24 Only fear the Lord, and serve him faithfully with all your heart; for consider what great things he has done for you.

[786] Revelation 22:1-2 Then the angel showed me the river of the water of life, bright as crystal, flowing from the throne of God and of the Lamb through the middle of the street of the city. On either side of the river is the tree of life with its twelve kinds of fruit, producing its fruit each month; and the leaves of the tree are for the healing of the nations.

[787] Psalm 32:5 Then I acknowledged my sin to you, and I did not hide my iniquity; I said, "I will confess my transgressions to the Lord," and you forgave the guilt of my sin.

[788] Psalm 25:6-7 Be mindful of your mercy, O Lord, and of your steadfast love, for they have been from of old. 7 Do not remember the sins of my youth or my transgressions; according to your steadfast love remember me, for your goodness' sake, O Lord!

[789] Ghaib is a concept that had historically had a metaphysical connotation. It refers to that which is absent, hidden, or concealed, such as the date of someone's death, who he/she would marry. In the Islamic context, al-Ghaib refers to what is only known to God. It is mentioned in sixty different places in the Qu'ran, in six different forms to cover basically three meanings: The Unknown or Hidden, something that took place in the absence of someone and the future. Various translators translated Ghaib in different ways, the most common is the unseen.

[790] Proverbs 2:6, For the Lord gives wisdom; from his mouth come knowledge and understanding;

a loss and expect that you will run into trouble, but it is they who will be overwhelmed by trouble. God hears everything[791] and knows everything. [98] Yet, there are also Bedouins who believe in God and the Last Day and regard everything they spend (in God's cause) to be means of drawing them closer to God and the Messenger's prayers. It will definitely bring them nearer to God, admitting them to His mercy. God is forgiving [792] and Merciful-to-all.[793] [99] It is the first of the early emigrants and supporters, as well as those who followed them in righteousness, with whom God is very pleased, and they are pleased with Him. He has prepared Gardens with flowing rivers for them, where they will stay forever. This is the ultimate victory. [100]

Among the Bedouins who live around you, some are hypocrites, as are some of the people of Medina, who have grown accustomed to hypocrisy. You do not (always) know them (but) We know them. We will cause them to suffer twice as much (in this world,) and then they will face a severe punishment. [101] And there are others, who, after having done both good and bad deeds, confessed their sins.[794] God may accept their repentance[795] because God is forgiving and Merciful-to-all. [102] Accept their offerings for the sake of God, that it may cleanse them and cause them to grow in purity, and pray for them. Your prayer will comfort them. God hears everything, [796]and He knows everything. [103] Do they not know that God alone can accept the repentance of His worshipers and is the (true) recipient of what is offered for His sake, and that God alone is the Acceptor of Repentance[797], the Merciful-to-all? [104] Say: "Act! And God will see your deeds, and so will His Messenger and the believers. (In the end), you will be brought before Him who knows the unknown and the known, and He will tell you what you have been doing." [105] And yet, there are others who are waiting for God's decree, either to punish them or to show them His mercy. God knows everything, and He is wise. [106]

(As for those hypocrites) who have established a (separate) house of worship in order to create trouble, causing unbelief and disunity among the believers, and providing a base for those who previously fought God and His Messenger. They will definitely swear, "We have only the best of intentions," while God testifies that they are lying. [107] (Prophet,) never pray in that mosque. Rather, you should pray only in a mosque founded from its very first day on consciousness of God. That is a place where men want to grow in purity. God

• • •

[791] Psalm 5:3 O Lord, in the morning you hear my voice; in the morning I plead my case to you, and watch.

[792] Psalm 130:1-4 Out of the depths I have cried to You, O Lord. Lord, hear my voice! Let Your ears be attentive. To the voice of my supplications. If You, Lord, should mark iniquities, O Lord, who could stand? But there is forgiveness with You, That You may be feared.

[793] Isaiah 54:7-8 For a brief moment I abandoned you, but with great compassion I will gather you. 8 In overflowing wrath for a moment I hid my face from you, but with everlasting love I will have compassion on you, says the Lord, your Redeemer.

[794] Proverbs 28:13 No one who conceals transgressions will prosper, but one who confesses and forsakes them will obtain mercy.

[795] Jeremiah 33:8 I will cleanse them from all the guilt of their sin against me, and I will forgive all the guilt of their sin and rebellion against me.

[796] Micah 7:7 But as for me, I will look to the Lord, I will wait for the God of my salvation; my God will hear me

[797] James 4:8 "Come near to God and he will come near to you. Wash your hands, you sinners, and purify your hearts, you double-minded."

loves everyone who purifies himself. [108] Which is better, one who has founded his building on God-consciousness and a desire for His acceptance, or he who has founded his building on the edge of a crumbling cliff that will tumble down with him into Hellfire? [798] God does not guide people who are (deliberately) unjust. [109] The building they built will always be a source of skepticism within their hearts until their hearts are torn to pieces. God knows everything, and He is wise. [110]

God has purchased the souls and possessions of the believers[799] promising them paradise in return. They fight in God's cause, and they kill and are killed. It is a true promise given by Him in the Torah, the Gospel, and the Qur'an. Who could be more faithful to his promise than God?[800] Rejoice in this good news! This is the bargain you have made with Him. This is the ultimate victory. [111] Those are the ones who turn to God in repentance, who worship and praise Him. They journey, bow before Him and prostrate themselves in adoration. They order what is obviously[801] right and forbid what is obviously wrong, and stay within the boundaries set by God. So, give good news to the believers. [112]

It is not for the Prophet and the believers to pray for forgiveness for the idolaters—even if they are related—after it has been made clear to them that those (sinners) are destined for Hell. [113] Abraham's prayer that his father would be forgiven was due to a promise that he had given his father. However, when it became clear to him that his father was one of God's enemies, he renounced him, even though Abraham was tender-hearted, tolerant. [114] God would not lead astray those He has already guided to the faith, unless He first makes it entirely clear to them what they should avoid. God knows everything. [115] To God, alone, belongs the kingdom of the heavens and the earth;[802] He, alone, has the power over life and death.[803] There is none besides Him who can protect you or help you.[804] [116]

God has forgiven the Prophet, as well as those emigrants and supporters who followed him in the hour of distress, after the hearts of some of them had

• • •

---

[798] Matthew 7:24-27 'Everyone then who hears these words of mine and acts on them will be like a wise man who built his house on rock. 25 The rain fell, the floods came, and the winds blew and beat on that house, but it did not fall, because it had been founded on rock. [26] And everyone who hears these words of mine and does not act on them will be like a foolish man who built his house on sand. [27] The rain fell, and the floods came, and the winds blew and beat against that house, and it fell—and great was its fall!'

[799] 1 Corinthians 6:19-20 Or do you not know that your body is a temple of the Holy Spirit within you, which you have from God, and that you are not your own? [20] For you were bought with a price; therefore, glorify God in your body.

[800] Psalm 109:21 But you, O Lord my Lord, act on my behalf for your name's sake; because your steadfast love is good, deliver me

[801] What is obviously right or wrong is time, place and culture sensitive.

[802] Isaiah 45:12 I made the earth, and created humankind upon it; it was my hands that stretched out the heavens, and I commanded all their host.

[803] 1 Samuel 2:6 The Lord kills and brings to life; he brings down to Sheol and raises up. Deuteronomy 32:39 See now that I, even I, am he; there is no god besides me. I kill and I make alive; I wound and I heal; and no one can deliver from my hand.

[804] Hosea 13:4 Yet I have been the Lord your God ever since the land of Egypt; you know no God but me, and besides me there is no savior.

hesitated. Then He forgave[805] them. He is compassionate, merciful.[806(117)] He also forgave the three[807] who stayed behind. They had (come to feel that) the earth, for all its vastness, was closing in on them, and that their souls were narrowing (as well), until they realized that the only refuge from God was to be with Him. He turned to them in mercy so that they would return to Him. God alone is the accepter of repentance and is merciful. [808(118)]

Believers, remain mindful of God and be among those who are truthful. [119]

It is not appropriate for the people of Medina and the Bedouins (who live) around them to stay behind (and refuse to follow) God's Messenger. Nor should they care about themselves more than they care for him. This is because a righteous deed is registered to their favor every time they suffer from thirst, weariness or hunger in God's cause, or take any step that angers the unbelievers, or cause any harm to any enemy. God never loses track of the rewards (due) those who do good. [120] They will spend no amount, large or small (for God's sake), nor cross any valley (in God's cause) that will not be credited to them. God will reward them according to the best of their deeds[809] [121]

The believers shouldn't all go to battle. From within every group, some should devote themselves to acquiring deeper knowledge of the Faith; to teach their people when they return. So they might be on their guard. [122] Believers, fight against the unbelievers who live nearer to you, and let them find you tough in your determination. Know that God is with those who are mindful of Him. [123]

Whenever a chapter is revealed, some ask, "Which of you has this increased in faith?" As for those who believe, it strengthens them in their faith, and they rejoice in the good news (it brings them).[810(124)] As for those who have diseased hearts,[811] (each new revelation) adds only (more) disbelief to their disbelief, and they die as unbelievers. [125] Do not they realize that they are being tested once or twice a year? Yet, they do not repent, nor do they remember [126] and whenever a chapter is revealed, they look at one another and say, "Is anyone watching you?" And then they leave. God has turned their hearts away from the truth because they are people who will not be able to understand. [127]

A messenger has come to you from among yourselves. Your suffering weighs heavily upon him. He is deeply concerned for you and full of compassion and mercy towards the believers. [128] If they turn away, say, "God is sufficient for me. There is no God but Him. In Him I have put my trust, for He is the Lord of the magnificent Throne of His majesty." [129]

• • •

[805] Jeremiah 33:8 I will cleanse them from all the guilt of their sin against me, and I will forgive all the guilt of their sin and rebellion against me.
[806] James 5:11 Indeed we call blessed those who showed endurance. You have heard of the endurance of Job, and you have seen the purpose of the Lord, how the Lord is compassionate and merciful.
[807] The classical commentators understood this to be a reference to Ka'b ibn Malik, Mararah ibn ar-Rabi' and Hilal ibn Umayyah (all of them from among the supporters).
[808] Psalm 73:28 But for me it is good to be near God; I have made the Lord God my refuge, to tell of all your works.
[809] Revelation 20:12 And I saw the dead, great and small, standing before the throne, and books were opened. Also another book was opened, the book of life. And the dead were judged according to their works, as recorded in the books.
[810] Psalm 32:11 Be glad in the Lord and rejoice, O righteous, and shout for joy, all you upright in heart.
[811] Jeremiah 17:9-10The heart is devious above all else; it is perverse—who can understand it? I the Lord test the mind and search the heart, to give to all according to their ways, according to the fruit of their doings.

CHAPTER **TEN**

YUNUS

THE PROPHET JONAH

THE **MECCA** PERIOD

Mecca Period
In the name of God, the Merciful-to-all, the Mercy Giver:
Alif Lam Ra [812]

These are the verses of the Wise Book. [01] Do people find it really amazing that We sent revelations to a man from among them, saying: "Warn all people, and give good news to those who believe that in the sight of their Lord, they are considered truthful." But the unbelievers say, "He is clearly a sorcerer!" [02]

Your Lord is God, who has created the heavens and the earth in six days. [813] He then settled on the throne of His majesty, governing everything that exists. [814] No one can intercede with Him unless He first gives His permission. [815] This is God, your Lord: worship Him. Will you not, then, keep this in mind? [03] You will all return to Him: [816] this is a true promise from God. He begins the process of creation, and then He repeats it so that He may justly reward all who believe and do good works. However, those who refuse to believe will have boiling drinks and grievous suffering because of their refusal to acknowledge the truth. [817] [04]

He has made the sun radiant light and the moon a source of enlightenment [818] for He has plotted out its phases [819] so that you may know how to calculate the

• • •

---

[812] Here and at the beginning of many chapters there are letters of unknown meaning called Al Muquatta'at. Numerous theories have been proposed, but there is no agreement on what they signify yet.

[813] Genesis 2:1-2 Thus the heavens and the earth were completed, and all their hosts.² And on the seventh day God finished the work that he had done, and he rested on the seventh day from all the work that he had done.

[814] Psalm 47:8 God reigns over the nations, God sits on His holy throne.

[815] Hebrews 6:3 And this we will do, if God permits.

[816] Romans 14:12 So then, each of us will be accountable to God

[817] Isaiah 50:11 But all of you are kindlers of fire, lighters of firebrands. Walk in the flame of your fire, and among the brands that you have kindled! This is what you shall have from my hand: you shall lie down in torment.

[818] Genesis 1:16 God made the two great lights—the greater light to rule the day and the lesser light to rule the night—and the stars.

[819] Genesis 1:17 God set them in the dome of the sky to give light upon the earth,

years and measure time.[820] There is a purpose to everything God created in Truth. He explains His messages to those who are willing to know.[821] (05) In the succession of night and day, and in all that God has created in the heavens and on the earth[822] there are signs for those who are aware of Him. (06) Those who do not believe that they are destined to meet Us—being content with their worldly life and unable to see beyond it, paying no attention to Our signs— (07) will have the fire for their home in return for all they have deserved. (08) As for those who believe and do righteous deeds, their Lord guides them because of their faith. Streams will flow at their feet in Gardens of pleasure (09) There they will call out, "Glory be to You, God," their greeting will be "Peace," and the last part of their prayer will be, "All praise is due to God, the Lord of the Worlds."[823](10)

Were God to rush punishment for people in the same way they rush toward what they consider good, their time would already be up. We will leave those who do not believe they are destined to meet Us to wander blindly in their arrogance. (11) When trouble afflicts man, he cries to Us, whether he is lying on his side, or sitting, or standing, but, as soon as We have freed him of his trouble, he carries on as though he had never called on Us to save him from his trouble. In this way the deeds of such overindulgent people seem right in their own eyes.[824] (12) We destroyed earlier generations when they transgressed in spite of the evidence of truth brought to them by their messengers, whom they refused to believe. This is how we punish those who force others to reject God's messages. (13) We then made you their successors on earth, so We could see what you would do. (14) Whenever Our messages are clearly conveyed to them, those who do not believe that they are destined to meet Us will say, "Bring us a different Qur'an, or change it." Say (Prophet), "It is not up to me to change it of my own accord; I follow only what is revealed to me. I fear the punishment of that Monumental Day (of Judgment) if I were to disobey my Lord." (15) Say, "If God had willed it, I would not have conveyed this (Book) to you, nor would He have brought it to your knowledge. I was among you for an entire lifetime before it came to me. Why cannot you not think?" (16)

Who could be more unjust than someone who makes up lies against God or denies His revelations? Those who force others to reject God's messages will never prosper,[825] (17) (nor will) they (who) worship things other than God—things

• • •

---

[820] Genesis 1:14 And God said, 'Let there be lights in the dome of the sky to separate the day from the night; and let them be for signs and for seasons and for days and years,

[821] Psalm 138:8 The Lord will fulfill his purpose for me; your steadfast love, O Lord, endures forever. Do not forsake the work of your hands.

[822] Isaiah 45:18 For thus says the Lord, who created the heavens (he is God!), who formed the earth and made it (he established it; he did not create it a chaos, he formed it to be inhabited!) I am the Lord, and there is no other.

[823] Revelation 19:1-2 After these things I heard something like a loud voice of a great multitude in heaven, saying, "Hallelujah! Salvation and glory and power belong to our God; 2 Because His judgements are true and righteous; for He has judged the great harlot who was corrupting the earth with her immorality, and He has avenged the blood of His bond-servants on her."

[824] Proverbs 21:2 Every man's way is right in his own eyes, But the Lord weighs the hearts.

[825] Jeremiah 22:21"I spoke to you in your prosperity; But you said, 'I will not listen!' This has been your practice from your youth, That you have not obeyed My voice."

that can neither harm nor benefit them[826]—saying, "These are our intercessors with God." Say, "Do you (think that you could) inform God about something in the heavens or on earth that He does not know?[827] May He be exalted in His glory, and far higher above all they associate with Him. [18] People were once a single community, [828] but later they began to hold divergent views. Had it not been for a prior decree from your Lord, their differences would already have been settled [19] They ask, "Why has his Lord never given him any miraculous sign?" Say, "The unknown belongs to God, so wait, and I will wait with you." [20] Whenever We let (such) people experience Our grace after they have endured hardship, they then turn to plot against Our messages. Say, "God plots even faster. Our (heavenly) messengers are tracking all of your plotting." [21]

He enables you to travel on land and sea, until—while they are sailing on ships and rejoicing in favorable winds—a storm arrives, and waves come towards them from all directions, so that you think you are facing death. Then they cry out to God in all sincerity, claiming faith in Him alone: "If You save us from this, We will be truly thankful!" [22] Once He has saved them, they return to being corruptive on earth[829] in defiance to the Truth. People! All your outrageous deeds will be counted against you; your enjoyment is limited to life in this world. Then you will return to Us, and We will confront you with everything You have done.[830] [23]

The example of life on earth is like rain that We send down, which stimulates the growth of plants that humans and animals eat. Then, (just) as the earth takes on its finest appearance and is beautifully adorned, and its people think they have power over it, Our judgment comes to it suddenly, by night or day, and We reduce it to stubble, as if it had not flourished just the day before. We make Our messages clear to people who reflect on them. [24]

God invites you to dwell in peace, and He guides whoever chooses to a straight path.[831] [25] For those who do good, there is ultimate good in store, and even more besides. No darkness or shame will overshadow their faces (on Resurrection Day). They are destined for Heaven, where they will remain forever. [26] As for those who have done evil deeds, one iniquity deserves another, shame will overshadow them, (and) they will have no one to protect them from God. Their faces will appear as if they were covered by the night's darkness. They are destined to live in the fire, and there they will remain. [27]

On the (Judgment) Day We will gather them all together, (and) We will say to those who associated other (beings) with God, "Stay where you are, you and

• • •

---

[826] Psalm 115:4-7, Their idols are silver and gold, the work of human hands. They have mouths, but do not speak; eyes, but do not see. They have ears, but do not hear; noses, but do not smell. They have hands, but do not feel; feet, but do not walk; they make no sound in their throats.

[827] Job 21:22 "Can anyone teach God knowledge, In that He judges those on high?

[828] Acts 17:26 From one ancestor he made all nations to inhabit the whole earth, and he allotted the times of their existence and the boundaries of the places where they would live,

[829] 2 Timothy 3:1-3 But realize this, that in the last days difficult times will come. [2] For men will be lovers of self, lovers of money, boastful, arrogant, revilers, disobedient to parents, ungrateful, unholy, [3] unloving, irreconcilable, malicious gossips, without self-control, brutal, haters of good.

[830] Ezekiel 24:14I, the Lord, have spoken; it is coming and I will act. I will not relent, and I will not pity and I will not be sorry; according to your ways and according to your deeds I will judge you," declares the Lord God.'"

[831] Proverbs 3:5-6 Trust in the Lord with all your heart, and do not rely on your own insight.

[6] In all your ways acknowledge him, and he will make straight your paths straight.

your associates." Then We will separate them from one another.[832] The partners will say, "You were not supposed to worship us. [28] God is witness enough between you and us. We were unaware that you were worshipping us." [29] There, every soul will answer for its past deeds, and they will all return to God, their true Supreme Lord, and all their false deities will desert them.[833] [30]

Say, "Who provides you with sustenance out of heaven and earth, or who has full power over hearing and sight? Who brings forward the living from the dead, and the dead from the living? Who administers all matters?"[834] They will say, "God." Then say, "will you not then be mindful of Him? [31] This is God, your Lord, the Ultimate Truth. What is beyond Truth except falsehood? How can you lose sight of the Truth?" [32] Thus, your Lord's word proved to be true against those who defiantly disobeyed Him; they will not believe. [33] Say, "Can any of your 'partners-gods' initiate creation, and then repeat it?" Say, "God initiates creation, and then repeats it. What falsehood are you preaching?" [34] Say, "Who among those 'partners-gods' you associated with Him guides you to the Truth?" Say, "It is God who guides to the Truth. Which is more worthy to be followed; He who guides you to the Truth, or he who cannot find the path unless he's guided? What is the matter with you? How do you judge?" [35] Most of them follow nothing but speculations, which can never substitute for the Truth. God has full knowledge of all that they do. [835] [36]

This Qur'an could have never been created by anyone but God as a confirmation of what is available to him from earlier revelations and a detailed explanation of the Book that—let there be no doubt—is from the Lord of all the worlds. [37] Or do they say, "He (the Prophet) has invented it?" Say, "Then produce a chapter of similar merit, and call on anyone you can other than God if what you say is true." [38] They are, in fact, denying what they cannot comprehend while its inner meaning has yet to become clear to them. In that same way, those who lived before them rejected belief, so reflect on the final fate of those who were unjust [39]

There are some among them who will eventually come to believe, just as there are some who will never believe. Your Lord is fully aware of those who cause corruption. [40] If they deny you, say, "I act based on my own belief, and your acts are based on yours. You are not accountable for what I do, and I am not accountable for whatever you do." [41] Some of them listen to you, but, can you cause the deaf to hear if they do not understand? [42] Some of them look at you, but can you show the blind[836] the right way even though they cannot see? [43] God does not wrong people at all but it is they who wrong themselves[837]. [44]

• • •

---

[832] Matthew 25:32 All the nations will be gathered before him, and he will separate people one from another as a shepherd separates the sheep from the goats

[833] Isaiah 55:6-7 Seek the Lord while he may be found, call upon him while he is near; [7] let the wicked forsake their way, and the unrighteous their thoughts; let them return to the Lord, that he may have mercy on them, and to our God, for he will abundantly pardon.

[834] Isaiah 42:5 Thus says God the Lord, Who created the heavens and stretched them out, Who spread out the earth and its offspring, Who gives breath to the people on it And spirit to those who walk in it,

[835] Psalm 44:21 Would not God find this out? For He knows the secrets of the heart

[836] Psalm 146:8 the Lord opens the eyes of the blind. The Lord lifts up those who are bowed down; the Lord loves the righteous.

[837] John 8:34 Everuone who sins is a slave to sin.

On the Day He gathers them together, it will be as if they have stayed (in this world) no longer than a single hour of the day, and they will recognize one another. Those who denied that they would ever meet God will be the losers, for they were not guided. (45) Whether We show you something of what We have promised them or retrieve you (first), they will still return to Us. Then God will be a witness to all that they have done (46) Every nation has had a messenger, and, only after their messenger appeared (and delivered his message) will they be justly judged; they will not be dealt with unfairly. (47) They ask, "When will this promise838 be fulfilled if you are telling the truth?" (48) Say, "I have no power to harm or help myself, except as God wills. An appointed time has been set for every nation839 and when they reach their appointed time, they can neither delay it by a single hour840 nor speed it up." (49) Say, "Have you ever considered how you would feel if His punishment were to befall you by night or by day? What part of it would those who force others to reject God's messages wish to speed up?" (50) Say, "Will you believe (only) when it actually befalls you. Now (at the Judgment, you believe), whereas (before) you tried to hasten it." (51) Then the wrongdoers will be told, "Taste eternal punishment. Why should you be repaid (with anything) other than what you have earned?" (52)

Some people ask you, "Is this really true?" Say, "Yes, by my Lord, it is definitely true, and you cannot prevent it." (53) Even if each soul that had done wrong possessed everything on earth, it would surely offer it (that day) in ransom. They will show remorse when they see the punishment; they will be judged justly, and they will not be treated unfairly. (54) Everything that is in the heavens and on earth belongs to God.841 God's promise always comes true,842 but most of them do not know this. (55) He's the One who grants life and deals death and you will all be returned to Him.843 (56) People, a lesson has now come to you from your Lord, and a cure for what is in your hearts, and guidance and grace to the believers. (57) Say, "It is grace and mercy from God, so let them rejoice;844 it is better than all (the wealth) that they have accumulated." (58) Say, "Have you considered the sustenance that God has sent down to you, some (of which) you have made unlawful and some lawful?" Say, "Has God given you permission (to do this), or are you inventing lies about God?" (59) What would those people who invent lies about God think on the Day of Resurrection?845 God's grace is limitless towards people, but most of them are ungrateful. (60)

• • •

---

838 2 Peter 3:4 and saying, 'Where is the promise of his coming? For ever since our ancestors died, all things continue as they were from the beginning of creation!'

839 Acts 17:26 From one ancestor he made all nations to inhabit the whole earth, and he allotted the times of their existence and the boundaries of the places where they would live,

840 Matthew 6:27 And can any of you by worrying add a single hour to your span of life?

841 Psalm 89:11 The heavens are yours, the earth also is yours; the world and all that is in it—you have founded them.

842 2 Peter 1:4 Thus he has given us, through these things, his precious and very great promises, so that through them you may escape from the corruption that is in the world because of lust, and may become participants in the divine nature.

843 Ecclesiastes 12:7 and the dust returns to the earth as it was, and the breath returns to God who gave it.

844 Psalm 32:11 Be glad in the Lord and rejoice, O righteous, and shout for joy, all you upright in heart.

845 Daniel 12:2 Many of those who sleep in the dust of the earth shall awake, some to everlasting life, and some to shame and everlasting contempt.

Whatever you (Prophet) are doing, or whatever part of the Qur'an you may be reciting, and whatever you (people) are doing, We are watching you when you are doing it. Not an atom's weight escapes your Lord on earth or in heaven,[846] nor is there anything even smaller or larger (that is not) recoded in a clear book. [(61)]

Truly, those who are loyal to God do not need to fear, and they will not grieve. [(62)] (For) those who believe and are ever mindful of God, [(63)] there is good news in the life of this world and the life to come. There is no changing the words of God; this is truly the supreme triumph. [(64)] And you (Prophet) should not be grieved by what they say. All might belongs entirely to God: He is All-Hearing,[847] All-Knowing.[848] [(65)] Verily, everyone in heaven and on earth belongs to God. Those who invoke other (beings) besides God are not really calling on His associates; they are only following their guess, and they only tell lies. [(66)] It is He who has made the night for you, so that you might rest, and the day, to give you sight. Truly there are messages in this for people who hear.[849] [(67)]

They say, "God has taken a son. May He be exalted in His glory. He is the self-sufficient beyond needs. Everything that is in the heavens and on earth belongs to Him.[850] You have no authority to say this. How dare you say about God what you do not know? [(68)] Say, "Those who invent lies about God will never prosper." [(69)] They may have brief enjoyment in this world, but they will return to Us, and We will make them taste severe suffering because of their denial of the truth. [(70)]

Tell them the story of Noah (Nuh), when he said to his people, "My people, if my presence (among you) and my reminding you of God's messages has become too much for you to bear, then my trust is really placed in God. So, decide with your 'partner-gods' what you want to do, and do not be hesitant; do with me whatever you decide, and do not keep me waiting. [(71)] If you turn away, I have asked for nothing from you; my reward is from God, for I was commanded to be among those who have surrendered themselves to Him." [(72)] (Nevertheless,) they denied him, so We rescued him and all those with him in the ark and made them successors,[851] while We drowned those who denied our messages.[852] See what happened to those who were forewarned. [(73)]

After him, We sent (other) messengers, each to his own people, who brought them evidence of the truth, but they were not going to believe anything they had already rejected. It is in this way that We seal the hearts of the transgressors.

• • •

[846] Proverbs 15:3 The eyes of the Lord are in every place, Watching the evil and the good.

[847] 1 John 5:14 And this is the boldness we have in him, that if we ask anything according to his will, he hears us.

[848] Psalm 33:13-15 The Lord looks down from heaven; he sees all humankind. 14 From where he sits enthroned he watches all the inhabitants of the earth— [15] he who fashions the hearts of them all, and observes all their deeds.

[849] Isaiah 32:3 Then the eyes of those who have sight will not be closed, and the ears of those who have hearing will listen

[850] Psalm 89:11 The heavens are Yours, the earth also is Yours; The world and all it contains, You have founded them.

[851] Genesis 9:1-2 God blessed Noah and his sons, and said to them, "Be fruitful and multiply, and fill the earth. [2] The fear and dread of you shall rest on every animal of the earth, and on every bird of the air, on everything that creeps on the ground, and on all the fish of the sea; into your hand they are delivered

[852] Genesis 7:23 Thus He blotted out every living thing that was upon the face of the land, from man to animals to creeping things and to birds of the sky, and they were blotted out from the earth; and only Noah was left, together with those that were with him in the ark.

(74) Afterward, We sent Moses (Musa) and Aaron with Our messages to Pharaoh and his inner circle, but they acted arrogantly because they had decided to severe all relations to God and to reject Him. (75) So, when the Truth came to them from Us, they said, "This is nothing but clear sorcery." (76) Moses said, "You are calling it sorcery when the Truth was being given to you? Sorcerers can never prosper." (77) They said, "Have you come to turn us away from what we found our forefathers believing so that the two of you might become supreme in this land? We do not believe in the two of you." (78) So Pharaoh commanded, "Bring every sorcerer of great knowledge before me." (79) When the sorcerers came, Moses said to them, "Throw whatever you may throw." (80) When they had thrown down, Moses said to them, "Everything you have done is sorcery, and God will show it to be false. God does not support the works of those who cause corruption.[853] (81) God confirms the Truth by His words, even though those who force others to reject God's messages hate it." (82) Only a handful of Moses' people declared their faith in him, (while others held back) for fear that Pharaoh would persecute them and their own people. Pharaoh was mighty on earth and prone to excesses. (83) Moses said, "My people, if you believe in God, place your trust in Him if you have (truly) surrendered yourselves to Him." (84) They answered, "We have placed our trust in God. Our Lord, do not make us an object of persecution for the people who do evil, (85) and save us, by Your grace, from people who deny the truth." (86)

We revealed to Moses and his brother, "Make homes for your people in Egypt and (tell them), 'Turn your houses into places of worship and be constant in prayer.' Give good news to the believers." (87)

Moses prayed, "Lord, You have given Pharaoh and his inner circle splendor and wealth in this life, and they are leading others astray from your path. Lord, wipe out their riches and harden their hearts, so that they will not attain faith until they see painful suffering." (88) God said, "Your (and Aaron's) prayer is accepted. Continue steadfastly on the right path[854] and do not follow the path of those who have no knowledge[855]." (89) We then brought the Children of Israel across the sea, and Pharaoh and his troops pursued them in arrogance and aggression, until, when he was about to drown, (Pharaoh) cried out, "I believe that there is no God except the one the Children of Israel believe in, and I am of those who surrender themselves to Him." (90) (And God said), "(Only) now? When (before) you rebelled and lived among those who caused corruption? (91) Today We will save only your body, so that you may be a sign to those who will come after you. Many people fail to heed Our signs." (92) We then settled the Children

• • •

[853] Exodus 7:9-13 When Pharaoh speaks to you, saying, 'Work a miracle,' then you shall say to Aaron, 'Take your staff and throw *it* down before Pharaoh, *that* it may become a serpent.'" [10] So Moses and Aaron came to Pharaoh, and thus they did just as the Lord had commanded; and Aaron threw his staff down before Pharaoh and his servants, and it became a serpent. [11] Then Pharaoh also called for *the* wise men and *the* sorcerers, and they also, the magicians of Egypt, did the same with their secret arts. [12] For each one threw down his staff and they turned into serpents. But Aaron's staff swallowed up their staffs. [13] Yet Pharaoh's heart was hardened, and he did not listen to them, as the Lord had said.

[854] Proverbs 4:25, Let your eyes look directly forwards, and your gaze be straight before you. Proverbs 3:6 In all your ways acknowledge him, and he will make straight your paths.

[855] Proverbs 5:5-6 Her feet go down to death; her steps follow the path to Sheol. 6 She does not keep straight to the path of life; her ways wander, and she does not know it

of Israel [856] in a good place and provided them[857] with good things to sustain them. And It was not until knowledge (of God's revelation) had come to them that they began to bicker among themselves. Your Lord will judge between them on Resurrection Day regarding all of their differences. (93)

So if you are in doubt about what We have revealed to you, ask those who have been reading the Book (revealed) before your time. The truth has certainly come to you from your Lord,[858] so don't be one of the doubters, (94) or (one of) those who deny God's messages, lest you be among the doomed. (95) Those against whom the words of your Lord are justly carried out will not believe, (96) even though every sign comes to them, until they see the agonizing suffering. (97) There had never been a single community that believed and benefited from its faith except Jonah's people. When they believed, We relieved them from the disgrace of suffering in the life of this world and allowed them to enjoy their life for a time.[859] (98) Had your Lord willed, all the people on earth would have believed, all of them entirely. Is it, then, up to you (Prophet) to compel People to believe? (99) No soul can ever believe except with God's permission, and He brings disgrace on those who will not use their reason. (100) Say, "Look at what there is in the heavens and on earth." But signs and warnings will not help the people who will not believe.[860] (101) What are they waiting for other than the punishment which came to those before them? Say, "Wait, then, and I will be waiting with you." (102) Then We will save Our Messengers and those who believe. It is incumbent upon us to save the believers (103)

Say, "People, if you are in doubt as to what my faith is, then (know that) I do not worship those you worship besides God, but I worship God alone, Who will eventually retrieve you back to Him, and I am commanded to be among the believers." (104) (Prophet,) set your face towards this faith, as a man inclined to the truth. Do not be among those who violate God's unity. (105) Do not call on any besides God who can neither benefit you nor harm you. If you do it, you will be among the unjust. (106)

If God inflicts harm on you, no one can remove it except for Him, and, if He intends good for you, no one can turn away His favor. He grants His bounty to any of His worshipers whom He wills. He alone is truly forgiving,[861] the true Purveyor of Mercy. (107)

Say, "People, the truth has come to you from your Lord. Whoever chooses to follow the path of guidance follows it for his own good, and whoever chooses to go astray does so to his own loss. I am not responsible for your conduct. (108)

. . .

---

[856] Psalm 135:12 and gave their land as a heritage, a heritage to his people Israel.

[857] Deuteronomy 31:20 For when I have brought them into the land flowing with milk and honey, which I promised on oath to their ancestors, and they have eaten their fill and grown fat, they will turn to other gods and serve them, despising me and breaking my covenant.

[858] Psalm 119:160 The sum of your word is truth; and every one of your righteous ordinances endures forever.

[859] Jonah 3:10 When God saw what they did, how they turned from their evil ways, God changed his mind about the calamity that he had said he would bring upon them; and he did not do it.

[860] Romans 1:20 Ever since the creation of the world his eternal power and divine nature, invisible though they are, have been understood and seen through the things he has made. So they are without excuse;

[861] Psalm 130:4 But there is forgiveness with you, so that you may be revered

Follow what is being revealed to you, and be patient in hard times until God gives His judgment.[862] He is the best of all judges.[863] (109)

•   •   •

---

[862] James 5:11 We count those blessed who endured. You have heard of the endurance of Job and have seen the outcome of the Lord's dealings, that the Lord is full of compassion and *is* merciful.
[863] Psalms 9:8 And He will judge the world in righteousness; He will execute judgment for the peoples with equity.

CHAPTER **ELEVEN**

HUD

THE PROPHET HUD

THE **MECCA** PERIOD

In the name of God, the Merciful-to-all, the Mercy Giver:

Alif. Lam. Ra, (this is) a Book whose verses are perfectly constructed, then detailed directly from the grace of the Wise, the Most Expert, [01] so that you may worship no one but God. I am sent to you from Him to warn you and to give you good news. [02] Ask your Lord to forgive your sins and turn towards Him in repentance.[864] He will let you enjoy a good life until a specified time, and He will give His grace to everyone who was graceful. But, if you turn away, I dread the suffering (which is bound to befall you) on that Mighty Day.[865] [03] You must all return to God, as He has power over everything. [04] See how they turn away, trying to hide from Him. Even when they cover themselves with their clothes, He knows all that they hide and what they reveal. He has full knowledge of what is in men's hearts.[866] [05]

Every living creature on earth depends on God[867] for sustenance and He knows where it lives and where it dies. It is all in a clear record.[868] [06]

He created the heavens and the earth in six days and the throne of His majesty of His Mightiness extended over the water.[869] (He created this) in order to test which of you is best in deeds. And If you (Prophet) say, "You will be resurrected after death," the unbelievers will answer, "This is clearly nothing but sorcery." [07] If We defer their suffering for a specified time, they are sure to say, "What is preventing it (from coming now)?" On the Day when it befalls them

• • •

---

[864] Isaiah 55:6-7 "Seek the Lord while he may be found; call on him while he is near. Let the wicked forsake his way and the evil man his thoughts. [7] Let him turn to the Lord, and he will have mercy on him, and to our God, for he will freely pardon."
[865] Revelation 20:15 and anyone whose name was not found written in the book of life was thrown into the lake of fire.
[866] Luke 16:15 And He said to them, "You are those who justify yourselves in the sight of men, but God knows your hearts; for that which is highly esteemed among men is detestable in the sight of God.
[867] Psalm 145:16 You open your hand, satisfying the desire of every living thing.
[868] Luke 10:20 Nevertheless, do not rejoice at this, that the spirits submit to you, but rejoice that your names are written in heaven.
[869] Psalm 24:2 for he has founded it on the seas, and established it on the rivers.

there will be nothing to divert it from them and they will be overwhelmed by the very thing they mocked. [08] If We let man taste some of Our mercy and then take it away from him, he will abandon all hope, forgetting all gratitude. [09] If We let him taste ease and plenty after hardship has touched him, he is sure to say, "Misfortune has gone away from me." He becomes overjoyed and boastful. [10] Except those who are patient in hard times and do righteous deeds: forgiveness of sins awaits them and a great reward. [870] [11]

Perhaps you are thinking about omitting part of what is being revealed to you, and you feel a tightness in your chest about it because they say, "If only a treasure were sent down to him, or an angel came with him (then we would believe)." (Prophet,) you are only a warner, it is God who is in charge of everything. [12] Or, they (may) say, "He invented it." Say, "Produce ten invented chapters of similar merit, and call in whoever you can besides God to help you, if what you say is true. [13] But if they (whom you called) do not respond to you, then know that (this Qur'an) has been revealed with God's knowledge and that there is no God but Him. Then will you submit to Him?" [14]

As for those who care only for the life of this world and its bounties, We will repay (them) fully for everything they did, and they will be given nothing less. [15] But, in the life to come, they will have nothing but the fire; their works will be fruitless, and their deeds futile. [16] Can they be compared to those who have clear evidence from their Lord, conveyed through (this) testimony from Him—as was the book previously revealed to Moses (Musa)—to be a guide and mercy (to humanity)? Those (who understand) believe in it, whereas those parties that deny its truth are promised the fire. Have no doubt about (this revelation); it is the Truth from your Lord, though most people do not believe so. [17]

Who could be more unjust than he who attributes his own lie to God? (Such people) will be arraigned before their Lord, and the witnesses will say, "They uttered lies about their Lord." God's rejection is what the unjust deserve [18] (those) who turn others away from the path of God-[871] trying to make it crooked[872]-and refuse to acknowledge the truth of the life to come. [19] They can never escape (their final reckoning, even if they remain unharmed) on earth; they will never find anyone who can protect them from God. Double suffering will be imposed on them for having lost the ability to hear (the truth) and failed to see (it).[873] [20] They have allowed themselves to be lost. All their invented gods will have deserted them. [21] Assuredly, in the life to come, they will lose the most. [22] (Only) those who believe and do righteous deeds and humble themselves[874] before their Lord are destined for heaven, where they will remain for eternity.[875] [23] These two groups are like the blind and deaf in comparison to those who see and hear. Can they be alike? How can you not pay attention? [24]

• • •

---

[870] Psalm 27:14 Wait for the Lord; Be strong and let your heart take courage; Yes, wait for the Lord.
[871] Matthew 23:13 'But woe to you, scribes and Pharisees, hypocrites! For you lock people out of the kingdom of heaven. For you do not go in yourselves, and when others are going in, you stop them.
[872] Acts 13:10 and said, "You who are full of all deceit and fraud, you son of the devil, you enemy of all righteousness, will you not cease to make crooked the straight ways of the Lord?
[873] Romans 2:9 There will be anguish and distress for everyone who does evil, the Jew first and also the Greek
[874] James 4:10 Humble yourselves before the Lord, and he will exalt you.
[875] Matthew 18:4 Whoever becomes humble like this child is the greatest in the kingdom of heaven.

(In like manner,) We have sent Noah to his people,[876] (saying,) "I come to you with the plain warning [(25)] that you may worship no one but God. I fear that you may suffer on a painful Day." [(26)] The notables among his people who denied the truth said, "We do not see anything in you but a mortal man like ourselves, and it is clear to see that only the worst among us follow you. We do not see that you could be superior to us in any way. On the contrary, we think you are a liar." [(27)] (Noah) said, "My people, have you considered that I might have a clear sign from my Lord, and that He has given me grace of His own even though it is not apparent to you? (In that case,) could we compel you to accept it against your will? [(28)] My people, I ask you no reward for it. My reward rests with none but God. I will not chase away the faithful. They know they are destined to meet their Lord, and I can see that you are foolish. [(29)] People, who could protect me from God if I chased (the faithful) away? Will you not take heed? [(30)] I do not say to you, 'God's treasures are with me,' nor (do I say), 'I have knowledge of what is hidden,' nor do I say, 'I am an angel,' nor do I say of those you hold in contempt, 'God will not grant them any good.' God is fully aware of what is in their hearts.[877] If I did this, I would be among the unjust." [(31)] (The notables) said, "Noah, you have argued with us for too long. Bring down on us the punishment with which you threaten us if you are a man of truth." [(32)] He answered, "Only God will bring it upon you, if He so wills and you will not escape it. [(33)] My advice will be no use to you if God wills that you remain lost in your delusions. He is your Lord, and to Him you must return."[878] [(34)]

Or do they (the idolaters) say he has invented this (story)?" Say (Muhammad) "If I have invented it, I am responsible for my own crime, but I am innocent of the crime of which you are guilty." [(35)]

It was revealed to Noah, "None of your people will believe other than those who have already done so. Do not be distressed by anything that they may do. [(36)] Build the Ark under Our observation and Our inspiration,[879] and do not appeal to Me on behalf of the transgressors. They are destined to be drowned." [(37)] (Noah) began to build the Ark, and every time the notables of his people passed by him, they mocked him. He said, "If you are mocking us now, we will come to mock you (and your ignorance) just as you are mocking us. [(38)] In time you will know who will receive a humiliating punishment, and on whom a lasting suffering will descend." [(39)] When Our judgment came, and waters gushed up,[880] We said, "Place on board this (Ark) a pair of each species, as well as your family—except those against whom the sentence has already been passed—and the

• • •

[876] Genesis 6-8 The story of Noah is told completely in these 3 chapters of Genesis

[877] Luke 16:15 And He said to them, "You are those who justify yourselves in the sight of men, but God knows your hearts; for that which is highly esteemed among men is detestable in the sight of God.

[878] Romans 14:12 So then, each of us will be accountable to God.

[879] Genesis 6:14-16 Make yourself an ark of cypress wood; make rooms in the ark, and cover it inside and out with pitch. [15] This is how you are to make it: the length of the ark three hundred cubits, its width fifty cubits, and its height thirty cubits. [16] Make a roof for the ark, and finish it to a cubit above; and put the door of the ark in its side; make it with lower, second, and third decks.

[880] Genesis 7:11 In the six hundredth year of Noah's life, in the second month, on the seventeenth day of the month, on that day all the fountains of the great deep burst forth, and the windows of the heavens were opened.

Believers,"[881] though only a few (of Noah's people) shared his faith.[882] [(40)] He said (to his followers), "Board this Ark[883]. In the name of God, it will sail and anchor. My Lord is much-forgiving, a dispenser of grace." [(41)] It sailed with them on waves[884] that were like mountains. Noah cried out to his son, who stayed behind, "Come aboard with us my son, and do not stay with the unbelievers." [(42)] (The son) answered, "I will take myself to a mountain[885] that will protect me from the waters." (Noah) said, "Today there is no protection (for anyone) from God's judgment, except (for) those who have earned (His) mercy." A wave rose up between them and (the son) was among those who drowned[886]. [(43)] Then it was said (by God), "Earth, swallow up your water, and sky, stop (your rain).[887] The waters sank into the earth,[888] and the will (of God) was done, and the ark came to rest on Mount Judi. It was said (by God), "Away with those evildoing folk." [(44)]

Noah called out to his Lord and said, "My Lord, my son was my family; Your promise always comes true, and You are the most just of all judges." [(45)] (God) answered, "Noah, he was not your family, because he was unrighteous in his conduct. Do not ask me for things you know nothing about. I am warning you not to be foolish." [(46)] (Noah) said, "My Lord, I seek refuge with You from ever (again) asking You anything about which I know nothing. Unless You forgive me and have mercy on me, I will be among the lost." [(47)] It was said (by God), "Noah, descend in peace from Us and with blessings on you [889] as well as on (some of the) nations[890] (that descend) from among those who are with you. (But as for) others (of their descendants), We will allow them to enjoy life (for a little while), and then a painful punishment from Us will afflict them." [(48)]

These accounts are part of what was beyond your knowledge (Muhammad). We revealed them to you. Neither you nor your people knew them, so be patient (like Noah) in hard times. The future belongs to those who are mindful of God.[891] [(49)]

• • •

[881] Genesis 7 The Great flood
[882] 1 Peter 3:20 who in former times did not obey, when God waited patiently in the days of Noah, during the building of the ark, in which a few, that is, eight people, were saved through water.
[883] Genesis 7:1 Then the Lord said to Noah, 'Go into the ark, you and all your household, for I have seen that you alone are righteous before me in this generation.
[884] Genesis 7:17 The flood continued for forty days on the earth; and the waters increased, and bore up the ark, and it rose high above the earth.
[885] Genesis 7:19 The waters swelled so mightily on the earth that all the high mountains under the whole heaven were covered;
[886] Genesis 7:21-22 And all flesh died that moved on the earth, birds, domestic animals, wild animals, all swarming creatures that swarm on the earth, and all human beings; [22] everything on dry land in whose nostrils was the breath of life died.
[887] Genesis 8:1-2 But God remembered Noah and all the wild animals and all the domestic animals that were with him in the ark. [2] And God made a wind blow over the earth, and the waters subsided; the fountains of the deep and the windows of the heavens were closed, the rain from the heavens was restrained,
[888] Genesis 8:3 and the waters gradually receded from the earth. At the end of one hundred and fifty days the waters had abated;
[889] Genesis 8:16 'Go out of the ark, you and your wife, and your sons and your sons' wives with you.
[890] Genesis 10 records the nations that emanated from Noah's family after the flood, ending with Genesis 10:32, These are the families of the sons of Noah, according to their genealogies, by their nations; and out of these the nations were separated on the earth after the flood
[891] Jeremiah 29:11 For surely I know the plans I have for you, says the Lord, plans for your welfare and not for harm, to give you a future with hope.

To (the tribe of) 'Ad,[892] (We sent) their brother Hud.[893] He said, "My people worship God (alone). You have no God other than Him. You are making up lies. [50] I ask no reward from you. My reward rests only with Him who created me. Why don't you use your common sense? [51] My people, ask your Lord to forgive your sins, and then turn towards Him in repentance[894]. He will shower you with abundant heavenly grace and will add strength to your strength. Do not turn away and be lost in sin." [52] They replied, "Hud, you have brought us no clear evidence (that you are a prophet), and we are not going to forsake our gods on the strength of your word alone, nor do we believe in you. [53] All we can say is that one of our gods has inflicted some harm on you." (Hud) answered, "I call God to witness, and you too are my witnesses, that I disown those to whom you ascribe divinity, [54] except for God. Plot (anything that you may wish) against me, and give me no respite. [55] I have placed my trust in God, (who is) my Lord and your Lord. There is no living creature that He does not control. My Lord's way is a straight path." [56] But if they turn away, then say, "I have delivered to you the messages with which I was sent, and my Lord will bring along another people to take your place, whereas you will in no way harm Him. My lord watches over all things." [57] When Our judgment came to pass, by Our grace We saved Hud and his fellow believers. We saved them from severe suffering (in the life to come) as well. [58] That was (the end of 'Ad, (who) rejected their Lord's messages, and rebelled against His Messengers, and followed the command of every arrogant enemy of the truth. [59] They were rejected in this world, and so will they be on the Day of Resurrection.[895] 'Ad denied their Lord. So away with 'Ad, the people of Hud. [60]

To (the tribe of) Thamud[896] (We sent) their brother Salih.[897] He said, "My people, worship God (alone). You have no God other than Him. He created you out of the earth and made you inhabit it. Ask Him to forgive your sins, and turn towards Him in repentance[898]. My Lord is near, and ready to answer (whoever calls to Him)." [61] They answered, "Salih, We used to have such great hopes in you. Would you forbid us to worship what our forefathers worshipped? We are in grave doubt, amounting to suspicion, about what you are asking us to do." [62] He retorted, "My people, just think, if I am taking my stand based on clear evidence from my Lord, and if He had given me mercy of His own, who could protect me from God if I disobeyed Him? You would only make my loss greater. [63] My people, this camel belongs to God; it will be a sign for you. Leave it to pasture on God's land and do her no harm, or you will soon be punished." [64] However, they cruelly slaughtered her. (Salih) said, "You will enjoy life in your homes for only three (more) days; this is a judgment which will not prove false."

• • •

[892] See ref. 615

[893] See ref. 616

[894] Isaiah 55:6-7 "Seek the Lord while he may be found; call on him while he is near. Let the wicked forsake his way and the evil man his thoughts [7] Let him turn to the Lord, and he will have mercy on him, and to our God, for he will freely pardon."

[895] Daniel 12:2 Many of those who sleep in the dust of the ground will awake, these to everlasting life, but the others to disgrace and everlasting contempt.

[896] See ref. 617

[897] See ref. 618

[898] Micah 7 18-19 Who is a God like you, who pardons sin and forgives the transgression of the remnant of his inheritance? [19] You do not stay angry forever but delight to show mercy.

(65) When Our command was fulfilled, We saved Salih and those who shared his faith as a mercy from us, and (We saved them) from the disgrace of (Our rejection on) that Day (of Resurrection). Your Lord alone is powerful, almighty. (66) The blast (of God's punishment) overtook the evildoers, and they lay lifeless in their homes and on the ground, (67) as though they had never lived there. Thamud denied their Lord, so away with Thamud. (68)

To Abraham, Our (heavenly) messengers brought good news.[899] They said, "Peace," and he answered, "(And upon you be) peace," and without delay he placed a roasted calf[900] before them. (69) When he saw that their hands did not reach out towards it, he found this strange and became apprehensive of them. They said, "Do not fear. We are sent against the people of Lot[901]." (70) His wife, standing (nearby), laughed (with happiness). We gave her the good news of (the birth of) Isaac[902] and, after Isaac, of (Isaac's son) Jacob. (71) She said, "Alas for me. How am I to bear a child when I am now an old woman, and this husband of mine is an old man[903]? That would be an astonishing thing." (72) (The messengers) said, "are you astonished at God's command?[904] May the mercy of God and His blessing be on you, people of this house. For He is worthy[905] all praise and Glory." (73) When the fear left Abraham and the good news had been conveyed to him, he began to plead with Us for Lot's people. [906] (74) Abraham was forbearing, tender-hearted, and devout. (75) (God's Messengers replied,) "Abraham, stop this (pleading). Your Lord's judgment has already passed. Punishment is coming to them, which cannot be turned back." (76)

When Our messengers came[907] to Lot, he was sad for (his people), seeing that it was beyond his power to protect them, and he said, "This is a truly terrible day." (78) His people came running to him;[908] they were accustomed to committing foul deeds. (Lot) said, "My people take my daughters instead. They are purer for you (than men). Fear God, and do not disgrace me with my

• • •

[899] Genesis 18:1-2,10 The Lord appeared to Abraham by the oaks of Mamre, as he sat at the entrance of his tent in the heat of the day. 2 He looked up and saw three men standing near him. When he saw them, he ran from the tent entrance to meet them, and bowed down to the ground. 10 Then one said, 'I will surely return to you in due season, and your wife Sarah shall have a son.' And Sarah was listening at the tent entrance behind him.

[900] Genesis 18:7-8 Abraham ran to the herd, and took a calf, tender and good, and gave it to the servant, who hastened to prepare it. 8 Then he took curds and milk and the calf that he had prepared, and set it before them; and he stood by them under the tree while they ate.

[901] Genesis 18:20-21 And the Lord said, "The outcry of Sodom and Gomorrah is indeed great, and their sin is exceedingly grave. 21 I will go down now, and see if they have done entirely according to its outcry, which has come to Me; and if not, I will know."

[902] Genesis 18:10 Then one said, 'I will surely return to you in due season, and your wife Sarah shall have a son.' And Sarah was listening at the tent entrance behind him.

[903] Genesis 18:12 So Sarah laughed to herself, saying, 'After I have grown old, and my husband is old, shall I have pleasure?

[904] Genesis 18:13,14 The Lord said to Abraham, 'Why did Sarah laugh, and say, "Shall I indeed bear a child, now that I am old?" 14 Is anything too wonderful for the Lord? At the set time I will return to you, in due season, and Sarah shall have a son.'

[905] 2 Samuel 22:4 I call upon the Lord, who is worthy to be praised, and I am saved from my enemies

[906] Genesis 18:32 Then he said, "Oh may the Lord not be angry, and I shall speak only this once; suppose ten are found there?" And He said, "I will not destroy it on account of the ten."

[907] Genesis 19:1 The two angels came to Sodom in the evening, and Lot was sitting in the gateway of Sodom. When Lot saw them, he rose to meet them, and bowed down with his face to the ground.

[908] Genesis 19:4 But before they lay down, the men of the city, the men of Sodom, both young and old, all the people to the last man, surrounded the house;

guests.[909] Is there not a single right-minded man among you?" They answered, "You have always known that we have no right to your daughters. You know very well what we want."[910] [(79)] (Lot) exclaimed, "If only I had the strength to defeat you or could rely on mightier support." [(80)] (The angels) said,[911] "Lot, we are messengers from your Lord. (Your enemies) will never reach you. Leave with your household in the dead of night[912] and do not look back.[913] (Take all of your family with you) with the exception of your wife[914]. The fate which will befall (the people of Sodom) will befall her (as well). Their appointed time is the morning. Is not the morning near?"[915] [(81)] When Our judgment came about, We turned those (sinful towns) upside down and rained down on them stones of hard clay,[916] layer after layer, (which were) [(82)] designated by your Lord (to punish sinners). (Such punishment) is never far from the unjust. [(83)]

To (the people of) Midian[917] (We sent) their brother Shu'ayb.[918] He said, "My people, worship God (alone). You have no God other than Him. Do not give (false) measure or weight (in your dealings with people). I see that you are prospering, but I fear for your suffering on a day that will encompass you (with doom). [(84)] Hence, my people, (always) give full measure and weight, with equity, and do not deprive people of what is rightfully theirs, and do not act wickedly on earth by spreading corruption. [(85)] What rests with God is best for you, if you are believers. I am not your keeper." [(86)] They said, "Shu'ayb, does your prayer really command you that we give up what our forefathers worshipped or to refrain from doing with our wealth whatever we please? You certainly sound like the perfect tolerant and right-minded man!" [(87)] He answered, "My people, what if I am acting on clear evidence from my Lord, and He Himself has given me good

• • •

[909] Genesis 19:7-8 and said, 'I beg you, my brothers, do not act so wickedly. [8] Look, I have two daughters who have not known a man; let me bring them out to you, and do to them as you please; only do nothing to these men, for they have come under the shelter of my roof.'

[910] Genesis 19:5 and they called to Lot, 'Where are the men who came to you tonight? Bring them out to us, so that we may know them.

[911] Genesis 19:10-11 But the men inside reached out their hands and brought Lot into the house with them, and shut the door. [11] And they struck with blindness the men who were at the door of the house, both small and great, so that they were unable to find the door.

[912] Genesis 19:12-13 Then the men said to Lot, 'Have you anyone else here? Sons-in-law, sons, daughters, or anyone you have in the city—bring them out of the place. [13] For we are about to destroy this place, because the outcry against its people has become great before the Lord, and the Lord has sent us to destroy it.'

[913] Genesis 19:17 When they had brought them outside, they said, 'Flee for your life; do not look back or stop anywhere in the Plain; flee to the hills, or else you will be consumed.'

[914] Genesis 19:26 But Lot's wife, behind him, looked back, and she became a pillar of salt.

[915] Genesis 19:15 When morning dawned, the angels urged Lot, saying, 'Get up, take your wife and your two daughters who are here, or else you will be consumed in the punishment of the city.'

[916] Genesis 19:24 Then the Lord rained on Sodom and Gomorrah sulphur and fire from the Lord out of heaven;

[917] The people of Madyan were Arabs who lived in a territory stretching along the lands of Al-Hijaz (Western Saudi Arabia) to the part of which today is greater Syria & surrounding regions, and east of the Gulf of Al-Aqaba They were a greedy people who did not believe that God existed and who led wicked lives. They gave short measure, praised their goods beyond their worth, and hid their defects. They lied to their customers, thereby cheating them.

[918] Prophet Shu'ayb armed with many miracles. Shu'ayb preached to them, begging them to be mindful of God's favors and warning them of the consequences of their evil ways, but they only mocked him. Shu'ayb remained calm as he reminded them of his kinship to them and that what he was doing was not for his personal gain. Shu'ayb is a prophet sent to Madyan people.

provision? I have no desire to differ from you concerning what I have forbidden you. I want no more than to set things right as much as I can. I cannot succeed without God's help. I have placed my trust in Him, and I always turn to Him. [88] My people, do not let (your) disagreement with me drive you into sin and bring upon you a fate similar to that of the people of Noah or Hud or Salih, and (remember that) the people of Lot did not live very far from you. [89] Ask your Lord to forgive your sins, and then turn towards Him in repentance.[919] My Lord is the Mercy-Giver and Most-Loving." [90] My Lord is the Mercy-Giver and Most-Loving." [90] (His people) said, "Shu'ayb, We cannot understand much of what you say. In fact, we find you weak (and poorly connected) among us, and, were it not for your clan, we would have stoned you to death, considering that you have no status among us." [91] He said, "My people, do you hold my clan in greater esteem than God, that you turned your backs on Him? My Lord is fully aware of all that you do. [92] Hence, do what you think is best, and I will do what I think is best. In time you will certainly know who will receive a punishment to disgrace him, and who is a liar. Watch (for what is coming). I will watch with you." [93] When Our judgment came to pass, by Our mercy We saved Shu'ayb and those who shared his faith, while the blast (of Our punishment) overtook those who had done wrong, and they lay lifeless in their homes [94] as though they had never lived there. Away with (the people of) Midian, as was done away with (the people of) Thamud. [95]

We sent Moses with Our messages and clear authority [96] to Pharaoh and his inner circle, but they followed Pharaoh's orders, and Pharaoh's orders were misguided. [97] On the Day of Resurrection, he will go before his people, having led them towards the fire. Miserable is the destination to which they are led. [98] They were pursued by (God's) rejection in this (world), and (will be overtaken by it) on the Day of Resurrection. What a rotten gift to be given. [99]

These are parts of the accounts of those (ancient) communities that We are relating to you; some still remain, and some are (extinct, like) a field mown down. [100] We did not wrong them; they wronged themselves.[920] When your Lord's judgment was ordained, those deities of theirs, which they called on instead of God, proved to be of no use to them and only increased their ruin. [101] Such is the punishment of your Lord when He decides to punish a community for their transgression. His punishment is painful and severe. [102]

In that is a sign for anyone who fears the suffering (which may befall them) in the Hereafter. That is the Day[921] on which people will be gathered together— that is a Day to be witnessed,[922] [103] (and) which We will not delay beyond a specified period. [104] When that Day comes, not a soul will speak except by His permission. Some will be miserable, and some will be blessed. [105] As for those

• • •

---

[919] Psalm 32:5-6 I acknowledged my sin to You, And my iniquity I did not hide; I said, "I will confess my transgressions to the Lord"; And You forgave the (guilt of my sin. [6] Therefore, let everyone who is godly pray to You in a time when You may be found. Micah 7 18-19 Who is a God like you, who pardons sin and forgives the transgression of the remnant of his inheritance? You do not stay angry forever but delight to show mercy.
[920] Revelation 2:23 and I will give to each one of you according to your deeds.
[921] Day of Judgment
[922] Zephaniah 3:8 "Therefore wait for Me," declares the Lord, "For the day when I rise up as a witness. Indeed, My decision is to gather nations, To assemble kingdoms, To pour out on them My indignation, all My burning anger; for all the earth will be devoured By the fire of My zeal.

who will have brought misery upon themselves, (they will live) in the fire, moaning and groaning, [106] where they will remain as long as the heavens and the earth endure, unless your Lord wills otherwise. Your Lord is the doer of what He wills.[923] [107] As for those who will be blessed, (they will live) in Heaven, to stay as long as the heavens and the earth endure, unless your Lord wills otherwise— an uninterrupted blessing. [108]

(Prophet), have no doubt about what these (misguided people) worship. They worship as their forefathers worshipped before them, and We will certainly give them their full share (for whatever good or evil they have earned), with no reduction. [109] We gave Moses the Book before you, but they were in dispute about it. Were it not for a prior decree from your Lord, it would have been settled between them. Still they had suspicious doubts about it[924] (the Torah). [110] Your Lord will give everyone their full due for whatever (good or evil) they may have done. He is aware of everything they do. [111] Remain steadfast, as you have been commanded (by God), together with all those along with you who have turned to Him. Do not let anyone overstep the limits, because He sees all that you do. [112] Do not incline towards those who do evil, lest the fire touch you. You will (then) have no one to protect you from God, nor will you be helped. [113] Be constant in prayer at the beginning and end of the day, as well as during parts of the night. Good deeds drive away evil deeds.[925] This is a reminder to the mindful. [114] Be patient in hard times. God does not fail to repay those who do good.[926] [115]

If only—among the generations before your time—there had been people with good sense to speak out against corruption on earth, (as did) the few of them whom We saved. (Instead,) the unjust only pursued pleasures that corrupted their entire beings, and that led them to sin [116] Your Lord would never destroy towns unjustly so long as their people behaved righteously (towards one another). [117] Had your Lord willed, He could have made all of humanity one single community, but (He willed it otherwise, and so) they continue to have divergent views, [118] except those on whom your Lord has mercy. To this end He created them. The word of your Lord will be fulfilled: "I will definitely fill Hell with both *jinn* and humans." [119]

So, (Prophet), We have relayed the accounts of the (earlier) messengers to you in order to make your heart firm. The Truth comes to you through these accounts, as well as lessons and reminders for the believers. [120] Say to those who will not believe, "Do anything that is within your power, while we labor (in God's way) [121] and wait (for what is coming). We are waiting too." [122] God alone comprehends the hidden reality of the heavens and the earth. Everything that exists goes back to Him, so worship Him and place your trust in Him alone. Your Lord is never unaware of what you (people) are doing. [123]

• • •

---

[923] Psalm 115:3 But our God is in the heavens; He does whatever He pleases.
[924] See Commentary (Tafseer) by Al Qurtubi https://en.wikipedia.org/wiki/Tafsir_al-Qurtubi
https://archive.org/details/TafseerEQurtubiArabicalJameAlAhkamAlQuran
[925] Ezekiel 18:21 "But if the wicked man turns from all his sins which he has committed and observes all My statutes and practices justice and righteousness, he shall surely live; he shall not die.
[926] Galatians 6:7-8 Do not be deceived, God is not mocked; for whatever a man sows, this he will also reap. 8 For the one who sows to his own flesh will from the flesh reap corruption, but the one who sows to the Spirit will from the Spirit reap eternal life.

CHAPTER TWELVE

YUSUF

THE PROPHET JOSEPH

THE **MECCA** PERIOD

In the name of God, the Merciful-to-all, the Mercy Giver:
Alif Lam. Ra, these are the verses of the Book that is awe-inspiringly clear. [01]
We have sent it down as an Arabic Qur'an, so that you might understand it. [02]
We tell you the best of stories in what We have revealed to you of this Qur'an,
seeing that you were among those who were unaware. [03]
Joseph said to his father, "Father, I saw (in a dream) eleven stars, as well as
the sun and the moon. I saw them bow before me."[928] [04] (Jacob) replied, "My
son, do not tell your brothers[929] your dream or they may plot to harm you (out
of envy). Satan is man's open enemy. [05] And thus Your Lord will choose you, and
will teach you to interpret some events, and will perfect His grace on you and on
the House of Jacob, just as He perfected it earlier upon your forefathers Abraham
and Isaac. Your Lord is All-Knowing,[930] All-Wise."[931] [06] In (the story of) Joseph
and his brothers, there are messages for all who search (for the truth). [07]
(Joseph's brothers) said (to one another), "Joseph and his brother (Benjamin)
are dearer to our father than we are,[932] even though we are so many. Our father
is clearly wrong." [08] (One of them said), "Kill Joseph[933] drive him away to some
(faraway) land, so that your father's attention will be free to turn to you. After
this is done, you will be (free to repent and to live once again as) righteous
people." [09] Another of them said, "Do not kill Joseph.[934] If you must do

•   •   •

[928] Genesis 37:9 He had another dream, and told it to his brothers, saying, 'Look, I have had another dream: the sun, the moon, and eleven stars were bowing down to me.
[929] Genesis 37:10 But when he told it to his father and to his brothers, his father rebuked him, and said to him, 'What kind of dream is this that you have had? Shall we indeed come, I and your mother and your brothers, and bow to the ground before you?'
[930] 1 John 3:20 whenever our hearts condemn us; for God is greater than our hearts, and he knows everything.
[931] Job 9:4 "Wise in heart and mighty in strength, Who has defied Him without harm?
[932] Genesis 37:11 So his brothers were jealous of him, but his father kept the matter in mind.
[933] Genesis 37:18 They saw him from a distance, and before he came near to them, they conspired to kill him.
[934] Genesis 37:21 But when Reuben heard it, he delivered him out of their hands, saying, 'Let us not take his life.'

something, throw him into the dark depths of this well, where some caravan may pick him up." [10] (They agreed on this course, and) they spoke (to Jacob), "Father, why don't you trust us with Joseph, seeing as we wish him well? [11] Let him go out with us tomorrow, so that he may play and enjoy himself, and We will protect him well." [12] (Jacob) said, "The thought of you taking him away with you worries me. I am afraid a wolf may eat him at a moment when you are not paying attention." [13] They said, "If the wolf were to devour him when there are so many of us, we would be the real losers. [14] When they went away with him and decided to throw him into the dark depths of a well, We inspired him, saying, "One day, you will remind them of their deed at a time when they will least expect it." [15] At nightfall they returned to their father, weeping, [935] [16] (and) said, "Father, we were racing with one another, and left Joseph behind with our things, and a wolf devoured him. (We know that) you will not believe us even though we are telling the truth," [17] and they produced his shirt deceptively stained with blood. [936] (Jacob) exclaimed, "Rather your souls have enticed you to something. But patience is beautiful and it is to God (alone) that I pray for strength to cope with what you are saying to me." [18]

A caravan came[937] and they sent someone to draw water. He sent down his bucket into the well, (and, when he saw Joseph) he said, "Good news, there is a boy." They hid him with the intention of selling him, but God had full knowledge of everything that they were doing. [19] They sold him for a small price[938] - a few pieces of silver: so little did they value him. [20] The man from Egypt that bought him[939] said to his wife, "Look after him well. He may be useful to us or we may adopt him as a son." In this way We gave Joseph a firm place on earth[940] and (We did this) so that We could teach him the inner meaning of things. God always prevails[941] in His purpose but most People do not know this. [21]

• • •

[935] Genesis 37:32 They had the long robe with sleeves taken to their father, and they said, 'This we have found; see now whether it is your son's robe or not

[936] Genesis 37:31 Then they took Joseph's robe, slaughtered a goat, and dipped the robe in the blood.

[937] Genesis 37:25 They had the long robe with sleeves taken to their father, and they said, 'This we have found; see now whether it is your son's robe or not ... Genesis 37:32 then they sat down to eat; and looking up they saw a caravan of Ishmaelites coming from Gilead, with their camels carrying gum, balm, and resin, on their way to carry it down to Egypt.

[938] Genesis 37:26-28 Then Judah said to his brothers, 'What profit is there if we kill our brother and conceal his blood? [27] Come, let us sell him to the Ishmaelites, and not lay our hands on him, for he is our brother, our own flesh.' And his brothers agreed. [28] When some Midianite traders passed by, they drew Joseph up, lifting him out of the pit, and sold him to the Ishmaelites for twenty pieces of silver. And they took Joseph to Egypt.

[939] Genesis 37:28,36, 39:1 When some Midianite traders passed by, they drew Joseph up, lifting him out of the pit, and sold him to the Ishmaelites for twenty pieces of silver. And they took Joseph to Egypt.

[36] Meanwhile the Midianites had sold him in Egypt to Potiphar, one of Pharaoh's officials, the captain of the guard. 39:1 Now Joseph was taken down to Egypt, and Potiphar, an officer of Pharaoh, the captain of the guard, an Egyptian, bought him from the Ishmaelites who had brought him down there.

[940] Genesis 39:2 The Lord was with Joseph, and he became a successful man; he was in the house of his Egyptian master.

[941] Isaiah 43:13 I am God, and also henceforth I am He; there is no one who can deliver from my hand; I work and who can hinder it?

When he reached full manhood, We gave him the ability to judge[942] (between right and wrong), as well as knowledge: We reward those who do good. [22] The woman in whose house he was living tried to seduce him;[943] and she bolted the doors and said, "Come to me." (Joseph) answered, "God forbid! My master has been good to me. No good can come of (such a) wrong." [23] She desired him and he desired her (and he would have succumbed) had he not seen evidence of his Lord's[944] truth. We did this in order to keep evil and indecency away from him. He was truly one of Our chosen worshipers. [24] They both rushed to the door and she tore his shirt[945] from behind and at the door they met her husband.[946] She said, "What, other than prison or painful punishment, should be the reward of someone who tried to dishonor your wife?" [25] (Joseph) said, "It was she who tried to seduce me." A member of her household suggested that, "If his shirt has been torn from the front; then she is telling the truth and he is a liar, [26] but if his shirt has been torn from behind, then she is lying and he is telling the truth." [27] When (her husband) saw that his shirt was torn from behind, he said, "This is another instance of women's treachery. Your treachery is truly great. [28] Joseph, overlook this. While you, (wife,) ask forgiveness for your sin—you are greatly at fault." [29]

Some women of the town said (to one another), "The governor's wife is trying to seduce her slave. Her love for him consumes her. We see that she is clearly lost." [30] When she heard about their gossip, she sent for them, and prepared a banquet for them, and handed each of them a knife. She said (to Joseph), "Come out before them." When the women saw him, they were awestruck (by his beauty) and (so flustered that) they cut their hands (with their knives), saying, "God save us. This is not a mortal man. He must be a precious angel." [31] She said, "Here is the one you blamed me for. I sought to seduce him, but he firmly refused. Now, if he does not do what I order, he will be put in prison and will be humiliated." [32] He said, "Lord, prison is more desirable to me than what these women are inviting me to do. If you do not protect me from their treachery, I might yield to their allure and so become one of the ignorant." [33] His Lord responded to his prayer and protected him from their treachery. He alone is All-Hearing, All-Knowing. [34]

It occurred to the governor and his household after they had seen all the signs (of Joseph's innocence), that they should imprison him[947] for a while.[35]

• • •

[942] Genesis 39:3-4 His master saw that the Lord was with him, and that the Lord caused all that he did to prosper in his hands. ⁴ So Joseph found favor in his sight and attended him; he made him overseer of his house and put him in charge of all that he had.

[943] Genesis 39:7 And after a time his master's wife cast her eyes on Joseph and said, 'Lie with me.'

[944] Genesis 39: 8-9 But he refused and said to his master's wife, 'Look, with me here, my master has no concern about anything in the house, and he has put everything that he has in my hand. ⁹ He is not greater in this house than I am, nor has he kept back anything from me except yourself, because you are his wife. How then could I do this great wickedness, and sin against God?'

[945] Genesis 39:12 she caught hold of his garment, saying, 'Lie with me!' But he left his garment in her hand, and fled and ran outside.

[946] Genesis 39:16-18 Then she kept his garment by her until his master came home, ¹⁷ and she told him the same story, saying, 'The Hebrew servant, whom you have brought among us, came in to me to insult me; ¹⁸ but as soon as I raised my voice and cried out, he left his garment beside me, and fled outside.'

[947] Genesis 39:20 And Joseph's master took him and put him into the prison, the place where the king's prisoners were confined; he remained there in prison.

Two young men happened to go to prison at the same time[948] as Joseph. One of them said, "I saw myself (in a dream) pressing wine."[949] The other said, "I saw myself (in a dream) carrying bread on my head, and birds were eating it." (They said to Joseph,) "Tell us the real meaning of this. We see that you are a knowledgeable man."[950] [36] (Joseph) answered, "I will inform you of the interpreted meaning of your dreams before your meal arrives, for this is (part) of the knowledge which my Lord has taught me. I have left behind the way of people who do not believe in God and who persistently deny the truth of the life to come, [37] and I follow the faith of my forefathers Abraham, Isaac and Jacob. It is not conceivable that we should ascribe divinity (to anything) beside God. Such is God's grace to us and all humanity, but most people are ungrateful. [38] Fellow prisoners, which is more reasonable: (belief in the existence of numerous divine) lords that are different from one another, or (in) the One God, who holds absolute power over all that exists? [39] All that you worship instead of God is nothing but (empty) names which you and your forefathers have invented, names for which God has sent down no authority. Judgment (as to what is right and what is wrong) rests with God alone, (and) He has ordered that you worship none but Him. This is the true faith, though most People do not realize it. [40] Fellow prisoners, (I will tell you the meaning of your dreams.) One of you will serve his master with wine to drink, but the other will be crucified, and birds will eat off of his head. [951] (Whatever your future holds,) the matter on which you asked my opinion has been decided (by God)." [41] (Joseph) said to the one he knew would be saved, "Mention me to your master[952] (when you are free)," but Satan caused him to forget to mention (Joseph) to his master and so he remained in prison for a few (more) years. [42]

(One day) the King said, "I saw (in a dream) seven fat cows[953] being devoured by seven (that were) lean;[954] and seven green spikes[955] (of grain) and (seven)

· · ·

[948] Genesis 40:1-3 Some time after this, the cupbearer of the king of Egypt and his baker offended their Lord the king of Egypt. [2] Pharaoh was angry with his two officers, the chief cupbearer and the chief baker, [3] and he put them in custody in the house of the captain of the guard, in the prison where Joseph was confined.

[949] Genesis 40:9-11 So the chief cupbearer told his dream to Joseph, and said to him, 'In my dream there was a vine before me, and [10] on the vine there were three branches. As soon as it budded, its blossoms came out and the clusters ripened into grapes. [11] Pharaoh's cup was in my hand; and I took the grapes and pressed them into Pharaoh's cup, and placed the cup in Pharaoh's hand.'

[950] Genesis 40:16-17 When the chief baker saw that the interpretation was favorable, he said to Joseph, 'I also had a dream: there were three cake baskets on my head, [17] and in the uppermost basket there were all sorts of baked food for Pharaoh, but the birds were eating it out of the basket on my head.'

[951] Genesis 40:18-19 And Joseph answered, 'This is its interpretation: the three baskets are three days; [19] within three days Pharaoh will lift up your head—from you! —and hang you on a pole; and the birds will eat the flesh from you.'

[952] Genesis 40:14 But remember me when it is well with you; please do me the kindness to make mention of me to Pharaoh, and so get me out of this place.

[953] Genesis 41:1-2 After two whole years, Pharaoh dreamed that he was standing by the Nile, [2] and there came up out of the Nile seven sleek and fat cows, and they grazed in the reed grass.

[954] Genesis 41:3-4 Then seven other cows, ugly and thin, came up out of the Nile after them, and stood by the other cows on the bank of the Nile. [4] The ugly and thin cows ate up the seven sleek and fat cows. And Pharaoh awoke.

[955] Genesis 41:5 Then he fell asleep and dreamed a second time; seven ears of grain, plump and good, were growing on one stalk.

others that were dry.[956] Noblemen, enlighten me about (the meaning of) my dream if you are able to interpret dreams."[957] They answered, [(43)] "These are confusing dreams and we have no deep knowledge of dream interpretation." [(44)] The prisoner who had been saved, (suddenly) remembered[958] (Joseph) after all that time and said, "I can inform you of the real meaning of this (dream), so send me forth." [(45)]

(He went to see Joseph in prison and said to him), "Truthful Joseph. Enlighten us about (the meaning of a dream in which) seven fat cows were being devoured by seven (that were) lean, and seven green spikes (of grain)and (seven) others that were dry, so that I may return (with your explanation) to the people (who sent me, and) inform them." [959] [(46)] (Joseph) replied, "You will sow for seven years as usual, but let all (the grain) that you harvest remain (untouched) in its spikes, except for a little that you may eat. [(47)] For, after that (period of seven good years) there will be seven years of hardship which will consume all[960] but a little of what you stored up for them. [(48)] After that there will come a year in which the People will have abundant rain and will press grapes." [(49)]

(As soon as Joseph's interpretation was conveyed to him,) the King said, "Bring him before me." When the (King's) messenger came to him, (Joseph) said, "Go back to your master and ask him (first to find out the truth) about those women who cut their hands—my Lord knows all about their treachery." [(50)] (The King sent for the women, and, when they came,) he asked, "What was it that you hoped to achieve when you tried to seduce Joseph?" The women answered, "God save us. We know nothing bad of him." The wife of Joseph's former master said, "Now the truth is out. It was I who tried to seduce him. He is an honest man." [(51)] (When Joseph learned what had happened, he said,) "I asked for this so that (my former master) can know that I did not betray him behind his back. God does not guide the mischief of the treacherous. [(52)] I am not trying to absolve

• • •

[956] Genesis 41:6-7 Then seven ears, thin and blighted by the east wind, sprouted after them. [7] The thin ears swallowed up the seven plump and full ears. Pharaoh awoke, and it was a dream.
[957] Genesis 41:8 In the morning his spirit was troubled; so he sent and called for all the magicians of Egypt and all its wise men. Pharaoh told them his dreams, but there was no one who could interpret them to Pharaoh.
[958] Genesis 41:9 Then the chief cupbearer said to Pharaoh, 'I remember my faults today.
[959] Genesis 41:17-24 Then Pharaoh said to Joseph, 'In my dream I was standing on the banks of the Nile; [18] and seven cows, fat and sleek, came up out of the Nile and fed in the reed grass. [19] Then seven other cows came up after them, poor, very ugly, and thin. Never had I seen such ugly ones in all the land of Egypt. [20] The thin and ugly cows ate up the first seven fat cows, [21] but when they had eaten them no one would have known that they had done so, for they were still as ugly as before. Then I awoke. [22] I fell asleep a second time and I saw in my dream seven ears of grain, full and good, growing on one stalk, [23] and seven ears, withered, thin, and blighted by the east wind, sprouting after them; [24] and the thin ears swallowed up the seven good ears. But when I told it to the magicians, there was no one who could explain it to me.'
[960] Genesis 41:25-32 Then Joseph said to Pharaoh, 'Pharaoh's dreams are one and the same; God has revealed to Pharaoh what he is about to do. [26] The seven good cows are seven years, and the seven good ears are seven years; the dreams are one. [27] The seven lean and ugly cows that came up after them are seven years, as are the seven empty ears blighted by the east wind. They are seven years of famine. [28] It is as I told Pharaoh; God has shown to Pharaoh what he is about to do. [29] There will come seven years of great plenty throughout all the land of Egypt. [30] After them there will arise seven years of famine, and all the plenty will be forgotten in the land of Egypt; the famine will consume the land. [31] The plenty will no longer be known in the land because of the famine that will follow, for it will be very grievous. [32] And the doubling of Pharaoh's dream means that the thing is fixed by God, and God will shortly bring it about.

myself. Man's inner soul incites him to evil unless my Lord shows mercy. My Lord is much-forgiving, a Dispenser of Grace." [53]

The King said, "Bring him to me.[961] I will have him serve me personally."[962] When he had spoken with him, (the King) said, "(From) now on you will have our trust and favor."[963] [54] (Joseph) replied, "Put me in charge of the nations' store-houses. I will be a good and wise keeper."[964] [55] We established Joseph securely in that land to live wherever he wished.[965] We grant Our grace upon whomever We will, and We do not fail to reward those who do good. [56] In the eyes of those who believe and have always been mindful of Us, a reward in the life to come is a far greater good (than any reward in this world). [57]

(After some years,) Joseph's brothers came (to Egypt) and presented themselves before him,[966] and he knew them (at once), but they did not recognize him.[967] [58] When he had provided them with their provisions,[968] he said, "(When you come here next,) bring me the brother of yours from your father's side. Have you not seen me giving generous measure and being the best of hosts?[969] [59] If you do not bring him to me, you will never again receive a single

• • •

[961] Genesis 41:14 Then Pharaoh sent for Joseph, and he was hurriedly brought out of the dungeon. When he had shaved himself and changed his clothes, he came in before Pharaoh.

[962] Genesis 41:46 Joseph was thirty years old when he entered the service of Pharaoh king of Egypt. And Joseph went out from the presence of Pharaoh, and went through all the land of Egypt.

[963] Genesis 41:40-44 You shall be over my house, and all my people shall order themselves as you command; only with regard to the throne will I be greater than you.' [41] And Pharaoh said to Joseph, 'See, I have set you over all the land of Egypt.' [42] Removing his signet ring from his hand, Pharaoh put it on Joseph's hand; he arrayed him in garments of fine linen, and put a gold chain around his neck. [43] He had him ride in the chariot of his second-in-command; and they cried out in front of him, 'Bow the knee!' Thus he set him over all the land of Egypt. [44] Moreover, Pharaoh said to Joseph, 'I am Pharaoh, and without your consent no one shall lift up hand or foot in all the land of Egypt.'

[964] Genesis 41:33-36 Now therefore let Pharaoh select a man who is discerning and wise, and set him over the land of Egypt. Let Pharaoh proceed to appoint overseers over the land, and take one-fifth of the produce of the land of Egypt during the seven plenteous years. Let them gather all the food of these good years that are coming, and lay up grain under the authority of Pharaoh for food in the cities, and let them keep it. That food shall be a reserve for the land against the seven years of famine that are to befall the land of Egypt, so that the land may not perish through the famine.

[965] Genesis 41:40 You shall be over my house, and all my people shall order themselves as you command; only with regard to the throne will I be greater than you.'

[966] Genesis 42:3-6 So ten of Joseph's brothers went down to buy grain in Egypt. [4] But Jacob did not send Joseph's brother Benjamin with his brothers, for he feared that harm might come to him. [5] Thus the sons of Israel were among the other people who came to buy grain, for the famine had reached the land of Canaan. [6] Now Joseph was governor over the land; it was he who sold to all the people of the land. And Joseph's brothers came and bowed themselves before him with their faces to the ground.

[967] Genesis 42:7-8 When Joseph saw his brothers, he recognized them, but he treated them like strangers and spoke harshly to them. 'Where do you come from?' he said. They said, 'From the land of Canaan, to buy food.' [8] Although Joseph had recognized his brothers, they did not recognize him.

[968] Genesis 42:25 Joseph then gave orders to fill their bags with grain, to return every man's money to his sack, and to give them provisions for their journey. This was done for them.

[969] Genesis 42:25-27 Joseph then gave orders to fill their bags with grain, to return every man's money to his sack, and to give them provisions for their journey. This was done for them. They loaded their donkeys with their grain, and departed. When one of them opened his sack to give his donkey fodder at the lodging-place, he saw his money at the top of the sack.

measure (of grain) from me, nor will you (be allowed to) come near me."[970] [(60)]
They answered, "We will try to persuade his father to part with him and We will
do (our best)." [(61)] (Joseph) said to his servants, "Place their merchandise in their
camel-packs, so that they may recognize them when they go back to their family,
and be eager to return. [(62)]

When they returned to their father, (Joseph's brothers) said, "Father, all
grain will be withheld from us[971] (in the future unless we bring Benjamin with
us). Send our brother with us so that we may be given another measure. We will
guard him carefully." [(63)] (Jacob) replied, "Will I trust you with him in the same
way I trusted you with his brother[972] (Joseph) before? No, but God's guardianship
is better[973] (than yours). He is the most Merciful to [974] those who show mercy."
[(64)] When they opened their packs, they discovered that their merchandise had
been returned to them, (and) they said, "Father, what more could we desire?
Here is our merchandise; it has been returned to us. (If you send Benjamin with
us,) We will (again) be able to bring food for our family, and will guard our
brother (well), and receive an additional camel-load of grain[975] - an extra measure
so easily achieved." [(65)] (Jacob) said, "I will not send him with you until you give
me a solemn pledge, before God, that you will bring him back to me, unless you
are overwhelmed (by enemies)." When they gave him their solemn pledge,
(Jacob) said, "God is witness to everything we say." [976] [(66)] He added, "My sons,

• • •

[970] Genesis 42:15-20 Here is how you shall be tested: as Pharaoh lives, you shall not leave this place unless
your youngest brother comes here! [16] Let one of you go and bring your brother, while the rest of you
remain in prison, in order that your words may be tested, whether there is truth in you; or else, a Pharaoh
lives, surely you are spies," [17] And he put them all together in prison for three days. [18] On the third day
Joseph said to them, "Do this and you will live, for I fear God: [19] if you are honest men, let one of your
brothers stay here where you are imprisoned. The rest of you shall go and carry grain for the famine of
your households, [20] and bring your youngest brother to me. Thus your words will be verified, and you shall
not die." And they agreed to do so.

[971] Genesis 43:3-5 But Judah said to him, 'The man solemnly warned us, saying, "You shall not see my face
unless your brother is with you." If you will send our brother with us, we will go down and buy you
food; but if you will not send him, we will not go down, for the man said to us, "You shall not see my face,
unless your brother is with you."'

[972] Genesis 42:36 And their father Jacob said to them, 'I am the one you have bereaved of children: Joseph
is no more, and Simeon is no more, and now you would take Benjamin. All this has happened to me!'

[973] Genesis 43:13, 14 Take your brother also, and be on your way again to the man; may God
Almighty grant you mercy before the man, so that he may send back your other brother and Benjamin. As
for me, if I am bereaved of my children, I am bereaved.'

[974] Psalm 116:5 Gracious is the Lord, and righteous; Yes, our God is compassionate. Luke 6:36 Be merciful,
just as your Father is merciful.

[975] Genesis 43:4-10 If you will send our brother with us, we will go down and buy you food; but if you will
not send him, we will not go down, for the man said to us, "You shall not see my face, unless your brother
is with you."' Israel said, 'Why did you treat me so badly as to tell the man that you had another
brother?' They replied, 'The man questioned us carefully about ourselves and our kindred, saying, "Is your
father still alive? Have you another brother?" What we told him was in answer to these questions. Could
we in any way know that he would say, "Bring your brother down"?' Then Judah said to his father Israel,
'Send the boy with me, and let us be on our way, so that we may live and not die—you and we and also
our little ones. I myself will be surety for him; you can hold me accountable for him. If I do not bring him
back to you and set him before you, then let me bear the blame for ever. If we had not delayed, we would
now have returned twice.'

[976] Genesis 43:8-9 Then Judah said to his father Israel, 'Send the boy with me, and let us be on our way,
so that we may live and not die—you and we and also our little ones. [9] I myself will be surety for him; you
can hold me accountable for him. If I do not bring him back to you and set him before you, then let me
bear the blame for ever.

do not enter (the town) through one gate, but enter through different gates. I cannot help you against the will of God. Judgment (as to what is to happen) rests with none but God. I have placed my trust in Him.[977] Everyone who has trust (in His existence) must place their trust in Him alone." [(67)] Although they entered (the town) in the way their father had told them,[978] it did not help them against the will of God, it merely satisfied a wish of Jacob's (to protect them). He knew well what We had taught him, though most people do not. [(68)]

When (the sons of Jacob) presented themselves before Joseph, he drew his brother (Benjamin)[979] to himself, saying (to him in secret), "I am your brother, so do not be saddened by their past actions." [(69)] (Later,) when he had provided them with their provisions, he placed the (king's) drinking-cup in his brother's camel-pack.[980] As (they were leaving the town,) a watchman called out, "People of the caravan, you are thieves."[981] [(70)] Turning towards the man and his companions, the brothers asked, "What is it that you are missing?" [(71)] They answered, "We are missing the King's cup[982] and he who produces it will receive a camel-load (of grain as a reward. I pledge myself to this (promise)." [(72)] (The brothers) said, "By God, you must know that We have not come to commit corrupt deeds in this land and that We have not been stealing."[983] [(73)] (The Egyptians) said, "What will be the penalty of this (deed) If you are (proved to be) liars?" [(74)] (The brothers) replied, "The penalty will be (the enslavement of) the person in whose bag the cup is found:[984] this is how we punish wrongdoers." [(75)] (They were brought before Joseph to be searched, and) he began with the bags of his half-brothers[985] before the bag of his brother (Benjamin). In the end he produced the drinking cup out of his brother's bag. In this way We schemed on Joseph's behalf—if God had not so willed, he could not have detained his brother as a penalty under the king's law. We raise the rank of whomever We will, but,

• • •

[977] Genesis 43:14 may God Almighty grant you mercy before the man, so that he may send back your other brother and Benjamin. As for me, if I am bereaved of my children, I am bereaved.

[978] Genesis 43:15 So the men took the present, and they took double the money with them, as well as Benjamin. Then they went on their way down to Egypt, and stood before Joseph.

[979] Genesis 43:16, 29 When Joseph saw Benjamin with them, he said to the steward of his house, 'Bring the men into the house, and slaughter an animal and make ready, for the men are to dine with me at noon.' 29 Then he looked up and saw his brother Benjamin, his mother's son, and said, 'Is this your youngest brother, of whom you spoke to me? God be gracious to you, my son!'

[980] Genesis 44:2 Put my cup, the silver cup, in the top of the sack of the youngest, with his money for the grain.' And he did as Joseph told him.

[981] Genesis 44:4-6 When they had gone only a short distance from the city, Joseph said to his steward, 'Go, follow after the men; and when you overtake them, say to them, "Why have you returned evil for good? Why have you stolen my silver cup? Is it not from this that my Lord drinks? Does he not indeed use it for divination? You have done wrong in doing this." 'When he overtook them, he repeated these words to them.

[982] Genesis 44:5 Is it not from this that my Lord drinks? Does he not indeed use it for divination? You have done wrong in doing this

[983] Genesis 44:7-8 They said to him, 'Why does my Lord speak such words as these? Far be it from your servants that they should do such a thing! Look, the money that we found at the top of our sacks, we brought back to you from the land of Canaan; why then would we steal silver or gold from your Lord's house?

[984] Genesis 44:9 Should it be found with any one of your servants, let him die; moreover, the rest of us will become my Lord's slaves.'

[985] Genesis 44:12 He searched, beginning with the eldest and ending with the youngest; and the cup was found in Benjamin's sack.

above everyone who is endowed with knowledge, there is One who knows everything. [76]

(As soon as the cup was produced from Benjamin's bag, the brothers) said, "If he is a thief, then his brother was a thief before him." Joseph said to himself, without revealing his thought to them, "You are far worse in this respect, and God is fully aware of what you are saying." [986] [77] They said, "Mighty governor, he has a father who is a very old man. Therefore, detain one of us instead. [987] We can see that you are a very good man." [78] (Joseph) answered, "May God preserve us from (the sin of) detaining anyone other than the person on whom we found our property; that would be unjust of us." [988] [79] When they lost all hope of (persuading) him, they withdrew to take counsel (among themselves). The eldest of them said, "Do not you remember that your father took a solemn pledge from you before God, and how before that you failed with regards to Joseph? I will not depart from this land until my father gives me leave, or God passes judgment in my favor. He is the best of all judges. [80] (As for you others,) return to your father and say, "Father, your son has stolen (the king's cup). We can tell you only what we saw. How could we guard against the unforeseen? [81] Ask in the town we were in (at the time), and the people of the caravan that we travelled with, and (you will find that) we are telling the truth." [82]

(When they returned to their father and told him what had happened,) he said, "No, your souls have enticed you to such a (terrible) thing. (As for me,) patience in hard times is most godly. [989]Perhaps God will bring them all (back) to me. All-Knowing, All-Wise." [83] He turned away from them and said, "Alas for Joseph," and his eyes clouded over with grief and he was filled with sorrow. [990] [84] (His sons) said, "By God. You will never stop remembering Joseph until you are broken in body and spirit, or are dead." [85] He answered, "It is only to God that I complain of my deep grief and sorrow. I know from God something that you do not know. [86] My sons, go and try to obtain some news of Joseph and his brother, and do not lose hope of God's mercy. Only the unbelievers lose hope of God's life-giving mercy." [87]

(The sons of Jacob went back to Egypt and to Joseph), and, when they presented themselves before him, they said, "Mighty governor, hardship has afflicted us and our family, and we have brought only a little merchandise, but give us full measure (of grain) and be charitable to us. God rewards those who give in charity." [88] He replied, "Do you remember what you did to Joseph and his brother when you were still ignorant?" [89] They said, "Could it be that you

•   •   •

[986] Genesis 44:15-16 Joseph said to them, 'What deed is this that you have done? Do you not know that one such as I can practice divination?' And Judah said, 'What can we say to my Lord? What can we speak? How can we clear ourselves? God has found out the guilt of your servants; here we are then, my Lord's slaves, both we and also the one in whose possession the cup has been found.'

[987] Genesis 44:33Now therefore, please let your servant remain as a slave to my Lord in place of the boy; and let the boy go back with his brothers

[988]Genesis 44:17 But he said, 'Far be it from me that I should do so! Only the one in whose possession the cup was found shall be my slave; but as for you, go up in peace to your father.'

[989] Galatians 5:22 By contrast, the fruit of the Spirit is love, joy, peace, patience, kindness, generosity, faithfulness,

[990] Genesis 42:36 And their father Jacob said to them, 'I am the one you have bereaved of children: Joseph is no more, and Simeon is no more, and now you would take Benjamin. All this has happened to me!'

are Joseph?" He said, "I am Joseph, [991] and this is my brother. God has been gracious to us. If one is mindful of Him and patient in hard times, God does not allow the reward of those who do good to be lost." [(90)] (The brothers) said, "By God. God has certainly raised you above us and we were sinners." [(91)] He said, "No blame will be uttered today against you.[992] May God forgive you for your sins.[993] He is the Most Merciful[994] of those who are merciful. [(92)] (Now) take this shirt of mine and lay it over my father's face and he will recover his sight. Then come (back) to me with all of your family."[995] [(93)]

As soon as the caravan (with which Jacob's sons were travelling) was on its way, their father said (to the people around him), "You may think I am senile, but I can smell Joseph." [(94)] They answered, "By God, you are still lost in that old illusion of yours." [(95)] But when the bearer of good news came (with Joseph's shirt), he laid it over his face, and he regained his sight[996] and said, "Did I not tell you, 'I know, from God, something that you do not know'?" [(96)] (His sons) answered, "Father, ask God to forgive us our sins. We were sinners." [(97)] He said, "I will ask my Lord to forgive you. He alone is truly forgiving, a true Purveyor of Mercy." [(98)]

When they (all arrived in Egypt and) presented themselves before Joseph, he drew his parent to him[997], saying, "Enter Egypt, if God wills, you will be secure."[998] [(99)] He raised his parents to the highest place of honor, and they (all) fell down before him, bowing. (Joseph) said, "My father, this is the real meaning of my dream long ago, which my Lord has made come true. He was good to me

• • •

[991] Genesis 45:2-4 And he wept so loudly that the Egyptians heard it, and the household of Pharaoh heard it. Joseph said to his brothers, 'I am Joseph. Is my father still alive?' But his brothers could not answer him, so dismayed were they at his presence. Then Joseph said to his brothers, 'Come closer to me.' And they came closer. He said, 'I am your brother Joseph, whom you sold into Egypt.

[992] Genesis 50:20 Even though you intended to do harm to me, God intended it for good, in order to preserve a numerous people, as he is doing today.

[993] Genesis 45:7-8 God sent me before you to preserve for you a remnant on earth, and to keep alive for you many survivors. So it was not you who sent me here, but God; he has made me a father to Pharaoh, and Lord of all his house and ruler over all the land of Egypt.

[994] Psalm 145:8 The Lord is gracious and merciful; Slow to anger and great in loving kindness.

[995] Genesis 45:18-19 Take your father and your households and come to me, so that I may give you the best of the land of Egypt, and you may enjoy the fat of the land." You are further charged to say, "Do this: take wagons from the land of Egypt for your little ones and for your wives, and bring your father, and come.

[996] Genesis 45:27 But when they told him all the words of Joseph that he had said to them, and when he saw the wagons that Joseph had sent to carry him, the spirit of their father Jacob revived.

[997] Genesis 46:29, 47:12 Joseph made ready his chariot and went up to meet his father Israel in Goshen. He presented himself to him, fell on his neck, and wept on his neck a good while. And Joseph provided his father, his brothers, and all his father's household with food, according to the number of their dependents.

[998] Genesis 47:6-11 The land of Egypt is before you; settle your father and your brothers in the best part of the land; let them live in the land of Goshen; and if you know that there are capable men among them, put them in charge of my livestock.' Then Joseph brought in his father Jacob, and presented him before Pharaoh, and Jacob blessed Pharaoh. Pharaoh said to Jacob, 'How many are the years of your life?' Jacob said to Pharaoh, 'The years of my earthly sojourn are one hundred and thirty; few and hard have been the years of my life. They do not compare with the years of the life of my ancestors during their long sojourn.' Then Jacob blessed Pharaoh, and went out from the presence of Pharaoh. Joseph settled his father and his brothers, and granted them a holding in the land of Egypt, in the best part of the land, in the land of Ramses, as Pharaoh had instructed.

when He freed me from the prison,[999] and (when) He brought you (all to me) from the desert after Satan sowed discord between me and my brothers.[1000] My Lord is most subtle in achieving whatever He wills. He alone is All-Knowing, All-Wise. [100] "My Lord, you have given me power, and have imparted to me some knowledge about the interpretation of dreams. Originator of the heavens and the earth,[1001] You are my protector in this world and in the life to come. Let me die as one who has surrendered himself to you, and allow me to join the righteous." [101]

(Prophet), We now reveal to you this account of something that was beyond your knowledge. You were not with Joseph's brothers when they decided what they were going to do and schemed (against him). [102] However eager you may be, most people will not believe (in this revelation), [103] although you do not ask them for any reward for (reciting) it. It is (God's) reminder to all people. [104] How many signs are there in the heavens and on earth which they pass by and on which they turn their backs? [105] Most of them do not even believe in God without associating others with Him. [106] Do they have assurances that the all-enveloping punishment of God's will evade them, or that the Last Hour [1002] will not come upon them suddenly, when they least expect it? [1003] [107]

(Prophet), Say, "This is my way: I and all who follow me call (people) to God based on the clear insight. May God be exalted in His glory! [1004] I am not one of those who associate others with Him." [108] (Even) before your time, We never sent (as Our Messengers) anyone except (mortal) men, whom We inspired, (and whom We always chose) from among the people of the (very) communities (to whom the message was to be brought). Have the (unbelievers) not travelled through the land and seen the end of those who went before them? Those who are mindful of God prefer the life to come. Do you (people) not use your reason? [109] (All the earlier messengers had to suffer persecution for a long time,) but, at last, when those messengers had lost all hope and saw themselves branded as liars, Our help came to them. We saved whomever We pleased, but Our punishment will not be turned away from those who force others to reject God's messages. [110] In the stories of these men, there is a lesson for those who understand. (As for this Qur'an), it could not possibly be a discourse invented (by the Prophet). No, it is a confirmation of what is available to him from prior

• • •

[999] Genesis 41:14 Then Pharaoh sent for Joseph, and he was hurriedly brought out of the dungeon. When he had shaved himself and changed his clothes, he came in before Pharaoh.

[1000] Genesis 37:18-20 They saw him from a distance, and before he came near to them, they conspired to kill him. They said to one another, 'Here comes this dreamer. Come now, let us kill him and throw him into one of the pits; then we shall say that a wild animal has devoured him, and we shall see what will become of his dreams.'

[1001] Genesis 1:1 In the beginning when God created the heavens and the earth.
Isaiah 45:18 For thus says the Lord, who created the heavens (He is the God who formed the earth and made it, He established it *and* did not create it a waste place, *but* formed it to be inhabited), "I am the Lord, and there is none else.

[1002] Revelation 14:7 He said in a loud voice, 'Fear God and give him glory, for the hour of his judgment has come; and worship him who made heaven and earth, the sea and the springs of water.'

[1003] Revelation 3:3 Remember then what you received and heard; obey it, and repent. If you do not wake up, I will come like a thief, and you will not know at what hour I will come to you.

[1004] Exodus 15:11 "Who is like you, O Lord, among the gods? Who is like you, majestic in holiness, awesome in splendor, doing wonders?

revelations, clearly spelling out everything, and (offering) guidance and mercy to people who will believe. [111]

CHAPTER THIRTEEN

AR-RA'D
THE THUNDER

THE **MEDINA** PERIOD

In the name of God, the Merciful-to-all, the Mercy Giver:

Alif Lam Meem Ra, These are the verses of the Book, and what has been sent down to you from your Lord is the Truth, yet most people will not believe. [01] It is God Who has raised the heavens [1004] without any visible supports and is established on the throne of His majesty. [1005] He has made the sun and the moon subservient (to His laws), each ordained by Him to run its course for an appointed time. [1006] He governs everything that exists. He clearly explains these messages, so that you can be sure that you are destined to meet your Lord (on Judgment Day). [02] He has spread [1007] the earth wide, placed firm mountains and running waters on it, [1008] and created two of every kind of fruit, [1009] (and He) causes the night to cover the day. [1010] Surely there are messages in all of this for People to contemplate. [1011] [03] There are, on earth, neighboring plots, gardens of vineyards, crops, date palm trees sharing the same root or alone. They are all watered with

• • •

[1004] Isaiah 40:22, "It is he who sits above the circle of the earth, and its inhabitants are like grasshoppers . . . who stretches out the heavens like a curtain, and spreads them like a tent to live in . . ."

[1005] Psalm 123:1, "To you I lift up my eyes, O you who are enthroned in the heavens!"

[1006] Genesis 1:14, "And God said, 'Let there be lights in the dome of the sky to separate the day from the night; and let them be for signs and for seasons and for days and years . . .'"

[1007] Isaiah 44:24, "Thus says the Lord, your Redeemer, who formed you in the womb: I am the Lord, who made all things, who alone stretched out the heavens, who by myself spread out the earth . . ."

[1008] Isaiah 41:18, "I will open rivers on the bare heights, and fountains in the midst of the valleys; I will make the wilderness a pool of water, and the dry land springs of water."

[1009] the reference may be to male and female plants

[1010] Psalm 19:2, 74:16, "Day to day pours forth speech, and night to night declares knowledge. 74:16 Yours is the day, yours also the night; you established the luminaries and the sun." Amos 5:8. "The one who made the Pleiades and Orion, and turns deep darkness into the morning, and darkens the day into night, who calls for the waters of the sea, and pours them out on the surface of the earth, the Lord is his name . . ."

[1011] Psalm 119:15-18 I will meditate on your precepts, and fix my eyes on your ways. [16] I will delight in your statutes; I will not forget your word. [17] Deal bountifully with your servant, so that I may live and observe your word. [18] Open my eyes, so that I may behold wondrous things out of your law.

the same water, yet We make some better tasting than others. Surely there are messages in all of this for people who use their reason [04]

And if you are astonished (at God's creation), then it is (equally) astonishing to hear them (doubters) say, "Once we are dust, will we (really) be created anew?" These are the ones who have denied the truth about their Lord, and who will have shackles around their necks, and are in the fire, where they will reside eternally. [05] They (the unbelievers) challenge you (Prophet), to hasten evil[1012] (in preference to) good, even though (they should know that) examples of punishments have (readily) occurred before. Your Lord is full of forgiveness [1013] for people in spite of their wrongdoing; nonetheless, your Lord is (also) severe in retribution. [06] And the unbelievers say, "Why has a sign [1014] not been sent down to him from his Lord?" You (Prophet) are there only to give warning, and for every people there has been a guide. [1015] [07]

God knows what every female bears and what the wombs carry for a shorter or a longer term. And everything with Him has a due measure. [08] (He is) Knower of all that is beyond human's perception, as well as all that can be witnessed by humans, the Grand, the Exalted. [09] It is the same (to Him) whether one among you will conceal (his) speech or speak openly, and whether one is hidden by night or conspicuous (among others) by day. [10] Each (person) has (angels arrayed) before and behind him to protect him by God's command. God does not change the condition of a people unless they change what is in themselves.[1016] And when God intends ill for a people, there is no avoiding it. Apart from Him, they have no protector. [11] It is He Who shows you lightning, (causing) fear and hope, and (Who) generates the heavy clouds.[1017] [12] The thunder glorifies and praises Him [1018] as do the angels in awe of Him. He sends thunderbolts and strikes therewith whom He wills while they stubbornly argue about God,[1019] while He alone has the power to do whatever He wills. [13] True prayer is to Him alone, and those who call upon anyone besides Him receive no response. (They are) like one who stretches his hands toward water hoping for it to reach his mouth, but it will not reach him. And the prayers of the unbelievers are simply lost. [14] Everything in

• • •

[1012] Meaning the punishment promised to the idol worshipers who reject the message to worship God only. See Commentary (Tafseer) by Ibn Katheer, section four page 433.
https://archive.org/search.php?query=subject%3A%22Tafsir+Ibn+Kathir+%2810+Volumes%29+-+alhamdulillah-library.blogspot.in.pdf%22

[1013] Psalm 65:3, "When deeds of iniquity overwhelm us, you forgive our transgressions." Isaiah 43:25.

[1014] Luke 11:16, "Others, to test him, kept demanding from him a sign from heaven." Mark 8:11, "The Pharisees came and began to argue with him, asking him for a sign from heaven, to test him." Matthew 16:1, "The Pharisees and Sadducees came, and to test Jesus they asked him to show them a sign from heaven."

[1015] God said in the Qur'an that He will not punish any people unless He sends a messenger to call these people to God. "We would never punish unless we had first sent a messenger." (17:15) There are twenty five prophets mentioned in the Qur'an out of thousands sent by God to various people at various times.

[1016] John 8:47 Whoever belongs to God hears what God says. The reason you do not hear is that you do not belong to God."

[1017] Jeremiah 10:13, "When he utters his voice, there is a tumult of waters in the heavens, and he makes the mist rise from the ends of the earth. He makes lightnings for the rain, and he brings out the wind from his storehouses."

[1018] Job 37:2, "Listen, listen to the thunder of his voice and the rumbling that comes from his mouth."

[1019] Isaiah 29:6, " . . . you will be visited by the Lord of hosts with thunder and earthquake and great noise, with whirlwind and tempest, and the flame of a devouring fire."

heaven and on earth submits to God, willingly or unwillingly, as do their shadows in the mornings and the evenings. [15]

Say, "Who is Lord of the heavens and earth?" Say, "God." Say, "Why do you then take protectors besides Him, who can neither benefit nor harm even themselves?" Say, "Are the blind the same as those who see? Or is ignorance equivalent to enlightenment?" Or, do they assign to God partners who have created a creation like His, so that the two creations appear similar to them? Say, "God is the Creator of all things, and He is the One, the All-Compelling." [1020] [16] He sends rain down from the sky and watercourses flow according to their capacity, and the torrent carries rising foam—like the foam that appears when people melt metal with fire to make ornaments or utensils. Thus God depicts Truth and falsehood. As for the foam, it vanishes, (being) cast off, but that which benefits human beings remains behind. In this way God presents analogies. [17] Those who respond to their Lord will (have) the best (reward), but those who do not respond to Him—(even) if they had all that is in the earth, and as much again—would give it to ransom themselves. They have terribly miscalculated; Hell will be their dwelling, a most evil place. [18]

Can the one who knows that what has been revealed to you from your Lord is the Truth be like one who is blind? Only people who are endowed with insight will keep this in mind. [19] Those who fulfill their commitment to God and do not break the covenant; [20] and those who join what God has ordered to be joined, and are in awe of their Lord, and fear a dire Reckoning; [21] and those who are patient, seeking the pleasure of their Lord, and establish prayer, and spend (both) secretly and publicly from what We have provided for them, and prevent evil with good[1021] - these will have the best reward, the Ultimate (Heavenly) Home, [22] the Gardens of Eden. Which they will enter with whoever was righteous among their forefathers, their spouses, and their descendants. The angels will go to them from every gate, (saying), [23] "Peace be upon you for what you patiently endured.[1022] How excellent is your Ultimate Home!" [24] But those who break the covenant of God after agreeing to it, and sever that which God has ordered to be joined, and spread corruption on earth—for them is the curse, and they will have the Worst Home (in Hell). [25] God extends or restricts sustenance to whom He wills. They rejoice in the life of this world, but it is simply a passing pleasure compared to the Hereafter. [26]

And the unbelievers say, "Why has a sign not been sent down to him from his Lord?" Say, "God lets go astray him who wills as He guides to Himself whoever turns (to Him). [1023][27] Those who have believed and whose hearts are assured by

●　　●　　●

[1020] Isaiah 44:24, "Thus says the Lord, your Redeemer, who formed you in the womb: I am the Lord, who made all things, who alone stretched out the heavens, who by myself spread out the earth . . . "

[1021] Romans 12:21, "Do not be overcome by evil, but overcome evil with good." 1 Peter 4:8, "Above all, maintain constant love for one another, for love covers a multitude of sins."

[1022] James 1:12, "Blessed is anyone who endures temptation. Such a one has stood the test and will receive the crown of life that the Lord has promised to those who love him."

[1023] 2 Chronicles 7:14 if my people who are called by my name humble themselves, pray, seek my face, and turn from their wicked ways, then I will hear from heaven, and will forgive their sin and heal their land.

the remembrance of God. Truly, hearts find peace only in the remembrance of God." [1024] [28] Those who have believed and done righteous deeds—joy and a blessed (final) return will await them. [1025] [29] Thus, We have sent you (Prophet) into a community that rejects the Merciful-to-all, to recite to them what We have revealed to you, (as we have sent other prophets) before to other communities who have come and gone. Say, "He (The Merciful) [1026] is my Lord; there is no God except Him. I put my trust in Him, and to Him I will return." [1027] [30] Even if there were a Qur'an which moved mountains or shattered the earth or the dead made to speak (they would not believe). In fact, God alone decides about all matters. Do the believers not know that, had God willed, He would have guided all human beings? As for the unbelievers—calamity will not cease to strike them for [1028] what they have done, nor (cease) to descend near their home(s), until the promise of God is fulfilled. God does not fail to keep His promise. [31] Messengers before you were ridiculed. I gave the unbelievers a little more time, and then I seized them. [1029] How terrible was My punishment. [32]

Is He who cares for every soul, according to what It deserves, (like any other?) And yet, they still associate partners to Him. Say, "Name them. Do you presume to tell Him something that He does not already know about the earth, or is this an empty display of words?" Rather, the unbelievers' ploy has been made to seem attractive to them, and so they have been diverted from the right path. Whomever God allows to stray, there will be no guide for him. [33] For them will be punishment in the life of (this) world, but the punishment of the Hereafter is more severe. And they will not have any protector from God. [1030] [34]

The likeness of Paradise, which the righteous have been promised: rivers flow through it, [1031] (and its) fruit and shade are everlasting. Such is the reward for the righteous, and the reward for the unbelievers is the Fire. [1032] [35] Those to whom We gave the Book rejoice at what has been sent down to you, but some of the opposing factions deny part of it. Say, "I have been commanded to worship God alone and not to associate anything with Him. To Him I invite others, and to Him

• • •

[1024] John 14:27, "Peace I leave with you; my peace I give to you. I do not give to you as the world gives. Do not let your hearts be troubled, and do not let them be afraid."

[1025] Matthew 5:6 Blessed are those who hunger and thirst for righteousness, for they will be filled.

[1026] Psalm 116:5 Gracious is the Lord, and righteous; our God is merciful.

[1027] Psalm 56:3-4, ". . . when I am afraid, I put my trust in you. [4] In God, whose word I praise, in God I trust; I am not afraid; what flesh do to me?"

[1028] Romans 9:16 – 18, "So it depends not on human will or exertion, but on God who shows mercy. For the scripture says to Pharaoh, 'I have raised you up for the very purpose of showing my power in you, so that my name may be proclaimed in all the earth.' So then he has mercy on whomsoever he chooses, and he hardens the heart of whomsoever he chooses."

[1029] Isaiah 26:21 For the Lord comes out from his place to punish the inhabitants of the earth for their iniquity;

[1030] Revelation 14:11, 20:10, "And the smoke of their torment goes up for ever and ever. There is no rest day or night for those who worship the beast and its image and for anyone who receives the mark of its name.' 20:10 And the devil who had deceived them was thrown into the lake of fire and sulphur, where the beast and the false prophet were, and they will be tormented day and night for ever and ever."

[1031] Revelation 22:1, "Then the angel showed me the river of the water of life, bright as crystal, flowing from the throne of God."

[1032] Matthew 25:41-43, "Then he will say to those at his left hand, 'You that are accursed, depart from me into the eternal fire prepared for the devil and his angels; [42] for I was hungry and you gave me no food, I was thirsty and you gave me nothing to drink, [43] I was a stranger and you did not welcome me, naked and you did not give me clothing, sick and in prison and you did not visit me.'"

I shall return." [36] And thus We have revealed it as an Arabic[1033] code of law. And if you should follow (your people's) whims and desires after knowledge has come to you, you would not have any ally or any protector from God. [37] We have already sent messengers before you and assigned to them wives and descendants. No messenger came with a sign except by permission of God. For every time period there has been a (suitable) revelation. [38] God eliminates or confirms (His earlier revelations) (as) He wills, and with Him is the source of all revelation. [39]

And whether We show you part of what We promise them (those who reject God) or cause you to die (before that time), your only responsibility is to deliver the message. Ours is (to deliver) the reckoning. [40] Have they not seen how We deal with the earth, eroding it at its extremities? God decides;[1034] no one can modify His decision. He is swift in calling to account. [41] And those (who lived) before them (your people who rejects God) schemed (against God's messengers), but the ultimate scheme belongs to God. He knows what every soul earns, and the unbelievers will soon know to whom the future belongs. [42] And those who have denied the truth say, "You are not a messenger." Say, "God is a sufficient Witness between you and me, and so is anyone else who has knowledge of the Book." [43]

• • •

[1033] The word Arabic can refer to the language or to its linguistic meaning which is perfect without mistakes.

[1034] Genesis 16:5 Then Sarai said to Abram, 'May the wrong done to me be on you! I gave my slave-girl to your embrace, and when she saw that she had conceived, she looked on me with contempt. May the Lord judge between you and me!'

CHAPTER FOURTEEN

IBRAHEEM

THE PROPHET ABRAHAM

THE **MECCA** PERIOD

In the name of God, the Merciful-to-all, the Mercy Giver:

Alif Lam Ra, a Book which We have sent down to you in order that you might, with your Lord's permission, bring people out of the depths of dark ignorance into enlightenment,[1035] onto the path that leads to the Almighty, the Praiseworthy[1036] (01) God, to Whom all that is in the heavens and all that is on earth belongs.[1037] And woe to the unbelievers for a severe punishment[1038] (02) awaits those who love the life of this world, preferring it to the life to come. They turn others away from the path[1039] of God and make it seem irrelevant. These people have gone far astray. (03) Every messenger whom We have sent used his own people's language, so that he might make (the Truth) clear to them, but God lets whoever wants to stray, go astray, and guides whoever wants (to be guided).[1040] He alone is Almighty, and The Wise. (04)

· · ·

[1035] Isaiah 9:2, The people who walked in darkness have seen a great light; those who lived in a land of deep darkness— on them light has shined. Colossians 1:13-14 He has rescued us from the power of darkness and transferred us into the kingdom of his beloved Son, in whom we have redemption, the forgiveness of sins.

[1036] 2 Samuel 22:4 I call upon the Lord, who is worthy to be praised, and I am saved from my enemies

[1037] Psalm 89:11, The heavens are yours, the earth also is yours; the world and all that is in it—you have founded them. Deuteronomy 10:14 Behold, to the Lord your God belong heaven and the highest heavens, the earth and all that is in it.

[1038] 2 Thessalonians 1:9 These will suffer the punishment of eternal destruction, separated from the presence of the Lord and from the glory of his might,

[1039] Matthew 23:13-15 "But woe to you, scribes and Pharisees, hypocrites, because you shut off the kingdom of heaven from people; for you do not enter in yourselves, nor do you allow those who are entering to go in. [14] Woe to you, scribes and Pharisees, hypocrites, because you devour widows' houses, and for a pretense you make long prayers; therefore you will receive greater condemnation.) [15] "Woe to you, scribes and Pharisees, hypocrites, because you travel around on sea and land to make one proselyte; and when he becomes one, you make him twice as much a son of hell as yourselves.

[1040] Romans 9:18 So then He has mercy on whom He desires, and He hardens whom He desires.

We sent Moses (Musa) with Our messages: "Lead your people out of the depths of dark ignorance into enlightenment,[1041] and remind them of the Days of God." In this there are messages for all who are patient and grateful. [(05)] Moses said to his people, "Remember the grace which God gave you when He saved you from Pharaoh's people who afflicted you with cruel suffering,[1042] and slaughtered your sons, and spared (only) your women,[1043] which was a severe test from your Lord. [(06)] (Remember the time) when your Lord promised, "If you are grateful, I will certainly give you more and more, but if you are ungrateful, My punishment[1044] will definitely be severe." [(07)] Moses added, "(even) If you, and whoever else lives on earth, (ever) deny the truth, God is rich beyond, worthy of all praise."[1045] [(08)]

Have you not heard of the stories of those who lived before you, the people of Noah, and of (the tribes of) Aad and Thamud, and of those who came after them, known only to God? A messenger came to them with all the evidence of the truth, but they covered their mouths with their hands and said, "We refuse to believe in the message with which you (claim to) have been entrusted, and we deeply suspect (the substance of) your call to us." [(09)] Their messengers answered, "Can there be any doubt about God, the Originator of the heavens and the earth?[1046] It is He who calls you, so that He may forgive you some of your sins and lets you enjoy your life until the appointed time."[1047] They said, "You are only mortal men like us. You want to turn us away from what our forefathers worshipped, well, then, bring us clear proof (that you are God's Messengers)." [(10)] Their messengers answered, "True, we are nothing but mortal men like you, but God favors whoever of His worshipers He chooses. It is not within our power to bring you proof, unless God permits it (so) let the believers place all of their trust in God.[1048] [(11)] How could we not place our trust in God, when it is He who has shown us our ways (to enlightenment). "We will be steadfast however much you harm us, for those who trust must place their trust in God."[1049] [(12)]

• • •

[1041] Exodus 3:10-12 So come, I will send you to Pharaoh to bring my people, the Israelites, out of Egypt.'
[11] But Moses said to God, 'Who am I that I should go to Pharaoh, and bring the Israelites out of Egypt?'
[12] He said, 'I will be with you; and this shall be the sign for you that it is I who sent you: when you have brought the people out of Egypt, you shall worship God on this mountain.'
[1042] Exodus 13:3 Moses said to the people, 'Remember this day on which you came out of Egypt, out of the house of slavery, because the Lord brought you out from there by strength of hand; no leavened bread shall be eaten.
[1043] Exodus 1:16 'When you act as midwives to the Hebrew women, and see them on the birthstool, if it is a boy, kill him; but if it is a girl, she shall live.'
[1044] 2 Thessalonians 1:9 These will suffer the punishment of eternal destruction, separated from the presence of the Lord and from the glory of his might,
[1045] Psalm 18:1-3 I love you, O Lord, my strength. [2] The Lord is my rock, my fortress, and my deliverer, my God, my rock in whom I take refuge, my shield, and the horn of my salvation, my stronghold. 3 I call upon the Lord, who is worthy to be praised; so I shall be saved from my enemies
[1046] Isaiah 45:18 For thus says the Lord, who created the heavens (he is God!), who formed the earth and made it (he established it; he did not create it a chaos, he formed it to be inhabited!): I am the Lord, and there is no other.
[1047] Psalm 91:16 With long life I will satisfy them, and show them my salvation.
[1048] Proverbs 3:5-6 Trust in the Lord with all your heart, and do not rely on your own insight. [6] In all your ways acknowledge him, and he will make straight your paths.
[1049] 1 Chronicles 4:10 Jabez called on the God of Israel, saying, "Oh that you would bless me and enlarge my border, and that your hand might be with me, and that you would keep me from hurt and harm!" And God granted what he asked.

The unbelievers said to their messengers, 'We will expel you from our land unless you return to our ways. But their Lord revealed to His Messengers, "We will destroy the unjust, [13] and We will let you dwell on earth (long) after they have passed away. This is (My promise) to all who are in awe of My presence, and stand in awe of My warning." [14] They prayed (to God for help) and each stubborn enemy of the truth failed, [15] with Hell awaiting him. (There) he will be made to drink the water of most bitter distress, [16] gulping it, little by little, but hardly able to swallow it. Death will creep in on him from every side, but he will not die, for more severe suffering lies ahead of him. [17] The example of those who insist on denying their Lord is that all their works are like ashes which blow about in a fierce wind on a stormy day:[1050] they have no power over anything they have gained. This is the farthest one can go astray. [18]

Are not you aware that God has created the heavens and the earth in accordance with Truth? He can, if He so wills, do away with you and bring forth a new creation:[1051] [19] That is not difficult for God.[1052] [20] All (people) will appear before God (on the Day of Judgment); the weak will say to those who had gloried in their arrogance, "We were your followers. Can you protect us from any of God's punishment?" They will say "If God had guided us, we would have guided you. It makes no difference now whether we rage or endure with patience: there is no escape for us." [1053] [21] And when everything had been decided, Satan will say: "God promised you the Truth. I also made promises to you, but I deceived [1054] you. I had no power at all over you, but I called you, and you responded to me. Hence, do not blame me, blame yourselves. I cannot be called to your aid, nor can you come to mine. I have (always) rejected[1055] the way you associated me with God." A grave suffering awaits all the unjust.[1056] [22] Those who believe and have done righteous deeds will be brought into Gardens through which running waters flow,[1057] where they will remain forever with their Lord's permission, and will be welcomed with the greeting, "Peace." [23]

Do you not see how God likens a good word to a good tree, firmly rooted, (reaching out) with its branches towards heaven, [24] yielding its fruit at all times [1058] by its Lord's permission? God gives such examples for people, so that they may reflect on them. [25] While the metaphor of a corrupt word is that of a rotten

• • •

[1050] Psalm 1:4 The wicked are not so, but are like chaff that the wind drives away.

[1051] Isaiah 65:17, 66:22 For I am about to create new heavens and a new earth; the former things shall not be remembered or come to mind. 66:22 For as the new heavens and the new earth, which I will make, shall remain before me, says the Lord, so shall your descendants and your name remain.

[1052] Luke 1:37 For nothing will be impossible with God.'

[1053] Romans 2:3 Do you imagine, whoever you are, that when you judge those who do such things and yet do them yourself, you will escape the judgment of God?

[1054] John 8:44 You are from your father the devil, and you choose to do your father's desires. He was a murderer from the beginning and does not stand in the truth, because there is no truth in him. When he lies, he speaks according to his own nature, for he is a liar and the father of lies.

[1055] James 2:19 You believe that God is one; you do well. Even the demons believe—and shudder.

[1056] 2 Thessalonians 1:9 These will suffer the punishment of eternal destruction, separated from the presence of the Lord and from the glory of his might,

[1057] Revelation 22:1-2 Then the angel showed me the river of the water of life, bright as crystal, flowing from the throne of God and of the Lamb through the middle of the street of the city. [2] On either side of the river is the tree of life with its twelve kinds of fruit, producing its fruit each month; and the leaves of the tree are for the healing of the nations.

[1058] Psalm 1:3, They are like trees planted by streams of water, which yield their fruit in its season, and their leaves do not wither. In all that they do, they prosper.

tree,[1059] uprooted from the face of the earth,[1060] unable to stand. [26] God gives steadfastness to those who believe[1061] through the unshakable word, both here and in the Hereafter. But He lets the unjust go astray:[1062] for God does whatever He wills.[1063] [27]

Do you not see those who, in exchange for God's favor, offer only ingratitude and make their people end up in the home of ruin, [28] Hell, where they will roast? What an evil place to be in. [29] They claimed that there are powers that could rival God, and so they strayed from His path. Say, "Enjoy yourselves, for your destination is the Fire." [30] Tell My worshipers who believe that they should perform the prayer and give secretly [1064] and openly, out of what We provide for them as sustenance. There will come a Day when there will be no bargaining [1065] and no friendship. [31]

It is God Who has created the heavens and the earth, and Who sends down water from the sky and brings forth fruit for your sustenance. He has made the ships useful to you, so that you may sail though the sea at His command and has made the rivers useful to you. [32] He has made the sun and the moon-- both of them constant in their courses-- useful to you and has made the night and the day useful to you. [33] He has given you some of everything for which you asked Him for. If you tried to count God's blessings, you could never do it. Indeed, humans are most persistent in wrongdoing and in their rejection of the truth [34]

Recall that Abraham said, "My Lord, make this land secure, and keep me and my children from ever worshipping idols[1066]- [35] because, my Lord, they[1067] have led my people astray. Hence, anyone who follows me is with me, but, for anyone who disobeys me, You are surely forgiving[1068] and Merciful-to-all."[1069] [36] Lord I have settled some of my children in an uncultivated valley,[1070] close to Your Sacred Sanctuary so that, oh our Lord, they might devote themselves to prayer.

• • •

[1059] Matthew 7:17-19 In the same way, every good tree bears good fruit, but the bad tree bears bad fruit. [18] A good tree cannot bear bad fruit, nor can a bad tree bear good fruit. [19] Every tree that does not bear good fruit is cut down and thrown into the fire.
[1060] Matthew 15:13 He answered, 'Every plant that my heavenly Father has not planted will be uprooted.
[1061] Galatians 3:9 For this reason, those who believe are blessed with Abraham who believed.
[1062] 2 Thessalonians 2:11 For this reason God sends them a powerful delusion, leading them to believe what is false,
[1063] Romans 9:18 So then He has mercy on whom He desires, and He hardens whom He desires.
[1064] Matthew 6:1-4 'Beware of practicing your piety before others in order to be seen by them; for then you have no reward from your Father in heaven. [2] 'So whenever you give alms, do not sound a trumpet before you, as the hypocrites do in the synagogues and in the streets, so that they may be praised by others. Truly I tell you, they have received their reward. [3] But when you give alms, do not let your left hand know what your right hand is doing, [4] so that your alms may be done in secret; and your Father who sees in secret will reward you.
[1065] 2 peter 3:7 But by the same word the present heavens and earth have been reserved for fire, being kept until the day of judgment and destruction of the godless.
[1066] Exodus 20:4-5: Thou shalt not make unto thee any graven image, or any likeness of any thing that is in heaven above, or that is in the earth beneath, or that is in the water under the earth. [5] You shall not bow down to them or worship them; for I the Lord your God am a jealous God,
[1067] 1 Corinthians 10:20 No, I imply that what pagans sacrifice, they sacrifice to demons and not to God. I do not want you to be partners with demons.
[1068] Psalm 65:3 When deeds of iniquity overwhelm us, you forgive our transgressions.
[1069] Luke 1:50 "And His merch is upon generation after generation toward those who fear Him.
[1070] Genesis 13:14-15 The Lord said to Abram, after Lot had separated from him, "Now lift up your eyes and look from the place where you are, northward and southward and eastward and westward; [15] for all the land which you see, I will give it to you and to your descendants forever.

Make some people's hearts drawn towards them, and provide them with sustenance, so that they may be grateful. [37] "Our Lord, You truly know all that we may hide (in our hearts), as well as all that we bring into the open: for nothing, on earth or in heaven, remains hidden from God.[1071] [38] "All praise is due to God, who has granted me Ishmael[1072] and Isaac[1073] in my old age.[1074] My Lord hears all prayer.[1075] [39] Lord, grant that I may perform prayer, and so may my children. "Lord accept my supplication [40] Grant Your forgiveness to me, and my parents, and all the believers, on the Day of Reckoning. [41]

Do not think (Prophet) that God is unaware of what the unjust do; He only gives them respite until the Day when eyes will stare in horror. [42] They run around confusedly, with their heads up, unable to look away, their hearts a gaping void.[1076] [43] Warn people of the Day when this suffering may befall them, and when the unjust will say, "Our Lord, grant us respite for a little more time, so that we might respond to Your call and follow the Messengers." (God will say,) "Did you not swear in the past that your power would have no end? [44] You have lived in the same places as those who wronged themselves, and it had become clear to you how We dealt with them and We gave you many examples." [45] They planned their schemes, but God was aware of their scheming, even when their schemes were such as to make mountains vanish. [46]

Do not ever think that God will fail to fulfill His promise[1077] to His Messengers: God is Almighty, Exactor of Revenge. [47] (It will be fulfilled) On the Day when the earth is changed[1078] to other than the earth, and the heavens too, and they all appear before God, the One, the All-Conquering. [48] For on that Day, you will see all those who force others to reject God's messages linked together in chains, [49] clothed in garments of tar, with fire veiling their faces. [50] (All will be judged on that Day,) so that God may reward every soul[1079] for what it earned: God is swift in His reckoning. [51]

This is a message to all people, so that they will be warned, and so they will know that He is One God. Let those of understanding be reminded. [52]

• • •

[1071] Psalm 69:5 O God, you know my folly; the wrongs I have done are not hidden from you. My frame was not hidden from you, when I was being made in secret, intricately woven in the depths of the earth.

[1072] Genesis 16:15 Hagar bore Abram a son; and Abram named his son, whom Hagar bore, Ishmael.

[1073] Genesis 21:3 Abraham gave the name Isaac to his son whom Sarah bore him.

[1074] Genesis 16:16, 21:5 Abram was eighty-six years old when Hagar bore him Ishmael. 21:5 Abraham was a hundred years old when his son Isaac was born to him.

[1075] Psalm 34:17 When the righteous cry for help, the Lord hears, and rescues them from all their troubles.

[1076] Isaiah 21:4 My mind reels, horror has appalled me; the twilight I longed for has been turned for me into trembling.

[1077] Hebrews 6:18 so that through two unchangeable things, in which it is impossible that God would prove false, we who have taken refuge might be strongly encouraged to seize the hope set before us.

[1078] Revelation 21:1 Then I saw a new heaven and a new earth; for the first heaven and the first earth had passed away, and the sea was no more

[1079] Revelation 22:12 'See, I am coming soon; my reward is with me, to repay according to everyone's work.

CHAPTER FIFTEEN

AL-HIIJR
THE ROCKY PLACE

THE **MECCA** PERIOD

In the name of God, the Merciful-to-all, the Mercy Giver:
Alif Lam Ra, these are the signs of the Book and a clear Qur'an. [01] Perhaps those who have rejected the truth will wish to submit themselves to God. [02] Let them eat and enjoy themselves[1080] and be preoccupied with (false) hope, for they will (one day) know.[1081] [03] We have never destroyed a town unless it had a known decree. [04] No nation can speed up (the end of) its time, nor defer it.[1082] [05] And (yet), they (who deny the truth) say, "You to whom the message has been sent down, you are crazy. [06] If you are honest, why do you not bring us angels?" [07] We do not send down the angels except in Truth and, (if We did so now, those who deny the truth)[1083] would have no reprieve [08] It is We who sent down this Reminder[1084] and We will preserve it.[1085] [09] We sent (messengers) before you, to earlier communities. [10] And every time a messenger came they mocked him.[1086] [11] In that way, We insert discord into the hearts of those who force others to reject Our messages. [12] They will not believe. This was what happened with those earlier people. [13] And (even) if We had opened a gate to the sky for them, and they had continued to ascend though it, [14] they would have said, "Our eyesight has only been befuddled," or, "We are under a spell." [15] We have placed constellations in the sky and have beautified it for the observers.[1087] [16] And We have secured it from every cursed satanic force. [17] Except for anyone who tries to eavesdropping (to learn the unknown)—he is

• • •

[1080] Matthew 24:37-38 For as the days of Noah were, so will be the coming of the Son of Man. [38] For as in those days before the flood they were eating and drinking, marrying and giving in marriage, until the day Noah entered the ark,
[1081] Ezekiel 6:14 I will stretch out my hand against them, and make the land desolate and waste, throughout all their settlements, from the wilderness to Riblah. Then they shall know that I am the Lord.
[1082] Acts 17:26 From one ancestor he made all nations to inhabit the whole earth, and he allotted the times of their existence and the boundaries of the places where they would live,
[1083] The truth here refers to God's promise of a Day of Judgment.
[1084] The Qur'an
[1085] Isaiah 40:8 " The grass weathers, the flower fades, but the word of our God stands forever"
[1086] Matthew 23:33-35 You snakes, you brood of vipers! [34] How can you escape being sentenced to hell? Therefore, I send you prophets, sages, and scribes, some of whom you will kill and crucify, and some you will flog in your synagogues and pursue from town to town, [35] so that upon you may come all the righteous blood shed on earth, from the blood of righteous Abel to the blood of Zechariah son of Barachiah, whom you murdered between the sanctuary and the altar.
[1087] Psalm 19:1 The heavens are telling the glory of God; and the firmament proclaims his handiwork.

pursued by a clear flame. [18] As for the earth - We have spread it[1088] wide and set firm mountains on it, and caused everything to grow in a well-balanced way.[1089] [19] And We put sustenance in it for both you and all creatures for whom you don't provide.[1090] [20] We have the storehouse of everything[1091] that exists, and We send it down only in a known measure. [21] We send the winds to fertilize, and we bring water from the sky for you to drink; but it is not you who control its sources [22] It is We who give life and cause death, and it is We alone who will inherit all. [23] We know very well those of you who have gone ahead and those who are still to come; [24] and, behold, it is your Lord who will gather them all together (on Judgment Day). Truly, He is the All-Wise[1092] and the All-Knowing![1093] [25] We have created man out of dried clay, formed from dark mud[1094] [26] and, before that, we had created jinn[1095] from a scorching firestorm. [27] And when Your Lord said to the angels: "Behold, I am about to create mortal man out of dried clay, formed from dark mud [28] and when I have fully formed him and breathed My spirit into him, fall down and prostrate (yourselves) before him!" [29] Then the angels prostrated themselves, all of them [30] except Iblīs.[1096] He refused to bow down with the others. [31] God said, "Iblīs! What prevents you from being among those who have prostrated themselves?" [32] (Iblīs) replied, "I will not bow down before a mortal man whom You have created out of dried clay, formed from dark mud!" [33] God said, "Be gone! You are expelled from Our grace [34] and you will be cursed until the Day of Reckoning!" [35] Iblīs said, "Then, my Lord, grant me relief until the Day when all will be raised again!" [36] God answered: "You will be granted relief [37] until the Day of the appointed time." [38] (Whereupon Iblīs) said, "Oh, my Lord! Since You led me on to this, I will make (all that is evil) on earth appear good to people, and will most certainly entice them into sin, [39] all except the sincere among your worshipers!" [40] God said: "(Devotion) is a straight path to Me. [41] Truly, you will have no power over My worshipers except for the misled who follow you [42] and Hell is the promised meeting place for all of you. [43] There will be seven gates leading into Hell, each gate receiving its allotted share." [44]

Truly, those who are ever mindful of God will be amid Gardens and springs, [45] "Enter it in peace, (safe and) secure!" [46] And We will remove whatever resentment may have been (lingering) in their hearts, brethren resting on couches facing one another [47] no weariness will ever touch them there, and they will never be made to leave. [48] Tell My worshipers that I am the

• • •

[1088] Isaiah 44:24 Thus says the Lord, your Redeemer, who formed you in the womb: I am the Lord, who made all things, who alone stretched out the heavens, who by myself spread out the earth;
[1089] Leviticus 26:4 I will give you your rains in their season, and the land shall yield its produce, and the trees of the field shall yield their fruit.
[1090] Psalm 145:15-16 The eyes of all look to you, and you give them their food in due season. [16] You open your hand, satisfying the desire of every living thing.
[1091] Psalm 33:7 He gathered the waters of the sea as in a bottle; he put the deeps in storehouses.
[1092] Proverbs 2:6 For the Lord gives wisdom; from his mouth come knowledge and understanding;
[1093] 1 John 3:20 whenever our hearts condemn us; for God is greater than our hearts, and he knows everything.
[1094] Genesis 2:7 then the Lord God formed man from the dust of the ground, and breathed into his nostrils the breath of life; and the man became a living being
[1095] Another kind of creatures with consciousness.
[1096] The Devil

Forgiving,[1097] The Mercy Giver;[1098] [(49)] and that my punishment[1099] is truly painful[(50)]
And tell them all (once again) about Abraham's guests. [1100(51)] When they entered his presence and greeted him with "Peace", he answered, " We are afraid of you!" [(52)] They said: "Fear not! We bring you the good news of (the birth of) a son who will be endowed with profound knowledge."[1101(53)] Abraham said: "Do you give me this good news despite the fact that I am overwhelmed with old age? [1102] What kind of good news is this?" [(54)] They answered: "We have given you the good news of truth so do not be among those who despair!") [1103] [(55)] He exclaimed): "And who - other than those who have utterly lost their way –could ever abandon the hope of his Lord's grace?"[1104] [(56)] He added: "And, heavenly messengers, what (else) might you have in mind?" [(57)] They answered: "We are sent to a people who already cut all relations to God and rejected his messages,[1105(58)] except for Lot's[1106] household. All of them will be saved,[1107(59)] except for Lot's wife,[1108] (God) has ordained that she should be among those who stay behind!" [(60)]
And when the messengers (of God) came to the house of Lot, [(61)] he said: "Who are you? I do not know you people!"[1109] [(62)] They said, "We have come to you with what they have always rejected but wondered whether it will happen to them," [(63)] and we bring you certainty (of its fulfillment), for we speak the Truth. " [(64)] Go, then with your family while it is still night, follow behind them

• • •

[1097] Isaiah 43:25 "I, even I, am the one who wipes out your transgressions for My own sake, And I will not remember your sins.
[1098] Isaiah 44:22 I have swept away your transgressions like a cloud, and your sins like mist; return to me, for I have redeemed you.
[1099] Ezekiel 25:17 I will execute great vengeance on them with wrathful punishments. Then they shall know that I am the Lord, when I lay my vengeance on them.
[1100] Genesis 18:1-2 The Lord appeared to Abraham by the oaks of Mamre, as he sat at the entrance of his tent in the heat of the day. ² He looked up and saw three men standing near him. When he saw them, he ran from the tent entrance to meet them, and bowed down to the ground.
[1101] Genesis 18:9-10 They said to him, 'Where is your wife Sarah?' And he said, 'There, in the tent.'
¹⁰ Then one said, 'I will surely return to you in due season, and your wife Sarah shall have a son.' And Sarah was listening at the tent entrance behind him.
[1102] Genesis 18:11 Now Abraham and Sarah were old, advanced in age; it had ceased to be with Sarah after the manner of women.
[1103] Genesis 18:12-14 So Sarah laughed to herself, saying, 'After I have grown old, and my husband is old, shall I have pleasure?' ¹³ The Lord said to Abraham, 'Why did Sarah laugh, and say, "Shall I indeed bear a child, now that I am old?" ¹⁴ Is anything too wonderful for the Lord? At the set time I will return to you, in due season, and Sarah shall have a son.'
[1104] Psalm 42: Why are you cast down, O my soul, and why are you disquieted within me? Hope in God; for I shall again praise him, my help and my God.
[1105] Genesis 18:20-21Then the Lord said, 'How great is the outcry against Sodom and Gomorrah and how very grave their sin! ²¹ I must go down and see whether they have done altogether according to the outcry that has come to me; and if not, I will know.'
[1106] Lot, nephew of Abraham
[1107] Genesis 19:15 When morning dawned, the angels urged Lot, saying, 'Get up, take your wife and your two daughters who are here, or else you will be consumed in the punishment of the city.'
[1108] Genesis 19:26 But Lot's wife, behind him, looked back, and she became a pillar of salt.
[1109] Genesis 19:1-2 The two angels came to Sodom in the evening, and Lot was sitting in the gateway of Sodom. When Lot saw them, he rose to meet them, and bowed down with his face to the ground. ² He said, 'Please, my Lords, turn aside to your servant's house and spend the night, and wash your feet; then you can rise early and go on your way.' They said, 'No; we will spend the night in the square.'

yourself;[1110] and do not permit anyone to look back,[1111] but go where you are told to go."[(65)] And We revealed unto him the decree: "The very last of those (sinners) will be wiped out by the morning." [1112] [(66)] The people of the town came (to Lot) hoping to have fun (with the strangers)[1113(67)] (Lot) said: "These are my guests. Do not bring shame on me,"[1114] [(68)] but fear God and do not disgrace me! [(69)] They answered, "Have we not forbidden you (to offer protection) to any kind of people?"[1115] [(70)] (Lot) said, "Take my daughters instead, if you must!"[1116] [(71)] "Do not pay attention to them (the messengers said), they are stumbling around in their wild intoxication!" [1117] [(72)] The blast (of Our punishment) overtook them around sunrise,[1118] [(73)] and We turned the town upside down,[1119] and rained down upon them stones of baked clay [(74)] Truly, there are messages in this for those who discern [(75)] (the town) is still there standing by a road that still exists. [(76)] Truly, there is a sign in this for all who believe. [(77)]

And the woods-dwellers were also unjust, [(78)] and so We inflicted Our retribution on them. Both of these (sinful communities) were on a highway, (still) plain to see. [(79)] And the people of Al-Hijr, likewise rejected our messengers [(80)] We gave them our signs, but they turned their backs to them. [(81)] They carved dwellings in the mountains, thinking themselves secure [(82)]) The blast (of Our punishment) overtook them early in the morning, [(83)] and all (the power) that they had acquired was of no use to them. [(84)]

We have not created the heavens and the earth[1120] and all that is between them without (an inner) truth; the Hour (when this will become clear to all) is yet to come. Hence, forgive (men's failings) gracefully. [(85)] Truly, your Lord is the All-Knowing Creator of all things! [(86)] And We have given you seven of the oft-repeated (verses), and this glorious Qur'an [(87)] (so) don't turn your eyes (longingly) towards what we have given some of them to enjoy. And neither

• • •

[1110] Genesis 19:12-13 Then the men said to Lot, 'Have you anyone else here? Sons-in-law, sons, daughters, or anyone you have in the city—bring them out of the place. [13] For we are about to destroy this place, because the outcry against its people has become great before the Lord, and the Lord has sent us to destroy it.'

[1111] Genesis 19:17 When they had brought them outside they said, "Flee for your life; do not look back or stop anywhere in the Plain: flee to the hills, or else you will be consumed."

[1112] Genesis 19:22, 23 Hurry, escape there, for I can do nothing until you arrive there.' [22] Therefore, the city was called Zoar. [23] The sun had risen on the earth when Lot came to Zoar.

[1113] Genesis 19:5 and they called to Lot, 'Where are the men who came to you tonight? Bring them out to us, so that we may know them.'

[1114] Genesis 19:7 and said, 'I beg you, my brothers, do not act so wickedly.

[1115] Genesis 19:9 But they said, "Stand aside." Furthermore, they said, "This one came in as an alien, and already he is acting like a judge; now we will treat you worse than them." So they pressed hard against Lot and came near to break the door.

[1116] Genesis 19:8 "Look, I have two daughters who have not know a man; let me bring them out to you, and do to them as you please; only do nothing to these men, for they have come under the shelter of my roof."

[1117] Genesis 19:11 And they struck with blindness the men who were at the door of the house, both small and great, so that they were unable to find the door.

[1118] Genesis 19:23-24 The sun had risen over the earth when Lot came to Zoar. [24] Then the Lord rained on Sodom and Gomorrah brimstone and fire from the Lord out of heaven,

[1119] Genesis 19:25 and He overthrew those cities, and all the valley, and all the inhabitants of the cities, and what grew on the ground.

[1120] Isaiah 42:5 Thus says God the Lord, Who created the heavens and stretched them out, Who spread out the earth and its offspring, Who gives breath to the people on it and spirit to those who walk in it,

grieve over those (who are rejecting your message), but spread your wings (of modesty and tenderness) over the believers, [88] and say, "I am the clear Warner! [89] Just as We have sent down warnings for the conspiring separatists [90] who reduced the Qur'an into fragments believing in some and rejecting others. [91] By your Lord! We will call them to account, one and all, [92] for whatever they have done! [93] Hence, proclaim openly all that you have been told (to say), and leave the idolaters alone. [94] Truly, We are sufficient for you against all who mock this revelation, [95] who associate another deity with God, for in time they will know. [96] And We know that your heart is distressed by the things they say: [97] but celebrate your Lord's limitless glory, praise Him, and be among those who prostrate themselves (before Him) in worship, [98] and worship your Lord until you die. [99]

CHAPTER **SIXTEEN**

AN-NAHAL
THE BEE

THE **MECCA** PERIOD

In the name of God, the Merciful-to-all, the Mercy Giver:
God's judgment is coming; do not try to hurry it. May He be exalted in His Glory! He is far above anything they associate with Him. ⁽⁰¹⁾ He sends down the angels with the Spirit that is of His command, on any of His worshipers, He may will, (saying) "Warn all (humanity) that there is no deity other than Me. Therefore, be mindful of me!"¹¹²¹ ⁽⁰²⁾ He has created heaven and earth in Truth.¹¹²² He is magnificently exalted above anything they associate with Him. ⁽⁰³⁾ He created the human being out of a (mere) sperm, and suddenly he is an open adversary.¹¹²³ ⁽⁰⁴⁾ And he creates livestock for you to provide warmth and other benefits and to eat. ⁽⁰⁵⁾ There is beauty in them for you, when you bring them home in the evenings and release them to pasture in the mornings. ⁽⁰⁶⁾ And they carry your cargoes to places that you would be unable to reach without great difficulties. Truly, your Lord is very compassionate, a purveyor of mercy!¹¹²⁴ ⁽⁰⁷⁾ And he creates horses, mules and donkeys for you to ride and as adornment. And He will continue to create what you do not know. ⁽⁰⁸⁾ It rests with God alone to show you the right path. However, many will deviate from it. Had he so willed it, he would have guided you all. ⁽⁰⁹⁾
It is He who sends the rains from the skies;¹¹²⁵ some you drink, and from it (grows) the shrubs on which you feed your cattle ⁽¹⁰⁾ And he causes your crops

• • •

---

¹¹²¹ Deuteronomy 6:4-5 Hear, O Israel: The Lord is our God, the Lord alone. ⁵ You shall love the Lord your God with all your heart, and with all your soul, and with all your might.
¹¹²² Isaiah 45:18 For thus says the Lord, who created the heavens (he is God!), who formed the earth and made it (he established it; he did not create it a chaos, he formed it to be inhabited!): I am the Lord, and there is no other.
¹¹²³ Human beings was endowed with consciousness and that gave them the ability to think, reflect, discuss, argue and challenge, which made him look like an open adversary.
¹¹²⁴ James 5:11 Indeed we call blessed those who showed endurance. You have heard of the endurance of Job, and you have seen the purpose of the Lord, how the Lord is compassionate and merciful.
¹¹²⁵ Deuteronomy 28:12 The Lord will open for you his rich storehouse, the heavens, to give the rain of your land in its season and to bless all your undertakings. You will lend to many nations, but you will not borrow.

167

to grow: olive trees, date-palm, grapes, and all other types of fruit. In that there is a message for people who think [11] He has made the night and the day subservient to you and the sun, the moon and the stars.[1126] There are messages in that for people who comprehend! [12] And all the beautiful colors that He has made for you on earth- in that, there is a message for people who consider.[1127] [13] And it is He who made the sea of benefit to you, so that you may eat from it fresh and tender meat and obtain ornaments which you may wear. You see ships cleaving through it, so that you may search for His abundant provision and so you may be grateful. [14] And He has placed solid mountains on the earth, so that it does not shift with you, and rivers and pathways, so that you can find your way, [15] as well as other landmarks-- for it is by the stars that men are able to find their way. [16] So, then, is He who creates like one who does not create? Will you not, then, consider? [17]

If you should ever try to count God's blessings, you could not count them,[1128] for God is truly forgiving and a purveyor of mercy[1129] [18] And God knows all that you keep secret and all that you declare. [19] Now, those they call on beside God cannot create anything,[1130] since they themselves are created. [20] They are in fact dead, not living, and they do not (even) know when they will be resurrected. [21] Your God is the One God, but, because of their arrogance, the hearts of those who do not believe in the Hereafter refuse to admit this (truth). [22] Truly God knows all they conceal and all they declare. He does not love the arrogant. [23]

And whenever (the arrogant) are asked, "What has your Lord sent down?" They say, "Ancient legends!". [24] So, on the Day of Resurrection they will carry the full weight of their own burdens as well as some of the burdens of those ignorant whom they have misled. How heavy will be the weight of their burden! [25] Those who lived before them also schemed and God destroyed their structure from its foundation and the roof fell on top of them. Suffering came at them suddenly from an unexpected source. [26] On the Day of Resurrection He will disgrace them and say, "Where are those associates, for whose sake you denied Me and became so hostile? Those given knowledge will say, "Truly, disgrace and desolation have come today on the unbelievers, [27] those who are wronging themselves while the angels gather them in death!" Then, the schemers will offer peace: "We did not do anything wrong!" (But they will hear an answer) "Yes you did, because God knows well what you were doing! [28] Now enter the gates of Hell to remain there forever! How evil, will be the abode of the arrogant." [29]

Those who are mindful of God were asked, "What has your Lord sent down?" They say, "Absolute goodness!" There is good in this word for those who do good, and the next world is even better. How wonderful is the abode of those who are ever mindful of God [30] They will enter Gardens of Eden. Running waters

• • •

[1126] Jeremiah 31:35 Thus says the Lord, Who gives the sun for light by day And the fixed order of the moon and the stars for light by night, Who stirs up the sea so that its waves roar; The Lord of Hosts is His name.
[1127] Psalm 19:1 The heavens are telling the glory of God; and the firmament proclaims his handiwork
[1128] Psalm 144:15 Happy are the people to whom such blessings fall; happy are the people whose God is the Lord
[1129] Isaiah 43:25 "I, even I, am the one who wipes out your transgressions for My own sake, And I will not remember your sins.
[1130] Isaiah 46:7 They lift it to their shoulders, they carry it, they set it in its place, and it stands there; it cannot move from its place. If one cries out to it, it does not answer or save anyone from trouble.

flow[1131] and there they will have all things they wish. This is how God will reward those who are mindful of Him. [31] Those who are gathered in death by the angels, being good, will be greeted with "Peace be upon you! Enter paradise by virtue of what you have done" [32]

Are the (unbelievers) expecting that the angels will appear or that God's judgment will be manifested? Those who lived before them behaved in the same way. God did not wrong them. They wronged themselves.[1132] [33] They were struck by the consequences of the evil they had done, and they were overtaken[1133] by the very thing they used to ridicule. [34]

Now the very ones who associate deities with God say, "Had God willed it so, we would have worshipped Him alone, and we would never have declared anything as forbidden unless he had commanded us to do so". This is just what those who lived before them did. Are the messengers required to do more than deliver the message clearly?[1134] [35] We sent a messenger to every nation, saying: "Worship God, and shun the powers of evil!" Some of them were guided by God, but others deserved to be misguided. Travel around the world and see what happened eventually to those who denied the truth. [36] However eager you are for them to be guided, God does not confer his guidance on any whom He judges to have gone astray,[1135] and they will have none to help them. [37] And so they swear by God, vowing most solemnly, "God will never raise the dead to life again!"[1136] But He will, for it is a binding promise that He will fulfill, but most people do not know [38] (On that day) He will make clear to them the things they differed about and the unbelievers will know that they were lying. [39] Whenever We will anything to be, we simply say, "Be!" and it is.[1137] [40] As for those who emigrated for God's sake after being persecuted, We will bless them with good fortune in this world, but their life in the Hereafter will be even greater still, if

• • •

[1131] Revelation 22:1-2 Then he showed me a river of the water of life, clear as crystal, coming from the throne of God and of the Lamb, in the middle of its street. 2 On either side of the river was the tree of life, bearing twelve kinds of fruit, yielding its fruit every month; and the leaves of the tree were for the healing of the nations.
[1132] Revelation 2:23 and I will strike her children dead. And all the churches will know that I am the one who searches minds and hearts, and I will give to each of you as your works deserve.
[1133] Deuteronomy 28:15 But if you will not obey the Lord your God by diligently observing all his commandments and decrees, which I am commanding you today, then all these curses shall come upon you and overtake you.
[1134] Ezekiel 33:6-9 But if the watchman sees the sword coming and does not blow the trumpet and the people are not warned, and a sword comes and takes a person from them, he is taken away in his iniquity; but his blood I will require from the watchman's hand.'7 "Now as for you, son of man, I have appointed you a watchman for the house of Israel; so you will hear a message from My mouth and give them warning from Me. 8 When I say to the wicked, 'O wicked man, you will surely die,' and you do not speak to warn the wicked from his way, that wicked man shall die in his iniquity, but his blood I will require from your hand. 9 But if you on your part warn a wicked man to turn from his way and he does not turn from his way, he will die in his iniquity, but you have delivered your life.
[1135] 2 Thessalonians 2:10 and every kind of wicked deception for those who are perishing, because they refused to love the truth and so be saved.
[1136] Acts 26:8 Why is it considered incredible among you people if God does raise the dead?
[1137] Genesis chapter one describes creation, and before each creative act is prefaced, "And God said" which is the English equivalent of "Be" in the Quran.

they only knew![1138] (41) They who, have been patient in hard times and placed their trust in their Lord.[1139] (42)

Even before your time (Prophet) we sent only men who were inspired, and if you have not yet realized this, ask the followers of earlier revelation. (43) (They brought) clear signs of the truth and books of divine wisdom. And we brought down to you this Reminder, so that you may clarify to people all that has been brought down to them, that they may reflect on it[1140] . (44)

Do those who conceive evil plans feel secure that God will not cause the earth to swallow them, or that suffering will not overtake them from whence they least expect it? (45) Or that He will not take them suddenly while they are coming and going—they being unable to escape him--[1141] (46) or that He will not take them gradually? Your Sustainer is most Merciful-to-all,[1142] a purveyor of mercy! (47) Have they not, then, ever considered the things that God has created—how even their shadows turn right or left, prostrating themselves before God, being absolutely submissive to His will? (48) For all that is in the heavens and on earth prostrates itself before God—[1143] every beast, and the angels— without any arrogance (49) They fear their Lord above them and do whatever they are commanded to do. (50)

And God said, "Do not worship two deities. There is only One god, so it is Me that you shall revere." (51) And to Him belongs all that is in heaven and on earth, and to Him alone be obedient, it is His right. Why, then, will you heed anyone but God?[1144] (52) For all good things come to you from God[1145] and whenever harm comes upon you, you cry to Him for help, (53) but as soon as He has relieved you of your hardship, some of you begin to associate others with Him. (54) They show their ingratitude for all that We have done for them! So, go ahead, enjoy your brief life, but eventually you will come to know (the Truth)! (55)

They assign a share in what We have given them for the (idols) about which they know nothing. By God, you will be asked about your lies! (56) They also ascribe daughters to God--May He be exalted in His glory--and they chose for themselves whatever they desire. (57) Whenever one of them is given the good

•   •   •

[1138] Mark 10:30 who will not receive a hundredfold now in this age—houses, brothers and sisters, mothers and children, and fields, with persecutions—and in the age to come eternal life.

[1139] Psalm 143: Let me hear of your steadfast love in the morning, for in you I put my trust. Teach me the way I should go, for to you I lift up my soul.

[1140] Luke 16:27-31 He said, 'Then, father, I beg you to send him to my father's house— 28 for I have five brothers—that he may warn them, so that they will not also come into this place of torment.' 29 Abraham replied, 'They have Moses and the prophets; they should listen to them.' 30 He said, 'No, father Abraham; but if someone goes to them from the dead, they will repent.' 31 He said to him, 'If they do not listen to Moses and the prophets, neither will they be convinced even if someone rises from the dead.' "

[1141] 1 Thessalonians 5:2-3 For you yourselves know very well that the day of the Lord will come like a thief in the night. 3 When they say, "There is peace and security," then sudden destruction will come upon them, as labor pains come upon a pregnant woman, and there will be no escape!

[1142] Exodus 34:6, Then the Lord passed by in front of him and proclaimed, "The Lord, the Lord God, compassionate and gracious, slow to anger, and abounding in loving kindness and truth;

[1143] Romans 14:11 For it is written, "As I live, says the Lord, every knee shall bow to me, and every tongue shall give praise to God."

[1144] Joshua 24:14, 'Now therefore revere the Lord, and serve him in sincerity and in faithfulness; put away the gods that your ancestors served beyond the River and in Egypt, and serve the Lord.1 Samuel 12:23-24

[1145] James 1:17 Every generous act of giving, with every perfect gift, is from above, coming down from the Father of lights, with whom there is no variation or shadow due to change.

news of a daughter's birth, his face darkens and he fills with bottled-up anger. [58] Ashamed, he avoids people because of the supposed bad news he has received, (and he debates with himself) should he keep her despite the disgrace (which he feels) or should he bury her in the ground? How dreadful is their judgment. [59] Those who do not believe in the Hereafter set the worst example, whereas God sets the highest example, for He alone is Almighty and Wise! [1146] [60] Now if God were to judge men immediately for all the evil they do on earth, He would not leave a single living creature alive. [1147] However, He gives them relief until a time appointed by Him, but when the end of their time approaches, they can neither delay it by a single second, nor can they hasten it. [1148][61] They attribute to God what they dislike, and (all the while) their tongues utter the lie that they deserve the best. Truly, they deserve the fire where they will be abandoned. [62]

By God, We sent messengers unto (various) nations before your time, but Satan made their own deeds look good to them, so he is their master now as before and painful punishment awaits them. [1149] [63] We sent down the Book to you, only to make clear to them the things about which they differ, and as guidance and mercy to people who will believe. [64]

And it is God who sends down water giving life to the earth, [1150] even after it has been lifeless. In this is a sign to those who will listen. [65] And there is a lesson for you in the grazing cattle: We give you drink from what is in their bellies - between dung and their blood- pure milk, pleasant to those who drink it. [66] And from the fruits of the palm trees and grapevines you obtain intoxicant as well as good provision. [1151] In this, too, there is a sign for people who think. [67] (And consider how) your Lord has so inspired the bee (saying): "Prepare for yourself dwellings in mountains and in trees, and in what people may build, [68] then eat all kinds of fruit, and follow humbly the paths ordained for you by your Lord." [1152] From there within these bees emerges a drink, of many colors, a healing food for man. In all this is a sign for people who reflect! [69]

And God has created you, and in time you will die, and some of you will come to an abject state in old age, ceasing to know anything that you once knew. God is All-knowing, All- Powerful! [1153] [70] And God has favored some of you in abundance over others. But those so favored will not share their wealth with those their right hands hold in trust, so (their dependents) will not be their

•   •   •

[1146] 1 Corinthians 1:25 For God's foolishness is wiser than human wisdom, and God's weakness is stronger than human strength.

[1147] Psalm 130:3 If you, O Lord, should mark iniquities, Lord, who could stand?

[1148] Matthew 6:27, And can any of you by worrying add a single hour to your span of life? Luke 12:25 And can any of you by worrying add a single hour to your span of life?

[1149] 2 peter 3:7 But by the same word the present heavens and earth have been reserved for fire, being kept until the day of judgment and destruction of the godless.

[1150] Isaiah 55:10 For as the rain and the snow come down from heaven, and do not return there until they have watered the earth, making it bring forth and sprout, giving seed to the sower and bread to the eater,

[1151] Psalm 104:14-16 You cause the grass to grow for the cattle, and plants for people to use, to bring forth food from the earth, [15] and wine to gladden the human heart, oil to make the face shine, and bread to strengthen the human heart. [16] The trees of the Lord are watered abundantly, the cedars of Lebanon that he planted.

[1152] Micah 6:8 He has told you, O mortal, what is good; and what does the Lord require of you but to do justice, and to love kindness, and to walk humbly with your God?

[1153] Job 42:2 'I know that you can do all things, and that no purpose of yours can be thwarted.

equals. Will they, then, renounce God's blessings? [71] And God has given you wives from among yourselves, and has given you, through your wives, children and grandchildren, and has provided for you all of the good things of life. Will they, then, continue to believe in falsehood and reject God's blessings? [72] And will they worship instead of God something that has no power whatsoever to provide them any sustenance from earth or heaven and can do nothing at all? [1154] [73] So, do not propose examples of what God is like! God knows and you do not. [1155] [74]

God set forth a parable (of two men): one is a slave, unable to do anything of his own accord, and the other a (free) man to whom We have given ample wealth, so that he can spend at will, both secretly and openly. Can these two be considered equal? All praise is due to God, but most people do not know. [75] And God provides another parable of two (other) men. One of them is mute, unable to do anything by himself, a burden to his caretaker. Whatever task he is directed to do, he accomplishes nothing beneficial. Can such a one be considered equal to one who commands justice (in his community), and is on the straight path? [76] It is God alone who possesses the hidden reality of the heavens and the earth. The matter of the Last Hour will be like the twinkling of an eye, or closer still, for God has the power to will anything. [77]

And God brought you out of your mothers' wombs[1156]— knowing nothing, and He has endowed you with hearing, and sight, and minds so that you might have cause to be grateful. [1157] [78] Have they not seen the birds,[1158] enabled by God to fly in mid-air,[1159] with none but God holding them aloft? In this there are messages for people who will believe! [79] And God made your homes places to rest and enabled you to make dwellings from cattle hides—light, and easy to carry, whether you travel or camp, and (has supplied you with) furnishings and goods from the animals' rough and soft wool and its hair (to use) for a time. [80] And, from what He has created, God has provided you with protection; (He has given you) shade (from the sun), places of refuge in the mountains, and gave you garments to protect you from the heat,[1160] as well as garments to protect you from your brutality towards each other. In this way He perfects His blessings on

• • •

[1154] Isaiah 45:20 Assemble yourselves and come together, draw near, you survivors of the nations! They have no knowledge— those who carry about their wooden idols, and keep on praying to a god that cannot save.

[1155] Isaiah 55:8-9 For my thoughts are not your thoughts, nor are your ways my ways, says the Lord. 9 For as the heavens are higher than the earth, so are my ways higher than your ways and my thoughts than your thoughts.

[1156] Psalm 139:13-14 For it was you who formed my inward parts; you knit me together in my mother's womb. 14 I praise you, for I am fearfully and wonderfully made. Wonderful are your works; that I know very well.

[1157] 1 Thessalonians 5:18 give thanks in all circumstances; for this is the will of God in Christ Jesus for you.

[1158] Matthew 6:26 Look at the birds of the air; they neither sow nor reap nor gather into barns, and yet your heavenly Father feeds them. Are you not of more value than they?

[1159] Proverbs 30:18-19 three things are too wonderful for me; four I do not understand 19 the way of an eagle in the sky, the way of a snake on a rock, the way of a ship on the high seas, and the way of a man with a girl.

[1160] Isaiah 25:4 For you have been a refuge to the poor, a refuge to the needy in their distress, a shelter from the rainstorm and a shade from the heat. When the blast of the ruthless was like a winter rainstorm,

you, so that you will surrender yourselves to Him.[1161] [81] But if you they turn away (Prophet), remember that your only responsibility is to deliver this revelation clearly. [82] They (who turn away) are fully aware of God's grace, but they nevertheless refuse to recognize it because they are used to denying the truth.[83]

The Day (of Judgment) will come when We will raise up a witness from every nation. On that day, the unbelievers will not be able to make excuses or to make amends. [84] And when those who were unjust see the suffering that awaits them, they will recognize that the severity of their punishment[1162] will not be lightened, nor will they be given any relief. [85] And when those who associated other beings with God see those they associated, they will say, "Our Lord these are our associates whom we used to call upon apart from You." But they will throw their words back at them: "You are liars" [86] and on that day they will freely submit to God, and all their idols will forsake them. [87] We will heap punishment upon punishment on all the unbelievers who turned others away from God's path, in return for the corruption they caused. [88]

On that day We will raise up from within each nation a witness against them, and We will bring you (Prophet) as a witness against them. We have sent down to you the Book as clarification for all things and as guidance and mercy and good news to all who would surrender themselves to God (Muslims). [89]

God orders justice, good works, and generosity to relatives and He forbids vice, evil, and oppression. He warns you so that you will keep all this in mind.[1163] [90] Fulfill the covenant of God whenever you commit to one. Do not break your oaths once they are confirmed,[1164] and you (will) have made God your guarantor. God knows all that you do. [91] And do not be like the woman who untwisted the thread she had firmly spun just to unravel it—do not use your oaths as means to deceive one another, because some of you are more powerful than others. God is testing you through all this, and on the Day of Resurrection He will make clear to you those things about which you disagreed. [92]

Had God so desired, he could surely have made you all the same nation, but He lets stray those who wish to reject His messages, and He guides rightly those who wish to be guided, and all of you will be called to account for all things you have done. [93] So do not use your oaths as a means of deceiving each other— or else your foot will slide after having been firmly in place, and you will then taste the miserable consequences of your having turned from God's path and incredible suffering will await you.[1165] [94] Do not exchange the covenant of God for a small price. What is with God is best for you, if you only knew. [95] All that

• • •

[1161] James 1:17 Every generous act of giving, with every perfect gift, is from above, coming down from the Father of lights, with whom there is no variation or shadow due to change. Psalm 13:6 I will sing to the Lord, because he has dealt bountifully with me.

[1162] Ezekiel 5:15 You shall be a mockery and a taunt, a warning and a horror, to the nations around you, when I execute judgments on you in anger and fury, and with furious punishments—I, the Lord, have spoken—

[1163] Deuteronomy 16:19 You must not distort justice; you must not show partiality; and you must not accept bribes, for a bribe blinds the eyes of the wise and subverts the cause of those who are in the right.

[1164] Numbers 30:2 When a man makes a vow to the Lord, or swears an oath to bind himself by a pledge, he shall not break his word; he shall do according to all that proceeds out of his mouth.

[1165] Ezekiel 25:17 I will execute great vengeance on them with wrathful punishments. Then they shall know that I am the Lord, when I lay my vengeance on them.

you currently have will come to an end,[1166] but that which God has is eternal. And We will most certainly grant to those who were patient their reward according to the best they ever did. [96] Whoever does good deeds, whether— man or woman—and is a believer, they will live a good life and will surely receive their reward in according with the best they have done. [97]

When you recite the Qur'an, seek refuge with God from Satan, the rebel expelled from God's mercy [98] He has no power over those who believe and who rely on their Lord. [1167][99] He has power only over those who ally themselves with him, and those who because of him associate others with God. [100] And if we replace one revelation with another- and God knows best what he confers (from heaven)- they say, "You made it all up!" Truly, most of them have no understanding. [101] Tell them, "The Holy Spirit has revealed it from your Lord in Truth, so that it might strengthen the believers, providing guidance and good news to all who have surrendered themselves to God (Muslims[1168])."[1169] [102] And We certainly know well what they say, "It is only a human being who is telling him what to say." The language of the one they allude to is a foreign one whereas this is in clear and lucid Arabic. [103] Truly, as for those who refuse to believe God's revelations, God does not guide them, and grievous suffering will await them.[1170] [104] It is only they who refuse to believe God's revelations, who speak these lies, and it is they who are lying. [105]

Whoever denies God after having once believed, (except for anyone who is forced to deny God while his heart remains true to his faith)- he who willingly opens up his heart to disbelief will have the wrath of God upon them and a grievous punishment awaiting them.[106] That is because they favored this worldly life over the Hereafter, and because God will not guide unbelieving people [107] The ones whose hearts, ears and eyes are sealed by God—it is they who are the heedless.[1171] [108] No doubt they will be doomed in the life to come. [109] As for those who migrated after they were persecuted and who then struggled and persevered, to them your Lord is so very forgiving, a purveyor of mercy! [110] On the Day when every soul will come to plead for itself, every soul will be fully rewarded for whatever it has done, and none will be wronged. [111] And God proposes to you this parable: (Imagine, if you will,) a town that was

•　•　•

[1166] 2 Corinthians 4:16-18, So we do not lose heart. Even though our outer nature is wasting away, our inner nature is being renewed day by day. [17] For this slight momentary affliction is preparing us for an eternal weight of glory beyond all measure, [18] because we look not at what can be seen but at what cannot be seen; for what can be seen is temporary, but what cannot be seen is eternal.

[1167] Luke 10:19, See, I have given you authority to tread on snakes and scorpions, and over all the power of the enemy; and nothing will hurt you.

[1168] The original meaning of the word 'Muslim' referred to those who were surrendered to God. Only later did it become equated with the followers of Mohammad, and eventually followers of Islam. However, it is used here in its original sense.

[1169] Romans 15:13 May the God of hope fill you with all joy and peace in believing, so that you may abound in hope by the power of the Holy Spirit.

[1170] Zephaniah 3:8 Therefore wait for me, says the Lord, for the day when I arise as a witness. For my decision is to gather nations, to assemble kingdoms, to pour out upon them my indignation, all the heat of my anger; for in the fire of my passion all the earth shall be consumed.

[1171] Isaiah 6:10 Make the mind of this people dull, and stop their ears, and shut their eyes, so that they may not look with their eyes, and listen with their ears, and comprehend with their minds, and turn and be healed.'

once safe and secure, with its provisions coming to it abundantly from all places. Then it denied God's grace. So God caused it to experience all-encompassing misery—hunger and fear as a result of what they had done. [112] And (imagine) that there had come a messenger from among them, but they denied him; so punishment overwhelmed them as they were unjust to themselves. [113]

Then eat of the lawful and good things that God has provided for you. And be grateful for the blessing of God, if it is Him whom you worship. [114] He has only prohibited you from eating carrion, and blood, and the flesh of pigs, and that which has been dedicated to other than God, unless one is compelled to eat it out of necessity, (and then) neither desiring it nor feeding to excess. Truly God is Merciful-to-all,[1172] the Mercy Giver. [115] So, do not lie by letting your tongues wag: "This is lawful and this is unlawful," thereby attributing your own lies to God. They who attribute their lies to God will never succeed! [116] A brief enjoyment, but grievous punishment awaits them. [117] We forbade to the Jews all that We have related to you previously. We did nothing wrong to them, but they wronged themselves. [118] Then to those who sin in ignorance and afterwards repent and live righteously, your Lord is Merciful-to-all, a purveyor of mercy. [119] Truly, Abraham was equal to a community in himself; he was devoted to obeying God. He turned from all that is wrong—and he was not among those idolaters.[120] He was grateful for the grace poured out on him by God—God had chosen him and guided him along a straight path.[121] And so We granted him favor in this world: truly, in the life to come he will be among the righteous. [122] And We have given you inspiration, (Prophet): "Follow the faith of Abraham, who turned from every false thing, and who was not among the idolaters."[123] The Sabbath[1173] was made obligatory only on those who differed about it. Your Lord will judge between them on the Day of Resurrection regarding to all matters about which they differed. [124]

Call people to the path of your Lord with wisdom and good advice and argue with them in the most courteous way[1174], for your Lord knows best who strays from His path, and knows best who is rightly guided. [125] If you want to retaliate to an attack make your response proportionate. But if you can be patient, it is always better to be patient. [126] (Prophet), be patient: your patience comes only from God. Do not grieve over the unbelievers, nor be distressed by their scheming, [127] for, truly, God stands with those who are mindful of Him and who do good.[128]

. . .

[1172] Psalm 103:8, The Lord is merciful and gracious, slow to anger and abounding in steadfast love.

[1173] Ezekiel 20:20, and hallow my Sabbaths that they may be a sign between me and you, so that you may know that I the Lord am your God.

[1174] 2 Timothy 2:25-26 correcting opponents with gentleness. God may perhaps grant that they will repent and come to know the truth, [26] and that they may escape from the snare of the devil, having been held captive by him to do his will.my strength.

CHAPTER SEVENTEEN

AL-ISRA
THE NIGHT JOURNEY

In the name of God, the Merciful-to-all, the Mercy Giver:

Glory be to Him who took His servant on a night journey from the Sacred Sanctuary (at Mecca) to the Remote House of Worship (Al-Aqsa Mosque at Jerusalem), whose surroundings we have blessed, [1176] so that We could show him some of Our signs--for truly, He is the All-Hearing, the All Seeing. [01] And We gave the Book [1177] to Moses (Musa), and we made it guidance for the Children of Israel, (saying) "Trust yourselves to no one but Me." [1178] [02] They are descendants from those whom we carried (in the ark) with Noah! [1179] He was (one of) Our most grateful worshipers. [03]

And we warned to the Children of Israel in the Book, "You will twice corrupt the earth, and you will rise to a great height." [04] When the first promise came true, We sent certain of Our servants against you, who were fierce in battle, and they ravaged your homes. It was a promise fulfilled. [05] And as time went on, We permitted you to prevail again against them, and We helped you with wealth and children, and We made you more numerous. [06] (And we said:) "If you do good, you do it for yourselves, and if you do evil, it will be returned to you." Then, when the final promise came, (We sent your enemies) to sadden your faces and to enter the place of worship, as they entered it the first time, and to destroy completely the structures that were the source of your pride [1180] [07] Your Lord may well show mercy to you; [1181] but if you turn back (to sinning), We will turn

• • •

[1176] Psalm 65:4 Happy are those whom you choose and bring near to live in your courts. We shall be satisfied with the goodness of your house, your holy temple.

[1177] Exodus 31:18 When God finished speaking with Moses on Mount Sinai, he gave him the two tablets of the covenant, tablets of stone, written with the finger of God.

[1178] Jeremiah 17:7 "Blessed are those who trust in the Lord, whose trust is the Lord."

[1179] Genesis 6:9 These are the descendants of Noah. Noah was a righteous man, blameless in his generation; Noah walked with God.

[1180] 2 Kings 25:8-9 In the fifth month, on the seventh day of the month—which was the nineteenth year of King Nebuchadnezzar, king of Babylon—Nebuzaradan, the captain of the bodyguard, a servant of the king of Babylon, came to Jerusalem. [9] He burned the house of the Lord, the king's house, and all the houses of Jerusalem; every great house he burned down.

[1181] Zechariah 1:3 Therefore say to them, Thus says the Lord of hosts: Return to me, says the Lord of hosts, and I will return to you, says the Lord of hosts.

back (to punishing you). And (do not forget) We have predestined that Hell will be a prison for all who reject Our promises.[1182] (08) Truly, this Qur'an shows the way of righteousness, and it brings good news to the believers who do good works that they will have a wonderful reward;[1183] (09) and We have prepared grievous punishment[1184] for those who do not believe in the life to come. (10) Human being is as hasty to pray for things that are wrong as he prays for things that are good. The human being is often hasty. (11) We have ordained night and day as two miracles. We have darkened the night and made the day visible,[1185] so that you will seek to acquire abundance from your Lord, and so that you may know the number of years and the count of time. We have made everything very clear. (12) We have tied every person's destiny about his neck and, on the Day of Judgment We will bring out a book for him, which he will find spread open in front of him. [1186] (13) And it will be said, "Read your book. Today you are a witness against yourself." (14)

Whoever chooses to follow the right path, it will be for the good of his soul, and whoever goes astray will (reap) his own hurt, and no bearer of burdens will bear the burdens of another. [1187] We would never punish unless we had first sent a messenger. (15) But when We decide to destroy a community, We first give Our final warning to all the decadent in it, but they defiantly disobey. Our sentence is justly carried out, and We then, destroy it utterly. (16) How many generations have We annihilated after Noah's time! Your Lord is sufficiently aware of His worshipers' sins, and all seeing. (17) As for anyone who prefers this momentary life, We readily grant whatever We will to whomever We will. Then We condemn him to the suffering of Hell which he will have to endure, disgraced and disowned! (18) But as for those who desire the life to come, and who endeavor earnestly to obtain it, and (demonstrate) that they truly believe—they are the ones who find favor (with God).[1188] (19) To both those (who are mindful of God in this life) as well as those (who are not) We give some of your Lord's gifts.[1189] Your Lord's giving is never restricted. (20) Observe how We give more abundance[1190] to some than to others, but (remember that) the life to come will be blessed with higher positions and greater favors. (21)

• • •

[1182] Matthew 25:41 Then he will say to those at his left hand, "You that are accursed, depart from me into the eternal fire prepared for the devil and his angels;

[1183] Hebrews 10:35 Do not, therefore, abandon that confidence of yours; it brings a great reward.

[1184] Ezekiel 5:15 You shall be a mockery and a taunt, a warning and a horror, to the nations around you, when I execute judgments on you in anger and fury, and with furious punishments— I, the Lord, have spoken—

[1185] Genesis 1:14 And God said, 'Let there be lights in the dome of the sky to separate the day from the night; and let them be for signs and for seasons and for days and years,

[1186] Revelation 20:12 And I saw the dead, great and small, standing before the throne, and books were opened. Also another book was opened, the book of life. And the dead were judged according to their works, as recorded in the books.

[1187] Ezekiel 18:20 The person who sins shall die. A child shall not suffer for the iniquity of a parent, nor a parent suffer for the iniquity of a child; the righteousness of the righteous shall be his own, and the wickedness of the wicked shall be his own. Galatians 6:5 "For every one shall bear his own burden.

[1188] Exodus 33:13 Now if I have found favor in your sight, show me your ways, so that I may know you and find favor in your sight. Consider too that this nation is your people."

[1189] Matthew 5:45 for he makes his sun rise on the evil and on the good, and sends rain on the righteous and on the unrighteous

[1190] Deuteronomy 10:15 yet the Lord set his heart in love on your ancestors alone and chose you, their descendants after them, out of all the peoples, as it is today.

Do not acknowledge any other deity alongside God,[1191] lest you (want) to find yourself discredited and abandoned. [(22)] Your Lord has decreed that you will worship none but Him, and show your parents[1192] tender kindness. Should one or both of them reach old age in your care,[1193] never say anything that shows impatience with them, never rebuke them, but (always) speak to them respectfully.[1194] [(23)] And spread the wing of mercy [1195] in humility over to them, and say, "My Lord! Have your mercy on them, just as they (had mercy on me) when they raised me as a child" [(24)] Your Lord is fully aware of what is in your hearts.[1196] If you seek (to live) righteously, (He will forgive your errors): He is Merciful-to-all[1197] who return to Him over and over. [(25)] Give what is due to your relatives, and the very poor, and to the traveler, and do not squander your money senselessly. [(26)] Those who misuse (their wealth) are (following) Satan in the same way that Satan proved to be ungrateful to his Sustainer. [(27)] But if you (must) turn away from the needy, while awaiting a blessing that you are hoping for from your Lord, at least speak kindly (to those in need). [(28)] Do not be either tightfisted or extend yourself to the point that you cannot even provide for yourself, so that you sit there blamed and impoverished. [(29)] Your Lord blesses abundantly, or gives in limited portion unto whomever He wills[1198] and is able. He is fully mindful of the needs of his creatures—seeing them all. [(30)]

Do not kill your children out of fear of poverty. We will provide for them and you. Killing them is truly a great sin. [(31)] And do not go anywhere near adultery [1199] because it is a disgrace and immoral. [(32)] And do not kill the soul which God has forbidden[1200]—unless in the pursuit of justice. If anyone has been killed unjustly,[1201] We have given legal recourse to his heir (to claim justice); but, even then, he should not be excessive in taking life. For he is helped (by God's law). [(33)] And do not approach an orphan's property before he reaches maturity,[1202] except with the best possible way. And be true to all you have committed to do,

• • •

[1191] Exodus 20: 3: Thou shalt have no other gods before me.
[1192] Deuteronomy 5:16 Honor your father and your mother, as the Lord your God commanded you, so that your days may be long and that it may go well with you in the land that the Lord your God is giving you.
[1193] Exodus 20: "Honor your father and your mother, that your days may be prolonged in the land which the Lord your God gives you.
[1194] Colossians 3:20 Children, obey your parents in everything, for this is your acceptable duty in the Lord.
[1195] 1 Peter 5:5 In the same way, you who are younger must accept the authority of the elders. And all of you must clothe yourselves with humility in your dealings with one another, for God opposes the proud, but gives grace to the humble.'
[1196] 1 Samuel 16:7 for the Lord does not see as mortals see; they look on the outward appearance, but the Lord looks on the heart.'
[1197] Psalm 145:8, The Lord is gracious and merciful, slow to anger and abounding in steadfast love.
[1198] Psalm 111:5 He provides food for those who fear him; he is ever mindful of his covenant.
[1199] Exodus 20:14 You shall not commit adultery.
[1200] Exodus 20:13 You shall not murder
[1201] Numbers 35:16-18 But anyone who strikes another with an iron object, and death ensues, is a murderer; the murderer shall be put to death. [17] Or anyone who strikes another with a stone in hand that could cause death, and death ensues, is a murderer; the murderer shall be put to death. [18] Or anyone who strikes another with a weapon of wood in hand that could cause death, and death ensues, is a murderer; the murderer shall be put to death.
[1202] Exodus 22:22 You shall not abuse any widow or orphan.

for truly (on the Day of Judgment), you will have to answer for every promise [1203] that you have made. [34] And whenever you measure, use accurate measurements and weigh with a level balance;[1204] this will be better and would be fairer. [35] And do not pursue matters about which you do not know anything: your hearing, sight and heart- all will be accounted for (on the Day of Judgment)! [36] Do not walk arrogantly about the earth; because, truthfully, you cannot tear up the earth or make yourself as tall as mountains. [37] All of this is evil and detested in your Lord's sight. [38]

This is part of the wisdom your Lord has revealed to you. So, do not equate any other deity with God,[1205] unless (you desire) to be thrown into Hell, self-condemned (by your actions) and rejected (by God). [39] Has your Lord chosen you to have sons, while He takes daughters from among the angels? What a grave thing for you to say! [40]

We have made things clear in this Qur'an, so (that) those (who deny the truth) might take it to heart, but it is only making them more distant from the truth [41] Say, "If there had been, as they say, other gods with Him, certainly they would have sought a way to the Lord of the Throne."[1206] [42] May He be exalted in His glory, far above what they say in greatness and sublimity. [43] The seven heavens and the earth, and everyone in them declare His glory.[1207] There is nothing which does not glorify Him with praise, but you humans fail to understand the manner of their glorification. He is All-Forbearing, Most-Forgiving[1208] [44]

And so it is (that) whenever you recite the Qur'an, We place an invisible veil between you and those who do not believe in the life Hereafter [45] for We have veiled their hearts[1209] to prevent them from understanding the meaning, and We have made their ears deaf.[1210] So, whenever you mention your Lord alone while you are reciting the Qur'an, they turn away in disdain. [1211] [46] We know best why they listen when they listen to you, for when they are in private these unjust people say (to one another): "You follow only a man bewitched." [47] See how they refer to you? They have strayed and cannot find the way! [48] And they say, "After we are but bones and dust, can we be resurrected to a new creation?" [49] Tell them: "Even if You have turned to stone or iron, [50] or any created thing, which, in your minds, is more difficult, (it is still possible). They will say, "Who

• • •

[1203] Numbers 30:2 When a man makes a vow to the Lord, or swears an oath to bind himself by a pledge, he shall not break his word; he shall do according to all that proceeds out of his mouth.

[1204] Proverbs 11:1 A false balance is an abomination to the Lord, but an accurate weight is his delight.

[1205] Exodus 20:3 you shall have no other gods before me.

[1206] Psalm 9:7 But the Lord sits enthroned forever, he has established his throne for judgment. Psalm 11:4 The Lord is in his holy temple; the Lord's throne is in heaven. His eyes behold, his gaze examines humankind. Psalm 47:8 God is king over the nations; God sits on his holy throne.

[1207] Psalm 148:1-4 Praise the Lord! Praise the Lord from the heavens; praise him in the heights! 2 Praise him, all his angels; praise him, all his host! 3 Praise him, sun and moon; praise him, all you shining stars! 4 Praise him, you highest heavens, and you waters above the heavens!

[1208] Ephesians 4:32 and be kind to one another, tender-hearted, forgiving one another, as God in Christ has forgiven you.

[1209] 2 Corinthians 3:15 Indeed, to this very day whenever Moses is read, a veil lies over their minds;

[1210] Isaiah 6:10 Make the mind of this people dull, and stop their ears, and shut their eyes, so that they may not look with their eyes, and listen with their ears, and comprehend with their minds, and turn and be healed.'

[1211] Titus 1:14 not paying attention to Jewish myths or to commandments of those who reject the truth.

will bring us back again?" Say: "He who brought you forth the first time." And (if) they shake their heads in disbelief, and ask you, "When will this happen?" Say, "It might be soon.[1212] (51) It will be the day when He calls you, and you respond by praising Him and think you have been there only a short time." (52)

Tell my worshipers always to say that which is best: truly, Satan is always ready to stir trouble among them [1213] — Satan is clearly man's enemy. (53) Your Lord knows you best. If He wills, He will give you mercy;[1214] and if He wills, He will punish you. And We have not sent you (Prophet) to be their protector, (54) your Lord knows best whoever is in the heavens and on earth. We favored some of the prophets over others, and, to David, We gave the Book of Psalms. (55) Say, "Call on those whom you claim to be deities beside Him. They do not have any power to remove or to avert any harm from you.[1215] (56) Those to whom they pray are themselves seeking a way to approach their Lord- striving to be nearest, hoping for His mercy, and fearing His punishment;[1216] your Lord's punishment is certainly something to be concerned about [1217] (57) We will destroy or chastise with severe suffering any community (if it proves sinful) before the Day of Resurrection. All of this is written in the Book. (58)

Nothing has prevented Us from sending down signs, except that people in the past denied them. We gave the (community of) Thamud the she-camel as a visible sign, and they sinned against it. We sent signs as a means of warning. (59) We have already told you (Muhammad) that your Lord knows all about human beings. The vision that We showed you—as well as the cursed tree (Hell) cursed in this Qur'an—are only a trial and temptation for men. We put Our fear in them but this only increases their tyranny. (60)

And we said to the angels, "Prostrate yourselves to Adam!" They all prostrated themselves except Iblīs, who said, "Will I prostrate myself to one whom you have created from mud?" [1218] (61) He then added, "Do You see this one that You have honored over me? If You will allow me time until the Day of Resurrection, I will unquestionably lead his descendants —all but a few—by the nose to obey me!" (62) God said, "Go! But as for those who will follow you, Hell will be the repayment for you all, a repayment in full![1219] (63) Stir up those you can with your voice. Rally all your horses and men against them, and share with them their worldly treasures and children. Make all kinds of promises to them, for they will not know that which Satan promises is only an illusion." (64) "Know

• • •

[1212] Revelation 22:7 'See, I am coming soon! Blessed is the one who keeps the words of the prophecy of this book.'

[1213] 1 Chronicles 21:1 Satan stood up against Israel, and incited David to count the people of Israel.

[1214] Romans 9:18 So then he has mercy on whomsoever he chooses, and he hardens the heart of whomsoever he chooses.

[1215] Isaiah 44:9 All who make idols are nothing, and the things they delight in do not profit; their witnesses neither see nor know. And so they will be put to shame.

[1216] Job 19:29 be afraid of the sword, for wrath brings the punishment of the sword, so that you may know there is a judgment.'

[1217] Isaiah 2:10, Enter into the rock, and hide in the dust from the terror of the Lord, and from the glory of his majesty

[1218] Genesis 2:7 then the Lord God formed man from the dust of the ground, and breathed into his nostrils the breath of life; and the man became a living being.

[1219] Ezekiel 5:15 You shall be a mockery and a taunt, a warning and a horror, to the nations around you, when I execute judgments on you in anger and fury, and with furious punishments—I, the Lord, have spoken—

that you will have no power over my worshipers; Your Lord suffices as their guardian." [65]

Your Lord is He who causes ships[1220] to move across the sea for you, so that you are able to seek His blessings. Truly He is the Mercy Giver to you. [66] And whenever you are in danger on the sea, all those you call upon vanish-except Him. But as soon as He brings you safely to shore,[1221] you turn away—for surely man is ungrateful.[1222] [67] Can you, then, ever feel secure that He will not cause a tract of dry land to swallow you, or release the deadly winds of a storm upon you, from which you will find no one to protect you? [68] Or can you even conceive of being certain that He will not make you go back to sea, and then release a raging hurricane upon you that will drown you for your lack of faith? You will find no one who will support you..[1223] [69] We have honored the children of Adam, and carried them over land and sea, and provided sustenance for them out of life's good things, and favored them to a far greater extent than most of Our creation.[1224] [70]

On that day We will call all human beings to judgment with their book of deeds. Those who are given their book in their right hand will read their book and will not be wronged not even by so much as a hair's breadth. [71] For whoever (refuses to see, and so) is blind in this world, will also be blind in the life to come, and still farther away from the (straight) path. [72]

(Prophet) they almost succeeded in tempting you to stray from (the Truth) that We have revealed to you, and to declare something else in Our name. In that case, they would have made you their friend. [73] Had We not kept you steadfast, you would have almost begun to lean a little towards them.[1225] [74] Had this happened, We would have made you doubly punished in life and doubly punished after death. You would have found no one to support you against Us! [75] And they stirred you up enough and almost succeeded in driving you away from the land, but had they succeeded, they would have remained   only briefly

• • •

[1220] Proverbs 30:18-19 Three things are too wonderful for me; four I do not understand: [19] the way of an eagle in the sky, the way of a snake on a rock, the way of a ship on the high seas, and the way of a man with a girl.

[1221] Psalm 107:23-28 Some went down to the sea in ships, doing business on the mighty waters; [24] they saw the deeds of the Lord, his wondrous works in the deep. [25] For he commanded and raised the stormy wind, which lifted up the waves of the sea. [26] They mounted up to heaven, they went down to the depths; their courage melted away in their calamity; [27] they reeled and staggered like drunkards, and were at their wits' end. [28] Then they cried to the Lord in their trouble, and he brought them out from their distress;

[1222] Job 8:13 Such are the paths of all who forget God; the hope of the godless shall perish.

[1223] Job 14:13 O that you would hide me in Sheol, that you would conceal me until your wrath is past, that you would appoint me a set time, and remember me!

[1224] Genesis 1:26-28 Then God said, 'Let us make humankind in our image, according to our likeness; and let them have dominion over the fish of the sea, and over the birds of the air, and over the cattle, and over all the wild animals of the earth, and over every creeping thing that creeps upon the earth.' [27] So God created humankind in his image, in the image of God he created them; male and female he created them. [28] God blessed them, and God said to them, 'Be fruitful and multiply, and fill the earth and subdue it; and have dominion over the fish of the sea and over the birds of the air and over every living thing that moves upon the earth.'

[1225] Psalm 5:7-8 But I, through the abundance of your steadfast love, will enter your house, I will bow down toward your holy temple in awe of you. [8] Lead me, O Lord, in your righteousness because of my enemies; make your way straight before me.

after you were gone.[76] Nothing has changed. It was this way with the messengers We sent before you. You will find no changes in Our ways.[1226] [77] Establish prayer from the time the sun declines until the darkening of the night, and also (remember) the (Qur'an) recitation at dawn. The dawn recitation is certainly witnessed (by Us). [78] Pray during the night, an extra voluntary prayer,[1227] as it may well be that your Lord will elevate you to a praiseworthy status. [79] Say, "My Lord, Cause me to enter (in all I do) with truth, and cause me to finish with truth, and grant me strength out of Your sustaining grace."[80] And say, "The Truth has come,[1228] and falsehood has vanished, for, falsehood is bound to vanish. [81]

We send down from the Qur'an what is a healing and mercy to the believers. And it only increases the unjust in their loss: [82] for, when We bless a human being, he turns away,[1229] and arrogantly distances himself; and when he encounters calamity he despairs. [83] Say, "Each one acts in a manner reflecting his own character. Your Lord is fully aware as to who is guided to the best path."[84]

And they will ask you about the spirit. Say, "The spirit is within my Lord's domain, and you have been given but little knowledge [85] And if We so desired, We could easily take away whatever We have revealed to you, and in that (case) you would not find anyone to plead your case with us [86] other than mercy from your Lord, His favor towards you is huge! [87] Say, "If all people and all Jinn would band together with the intent of generating the likes of this Qur'an, they, would never be able to come out with anything like it, even if they backed each other up. [88] We have mentioned in this Qur'an every kind of example to benefit people.[1230] However, most of the people persist in rejecting the truth.[1231] [89] And so they say, "We will not believe you (Prophet) until you cause a spring to gush up from the earth; [90] or, unless you have a garden of dates and grapes and cause rivers to pour through it abundantly. [91] Or, until the skies fall down upon us— crushing us, as you have threatened to do. Or (until) you bring God and the angels face to face before us, [92] or, to have a house of gold or you go to heaven—but we would not even believe in your ascension unless you return with a book that we can read! "Say, "May my Lord be exalted in His glory, am I other than a man appointed as a messenger?" [93] Yet nothing has prevented people from believing whenever guidance was sent to them, except for their saying, "Has God sent a mere mortal man as His Messenger?" [94] Say, "If angels walked the earth feeling at home, We would have then sent down an angel from heaven

• • •

[1226] Numbers 23:19 God is not a human being, that he should lie, or a mortal, that he should change his mind. Has he promised, and will he not do it? Has he spoken, and will he not fulfill it?

[1227] Psalm 119:62, 164 At midnight I rise to praise you, because of your righteous ordinances. [164] Seven times a day I praise you for your righteous ordinances.

[1228] John 8:12 The truth will set you free.

[1229] Judges 3:7 The Israelites did what was evil in the sight of the Lord, forgetting the Lord their God, and worshipping the Baals and the Asherahs.

[1230] Proverbs 1:2-6 For learning about wisdom and instruction, for understanding words of insight, [3] for gaining instruction in wise dealing, righteousness, justice, and equity; [4] to teach shrewdness to the simple, knowledge and prudence to the young— [5] let the wise also hear and gain in learning, and the discerning acquire skill, [6] to understand a proverb and a figure, the words of the wise and their riddles.

[1231] Mark 7:9 Then he said to them, "You have a fine way of rejecting the commandment of God in order to keep your tradition!

as Our Messenger." [95] Say, "God is sufficient witness between you and me; truly, he is fully aware of His worshipers and He sees all." [96]

Whoever God guided, is truly guided,[1232] but for those whom God allows to stray[1233] you will not find any protection for them apart from Him. We will gather them on the Day of Resurrection, flat on their faces, blind, dumb and deaf, with Hell as their (ultimate) dwelling; Whenever the fire subsides, We will increase it for them. [97] This will be their reward for having rejected Our signs and for having said, "After We will have become bones and dust, will we, be raised up then as a new creation?" [98] Don't they see that God, Who created the heavens and the earth, has the power to create another just like them, and to assign a fixed term for them of which there is no doubt?" But the unjust refuse to accept anything except to reject the truth. [99] Say, "If you were to possess the vast storehouses of my Lord's mercy, you would still hold on to them, fearing they run out. Man has always been tightfisted [100]

We gave Moses nine self-evident signs.[1234] So, ask the Children of Israel (to tell you what happened) when Moses came to them (appealing to Pharaoh on their behalf), and Pharaoh responded to him, "Truly, Moses, I think you are engaged in witchcraft." [101] And (Moses) answered: "You know very well that no one but the Lord of heavens and earth can produce such miracles, as evidence so that you may see. So, Pharaoh, (since you have chosen rather to reject what you see), I know you are utterly lost." [102] And then Pharaoh wanted to wipe (the Children of Israel) from the face of the earth, and We subsequently caused Pharaoh and all who joined him to drown.[1235] [103] And after that, We told the Children of Israel, "Dwell safely on earth, but always (remember that) when the promise of the Last Day is due, We will bring you forth as (a part of) a diverse multitude." [104]

We sent down the Qur'an with the Truth and with Truth it has come down. We only sent you (Prophet) to bring good news and to give a warning [105] with a Qur'an which We have revealed gradually, so that you may read it to the people slowly, with reflection. We have sent it down with the actual words of God in the format that He chose. [106] Say, "Believe it or do not believe it." When it is recited to those who have been given knowledge before, they fall down on their faces in prostration, [107] saying, 'May our Lord be exalted in His glory! Truly, our Lord has fulfilled His promise' [108] and they fall down, weeping. It (the Qur'an) fills them with humility" [109]

Say, "Call on God; or call on the Merciful-to-all.[1236] By whichever name you call upon (Him), the most beautiful names are His! And pray, not screaming or

• • •

[1232] Isaiah 48:17 Thus says the Lord, your Redeemer, the Holy One of Israel: I am the Lord your God, who teaches you for your own good, who leads you in the way you should go.

[1233] 2 Thessalonians 2:11 For this reason God sends them a powerful delusion, leading them to believe what is false,

[1234] The story of Moses and Pharaoh is detailed in Exodus 7 - 14

[1235] Exodus 14:26-28 Then the Lord said to Moses, 'Stretch out your hand over the sea, so that the water may come back upon the Egyptians, upon their chariots and chariot drivers.' [27] So Moses stretched out his hand over the sea, and at dawn the sea returned to its normal depth. As the Egyptians fled before it, the Lord tossed the Egyptians into the sea. [28] The waters returned and covered the chariots and the chariot drivers, the entire army of Pharaoh that had followed them into the sea; not one of them remained.

[1236] Isaiah 55:1 The Free Offer of Mercy "Ho! Everyone who thirsts, come to the waters; And you who have no money come, buy and eat. Come, buy wine and milk Without money and without cost.

whispering, but in a moderate voice, [110] and say, "All praise be to God, who has had no son and who has no partner in His kingdom, and who needs no protector from disgrace!" And proclaim His immeasurable greatness. [111]

CHAPTER EIGHTEEN

AL-KAHF

THE CAVE

THE **MECCA** PERIOD

In the Name of God, the Merciful-to-all, the Mercy Giver:

All praise is (due) to God, who has sent down the Book to His servant and allowed no crookedness in it, [01] but unerringly straight, [1236] to warn of severe punishment from Him and to give good news to the believers who do righteous deeds, that they will have excellent reward[1237] [02] where they will remain forever.[1238] [03] And to warn those who say, "God has taken a son." [04] They have no knowledge of this, nor had their forefathers. The word that comes out of their mouths is grievous; they say nothing but a lie. [05] Then perhaps you are going to worry yourself to death chasing after them, if they do not believe in this message. [06]

We have adorned the earth with attractive things[1239] so that We may test people (as to) who will do best [07] but We will (later) reduce all of it into a wasteland. [08] Or did you think that the fellows of the cave and (their devotion to) the scriptures were among our amazing signs? [09] The young men retreated to a cave and said, "Our Lord, grant us Your mercy and help us see our way clear out of this ordeal." [10] So, We sealed their ears in the cave for a number of years. [11] Then We awakened them to know which of the two groups was better able to calculate the time they had stayed there. [12]

We now relate to you their story in Truth. They were young people who believed in their Lord, and We deepened their understanding. [13] We

• • •

[1236] Psalm 19:9 the fear of the Lord is pure, enduring for ever; the ordinances of the Lord are true and righteous altogether.
[1237] 1 Samuel 26:2 So Saul rose and went down to the Wilderness of Ziph, with three thousand chosen men of Israel, to seek David in the Wilderness of Ziph.
[1238] Matthew 25:46 And these will go away into eternal punishment, but the righteous into eternal life.'
[1239] 30 God said, 'See, I have given you every plant yielding seed that is upon the face of all the earth, and every tree with seed in its fruit; you shall have them for food. And to every beast of the earth, and to every bird of the air, and to everything that creeps on the earth, everything that has the breath of life, I have given every green plant for food.' And it was so. 31 God saw everything that he had made, and indeed, it was very good. And there was evening and there was morning, the sixth day.

emboldened them when they stood up (to their people) and said, "Our Lord is the Lord of the heavens and the earth. Never will we invoke any deity other than Him, for that would be a deplorable thing to do. [14] Our people have taken gods besides Him. Why, can they not produce any clear evidence for their beliefs? Who, then, could be more unjust than someone who makes up lies about God"? [1240] [15] "Now that you have withdrawn from them and that which they worship instead of God, take refuge in that cave. Your Lord will spread out His mercy for you and will help you find the best way out of your predicament." [16]

And (had you been present), you would have seen the sun, when it rose, veering away from their cave towards the right, and, when it set, passing away from them to the left, while they lay within an opening of that cave. This is one of God's signs. He whom God guides is the rightly guided,[1241] he whom God leaves to stray, you will not find for him a guiding protector [1242] [17] And you would have thought that they were awake, whereas they were really asleep. And We turned them to the right side and to the left side, while their dog stretched his forelegs at the entrance. If you had looked at them, you would have turned and run away and been very afraid of them. [18]

In time We awakened them, so they may ask one another. One of them said: "How long have you remained here?" They said, "We have been here a day or part of a day." They said, "Your Lord knows best how long You have been here. So send one of you with this silver coin of yours to the town and let him find the best food, and bring some back to you, but let him be cautious. And let no one be aware of you. [19] If they come to know, about you, they will stone you or force you to return to their religion. And then you would never succeed, ever." [20] It is in this way that we caused them to be found, so that people would know that the promise of God is true and that there is no doubt about the Hour[1243] (of Resurrection). AS they were arguing among themselves about them, some said, "Build a structure over them. Their Lord knows best about them."[1244] But those who prevailed in the matter said: "We will build a place of worship over them." [21] Some will say there were three (sleepers), the fourth one being their dog; while others will say there were five, the sixth one being their dog - Just guessing at the unknown. Still others will say there were seven, and the eighth one was their dog. Say, "My Lord knows their number best.[1245] Very few know (the truth) about them, so do not argue about them except in relation to what is clearly known, and do not seek the opinion of any of these people about them." [22] Never say of anything, "I will do that tomorrow," [23] without adding, "God willing."[1246] And whenever you forget, remember your Lord and say, "I pray that my Lord will guide me closer to what is right." [24] And they remained in their cave

• • •

[1240] Psalm 5:6 You destroy those who speak lies; the Lord abhors the bloodthirsty and deceitful.

[1241] Psalm 73:24 You guide me with your counsel, and afterwards you will receive me with honor

[1242] 2 Thessalonians 2:11 For this reason God sends them a powerful delusion, leading them to believe what is false,

[1243] John 5:28 Do not be astonished at this; for the hour is coming when all who are in their graves will hear his voice

[1244] 2 Timothy 2:19 But God's firm foundation stands, bearing this inscription: 'The Lord knows those who are his', and, 'Let everyone who calls on the name of the Lord turn away from wickedness.'

[1245] 1 John 3:20 whenever our hearts condemn us; for God is greater than our hearts, and he knows everything.

[1246] James 4:15 Instead you ought to say, 'If the Lord wishes, we will live and do this or that.'

for three hundred years plus an additional nine. [25] Say, "God knows best how long they remained. All that is beyond our senses, in the heavens and on the earth belongs to Him.[1247] How perfectly He sees, and how perfectly He Hears! They have no protector besides Him, and He does not share His rule with anyone."[1248] [26]

Recite what has been revealed to you from your Lord's Book. No one can change His words, and you will never find any refuge except with Him. [1249] [27] And patiently stay with those who call upon their Lord morning and evening, seeking His approval.[1250] And let not your eyes turn away from them, desiring worldly attractions.[1251] Do not obey anyone whose heart We have made oblivious of Our remembrance, who follows his own whims and desires, and who abandons all that is good. [28] And say, "The Truth is from your Lord.[1252] Whoever wills - let him believe; and whoever wills - let him deny the truth." We have prepared a fire for the unjust whose walls will surround them. And if they call for relief, they will be relieved with water like molten brass, which scalds their faces. Terrible is that drink, and evil is that resting place. [29] As for those who have believed and done righteous deeds - We do not let the reward – of anyone who does a good deed go to waste.[1253] [30] They will have Gardens of Eden; beneath them rivers will flow. They will be adorned with bracelets of gold, and will wear green garments of fine silk and brocade, and recline on couches. What an excellent reward, and what a wonderful resting place! [31]

And present to them the parable of two men. To one of them, We gave two gardens of grapevines, and surrounded them with palm trees, and placed fields of crops between them. [32] Each of the two gardens produced its fruit and did not fall short[1254] in anything. And We made a gushing river flow right through them. [33] And he had plenty of fruit, so he said to his neighbor while conversing with him, "I am greater than you in wealth and mightier in (numbers of) men."[1255] [34] He entered his garden and did himself harm by saying: "I do not think that this will ever perish. [35] And neither do I think that the Hour will come.[1256] But even if I should be brought back to my Lord, I will surely get something better in

• • •

[1247] 1 Chronicles 29:11 Yours, O Lord, are the greatness, the power, the glory, the victory, and the majesty; for all that is in the heavens and on the earth is yours; yours is the kingdom, O Lord, and you are exalted as head above all.
[1248] Deuteronomy 6:13 The Lord your God you shall fear; him you shall serve, and by his name alone you shall swear.
[1249] Psalm 73:28 But for me it is good to be near God; I have made the Lord God my refuge, to tell of all your works.
[1250] Psalm 27:8 'Come,' my heart says, 'seek his face!' Your face, Lord, do I seek.
[1251] 1 John 2:15-17 Do not love the world or the things in the world. The love of the Father is not in those who love the world; [16] for all that is in the world—the desire of the flesh, the desire of the eyes, the pride in riches—comes not from the Father but from the world. [17] And the world and its desire are passing away, but those who do the will of God live forever.
[1252] John 8:32 The truth will set you free.
[1253] 2 Timothy 1:12 and for this reason I suffer as I do. But I am not ashamed, for I know the one in whom I have put my trust, and I am sure that he is able to guard until that day what I have entrusted to him.
[1254] Luke 12:16-17 Then he told them a parable: 'The land of a rich man produced abundantly. 17 And he thought to himself, "What should I do, for I have no place to store my crops?"
[1255] Luke 12:18 Then he said, "I will do this: I will pull down my barns and build larger ones, and there I will store all my grain and my goods.
[1256] Luke 12:19 And I will say to my soul, Soul, you have ample goods laid up for many years; relax, eat, drink, be merry."

return."[1257] [36] His neighbor said to him in the course of the conversation: "Have you no faith [1258] in Him who created you from dust,[1259] and then from a sperm-drop and then shaped you into a man? [37] As for me, He is my Lord, and I don't associate anyone with my Lord. [38] if only, you had said, when you entered your garden, 'It is all God's will; there is no power except in God'?[1260] Although you see me possessing less than you in wealth and children, [39] it may well be that my Lord will give me something better than your garden and send down on it thunderbolts from the sky so that it becomes a heap of barren dust, [40] or its water sinks deep into the ground, so that you will never be able to attain it." [41] And (thus it happened): his fruitful garden was surrounded (by ruin), and there he was, wringing his hands in grief over what he had spent on it, while it had collapsed upon its trellises. He said, "Oh, I wish I had not associated anyone with my Lord," [42] for now there was no one other than God to help him, nor could he help himself. [43] Thus it is, all protection there belongs to God, the Truth. He gives the best reward and the best outcome. [44]

Cite for them the parable of the life of this world, it is like water that We send down from the sky[1261] and is absorbed by the plants of the earth. But in time it becomes dry chaff,[1262] scattered by the winds. And it is God who has absolute power over all things. [45] Wealth and children are adornments of this worldly life, but the enduring good deeds produce a greater reward from your Lord and a better hope.[1263] [46] On the Day We will set the mountains in motion, and you see the earth emerging, and We will gather them all, leaving not a single one behind. [47] They will be lined up before your Lord, (and He will say) "You have come to Us just as We created you in the first instance. Even though you claimed that We will not make such an appointment for you." [48] And the Book (of deeds) will be laid (open)[1264] and you will see those who forced others to reject God's messages filled with dread at what is in it, and they will say, "Alas for us! What a record is this! It leaves out no deeds, small or great, but accounts for it!" They will find everything they ever did present (before them). Your Lord will not be unjust to anyone. [49]

And (mention) when We told the angels, "Prostrate yourselves before Adam," and they all prostrated themselves, except for Iblīs.[1265] He was of the

• • •

[1257] Luke 12:20 But God said to him, "You fool! This very night your life is being demanded of you. And the things you have prepared, whose will they be?"

[1258] Hebrews 11:1 Now faith is the assurance of things hoped for, the conviction of things not seen.

[1259] Genesis 2:7 then the Lord God formed man from the dust of the ground, and breathed into his nostrils the breath of life; and the man became a living being.

[1260] Deuteronomy 8:17-18 Do not say to yourself, 'My power and the might of my own hand have gained me this wealth.' [18] But remember the Lord your God, for it is he who gives you power to get wealth, so that he may confirm his covenant that he swore to your ancestors, as he is doing today.

[1261] Matthew 5:45 so that you may be children of your Father in heaven; for he makes his sun rise on the evil and on the good, and sends rain on the righteous and on the unrighteous.

[1262] Matthew 6:30, But if God so clothes the grass of the field, which is alive today and tomorrow is thrown into the oven, will he not much more clothe you—you of little faith?, Psalm 1:4 The wicked are not so, but are like chaff that the wind drives away.

[1263] Psalm 39:7 "And now, O Lord, what do I wait for? My hope is in you.

[1264] Revelation 20:12 And I saw the dead, great and small, standing before the throne, and books were opened. Also another book was opened, the book of life. And the dead were judged according to their works, as recorded in the books.

[1265] See Glossary

jinn, but he disobeyed his Lord's command. Do you (seriously consider) choosing him and his descendants as allies instead of Me, when they are your enemies? How despicable a bargain this is for the unjust? [50] I did not make them witness to the creation of the heavens and earth, nor to their own creation, and neither do I have any need to take those who lead others astray as my helpers. [51] And (warn of) the Day when He will say, "Call 'My partners' whom you claimed," and they (the unjust) will call on them, but they (the partners) will not respond to them, for we shall place an unbridgeable divide between them. [52] And those who forced others to reject Our messages will see the Fire, and they will know that they are bound to fall into it, and they will not find any escape from it. [53]

We have mentioned in this Qur'an all kind of examples for the benefit of people, but, more than anything else, man is argumentative! [54] Now that guidance has come to them, What could it be that is preventing people from believing or from asking their Lord for forgiveness, other than that the fate of earlier generations has not yet befallen them, or the punishment has not yet come upon them. [55] We sent Our message-bearers only to bring good news and to give warning, yet the unbelievers seek to refute the Truth with false arguments[1266] and mock My signs and warnings. [56] And who is more unjust than one who is reminded of his Lord's messages but turns away from them, forgetting what he has done? We have placed veils over their hearts, lest they understand, and deafness in their ears.[1267] If you ask them to be guided, they will never be guided. [57] Yet your Lord is the Most-Forgiving and full of mercy. Were He to take them to task for what they deserved, He would have hastened their punishment[1268] Rather, they have an appointed time from which they will never find an escape,[58] as (was the case with) those communities that We destroyed when they did wrong:[1269] We made an appointed time for their destruction.[1270] [59]

Recall when Moses said to his servant, "I will not give up until I reach the junction of the two seas, even if I must press on for years." [60] But when they reached the junction where the two seas meet, they forgot their fish, which made its way into the sea and swam away. [61] So when they had moved on, (Moses) said to his servant, "Bring us our lunch. We have certainly suffered hardship on this journey." [62] He (the servant) said, "Remember when we rested by the rock? I forgot the fish there. And it was Satan who made me forget to pay attention to it. And amazingly, it found its way into the sea." [63] (Moses) said, "That is what we were seeking." So they returned, following their own footprints.

• • •

[1266] 1 Timothy 1:6 Some people have deviated from these and turned to meaningless talk,
[1267] Jeremiah 6:10 To whom shall I speak and give warning, that they may hear? See, their ears are closed, they cannot listen. The word of the Lord is to them an object of scorn; they take no pleasure in it.
[1268] Matthew 25:41 Then he will say to those at his left hand, "You that are accursed, depart from me into the eternal fire prepared for the devil and his angels;
[1269] Genesis 18:20-21 Then the Lord said, 'How great is the outcry against Sodom and Gomorrah and how very grave their sin! 21 I must go down and see whether they have done altogether according to the outcry that has come to me; and if not, I will know.' Genesis 19:24- 25 Then the Lord rained on Sodom and Gomorrah sulphur and fire from the Lord out of heaven; and he overthrew those cities, and all the Plain, and all the inhabitants of the cities, and what grew on the ground.
[1270] Matthew 10:15 Truly I tell you, it will be more tolerable for the land of Sodom and Gomorrah on the day of judgment than for that town.

[64] There, they found one of Our servants, whom We had blessed with mercy from Us, and unto whom We had imparted knowledge of our Own [65] Moses said to him, "May I follow you, so that you will teach me some of the right guidance You have been taught?" [66] He said, "You will not be able to wait patiently with me, [67] for how can you have patience for what you do not understand?" [68] (Moses) said, "You will find me, God willing, patient, and I will not disobey you in (any) way."[1271] [69] He said, "Then if you follow me, do not ask me about anything until I mention it to you." [70]

So they set out, until, when they had embarked on the ship, the man made a hole in it. (Moses) said "Did you knock a hole in it to drown its passengers? You have certainly done a dreadful thing." [71] The man said, "Didn't I tell you that you would not be able to wait patiently with me?" [72] (Moses) said, "Forgive me for forgetting, and don't be too harsh with me." [73] So they set out, until they met a boy, whom the man killed. (Moses) said, "You killed an innocent soul who never killed anyone. You have certainly done a deplorable thing." [74] The man said, "Didn't I tell you that you would not be able to wait patiently with me?" [75] (Moses) said, "If I should ask you about anything after this, then you should no longer let me accompany you. You have a good excuse not to put up with me." [76] So they set out, until they reached the inhabitants of a town and they asked them for food, but they refused to entertain them as guests. Then they found a wall about to collapse, so the man restored it. (Moses) said, "If you wished, you could have been paid for (fixing) it." [77] He said, "This is where you and I will part company. I will tell you the interpretation of what you could not wait for patiently. [78] As for the ship, it belonged to poor people working at sea. I damaged it because there was a king after them who seized every (good) ship by force. [79] And as for the boy, his parents were believers, and we had reasons to fear that he would cause them extreme distress by transgression and unbelief. [80] So, we wished that their Lord would give them a son better in purity and closer to mercy. [81] As for the wall, it belonged to two orphan boys (living) in town, and there was a treasure beneath it belonging to them. Their father was a righteous man. So your Lord intended that they reach maturity and then to unearth their treasure as a mercy from your Lord. And I did not do (any of this) of my own accord. This is the interpretation of what you were not able to wait for patiently." [82]

And they ask you, about the Zul-Qarnayn (Two-Horned One).[1272] "I will tell you something about him." [83] We gave him power and authority on earth, and We gave him a way to achieve anything. [84] So he chose a way [85] until, when he reached the setting of the sun, he found it (as if) setting in a dark, muddy spring, and nearby he found some people. We said, "O Zul-Qarnayn, either cause (them) to suffer or treat them with kindness." [86] He said, "We will punish the unjust. Then he will return to his Lord, and He will punish him with unspeakable suffering.[1273] [87] But as for the one who believes and does righteousness, he will

• • •

[1271] Psalm 143:10 Teach me to do your will, for you are my God. Let your good spirit lead me on a level path.
[1272] Daniel 11:3 Then a warrior king shall arise, who shall rule with great dominion and take action as he pleases.
[1273] Matthew 25:41 Then he will say to those at his left hand, "You that are accursed, depart from me into the eternal fire prepared for the devil and his angels;

have the best of rewards.[1274] require him to do only easy things." [88] Then he followed a path [89] until he came to the rising of the sun. He found it rising on a people for whom We had provided no shade. [90] And so it was, Our knowledge encompassed all that happened to him. [91]

Then he followed a path [92] until he reached a pass between two mountains, where he found a people who could hardly understand a word he was saying. [93] They said, "O Zul-Qarnayn, Gog and Magog[1275] are corrupting this land. Can we pay you to erect a barrier between us and them? [94] He said, "What my Lord has given me is better (than any compensation). Just give me a strong helping hand and I will build a solid barrier between you and them. [95] Bring me chunks of iron." When he had filled in (the gap) between the two mountain-sides, he said, "Blow!" When he had made (the iron) as red hot as fire, he said, "Bring me molten copper to pour over it." [96] So (Gog and Magog) were able neither to scale the barrier, nor were they able to pierce it. [97] He said, "This is a mercy from my Lord; but when the promise of my Lord comes, He will crush it (the barrier). The promise of my Lord is surely true."[1276] [98] And on that Day We will let them surge like waves over each other, and (then) the Horn will be blown,[1277] and We will gather them all together. [99] On that Day We shall display Hell plainly to the unbelievers, [100] those whose eyes had been veiled from My message, and who could not hear it. [101] Do those who have denied the truth think that they can take My servants as protectors instead of Me? We have prepared Hell for the unbelievers as their lodging place. [102]

Say, "Shall we tell you who are the most failing in whatever they do? [103] They are those whose efforts are lost in worldly pursuits, while they think that they are doing good work." [104] Those are the ones who deny the signs of their Lord and deny that they will meet Him. Their actions will come to nothing and on the Day of Resurrection they will be of no consequence.[1278] [105] Hell is their recompense for having denied the truth, and ridiculed My signs and My messengers.[106] Those who have believed and done righteous deeds will have

• • •

[1274] John 14:1-3 'Do not let your hearts be troubled. Believe in God, believe also in me. [2] In my Father's house there are many dwelling-places. If it were not so, would I have told you that I go to prepare a place for you? [3] And if I go and prepare a place for you, I will come again and will take you to myself, so that where I am, there you may be also.

[1275] Ezekiel 38:2-3 Mortal, set your face towards Gog, of the land of Magog, the chief prince of Meshech and Tubal. Prophesy against him 3 and say: Thus says the Lord GOD: I am against you, O Gog, chief prince of Meshech and Tubal;

[1276] 2 Samuel 22:31 This God—his way is perfect; the promise of the Lord proves true; he is a shield for all who take refuge in him.

[1277] 1 Corinthians 15:52 in a moment, in the twinkling of an eye, at the last trumpet. For the trumpet will sound, and the dead will be raised imperishable, and we will be changed.

[1278] 1 Corinthians 3:12-15 Now if anyone builds on the foundation with gold, silver, precious stones, wood, hay, straw—[13] the work of each builder will become visible, for the Day will disclose it, because it will be revealed with fire, and the fire will test what sort of work each has done. [14] If what has been built on the foundation survives, the builder will receive a reward. If the work is burned, the builder will suffer loss; the builder will be saved, but only as through fire.

Paradise[1279] for their lodging, [(107)] where they will abide eternally,[1280] never wishing to leave. [(108)]

Say, "If the sea were ink for (writing) the words of my Lord, the sea would run out long before the words of my Lord ran out, even if We were to add another sea to it. [(109)] Say, "I am only a man like you, to whom has been revealed that your god is one God.[1281] So, whoever looks forward with hope to meet his Lord, let him do righteous deeds[1282] and in the worship of his Lord not associate anyone with him." [(110)]

• • •

[1279] Revelation 22:1-5 Then the angel showed me the river of the water of life, bright as crystal, flowing from the throne of God and of the Lamb [2] through the middle of the street of the city. On either side of the river is the tree of life with its twelve kinds of fruit, producing its fruit each month; and the leaves of the tree are for the healing of the nations. [3] Nothing accursed will be found there any more. But the throne of God and of the Lamb will be in it, and his servants will worship him; [4] they will see his face, and his name will be on their foreheads. [5] And there will be no more night; they need no light of lamp or sun, for the Lord God will be their light, and they will reign for ever and ever

[1280] Matthew 25:34 Then the king will say to those at his right hand, "Come, you that are blessed by my Father, inherit the kingdom prepared for you from the foundation of the world.

[1281] Mark 12:29-30 Jesus answered, "The foremost is, 'Hear, o israel! the Lord our God is one Lord; [30] and you shall love the Lord your God with all your heart, and with all your soul, and with all your mind, and with all your strength.'

[1282] Mark 12:31 "The second is this, 'You shall love your neighbor as yourself.' There is no other commandment greater than these."

CHAPTER NINETEEN

Maryam

MARY

THE **MECCA** PERIOD

In the Name of God, the Merciful-to-all, the Mercy Giver:

Kaf Ha Ya 'Ayn Sad.[1283] [01] Recount your Lord's mercy on His servant [1284] Zechariah[1285] [02] When he called to His Lord silently [03] he said, "My Lord, my bones have weakened, and my head shimmers with grey hair, but never, Lord, have I failed to be blessed in praying to you. [04] And I fear what my kinsfolk (will do) after I am gone. My wife has been barren, so give me an heir as a gift from You [05] one who will receive my inheritance and he will be an heir to the family of Jacob. And make him, my Lord, pleasing to You." [06] "O Zechariah, We bring you good news of a son whose name will be John,[1286] a name We have never given to anyone else before." [07] (Zechariah) said, "My Lord, how will I have a son when my wife has been barren and I have reached advanced old age?" [08] He said, "It will be so. Your Lord says: 'It is easy for Me, for I created you before, when you were nothing.' "[09] (Zechariah) said, "My Lord, give me a sign." He said, "Your sign is that you will not speak to people for three full nights." [10] So he came out from the sanctuary and signaled his people to glorify (God) in the morning and in the evening. [11]

"John,[1287] take hold of the Book with steadfastness." And We gave him wisdom (while he was still) a boy [12] as well as affection from Us and purity, and he was always mindful of Us [13] and full of kindness towards his parents, and he was not domineering or rebellious.[14] (God's) peace was upon him on the day he

• • •

[1283] Here and at the beginning of many chapters there are letters of unknown meaning called Al Muquatta'at. Numerous theories have been proposed, but there is no agreement on what they signify yet.

[1284] Servant" is much more common in English than the word "slave," but both this Arabic word /abd / and the corresponding words in the Law /abd/ and the Gospel /doulos/ are stronger than this. This word means both slave and worshiper. All the holy books call the believers slaves of God, but I prefer worshiper.

[1285] Zechariah. See Glossary. Luke 1:5 In the days of King Herod of Judea, there was a priest named Zechariah, who belonged to the priestly order of Abijah. His wife was a descendant of Aaron, and her name was Elizabeth

[1286] Luke 1:13 But the angel said to him, 'Do not be afraid, Zechariah, for your prayer has been heard. Your wife Elizabeth will bear you a son, and you will name him John.

[1287] John the Baptist

was born and the day of his death, and it will be upon him on the day he is raised alive. [15]

Mention in the Book the story of Mary,[1288] when she withdrew from her family to a place toward the east, [1289] [16] and secluded herself from them. We then sent to her Our Spirit, who appeared to her in the shape of a perfect human being. [1290] [17] She said, "I seek refuge from you in the Merciful, [1291] (leave me alone) if you are God fearing." [18] He said, "I am only the messenger of your Lord, (who says,) 'I will give you a son endowed with purity.'" [1292] [19] She said, "How can I have a son when no man has touched me and I have not been a promiscuous woman?"[1293] [20] He said, "It will be so. Your Lord says, 'It is easy for Me, and We will make him a sign to people and a mercy from Us. The matter is already determined.'"[21] So she conceived him, and she withdrew with him to a remote place. [22] Then the pains of childbirth drove her to the trunk of a palm tree. She said, "Oh, I wish I had been dead and forgotten before all this." [23] But a voice called to her from below, "Do not grieve; your Lord has provided a stream beneath you. [24] Shake the trunk of the palm tree toward you; it will drop ripe, fresh dates to you. [25] So eat and drink and be satisfied and say to anyone you may see, I have made a vow of silence to the Lord of Mercy and I will not talk to anyone today." [26]

Then she went back to her people, carrying him. They said, "Mary, you have done an unthinkable thing. [27] Sister of Aaron,[1294] your father was not a bad man, nor was your mother a loose woman." [28] She pointed to him. They said, "How can we speak to a child in the cradle?" [29] (Jesus) said, "I am the servant of God. He has given me the Book and made me a prophet.[1295] [30] And He has made me blessed[1296] wherever I am and directed me to pray and to give charitable gifts as long as I live [31] And to be full of kindness toward my mother, and He has not made me domineering or rebellious. [32] And (God's) peace was upon me [1297] the day I was born and the day I will die and it will be upon me the day I am raised alive." [33]

Such is Jesus (Esa), the son of Mary – the Word of Truth about which they are in dispute. [34] It does not befit God to have a son; may He be exalted in His glory! When He decides on something, He simply says to it, "Be!" and it is.[1298] [35] (Jesus

• • •

[1288] Mother of Jesus

[1289] Luke 1:39-40 In those days Mary set out and went with haste to a Judean town in the hill country, [40] where she entered the house of Zechariah and greeted Elizabeth.

[1290] Luke 1:26-27 In the sixth month the angel Gabriel was sent by God to a town in Galilee called Nazareth, [27] to a virgin engaged to a man whose name was Joseph, of the house of David. The virgin's name was Mary.

[1291] Psalm 145:8 The Lord is gracious and merciful, slow to anger and abounding in steadfast love.

[1292] Luke 1:28-31 And he came to her and said, 'Greetings, favored one! The Lord is with you.' [29] But she was much perplexed by his words and pondered what sort of greeting this might be. [30] The angel said to her, 'Do not be afraid, Mary, for you have found favor with God. [31] And now, you will conceive in your womb and bear a son, and you will name him Jesus.

[1293] Luke 1:34 Mary said to the angel, 'How can this be, since I am a virgin?'.

[1294] Mary is a descendant of Aaron and to call her sister of Aaron is a figure of speech.

[1295] Jesus mentioned in the Qur'an as a prophet from birth.

[1296] Jesus mentioned in the Qur'an as a /mubarak/ (blessed) . . .

[1297] Jesus mentioned in the Qur'an as he pronounces peace upon himself.

[1298] Psalm 33: 9 For he spoke, and it came to be; he commanded, and it stood firm.

continued): "God is my Lord and your Lord, so worship Him.[1299] That is a straight path."[1300] [(36)] Then, the sects differed among themselves (concerning the nature of Jesus), so woe to those who reject the truth when they witness that awesome Day. [(37)] How (clearly) they will hear and see on the Day they will come before Us. Today, however, they are in clear error. [(38)] Warn them of the Day of Regret, when everything will have been decided; and (yet), they are heedless, and they do not believe. [(39)] It is We who will inherit the earth and all those on it, and to Us they will be returned. [(40)]

And mention in the Book (the story of) Abraham. He was a man of truth and a prophet.[1301] [(41)] He said to his father, "O my father, why do you worship that which does not hear and does not see and will not benefit you at all? [(42)] Father, I have received knowledge which has not come to you, so follow me; I will guide you to an even path. [(43)] O my father, do not worship Satan. Satan was disobedient to the Merciful. [(44)] Father, I fear that a punishment from the Merciful will afflict you so that you will be Satan's companion (in Hell)." [(45)] (His father) said, "Are you forsaking my gods, Abraham? If you do not stop this, I will surely stone you. Now get away from me and don't come back." [(46)] He said, "Peace be upon you. I will ask my Lord to forgive you. He is always gracious to me [(47)] and I will leave you and those you call upon other than God and will call upon my Lord. Perhaps in calling on my Lord, I will be blessed." [(48)] So when he had left them and those they worshipped other than God, We gave him Isaac and Jacob, and each (of them) We made a prophet. [(49)] And We endowed them with Our mercy, and we made them highly honored [(50)]

And mention in the Book, Moses (Musa).[1302] He was sincere, and he was a messenger and a prophet. [(51)] We called out to him from the right hand side of the mount and We brought him near to Us in close communication [(52)] and out of Our mercy We gave him his brother Aaron as a prophet.[1303] [(53)] And mention in the Book, Ishmael.[1304] He was true to his promise, and he was a messenger and a prophet. [(54)] He used to order his people to pray and to give the purifying alms and he found favor with His Lord [(55)] And mention in the Book, Enoch

• • •

[1299] Mark 12:29 Jesus answered, 'The first is, "Hear, O Israel: the Lord our God, the Lord is one; John 20:17 Jesus said to her, 'Do not hold on to me, because I have not yet ascended to the Father. But go to my brothers and say to them, "I am ascending to my Father and your Father, to my God and your God."'

[1300] Proverbs 3:6 In all your ways acknowledge him, and he will make straight your paths.

[1301] Genesis 12:1-3 Now the Lord said to Abram, 'Go from your country and your kindred and your father's house to the land that I will show you. [2] I will make of you a great nation, and I will bless you, and make your name great, so that you will be a blessing. [3] I will bless those who bless you, and the one who curses you I will curse; and in you all the families of the earth shall be blessed.'

[1302] Exodus 2:10 When the child grew up, she brought him to Pharaoh's daughter, and she took him as her son. She named him Moses, 'because', she said, 'I drew him out of the water.' – Deuteronomy 34:5 Then Moses, the servant of the Lord, died there in the land of Moab, at the Lord's command.

[1303] Exodus 4:14-16 Then the anger of the LORD was kindled against Moses and he said, 'What of your brother Aaron the Levite? I know that he can speak fluently; even now he is coming out to meet you, and when he sees you his heart will be glad. [15] You shall speak to him and put the words in his mouth; and I will be with your mouth and with his mouth, and will teach you what you shall do. [16] He indeed shall speak for you to the people; he shall serve as a mouth for you, and you shall serve as God for him.

[1304] Genesis 16:15-16 Hagar bore Abram a son; and Abram named his son, whom Hagar bore, Ishmael. [16] Abram was eighty-six years old when Hagar bore him Ishmael. The extensive history of Ishmael is covered in Genesis 16, 17, 21 and 25.

(Idris).[1305] He was a man of truth and a prophet [56] and We raised him to a high position.[1306] [57]

These are some of the prophets whom God has blessed - from among the descendants of Adam, and those We carried with Noah, and the descendants of Abraham and Israel, and those whom We guided and chose. When the verses of the Merciful were recited to them, they fell down prostrating and weeping. [58] But they were succeeded by generations who neglected prayer and pursued their own desires so they will meet with utter disillusionment[59] except for those who repent, believe and do righteous deeds; they will enter Paradise and will not be wronged in any way. [60] (They will be in) the Gardens of Eden which the Merciful has promised His worshipers in a realm which is beyond the reach of human perception. His promise will be fulfilled. [61] There they will hear no ill speech - only (greetings of) peace - and there they will have their provisions, morning and evening. [62] Such is Paradise, which We give as an inheritance to those of Our worshipers who were ever mindful of God. [63]

And (the angels said), "We descend only at your Lord's command. To Him belongs what is before us and behind us and in between. And your Lord is never forgetful - [64] (He is) Lord of the heavens and the earth and whatever is between them - so worship Him and persevere in His worship. Do you know of anyone equal to Him?" [65]

Yet the human being continues to ask, "When I am dead, will I then be brought out alive again?" [66] Does the human being not remember that We created him before, when he was nothing[1307]? [67] So by your Lord, We will surely round them up along with the devils, and then We will bring them around Hell on their knees. [68] Then from every sect, We will drag out those who were the most defiant towards the Merciful. [69] Surely, We know best who most deserves the fire of Hell. [70] And all of you will go through it. This is a decree from your Lord that must be fulfilled. [71] Then We will save those who were mindful of God and leave the unjust on their knees. [72]

And when Our verses, which are perfectly clear, are recited to them, the unbelievers say to those who believe, "Which of (our) two parties is in the better position and enjoys superior influence?" [73] And yet how many generations have We destroyed before them who surpassed them in possessions and (outward) appearance? [74] Say, "As for him who is lost, let the Merciful-to-all lengthen the span of his days until they see what they were promised, punishment either (in this world) or at the Hour [1308] (of Judgment). Then they will clearly see who is worse in possessions and who has the weaker forces." [75] To those rightly guided, God increases guidance, and the good deeds that will last are those that are deemed best and most rewarding in your Lord's sight. [76] Have you considered

• • •

[1305] Genesis 5:24, Enoch walked with God; then he was no more, because God took him.

[1306] Hebrews 11:5. By faith Enoch was taken so that he did not experience death; and 'he was not found, because God had taken him.' For it was attested before he was taken away that 'he had pleased God.'

[1307] Matthew 22:31-32 "But regarding the resurrection of the dead, have you not read what was spoken to you by God: [32] 'I am the God of Abraham, and the God of Isaac, and the god of Jacob'? He is not the God of the dead but of the living." [33] When the crowds heard this, they were astonished at His teaching.

[1308] Revelation 14:7 He said in a loud voice, 'Fear God and give him glory, for the hour of his judgment has come; and worship him who made heaven and earth, the sea and the springs of water.'

the man who denies the truth of Our signs and says, "I will surely be given wealth and children." [77] Has he received extrasensory knowledge, or has he received a pledge from the Merciful? [78] No! We will record what he says and extend the duration of his punishment. [79] And We will inherit from him the things he's talks about, and he will come to Us alone. [80]

And they have taken gods other than God, hoping that they would be (a source of) strength for them. [81] No! Those deities will reject their worship and will even turn against them. [82] Do you not see that We have sent the devils to the unbelievers, inciting them to sin? [83] So do not try to expedite their punishment. We are simply counting down the number of their days. [84] On the Day (of Judgment,) We will gather all the righteous as (an honored) delegation to the Merciful [85] and will drive those who forced others to reject Our messages to Hell like a thirsty herd. [86] None will have (power to) intercede on their behalf except him who has received permission from the Merciful. [87]

And they say, "The Merciful-to-all has taken (for Himself) a son." [88] You have done an atrocious thing. [89] It almost causes the heavens to rupture, the earth to split open and the mountains to collapse in devastation [90] that they attribute a son to the Merciful. [91] It does not befit the Merciful to take a son. [92] There is no one in the heavens and earth who will not come as a servant to the Merciful.[1309] [93] He has numbered them and counted them precisely [94] so that every one of them will appear alone before Him on the Day of Resurrection. [95]

The Merciful-to-all will bestow His affection on those who have believed and done righteous deeds. [96] And We have made (this Qur'an) easy to recite (Prophet) so that you may give good news to the righteous and warning to stubborn people. [97] How many generations have We destroyed before them? Do you see any one of them or even hear from them even a whisper? [98]

•   •   •

[1309] Psalm 119:91 By your appointment they stand today, for all things are your servants

CHAPTER **TWENTY**

TA HA

TAHA

THE **MECCA** PERIOD

In the name of God, the Merciful-to-all, the Mercy Giver:
Ta Ha.[1310] (01)
We have not sent down the Qur'an for you to be distressed, (02) but only as a reminder to all who stand in awe (of God) (03) a revelation that was sent down gradually from Him who created the earth and highest heavens, (04) the Merciful-to-all (who is) established on the throne of His majesty.[1311] (05) To Him belongs what is in the heavens and what is on the earth, and what is between them, and what is beneath the soil. (06) Whether or not you speak aloud, He knows what is secret as well as what is (even) more hidden. (07) God there is no god except Him. All the attributes of perfection belong to Him. (08)
And has the story of Moses reached you? (09) When he saw a fire and said to his family, "Wait here. I can see a fire; perhaps I will bring you a piece of it, or maybe I will find guidance there."[1312] (10) But when he came to the fire, he was called, "Moses, (11) I am truly your Lord, so remove your sandals. You are in the sacred valley of Tuwa.[1313] (12) and I have chosen you,[1314] so listen to what is revealed. (13) Verily I am God.[1315] There is no God except Me, so worship Me and

• • •

[1310] Here and at the beginning of many chapters there are letters of unknown meaning called Al Muquatta'at. Numerous theories have been proposed, but there is no agreement on what they signify yet.
[1311] Psalm 103:19 The Lord has established his throne in the heavens, and his kingdom rules over all.
[1312] Exodus 3:3 Then Moses said, 'I must turn aside and look at this great sight, and see why the bush is not burned up.'
[1313] Exodus 3:5 Then he said, 'Come no closer! Remove the sandals from your feet, for the place on which you are standing is holy ground.'
[1314] Exodus 3:10 So come, I will send you to Pharaoh to bring my people, the Israelites, out of Egypt.'
[1315] Exodus 3:6, 14 He said further, 'I am the God of your father, the God of Abraham, the God of Isaac, and the God of Jacob.' And Moses hid his face, for he was afraid to look at God. [14] God said to Moses, 'I am who I am.' He said further, 'Thus you shall say to the Israelites, "I am has sent me to you."'

establish prayer to remember Me. [14] The Hour[1316] (of Judgment) is coming-though I have chosen to obscure it-when every soul may be rewarded according to its deeds. [15] Do not let your focus be diverted from it by anyone who does not believe in its coming and follows his own whim, lest you perish. [16]

(God said) and what is that in your right hand,[1317]Moses?" [17] "It is my staff; I lean upon it, I bring down leaves for my sheep and I have other uses for it." [18] (God said,) "Throw it down, Moses." [19] So he threw it down, and - behold - it turned into a snake, moving swiftly.[1318] [20] (God) said, "Pick it up[1319] and do not be afraid; We will return it to its former condition. [21] Now draw your hand to your side; it will come out white, though unharmed - another sign,[1320] [22] so that We may show you (some) of Our greater signs.[1321] [23] Go to Pharaoh. He has transgressed all bounds."[1322] [24] (Moses) said, "My Lord, put my heart at ease [25] and ease my task for me [26] and untie the knot from my tongue [27] so that they may understand my speech,[1323] [28] and appoint for me a minister from my family[1324] [29] Aaron, my brother. [30] Increase my strength through him[1325] [31] and let him share my task[1326] [32] so that we may glorify You much [33] and remember You much. [34] You see and know all about us." [35]

(God) said, "You have been granted your request,[1327] Moses. [36] And We have already favored you in a previous time, [37] when We inspired your mother with this:[1328] [38] "Put him into the chest and cast it into the river.[1329] Let the river wash

• • •

[1316] Revelation 14:7 He said in a loud voice, 'Fear God and give him glory, for the hour of his judgment has come; and worship him who made heaven and earth, the sea and the springs of water.'

[1317] Exodus 4:2 The Lord said to him, 'What is that in your hand?' He said, 'A staff.'

[1318] Exodus 4:3 And he said, 'Throw it on the ground.' So he threw the staff on the ground, and it became a snake; and Moses drew back from it.

[1319] Exodus 4:4 Then the Lord said to Moses, 'Reach out your hand, and seize it by the tail'—so he reached out his hand and grasped it, and it became a staff in his hand—

[1320] Exodus 4:6-7 Again, the Lord said to him, 'Put your hand inside your cloak.' He put his hand into his cloak; and when he took it out, his hand was leprous, as white as snow. 7 Then God said, 'Put your hand back into your cloak'—so he put his hand back into his cloak, and when he took it out, it was restored like the rest of his body.

[1321] Exodus 4:8-9 'If they will not believe you or heed the first sign, they may believe the second sign. 9 If they will not believe even these two signs or heed you, you shall take some water from the Nile and pour it on the dry ground; and the water that you shall take from the Nile will become blood on the dry ground.'

[1322] Exodus 3:10 So come, I will send you to Pharaoh to bring my people, the Israelites, out of Egypt.'

[1323] Exodus 4:10-12 But Moses said to the Lord, 'O my Lord, I have never been eloquent, neither in the past nor even now that you have spoken to your servant; but I am slow of speech and slow of tongue.' 11 Then the Lord said to him, 'Who gives speech to mortals? Who makes them mute or deaf, seeing or blind? Is it not I, the Lord? 12 Now go, and I will be with your mouth and teach you what you are to speak.'

[1324] Exodus 4:13 But he said, 'O my Lord, please send someone else.'

[1325] Exodus 4:14 Then the anger of the Lord was kindled against Moses and he said, 'What of your brother Aaron the Levite? I know that he can speak fluently; even now he is coming out to meet you, and when he sees you his heart will be glad.

[1326] Exodus 4:15 You shall speak to him and put the words in his mouth; and I will be with your mouth and with his mouth, and will teach you what you shall do.

[1327] Exodus 4:16 He indeed shall speak for you to the people; he shall serve as a mouth for you, and you shall serve as God for him.

[1328] Hebrews 11:23 By faith Moses was hidden by his parents for three months after his birth, because they saw that the child was beautiful; and they were not afraid of the king's edict.

[1329] Exodus 2:3 When she could hide him no longer she got a papyrus basket for him, and plastered it with bitumen and pitch; she put the child in it and placed it among the reeds on the bank of the river.

it to the bank, where he will be taken by an enemy of Mine and his."[1330] And I bestowed upon you My love, so that you would be brought up under My watchful eye. [39] Then your sister walked by and said, "Shall I direct you to someone who will take care of him?"[1331] So We returned you to your mother[1332] so that she could rejoice and not grieve. Later, you killed someone,[1333] but We rescued you from distress[1334] but put you through other severe tests. And you remained some years among the people of Midian.[1335] Then you came (here) at the time as I ordained,[1336] Moses. [40] And I have chosen you for Myself. [41] Go, you and your brother, with My signs and do not falter in remembering Me. [42] Go, both of you, to Pharaoh. He has overstepped all My limits.[1337] [43] And speak to him gently that perhaps he may remember or fear (God)." [44] They said, "Our Lord, we are afraid that He will quickly do us harm or that he will overstep all boundaries." [45] God said, "Fear not. I am with you both; I hear and I see. [46] Go to him and tell him: "We are messengers of your Lord, so send the Children of Israel with us, and do not punish them.[1338] We have come to you with a sign from your Lord. And peace will be upon him who follows His guidance. [47] It has been revealed to us that punishment will come upon whoever rejects the truth and turns away."[1339] [48]

(Pharaoh) said, "So who is the Lord of you two, Moses?"[1340] [49] He said, "Our Lord is He who gave each thing its form and then guided (it)." [50] (Pharaoh) said, "Then what about the former generations?" [51] He said, "Their knowledge is with my Lord in a record. My Lord neither errs nor forgets." [52] It is He who has made

• • •

[1330] Exodus 2:5-6 The daughter of Pharaoh came down to bathe at the river, while her attendants walked beside the river. She saw the basket among the reeds and sent her maid to bring it. ⁶When she opened it, she saw the child. He was crying, and she took pity on him. 'This must be one of the Hebrews' children,' she said

[1331] Exodus 2:7 Then his sister said to Pharaoh's daughter, 'Shall I go and get you a nurse from the Hebrew women to nurse the child for you?'

[1332] Exodus 2:8-9 Pharaoh's daughter said to her, 'Yes.' So the girl went and called the child's mother. ⁹ Pharaoh's daughter said to her, 'Take this child and nurse it for me, and I will give you your wages.' So the woman took the child and nursed it.

[1333] Exodus 2:12 He looked this way and that, and seeing no one he killed the Egyptian and hid him in the sand.

[1334] Exodus 2:15 When Pharaoh heard of it, he sought to kill Moses. But Moses fled from Pharaoh. He settled in the land of Midian, and sat down by a well.

[1335] Exodus 3:1 Moses was keeping the flock of his father-in-law Jethro, the priest of Midian; he led his flock beyond the wilderness, and came to Horeb, the mountain of God.

[1336] Exodus 3:14 God said to Moses, 'I am who I am' He said further, 'Thus you shall say to the Israelites, "I am has sent me to you."'

[1337] Exodus 3:10, 4:21, 6:12 So come, I will send you to Pharaoh to bring my people, the Israelites, out of Egypt. 4:21 And the Lord said to Moses, 'When you go back to Egypt, see that you perform before Pharaoh all the wonders that I have put in your power; but I will harden his heart, so that he will not let the people go. 6:12 But Moses spoke to the Lord, 'The Israelites have not listened to me; how then shall Pharaoh listen to me, poor speaker that I am?'

[1338] Exodus 4:22-23, 5:1 Then you shall say to Pharaoh, "Thus says the Lord: Israel is my firstborn son. ²³ I said to you, 'Let my son go that he may worship me.' But you refused to let him go; now I will kill your firstborn son."' 5:1 Afterwards Moses and Aaron went to Pharaoh and said, 'Thus says the Lord, the God of Israel, "Let my people go, so that they may celebrate a festival to me in the wilderness." '

[1339] Exodus 4:23 I said to you, "Let my son go that he may worship me." But you refused to let him go; now I will kill your firstborn son."'

[1340] Exodus 5:2 But Pharaoh said, 'Who is the Lord, that I should heed him and let Israel go? I do not know the Lord, and I will not let Israel go.

the earth as a cradle for you and traced pathways for you through it and sent down rain from the sky, with which We bring forth various kinds of plants [53] to eat as well as pasture for your cattle. In this there are signs for intelligent beings. [54] From earth We created you, and to it We will return you, and from it[1341] We will bring you forth once again. [55] And We certainly showed Pharaoh all of Our signs,[1342] but he denied (them) and refused (to believe).[1343] [56]

(Pharaoh) said, "Have you come to us to drive us out of our land with your magic, Moses? [57] Then we will surely bring you magic like it.[1344] So let's set a time that neither (of us) will fail to keep in a mutually agreed-upon place." [58] (Moses) said, "Your appointment is on the day of the festival, when the people assemble at mid-morning." [59]

So Pharaoh turned away, decided on his scheme, and then he returned. [60] Moses said to the magicians summoned by Pharaoh, "Beware! Do not invent lies against God or He will afflict you with a grievous punishment. He who lies shall fail." [61] So (the magicians) argued among themselves over their plan but kept their conversation secret. [62] They said, "these are two magicians who want to drive you out of your land with their magic and to abolish your most exemplary way of life. [63] So gather your resources and line up for the contest. And whoever succeeds today will prosper." [64] They said, "Moses, either you throw, or we will be the first to throw." [65] He said, "No, you throw." And, behold! Their ropes and staffs seemed to him from their sorcery to move (like snakes).[1345] [66] Moses felt fear within himself [67] but God said, "Have no fear. You will have the upper hand. [68] And throw what is in your right hand; it will swallow up what They have crafted,[1346] for what they have crafted is a magician's trick, and the magician will not succeed in whatever he tries." [69]

(So it was, and) the magicians, fell down in prostration. They said, "We believe in the Lord of Aaron and Moses."[1347] [70] (Pharaoh) said, "How dare you believe him before I gave you permission? He must be your leader who has taught you magic. So I will surely cut off your hands and your feet on opposite sides, and I will crucify you on the trunks of palm trees, and you will surely know which of us is more severe in punishment and more enduring." [71] They said, "Never will we prefer you over the clear proof that has come to us as nor (over) Him who created us. So, decree whatever you will. You can decree only for this worldly life. [72] We have believed in our Lord, so that He may forgive us our sins

• • •

[1341] Genesis 3:19 By the sweat of your face you shall eat bread until you return to the ground, for out of it you were taken; you are dust, and to dust you shall return.'

[1342] Exodus 7:11-12 Then Pharaoh summoned the wise men and the sorcerers; and they also, the magicians of Egypt, did the same by their secret arts. 12 Each one threw down his staff, and they became snakes; but Aaron's staff swallowed up theirs.

[1343] Exodus 7:13 Still Pharaoh's heart was hardened, and he would not listen to them, as the Lord had said.

[1344] Exodus 7:11-12, 22 Then Pharaoh summoned the wise men and the sorcerers; and they also, the magicians of Egypt, did the same by their secret arts. 12 Each one threw down his staff, and they became snakes; but Aaron's staff swallowed up theirs. 22 But the magicians of Egypt did the same by their secret arts; so Pharaoh's heart remained hardened, and he would not listen to them, as the Lord had said.

[1345] Exodus 7:11 Then Pharaoh summoned the wise men and the sorcerers; and they also, the magicians of Egypt, did the same by their secret arts. Each one threw down his staff, and they became snakes;

[1346] Exodus 7:12 but Aaron's staff swallowed up theirs.

[1347] Exodus 8:19 And the magicians said to Pharaoh, 'This is the finger of God!' But Pharaoh's heart was hardened, and he would not listen to them, just as the LORD had said.

and the magic that you forced us to perform. God is better and more enduring." [73] Whoever comes to his Lord as an evildoer is destined for Hell where he will neither die nor live. [74] But whoever comes to Him as a believer, having done righteous deeds will be the highest ranks and [75] Gardens of Eden beneath which rivers flow,[1348] where they will dwell eternally. And that is the reward for one who purifies himself. [76]

We revealed to Moses, "Travel by night[1349] with My worshipers and strike[1350] a dry path[1351] through the sea for them, do not fear being overtaken (by Pharaoh) or fear (drowning)."[1352] [77] So Pharaoh pursued them with his soldiers,[1353] and they were utterly overwhelmed by the sea[1354] [78] Pharaoh led his people astray and did not guide (them). [79]

O Children of Israel, We delivered you from your enemy, and We made a covenant with you on the right side of the mountain, and We repeatedly sent down manna and quail to you, [80] (saying), "Eat from the good things which We have provided you, but do not abuse them or I will be angry with you. And he with whom I am angry will certainly fall." [81] Yet I am most forgiving[1355] towards those who repent, believe, do righteous deeds, and stay on the right path.' [82]

(God) said, "Moses, what made you come in such haste ahead of your people?" [83] He said, "They are following closely upon my heels, and I rushed to You, my Lord, so that You might be pleased." [84] (God) said, "But We have tested your people after you (departed), and the Samaritan has led them astray."[1356] [85] So Moses returned to his people, angry and grieved.[1357] He said, "My people, did not your Lord make you a gracious promise? Did the fulfillment (of the covenant)

•   •   •

[1348] Revelation 22:1-2 Then the angel showed me the river of the water of life, bright as crystal, flowing from the throne of God and of the Lamb through the middle of the street of the city. 2 On either side of the river is the tree of life with its twelve kinds of fruit, producing its fruit each month; and the leaves of the tree are for the healing of the nations.

[1349] Exodus 12:31 Then he summoned Moses and Aaron in the night, and said, 'Rise up, go away from my people, both you and the Israelites! Go, worship the Lord, as you said.

[1350] Exodus 14:16 But you lift up your staff, and stretch out your hand over the sea and divide it, that the Israelites may go into the sea on dry ground.

[1351] Exodus 14:22 The Israelites went into the sea on dry ground, the waters forming a wall for them on their right and on their left.

[1352] Exodus 14:13-14 But Moses said to the people, 'Do not be afraid, stand firm, and see the deliverance that the Lord will accomplish for you today; for the Egyptians whom you see today you shall never see again. 14 The Lord will fight for you, and you have only to keep still.'

[1353] Exodus 14:23-25 The Egyptians pursued, and went into the sea after them, all of Pharaoh's horses, chariots, and chariot drivers. 24 At the morning watch the LORD in the pillar of fire and cloud looked down upon the Egyptian army, and threw the Egyptian army into panic. 25 He clogged their chariot wheels so that they turned with difficulty. The Egyptians said, 'Let us flee from the Israelites, for the Lord is fighting for them against Egypt.'

[1354] Exodus 14:26-28 Then the Lord said to Moses, 'Stretch out your hand over the sea, so that the water may come back upon the Egyptians, upon their chariots and chariot drivers.' 27 So Moses stretched out his hand over the sea, and at dawn the sea returned to its normal depth. As the Egyptians fled before it, the Lord tossed the Egyptians into the sea. 28 The waters returned and covered the chariots and the chariot drivers, the entire army of Pharaoh that had followed them into the sea; not one of them remained.

[1355] Psalm 65:3 When deeds of iniquity overwhelm us, you forgive our transgressions.

[1356] Exodus 32:7 The Lord said to Moses, 'Go down at once! Your people, whom you brought up out of the land of Egypt, have acted perversely;

[1357] Exodus 32:15 Then Moses turned and went down from the mountain, carrying the two tablets of the covenant in his hands, tablets that were written on both sides, written on the front and on the back.

seem too long to you,[1358] or did you want anger of the Lord to fall on you,[1359] so you broke your promise to me?" [86] They said, "We did not break our promise to you deliberately, but we were weighed down with the heavy burden of the people's jewelry[1360] so we threw them (into the fire), following what the Samaritan did." [87] The Samaritan made them (a statue of) a calf [1361] which had a lowing sound, so they said (to each other), "This is your god and the god of Moses, but he has forgotten (his past)." [88] Did they not see that it did not respond to them and that it had no power to either harm or benefit them? [1362] [89] Aaron had already told them before (the return of Moses), "My people, you are only being tested by it, and your Lord is the Merciful-to-all, so follow me and obey my order."[1363] [90] They said, "We will never cease being devoted to the calf until Moses returns to us." [91]

(Moses) said, "Aaron, what prevented you, when you saw them going astray, [92] from following me? Have you then disobeyed my order?"[1364] [93] (Aaron) said, "son of my mother, do not seize (me) by my beard or by my head.[1365] I feared that you would say, You caused division among the Children of Israel, and you did not remember my words.' " [94] (Moses) said, "And what is the matter with you Samaritan?" [95] He said, "I gained insight into what they did not see, so I took a handful (of dust) from the messenger's track and threw it in. This is what my soul tempted me to do." [96] (Moses) said, "Get out of here. All that you can ask for in this life is not to be physically harmed. But you have an appointment (in the Hereafter) you will not fail to keep. Look at your 'god' to which you remained devoted. We will burn it up and we will scatter its dust into the sea.[1366] [97] (People) your true god is God; there is no god but Him.[1367] His knowledge encompasses all things. " [98]

In this way We tell you (Prophet) the news of what has happened before, and We have given you a Reminder directly from Us. [99] Whoever turns away from it will bear a heavy burden on the Day of Resurrection, [100] carrying it eternally. What a terrible burden to carry on the Day of Resurrection. [101] On that Day the

• • •

[1358] Exodus 32:1 When the people saw that Moses delayed to come down from the mountain, the people gathered around Aaron and said to him, 'Come, make gods for us, who shall go before us; as for this Moses, the man who brought us up out of the land of Egypt, we do not know what has become of him.'

[1359] Exodus 32:10 Now let me alone, so that my wrath may burn hot against them and I may consume them; and of you I will make a great nation.'

[1360] Exodus 32:2-3 Aaron said to them, 'Take off the gold rings that are on the ears of your wives, your sons, and your daughters, and bring them to me.' ³ So all the people took off the gold rings from their ears, and brought them to Aaron.

[1361] Exodus 32:24 So I said to them, "Whoever has gold, take it off"; so they gave it to me, and I threw it into the fire, and out came this calf!'

[1362] Psalm 115:4-7 Their idols are silver and gold, the work of human hands. ⁵ They have mouths, but do not speak; eyes, but do not see. ⁶ They have ears, but do not hear; noses, but do not smell. ⁷ They have hands, but do not feel; feet, but do not walk; they make no sound in their throats.

[1363] Luke 1:50 His mercy is for those who fear him from generation to generation.

[1364] Exodus 32:21 Moses said to Aaron, 'What did this people do to you that you have brought so great a sin upon them?'

[1365] Exodus 32:22 And Aaron said, 'Do not let the anger of my Lord burn hot; you know the people, that they are bent on evil.

[1366] Exodus 32:20 He took the calf that they had made, burned it with fire, ground it to powder, scattered it on the water, and made the Israelites drink it.

[1367] Deuteronomy 6:4 Hear, O Israel: The Lord is our God, the Lord alone.

Horn will be blown and We will gather those who force others to reject Our messages, blinded (with terror). (102) and they will whisper to each other, "You have spent only ten (days)." (103) We know best what they will say when the most perceptive (among them) will say, "(In fact) you have spent only one day." (104)

And (should) they ask you (Prophet) about the mountains, say, "My Lord will blow them away into dust (105) and He will level them into empty plains; (106) where you will not see a dip or an elevation." (107) On that Day, everyone will follow the Caller from whom there is no escape. Then, all voices will be quieted before the Merciful-to-all and only whispers will be heard.1368 (108) On that Day, no intercession will be of value except from one to whom the Merciful-to-all has given permission and was pleased with his speech. (109) God knows what is before them and what will be after them, but they cannot contain Him with their knowledge.1369 (110)

And (on that day all) faces will be humbled before the Ever-Living, the Sustainer of existence. And he who bears injustice will despair. (111) But he who does righteous deeds while he is a believer he will fear neither injustice nor deprivation. (112) And thus We have sent down (this revelation) as a perfect Arabic Qur'an and have given warnings that perhaps they will remain mindful of Us, or that it might give them a new awareness. (113) Know then, that God, the Ultimate Sovereign, the Ultimate Truth is So exalted. (Prophet) do not rush ahead with the Qur'an before its revelation to you is complete, and say, "My Lord, increase me in knowledge." (114)

And We had already made a covenant with Adam, but he forgot (it); and We found him lacking in steadfastness. (115) And (mention) when We said to the angels, "Bow down before Adam," and they bowed, except Iblīs; he refused. (116) So We said, "O Adam, this is an enemy to you and to your wife. Do not let him drive you out of the Garden and make you suffer. (117) In the Garden you will never go hungry or go naked, (118) nor will you go thirsty or suffer the heat of the sun." (119) Then Satan whispered to him, saying, "Adam, shall I show you the tree of immortality and a kingdom that will never decay?"1370 (120) And they both ate from it, then their nakedness became apparent to them, and they began to cover themselves with the leaves of the Garden.1371 Adam disobeyed his Lord and was led astray.1372 (121) But later, his Lord chose to bring him closer, accepted his repentance, and guided him. (122) (God) said, "Go down from it, all of you, as enemies to one another. But when guidance comes to you from Me, then whoever follows My guidance will neither go astray (in this world) nor suffer (in the Hereafter). (123) But whoever turns away from remembering Me, he will have a life of great hardship, and We will raise him blind on the Day of Resurrection."

• • •

1368 Romans 14:11 "As I live, says the Lord, every knee shall bow to me, and every tongue shall give praise to God
1369 Isaiah 55:9 For as the heavens are higher than the earth, so are my ways higher than your ways and my thoughts than your thoughts
1370 Genesis 3:4-5 But the serpent said to the woman, 'You will not die; 5 for God knows that when you eat of it your eyes will be opened, and you will be like God, knowing good and evil.'
1371 Genesis 3:7 Then the eyes of both were opened, and they knew that they were naked; and they sewed fig leaves together and made loincloths for themselves.
1372 Genesis 3:11-12 He said, 'Who told you that you were naked? Have you eaten from the tree of which I commanded you not to eat?' 12 The man said, 'The woman whom you gave to be with me, she gave me fruit from the tree, and I ate.'

[124] He will say, "My Lord, why have you raised me blind whereas I was able to see before?" [125] (God) will say, "Just as Our Signs came to you and you forgot them, in the same way, you too will this Day will be forgotten."[1373] [126] This is how We repay him who goes too far and does not believe in the signs of his Lord. And the punishment[1374] of the Hereafter is more severe and most enduring.[127]

Has it not become clear to them how many generations We destroyed before them, in whose ruined dwellings they now walk? There are signs in this for those with understanding. [128] And were it not for a prior word from your Lord, setting an appointed term, (their punishment) would necessarily have come immediately. [129] So (Prophet) be patient with what they say and exalt your Lord's limitless glory and praise Him before the rising of the sun[1375] and before its setting; and exalt His limitless glory during periods of the night and the day, so that you may be content. [130] And do not gaze longingly toward what We have given some of them to enjoy, (it is merely) the splendor of worldly life by which We test them, but the provision of your Lord is better and more enduring. [131] Order your people to pray and be steadfast yourself. We are not asking you for provision; We provide for you, and the (best) end (comes through) being mindful of God. [132] And they say, "If he would only bring us a sign from his Lord?" Has not clear evidence come to them in the earlier texts? [133] And if We had destroyed them with a punishment before this, they would have said, "Our Lord, if You had only sent us a messenger, we could have followed Your signs before we were humiliated and disgraced." [134] Say, "Each is expectantly waiting; so wait with your expectations. For you will eventually know who is on the path of equity and who is rightly guided." [135]

. . .

[1373] Hosea 4:6 My people are destroyed for lack of knowledge; because you have rejected knowledge, I reject you from being a priest to me. And since you have forgotten the law of your God, I also will forget your children

[1374] Isaiah 10:3 What will you do on the day of punishment, in the calamity that will come from far away? To whom will you flee for help, and where will you leave your wealth,

[1375] Psalm 5:3 O Lord, in the morning you hear my voice; in the morning I plead my case to you, and watch.

CHAPTER TWENTY ONE

AL-ANBIYA
THE PROPHETS

In the name of God, the Merciful-to-all, the Mercy Giver:

People's reckoning draws closer, but they turn away without paying any attention.[1376] [01] Every time a new message comes to them from their Lord, they listen to it while they play, [02] with their hearts distracted. Those bent on wrongdoing conceal their private conversation, (saying), "Is he not (Muhammad) just a man like you? Do you succumb to magic with your eyes wide open?" [03] He said, "My Lord knows whatever is said throughout the heaven and earth, and He is the All-Hearing, the All-knowing."[1377] [04] But they continue to quibble, "These (revelations) are only confused dreams," or, "He has just invented it," or, "He is merely a poet." "So (they say) let him bring us a sign like those who were sent previously." [05] We destroyed the communities before them who did not believe, so will they believe? [06] Those We have sent before you were only men whom We inspired. So, tell those who deny of the truth: "if you do not know this, ask the people of earlier revelations." [07] And We did not give the prophets bodies that did not eat food, nor were they immortal. [08] Then We fulfilled Our promise to them and We saved those We willed, and destroyed those who exceeded all bounds.[1378] [09]

•   •   •

[1376] Isaiah 48:17,18 Thus says the Lord your Redeemer, the Holy One of Israel: I am the Lord your God, who teaches you for your own good, who leads you in the way you should go. [18] O that you had paid attention to my commandments! Then your prosperity would have been like a river, and your success like the waves of the sea

[1377] Daniel 2:22 He reveals deep and hidden things; he knows what is in the darkness, and light dwells with him.

[1378] Deuteronomy 13:13-16 some worthless men have gone out from among you and have seduced the inhabitants of their city, saying, 'Let us go and serve other gods' (whom you have not known), [14] then you shall investigate and search out and inquire thoroughly. If it is true and the matter established that this abomination has been done among you, [15] you shall surely strike the inhabitants of that city with the edge of the sword, utterly destroying it and all that is in it and its cattle with the edge of the sword. [16] "Then you shall gather all its booty into the middle of its open square and burn the city and all its booty with fire as a whole burnt offering to the Lord your God; and it shall be a ruin forever. It shall never be rebuilt.

We have sent down to you a Book containing all that you ought to bear in mind. Will you not reason, then? [10] And how many communities of unjust people have We destroyed, raising up other people in their place? [11] When they felt the might of Our punishment, they fled at once. [12] "Do not flee, but return to the life of luxury you enjoyed and to your homes, so that you may be questioned." [13] They said, "Woe to us! we were truly wrongdoers." [14] And that cry of theirs did not cease until We made them like stubble, silent and still [15]

We did not create the heavens and the earth and all that is between them in play; [16] had We wished for amusement, We could have found it within Ourselves- had We so willed. [17] Instead, We hurl the Truth after falsehood, and the Truth destroys it, and it withers away. But woe to you for all your (attempts to) define (God). [18] To Him belongs everything in the heavens and on earth. And those near Him are never too proud to worship Him, nor do they tire (of doing so). [19] They exalt His limitless glory day and night, (and) do not grow weary.[1379][20]

Or have they taken for themselves earthly gods who resurrect the dead? [21] Had there been in heaven or on earth any deities other than God, they would both be ruined. But exalted be God in His limitless glory, Lord of the Throne, Who is far above anything they describe. [22] He will not be questioned about what He does, but they will be questioned. [23] Or have they taken gods besides Him? Say, "Produce your proof.[1380] This is the message for those with me and the message of those before me."[1381] But most of them do not know the Truth, so they turn away. [24] We never sent any messenger before you (Prophet) without revealing to him that "There is no god except Me, so worship Me." [25] And yet, some say, "The Merciful-to-all has taken a son!" May He be exalted in His glory! " No! They are only His honored worshipers. [26] They do not speak before He does, and they act only on His command. [27] He knows what is before them and what is behind them, and they cannot intercede (for anyone) except with His approval,[1382] as they are in reverent awe of Him. [28] Where any of them say, "I am a god besides Him"— that one We would repay with Hell. This is how We repay the transgressors [29]

· · ·

[1379] Revelation 7:15 For this reason they are before the throne of God, and worship him day and night within his temple, and the one who is seated on the throne will shelter them.
Psalm 30:12 so that my soul may praise you and not be silent. O Lord my God, I will give thanks to you forever.
[1380] Isaiah 45:21 Declare and present your case; let them take counsel together! Who told this long ago? Who declared it of old? Was it not I, the Lord? There is no other god besides me, a righteous God and a Savior; there is no one besides me.
[1381] Revelation 1:8 'I am the Alpha and the Omega', says the Lord God, who is and who was and who is to come, the Almighty.
[1382] 1 John 3:20 whenever our hearts condemn us; for God is greater than our hearts, and he know everything.

Are the unbelievers not aware that the heavens and the earth were one mass,[1383] before We separated them[1384] and made every living thing from water?[1385] Will they not believe, then? [30] And We placed within the earth firmly set mountains, lest it should shake with them, and We made valleys, as roadways as roadways that they might be guided (through them) [31] and We made the sky a protected roof, yet still, they turn away from its signs. [32] And It is He who created the night and the day[1386] and the sun and the moon;[1387] each floating in its orbit.[1388] [33] (Prophet) We did not grant immortality to any human being before you; so if you die, would they live forever? [34] Every soul is bound to taste death. We test you with evil and with good as a trial[1389] and to Us you will all return.[1390] [35] And when the unbelievers see you, they laugh at you, (saying), "Is this the one who keeps talking about your gods?" Yet when the Merciful-to-all is mentioned, they reject Him. [36]

Human beings were created hasty by nature. I will show you My signs soon, so do not ask Me to show them sooner. [37] And they say, "When will this promise be fulfilled, if you are telling the truth?" [38] If the unbelievers only knew the time when they will not be able to divert the Fire from their faces or from their backs, and they will find no help. [39] Rather, it will come to them unexpectedly and bewilder them, and they will not be able to repel it, nor will they be reprieved.[40]

Messengers before you were also mocked, but those who mocked them were overwhelmed by the very thing they mocked. [41] Say, "Who can protect you by night or day from the Merciful-to-all?" Yet they turn away when their Lord is mentioned.[1391] [42] Or, do they have gods to defend them from Us? They

• • •

[1383] Genesis 1:6-7 And God said, 'Let there be a dome in the midst of the waters, and let it separate the waters from the waters.' [7] So God made the dome and separated the waters that were under the dome from the waters that were above the dome. And it was so.

[1384] Genesis 1:8-9 God called the dome Sky. And there was evening and there was morning, the second day. [9] And God said, 'Let the waters under the sky be gathered together into one place, and let the dry land appear.' And it was so.

[1385] Genesis 1:10-12 God called the dry land Earth, and the waters that were gathered together he called Seas. And God saw that it was good. [11] Then God said, 'Let the earth put forth vegetation: plants yielding seed, and fruit trees of every kind on earth that bear fruit with the seed in it.' And it was so. [12] The earth brought forth vegetation: plants yielding seed of every kind, and trees of every kind bearing fruit with the seed in it. And God saw that it was good.

[1386] Genesis 1:5 God called the light Day, and the darkness he called Night. And there was evening and there was morning, the first day.

[1387] Genesis 1:14-16 And God said, 'Let there be lights in the dome of the sky to separate the day from the night; and let them be for signs and for seasons and for days and years, [15] and let them be lights in the dome of the sky to give light upon the earth.' And it was so. [16] God made the two great lights—the greater light to rule the day and the lesser light to rule the night—and the stars.

[1388] Genesis 1:17-18, God set them in the dome of the sky to give light upon the earth, [18] to rule over the day and over the night, and to separate the light from the darkness. And God saw that it was good. Psalm 19:4-5 yet their voice goes out through all the earth, and their words to the end of the world. In the heavens he has set a tent for the sun, [5] which comes out like a bridegroom from his wedding canopy, and like a strong man runs its course with joy.

[1389] Psalm 11:5 The Lord tests the righteous and the wicked, and his soul hates the lover of violence.

[1390] Joel 2:12 Yet even now, says the Lord, return to me with all your heart, with fasting, with weeping, and with mourning [13] rend your hearts and not your clothing. Return to the Lord, your God, for he is gracious and merciful, slow to anger, and abounding in steadfast love, and relents from punishing.

[1391] 2 Timothy 4:3-4 For the time is coming when people will not put up with sound doctrine, but having itching ears, they will accumulate for themselves teachers to suit their own desires, [4] and will turn away from listening to the truth and wander away to myths.

are unable (even) to help themselves, nor can they be protected from Us? [43] We have allowed these people and their fathers to enjoy life for a long time, until life seemed long and good to them. Do they not see how We come upon the land, eroding it from its extremities? Will they prevail then? [44] Say: "I can only warn you through Revelation," but the deaf cannot hear the call when they are warned. [45] Yet, if but a whiff of your Lord's punishment should touch them, they would surely say, "Woe to us! We have been unjust." [46] And We place the scales of justice for the Day of Resurrection, so that no soul will be wronged in the least for though there be (only) the weight of a mustard seed, We will bring it forth. It suffices that We will do the reckoning. [47]

And We gave Moses (Musa) and Aaron the Furqan (a standard by which to judge right from wrong) a light and a reminder for those who are ever mindful of God- [48] those who stand in awe of their Lord, though He is unseen, and who fear the Hour.[1392] [49] And this (Qur'an) too is a blessed message that We have sent down. Will you then ignore it? [50] Before (Moses) We gave Abraham sound judgment, [1393] and We knew him well,[51] when he said to his father and his people, "What are these statues to which you are devoted?" [52] They said, "We found our fathers worshipping them." [53] He said, "You and your fathers have obviously gone astray." [54] They said, "Have you come to us with the Truth, or are you playing games?" [55] He said, "(No), rather, your Lord, who created them, is the Lord of the heavens and the earth,[1394] and I am a witness to that. [56] And, by God, I will surely plot against your idols after You have turned your backs and gone away." [57] So he broke them into pieces, except for the largest one among them, so that they might return to it (and question). [58] They said, "Who has done this to our gods? He is unjust." [59] Some said, "We heard a young man mention them; they call him Abraham." [60] They said, "Then bring him before the eyes of the people, so that they may be witnesses." [61] They said, "Have you done this to our gods, Abraham?" [62] He said, "Rather, this one, the largest of them, did it, so ask them, if they are able to speak." [63] So they turned on one another, saying, "It is you who are the unjust." [64] Then, they reversed themselves, (saying), "You (Abraham) knew that these (idols) do not speak!" [65] He said, "Then do you worship what does not help or harm you at all instead of God? [66] Shame on you, and shame on what you worship instead of God.[1395] Will you not use reason then?" [67] They said, "Burn him and support your gods—if you are to act." [68] But We said, "Fire, be coolness and peace for Abraham." [69] And they intended to harm him, but We made them the greatest losers. [70] And

•   •   •

[1392] Revelation 14:7 He said in a loud voice, 'Fear God and give him glory, for the hour of his judgment has come; and worship him who made heaven and earth, the sea and the springs of water.'
[1393] Genesis 12:1 Now the Lord said to Abram, 'Go from your country and your kindred and your father's house to the land that I will show you.
[1394] Isaiah 45:18 For thus says the Lord, who created the heavens (he is God!), who formed the earth and made it (he established it; he did not create it a chaos, he formed it to be inhabited!): I am the Lord, and there is no other.
[1395] Isaiah 44:20 He feeds on ashes; a deluded mind has led him astray, and he cannot save himself or say, "Is not this thing in my right hand a fraud?

We delivered him [1396] and Lot[1397] to the land which We had blessed for all people. [71] And We gave him Isaac and Jacob as an additional gift, and all (of them) We made righteous.[72] We made them leaders guiding others by Our command. And We inspired them to do good deeds, to establish prayer, and to give the purifying alms; they were our true worshippers. [73] And to Lot We gave sound judgment and knowledge, and We saved him from the town that was committing wicked deeds.[1398] They were evil, who were perverse people.[1399] [74] And We admitted him into Our mercy. He was of the righteous.[1400] [75]

Long before that, We answered Noah when he called to Us, so We responded to him, and saved him and his family from the great calamity.[1401] [76] And We helped him against the people who denied Our signs. They were an evil people, so We drowned them, all together. [1402] [77]

And David and Solomon, when they gave judgment concerning the field into which some people's sheep had strayed (at night). We were witness to their judgment [78] and We gave understanding of the case to Solomon,[1403] and to each (of them) We gave sound judgment and knowledge. And We caused the mountains[1404] and the birds to join David in extolling Our limitless glory,[1405] for We are able to do (all things). [79] And We taught him to fashion coats of armor to protect you from your (enemy in) battle. But are you grateful? [1406] [80] And to Solomon We subjected the wind, which aped at his command toward the land that We had blessed. It is We who have knowledge of everything. [1407] [81] And among the (devils) rebellious creatures, who dove into the sea for him and did other work, but it was We who kept watch over them. [82]

• • •

[1396] Genesis 19:29, 13:14-15 So it was that, when God destroyed the cities of the Plain, God remembered Abraham, and sent Lot out of the midst of the overthrow, when he overthrew the cities in which Lot had settled. 13:14-15 The Lord said to Abram, after Lot had separated from him, 'Raise your eyes now, and look from the place where you are, northwards and southwards and eastwards and westwards; [15] for all the land that you see I will give to you and to your offspring for ever

[1397] Nephew of Abraham

[1398] Sodom

[1399] Genesis 13:13 Now the people of Sodom were wicked, great sinners against the Lord.

[1400] 2 Peter 2:7 and if he rescued Lot, a righteous man greatly distressed by the licentiousness of the lawless

[1401] The complete story of Noah is contained in Genesis 6-9.

[1402] Genesis 7:21 And all flesh died that moved on the earth, birds, domestic animals, wild animals, all swarming creatures that swarm on the earth, and all human beings;

[1403] 1 Kings 3:9-14 Give your servant therefore an understanding mind to govern your people, able to discern between good and evil; for who can govern this your great people?' [10] It pleased the Lord that Solomon had asked this. [11] God said to him, 'Because you have asked this, and have not asked for yourself long life or riches, or for the life of your enemies, but have asked for yourself understanding to discern what is right, [12] I now do according to your word. Indeed, I give you a wise and discerning mind; no one like you has been before you and no one like you shall arise after you. [13] I give you also what you have not asked, both riches and honor all your life; no other king shall compare with you. [14] If you will walk in my ways, keeping my statutes and my commandments, as your father David walked, then I will lengthen your life.'

[1404] Psalm 148:9 Mountains and all hills, fruit trees and all cedars!

[1405] Luke 19:40 He answered, 'I tell you, if these were silent, the stones would shout out.'

[1406] 2 Timothy 3:2-3 For people will be lovers of themselves, lovers of money, boasters, arrogant, abusive, disobedient to their parents, ungrateful, unholy, [3] inhuman, implacable, slanderers, profligates, brutes and haters of good.

[1407] Ecclesiastes 11:5 Just as you do not know how the breath comes to the bones in the mother's womb, so you do not know the work of God, who makes everything.

And (mention) Job, when he cried to his Lord, "Great harm has afflicted me, and you are the Most Merciful of the Merciful."[1408] (83) So We responded to him and removed the harm that afflicted him.[1409] And We restored his family [1410] and their like with them, as a mercy from Us and a reminder for God's worshippers. (84) And (mention) Ishmael and Enoch (Idris)[1411] and Dhul-Kifl;[1412] all were all steadfast (85) And We admitted them into Our mercy for they were truly righteous. (86) And (Jonah) Zun-nun[1413] when he went[1414] off in anger[1415] and thought that We would not punish him. Then he called out from the deep darkness,[1416] "There is no God except You; May You be exalted in Your glory. I have been among the unjust."[1417] (87) We responded to him and saved him from his grief. This is how We save the believers.[1418] (88) And Zechariah, when he called to his Lord, "My Lord, do not leave me childless, for you are the best of heirs."[1419] (89) We responded to him, gave him John,[1420] and healed his wife for him.[1421] They were always eager to do good deeds,[1422] calling out to Us in hope and fear, and they humbled themselves before Us. (90) And (mention Mary) the one who guarded her chastity. We breathed into her[1423] from Our Spirit[1424] and made her and her son[1425] a sign for all people.[1426] (91)

This is your community, a single community (of believers), and I am your Lord, so worship Me. (92) And (yet), they later disagreed and became divided, (but) they are all destined to return to Us. (93) So whoever does righteous deeds while he is

• • •

[1408] Psalm 11:4 The Lord is in His holy temple; the Lord's throne is in heaven; His eyes behold, His eyelids test the sons of men.
[1409] Job 42:10 And the Lord restored the fortunes of Job when he had prayed for his friends; and the Lord gave Job twice as much as he had before.
[1410] Job 42:13-14 He also had seven sons and three daughters. 14 He named the first Jemimah, the second Keziah, and the third Keren-happuch.
[1411] Enoch
[1412] Ezekiel
[1413] Jonah (Yunis)
[1414] Jonah 1:3 But Jonah set out to flee to Tarshish from the presence of the Lord. He went down to Joppa and found a ship going to Tarshish; so he paid his fare and went on board, to go with them to Tarshish, away from the presence of the Lord.
[1415] Jonah 4:1 But this was very displeasing to Jonah, and he became angry.
[1416] Jonah 2:1-2 Then Jonah prayed to the Lord his God from the belly of the fish, 2 saying, 'I called to the Lord out of my distress, and he answered me; out of the belly of Sheol I cried, and you heard my voice.
[1417] Jonah 2:9 But I with the voice of thanksgiving will sacrifice to you; what I have vowed I will pay. Deliverance belongs to the Lord!'
[1418] Jonah 2:10 Then the Lord spoke to the fish, and it spewed Jonah out upon the dry land.
[1419] Luke 1:13 But the angel said to him, 'Do not be afraid, Zechariah, for your prayer has been heard. Your wife Elizabeth will bear you a son, and you will name him John.
[1420] John the Baptist
[1421] Luke 1:24 After those days his wife Elizabeth conceived, and for five months she remained in seclusion. She said,
[1422] Luke 1:5-6 In the days of King Herod of Judea, there was a priest named Zechariah, who belonged to the priestly order of Abijah. His wife was a descendant of Aaron, and her name was Elizabeth. 6 Both of them were righteous before God, living blamelessly according to all the commandments and regulations of the Lord.
[1423] Mary, the mother of Jesus
[1424] Luke 1:35 The angel said to her, 'The Holy Spirit will come upon you, and the power of the Most High will overshadow you; therefore, the child to be born will be holy.
[1425] Jesus
[1426] Luke 1:34 Mary said to the angel, 'How can this be, since I am a virgin?'

a believer—his effort will not be ignored, and We shall record it in his favor. (94) No community that We have destroyed can possibly return (95) until Gog and Magog are let loose and they rush down from the heights, (96) Then, the true promise will approach and the eyes of the unbelievers will stare (in horror, while they say), "Woe to us; we were oblivious to this; rather, we were unjust." (97) You and what you worship other than God are the firewood of Hell. You will be coming to it. (98) Had these (false deities) been (actual) gods, they would not have come to it, but each one of them will stay there (in Hell) forever. (99) In it they will be wailing and they will not be able to hear. (100)

As for those for whom We have decreed the best (reward)—they will be kept far removed from Hell. (101) They will not hear its sound, while they abide eternally in whatever their souls desire. (102) They will not be grieved by the greatest horror and the angels will greet them, (saying), "This is your Day which you have been promised"[1427] (103) the Day when We will roll up the heavens as one rolls up a written scroll.[1428] Just as We produced the first creation, (so) We will repeat it.[1429] This is a binding promise on Us. We will do it. (104)

We have written in the Zabour (Psalms) as We did in previous Scriptures,[1430] that My righteous worshipers shall inherit the earth.[1431] (105) Truly there is a message in this for people who worship! (106) We have only sent you (Prophet) as a mercy to humanity. (107) Say, "It is revealed to me that your god is but one God- so, will you be submissive[1432] to Him?" (108) But, if they turn away, then say, "I have proclaimed the message equally to (all of) you. And I do not know if what you have been promised is near or far. (109) He knows what is revealed when you speak, and He knows what you conceal. (110) For all I know (this delay in God's judgment) may be a trial for you and you will have enjoyment for a while." (111) Say (Prophet) "My Lord, judge (between us) in Truth. Our Lord is the Merciful- to-all,[1433] the one whose help is ever sought against that which you unbelievers speak." (112)

• • •

[1427] John 14:1-3 'Do not let your hearts be troubled. Believe in God, believe also in me. ² In my Father's house there are many dwelling-places. If it were not so, would I have told you that I go to prepare a place for you? ³ And if I go and prepare a place for you, I will come again and will take you to myself, so that where I am, there you may be also.

[1428] Hebrews 1:10-12 And, 'In the beginning, Lord, you founded the earth, and the heavens are the work of your hands; ¹¹ they will perish, but you remain; they will all wear out like clothing; ¹² like a cloak you will roll them up, and like clothing they will be changed. But you are the same, and your years will never end.'

[1429] Revelation 21:5 And the one who was seated on the throne said, 'See, I am making all things new.' Also he said, 'Write this, for these words are trustworthy and true.'

[1430] Here the previous Scriptures refers to the book before the Zabur, i.e. the Torah.

[1431] 1 Peter 1:4-5 and into an inheritance that is imperishable, undefiled, and unfading, kept in heaven for you, ⁵ who are being protected by the power of God through faith for a salvation ready to be revealed in the last time.

[1432] See Glossary for Islam or Submission.

[1433] Psalm 111:2-4, Great are the works of the Lord, studied by all who delight in them. ³ Full of honor and majesty is his work, and his righteousness endures forever. ⁴ He has gained renown by his wonderful deeds; the Lord is gracious and merciful

CHAPTER TWENTY TWO

AL-HAJJ
THE PILGRIMAGE

THE **MEDINA** PERIOD

In The Name of God, The Merciful-to-all, the Mercy Giver:

People, be ever mindful of your Lord. The tremor of the (final) Hour is a mighty thing. [01] On the Day you see it every nursing mother will be distracted from the child she is nursing, and every pregnant woman will abort her pregnancy, and you will think that people are drunk while they are not-but God's punishment is severe [1435] [02] Yet some people still argue about God[1436] without knowledge, following every rebellious devil [03] who is destined to lead astray those who ally themselves with him,[1437] and guide them toward the suffering of the blazing flame. [04]

People-If you should be in doubt about the Resurrection,[1438] then (consider that) We created you from dust,[1439] then from a drop of sperm, then a clinging

. . .

[1435] Mark 13:17 - 20 Woe to those who are pregnant and to those who are nursing infants in those days! [18] Pray that it may not be in winter. [19] For in those days there will be suffering, such as has not been from the beginning of the creation that God created until now, no, and never will be. [20] And if the Lord had not cut short those days, no one would be saved; but for the sake of the elect, whom he chose, he has cut short those days.

[1436] 2 Timothy 2:16-18 Avoid profane chatter, for it will lead people into more and more impiety, [17] and their talk will spread like gangrene. Among them are Hymenaeus and Philetus, [18] who have swerved from the truth by claiming that the resurrection has already taken place. They are upsetting the faith of some.

[1437] 2 Timothy 2:25-26 correcting opponents with gentleness. God may perhaps grant that they will repent and come to know the truth, [26] and that they may escape from the snare of the devil, having been held captive by him to do his will.

[1438] Matthew 22:31-32 And as for the resurrection of the dead, have you not read what was said to you by God, 32 "I am the God of Abraham, the God of Isaac, and the God of Jacob"? He is God not of the dead, but of the living.'

[1439] Genesis 2:7 then the Lord God formed man from the dust of the ground, and breathed into his nostrils the breath of life; and the man became a living being.

clot, and then a lump of flesh,[1440] formed and unformed[1441] so We may show you (our power).[1442] And We settle in the womb[1443] whom We will for a specified term, then We bring you forth as an infant, and then you may grow to reach maturity. And among you some will die, and some will reach the most decrepit age in which he no longer knows what he once knew.[1444] You see the earth barren, yet when We send down rain,[1445] it shakes and swells and produces every kind of beautiful plant.[1446] [05] That is because God is the Ultimate Truth and because He alone brings the dead to life and because He is competent over all things. [06] And (that they may know) that the Hour is coming; no doubt about it, and that God will resurrect all those in the graves.[1447] [07]

Yet among men there is he who argues about God without knowledge or guidance or an enlightening Book, [08] turning away (from the truth) in his arrogance to lead (people) astray from the path of God. For him there is only disgrace in the world, and We will make him taste the punishment of the burning fire on the Day of Resurrection[1448] [09] (He will be told) "This is for what you have done. God is never unfair to His servants." [10] And among people you would find one who worship God with shaky faith.[1449] If good befalls him, he is reassured by it; but if he is tested, he reverts to his old ways,[1450] (thereby) losing both (this) world and the next. That is a manifest loss. [11] Instead of God, he calls upon what can neither harm him nor benefit him.[1451] That is the ultimate misguidance. [12] He calls on one who is more likely to harm than to benefit (him). How miserable are both the protector and the companion. [13]

• • •

[1440] Job 10:10 Did you not pour me out like milk and curdle me like cheese? Psalm 139:13-16 For it was you who formed my inward parts; you knit me together in my mother's womb. [14] I praise you, for I am fearfully and wonderfully made. Wonderful are your works; that I know very well. [15] My frame was not hidden from you, when I was being made in secret, intricately woven in the depths of the earth. [16] Your eyes beheld my unformed substance. In your book were written all the days that were formed for me, when none of them as yet existed.

[1441] Job 10:11 You clothed me with skin and flesh, and knit me together with bones and sinews.

[1442] Psalm139:14 I praise you, for I am fearfully and wonderfully made. Wonderful are your works; that I know very well.

[1443] Isaiah 49:5 And now the Lord says, who formed me in the womb to be his servant, to bring Jacob back to him, and that Israel might be gathered to him, for I am honored in the sight of the Lord, and my God has become my strength—

[1444] Ecclesiastes 12:1-3 Remember your creator in the days of your youth, before the days of trouble come, and the years draw near when you will say, 'I have no pleasure in them'; [2] before the sun and the light and the moon and the stars are darkened and the clouds return with the rain; [3] on the day when the guards of the house tremble, and the strong men are bent, and the women who grind cease working because they are few, and those who look through the windows see dimly;

[1445] Job 5:10 He gives rain on the earth and sends waters on the fields;

[1446] Isaiah 55:10 For as the rain and the snow come down from heaven, and do not return there until they have watered the earth, making it bring forth and sprout, giving seed to the sower and bread to the eater,

[1447] John 5:28-30 Do not be astonished at this; for the hour is coming when all who are in their graves will hear his voice 29 and will come out—those who have done good, to the resurrection of life, and those who have done evil, to the resurrection of condemnation.

[1448] 2 peter 3:7 But by the same word the present heavens and earth have been reserved for fire, being kept until the day of judgment and destruction of the godless.

[1449] Revelation 3:16 So, because you are lukewarm, and neither cold nor hot, I am about to spit you out of my mouth.

[1450] Matthew 13:21 yet such a person has no root, but endures only for a while, and when trouble or persecution arises on account of the word, that person immediately falls away.

[1451] Isaiah 41:23 Tell us what is to come hereafter, that we may know that you are gods; do good, or do harm, that we may be afraid and terrified.

But God will admit those who believe and do righteous deeds to Gardens with rivers flowing through them.[1452] God does what He wills. [14] Anyone who thinks that God will not help him[1453] (the Prophet) in this world and in the Hereafter, let him find a way to reach out to heaven, then try to make headway, and see if his scheme will eliminate what enrages him. [15] And thus have We sent the Qur'an down as verses of clear evidence, for God guides those who want to be guided. [16] As for those who believed, the Jews, the Sabeans, the Christians[1454], the Magians[1455] and those ascribing divinity to other than God- God will judge between them on the Day of Resurrection. God witnesses all things [17] Do you not see that everyone in the heavens and everyone on earth and the sun, the moon, the stars, the mountains, the trees, the moving creatures [1456] and many human beings bow down before God? But for many others their punishment is justified. [1457] And he who is disgraced by God cannot have his honor restored by anyone. God does whatever He wills [1458] [18]

These are two adversaries who have disputed over their Lord. But the unbelievers will have cut out garments of fire cut out for them, and boiling water will be poured over their heads- [19] which will melt the contents of their bellies as well as their skin- [20] and they shall be held by iron grips. [21] Every time they try to escape (the fire) of it in their anguish, they will be returned to it, and (it will be said), "Taste the punishment of the Burning Fire!" [1459] [22]

As for those who believe and do righteous deeds, God will admit them to Gardens with rivers flowing through them.[1460] They will be adorned with bracelets of gold and pearls, and their garments will be silk, [23] for they were (willing to be) guided (in this life) to speak the best words, and so they were guided to the path that leads to Him Who is Worthy of (all) Praise. [24]

As for the unbelievers who divert (others) from the path of God [1461] and (from) the Sacred House, which We made for all People equally-(both) those who

• • •

[1452]Genesis 2:10 A river flows out of Eden to water the garden, and from there it divides and becomes four branches.

[1453] See Al Cortobi and Al Jalalein commentary.

[1454] The word Christians (in Arabic Maseheein) is never mentioned in the Qur'an. Instead the Qur'an mentions the word /nasara/ and it is historically equated by Muslim commentators to Christians but its origins are not clear. Some have suggested that the word is derived from Nazareth, the town where Jesus was brought up, as it is implied in the Gospel, (Matthew 2:23, Acts 24:5). Others believe that it is because the Arabic word /ansaar/ (helpers/supporters) (root: nasr) refers to the followers of Jesus who are called supporters of God in the Qur'an (61:14, 3:52).

[1455] Member of the Zoroastrian priestly caste of the Medes and Persians. Magus In the New Testament, one of the wise men from the East, traditionally held to be three, who traveled to Bethlehem to pay homage to the infant Jesus.

[1456] Psalm 150:5 Praise him with clanging cymbals; praise him with loud clashing cymbals!

[1457] 2 Peter 2:1 But false prophets also arose among the people, just as there will be false teachers among you, who will secretly bring in destructive opinions. They will even deny the Master who bought them— bringing swift destruction on themselves.

[1458] Psalm 115:3 Our God is in the heavens; he does whatever he pleases.

[1459] Revelation 20:10 And the devil who had deceived them was thrown into the lake of fire and sulphur, where the beast and the false prophet were, and they will be tormented day and night for ever and ever.

[1460] Genesis 2:10 A river flows out of Eden to water the garden, and from there it divides and becomes four branches.

[1461] Matthew 23:13 'But woe to you, scribes and Pharisees, hypocrites! For you lock people out of the kingdom of heaven. For you do not go in yourselves, and when others are going in, you stop them.

dwell there, and those who come from abroad – We will let those who desire to profane it with wrongdoing taste a painful punishment.[1462] (25)

For when We showed Abraham the site of the House, (We told him), "Do not associate anything with Me and purify My House for those who will circle around it, and those who stand to pray and those who bow down and prostrate themselves. (26) "And proclaim the Pilgrimage to all people: they will come to you on foot and on every kind of swift and lean mount, through distant passes; (27) so that they may receive benefits for themselves and to celebrate God's name on appointed days. He has provided (sacrificial) animals for their purposes. So eat of them and feed the miserable and poor. (28) So let the pilgrims perform their acts of purification and fulfill their vows. And then circle around the Ancient House." (29) All of that (has been commanded). As for anyone who honors the sacred ordinances of God, it is good for him in the sight of his Lord. Livestock have been permitted to you, except what has been explicitly forbidden. So turn away from the filth of idols,[1463] and turn away from telling lies (30) inclining (only) to God, not associating (anything) with Him. And he who associates others with God- it is as though he had fallen from the sky and was snatched by the birds or the wind carried him down into a remote place.[1464] (31) Thus it is; and whoever venerates the sacred rites of God—(their acts) proceed from a pious heart. (32) You have benefits in these animals marked for sacrifice for a specified time; then, their place of sacrifice is at the Ancient House. (33) We have appointed a rite (of sacrifice) for every nation, so that they may mention the name of God over whatever (sacrificial) animals He has provided them. Your god is one God, so submit to Him. And, give good news to the humble of heart- (34) those whose hearts tremble[1465] when God is mentioned, and those who patiently persevere over what has afflicted them,[1466] and those who perform prayer and those who spend from what We have provided them. (35)

We have appointed sacrificial animals for you among the rituals of God. There is much good for you in them, so mention God's name over them when they lined up (for sacrifice), and, when they are (lifeless) on their sides, then eat from them and feed the needy and the beggar. Thus We have subjected them to you so that hopefully you may be grateful. (36) It is neither their meat nor their blood that reaches Good: what reaches Him is your piety.[1467] Thus He has made them

• • •

[1462] 2 Peter 2:1 But false prophets also arose among the people, just as there will be false teachers among you, who will secretly bring in destructive opinions. They will even deny the Master who bought them—bringing swift destruction on themselves
[1463] Deuteronomy 7:25 The images of their gods you shall burn with fire. Do not covet the silver or the gold that is on them and take it for yourself, because you could be ensnared by it; for it is abhorrent to the Lord your God.
[1464] Psalm 1:4 The wicked are not so, but are like chaff that the wind drives away.
[1465] Psalm 114:7 Tremble, O earth, at the presence of the Lord, at the presence of the God of Jacob,
[1466] Romans 12:12, Rejoice in hope, be patient in suffering, persevere in prayer. Romans 5:3-5 And not only that, but we also boast in our sufferings, knowing that suffering produces endurance, [4] and endurance produces character, and character produces hope, [5] and hope does not disappoint us, because God's love has been poured into our hearts through the Holy Spirit that has been given to us.
[1467] Psalm 51:17 The sacrifice acceptable to God is a broken spirit; a broken and contrite heart, O God, you will not despise.

subject to you, so that you may glorify God for having guided you.[1468] And give good news to those who do their best at whatever they do. (37)

God will defend the believers. God does not like the treacherous and ungrateful.[1469] (38) Permission (to fight) has been given to those against whom war is being waged wrongfully, because they were wronged. And God is surely capable of giving them victory.[1470] (39) (They are) those who have been driven from their homes unjustly, for saying only that "Our Lord is God." And, if God did not intervene by using some people to drive out others, many monasteries, churches, synagogues, and mosques, where God's name is much remembered, would have been destroyed. God is sure to help [1471] those who help His cause, for truly God is strong and mighty. (40) (And they are) those who, if We give them authority in the land, establish prayer, and give the purifying alms, and order what is obviously[1472] right, and forbid what is obviously wrong. And to God belongs the outcome of (all) matters.[1473](41)

And if they deny you (Prophet), so, did the people of Noah and Aad and Thamud deny (their prophets), (42) as did the people of Abraham and the people of Lot[1474] (43) and the inhabitants of Midian. And Moses was called a liar. So, I indulged the unbelievers for a time, and then I seized them, and how (terrible) was My reproach. (44) And how many a town did We destroy while it was committing wrong, so It is (now) fallen into ruin, and (how many) an abandoned well, and (how many) a lofty palace? (45) Have they not traveled through the land, so that their hearts gain wisdom and their ears learn to listen? For it is not the eyes that are blind, but the hearts within the breasts[1475]. (46) They challenge you (Prophet) to bring on their punishment (if you can). But God will never fail to deliver His promise.[1476] A day with your Lord is like a thousand years as you count them.[1477] (47) And how many a community did I indulge while it was unjust?[1478] Then I seized it, and their (final) destination is up to Me. (48)

• • •

[1468] Psalm 78:52,72 Then he led out his people like sheep, and guided them in the wilderness like a flock. [72] With upright heart he tended them, and guided them with skilful hand.

[1469] Proverbs 6:16-19 There are six things that the Lord hates, seven that are an abomination to him: [17] haughty eyes, a lying tongue, and hands that shed innocent blood, [18] a heart that devises wicked plans, feet that hurry to run to evil, [19] a lying witness who testifies falsely, and one who sows discord in a family.

[1470] 2 Chronicles 14:11 "Asa cried to the Lord his God, "O Lord, there is no difference for you between helping the mighty and the weak. Help us, O Lord our God, for we rely on you, and in your name we have come against this multitude. O Lord, you are our God; let no mortal prevail against you."

[1471] Isaiah 50:9-10 It is the Lord God who helps me; who will declare me guilty? All of them will wear out like a garment; the moth will eat them up. [10] Who among you fears the Lord and obeys the voice of his servant, who walks in darkness and has no light, yet trusts in the name of the Lord and relies upon his God?

[1472] What is obviously right or wrong is time, place and culture sensative.

[1473] Psalm 62:11 Once God has spoken; twice have I heard this: that power belongs to God,

[1474] nephew of Abraham.

[1475] Exodus 10:23 states, "They saw not one another" Rabbinic sages explain that the Ninth Plague – the plague of Darkness – did not represent an actual darkening of the sky, but rather a darkness of the heart, a communal blindness, a plague which has afflicted human societies from time immemorial.

[1476] Numbers 23:19 God is not a human being, that he should lie, or a mortal, that he should change his mind. Has he promised, and will he not do it? Has he spoken, and will he not fulfil it?

[1477] 2 Peter 3:8 But do not ignore this one fact, beloved, that with the Lord one day is like a thousand years, and a thousand years are like one day.

[1478] Acts 17:30 While God has overlooked the times of human ignorance, now he commands all people everywhere to repent,

Say (Prophet), "O People, I am sent only to deliver a clear warning to you." (49) And those who have believed and done righteous deeds - for them is forgiveness and generous rewards. (50) But those who oppose Our message, (seeking) in vain to cause it to fail-those are the companions of Hell. (51) Yet, whenever We sent a messenger or a prophet ahead of you, and he was hoping (that his warning will be heeded), Satan would cast (doubt) on his hopes. But God destroys that what Satan insinuates, and God confirms His messages, for God is All-Knowing and All-Wise. (52) He makes what Satan spews forth a temptation[1479] only to those whose hearts are sick or hardened-surely the unjust are profoundly opposed to the Truth. (53) So that those who have been given knowledge may understand that it is the Truth from your Lord and believe in Him, while their hearts humbly submit to Him. God will guide the believers[1480] to a straight path,[1481] (54) but the unbelievers will continue to be in doubt about it until the Hour comes suddenly[1482] on them or punishment strikes them on the Day of desolation.[1483] (55) (All) sovereignty on that Day will belong to God;[1484] He will judge between them. So, those who believed and did righteous deeds will be in the Gardens of Delight. (56) While the unbelievers and those who reject Our signs will receive a humiliating punishment. (57)

And those who emigrated for the cause of God and then were killed or died-God will surely provide for them handsomely, for God is surely the best of providers.[1485] (58) He will surely admit them into a place that well pleases them, for God is Knowing[1486] and Forbearing. (59) That (is so); and whoever responds (to an act of aggression) only with an equivalent force and is then wronged again, God will surely help him. God is pardoning and forgiving. (60) Thus it is, because God merges the night into day and merges the day into night, and because God is All-Hearing and All-Seeing. (61) Thus it is, because God is the Ultimate Truth, and anything they call upon other than Him is falsehood, because God is the Most High, the Most Great. (62) Do you not see that God has sent down rain from the sky, and then the earth becomes green? God is Most-Subtle, All-Aware. (63) To Him belongs all that is in the heavens and on earth, God is the Rich Beyond Need; the Praiseworthy. (64) Do you not see that God has made everything on the earth of service to you-including the ships that run through the sea by His command- and that He prevents heaven from falling on the earth without His

• • •

[1479] James 1:13 No one, when tempted, should say, 'I am being tempted by God'; for God cannot be tempted by evil and he himself tempts no one.
[1480] Psalm 23:3 he restores my soul. He leads me in right paths for his name's sake.
[1481] Proverbs 3:6 In all your ways acknowledge him, and he will make straight your paths
[1482] 1 Thessalonians 5:1,2 Now concerning the times and the seasons, brothers and sisters, you do not need to have anything written to you. ² For you yourselves know very well that the day of the Lord will come like a thief in the night.
[1483] Ezekiel 30:3 For a day is near, the day of the Lord is near; it will be a day of clouds, a time of doom for the nations.
[1484] Revelation 11:15 Then the seventh angel blew his trumpet, and there were loud voices in heaven, saying, 'The kingdom of the world has become the kingdom of our Lord and of his Messiah, and he will reign for ever and ever.'
[1485] Matthew 6:26 Look at the birds of the air; they neither sow nor reap nor gather into barns, and yet your heavenly Father feeds them. Are you not of more value than they?
[1486] 1 John 3:20 whenever our hearts condemn us; for God is greater than our hearts, and he knows everything.

permission? God is most compassionate and most Merciful-to-all people. [1487] (65) He is the One Who gave you life, and then will cause you to die, and then will bring you back to life. Human beings however are ungrateful. (66)

We have appointed acts of worship for every nation, which they (are to) observe. So, let the unbelievers not contend with you over the matter, but invite them to your Lord. You are on the straight path, [1488] (67) and if they argue with you, then say, "God knows best what you are doing. (68) On the Day of Resurrection, God will judge between you regarding your differences." (69) Do you not know that God knows what is in the heaven and earth? All this is written in a Record. This is easy for God. (70)

Nevertheless, they worship others besides God, something for which He has granted no authority, and about which they have no knowledge. There will not be any helper for the unjust. [1489] (71) And when Our verses are recited to them as clear evidence, you will detect disapproval in the faces of the unbelievers. They all but assault those who recite Our verses. Say, "Shall I inform you of (what is) worse than that? (It is) the Fire that God has promised the unbelievers. How miserable is their destination." (72)

People, an example is presented, so listen to it. Those you call on besides God will never be able to create (as much as) a fly, even if they all gathered together for that purpose. And if the fly robs them of anything, they will not be able to retrieve it. How feeble are the petitioners and those they petition. (73) They do not give God His due esteem. God is omnipotent, almighty. (74)

God chooses messengers from among the angels and people. God is All-Hearing and All- Seeing. (75) He knows what lies before them and what is behind them, for all matters will go back to God. (76) Believers: bow, and prostrate[1490], and worship your Lord and do good, so that you may succeed. (77) And strive for God as He deserves.[1491] He has chosen you and has not imposed hardships on you in religion- the faith of your father, Abraham. He named you "Muslims" (submitters) before (in former Books) and in this (revelation), so that the Messenger may be a witness over you, and you may be witnesses over other human beings. So, perform prayer, and give the purifying alms and hold fast to God. He is your protector, and how excellent is this protector, how excellent this helper.[1492] (78)

• • •

[1487] James 5:11 Indeed we call blessed those who showed endurance. You have heard of the endurance of Job, and you have seen the purpose of the Lord, how the Lord is compassionate and merciful.
[1488] Psalm 25:10 All the paths of the Lord are steadfast love and faithfulness, for those who keep his covenant and his decrees
[1489] Isaiah 48:22 'There is no peace', says the Lord, 'for the wicked.'
[1490] Exodus 34:8 'Then Moses quickly went down on his face in worship.' Joshua 5:14 '. . . Then Joshua, falling down with his face to the earth in worship . . .' Matthew 26:39 'And he (Jesus) went forward a little and falling down on his face in prayer . . .'
[1491] 2 Samuel 22:4 I call upon the Lord, who is worthy to be praised, and I am saved from my enemies.
[1492] Psalm 68:5 Father of orphans and protector of widows is God in his holy habitation

CHAPTER TWENTY THREE

AL-MU'MINUN
THE BELIEVERS

THE **MECCA** PERIOD

In the name of God, the Merciful-to-all, the Mercy Giver:

The Believers have prospered.[1492] [(01)] They are those who humble themselves in prayer, [(02)] who turn away from meaningless talk, [(03)] pay the purifying alms, [(04)] and who protect their chastity [(05)] except with their wives or with those whom their right hands held in trust, for which they will not be blamed. [(06)] Those who desire anything beyond that are transgressors, [(07)] whereas those who honor their trusts and their promises [(08)] and who keep up their prayers, [(09)] those are the inheritors [1493][(10)] who will inherit Paradise of Ferdous, where they will dwell for eternity.[1494] [(11)]

And We did certainly create man from an extract of clay.[1495] [(12)] and then We placed him as a drop of sperm in a safe place, [(13)] and then We transformed the drop of sperm into a clinging clot, and the clot into a lump (of flesh),[1496] and (from) the lump, We created bones, and We covered the bones with flesh, and then We structured him into yet another creation. Blessed is God, the best of creators.[1497] [(14)] Then, after that, you will surely die. [(15)] Then, on the Day of Resurrection, you will be resurrected. [(16)]

And We have created above you seven heavenly dimensions, and We have never abandoned (Our) creation. [(17)] And We have sent down rain from the sky in a measured amount and we settle it into the earth, (although) We have the

• • •

[1492] Joshua 1:8 This book of the law shall not depart out of your mouth; you shall meditate on it day and night, so that you may be careful to act in accordance with all that is written in it. For then you shall make your way prosperous, and then you shall be successful. Matthew 6:7 And when you pray, do not keep on babbling like pagans, for they think they will be heard because of their many words.

[1493] Psalm 37:9 For the wicked shall be cut off, but those who wait for the Lord shall inherit the land.

[1494] Matthew 5:10 'Blessed are those who are persecuted for righteousness' sake, for theirs is the kingdom of heaven.

[1495] Genesis 2:7 then the Lord God formed man from the dust of the ground, and breathed into his nostrils the breath of life; and the man became a living being.

[1496] Psalm 139:13-14 For it was you who formed my inward parts; you knit me together in my mother's womb. [13] I praise you, for I am fearfully and wonderfully made. [14] Wonderful are your works; that I know very well.

[1497] Psalm 103:1 Of David. "Bless the Lord, O my soul, and all that is within me, bless his holy name."

power to withdraw it. ⁽¹⁸⁾ With (water) We bring forth gardens of palm trees, and vines with abundant fruit for you¹⁴⁹⁸ from which you may eat, ⁽¹⁹⁾ and a tree growing out of Mount Sinai that produces oil and relish for those who eat. ⁽²⁰⁾ And there is a lesson for you in livestock, we give you milk to drink from their bellies, (you derive) numerous other benefits from them: you eat (their meat) (23:21) and ride upon them as you do on ships. ⁽²²⁾

We sent Noah to his people, and he said, "My people, worship God; you have no gods before Him. Will you not be aware of Him?" ⁽²³⁾ But their leaders, who were among the unbelievers from his people said, "He is but a human being like you, trying to gain dominance over you; if God had so willed, He would have sent down angels. We have never heard of anything like this from our forefathers. ⁽²⁴⁾ He is only a man possessed, so put up with him for a while, and let's see what happens to him." ⁽²⁵⁾ (Noah) said, "My Lord, help me, because they have accused me of lying." ⁽²⁶⁾ So We instructed him, "Build the Ark¹⁴⁹⁹ under Our watchful eyes and (according to) Our revelation. When Our command comes and the valley overflows, take on board pairs of every species¹⁵⁰⁰ and your family, except for those among them against whom judgment has been proclaimed.¹⁵⁰¹ And do not plead with Me on behalf of the unjust; they will all be drowned.¹⁵⁰² ⁽²⁷⁾ When you and those with you are settled on the Ark,¹⁵⁰³ then say, 'All praise is due to God, who has delivered us from the oppressive people.' ⁽²⁸⁾ And say, 'My Lord, let me land at a blessed landing place, as You are the best to provide.'" ⁽²⁹⁾ There are signs in all this, and We are always putting people to the test. ⁽³⁰⁾

Then, after those people, We raised up a new generation. ⁽³¹⁾ And We sent them a messenger from among them, (saying), "Worship God¹⁵⁰⁴ for you have no god before Him; Will you not, then, be aware of Him?" ⁽³²⁾ But the leaders among his people, who denied the truth and denied the encounter with the Hereafter, and to whom We had given ease and plenty in this worldly, life said, "This is only a man like you, who eats what you eat and drinks what you drink ⁽³³⁾ and, if you should obey a human being like yourselves, you would then fail. ⁽³⁴⁾ Does he promise you that when you have died and become dust and bones that you will be brought forth (to a new life)? ⁽³⁵⁾ What You have been promised is sheer nonsense. ⁽³⁶⁾ Life is only our worldly life: we live and die, but we will not be resurrected. ⁽³⁷⁾ He is just a man who has invented a lie about God, and We will never believe him." ⁽³⁸⁾ He said, "My Lord, help me because they call me a liar." ⁽³⁹⁾ (God) said, "After a little while, they will surely regret (what they have

• • •

¹⁴⁹⁸ Isaiah 55:10 For as the rain and the snow come down from heaven, and do not return there until they have watered the earth, making it bring forth and sprout, giving seed to the sower and bread to the eater,
¹⁴⁹⁹ Genesis 6:14 Make yourself an ark of cypress wood; make rooms in the ark, and cover it inside and out with pitch.
¹⁵⁰⁰ Genesis 6:19 And of every living thing, of all flesh, you shall bring two of every kind into the ark, to keep them alive with you; they shall be male and female.
¹⁵⁰¹ Genesis 6:17 For my part, I am going to bring a flood of waters on the earth, to destroy from under heaven all flesh in which is the breath of life; everything that is on the earth shall die.
¹⁵⁰² Genesis 7:21-22 And all flesh died that moved on the earth, birds, domestic animals, wild animals, all swarming creatures that swarm on the earth, and all human beings; ²² everything on dry land in whose nostrils was the breath of life died.
¹⁵⁰³ Genesis 7:7 And Noah with his sons and his wife and his sons' wives went into the ark to escape the waters of the flood.
¹⁵⁰⁴ Exodus 20:1-3 Then God spoke all these words: ² I am the Lord your God, who brought you out of the land of Egypt, out of the house of slavery; ³ you shall have no other gods before me.

said)." [(40)] So the blast justly struck them, and We swept them away like scum. Away then with the oppressive people. [(41)] After them, We gave rise to new generations. [(42)] No community can speed up or hold back its appointed destiny.[1505] [(43)] Then We sent Our messengers in succession. Whenever a messenger came to a community he was invariably rejected,[1506] so We destroyed them one after the other, until they became mere tales. Away, then, with the people who do not believe.[1507] [(44)]

Then We sent Moses and his brother Aaron with Our signs and a clear authority[1508] [(45)] to Pharaoh and his inner circle, but they were an arrogant, haughty people. [1509] [(46)] They said, "Should we believe two human beings like us while their people are serving us?" [(47)] So they called them both liars, and were consequently destroyed.[1510] [(48)] And We gave Moses the Book[1511] so that he might be guided. [(49)] And We made the son of Mary[1512] and his mother[1513] a sign and sheltered them within a hill where there was a meadow and a flowing spring.[(50)]

(God said), "O Messengers, eat good things and do good. I know all that you do. [(51)] This community of yours is one community, and I am your Lord, so be ever conscious of Me." [(52)] Yet (your followers) tore their unity piece by piece, each faction rejoicing in what it has. [(53)] So, leave them in their confusion for a while. [(54)] Do they think that We provide them wealth and children [(55)] because We rush to give them good things? No, but they are oblivious (to what is going on). [(56)] Those who stand in awe of their Lord [(57)] who believe in the messages of their Lord [(58)] who do not associate anything with their Lord, [(59)] and who give whatever they can while their hearts tremble at the thought that they will be returning to their Lord, [1514(60)] these are the ones who vie to do good deeds, and they will be the first to attain them. [(61)]

We do not burden any soul with more than it can bear.[1515] There is a record with Us which speaks the Truth and they will not be treated unjustly. [(62)] However, the (unbelievers') hearts are in confusion about this (message), and

• • •

[1505] Matthew 6:27 And can any of you by worrying add a single hour to your span of life?

[1506] Matthew 21:42 Jesus said to them, 'Have you never read in the scriptures: "The stone that the builders rejected has become the cornerstone; this was the Lord's doing, and it is amazing in our eyes"?

[1507] 2 Thessalonians 2:12 so that all who have not believed the truth but took pleasure in unrighteousness will be condemned.

[1508] Exodus 4:21 And the Lord said to Moses, 'When you go back to Egypt, see that you perform before Pharaoh all the wonders that I have put in your power; but I will harden his heart, so that he will not let the people go.

[1509] Exodus 5:2 But Pharaoh said, 'Who is the LORD, that I should heed him and let Israel go? I do not know the Lord, and I will not let Israel go.'

[1510] Hebrews 11:29 By faith the people passed through the Red Sea as if it were dry land, but when the Egyptians attempted to do so they were drowned.

[1511] Exodus 31:18 When God finished speaking with Moses on Mount Sinai, he gave him the two tablets of the covenant, tablets of stone, written with the finger of God.

[1512] Jesus

[1513] Mary, mother of Jesus

[1514] Job 37:1-3 At this also my heart trembles, and leaps out of its place. [2] Listen, listen to the thunder of his voice and the rumbling that comes from his mouth. [3] Under the whole heaven he lets it loose, and his lightning to the corners of the earth.

[1515] 1 Corinthians 10:13 No testing has overtaken you that is not common to everyone. God is faithful, and he will not let you be tested beyond your strength, but with the testing he will also provide the way out so that you may be able to endure it.

they do even do worse deeds, ⁽⁶³⁾ until We bring those corrupted with opulence for punishment. Only then will they suddenly start crying (to God) for help. ⁽⁶⁴⁾ "Do not cry out today. You will not get any help from Us. ⁽⁶⁵⁾ For (every time) My verses were recited to you, you turned away from them ⁽⁶⁶⁾ in arrogance, amusing yourself by talking nonsense about them far into the night." ⁽⁶⁷⁾

Have they not thought about what We tell them, or has something come to them that did not come to their forefathers? ⁽⁶⁸⁾ Or do they not recognize their messenger? Is that why they do not acknowledge him? ⁽⁶⁹⁾ Or do they say, "He is crazy?" when in fact he brought them the Truth. But most of them hate the Truth. ^{1516 (70)} If the Truth conformed to their desires, truly, the heavens, and the earth, and whoever is in them would have been corrupted. Instead, We have given them their Reminder, but they turn away from it. ⁽⁷¹⁾ Or (do they think that) you are asking them for compensation, when your Lord's compensation is best? He is the Best of Providers. ⁽⁷²⁾ You call them to a straight path, ^{1517 (73)} but those who do not believe in the Hereafter deviate from that path. ⁽⁷⁴⁾ Even if We were to show them mercy and relieve them of the harm afflicting them, they would persist in their blind transgression. ⁽⁷⁵⁾ Even when We afflicted them with suffering (as a warning), they did not humble themselves to their Lord, nor were they submissive, ⁽⁷⁶⁾ but when We open a gate of severe punishment to them, they will immediately be crushed with despair. ⁽⁷⁷⁾

And it is He who created your hearing and vision and hearts; how seldom are you grateful. ⁽⁷⁸⁾ And it is He who spread you over the earth, ¹⁵¹⁸ and to Him you will be gathered. ^{1519 (79)} And It is He Who gives life and causes death, ¹⁵²⁰ and to Him is due the alternation of night and day. Will you not then use your reason? ⁽⁸⁰⁾ However, they are content to say what their ancestors said. ⁽⁸¹⁾ They said, "When we die and become dust and bones, are we to be resurrected? ⁽⁸²⁾ We have been promised this before, and so were our forefathers. These are just ancient legends." ⁽⁸³⁾ Say, "To whom belongs the earth and all that is in it, if you know?"^{1521 (84)} They will say, "To God." Say, "Then will you not take heed?" ⁽⁸⁵⁾ Say, "Who is Lord of the seven heavens and Lord of the Mighty Throne?" ⁽⁸⁶⁾ They will say, "(They belong) to God." Say, "Then will you not be mindful?" ⁽⁸⁷⁾ Say, "In whose hand is the dominion over all things. Who protects, while none can protect against Him, ¹⁵²² if you happen to know?" ⁽⁸⁸⁾ They will say, "(All belongs) to God." Say, "Then how can you be so mislead?" ⁽⁸⁹⁾ In fact, We have sent them the Truth, but they lie. ⁽⁹⁰⁾ God has not taken any son, nor has there ever been any other god but Him. (Had there been), then each god would have taken aside what it created, and sought to overcome the others. May God be exalted in His

• • •

¹⁵¹⁶ Amos 5:10 They hate the one who reproves in the gate, and they abhor the one who speaks the truth.
¹⁵¹⁷ Psalm 23:3 he restores my soul. He leads me in right paths for his name's sake.
¹⁵¹⁸ Isaiah 9:3 You have multiplied the nation, you have increased its joy; they rejoice before you as with joy at the harvest, as people exult when dividing plunder.
¹⁵¹⁹ Matthew 25:32 All the nations will be gathered before him, and he will separate people one from another as a shepherd separates the sheep from the goats,
¹⁵²⁰ 1 Samuel 2:6, The Lord kills and brings to life; he brings down to Sheol and raises up. Deuteronomy 32:39 See now that I, even I, am he; there is no god besides me. I kill and I make alive; I wound and I heal; and no one can deliver from my hand.
¹⁵²¹ Deuteronomy 10:14 Although heaven and the heaven of heavens belong to the Lord your God, the earth with all that is in it,
¹⁵²² 1 John 5:18 We know that those who are born of God do not sin, but the one who was born of God protects them, and the evil one does not touch them.

glory, far above what they ascribed to Him. [91] The Knower of all that is beyond human perception, as well as all that can be witnessed by humans. May He be exalted above all whom they associate with Him! [92] Say, "My Lord, if You are going to show me what you have promised them, [93] then, My Lord, do not place me among such unjust people." [94] We are surely able to show you what We have promised them. [95] Overcome evil with good[1523]- We are well aware of what they are saying. [96] And say, "My Lord, I seek refuge in You from the incitements of the devils,[1524] [97] And I seek refuge in You, my Lord, so they may not come near me." [98]

When death comes to one of them, he says, "My Lord, send me back [99] so that I may make amends for what I left undone." Never! This is but a word he is saying; for behind them there is a (dimensional) barrier until the Day when all will be resurrected! [100] So when the Horn is blown, no ties of kinship will bind them on that Day, nor will they ask about one another. [101] And those whose balance (of good deeds) is heavy, it is they who will be successful; [102] but those whose balance is light, those are the ones who have lost their souls and will remain in Hell forever. [103] The Fire will sear their faces, distorting them horribly and painfully. [104] "Were not My verses recited to you and did you not reject them?" [105] They will say, "Our Lord, our defiance overcame us, and we were led astray. [106] Our Lord, get us out of here, and, if we go back to our evil ways, we would be unjust." [107] He will say, "Remain despised where you are and do not speak to Me. [108] Among My worshipers there were those who used to say, 'Our Lord, We have believed, so forgive us and have mercy on us, for You are the most Merciful.' [109] But you were so preoccupied with mocking them that you forgot about Me, while you were laughing at them. [110] I have rewarded them this Day for their patient endurance – they are the successful." [111] He said: "How many years were you on earth?" [112] They will say, "We were there a day or part of a day; ask those who keep track of it." [113] He will say, "You stayed but a little, if only you had known. [114] Did you think, then, that We created you in vain, or that you would not be returned to Us?" [115]

How sublimely exalted is God, the Ultimate Sovereign, the Ultimate Truth; there is no deity except Him, Lord of the Noble Throne of His majesty.[1525] [116] Whoever calls another deity besides God with no evidence for its existence, then his reckoning will be with his Lord. the unbelievers will never triumph. [117] And, say, "My Lord, forgive and have mercy; and You are the most Merciful-to-all."[1526] [118]

• • •

[1523] Romans 12:21 Do not be overcome by evil, but overcome evil with good. Matthew 7:12 "In everything do to others as you would have them do to you; for this is the law and the prophets."
[1524] John 17:15 I am not asking you to take them out of the world, but I ask you to protect them from the evil one.
[1525] Revelation 7:11 And all the angels stood around the throne and around the elders and the four living creatures, and they fell on their faces before the throne and worshipped God.
[1526] Psalm 116:5 Gracious is the Lord, and righteous; our God is merciful.

CHAPTER TWENTY FOUR

AN-NUR
THE LIGHT

THE **MECCA** PERIOD

In the name of God, the Merciful-to-all, the Mercy Giver:
(This is) a chapter which We have sent down and made it obligatory, revealing clear messages so that you might take heed.[1528] [(01)]
The (unmarried) woman or man found guilty of adultery, lash each one of them with a hundred lashes, and do not let compassion for them prevent you from obeying God's religion, if you believe in God and the Last Day. And let a group of the believers witness their punishment. [(02)] The adulterer shouldn't marry except an adulteress or idolatress, and let none marry her except an adulterer or an idolater. Such behavior is forbidden to believers. [(03)] And as for those who accuse a chaste women and then do not produce four witnesses, lash each with eighty lashes, and do not accept their testimony again, for they are deviators from the truth,[1529] [(04)] except for those who repent later and reform, for God is most forgiving and Merciful-to-all. [(05)] As for those who accuse their own wives (of adultery) and have no witnesses except themselves, let each call on God four times to witness that he is telling the truth, [(06)] and the fifth (testimony will be) that the curse of God be upon him should he be lying. [(07)] But she will not be punished if she gives four testimonies with God as her witness that he is lying, [(08)] and the fifth (testimony will be) that the wrath of God be upon her should he be truthful. [(09)] Were it not for God's favor to you and His mercy, and because God is accepting of repentance and Wise . . .! [(10)]

• • •

[1528] Numbers 15:40 So you shall remember and do all my commandments, and you shall be holy to your God.
[1529] Deuteronomy 19:16-21 If a malicious witness comes forward to accuse someone of wrongdoing, [17] then both parties to the dispute shall appear before the Lord, before the priests and the judges who are in office in those days, [18] and the judges shall make a thorough inquiry. If the witness is a false witness, having testified falsely against another, [19] then you shall do to the false witness just as the false witness had meant to do to the other. So you shall purge the evil from your midst. [20] The rest shall hear and be afraid, and a crime such as this shall never again be committed among you. Show no pity: life for life, eye for eye, tooth for tooth, hand for hand, foot for foot.

There is a group among you who spread slander. Do not think it bad for you; rather It is a good thing. Every one of them shall bear the sin that he has earned,[1530] and he who took the greatest part in it will have a painful punishment.[1531] (11) When you heard about it, why did the believers-men and women-not think well of one another and say "This is an obvious lie?" (12) And why did they not produce four witnesses to it? When accusers do not produce four witnesses, then in God's sight it is they who are the liars. (13) And had it not been for God's favor upon you and His mercy in this world and the Hereafter, you would have already been afflicted by terrible suffering for indulging in such talk. (14) When you received it on your tongues and your mouths uttered things about which you had no knowledge, you thought it a trivial matter, while in God's sight it was most serious. (15) And why, when you heard it, did you not say, "It does not behoove us to speak about this. May you (O God) be exalted in Your glory; this is a great slander?" (16) God warns you never to repeat this (conduct), if you are true believers. (17) God makes His messages clear to you, for God is All-knowing and All-Wise.[1532] (18) Those who enjoy hearing that immorality has spread among the believers will have a painful punishment both in this world and the Hereafter. God knows and you do not. (19) Were it not for God's favor to you and His mercy, and because God is compassionate and Merciful-to-all.[1533] (20)

Believers, do not follow Satan's footsteps, for he who follows Satan's footsteps joins immorality and wrongdoing. Were it not for God's favor to you and His mercy, not one of you would have been purified,[1534] ever, but God purifies whom He wills, for God is All-Hearing and All-Knowing. (21) Let not those among you who possess affluence and wealth swear against giving to their relatives, the needy, and the emigrants for God's sake, but let them pardon and forgive. Would you not like for God to forgive[1535] you? God is forgiving and Merciful-to-all.[1536] (22)

Those who (falsely) accuse chaste women (who are) incautious but believing are cursed in this world and the Hereafter; they will have a great punishment (23) on the Day when their tongues, their hands and their feet will bear witness against them regarding what they used to do. (24) On that Day, God will pay them in full their just due,[1537] and they will know that God is the Manifest Truth. (25) Wicked women are for wicked men, and wicked men are for wicked women. Good women are for good men, and good men are for good women. The good (men and women) are innocent of what has been said against them; they will have forgiveness and a generous provision. (26)

• • •

[1530] Ezekiel 18:20 The person who sins shall die. A child shall not suffer for the iniquity of a parent, nor a parent suffer for the iniquity of a child; the righteousness of the righteous shall be his own, and the wickedness of the wicked shall be his own.

[1531] Matthew 25:46 And these will go away into eternal punishment, but the righteous into eternal life.'

[1532] 1 Corinthians 1:25 For God's foolishness is wiser than human wisdom, and God's weakness is stronger than human strength.

[1533] Psalm 116:5 Gracious is the Lord, and righteous; our God is merciful.

[1534] Ecclesiastes 7:20, Surely there is no one on earth so righteous as to do good without ever sinning.

[1535] Mathew 6:14 For if you forgive others their trespasses, your heavenly father will forgive you;

[1536] Luke 1:50 His mercy is for those who fear him from generation to generation.

[1537] Isaiah 59:18 According to their deeds, so will he repay; wrath to his adversaries, requital to his enemies; to the coastlands he will render requital.

Believers do not enter houses other than your own until you have asked permission to do so and greeted their residents. That is best for you, so that you will be reminded (of each other's rights). [27] And if you do not find anyone in, do not enter until permission has been granted, and, if It is said to you, "Go away," then go away. This is purer for you, for God knows well what you do. [28] (However) there is no blame on you for entering houses not inhabited but serve a purpose useful to you. God knows what you reveal and what you conceal. [29]

Tell believing men to lower their gaze and guard their private parts. That is purer for them. God is acquainted with what they do. [30] And tell the believing women to lower their gaze and guard their private parts and not expose their charms, beyond what may be (acceptable to) display. [1538] Let them drape (a portion of) their head coverings over their breasts, and not reveal their charms except to their husbands, their fathers, their husbands' fathers, their sons, their husbands' sons, their brothers, their brothers' sons, their sisters' sons, their womenfolk, their slaves, or those male attendants having no sexual desire, or children who are not yet aware of women's private parts. And let them not stamp their feet to make known what they conceal of their charms. And believers-all of you-turn to God in repentance, [1539] that you may succeed. [31]

Marry off those among you who are unmarried and those who are righteous among your male and female slaves. If they should be poor, God will enrich them from His favor; God is All- Encompassing and All-Knowing. [32] Those who are unable to marry should keep chaste until God gives them sufficiently from His favor. If any of those whom your right hands held in trust seek a contract then, draw one with them if you know there is goodness within them, and share with them the wealth that God has given you. Do not compel your girls against their will to prostitution, out of your desire for the short-term gains of this world, if they want to be married. If they however are compelled, God will be forgiving and merciful to them. [33]

We have sent down to you clarifying messages and examples from those who passed on before you, and an admonition for those who are ever mindful of God. [34]

God is the illuminator [1540] of the heavens and the earth. His light may be likened to (the light emanating from) a niche containing a lamp, [1541] that is enclosed in glass, the glass (is shining) like a brilliant star fueled from a blessed tree, an olive tree that is neither of the east nor of the west-its oil is nearly luminous even if untouched by fire. Light upon light. [1542] God guides to His enlightenment whoever wills (to be guided). God presents such examples to

• • •

[1538] 1 Timothy 2:9-10 I also want women to dress modestly, with decency and propriety, not with braided hair or gold or pearls or expensive clothes, [10] but with good deeds, appropriate for women who profess to worship God.

[1539] Isaiah 55:6-7 "Seek the Lord while he may be found; call on him while he is near. Let the wicked forsake his way and the evil man his thoughts. [7] Let him turn to the Lord, and he will have mercy on him, and to our God, for he will freely pardon."

[1540] 1 John 1:5 This is the message we have heard from him and proclaim to you, that God is light and in him there is no darkness at all.

[1541] Psalm 119:105 Your word is a lamp to my feet and a light to my path.

[1542] Isaiah 42:16 I will lead the blind by a road they do not know, by paths they have not known I will guide them. I will turn the darkness before them into light, the rough places into level ground These are the things I will do, and I will not forsake them.

people, since God (alone) has full knowledge of all things. [35] In houses of worship that God has allowed to be raised, where His Name will be remembered and where His limitless glory is celebrated morning and evenings [36] (by) men whom neither commerce nor business can distract from the remembrance of God, performance of prayer, and the payment of the purifying alms. They fear a Day when hearts and eyes will be convulsed [37] hoping that God may reward them according to the best of what they did,[1543] and give them more from His favor. God provides limitlessly for anyone He will. [38]

But the unbelievers, their deeds are like a mirage in a desert that the thirsty mistake for water until, when he comes to it, he finds it is nothing. Instead, he finds only God there, and God will pay him his full due, for God is quick to take account. [39] Or (their deeds are) like darkness over a stormy sea covered by waves, over waves, over which are dark clouds, layer upon layer of darkness. If one holds out his hand, he can hardly see it.[1544] For him to whom God gives no enlightenment, there is no enlightenment.[1545] [40]

Do you not see that God's limitless glory is exalted by all in the heavens and the earth, even by the birds with wings outspread (in flight)? Each (of them) knows how to pray to and glorify (Him), and God well knows that they do. [41] To God belongs the dominion of the heavens and the earth, and to God (all things) ultimately return.[1546] [42] Do not you see that God drives the clouds, then brings them together, and then piles them into heaps until you see rain come pouring from them?[1547] He sends down from the sky mountains (of clouds) filled with hail, striking with it whom He wills [1548] and averting it from whom He wills.[1549] The flash of its lightening almost blinds the eyes. [43] God revolves night and day.[1550] In (all) this is a lesson for those who are insightful. [44] God has created every living creature from water. Some of them creep on their bellies, some walk on two legs, and some walk on four. God creates what He wills for God is surely able to do all things. [45] We have indeed sent down messages clarifying everything. God guides [1551] to a straight path whoever wills (to be guided). [46]

Some declare, "We believed in God and the Messenger, and we obey," but then, a group of them turn away. Such people are not true believers. [47] When they are called to God and His Messenger to judge between them, some of them turn away, [48] but if they think that the right is on their side, they then come to

•   •   •

[1543] Luke 14:14 And you will be blessed, because they cannot repay you, for you will be repaid at the resurrection of the righteous.
[1544] Matthew 22:13Then the king said to the attendants, "Bind him hand and foot, and throw him into the outer darkness, where there will be weeping and gnashing of teeth."
[1545] Psalm 36:8-9 They feast on the abundance of your house, and you give them drink from the river of your delights. 9 For with you is the fountain of life; in your light we see light.
[1546] Matthew 4:17 From that time Jesus began to proclaim, 'Repent, for the kingdom of heaven has come near.'
[1547] Matthew 5:45 so that you may be children of your Father in heaven; for he makes his sun rise on the evil and on the good, and sends rain on the righteous and on the unrighteous.
[1548] Exodus 9:22 The Lord said to Moses, 'Stretch out your hand towards heaven so that hail may fall on the whole land of Egypt, on humans and animals and all the plants of the field in the land of Egypt.'
[1549] Exodus 9:26 Only in the land of Goshen, where the Israelites were, there was no hail.
[1550] Genesis 1:14-15 And God said, 'Let there be lights in the dome of the sky to separate the day from the night; 15 and let them be for signs and for seasons and for days and years, and let them be lights in the dome of the sky to give light upon the earth.' And it was so.
[1551] Psalm 23:3 he restores my soul. He leads me in right paths for his name's sake.

him (the Prophet) in prompt obedience. [49] Is there a sickness in their hearts? [1552] Or are they in doubt? Or do they fear that God and His Messenger will be unjust to them? Rather, it is they who are the unjust. [1553] [50] When the believers are called to God and His Messenger to judge between them, they respond "We hear and we obey." Those are the achievers, [51] for whoever obeys God and His Messenger, and is in awe of God and is ever mindful of Him, it is they who are the successful. [1554] [52] (Others) solemnly swear by God that if you (Prophet) ordered them, they would go forth (in God's cause). Say, "Do not swear. (Such) obedience is (expected). God is well aware of all you do." [53] Say, "Obey God and obey the Messenger; but if you turn away, he is responsible only for what he has been given to do, and you are responsible for what you have been given. [1555] If you obey him, you will be (rightly) guided, but the Messenger's duty is only to deliver the Message clearly." [54]

God has promised those among you who have believed and done righteous deeds that He will make them successors upon the earth just as He did those before them, and that He will establish for them the faith that He has chosen for them. He will exchange the fear they have experienced with security, [1556] (for) they worship Me (alone), not associating anything with Me. But whoever denies the truth after (having understood) this, then those are the defiantly disobedient. [55] Establish prayer, and give the purifying alms, and obey the Messenger, so that you may receive mercy. [1557] [56] Do not ever think that the unbelievers can ever escape God on earth. Their refuge will be the Fire. What an evil destination. [57]

Believers, let your slaves and those who have not (yet) reached puberty among you ask permission of you (before entering your presence) at three times of the day: before the dawn prayer, and when you take off your clothing (for rest) at noon, and after the evening prayer. (These are) three times of privacy for you. At other times, there is no blame on you or them if you move about freely, tending to each other's needs. In this way does God make the message clear to you, for God is All-Knowing and All-Wise. [1558] [58] And when your children reach puberty, let them ask your permission to enter, just as those before them have done. In this way God makes His messages clear to you, for God is All-Knowing and All-Wise. [59] As for elderly women who have no desire to marry-there is no blame upon them if they remove their outer garments without displaying their

• • •

[1552] Jeremiah 17:9-10 The heart is devious above all else; it is perverse—who can understand it? [10] I the Lord test the mind and search the heart, to give to all according to their ways, according to the fruit of their doings.

[1553] Proverbs 29:27 The unjust are an abomination to the righteous, but the upright are an abomination to the wicked.

[1554] Ecclesiastes 12:13 The end of the matter; all has been heard. Fear God, and keep his commandments; for that is the whole duty of everyone.

[1555] Galatians 6:4-5 All must test their own work; then that work, rather than their neighbor's work, will become a cause for pride. [5] For all must carry their own loads.

[1556] 2 Corinthians 5:6-8 So we are always confident; even though we know that while we are at home in the body we are away from the Lord— [7] for we walk by faith, not by sight. [8] Yes, we do have confidence, and we would rather be away from the body and at home with the Lord.

[1557] Matthew 5:7 'Blessed are the merciful, for they will receive mercy.

[1558] Job 9:4 He is wise in heart, and mighty in strength —who has resisted him, and succeeded? —

charms, but, to modestly refrain (from that) is better for them, for God is All-Hearing and All-Knowing.[1559] [(60)]

There is not any restriction on the blind, the lame, the ill or yourselves when you eat from your (own) houses or the houses of your fathers, your mothers, your brothers, your sisters, your father's brothers, your father's sisters, your mother's brothers, your mother's sisters or (from houses) whose keys you possess, or from any of your friends' houses. There is nothing wrong with your eating (either) together or separately, but, when you enter any house, give greetings of peace upon each other, a greeting from God, blessed and good.[1560] In this way God makes His messages clear to you so that you may understand.[(61)]

The Believers are those who believe in God and His Messenger, and who, when they meet with him about some matter of common concern, do not depart until they have asked his permission. (Prophet), those who ask your permission are the ones who (truly) believe in God and His Messenger. So, when they ask your permission to attend to their affairs, then give permission to any among them you will, and ask God to forgive them. God is Ever-Forgiving[1561] and Merciful-to-all.[1562] [(62)] (Believers), do not call the Messenger as you call one another. God knows those of you who slip away, (from meetings with the Prophet) stealthily, so let those who dissent from the Prophet's order beware, lest some trial befall them (in this life) or a painful punishment (in the next). [(63)]

To God belongs everything in the heavens and earth. He knows what you stand for, and one Day, when all return to Him, He will inform them what they have done, for God knows all things. [(64)]

● ● ●

[1559] Daniel 2:22 He reveals deep and hidden things; he knows what is in the darkness, and light dwells with him.
[1560] Matthew 10:12-13 "As you enter the house, give it your greeting. [13] "If the house is worthy, give it your blessing of peace.
[1561] Daniel 9:9 To the Lord our God belong mercy and forgiveness, for we have rebelled against him,
[1562] Romans 11:29-31 for the gifts and the calling of God are irrevocable. [30] Just as you were once disobedient to God but have now received mercy because of their disobedience, [31] so they have now been disobedient in order that, by the mercy shown to you, they too may now receive mercy.

CHAPTER TWENTY FIVE

AL-FURGAN
THE DIFFERENTIATOR

THE **MECCA** PERIOD

In the name of God, the Merciful-to-all, the Mercy Giver:

Blessed is He who sent down to His Servant [1563] the Furqan (the Standard by which we judge right from wrong), so that he may be a Warner to all people. [01] It is He to whom belongs the dominion over the heavens and the earth, and who has not taken a son and has no associate in His dominion, for He has created all things according to precise measures. [1564] [02] Yet some have chosen to worship gods other than Him, gods who cannot create but are themselves created, who have no power to protect themselves from harm or benefit themselves, and who have no power over death, or life, or resurrection. [1565] [03]

And the unbelievers say, "This is but a lie he has devised, made possible with the help of other people." In truth, they have committed injustice and falsehood. [04] They (also) say, "These are just legends of the ancients that he (directed to be) written down and dictated to him morning and evening." [05] Say, "It has been sent down by Him who knows (every) secret [1566] within the heavens and the earth. He is ever-forgiving [1567] and Merciful-to-all." [1568] [06] And they also say, "What sort of messenger eats food and walks in the markets? Should not at least

• • •

[1563] "Servant" is much more common in English than the word "slave," but both this Arabic word /abd/ and the corresponding words in the Law /abd/ and the Gospel /doulos/ are stronger than this. This word means both slave and worshiper. All the holy books call the believers slaves of God.

[1564] Isaiah 45:7-8 I form light and create darkness, I make weal and create woe; I the Lord do all these things. Shower, O heavens, from above, and let the skies rain down righteousness; let the earth open, that salvation may spring up, and let it cause righteousness to sprout up also; I the Lord have created it.

[1565] Psalm 115:4-7 Their idols are silver and gold, the work of human hands. [5] They have mouths, but do not speak; eyes, but do not see. [6] They have ears, but do not hear; noses, but do not smell. [7] They have hands, but do not feel; feet, but do not walk; they make no sound in their throats.

[1566] Daniel 2:47 The king said to Daniel, 'Truly, your God is God of gods and Lord of kings and a revealer of mysteries, for you have been able to reveal this mystery!'

[1567] Psalm 79:9 Help us, O God of our salvation, for the glory of your name; deliver us, and forgive our sins, for your name's sake.

[1568] Exodus 34:6 The Lord passed before him, and proclaimed, 'The LORD, the LORD, a God merciful and gracious, slow to anger, and abounding in steadfast love and faithfulness,

an angel have been sent down to him, to help him with his warning?" [07] Or, "Why hasn't he been given a treasure?" Or, "Why he does not have a garden from which he eats?" And the unjust say, "The man you follow is simply bewitched." [08] Look at the examples they are using to describe you, (Prophet) but they have strayed and now cannot find their way. [09] Blessed is He Who, if He wishes, can give you (Prophet) better than these; Gardens with rivers flowing through them and can grant you palaces. [10]

Denying that there is an Hour (of resurrection)[1569] is actually their main issue. (Hence), We have prepared a blazing fire for those who deny the Hour. [11] When (Hell) sees them from a distance, they will hear its fury and roaring, [12] and when they are thrown, shackled together, into a narrow place therein, they will pray for death. [13] (They will be told) "Do not pray today for one death, but pray for many deaths." [14] Say, "Is that (fate) better for you, or is the Garden of Eternity, which is promised to those that were ever mindful of God, better? For them, It will be a reward and a destination. [15] Where they can have whatever they wish forever. This is a binding promise from your Lord. [16] And on the Day He will gather them (the unjust) along with those they worship beside God, and (He) will say, "Was it you who misled My servants, or did they stray from the path by themselves?" [17] They will say, "May You be exalted in Your glory! It was not for us to take any protectors beside You. But You provided comforts for them and their fathers until they forgot your message and became a worthless people." [18] (God will say) "They (whom you claimed as divine), are refuting you and what you claim. Hence, you cannot avoid (punishment) or (find) help. And whoever commits injustice among you, We will make him suffer great punishment."[1570][19]

(Prophet) Every messenger we ever sent before you ate food and walked in the markets. But We have made some of you a test for others to see if you will be steadfast? For your Lord is ever insightful. [20]

Those who do not expect that they are destined to meet Us say, "Why were not angels sent down to us, or (why) do we (not) see our Lord?" They have certainly become too proud of themselves and excessively insolent.[1571] [21] On the day they see the angels, there won't be any good news for those who denied God, and (the angels guarding the gate to paradise) will say, "Stop, stay out." [22] We will examine their deeds and scatter them like dust, [23] Meanwhile those who are destined for paradise will, on that Day, be securely settled in the best resting place.[1572] [24] The Day when heaven will split open with clouds (emerging), and the angels are sent down successively in streams. [25] True sovereignty, on that Day, will belong to the Merciful-to-all.[1573] For unbelievers, it will be a day of distress; [26] on that Day the one who was unjust to himself will bite his hands (in regret) and will say, "How I wish I had followed the way of the Messenger. [27] Woe to me! I wish I had not taken so and so as a friend. [28] He led me away from

• • •

[1569] Revelation 14:7 He said in a loud voice, 'Fear God and give him glory, for the hour of his judgment has come; and worship him who made heaven and earth, the sea and the springs of water.'
[1570] 2 Thessalonians 1:9 These will suffer the punishment of eternal destruction, separated from the presence of the Lord and from the glory of his might,
[1571] 2 Chronicles 26:16 But when he had become strong he grew proud, to his destruction. For he was false to the LORD his God, and entered the temple of the Lord to make offering on the altar of incense.
[1572] Revelation 2:7 Let anyone who has an ear listen to what the Spirit is saying to the churches. To everyone who conquers, I will give permission to eat from the tree of life that is in the paradise of God.
[1573] Romans 11:32 For God has imprisoned all in disobedience so that he may be Merciful-to-all.

the remembrance (of God) after it had come to me. Satan, has always let man down." (29)

The Messenger will say, "My Lord, This Qur'an was abandoned by my people," (30) and thus have We assigned to every prophet an enemy; those, who force others to reject Our messages. But your Lord is sufficient as a guide and a helper.1574 (31) And the unbelievers say, "Why was the Qur'an not sent to him in one single revelation?" (It was revealed in stages) so that We may strengthen your heart. And We revealed it in well-organized portions. (32) And every time they come to you with an argument, We will give you the (full) Truth and the best explanation. (33) As for those who are dragged facedown to Hell, they will be in the worst place as they are the most misguided from the path. (34)

And We gave Moses the Book and appointed his brother Aaron to help him.1575 (35) We said, "Go together to the people who have rejected Our signs." Then We destroyed them completely. (36) And the people of Noah-when they denied the messengers, We drowned them,1576 and We made them a sign for people to come. And We have prepared a painful punishment for the unjust.1577 (37) (And the people of) Aad and Thamud, the people of the Al Rass and many generations in between. (38) In each case, We (warn them with) examples, and each We utterly destroyed. (39) They must surely have come upon the town that was showered with a horrible rain; have they not seen it? But they do not expect resurrection. (40) And whenever they see you (Prophet) they ridicule you, (saying), "Is this the one God sent as a messenger? (41) He would almost have misled us from our gods had we not stood firmly by them." But soon, when they see the punishment, they will know who is the most misguided. (42) Have you seen the one who has taken his own whims as his god? 1578 Are you responsible for him? (43) And do you think that most of them hear or understand? They are just like cattle; indeed, they are (even) more lost. (44)

Have you not considered how your Lord lengthens the shadow (when), had He so willed, He could have made it stationary? (Instead), We have made the sun its guide, (45) and We draw it back toward us gradually. (46) It is He who made the night a veil for you and sleep for rest, and the day a time for rising. (47) And it is He who sends forth the winds, bringing good news of His mercy. And We send down from the sky pure water, (48) so that We may bring dead land to life and provide drink for the multitude of beings, animals and people, We have created.

• • •

1574 2 Corinthians 12:9 but he said to me, 'My grace is sufficient for you, for power is made perfect in weakness.' So, I will boast all the more gladly of my weaknesses, so that the power of Christ may dwell in me.
1575 Exodus 4:28-30 Moses told Aaron all the words of the LORD with which he had sent him, and all the signs with which he had charged him. 29 Then Moses and Aaron went and assembled all the elders of the Israelites. 30 Aaron spoke all the words that the LORD had spoken to Moses, and performed the signs in the sight of the people.
1576 Genesis 7:23-24 He blotted out every living thing that was on the face of the ground, human beings and animals and creeping things and birds of the air; they were blotted out from the earth. Only Noah was left, and those that were with him in the ark. And the waters swelled on the earth for one hundred and fifty days.
1577 Matthew 25:41,46 Then he will say to those at his left hand, "You that are accursed, depart from me into the eternal fire prepared for the devil and his angels; 46 And these will go away into eternal punishment, but the righteous into eternal life.'
1578 Philippians 3:19 Their end is destruction; their god is the belly; and their glory is in their shame; their minds are set on earthly things.

(49) Indeed, We have distributed it among them so that they might take heed, but most people continue in their denial of the truth. (50) And if We had willed, We could have sent a warner to every town, (51) so do not go along with the unbelievers, but strove hard against them with this (Qur'an). (52) He is the one who has merged the two seas, one fresh and sweet, the other salty and bitter, and He placed between them an insurmountable barrier. (53) He created human beings from water and made them kin by blood and marriage. Your Lord is able to do all things. (54) Yet, instead of God, they worship what can neither benefit nor harm them. The unbeliever is always biased, against his Lord.[1579] (55) We have sent you (Prophet) only to bring good news and deliver a warning. (56) Say, "I ask you no payment for doing this- only that whoever wills may take a path to his Lord." (57) Put your trust in the Everlasting who does not die, glorify Him and celebrate His praise. For it is sufficient that none knows His worshipers' sins as fully as does He (58) Who created the heavens and the earth and everything in between them in six days,[1580] and then established Himself above the Throne of His majesty- the Merciful-to-all![1581] Ask about Him, then, the well informed. (59) Yet, when they are told, "Prostrate yourselves before the Merciful-to-all," they say, "And who is the 'Merciful-to-all'? Should we prostrate ourselves before whatever you order us (to worship)?" And they turn farther away. (60) Blessed is He who has placed constellations in the sky, a radiant light and glowing moon.[1582] (61) And It is He who has made night and day succeed each other,[1583] (revealing Himself to) for anyone who wishes to be mindful or show gratitude. (62) The worshipers of the Merciful-to-all are those who walk upon the earth with humility, and when the ignorant address them, reply with "peace";[1584] (63) those who spend the night prostrating themselves and standing before their Lord; (64) and those who say "Our Lord, spare us the punishment of Hell.[1585] Its punishment is dreadful; (65) It is an evil abode and resting-place." (66) They are those who, when they spend, are neither wasteful nor tightfisted, but maintain balanced spending habits, (67) (as well as) those who never invoke another god alongside God nor kill the soul that God has forbidden (to be killed), except in the pursuit

• • •

[1579] 2 Kings 17:15 They despised his statutes, and his covenant that he made with their ancestors, and the warnings that he gave them. They went after false idols and became false; they followed the nations that were around them, concerning whom the Lord had commanded them that they should not do as they did. Job 42:2 'I know that you can do all things, and that no purpose of yours can be thwarted.

[1580] Genesis 1:31, 2:1 God saw everything that he had made, and indeed, it was very good. And there was evening and there was morning, the sixth day. 2:1 Thus the heavens and the earth were finished, and all their multitude.

[1581] Hebrews 4:16 Let us therefore approach the throne of grace with boldness, so that we may receive mercy and find grace to help in time of need.

[1582] Genesis 1:16 God made the two great lights—the greater light to rule the day and the lesser light to rule the night—and the stars.

[1583] Genesis 1:14-15 And God said, 'Let there be lights in the dome of the sky to separate the day from the night; and let them be for signs and for seasons and for days and years, and let them be lights in the dome of the sky to give light upon the earth.' And it was so.

[1584] Matthew 5:5 Blessed are the meek, for they will inherit the earth. Philippians 2:3-4 Do nothing from selfish ambition or conceit, but in humility regard others as better than yourselves. ⁴ Let each of you look not to your own interests, but to the interests of others.

[1585] 1Chronicles 16:35 Say also: 'Save us, O God of our salvation, and gather and rescue us from among the nations, that we may give thanks to your holy name, and glory in your praise.

of justice, nor commit unlawful sexual intercourse.[1586] Whoever does these things will face a penalty [(68)] that will be multiplied for him on the Day of Resurrection, and he will remain in humiliation forever, [(69)] except those who repent, believe and do righteous work, (in that case) God will replace their evil deeds with good ones for God is ever-forgiving [1587] and Merciful-to-all[1588]. [(70)] Whoever repents and act righteously has truly returned to God in repentance.[(71)]

Those who do not testify to falsehood[1589], and, when they pass near ill speech, pass by with dignity; [(72)] and those who, when reminded of their Lord's revelations, do not turn a deaf ear or a blind eye; [(73)] and those who say, "Our Lord, give us joy in our spouses and offspring, and make us a good example for those who are ever mindful of You."[1590] [(74)] All of them will be awarded the highest paradise for what they patiently endured and they will be received with greetings of peace, [(75)] and will live there for eternity. What an excellent home and place of rest. [(76)] Say (to unbelievers), "What would my Lord care for you if not for your prayers to Him?" But since you have denied the truth as lies, (punishment) will inevitably befall you. [(77)]

• • •

[1586] Galatians 5:19 Now the works of the flesh are obvious: fornication, impurity, licentiousness, 1 Corinthians 6:18 Shun fornication! Every sin that a person commits is outside the body; but the fornicator sins against the body itself.
[1587] Psalm 65:3 When deeds of iniquity overwhelm us, you forgive our transgressions.
[1588] Psalm 116:5 Gracious is the LORD, and righteous; our God is merciful. Psalm 32:1-2 Happy are those whose transgression is forgiven, whose sin is covered. [2] Happy are those to whom the Lord imputes no iniquity, and in whose spirit there is no deceit.
[1589] Exodus 20:16: You shalt not bear false witness against your neighbour.
[1590] Proverbs 5:18 Let your fountain be blessed, and rejoice in the wife of your youth, Psalm 128:3 Your wife will be like a fruitful vine within your house; your children will be like olive shoots around your table.

CHAPTER TWENTY SIX

ASH-SHU'ARA
THE POETS

THE **MECCA** PERIOD

In the name of God, the Merciful-to-all, the Mercy Giver:
Ta Seen Meem,^{1590 (01)}
These are the verses of the Book that makes everything clear. ⁽⁰²⁾ Perhaps, (Prophet) you punish yourself with grief because they will not believe. ⁽⁰³⁾ If We so will, We can send down from heaven a miracle that will force their necks to remain bowed in humility. ⁽⁰⁴⁾ Whenever a new revelation comes to them from the Merciful-to-all,¹⁵⁹¹ they turn away. ⁽⁰⁵⁾ They have already denied the truth, but the news of what they used to ridicule will come back to (haunt) them. ⁽⁰⁶⁾ Do not they see the earth, and how many kinds of noble pairs of plants, We have caused to grow in it? ⁽⁰⁷⁾ There is a sign in this, but most of them will not believe. ⁽⁰⁸⁾ Truly your Lord is the Almighty¹⁵⁹² the Merciful-to-all.^{1593 (09)}
When your Lord called on Moses (Musa), (saying), "Go to the unjust People, ⁽¹⁰⁾ The People of Pharaoh.¹⁵⁹⁴ Will they not be mindful of Me?" ⁽¹¹⁾ He said, "My Lord, I fear that they will call me a liar^{1595 (12)} and that my breast will tighten, and my tongue will be tied,¹⁵⁹⁶ so send for Aaron.^{1597 (13)} Besides, they have a charge

•   •   •

---

¹⁵⁹⁰ Here and at the beginning of many chapters there are letters of unknown meaning called Al Muquatta'at. Numerous theories have been proposed, but there is no agreement on what they signify yet.
¹⁵⁹¹ Titus 3:5 he saved us, not because of any works of righteousness that we had done, but according to his mercy, through the water of rebirth and renewal by the Holy Spirit.
¹⁵⁹² Psalm 93:4 More majestic than the thunders of mighty waters, more majestic than the waves of the sea, majestic on high is the Lord!
¹⁵⁹³ Psalm 103:8 The Lord is gracious and merciful, slow to anger and abounding in steadfast love.
¹⁵⁹⁴ Exodus 3:10 So come, I will send you to Pharaoh to bring my people, the Israelites, out of Egypt.'
¹⁵⁹⁵ Exodus 3:11 But Moses said to God, 'Who am I that I should go to Pharaoh, and bring the Israelites out of Egypt?'
¹⁵⁹⁶ Exodus 4:10 But Moses said to the Lord, 'O my Lord, I have never been eloquent, neither in the past nor even now that you have spoken to your servant; but I am slow of speech and slow of tongue.'
¹⁵⁹⁷ Exodus 4:13 But he said, 'O my Lord, please send someone else.'

against me, so I fear that they will kill me."[1598] [(14)] (God) said, "No. Go both of you with Our signs;[1599] We are with you, listening.[1600] [(15)] Go to Pharaoh and say, "We are the messenger from the Lord of the worlds,[1601] [(16)] the Children of Israel go with us."[1602] [(17)]

(Pharaoh) said, "Did we not raise you among us as a child, and you lived among us for many years?[1603] [(18)] (Then) you committed that crime of yours, you were so ungrateful."[1604] [(19)] (Moses) said, "At the time I did it, I was of the misguided. [(20)] So I fled from you because I feared you.[1605] Then my Lord gave me wisdom and made me one of the messengers.[1606] [(21)] As for that favor of which you remind me, was it not because you enslaved the Children of Israel?"[1607] [(22)]

Pharaoh said, "But what is the Lord of the worlds?"[1608] [(23)] He said, "The Lord of the heavens and earth and all that between them, if you only knew." [(24)] (Pharaoh) said to those around him, "Do you hear (what he said)?" [(25)] (Moses went on), "Your Lord and the Lord of your forefathers." [(26)] (Pharaoh) said, "This messenger who has been sent to you is really mad." [(27)] (Moses) said, "Lord of the east and the west and that between them, if you (would just use your) reason." [(28)] (Pharaoh) said, "If you take a god other than me, I will surely

• • •

[1598] Exodus 2:12-15 He looked this way and that, and seeing no one he killed the Egyptian and hid him in the sand. [13] When he went out the next day, he saw two Hebrews fighting; and he said to the one who was in the wrong, 'Why do you strike your fellow Hebrew?' [14] He answered, 'Who made you a ruler and judge over us? Do you mean to kill me as you killed the Egyptian?' Then Moses was afraid and thought, 'Surely the thing is known.' [15] When Pharaoh heard of it, he sought to kill Moses. But Moses fled from Pharaoh. He settled in the land of Midian, and sat down by a well.

[1599] Exodus 3:12 He said, 'I will be with you; and this shall be the sign for you that it is I who sent you: when you have brought the people out of Egypt, you shall worship God on this mountain.'

[1600] Exodus 4:11-12 Then the LORD said to him, 'Who gives speech to mortals? Who makes them mute or deaf, seeing or blind? Is it not I, the Lord? [12] Now go, and I will be with your mouth and teach you what you are to speak.'

[1601] Exodus 3:10, 14 So come, I will send you to Pharaoh to bring my people, the Israelites, out of Egypt.' God said to Moses, 'I am who I am'. He said further, [14] 'Thus you shall say to the Israelites, "I am has sent me to you." '

[1602] Exodus 3:18 They will listen to your voice; and you and the elders of Israel shall go to the king of Egypt and say to him, "The Lord, the God of the Hebrews, has met with us; let us now go a three days' journey into the wilderness, so that we may sacrifice to the Lord our God."

[1603] Exodus 2:5-10 The daughter of Pharaoh came down to bathe at the river, while her attendants walked beside the river. She saw the basket among the reeds and sent her maid to bring it. [6] When she opened it, she saw the child. He was crying, and she took pity on him. 'This must be one of the Hebrews' children,' she said. [7] Then his sister said to Pharaoh's daughter, 'Shall I go and get you a nurse from the Hebrew women to nurse the child for you?' [8] Pharaoh's daughter said to her, 'Yes.' So the girl went and called the child's mother. [9] Pharaoh's daughter said to her, 'Take this child and nurse it for me, and I will give you your wages.' So the woman took the child and nursed it. [10] When the child grew up, she brought him to Pharaoh's daughter, and she took him as her son. She named him Moses, 'because', she said, 'I drew him out of the water.'

[1604] Exodus 2:11-12 One day, after Moses had grown up, he went out to his people and saw their forced labor. He saw an Egyptian beating a Hebrew, one of his kinsfolk. [12] He looked this way and that, and seeing no one he killed the Egyptian and hid him in the sand.

[1605] Exodus 2:15 When Pharaoh heard of it, he sought to kill Moses. But Moses fled from Pharaoh. He settled in the land of Midian, and sat down by a well.

[1606] Exodus 3:10 So come, I will send you to Pharaoh to bring my people, the Israelites, out of Egypt.'

[1607] Exodus 3:9 The cry of the Israelites has now come to me; I have also seen how the Egyptians oppress them.

[1608] Exodus 5:2 But Pharaoh said, 'Who is the Lord, that I should heed him and let Israel go? I do not know the LORD, and I will not let Israel go.'

imprison you." [29] (Moses) said, "Even if I show you undeniable proof?" [30] (Pharaoh) said, "Bring it, then, if you are telling the truth."[1609] [31] So (Moses) threw down his staff, and-behold-it was an undeniable snake.[1610] [32] Then he drew out his hand, and-behold-it was (shining) white for all to see.[1611] [33] (Pharaoh) said to the notables around him, "This is a skilled magician. [34] He wants to drive you out of your land with his magic, so what do you recommend?" [35] They said, "Let him and his brother wait for a while, and (meanwhile) send marshals to all the cities [36] to bring every skilled magician." [37] So the magicians were assembled [1612] at the appointed time on the appointed day. [38] It was said to the People, "Have you assembled [39] so that we might follow the magicians if they win?" [40] When the magicians arrived, they said to Pharaoh, "Is there a reward for us if we win?" [41] He said, "Yes. You will be in my inner circle." [42] Moses said to them, "Throw whatever you will throw." [43] So they threw their ropes and their staffs, and said, "By the might of Pharaoh, We will surely win." [44] Then Moses threw down his staff, and it devoured their deceptions.[1613] [45] And down fell the magicians in prostration (to God), [46] saying, "we believe in the Lord of the Worlds,[1614] [47] the Lord of Moses and Aaron." [48] (Pharaoh) said, "How dare you believe in Him before I have given you permission? He (Moses) must be your leader who has taught you magic. But soon you will know. I will cut off your hands and feet on opposite sides, and I will crucify all of you." [49] They said, "We do not care! We will be returning to our Lord. [50] We hope that our Lord will forgive us our sins, because we were the first believers." [51]

We later revealed to Moses, "Travel by night with My worshipers,[1615] for you will be pursued."[1616] [52] Then Pharaoh sent his marshals to the cities, [53] (saying), "(The Children of Israel) are a small band, [54] but they are offending us, [55] and we are a vigilant society."[56] So We expelled them from (their) gardens and springs [57] treasures and honored estates. [58] Thus it was. (In time), We caused the Children of Israel to inherit all of this. [59] So, they (the Egyptians) pursued them at sunrise,[1617] [60] and when the two sides sighted one another, Moses'

• • •

1609 Exodus 7:9 'When Pharaoh says to you, "Perform a wonder", then you shall say to Aaron, "Take your staff and throw it down before Pharaoh, and it will become a snake." '

1610 Exodus 7:10 So Moses and Aaron went to Pharaoh and did as the LORD had commanded; Aaron threw down his staff before Pharaoh and his officials, and it became a snake.

1611 Exodus 4:6 Again, the Lord said to him, 'Put your hand inside your cloak.' He put his hand into his cloak; and when he took it out, his hand was leprous, as white as snow.

1612 Exodus 7:11 Then Pharaoh summoned the wise men and the sorcerers; and they also, the magicians of Egypt, did the same by their secret arts.

1613 Exodus 7:12 Each one threw down his staff, and they became snakes; but Aaron's staff swallowed up theirs.

1614 Exodus 8:19 And the magicians said to Pharaoh, 'This is the finger of God!' But Pharaoh's heart was hardened, and he would not listen to them, just as the Lord had said.

1615 Exodus 12:31Then he summoned Moses and Aaron in the night, and said, 'Rise up, go away from my people, both you and the Israelites! Go, worship the Lord, as you said.

1616 Exodus 14:4 I will harden Pharaoh's heart, and he will pursue them, so that I will gain glory for myself over Pharaoh and all his army; and the Egyptians shall know that I am the Lord.' And they did so.

1617 Exodus 14:5-8 When the king of Egypt was told that the people had fled, the minds of Pharaoh and his officials were changed towards the people, and they said, 'What have we done, letting Israel leave our service?' 6 So he had his chariot made ready, and took his army with him; 7 he took six hundred picked chariots and all the other chariots of Egypt with officers over all of them. 8 The Lord hardened the heart of Pharaoh king of Egypt and he pursued the Israelites, who were going out boldly.

companions' said, " We will be overtaken!" [1618] [61] (Moses) said, "No! my Lord is with me; He will guide me."[1619] [62] Then, We revealed to Moses, "Strike with your staff the sea."[1620] It parted,[1621] and each part looked like a mountain.[1622] [63] We brought the pursuers right into it,[1623] [64] and We saved Moses and all who were with him,[1624] [65] and We drowned the others.[1625] [66] There is a sign in this, but most of them will not believe. [67] Truly your Lord is the Almighty,[1626] the Merciful-to-all.[1627] [68]

Tell them the story of Abraham, [69] when he said to his father and his People, "What do you worship?" [70] They said, "We worship idols,[1628] and we are always attend to them." [71] He asked, "Do they hear you when you call on them?[1629] [72] Or do they benefit you, or harm you?"[1630] [73] They said, "But this is what we found our fathers doing." [74] He said, "Have you really thought about what You have been worshipping, [75] you and your forefathers? [76] They are enemies to me. (I worship none) except the Lord of the worlds, [1631][77] Who created me. It is He Who guides me. [78] and He who feeds me and gives me drink, [79] and He who

• • •

[1618] Exodus 14:9-12 The Egyptians pursued them, all Pharaoh's horses and chariots, his chariot drivers and his army; they overtook them camped by the sea, by Pi-hahiroth, in front of Baal-zephon. [10] As Pharaoh drew near, the Israelites looked back, and there were the Egyptians advancing on them. In great fear the Israelites cried out to the Lord. [11] They said to Moses, 'Was it because there were no graves in Egypt that you have taken us away to die in the wilderness? What have you done to us, bringing us out of Egypt? [12] Is this not the very thing we told you in Egypt, "Let us alone and let us serve the Egyptians"? For it would have been better for us to serve the Egyptians than to die in the wilderness.'

[1619] Exodus 14:13-14 But Moses said to the people, 'Do not be afraid, stand firm, and the deliverance that the Lord will accomplish for you today; for the Egyptians whom you today you shall never again. [14] The LORD will fight for you, and you have only to keep still.'

[1620] Exodus 14:15-16 Then the Lord said to Moses, 'Why do you cry out to me? Tell the Israelites to go forward. [16] But you lift up your staff, and stretch out your hand over the sea and divide it, that the Israelites may go into the sea on dry ground.

[1621] Exodus 14:21 Then Moses stretched out his hand over the sea. The Lord drove the sea back by a strong east wind all night, and turned the sea into dry land; and the waters were divided.

[1622] Exodus 14:22 The Israelites went into the sea on dry ground, the waters forming a wall for them on their right and on their left.

[1623] Exodus 14:23 The Egyptians pursued, and went into the sea after them, all of Pharaoh's horses, chariots, and chariot drivers.

[1624] Exodus 14:29-30 But the Israelites walked on dry ground through the sea, the waters forming a wall for them on their right and on their left. [30] Thus the Lord saved Israel that day from the Egyptians; and Israel saw the Egyptians dead on the seashore.

[1625] Exodus 15:4-5 Pharaoh's chariots and his army he cast into the sea; his picked officers were sunk in the Red Sea. [5] The floods covered them; they went down into the depths like a stone.

[1626] Deuteronomy 10:17 For the Lord your God is God of gods and Lord of Lords, the great God, mighty and awesome, who is not partial and takes no bribe.

[1627] Psalm 103:8 The Lord is gracious and merciful, slow to anger and abounding in steadfast love.

[1628] Psalm 115:4 Their idols are silver and gold, the work of human hands.

[1629] Psalm 115:6 They have ears, but do not hear; noses, but do not smell.

[1630] Jeremiah 10:5 Their idols are like scarecrows in a cucumber field, and they cannot speak; they have to be carried, for they cannot walk. Do not be afraid of them, for they cannot do evil, nor is it in them to do good.

[1631] Nehemiah 9:5-6 Then the Levites, Jeshua, Kadmiel, Bani, Hashabneiah, Sherebiah, Hodiah, Shebaniah, and Pethahiah, said, "Stand up and bless the Lord your God from everlasting to everlasting. Blessed be your glorious name, which is exalted above all blessing and praise." [6] And Ezra said: "You are the Lord, you alone; you have made heaven, the heaven of heavens, with all their host, the earth and all that is on it, the seas and all that is in them. To all of them you give life, and the host of heaven worships you.

heals me when I am ill,[1632] [(80)] and He who will cause me to die and then bring me back to life,[1633] [(81)] and who I hope will forgive my sins[1634] on the Day of Judgment." [(82)] (Abraham then said), "My Lord, grant me wisdom and allow me to join with the righteous,[1635] [(83)] and grant me a lasting mention as one who told the truth among later generations.[1636] [(84)] And make me among those who will inherit the Garden of Bliss. [(85)] Forgive my father, for he has been of those who were misguided, [(86)] and do not disgrace me on the Day they are (all) resurrected, [(87)] the Day when neither wealth nor children will benefit (anyone) [(88)] except the one who comes to God with a flawless heart."[1637] [(89)]

(On that day), Paradise will be brought near to those who were mindful of God, [(90)] and Hell will be brought forth for those who were misled. [(91)] It will be said to them, "Where are those you used to worship [(92)] other than God? Can they help you or help themselves?" [(93)] So They will be hurled into Hell with those who misled them [(94)] with Iblīs' helpers, all together.[1638] [(95)] While bickering with each other they will say, [(96)] "By God, we were obviously misguided [(97)] when we equated you with the Lord of the worlds. [(98)] No one misguided us except those who forced us to reject God's messages. [(99)] So now we have no intercessors, [(100)] nor a devoted friend. [(101)] If we can only go back (to the world), we will be believers." [(102)] There is a sign in this, but most of them will not believe. [(103)] Truly your Lord is the Almighty,[1639] the Merciful-to-all. [(104)]

The People of Noah denied the messengers[1640] [(105)] when their brother Noah said to them, "Will you not be mindful of God? [(106)] I am a trustworthy messenger[1641] to you. [(107)] So be mindful of God and obey me. [(108)] I ask no reward from you for doing this; my reward comes only from the Lord of the worlds. [(109)] So be mindful of God, and obey me." [(110)] They said, "How can we believe you when you are followed mostly by the lowest (class of People)?" [(111)] He said, "What do I know about what they have been doing? [(112)] It is for my Lord alone to bring them to account, if you (could) only understand. [(113)] I am not one to drive away the believers. [(114)] I am only a clear warner." [(115)] They said, "If you do not desist, Noah, you will surely be stoned." [(116)] He said, "My Lord, my people

• • •

[1632] Jeremiah 17:14 Heal me, O Lord, and I shall be healed; save me, and I shall be saved; for you are my praise.
[1633] Psalm 103:4 who redeems your life from the Pit, who crowns you with steadfast love and mercy,
[1634] Psalm 103:3 who forgives all your iniquity, who heals all your diseases,
[1635] 2 Chronicles 1:10 Give me now wisdom and knowledge to go out and come in before this people, for who can rule this great people of yours?'
[1636] Psalm 101:2-3 I will study the way that is blameless. When shall I attain it? I will walk with integrity of heart within my house; [3] I will not set before my eyes anything that is base. I hate the work of those who fall away; it shall not cling to me.
[1637] Psalm 24:3-5 Who shall ascend the hill of the Lord? And who shall stand in his holy place? [4] Those who have clean hands and pure hearts, who do not lift up their souls to what is false, and do not swear deceitfully. [5] They will receive blessing from the Lord, and vindication from the God of their salvation.
[1638] Revelation 20:10,14,15 And the devil who had deceived them was thrown into the lake of fire and sulphur, where the beast and the false prophet were, and they will be tormented day and night for ever and ever. [14] Then Death and Hades were thrown into the lake of fire. This is the second death, the lake of fire; [15] and anyone whose name was not found written in the book of life was thrown into the lake of fire.
[1639] Revelation 18:8 therefore her plagues will come in a single day—pestilence and mourning and famine—and she will be burned with fire; for mighty is the Lord God who judges her.'
[1640] Ephesians 2:4 But God, who is rich in mercy, out of the great love with which he loved us
[1641] Genesis 6:8 But Noah found favor in the sight of the Lord.

have denied me. [117] Judge between us decisively, and save me and those believers with me." [118] So We saved him and those with him in the laden ark, [1642] [119] and then We drowned the rest. [120] There is a sign in this, but most of them will not believe. [121] Truly your Lord is the Almighty, the Merciful-to-all. [122]

(The people of) Aad denied the Messengers [123] when their brother Hud said to them, "Will you not be mindful of God? [124] I am a trustworthy messenger to you, [125] so be mindful of God, and obey me. [126] I ask no reward from you for doing this; my reward is only from the Lord of the worlds. [127] Do you build a tower on every hill just to amuse yourselves, [128] and construct for yourselves mighty castles hoping to live there eternally? [129] And when you attack, why do you attack like tyrants. [130] So be mindful of God, and obey me, [131] and be mindful of Him Who provided you with everything you know- [132] grazing livestock and children, [133] gardens and springs. [134] I fear for you the punishment of a terrible day." [1643] [135] They said, "It is all the same to us whether you preach or not; [136] this is only what our forefathers used to do. [137] We will not be punished." [138] They denied him, so We destroyed them. There is a sign in this, but most of them will not believe. [139] Truly your Lord is the Almighty, the Merciful-to-all. [140]

(The people of) Thamud [1644] denied the Messengers [141] when their brother Salih said to them, "Will you not be mindful of God? [142] I am a trustworthy messenger to you, [143] so be mindful of God, and obey me. [144] I ask no reward from you for doing this; my reward (comes) only from the Lord of the worlds. [145] Do you think that you will be left secure in what you have here, [146] (your) gardens and springs, [147] fields of crops and palm trees with softened fruit? [148] And your fine homes that you skillfully carve out of the mountains? [149] Be mindful of God and obey me, [150] and do not obey those given to excess, [151] who spread corruption on earth and do not set things right." [152] They said, "You are bewitched. [153] You are only a man like us, so bring a sign, if you are telling the truth." [154] He said, "This is a camel. She will have a time to drink, and you will have a time, (each) on an appointed day. [155] Do not harm her, unless you want to be seized by the punishment of a terrible day." [156] But they hamstrung her and woke up fully regretful, [157] and the punishment seized them. There is a sign in this, but most of them will not believe. [158] Truly your Lord is the Almighty, the Merciful-to-all. [1645] [159]

The People of Lot [1646] denied the messengers [1647] [160] When their brother Lot said to them, "Will you not be mindful of God? [1648] [161] I am a trustworthy messenger to you, [162] So be mindful of God, and obey me. [163] I ask no reward

• • •

[1642] Genesis 7:23 He blotted out every living thing that was on the face of the ground, human beings and animals and creeping things and birds of the air; they were blotted out from the earth. Only Noah was left, and those that were with him in the ark.

[1643] Matthew 25:46 And these will go away into eternal punishment, but the righteous into eternal life.'

[1644] See Glossary

[1645] Psalm 145:8 The Lord is gracious and merciful, slow to anger and abounding in steadfast love

[1646] Lot, nephew of Abraham

[1647] Genesis 19:9 But they replied, 'Stand back!' And they said, 'This fellow came here as an alien, and he would play the judge! Now we will deal worse with you than with them.' Then they pressed hard against the man Lot, and came near the door to break it down.

[1648] Genesis 19:7-8 and said, 'I beg you, my brothers, do not act so wickedly. Look, I have two daughters who have not known a man; let me bring them out to you, and do to them as you please; only do nothing to these men, for they have come under the shelter of my roof.'

from you for doing this; my reward comes only from the Lord of the worlds. [164] Why do you get intimate with men[1649] [165] and leave the mates your Lord has created for you? You people have transgressed all bounds." [166] They said, "If you do not stop this, Lot, you will surely be kicked out."[1650] [167] He said, "I despise your actions. [168] My Lord, save me and my family from (the consequence of) what they do." [169] So We saved him and his family, all of them,[1651] [170] except for an old woman who stayed behind.[1652] [171] Then, We destroyed the others.[1653] [172] We poured upon them a rain of destruction. How terrible is such rain [1654] on those who had been forewarned. [173] There is a sign in this, but most of them will not believe.[1655] [174] Truly your Lord is the Almighty, the Merciful-to-all. [175]

The woods-dwellers denied the messengers. [176] When Shu'ayb[1656] said to them, "Will you not be mindful of God? [177] I am a trustworthy messenger to you,[1657] [178] so be mindful of God, and obey me. [179] I ask no reward from you for doing this; my reward comes only from the Lord of the worlds. [180] Give full measure, and do not cheat. [181] Weigh with an even scale, [182] and do not mislead people into thinking that their goods are worth less than their real value, and do not spread corruption on earth. [183] Fear Him who created you and the former generations." [184] They said, "You are surely bewitched. [185] You are a man like us, and we think you are a liar. [186] Make a fragment of the sky fall on us, if you are telling the truth." [187] He said, "My Lord knows best what you are doing." [188] But they did not believe him, and the punishment [1658] of the day of shadow seized them truly, the punishment of a terrible day. [189] There is a sign in this, but most of them will not believe. [190] Truly your Lord is the Almighty, the Merciful-to-all. [191]

This (Qur'an) is the revelation sent as you received it from the Lord of the worlds, [192] and brought down by The Trustworthy Spirit [193] to your heart, that you may (Prophet) be of the warners [194] in a clear perfected (Arabic) tongue. [195] It is mentioned in the scriptures of the ancients. [196] Is it not a sign that the

• • •

[1649] Jude 7 Likewise, Sodom and Gomorrah and the surrounding cities, which, in the same manner as they, indulged in sexual immorality and pursued unnatural lust, serve as an example by undergoing a punishment of eternal fire. Romans 1:27 and in the same way also the men, giving up natural intercourse with women, were consumed with passion for one another. Men committed shameless acts with men and received in their own persons the due penalty for their error.

[1650] Genesis 19:29, 13:14-15 So it was that, when God destroyed the cities of the Plain, God remembered Abraham, and sent Lot out of the midst of the overthrow, when he overthrew the cities in which Lot had settled. 13:14 The Lord said to Abram, after Lot had separated from him, 'Raise your eyes now, and look from the place where you are, northwards and southwards and eastwards and westwards; 15 for all the land that you see I will give to you and to your offspring for ever.

[1651] Genesis 19:29 So it was that, when God destroyed the cities of the Plain, God remembered Abraham, and sent Lot out of the midst of the overthrow, when he overthrew the cities in which Lot had settled.

[1652] Genesis 19:26 But Lot's wife, behind him, looked back, and she became a pillar of salt.

[1653] Luke 17:29 but on the day that Lot left Sodom, it rained fire and sulphur from heaven and destroyed all of them

[1654] Genesis 19:24 Then the Lord rained on Sodom and Gomorrah sulphur and fire from the Lord out of heaven;

[1655] Psalm 78:32 In spite of all this they still sinned; they did not believe in his wonders.

[1656] Jethro

[1657] 2 Chronicles 36:15 The Lord, the God of their ancestors, sent persistently to them by his messengers, because he had compassion on his people and on his dwelling-place;

[1658] Habakkuk 1:12 Are you not from of old, O Lord my God, my Holy One? You shall not die. O Lord, you have marked them for judgment; and you, O Rock, have established them for punishment.

scholars of the Children of Israel knew it? [197] Yet even if We had revealed it to a non-Arab, [198] and he had recited it to them, they would still not believe in it. [199] This is how We make it go unheeded through the hearts of those who force others to reject Our messages; [200] they will not believe until they see the painful punishment [201] that will come upon them suddenly, when they do not expect it. [1659] [202] They will say, "May we have more time?" [203] Why do they ask that we hasten Our punishment? [204] Do you see that, if We gave them years of enjoyment, [205] then inflicted the punishment as promised, [206] what good would the years of enjoyment be to them? [207] We have never destroyed a town without sending messengers to warn [208] and remind it, for We have never been unjust [209]

The devils did not bring it (this Qur'an) down. [210] They are not able, nor are they capable. [211] As they are indeed barred from hearing (what goes on around the throne of His majesty). [212] So do not invoke another deity beside God, or you will incur punishment. [213] Warn your closest relatives, [214] and be humble and kind to the believers who follow you, [215] but, if they disobey you, then say, "I am not responsible for what you are doing." [216] And rely upon the Almighty, [1660] the Merciful-to-all, [1661] [217] Who sees you when you arise [1662] [218] and when you move among those who prostrate themselves. [219] He is the All-Hearing, the All-Knowing. [1663] [220] Shall I inform you upon whom the devils descend? [1664] [221] They descend upon every sinful liar [222] who readily lends an ear, but most of them are liars. [223] As for the poets, (only) the perverse follow them; [224] Do you not see that they wander aimlessly in every valley [225] and say what they do not do? [226] But except those (poets) who believe, do righteous deeds, remember God often, and defend themselves after they were wronged. Those who do wrong will soon know the kind of reversal they will receive! [227]

• • •

[1659] 1 Thessalonians 5:2-3 For you yourselves know very well that the day of the Lord will come like a thief in the night. [3] When they say, 'There is peace and security', then sudden destruction will come upon them, as labor pains come upon a pregnant woman, and there will be no escape!
[1660] Psalm 93:4 More majestic than the thunders of mighty waters, more majestic than the waves of the sea, majestic on high is the Lord!
[1661] Exodus 34:6 The Lord passed before him, and proclaimed, 'The Lord, the Lord, a God merciful and gracious, slow to anger, and abounding in steadfast love and faithfulness,
[1662] Psalm 139:2-3 You know when I sit down and when I rise up; you discern my thoughts from far away. [3] You search out my path and my lying down, and are acquainted with all my ways.
[1663] 1 John 3:20 whenever our hearts condemn us; for God is greater than our hearts, and he knows everything.
[1664] 1 Peter 5:8 Discipline yourselves; keep alert. Like a roaring lion your adversary the devil prowls around, looking for someone to devour.

CHAPTER TWENTY SEVEN

AN-NAML
THE ANTS

THE **MECCA** PERIOD

In the name of God, the Merciful-to-all, the Mercy Giver:
Ta, Seen.[1665]
These are the verses of the Qur'an, a book that makes everything clear, [01] a
guidance[1666] and good news for the believers [02] who perform prayer and give
the purifying alms, and are certain of the Hereafter. [03] As for those who do not
believe in the Hereafter, We have made their deeds seem right in their own eyes,
so they will wander blindly.[1667] [04] It is they who will receive the worst
punishment,[1668] and in the Hereafter, they are the most failing. [05] You have
received the Qur'an from the Grace of the All-Wise[1669] and All-Knowing.[1670] [06]
(Mention) when Moses (Musa) said to his family, "I think I see a fire. I will
bring you information or will bring you a burning torch that you may warm
yourselves."[1671] [07] But when he reached it, a voice called to him: "Blessed is He
who is in the fire and whoever is around it. And may God be exalted in His Glory,
the Lord of the Worlds.[1672] [08] Moses, It is I - God, the Almighty,[1673] the Wise" [09]

• • •

[1665] Here and at the beginning of many chapters there are letters of unknown meaning called
Al Muquatta'at. Numerous theories have been proposed, but there is no agreement on what
they signify yet.
[1666] Psalm 119:105 Your word is a lamp to my feet and a light to my path.
[1667] 2 Thessalonians 2:11 For this reason God sends them a powerful delusion, leading them
to believe what is false,
[1668] Matthew 25:46 And these will go away into eternal punishment, but the righteous into eternal life.'
[1669] Job 9:4 He is wise in heart, and mighty in strength—who has resisted him, and succeeded? —
[1670] Psalm 37:18 The Lord knows the days of the blameless, and their heritage will abide for ever;
[1671] Exodus 3:3-4 Then Moses said, 'I must turn aside and look at this great sight, and see why the bush is
not burned up.' 4 When the Lord saw that he had turned aside to see, God called to him out of the bush,
'Moses, Moses!' And he said, 'Here I am.'
[1672] 2 Kings 19:15 And Hezekiah prayed before the Lord, and said: 'O Lord the God of Israel,
who are enthroned above the cherubim, you are God, you alone, of all the kingdoms of the earth;
you have made heaven and earth.
[1673] Genesis 35:11 God said to him, 'I am God Almighty: be fruitful and multiply; a nation and a company
of nations shall come from you, and kings shall spring from you.

"Throw down your staff."[1674] But when he saw it moving as if it were a snake, he ran away and did not turn. (God said), "Moses, do not be afraid.[1675] In My presence the messengers do not have anything to fear [(10)] I am Forgiving[1676] and Merciful to him[1677] who does wrong but (who then) replaces his bad deeds with good ones. [(11)] And put your hand in your garment; it will come out white yet unharmed[1678]-One of nine signs (you will take) to Pharaoh and his people.[1679] They have been disobedient people." [(12)]

But when Our enlightening signs came to them, they said, "This is clearly magic." [(13)] Even though they were convinced, they rejected them out of spite and pride.[1680] So consider what happen to those who spread corruption. [(14)]

We gave knowledge to David and Solomon,[1681] and they said, "Praise God, who has favored us over many of His believing servants."[1682] [(15)] And Solomon was David's heir. He said, "People, we have been taught the language of birds, and we have been given a share of everything. This is clearly a blessing."[1683] [(16)] Then one day, Solomon's troops of jinn and men and birds were assembled before him, and they were (marching) in rows. [(17)] When they came upon the valley of the ants, one of the ants said, "Ants enter your dwellings so that you will not be crushed by Solomon and his soldiers without their knowing it." [(18)] Solomon smiled, amused at what she said, and said, "My Lord, enable me to be grateful for the blessings You have given me and my parents, and that I may do righteous deeds accepted by You. And admit me by Your mercy into (the ranks of) Your righteous worshipers." [(19)]

(One day) he inspected the birds and said, "Why do I not see the hoopoe[1684] - or is he absent without permission? [(20)] I will surely punish him severely or kill him unless he brings me a convincing excuse." [(21)] But the hoopoe did not stay away for long. It said, "I learned something that you do not know, and I have brought you news from Sheba. [(22)] I found a woman ruling them. She has been

● ● ●

[1674] Exodus 4:2-3 The LORD said to him, 'What is that in your hand?' He said, 'A staff.' ³ And he said, 'Throw it on the ground.' So he threw the staff on the ground, and it became a snake; and Moses drew back from it.

[1675] Exodus 4:13-15 But he said, 'O my Lord, please send someone else.' ¹⁴ Then the anger of the Lord was kindled against Moses and he said, 'What of your brother Aaron the Levite? I know that he can speak fluently; even now he is coming out to meet you, and when he sees you his heart will be glad. ¹⁵ You shall speak to him and put the words in his mouth; and I will be with your mouth and with his mouth, and will teach you what you shall do.

[1676] Psalm 65:3 When deeds of iniquity overwhelm us, you forgive our transgressions.

[1677] Psalm 103:8 The Lord is merciful and gracious, slow to anger and abounding in steadfast love.

[1678] Exodus 4:6 Again, the Lord said to him, 'Put your hand inside your cloak.' He put his hand into his cloak; and when he took it out, his hand was leprous, as white as snow.

[1679] Exodus 4:7-8 Then God said, 'Put your hand back into your cloak'—so he put his hand back into his cloak, and when he took it out, it was restored like the rest of his body— ⁸ 'If they will not believe you or heed the first sign, they may believe the second sign.

[1680] Exodus 8:32 But Pharaoh hardened his heart this time also, and would not let the people go.

[1681] 1 Kings 4:32 He composed three thousand proverbs, and his songs numbered a thousand and five.

[1682] "Servant" is much more common in English than the word "slave," but both this Arabic word /abd/ and the corresponding words in the Law /abd/ and the Gospel /doulos/ are stronger than this. This word means both slave and worshiper. All the holy books call the believers slaves of God.

[1683] 1 Kings 4:33-34 He would speak of trees, from the cedar that is in the Lebanon to the hyssop that grows in the wall; he would speak of animals, and birds, and reptiles, and fish. ³⁴ People came from all the nations to hear the wisdom of Solomon; they came from all the kings of the earth who had heard of his wisdom.

[1684] The hoopoe is a bird common in Palestine and Yemen, as well as elsewhere in Eurasia and Africa.

given (an abundance) of all things, and she has a magnificent throne. [23] I found that she and her people bow to the sun instead of God. Satan has made their deeds seem right to them and has turned them away from the right path, so they cannot find their way. [24] Should they not bow to God, who brings forth what is hidden within the heavens and the earth, and who knows what you conceal and what you declare? [1685] [25] He is God - there is no god except Him, Lord of the Awesome Throne.[1686] [26] (Solomon) said, "We will see whether you told the truth or were a liar. [27] Take this letter of mine and deliver it to them. Then withdraw but see what response they will have." [28]

The Queen said, "Counselors, a gracious letter has been delivered to me. [29] It is from Solomon, and it is, 'In the name of God, the Merciful-to-all, the Mercy Giver, [30] Do not allow yourself to think that you are above me, come to me in submission.' "[1687] [31] She said, "Council, advise me on the matter before me. I will not decide on a matter unless I hear from you." [32] They said, "We are powerful and have great military might, but the decision is yours, and we stand ready to follow your orders." [33] She said, "When kings enter a town, they ruin it and humiliate its proudest inhabitants. This is what they do. [34] I am sending them a gift, [1688] and I will see what the messengers bring back." [35]

So when her messengers gained an audience with Solomon (and presented the gift), Solomon said, "Do you bring me wealth, when what God has given me is better than what He has given you? It is people like you who will rejoice in a gift like this. [36] Go back (and tell) them, that we will come to them with soldiers whom they will be unable to face, and We will expel them from their land in humiliation, and disgrace." [37] Then he said, "Council, which of you will bring me her magnificent throne before they come to me in submission?" [38] A daring one from among the jinn said, "I will bring it to you before you rise from your council. I am strong enough to do it and can be trusted." [39] But one who had knowledge from the Book said, "I will bring it to you before your glance returns to you." And when (Solomon) saw it placed before him, he said, "This is a favor of my Lord to test me whether I will be grateful or not. And whoever is grateful, it is for his own good. As for the ungrateful, then my Lord is rich beyond need and generous." [40] Then he said, "Disguise her throne; We will see whether she will allow herself to be guided (to truth) or will be among those who reject guidance." [41]

So when she arrived, she was asked, "Is your throne like this?" She said, "It is as if it were the same." (Solomon thought), "We were given knowledge before her, and we have been submissive to God. [42] While what she worshiped beside God prevented her from believing, as she is from a people who deny the truth." [43] She was told, "Enter the courtyard." But when she saw it, she thought it was a pool and uncovered her legs. He said, "It is a courtyard paved with smooth

• • •

[1685] Matthew 10:26 There is nothing concealed that will not be disclosed, or hidden that will not be made known. Luke 12:3 Therefore whatever you have said in the dark will be heard in the light, and what you have whispered behind closed doors will be proclaimed from the housetops.

[1686] Revelation 20:11 Then I saw a great white throne and the one who sat on it; the earth and the heaven fled from his presence, and no place was found for them.

[1687] James 4:7 Submit yourselves therefore to God. Resist the devil, and he will flee from you.

[1688] 1 Kings 10:10 Then she gave the king one hundred and twenty talents of gold, a great quantity of spices, and precious stones; never again did spices come in such quantity as that which the queen of Sheba gave to King Solomon.

glass." She said, "My Lord, I have been wrong (because of my limited knowledge), and I submit with Solomon to God, Lord of the Worlds." [44]

And We had sent to Thamud[1689] their brother Salih,[1690] (saying), "Worship God," but they were split into rival factions. [45] He said, "My people, why are you so anxious to rush toward evil instead of to good?[1691] Why you do not ask God for forgiveness, so that maybe you will receive mercy?"[1692] [46] They said, "We consider you to be a bad omen, you and those with you." He said, "Your omen is with God. Rather, it is you who are being tested." [47] And in the town there were heads of nine clans who spread mischief in the land and did no good. [48] They said to each other, "Let's take an oath by God that we will kill him and his family tonight. Then we will say to his protector, 'we did not witness the destruction of his family, and we are truthful.'" [49] So they devised their plan, and We too had a plan, but they were not aware of what We were planning. [50] Look, then, at the outcome of their plan: We destroyed them and all their people. [51] Here are their houses, desolate because they were unjust. There is a sign in that for people who know. [52] And We saved those who believed and were mindful of God. [53]

And Lot,[1693] when he said to his people, "How can you commit this indecent act with your eyes wide open?[1694] [54] You lust after men instead of women? You are ignorant people." [55] But his people's answer was "Expel Lot and his family from your town. They are people who keep themselves pure." [56] So We saved him and his family,[1695] except for his wife; We determined she would be with those who stayed behind.[1696] [57] And We rained upon them a rain. Horrible was the rain for those who were forewarned.[1697] [58]

Say, "Praise be to God, and peace be on His worshipers whom He has chosen.[1698] Is not God better than those they associate with Him?" [59] Is He (not best) who created the heavens and the earth?[1699] Who sent down rain from the sky for you, causing gardens full of beauty to grow; you could not have grown the trees on your own. Is there another god alongside God? (No), but there are people who take others to be equal to Him. [1700] [60] Is He (not best) who made

• • •

[1689] See Glossary

[1690] Ibid.

[1691] 1 Kings 14:9 but you have done evil above all those who were before you and have gone and made for yourself other gods, and cast images, provoking me to anger, and have thrust me behind your back;

[1692] Psalm 130:4 But there is forgiveness with you, so that you may be revered.

[1693] Lot, nephew of Abraham

[1694] Genesis 19:5-7 and they called to Lot, 'Where are the men who came to you tonight? [6] Bring them out to us, so that we may know them.' [7] Lot went out of the door to the men, shut the door after him, and said, 'I beg you, my brothers, do not act so wickedly.

[1695] See Genesis 19:15-22

[1696] Genesis 19:26 But Lot's wife, behind him, looked back, and she became a pillar of salt.

[1697] Genesis 19:24-25 Then the Lord rained on Sodom and Gomorrah sulphur and fire from the Lord out of heaven; [25] and he overthrew those cities, and all the Plain, and all the inhabitants of the cities, and what grew on the ground.

[1698] Luke 2:14 'Glory to God in the highest heaven, and on earth peace among those whom he favors!'

[1699] Isaiah 42:5 Thus says God, the Lord, who created the heavens and stretched them out, who spread out the earth and what comes from it, who gives breath to the people upon it and spirit to those who walk in it:

[1700] Isaiah 44:6 Thus says the Lord, the King of Israel and his Redeemer, the Lord of hosts: I am the first and I am the last; besides me there is no god.

the earth a stable ground, and placed rivers[1701] within it, and set mountains firmly on it, and placed a barrier between the two seas? Is there a god with God? (No,) but most of them do not know. [61] Is He (not best) Who responds to the desperate when he calls upon Him,[1702] and Who removes his distress and makes you successors on earth?[1703] Is there a god with God? Little do you remember? [62] Is He (not best) Who guides[1704] Who guides you through the darkness of land and sea and who sends the winds, bringing advance news of His mercy? Is there a god with God? Exalted is God above whatever they associate with Him.[1705] [63] Is He (not best) Who begins creation[1706] and then repeats it, and who provides for you from the heaven and the earth?[1707] Is there a god with God? Say, "Show me your evidence, if you are truthful." [64]

Say, "None in the heavens and earth knows what lies beyond our senses except God,[1708] and they do not know when they will be resurrected." [65] Rather, their knowledge cannot comprehend the Hereafter. They are in doubt about it; they are in fact blind to it. [66] So the unbelievers say, "When we and our fathers become dust, will we then be brought out of the graves? [67] We and our forefathers have been promised this before. This is only a legend of an ancient people." [68] Say, "Travel around the earth and observe the fate of those who are guilty of forcing others to reject God's messages." [69] (Prophet,) do not grieve over them or be distressed by what they conspire. [70] They say, "When is (the fulfillment of) this promise,[1709] if you are truthful?" [71] Say, "Perhaps some of what you seem eager for is closer than you think. [72] Verily your Lord is bountiful to people, but most of them do not show gratitude." [73] Certainly your Lord knows what their hearts conceal and what they declare, [74] for there is nothing (so) hidden in heaven and earth that it is not in a clear record. [75]

This Revelation (The Qur'an) explains to the Children of Israel most of what they differ about. [76] And it is guidance and mercy for the Believers. [77] Your Lord will judge between them by His (wise) judgment, for He is the Almighty,[1710] the All-Knowing.[1711] [78] So put your trust in God; you are on the path of clear Truth. [79] You will not make the dead hear, nor will you make the deaf listen to the call

• • •

[1701] Psalm 24:1-2 The earth is the Lord's and all that is in it, the world, and those who live in it; for he has founded it on the seas, and established it on the rivers.
[1702] Mark 11:24 So I tell you, whatever you ask for in prayer, believe that you have received it, and it will be yours.
[1703] Genesis 1:28 God blessed them, and God said to them, 'Be fruitful and multiply, and fill the earth and subdue it; and have dominion over the fish of the sea and over the birds of the air and over every living thing that moves upon the earth.'
[1704] Psalm 23:3 he restores my soul. He leads me in right paths for his name's sake
[1705] Psalm 108:5 Be exalted, O God, above the heavens, and let your glory be over all the earth. Isaiah 33:5 The Lord is exalted, he dwells on high; he filled Zion with justice and righteousness;
[1706] Genesis 1:1 In the beginning when God created the heavens and the earth,
[1707] 1 Timothy 6:17 As for those who in the present age are rich, command them not to be haughty, or to set their hopes on the uncertainty of riches, but rather on God who richly provides us with everything for our enjoyment.
[1708] Isaiah 66:18 For I know their works and their thoughts, and I am coming to gather all nations and tongues; and they shall come and shall see my glory,
[1709] 2 Peter 3:4 and saying, 'Where is the promise of his coming? For ever since our ancestors died, all things continue as they were from the beginning of creation!'
[1710] Job 11:7 Can you find out the deep things of God? Can you find out the limit of the Almighty?
[1711] 1 Samuel 2:3 Talk no more so very proudly, let not arrogance come from your mouth; for the Lord is a God of knowledge, and by him actions are weighed.

when they have turned their backs and gone away, [80] and you cannot guide the blind away from their error. You cannot make anyone hear you except those who believe in Our signs and submit to (Us).[1712] [81] And when the judgment comes against them, We will bring forth a beast from the earth to tell[1713] them that, truly people had no true faith in Our Signs [82] And (warn of) the Day when We will gather from every nation a crowd of those who deny Our messages, and they will be formed into groups, [83] until, when they arrive (at the place of Judgment), He will say, "Did you deny My messages without even trying to understand them? What were you doing?" [84] The verdict will be handed down for their wrongdoing, and they will not speak. [85]

Do they not see that We made the night for them to rest and the day to see? There are signs in that for people who believe. [86] And (warn of) the Day on which the Horn will be blown, and everyone in the heavens and on earth will be terrified [1714] except whom God wills, and all will come to Him completely humbled. [87] And you will see the mountains, thinking they are solid, going by like clouds.[1715] (It is) the work of God, who perfected all things; He is well aware of all you do. [88] Whoever comes (at Judgment) with a good deed will be rewarded with something better, and they will be safe from the terror of that Day. [89] And whoever comes with an evil deed, they will be cast face down into the Fire.[1716] (and will be asked) "Are you being repaid for anything except what you have done?" [90]

(Say), "I have simply been ordered to worship the Lord of this town, Who made it sacred and to Whom all things belong. And I have been ordered to be one of those who submit to God[1717] [91] and recite the Qur'an." Whoever is guided is guided only for his own good, and to whoever strays, say, "I am only one who gives warning." [92] And say, "All praise is due to God.[1718] (In time) He will show you His signs, and you will recognize them. Your Lord is never unaware of what you do."[1719] [93]

■   ■   ■

[1712] James 4:7 Submit yourselves therefore to God. Resist the devil, and he will flee from you.

[1713] Revelation 13:11 Then I saw another beast that rose out of the earth; it had two horns like a lamb and it spoke like a dragon.

[1714] Revelation 11:15 Then the seventh angel blew his trumpet, and there were loud voices in heaven, saying, 'The kingdom of the world has become the kingdom of our Lord and of his Messiah, and he will reign for ever and ever.'

[1715] Revelation 16:20 And every island fled away, and no mountains were to be found;

[1716] Matthew 25:46 And these will go away into eternal punishment, but the righteous into eternal life.'

[1717] James 4:7 Submit yourselves therefore to God. Resist the devil, and he will flee from you.

[1718] Psalm 66: 1-4 Make a joyful noise to God, all the earth; [2] sing the glory of his name; give to him glorious praise. [3] Say to God, "How awesome are your deeds! Because of your great power, your enemies cringe before you. [4] All the earth worships you; they sing praises to you, sing praises to your name."

[1719] 1 John 3:20 whenever our hearts condemn us; for God is greater than our hearts, and he knows everything.

CHAPTER TWENTY EIGHT

AL-QASAS
THE STORIES

THE **MECCA** PERIOD

In the name of God, the Merciful-to-all, the Mercy Giver:
Ta Seen Meem, [1720] [01]
These are the verses of the Book that makes everything clear. [02] We recite to you from the story of Moses (Musa) and Pharaoh[1721] setting out the truth for people who believe. [03] Pharaoh exalted himself [1722] and divided the people into factions: oppressing a segment of them,[1723] slaughtering their sons while sparing the women.[1724] He was one of those who spread corruption. [04] But, We wanted to favor those who were oppressed in the land, and make them leaders and make them inheritors of the land [05] and to empower them and show Pharaoh, Haman and their soldiers through them the very thing that they feared [06]
So, We inspired Moses' mother, "Nurse him for now;[1725] but when you fear for his safety, put him into the river;[1726] do not be afraid and do not grieve. We

• • •

[1720] Here and at the beginning of many chapters there are letters of unknown meaning called Al Muquatta'at. Numerous theories have been proposed, but there is no agreement on what they signify yet.
[1721] See Exodus 5-12 the complete story of Moses and Pharaoh is recorded.
[1722] Exodus 5:2 But Pharaoh said, 'Who is the Lord, that I should heed him and let Israel go? I do not know the Lord, and I will not let Israel go.'
[1723] Exodus 3:7 Then the Lord said, 'I have observed the misery of my people who are in Egypt; I have heard their cry on account of their taskmasters. Indeed, I know their sufferings,
[1724] Exodus 1:16-20 'When you act as midwives to the Hebrew women, and see them on the birthstool, if it is a boy, kill him; but if it is a girl, she shall live.' [17] But the midwives feared God; they did not do as the king of Egypt commanded them, but they let the boys live. [18] So the king of Egypt summoned the midwives and said to them, 'Why have you done this, and allowed the boys to live?' [19] The midwives said to Pharaoh, 'Because the Hebrew women are not like the Egyptian women; for they are vigorous and give birth before the midwife comes to them.' [20] So God dealt well with the midwives; and the people multiplied and became very strong.
[1725] Exodus 2:1-2 Now a man from the house of Levi went and married a Levite woman. [2] The woman conceived and bore a son; and when she saw that he was a fine baby, she hid him for three months.
[1726] Exodus 2:3 When she could hide him no longer she got a papyrus basket for him, and plastered it with bitumen and pitch; she put the child in it and placed it among the reeds on the bank of the river.

will return him to you[1727] and will make him a messenger."[1728] [07] And Pharaoh's people picked him up, to become later an enemy to them and a source of grief, (since) Pharaoh and Haman and their soldiers were sinners. [08] Pharaoh's wife said, "He will be a delight for my eyes and yours. Do not kill him; He may be useful to us, or we may adopt him as a son." [1729] They did not realize (the consequences of) what was going on. [09] (Later) Moses' mother felt her heart totally empty. She was about to disclose the matter had We not strengthened her heart that she would be counted among the believers. [10] And she said to his sister, "Follow him,"[1730] so she watched him from a distance without being noticed. [11] And We made him reject all wet nurses, so she said, "Shall I tell you about a household that will feed him for you and be good to him?"[1731] [12] And We returned him to his mother so that she might delight her eyes with him, not grieve and know that God's promise is true. But most people do not know. [13]

And when he attained his full strength and maturity, We gave him judgment and knowledge. And thus We reward those who do of good.[1732] [14] (One day) he entered the town unnoticed and found two men fighting, one from his own people and the other from his enemy.[1733] The one from his own people cried out to him for help against the enemy, so Moses struck him and killed him.[1734] (Moses) said, "This must be from Satan's doing. He is clearly an enemy who clearly leads (people) astray." [15] He said, "My Lord, I have done wrong. Please forgive me," and He forgave him. He is the Forgiving,[1735] the Merciful-to-all.[1736] [16] (Moses) said, "My Lord, with all of Your blessings to me, I will never support those who do evil." [17]

Next morning, he entered the town, fearful and anxious, when suddenly the man who sought his help the previous day cried out to him again for help. Moses said to him, "You are clearly a troublemaker."[1737] [18] As (Moses) was about to strike the one who was an enemy to both of them, (the man) said, "Moses, do you want to kill me as you killed that man yesterday?[1738] You want only to be an oppressor in the land and do not want to put things right." [19] And a man came

• • •

[1727] Exodus 2:7-9 Then his sister said to Pharaoh's daughter, 'Shall I go and get you a nurse from the Hebrew women to nurse the child for you?' Pharaoh's daughter said to her, 'Yes.' So the girl went and called the child's mother. Pharaoh's daughter said to her, 'Take this child and nurse it for me, and I will give you your wages.' So the woman took the child and nursed it.

[1728] Exodus 3:10 So come, I will send you to Pharaoh to bring my people, the Israelites, out of Egypt.'

[1729] Exodus 2:10 When the child grew up, she brought him to Pharaoh's daughter, and she took him as her son. She named him Moses, 'because', she said, 'I drew him out of the water.'

[1730] Exodus 2:4 His sister stood at a distance, to what would happen to him.

[1731] Exodus 2:7 Then his sister said to Pharaoh's daughter, 'Shall I go and get you a nurse from the Hebrew women to nurse the child for you?'

[1732] Acts 7:22 So Moses was instructed in all the wisdom of the Egyptians and was powerful in his words and deeds.

[1733] Exodus 2:11 One day, after Moses had grown up, he went out to his people and saw their forced labor. He saw an Egyptian beating a Hebrew, one of his kinsfolk.

[1734] Exodus 2:12 He looked this way and that, and seeing no one he killed the Egyptian and hid him in the sand.

[1735] Psalm 65:3 When deeds of iniquity overwhelm us, you forgive our transgressions.

[1736] Psalm 103:8 The Lord is merciful and gracious, slow to anger and abounding in steadfast love.

[1737] Exodus 2:13 When he went out the next day, he saw two Hebrews fighting; and he said to the one who was in the wrong, 'Why do you strike your fellow Hebrew?'

[1738] Exodus 2:14 He answered, 'Who made you a ruler and judge over us? Do you mean to kill me as you killed the Egyptian?' Then Moses was afraid and thought, 'Surely the thing is known.'

from the far end of the town, running. He said, "Moses, they are talking about killing you,[1739] so leave; I am giving you a good advice." [(20)] So (Moses) left the town, fearful and on his guard. He said, "My Lord, save me from these oppressive people." [(21)]

And he made his way toward Midian,[1740] he was saying, "Perhaps my Lord will guide me in the right way." [(22)] When he came to the well of Midian, he found there a crowd of people watering (their flocks), and beside them he found two women[1741] holding back their flocks. He said, "What is going on?" They said, "We cannot water until the shepherds take their flocks away,[1742] and our father is an old man."[(23)] So he watered their flocks for them.[1743] Then he went back to the shade and said, "My Lord, I am very much in need for whatever good You might send down to me." [(24)] Then, one of the two women came walking toward him shyly and said, "My father would like to pay you for having watered (our flock) for us."[1744]

So when Moses came to him and told him his story, he said, "Don't be afraid. You have escaped from those oppressive people." [(25)] One of the women said, "Father, hire him. A strong and trustworthy man is the best that you can hire." [(26)] He said, "I want to marry one of these two daughters of mine to you, on (condition) that you work for me for eight full years;[1745] but if you complete ten, it will be seen (as a favor) from you. I do not wish to make things difficult for you. You will find me to be, God willing, a fair man." [(27)] (Moses) said, "That is a deal between us. Whichever of the two terms I complete, there should be no bad feelings toward me. May God be Witness over what we say." [(28)]

When Moses completed the term and was traveling with his family,[1746] he noticed a fire from the direction of the mountain.[1747] He said to his family, "Stay here; I have seen a fire.[1748] Perhaps I will bring you from there (some) information or burning wood from the fire that you may warm yourselves." [(29)]

•   •   •

[1739] Exodus 2:15 When Pharaoh heard of it, he sought to kill Moses. But Moses fled from Pharaoh. He settled in the land of Midian, and sat down by a well.

[1740] See the Glossary

[1741] Exodus 2:16-17 The priest of Midian had seven daughters. They came to draw water, and filled the troughs to water their father's flock. [17] But some shepherds came and drove them away. Moses got up and came to their defense and watered their flock.

[1742] Genesis 29:8 But they said, 'We cannot until all the flocks are gathered together, and the stone is rolled from the mouth of the well; then we water the sheep.'

[1743] Genesis 29:10 They said, 'An Egyptian helped us against the shepherds; he even drew water for us and watered the flock.'

[1744] Exodus 2:20 He said to his daughters, 'Where is he? Why did you leave the man? Invite him to break bread.'

[1745] Exodus 2:21 Moses agreed to stay with the man, and he gave Moses his daughter Zipporah in marriage.

[1746] Exodus 3:1 Moses was keeping the flock of his father-in-law Jethro, the priest of Midian; he led his flock beyond the wilderness, and came to Horeb, the mountain of God.

[1747] Exodus 3:2 There the angel of the Lord appeared to him in a flame of fire out of a bush; he looked, and the bush was blazing, yet it was not consumed.

[1748] Exodus 3:3 Then Moses said, 'I must turn aside and look at this great sight, and why the bush is not burned up.'

But when he came to the fire, a voice called from the right side of the valley from the tree on the blessed spot,[1749] "Moses, I am God, Lord of the worlds."[1750] (30) "Throw down your staff."[1751] But when he saw it moving as if it were a snake, he fled in fear and would not return.[1752] "Moses (he was called again), come back and do not be afraid. You are one of those who are safe.[1753] (31) Insert your hand into your garment; it will come out white, but unharmed.[1754] And hug your arms to your sides to still your fear, for those are two proofs from your Lord to Pharaoh and his circle.[1755] They have been defiant and disobedient people." (32) He said, "My Lord, I killed one of them, and I fear they will kill me. (33) My brother Aaron can speak better than I, so send him with me to support me and confirm my words. I fear they call me a liar." [1756] (34) (God) said, "We will strengthen you through your brother and We shall give you both power so that they cannot touch you. With our signs,[1757] you and those who follow you will be victorious."(35)

· · ·

[1749] Exodus 3:4 When the Lord saw that he had turned aside to, God called to him out of the bush, 'Moses, Moses!' And he said, 'Here I am.'
[1750] Exodus 3:5-6 Then he said, 'Come no closer! Remove the sandals from your feet, for the place on which you are standing is holy ground.' He said further, 'I am the God of your father, the God of Abraham, the God of Isaac, and the God of Jacob.' And Moses hid his face, for he was afraid to look at God.
[1751] Exodus 4:2-3 The Lord said to him, 'What is that in your hand?' He said, 'A staff.' And he said, 'Throw it on the ground.' So he threw the staff on the ground, and it became a snake; and Moses drew back from it.
[1752] Exodus 4:3 And he said, 'Throw it on the ground.' So he threw the staff on the ground, and it became a snake; and Moses drew back from it.
[1753] Exodus 4:4 Then the Lord said to Moses, 'Reach out your hand, and seize it by the tail'—so he reached out his hand and grasped it, and it became a staff in his hand—
[1754] Exodus 4:6 Again, the Lord said to him, 'Put your hand inside your cloak.' He put his hand into his cloak; and when he took it out, his hand was leprous, as white as snow.
[1755] Exodus 4:8 'If they will not believe you or heed the first sign, they may believe the second sign.'
[1756] Exodus 4:10-16 But Moses said to the Lord, 'O my Lord, I have never been eloquent, neither in the past nor even now that you have spoken to your servant; but I am slow of speech and slow of tongue.' [11] Then the Lord said to him, 'Who gives speech to mortals? Who makes them mute or deaf, seeing or blind? Is it not I, the Lord? [12] Now go, and I will be with your mouth and teach you what you are to speak.' [13] But he said, 'O my Lord, please send someone else.' [14] Then the anger of the Lord was kindled against Moses and he said, 'What of your brother Aaron the Levite? I know that he can speak fluently; even now he is coming out to meet you, and when he sees you his heart will be glad. [15] You shall speak to him and put the words in his mouth; and I will be with your mouth and with his mouth, and will teach you what you shall do. [16] He indeed shall speak for you to the people; he shall serve as a mouth for you, and you shall serve as God for him.
[1757] Exodus 4:12,17 Now go, and I will be with your mouth and teach you what you are to speak.' [17] Take in your hand this staff, with which you shall perform the signs.'

But when Moses came to them with Our clear signs, they said, "This is only false magic.[1758] We have not heard of this from our forefathers." [36] Moses said, "My Lord knows best who has come with guidance from Him and whose end will be best in the Hereafter. Those who are unjust do not succeed." [37] Pharaoh said, "Counselors, I have not known you to have a god other than Me. Haman, light me a fire to bake clay, and then build me a tower that I may climb up to Moses' God. I think he's a liar." [38]

He and his soldiers behaved arrogantly in the land, as they did not know the Truth, and they thought that they would not return to Us. [39] So, We took him and his soldiers and threw them into the sea.[1759] See what became of the unjust. [40] We made them leaders calling (others) to the Fire, and on the Day of Resurrection they will receive no help. [41] And We pursued them with a curse in this world, and, on the Day of Resurrection, they will be among the despised. [42] After We had destroyed the earlier generations, We gave Moses the Book[1760] as enlightenment to the people, and as guidance and mercy so that they might be reminded. [1761] [43]

You (Prophet), were not on the western side (of the mount) when We gave Our command to Moses, and you were not a witness. [44] But We produced (many) generations (after Moses), and life dragged on for them. You were not dwelling among the people of Midian, reciting Our verses to them, but We have always sent messages to people. [45] Nor were you on the side of the mount when We called (Moses), but (you were sent) as a mercy from your Lord to warn a people to whom no messenger had come before, so that they might be reminded, [46] that if a disaster should strike them for what they have done, they would not be able to say, "Our Lord, if You had only sent a messenger to us so we could have followed Your instructions and became believers." [47] But even when the Truth came to them from Us, they said, "Why Was (the Prophet) not given signs like those given to Moses?" Did they not previously deny what Moses was given? They said, "(These are just) two magicians supporting each other, and we are denying each of them." [48] Say, "If you are truthful, then bring a Book from God that gives better guidance than either of them that I may follow it." [49] But if they do not respond to you, then know that they are only following their

• • •

[1758] Exodus 7:10-12 So Moses and Aaron went to Pharaoh and did as the LORD had commanded; Aaron threw down his staff before Pharaoh and his officials, and it became a snake. [11] Then Pharaoh summoned the wise men and the sorcerers; and they also, the magicians of Egypt, did the same by their secret arts. [12] Each one threw down his staff, and they became snakes; but Aaron's staff swallowed up theirs.

[1759] Exodus 14:26-31 Then the Lord said to Moses, 'Stretch out your hand over the sea, so that the water may come back upon the Egyptians, upon their chariots and chariot drivers.' [27] So Moses stretched out his hand over the sea, and at dawn the sea returned to its normal depth. As the Egyptians fled before it, the Lord tossed the Egyptians into the sea. [28] The waters returned and covered the chariots and the chariot drivers, the entire army of Pharaoh that had followed them into the sea; not one of them remained. [29] But the Israelites walked on dry ground through the sea, the waters forming a wall for them on their right and on their left. [30] Thus the Lord saved Israel that day from the Egyptians; and Israel saw the Egyptians dead on the seashore. [31] Israel saw the great work that the Lord did against the Egyptians. So the people feared the Lord and believed in the Lord and in his servant Moses.

[1760] Exodus 31:18 When God finished speaking with Moses on Mount Sinai, he gave him the two tablets of the covenant, tablets of stone, written with the finger of God.

[1761] Deuteronomy 4:39 So acknowledge today and take to heart that the Lord is God in heaven above and on the earth beneath; there is no other.

whims and desires. And who is more lost than one who follows his own whims and desires without guidance from God?[1762] God does not guide unjust people[(50)] We have continuously conveyed the Word to them that they might take heed. [(51)] Those to whom We gave the Book before (are bound to) believe it. [(52)] When it is recited to them, they say, "We believe in it. It is the Truth from our Lord. We had devoted ourselves to God even before this came to us." [(53)] They will be given their reward twice for what they patiently endured, and (because) they ward off evil with good, and give from what we have provided for them. [(54)] When they hear worthless talk, they turn away from it and say, "We have our deeds, and you have your deeds. Peace be with you; we do not seek the company of the ignorant." [(55)]

"You cannot guide (to the Truth) whom you love, but God guides him who wants to be guided. And He knows best those who are guided". [(56)] They say, "If we were to follow the guidance with you, we would be torn from our land." Have we not established for them a safe sanctuary, to which are brought all kind of fruits, as provisions from Us? But most of them do not understand. [(57)] How many towns have We destroyed which lived in ease and plenty but were ungrateful? Here are their dwellings, virtually uninhabited since their time. We have inherited them. [(58)] Your Lord never destroys cities unless He (first) sends a messenger in their midst reciting Our verses, nor would We destroy cities unless their inhabitants were evil. [(59)] (People) whatever you are given is only for the (passing) enjoyment and vanity of this life, but what is with God is better and more lasting. Will you not, then, use reason? [(60)]

Is the one who sees the fulfillment of the good promise We gave him (about the Hereafter) like the one We provided with worldly enjoyment (but) who, on the Day of Resurrection, is summoned (for punishment)? [(61)] On that Day, He will call them and say, "Where are My partners whom you used to claim?" [(62)] Those against whom the charge will be proved will say, "Our Lord, these are the people we led astray, just as we, too, were led astray. We declare our innocence to You; it was not us they were worshipping. [(63)] It will be said to them, "Call those 'partners.'" They will call them, but they will not respond to them, and they will see the punishment (that awaits). If only they had followed Our guidance! [(64)] On that day He will call them and say, "How did you respond to My Messengers?" [(65)] All their usual arguments will be of no use to them that Day, and they will not (be able to) ask one another. [(66)] As for the one who has repented, believed, and done righteous deeds, he can hope that to be counted among the successful. [(67)] Your Lord creates whatever He wills and chooses; The choice is never theirs. May God be exalted in His Glory and far above all they associate with Him. [(68)] Your Lord knows what their hearts conceal and what they declare. [(69)] He is God; there is no god except Him. (All) praise belongs to Him in this world and the next. The judgment is His, and to Him you will be returned [(70)]

Say, "Just think, if God were to make the night continuous for you until the Day of Resurrection, what god other than God could bring you light? Will you not listen?" [(71)] Say, "Just think, what if God should make daylight continuous for you until the Day of Resurrection, what god other than God could bring you the night in which to rest? Will you not see?" [(72)] But, out of His mercy, He made the night

• • •

[1762] 2 Timothy 4:3 For the time is coming when people will not put up with sound doctrine, but having itching ears, they will accumulate for themselves teachers to suit their own desires,

and the day[1763] for you so that you may rest, and seek from His favor, and perhaps give thanks.[1764] (73) On the Day He will call them and say, "Where are those you used to claim as My partners?" (74) We will pull out a witness from every nation and say, "Produce your evidence."[1765] They will then know that the truth belongs to God alone, and (the gods) they have invented have forsaken them. (75)

Korah (Qarun) was one of Moses' people, but he exploited them.[1766] We allowed him to have treasures, the keys to which would burden even a band of strong men. When his people told him, "Don't gloat.[1767] God does not like it, when people gloat,[1768] (76) seek the Hereafter with what God has given you, but do not neglect your share of this world. Do good as God has done good to you.[1769] Do not seek to cause corruption in the land, for God does not like those who spread corruption." (77) His answer was, "I was able to obtain this (wealth) because of knowledge I have." Did he not know that God had destroyed many generations before him, who had greater power than he, and greater wealth? But the criminals will not even be asked about their sins. (78) So he came out, in his splendor, before his people. Those who desired this worldly life said,[1770] "How we wish to have been given like what Korah had been given; he is truly a most fortunate man." (79) But those who had been given knowledge said, "You are wrong! God's reward is better for him who believes and does good deeds; only those with great patience will obtain this."[1771] (80) And We caused the earth to

• • •

[1763] Genesis 1:14-19 And God said, 'Let there be lights in the dome of the sky to separate the day from the night; and let them be for signs and for seasons and for days and years, [15] and let them be lights in the dome of the sky to give light upon the earth.' And it was so. [16] God made the two great lights—the greater light to rule the day and the lesser light to rule the night—and the stars. [17] God set them in the dome of the sky to give light upon the earth, [18] to rule over the day and over the night, and to separate the light from the darkness. And God saw that it was good. [19] And there was evening and there was morning, the fourth day.

[1764] Psalm 9:1-2 I will give thanks to the Lord with my whole heart; I will tell of all your wonderful deeds. [2] I will be glad and exult in you; I will sing praise to your name, O Most High.

[1765] Isaiah 45:21 Declare and present your case; let them take counsel together! Who told this long ago? Who declared it of old? Was it not I, the Lord? There is no other god besides me, a righteous God and a Savior; there is no one besides me.

[1766] Numbers 16:1-3 Now Korah son of Izhar son of Kohath son of Levi, along with Dathan and Abiram sons of Eliab, and On son of Peleth—descendants of Reuben—took two [2] hundred and fifty Israelite men, leaders of the congregation, chosen from the assembly, well-known men, and they confronted Moses. [3] They assembled against Moses and against Aaron, and said to them, 'You have gone too far! All the congregation are holy, every one of them, and the Lord is among them. So why then do you exalt yourselves above the assembly of the Lord?'

[1767] Jeremiah 9:23-24 Thus says the LORD: Do not let the wise boast in their wisdom, do not let the mighty boast in their might, do not let the wealthy boast in their wealth; [24] but let those who boast boast in this, that they understand and know me, that I am the Lord; I act with steadfast love, justice, and righteousness in the earth, for in these things I delight, says the Lord.

[1768] James 4:6 But he gives all the more grace; therefore, it says, 'God opposes the proud, but gives grace to the humble.'

[1769] 1 Timothy 6:17-18 As for those who in the present age are rich, command them not to be haughty, or to set their hopes on the uncertainty of riches, but rather on God who richly provides us with everything for our enjoyment. [18] They are to do good, to be rich in good works, generous, and ready to share,

[1770] 1 Timothy 6:9 But those who want to be rich fall into temptation and are trapped by many senseless and harmful desires that plunge people into ruin and destruction.

[1771] Matthew 24:13 But anyone who endures to the end will be saved.

swallow him and his house.[1772] There was no one to help him against God, nor could he help himself. [81] And those who had wished in the previous day to be in his place said, "As if God gives abundantly or sparingly, to whomever He wishes of His servants. Oh! If God had not been gracious to us, He would have caused the earth to swallow us too.[1773] Alas, those who deny the truth will never succeed." [82]

We grant a home in the Hereafter to those who do not desire superiority on earth or to spread corruption, for the (best) outcome is for those who are mindful of God. [83] Whoever comes (on the Day of Judgment) with a good deed will have a better reward, and whoever comes with an evil deed will be punished only for what they have done.[1774] [84] He who ordained the Qur'an for you (Prophet) will see you back to your destination. Say, "My Lord best knows he who brought true guidance, and he who is clearly lost." [85] You (Prophet) could not have expected that the Book would be conveyed to you, but (It is) a mercy from your Lord. So do not back up the unbelievers, [86] and never let them turn you away from God's revelations after they have been revealed to you. (Instead), invite people to your Lord. Never be one of those who associate others with God, [87] and do not invoke another god besides God; there is no god except Him. All things will perish except His Face. Judgment belongs to Him, and to Him you will be returned.[1775] [88]

• • •

[1772] Numbers 16:31-33 As soon as he finished speaking all these words, the ground under them was split apart. [32] The earth opened its mouth and swallowed them up, along with their households— everyone who belonged to Korah and all their goods. [33] So they with all that belonged to them went down alive into Sheol; the earth closed over them, and they perished from the midst of the assembly.

[1773] Numbers 16:34 All Israel around them fled at their outcry, for they said, 'The earth will swallow us too!'

[1774] Colossians 3:25 For the wrongdoer will be paid back for whatever wrong has been done, and there is no partiality.

[1775] Romans 14:12 So then, each of us will be accountable to God.

CHAPTER TWENTY NINE

AL-'ANKABUT
THE SPIDER

THE **MECCA** PERIOD

In the name of God, the Merciful-to-all, the Mercy Giver:

Alif Lam Meem,[1777] [(01)] Do people think that they will be left to say, "We believe," without being tested? [(02)] We have tested those who lived before them[1778] so God will note those who prove to be truthful, and will note the liars. [(03)] Or do those who do bad deeds think they can escape Us? (That is) bad judgment on their part. [(04)] As for those who look forward to meeting God, God's appointed time is coming. He is the All-Hearing,[1779] the All-knowing.[1780] [(05)] And whoever strives, strives only to benefit himself, for God is rich beyond any needs of the worlds. [(06)] As for those who believe and do good deeds, We will remove their bad deeds and will reward them according to the best of what they have done. [(07)] We have commanded people to honor their parents;[1781] of which you have no knowledge, for you will all return to me, and I will tell you about everything you have done. [(08)] Those who believe and do good deeds, We will admit them with the righteous (into Paradise).[1782] [(09)]

Some people say, "We believe in God," but when one (of them) is harmed for God's sake, they consider human persecution to be as severe as God's punishment. But if victory comes from your Lord, they say, "We were always

• • •

[1777] Here and at the beginning of many chapters there are letters of unknown meaning called Al Muquatta'at. Numerous theories have been proposed, but there is no agreement on what they signify yet.

[1778] Psalm 66:10-12 For you, O God, have tested us; you have tried us as silver is tried. [11] You brought us into the net; you laid burdens on our backs; [12] you let people ride over our heads; we went through fire and through water; yet you have brought us out to a spacious place.

[1779] Psalm 4:3 But know that the Lord has set apart the faithful for himself; the Lord hears when I call to him.

[1780] Psalm 44:21 would not God discover this? For he knows the secrets of the heart.

[1781] Exodus 20:12 Honor your father and your mother, so that your days may be long in the land that the Lord your God is giving you.

[1782] James 2:24 You that a person is justified by works and not by faith alone.

with you." Does God not know what is in everyone's heart?[1783] [(10)] God will surely note the believers, and will note the hypocrites. [(11)] The unbelievers said to the believers, "Follow our way, and We will bear your sins." But they will not bear any of their sins. They are liars. [(12)] They will surely carry their own burdens,[1784] and other burdens along with their burdens, and they will be questioned on the Day of Resurrection about their false assertions [(13)]

We sent Noah to (call) his people (to God). He remained among them a thousand years minus fifty,[1785] and the flood seized them while they were unjust.[1786] [(14)] But We saved him and the ark's occupants,[1787] and We made it a sign for the worlds.[1788] [(15)] And (We sent)[1789] Abraham, who called on his people, "Worship God and be always mindful of Him. That is best for you if you should know. [(16)] You worship mere idols instead of God; they are man-made lies. Those you worship instead of God do not have the ability to provide for you. So seek provision from God[1790] and worship Him and be grateful to Him. You will all be returned to Him." [(17)] If you deny (Our message), there are nations before you who have denied it. The Messenger is only responsible for clear transmission [(18)]

Haven't they considered how God begins creation and then repeats it? That, for God, is easy.[1791] [(19)] Say, "Travel throughout the earth and observe how He brings life into being. Then God will bring the next life into being, for God has power over all things." [(20)] He punishes whom He wills and has mercy on whom He wills,[1792] and you will all be returned to Him. [(21)] You will never be beyond His reach on earth or in the heaven, and you have none other than God to protect you or help you.[1793] [(22)] Those who deny God's signs and their preordained meeting with Him—they have lost hope of My mercy, and they will have a painful punishment.[1794] [(23)]

The only answer of (Abraham's) people was "Kill him or burn him," but God saved him from the fire. In that there are signs for people who believe. [(24)]

● ● ●

[1783] Luke 16:15 So he said to them, 'You are those who justify yourselves in the sight of others; but God knows your hearts; for what is prized by human beings is an abomination in the sight of God.
[1784] Galatians 6:5 For all must carry their own loads.
[1785] Genesis 9:29 All the days of Noah were nine hundred and fifty years; and he died.
[1786] Genesis 7:23 He blotted out every living thing that was on the face of the ground, human beings and animals and creeping things and birds of the air; they were blotted out from the earth. Only Noah was left, and those that were with him in the ark.
[1787] Genesis 8:18 So Noah went out with his sons and his wife and his sons' wives.
[1788] Genesis 9:12 God said, 'This is the sign of the covenant that I make between me and you and every living creature that is with you, for all future generations:
[1789] Genesis 12:1-3 Now the Lord said to Abram, 'Go from your country and your kindred and your father's house to the land that I will show you. ² I will make of you a great nation, and I will bless you, and make your name great, so that you will be a blessing. ³ I will bless those who bless you, and the one who curses you I will curse; and in you all the families of the earth shall be blessed.'
[1790] Psalm 81:10 I am the Lord your God, who brought you up out of the land of Egypt. Open your mouth wide and I will fill it.
[1791] Isaiah 65:17 For I am about to create new heavens and a new earth; the former things shall not be remembered or come to mind.
[1792] Romans 9:18 So then he has mercy on whomsoever he chooses, and he hardens the heart of whomsoever he chooses.
[1793] Hosea 13:4 Yet I have been the Lord your God ever since the land of Egypt; you know no God but me, and besides me there is no savior.
[1794] Matthew 25:41 Then he will say to those at his left hand, "You that are accursed, depart from me into the eternal fire prepared for the devil and his angels;

(Abraham) said, "You have chosen (to worship) idols other than God, but your bond of affection with them will be only in this worldly life. On the Day of Resurrection, you will deny and curse one another, and your refuge will be the Fire, (where) you will have no helpers." [25] Lot[1795] believed him. He said, "I will flee to my Lord, He is the Almighty,[1796] the Wise."[1797] [26] And We gave Isaac[1798] and Jacob[1799] to Abraham, and placed prophets and the Book among his descendants. We gave him his reward in this world, and he is in the Hereafter among the righteous.[1800] [27]

And Lot, when he said to his people, "You commit such outrageous immoral acts that no one else in the world ever committed before you. [28] You lust after men, obstruct nature's way, and commit (every) shameful act in your gatherings." His people's answer was: "Bring us God's punishment if what you say is true." [29] He said, "My Lord, support me against these wicked people." [30]

And when Our messengers came to Abraham with the good news, (of Isaac's birth) [1801] they also said, "We will destroy the people of that town. Its people have been wicked."[1802] [31] (Abraham) said, "But Lot is there." They said, "We know who is there better than you do. We will save him and his family, except for his wife. She is to be among those who remain behind." [32] And when Our Messengers came to Lot, they were mistreated, and he was troubled and distressed on their account, because he felt powerless to protect them. They said, "Fear not, nor grieve. We will save you and your family, except your wife; she's among those who will remain behind. [33] We will bring down punishment from the sky on the people of this town because they have deviated (from God's orders)."[1803] [34] We have a remnant of that town as clear evidence for people who use their reason. [35]

And to Midian (We sent) their brother Shu'ayb,[1804] who told them, "My people, worship God, and look forward to the Last Day, and do not spread

• • •

[1795] Lot, nephew of Abraham

[1796] Psalm 93:4 More majestic than the thunders of mighty waters, more majestic than the waves of the sea, majestic on high is the Lord!

[1797] Job 9:4 He is wise in heart, and mighty in strength—who has resisted him, and succeeded? —

[1798] Genesis 21:3 Abraham gave the name Isaac to his son whom Sarah bore him.

[1799] Genesis 25:26 Afterwards his brother came out, with his hand gripping Esau's heel; so he was named Jacob. Isaac was sixty years old when she bore them.

[1800] Hebrews 11:8-13 By faith Abraham obeyed when he was called to set out for a place that he was to receive as an inheritance; and he set out, not knowing where he was going. ⁹ By faith he stayed for a time in the land he had been promised, as in a foreign land, living in tents, as did Isaac and Jacob, who were heirs with him of the same promise. ¹⁰ For he looked forward to the city that has foundations, whose architect and builder is God. ¹¹ By faith he received power of procreation, even though he was too old—and Sarah herself was barren—because he considered him faithful who had promised. ¹² Therefore, from one person, and this one as good as dead, descendants were born, 'as many as the stars of heaven and as the innumerable grains of sand by the seashore.' ¹³ All of these died in faith without having received the promises, but from a distance they saw and greeted them. They confessed that they were strangers and foreigners on the earth,

[1801] Genesis 18:10 Then one said, 'I will surely return to you in due season, and your wife Sarah shall have a son.' And Sarah was listening at the tent entrance behind him.

[1802] Genesis 18:20-21 Then the Lord said, 'How great is the outcry against Sodom and Gomorrah and how very grave their sin! ²¹ I must go down and see whether they have done altogether according to the outcry that has come to me; and if not, I will know.'

[1803] Genesis 19:13 For we are about to destroy this place, because the outcry against its people has become great before the Lord, and the Lord has sent us to destroy it.'

[1804] See Glossary

wickedness on the earth." [36] But they rejected him, so an earthquake seized them, and next morning they lay dead in their homes. [37] And Aad [1805] and Thamud[1806]- what happen to them is obvious to you from their (ruined) dwellings. Satan made their deeds pleasing to them and diverted them from the path[1807] (of God) even though they had been able to see the truth. [38] (The same fate befell) Korah (Qarun), [1808] Pharaoh[1809] and Haman[1810] Moses came to all of them with clear evidence, but they chose to be arrogant on earth, and they couldn't escape Our punishment. [39] So We seized each of them for their wrong doing: upon some We sent a storm of stones, and some were seized by a blast (from the sky), and some We caused the earth to swallow,[1811] and some We drowned.[1812] It was not God who did them an injustice, they did themselves an injustice. [40]

The example of those who take protectors other than God is like that of the spider that made itself a home, for the weakest of homes is the spider's home. If they only knew. [41] God knows whatever they call upon other than Him, for He is the Almighty,[1813] the Wise. [1814] [42] Such examples We offer to people, but only those with knowledge will grasp their meaning.[1815] [43] God created the heavens and the earth in Truth. There is in that is a sign for the believers.[1816(44)]

Recite what has been revealed to you of the Book, and pray. Prayer restrains indecency and wrongdoing, and enhances the remembrance of God. God knows all that you do. [45] If you argue with the People of the Book, then argue only in

• • •

[1805] see ref. 615

[1806] See ref. 617

[1807] Deuteronomy 11:16 Take care, or you will be seduced into turning away, serving other gods and worshipping them,

[1808] Numbers 16:32 The earth opened its mouth and swallowed them up, along with their households— everyone who belonged to Korah and all their goods.

[1809] Exodus 3:9-10 The cry of the Israelites has now come to me; I have also seen how the Egyptians oppress them. [10] So come, I will send you to Pharaoh to bring my people, the Israelites, out of Egypt.'

[1810] Pharaoh's chief adviser

[1811] Numbers 16:31-35 As soon as he finished speaking all these words, the ground under them was split apart. [32] The earth opened its mouth and swallowed them up, along with their households—everyone who belonged to Korah and all their goods. [33] So they with all that belonged to them went down alive into Sheol; the earth closed over them, and they perished from the midst of the assembly. [34] All Israel around them fled at their outcry, for they said, 'The earth will swallow us too!' [35] And fire came out from the Lord and consumed the two hundred and fifty men offering the incense.

[1812] Exodus 14:28 The waters returned and covered the chariots and the chariot drivers, the entire army of Pharaoh that had followed them into the sea; not one of them remained.

[1813] Psalm 24:8 Who is the King of glory? The LORD, strong and mighty, the Lord, mighty in battle.

[1814] 1 Corinthians 1:25 For God's foolishness is wiser than human wisdom, and God's weakness is stronger than human strength

[1815] Matthew 13:13-17 The reason I speak to them in parables is that "seeing they do not perceive, and hearing they do not listen, nor do they understand." [14] With them indeed is fulfilled the prophecy of Isaiah that says: "You will indeed listen, but never understand, and you will indeed look, but never perceive. [15] For this people's heart has grown dull, and their ears are hard of hearing, and they have shut their eyes; so that they might not look with their eyes, and listen with their ears, and understand with their heart and turn— and I would heal them." [16] But blessed are your eyes, for they see, and your ears, for they hear. [17] Truly I tell you, many prophets and righteous people longed to see what you see, but did not see it, and to hear what you hear, but did not hear it.

[1816] Romans 1:20 Ever since the creation of the world his eternal power and divine nature, invisible though they are, have been understood and seen through the things he has made. So they are without excuse;

the kindest way, except with those among them who are unjust, and say, "We believe in what was revealed to us and in what was revealed to you. Our God and your God is one; and we are submissive to Him."[1817] [(46)] Hence, We have sent down the Book to you (Prophet). Those to whom We previously gave the Book believe in it, and so do some of these (other) people. No one rejects Our revelations except those who deny an obvious truth. [(47)]

You never recited any Book before We revealed this one to you, nor did you ever write one with your own hand. Otherwise, those who try to disprove the truth would have had cause for doubt. [(48)] Rather, the Qur'an is a clear message to the hearts of those who have been given knowledge. No one knowingly rejects Our verses except those who are unjust (to themselves). [(49)] But they say, "Why have no miracles been sent down to him from his Lord?" Say, "The miracles are only with God, and I am only sent to give you a clear warning" [(50)] Isn't it enough for them that We inspired you to recite the Book to them? There is a mercy in this and a reminder for believing people. [(51)] Say, "God is sufficient witness between you and me. He knows what is in the heavens and earth. Those who believe in falsehood and deny God will be the losers." [(52)]

They dare you to hasten judgment against them. They would already have received a punishment had its time not already been set [1818] (by God), but it will surely come to them suddenly, when they least expect it. [(53)] They dare you to hasten their punishment, but Hell will surely encompass the unbelievers [(54)] on the Day when the punishment [1819] will overwhelm them from above them and from beneath their feet, and He will say, "Taste (the result of) what you have done." [(55)]

My worshipers who have believed My earth is spacious, so worship only Me. [(56)] Every soul will taste death. Then you will be returned to Us.[1820] [(57)] To those who have believed and done righteous deeds, We will assign mansions [1821] in Paradise through which rivers flow, where they will remain forever-an excellent reward for those who do good work, [(58)] who have been patient, and who have put their trust in their Lord. [(59)] How many a creature gives no thought to their (own) sustenance, but God provides for them and for you.[1822] He is the All-

• • •

[1817] James 4:7 Submit yourselves therefore to God. Resist the devil, and he will flee from you.
[1818] Revelation 14:15 Another angel came out of the temple, calling with a loud voice to the one who sat on the cloud, 'Use your sickle and reap, for the hour to reap has come, because the harvest of the earth is fully ripe.'
[1819] 2 Thessalonians 1:9 These will suffer the punishment of eternal destruction, separated from the presence of the Lord and from the glory of his might,
[1820] Hebrews 9:27 And just as it is appointed for mortals to die once, and after that the judgment,
[1821] John 14:2 In my Father's house there are many dwelling places. If it were not so, would I have told you that I go to prepare a place for you
[1822] Matthew 6:25-34 Do Not Worry 'Therefore I tell you, do not worry about your life, what you will eat or what you will drink, or about your body, what you will wear. Is not life more than food, and the body more than clothing? [26] Look at the birds of the air; they neither sow nor reap nor gather into barns, and yet your heavenly Father feeds them. Are you not of more value than they? [27] And can any of you by worrying add a single hour to your span of life? [28] And why do you worry about clothing? Consider the lilies of the field, how they grow; they neither toil nor spin, [29] yet I tell you, even Solomon in all his glory was not clothed like one of these. [30] But if God so clothes the grass of the field, which is alive today and tomorrow is thrown into the oven, will he not much more clothe you—you of little faith? [31] Therefore, do not worry, saying, "What will we eat?" or "What will we drink?" or "What will we wear?" [32] For it is the Gentiles who strive for all these things; and indeed your heavenly Father knows that you need all these things. [33] But strive first for the kingdom of God and his righteousness, and all these things will be given to

Hearing, the All-Knowing.[1823] [(60)] If you asked them, "Who created the heavens and earth and made the sun and the moon subservient (to his laws)?"[1824] they will say, "God." Then why do they lie about it? [(61)] God gives plenty to anyone He wants, and gives little to anyone He wants. God knows everything. [(62)] And if you asked them, "Who sends down rain from the sky[1825] to give life to the earth after it was dead?" they would surely say "God." Say, "Praise be to God;"[1826] but most of them do not think. [(63)]

The life of this world is only diversion and amusement.[1827] whereas the true life is in the Hereafter, if they only knew.[1828] [(64)] When they board a ship, they pray to God, dedicating their faith to him alone, but when He delivers them safely to shore, at once they associate others with Him. [(65)] So let them deny what We have given them, and let them enjoy themselves, they will soon know. [(66)] Do they not see that We have made (Mecca) a secure sanctuary, while, all around them, people are being taken away? How is it possible that they still believe in falsehood and deny the blessings of God? [(67)] Who is more unjust than one who invents lies about God or denies the Truth when it has come to him?[1829] Is there not (sufficient) room in Hell for the unbelievers? [(68)] But those who strive for Our cause, We will surely guide them in Our ways.[1830] Truly, God is with those who do good.[1831] [(69)]

• • •

you as well. [34] 'So do not worry about tomorrow, for tomorrow will bring worries of its own. Today's trouble is enough for today.

[1823] 1 John 3:20 whenever our hearts condemn us; for God is greater than our hearts, and he knows everything.

[1824] Genesis 1:1 In the beginning when God created the heavens and the earth,

[1825] Job 5:10 He gives rain on the earth and sends waters on the fields;

[1826] 2 Samuel 22:4 I call upon the Lord, who is worthy to be praised, and I am saved from my enemies Psalm 18:3. Psalm 35:28 Then my tongue shall tell of your righteousness and of your praise all day long.

[1827] 2 Corinthians 4:18 because we look not at what can be seen but at what cannot be seen; for what can be seen is temporary, but what cannot be seen is eternal

[1828] 1 Timothy 6:19 thus storing up for themselves the treasure of a good foundation for the future, so that they may take hold of the life that really is life.

[1829] Romans 1:18 For the wrath of God is revealed from heaven against all ungodliness and wickedness of those who by their wickedness suppress the truth.

[1830] Psalm 48:14 that this is God, our God for ever and ever. He will be our guide for ever.

[1831] Proverbs 15:9 The way of the wicked is an abomination to the Lord, but he loves the one who pursues righteousness.

CHAPTER THIRTY

AR-RUM

THE BYZANTINES

THE **MECCA** PERIOD

Alif Lam Meem,[1831] [(01)]

The Byzantines[1832] have been defeated [(02)] in a nearby land, but, after their defeat, they will be victorious [(03)] within few years. To God belongs the decision, from beginning to end. On that day (of victory) the Believers will rejoice [(04)] in God's victory. He gives victory to whoever He wills;[1833] He is the Almighty,[1834] the Merciful-to-all.[1835] [(05)] This is God's promise. God never breaks His promise,[1836] but most people do not know.[(06)] They only know the outward aspect of this worldly life,[1837] but they are unaware of the Hereafter.[(07)] Have they not considered in their own minds that God created the heavens, and the earth, and everything between them in Truth [1838] and for an appointed time?[1839] Yet many people deny that they will meet their Lord.[1840] [(08)]

Have they[1841] not traveled through the land and seen the final fate of those before them? They were greater in power than they are, cultivated the land, and built it up more than these have, and their messengers came to them with clear

• • •

[1831] Here and at the beginning of many chapters there are unvowelled letters of unknown meaning. Numerous theories have been proposed, but there is no agreement on the subject.

[1832] Roman Empire

[1833] Proverbs 21:31 The horse is made ready for the day of battle, but the victory belongs to the Lord.

[1834] Deuteronomy 3:24 'O Lord God, you have only begun to show your servant your greatness and your might; what god in heaven or on earth can perform deeds and mighty acts like yours!

[1835] Psalm 103:8, 145:8 The Lord is merciful and gracious, slow to anger and abounding in steadfast love.

[1836] Numbers 23:19 God is not a human being, that he should lie, or a mortal, that he should change his mind. Has he promised, and will he not do it? Has he spoken, and will he not fulfil it?

[1837] James 4:14 Yet you do not even know what tomorrow will bring. What is your life? For you are a mist that appears for a little while and then vanishes.

[1838] 2 Kings 19:15And Hezekiah prayed before the LORD, and said: 'O Lord the God of Israel, who are enthroned above the cherubim, you are God, you alone, of all the kingdoms of the earth; you have made heaven and earth.

[1839] Ecclesiastes 3:11 He has made everything suitable for its time; moreover, he has put a sense of past and future into their minds, yet they cannot find out what God has done from the beginning to the end.

[1840] Romans 14:10 Why do you pass judgment on your brother or sister? Or you, why do you despise your brother or sister? For we will all stand before the judgment seat of God.

[1841] The people you are calling to believe in this message.

evidence. God would never have wronged them, but they did themselves wrong. [09] The final fate of those who did evil was the worst, then, because they denied and ridiculed the signs of God. [10] God brings creation into being; then, He reproduces it; then you will be returned to Him. [11]

On the day the hour comes, [1842] who force others to reject God's messages will be in despair. [12] None of the partners they ascribed to God will intercede for them, so they will deny their partners [13] On the Day the Hour comes-on that Day, they will be sorted out. [1843] [14] Those who believed and did good deeds, they will be jubilant in a (lovely) meadow. [15] While those who denied the truth and denied Our signs and the meeting of the Hereafter, they will be delivered into everlasting punishment. [1844] [16]

So celebrate God's glory in the evening and in the morning, [1845] [17] for to Him alone is praise due throughout the heavens and the earth, at night and at noon. [18] He brings forth the living from the dead, and brings forth the dead from the living. He brings life to the earth after it has been dead. And you will be brought forth in the same way. [19] Among His signs is that He created you from dust, [1846] and you became human beings, spread far and wide. [20] And among His signs is that He created spouses for you from among yourselves, [1847] so that you may find peace with them, and He has placed affection and mercy [1848] between you. In this there are signs for people who think. [21] And among His signs is the creation of the heavens and the earth, and the diversity of your languages [1849] and your colors. These are signs for those who know. [22] And among His signs is your (ability to) sleep by night and day, and to seek His bounties. These are signs for people who listen. [23] And among His signs is (that) He shows you the lightening, [1850] (causing) fear and hope, and He sends down rain from the sky to

• • •

[1842] John 5:28 Do not be astonished at this; for the hour is coming when all who are in their graves will hear his voice
[1843] Matthew 25:32 All the nations will be gathered before him, and he will separate people one from another as a shepherd separates the sheep from the goats,
[1844] Habakkuk 1:12 Are you not from of old, O Lord my God, my Holy One? You shall not die. O Lord, you have marked them for judgment; and you, O Rock, have established them for punishment.
[1845] Psalm 66: 1-4 Make a joyful noise to God, all the earth; [2] sing the glory of his name; give to him glorious praise [3] Say to God, "How awesome are your deeds! Because of your great power, your enemies cringe before you. [4] All the earth worships you; they sing praises to you, sing praises to your name."
[1846] Genesis 2:7 then the Lord God formed man from the dust of the ground, and breathed into his nostrils the breath of life; and man became a living being.
[1847] Genesis 2:21-24 So the Lord God caused a deep sleep to fall upon the man, and he slept; then he took one of his ribs and closed up its place with flesh. [22] And the rib that the Lord God had taken from the man he made into a woman and brought her to the man. [23] Then the man said, 'This at last is bone of my bones and flesh of my flesh; this one shall be called Woman, for out of Man this one was taken.' [24] Therefore, a man leaves his father and his mother and clings to his wife, and they become one flesh.
[1848] Hebrews 4:16 Let us therefore approach the throne of grace with boldness, so that we may receive mercy and find grace to help in time of need.
[1849] Genesis 11:5-9 The Lord came down to see the city and the tower, which mortals had built. 6 And the LORD said, 'Look, they are one people, and they have all one language; and this is only the beginning of what they will do; nothing that they propose to do will now be impossible for them. [7] Come, let us go down, and confuse their language there, so that they will not understand one another's speech.' [8] So the Lord scattered them abroad from there over the face of all the earth, and they left off building the city. [9] Therefore, it was called Babel, because there the Lord confused the language of all the earth; and from there the Lord scattered them abroad over the face of all the earth.
[1850] Job 37:11 He loads the thick cloud with moisture; the clouds scatter his lightning.

revive the earth to life after it had been dead.[1851] These are signs for people who understand. [24] And among His signs is that the heaven and the earth are sustained by His command.[1852] Then when He calls you forth from the earth, you will emerge immediately. [25] To Him belongs whoever is in the heavens and earth; [1853] all are submissive to Him.[1854] [26] It is He who brings forth creation, then He reproduces it, and that is easy for Him, for He is above all comparisons in the heavens and earth. He is the Almighty,[1855] The Wise.[1856] [27]

God gives you an example based on your lives: Do you make those whom your right hands held in trust your full partners with the wealth We have provided you, so that all of you own it equally? And do you fear (to use it without consulting) them, just as you might fear your equals? (No.) This is how We explain the verses for people who can understand, [28] but those who persist on being evildoers follow their (own) whims and desires without knowledge.[1857] Who can guide those whom God allows to stray?[1858] They will have no helpers.[1859] [29] So stand firm in your devotion to the faith, inclining to truth, (according to) the innate nature God has instilled in (all) people.[1860] There is no changing God's creation. This is the correct religion, but most people do not know it, [30] turning to Him, being ever mindful of Him, performing prayer, and neither be from those who associate others with God, [31] (Or) of those who have split up their faith and divided into sects, every faction rejoicing in what it has.[32]

When harm touches people, they call on their Lord, turning to Him for help. Then right after He gives them a taste of His mercy, some of them associate others with their Lord, [33] (as if) to show their ingratitude for all that We have granted them. Enjoy your (brief) life, then, for you will soon know. [34] Have We sent down to them an authority, that sanctions the partners they were associating with Him?[1861] [35] When We give people a taste of mercy, they rejoice, but if something bad happens to them because of their own misdeeds, they immediately lose all hope. [36] Do they not see that God gives much to anyone He wills or restricts it?[1862] In that are signs for people who believe. [37] So give

• • •

[1851] Isaiah 44:3 For I will pour water on the thirsty land, and streams on the dry ground; I will pour my spirit upon your descendants, and my blessing on your offspring.

[1852] Psalm 119:89-90 The Lord exists for ever; your word is firmly fixed in heaven. 90 Your faithfulness endures to all generations; you have established the earth, and it stands fast.

[1853] Psalm 89:11 The heavens are yours, the earth also is yours; the world and all that is in it—you have founded them.

[1854] Psalm 119:91 By your appointment they stand today, for all things are your servants.

[1855] Psalm 93:4 More majestic than the thunders of mighty waters, more majestic than the waves of the sea, majestic on high is the Lord!

[1856] Job 9:4 He is wise in heart, and mighty in strength—who has resisted him, and succeeded?—

[1857] Romans 8:7 For this reason the mind that is set on the flesh is hostile to God; it does not submit to God's law—indeed it cannot,

[1858] 2 Thessalonians 2:11 For this reason God sends them a powerful delusion, leading them to believe what is false,

[1859] Hosea 13:4 Yet I have been the Lord your God ever since the land of Egypt; you know no God but me, and besides me there is no savior.

[1860] Romans 1:19-20 For what can be known about God is plain to them, because God has shown it to them. Ever since the creation of the world his eternal power and divine nature, invisible though they are, have been understood and seen through the things he has made. So they are without excuse;

[1861] Isaiah 44:8 Do not fear, or be afraid; have I not told you from of old and declared it? You are my witnesses! Is there any god besides me? There is no other rock; I know not one.

[1862] 1 Samuel 2:7 The Lord makes poor and makes rich; he brings low, he also exalts.

relatives their due, as well as the needy and the traveler.[1863] That is best for those who seek the pleasure of God; It is they who will prosper. (38) And (remember): what you lend in usury aiming to increase it from people's wealth will not increase in God's sight, but what you give in purifying alms, seeking God's approval, will multiply its rewards.[1864] (39) It is God who created you, then provided for you,[1865] Who will cause you to die and then will give you life again.[1866] Can any of your "partners" do any of those things?[1867] May He be exalted in His glory and high above anything they associate with Him.[1868] (40) Corruption has appeared throughout the land and sea as a result of people's actions,[1869] so He will make them taste (the consequences of) some of their actions, so that perhaps they will return (to righteousness). (41) Say, "Travel through the land and observe the final fate of those who came before; most of them were idolaters. (42) So stand firm in your devotion to the upright religion, before a Day comes from God that no one can stop. On that Day, they will be broken.[1870] (43) Whoever denies the truth, his denial is against him; And whoever does good deeds, they are preparing the way for themselves,[1871] (44) so, that He may reward, out of His bounty, those who have believed and done good deeds. He truly does not like the unbelievers. (45)

And of His signs the winds that bear good news,[1872] to give you a taste of His mercy, and set ships to sail at His command, to enable you to seek His favor and, perhaps be thankful. (46) We have already sent messengers to the people who came before you, and they came to them with clear evidence. Then, We imposed retribution on those who severed relations with Us, for We have taken it upon Ourselves to help the believers. (47) It is God who sends the winds to raise the clouds. Then, He spreads them about the sky however He wills, and He makes

• • •

[1863] Deuteronomy 24:14 You shall not withhold the wages of poor and needy laborers, whether other Israelites or aliens who reside in your land in one of your towns.

[1864] Proverbs 19:17 Whoever is kind to the poor lends to the Lord, and will be repaid in full.

[1865] Matthew 6:25-26 'Therefore I tell you, do not worry about your life, what you will eat or what you will drink, or about your body, what you will wear. Is not life more than food, and the body more than clothing? 26 Look at the birds of the air; they neither sow nor reap nor gather into barns, and yet your heavenly Father feeds them. Are you not of more value than they?

[1866] Revelation 20:12 And I saw the dead, great and small, standing before the throne, and books were opened. Also another book was opened, the book of life. And the dead were judged according to their works, as recorded in the books.

[1867] Isaiah 41:21-23 Set forth your case, says the Lord; bring your proofs, says the King of Jacob. 22 Let them bring them, and tell us what is to happen. Tell us the former things, what they are, so that we may consider them, and that we may know their outcome; or declare to us the things to come. 23 Tell us what is to come hereafter, that we may know that you are gods; do good, or do harm, that we may be afraid and terrified.

[1868] Isaiah 41:24 You, indeed, are nothing and your work is nothing at all; whoever chooses you is an abomination.

[1869] Isaiah 24:5 The earth lies polluted under its inhabitants; for they have transgressed laws, violated the statutes, broken the everlasting covenant.

[1870] Matthew 25:32 All the nations will be gathered before him, and he will separate people one from another as a shepherd separates the sheep from the goats,

[1871] John 5:29, "and will come out—those who have done good, to the resurrection of life, and those who have done evil, to the resurrection of condemnation." 2 Timothy 1:12

[1872] John 3:8 The wind blows where it chooses, and you hear the sound of it, but you do not know where it comes from or where it goes. So it is with everyone who is born of the Spirit.'

them break up so you see the rain fall through them;[1873] and when He causes rain to fall on whomever of His worshipers He wills,[1874] as they rejoice[(48)] even though, before it was sent down upon them they were in despair. [(49)] So observe the effects of the God's mercy, how He gives life to the earth after it had been dead.[1875] He is the One who brings the dead to life;[1876] He has power over all things.[1877] [(50)] But if We should (then) send a (bad) wind and they see (their crops turn) yellow, they would continue to deny the truth. [(51)] Truly, you cannot make the dead hear, nor can you make the deaf hear the call when they turn their backs and go away, [(52)] and you cannot guide the blind[1878] (of heart) away from their misguidance. You can make none hear you except those who believe in Our messages and thus submit themselves to us.[1879] [(53)] It is God who creates you weak, then gives you strength, then after (a period of) strength, he ordains weakness and white hair.[1880] He creates what He wills. He is the All-Knowing,[1881] the All Powerful.[1882] [(54)]

On the Day the Hour comes, those who forced others to reject God's messages will swear they had idled (on earth) for only an hour, for they had always deluded themselves, [(55)] but those who were given knowledge and faith will say, "You idled according to God's decree until the Day of Resurrection, and this is the Day of Resurrection, but you were determined not to know it." [(56)] On that Day, the excuses of those who wronged (themselves) will not benefit them, nor will they be allowed to make amends.[1883] [(57)]

We have certainly presented to humanity all kind of parables in this Qur'an. Yet, if you (Prophet) should bring them a sign, the unbelievers will say, "You are all full of falsehood." [(58)] This is how God seals the hearts of those who do not

•　•　•

[1873] Isaiah 30:23 He will give rain for the seed with which you sow the ground, and grain, the produce of the ground, which will be rich and plenteous. On that day your cattle will graze in broad pastures;

[1874] Matthew 5:45 so that you may be children of your Father in heaven; for he makes his sun rise on the evil and on the good, and sends rain on the righteous and on the unrighteous.

[1875] Job 5:10 He gives rain on the earth and sends waters on the fields;

[1876] Mark 10:27 Jesus looked at them and said, 'For mortals it is impossible, but not for God; for God all things are possible.'

[1877] Job 42:2 'I know that you can do all things, and that no purpose of yours can be thwarted.

[1878] Romans 2:19 and if you are sure that you are a guide to the blind, a light to those who are in darkness,

[1879] James 4:7 Submit yourselves therefore to God. Resist the devil, and he will flee from you.

[1880] Ecclesiastes 12:2-7 before the sun and the light and the moon and the stars are darkened and the clouds return with the rain; [3] on the day when the guards of the house tremble, and the strong men are bent, and the women who grind cease working because they are few, and those who look through the windows see dimly; [4] when the doors on the street are shut, and the sound of the grinding is low, and one rises up at the sound of a bird, and all the daughters of song are brought low; [5] when one is afraid of heights, and terrors are in the road; the almond tree blossoms, the grasshopper drags itself along and desire fails; because all must go to their eternal home, and the mourners will go about the streets; [6] before the silver cord is snapped, and the golden bowl is broken, and the pitcher is broken at the fountain, and the wheel broken at the cistern, [7] and the dust returns to the earth as it was, and the breath returns to God who gave it.

[1881] Psalm 44:21 Would not God find this out? For He knows the secrets of the heart

[1882] Job 42:2 'I know that you can do all things, and that no purpose of yours can be thwarted.

[1883] Revelation 20:12-13 And I saw the dead, great and small, standing before the throne, and books were opened. Also another book was opened, the book of life. And the dead were judged according to their works, as recorded in the books. [13] And the sea gave up the dead that were in it, Death and Hades gave up the dead that were in them, and all were judged according to what they had done.

know.[1884] [(59)] Be patient.[1885] God's promise is Truth, and do not let those who have no certainty in God dishearten you. [(60)]

• • •

[1884] Romans 9:18 So then he has mercy on whomsoever he chooses, and he hardens the heart of whomsoever he chooses.
[1885] James 5:7-8 Be patient, therefore, beloved, until the coming of the Lord. The farmer waits for the precious crop from the earth, being patient with it until it receives the early and the late rains. You also must be patient. Strengthen your hearts, for the coming of the Lord is near.

CHAPTER THIRTY ONE

LUGMAN

LUGMAN

In the name of God, the Merciful-to-all, the Mercy Giver:

Alif Lam Meem,[1887 (01)]

These are verses of the wise Book,[1888 (02)] a guidance and mercy for those who do good [(03)] who establish prayer and give the purifying alms, and who are certain of the Hereafter [1889 (04)] They are rightly guided by their Lord, and they are the successful.[1890 (05)] Some people prefer idle talk (over God's message) in order to lead those without knowledge away from God's path, and to ridicule it. They will have a humiliating punishment.[1891 (06)] And when our verses are recited to him, he turns away arrogantly, as if he had not heard, as if there was deafness in his ears, so give him news of a painful punishment.[(07)] Those who believe and do good deeds will have Gardens of Delight,[(08)] where they will remain forever.[1892] this is the true promise of God, for He is the Almighty,[1893] the Wise.[1894 (09)] He created the heavens without visible pillars, and firmly set mountains on earth, in case it should move under you, and spread every kind of creature over it. And

.   .   •   •   •   .

[1887] Here and at the beginning of many chapters there are letters of unknown meaning called Al Muquatta'at. Numerous theories have been proposed, but there is no agreement on what they signify yet.

[1888] Proverbs 1:2-6 For learning about wisdom and instruction, for understanding words of insight, 3 for gaining instruction in wise dealing, righteousness, justice, and equity; 4 to teach shrewdness to the simple, knowledge and prudence to the young— 5 let the wise also hear and gain in learning, and the discerning acquire skill, 6 to understand a proverb and a figure, the words of the wise and their riddles.

[1889] John 5:24 Very truly, I tell you, anyone who hears my word and believes him who sent me has eternal life, and does not come under judgment, but has passed from death to life.

[1890] Joshua 1:8 This book of the law shall not depart out of your mouth; you shall meditate on it day and night, so that you may be careful to act in accordance with all that is written in it. For then you shall make your way prosperous, and then you shall be successful.

[1891] Matthew 25:46 And these will go away into eternal punishment, but the righteous into eternal life.'

[1892] John 4:14 but those who drink of the water that I will give them will never be thirsty. The water that I will give will become in them a spring of water gushing up to eternal life.'

[1893] Psalm 62:7 On God rests my deliverance and my honor; my mighty rock, my refuge is in God.

[1894] Job 9:4 He is wise in heart, and mighty in strength —who has resisted him, and succeeded? —

We send down rain from the sky and make every kind of good plant grow. [10] This is God's creation. Show me, then, what your other gods have created. Truly, the unjust are clearly lost. [11]

We gave Luqman Wisdom, "Be grateful to God.[1895] Whoever is grateful does so only for his own good, (whereas) whoever is ungrateful (should know that) God is rich beyond need and praiseworthy.[1896] [12] Luqman said to his son while instructing him, "O my son, do not attribute any partners to God. Associating others with him is a great transgression." [13] And We have commanded the human being to care for his parents. His mother carried him in weakness,[1897] and his weaning is in two years. Be grateful to Me and to your parents; all will return to Me. [14] But if they try to make you associate with Me other partners whom you don't know, do not obey them. Do, however, (continue to) keep them company in (this) world according to what is right, but follow the way of those who turn towards Me. Then you will all return to me, and I will make you understand all that you have done [15] "My son, if something weighs as little as a mustard seed[1898] and should be within a rock or (anywhere) in the heavens or in the earth, God will bring it forth. God is Most-Subtle, All-Aware. [16] My son, keep up prayer, order what is obviously[1899] right, forbid what is obviously wrong, and be patient (in the face of) all that happens to you. Surely, these acts require courage. [17] And do not turn your cheek (in contempt) away from people, and do not walk in arrogance, for God does not like any vain and boastful person.[1900] [18] And be moderate[1901] in your pace and lower your voice; the most disagreeable of sounds is the braying of donkeys." [19]

Do you not see that God has made everything in heaven and on earth subject to you, and has abundantly showered you with His favors, (both) seen and unseen? Yet some people argue about God in ignorance[1902] without guidance or illuminating Scripture. [20] And when they are told, "Follow what God has revealed," they say, " We will follow what we found our fathers doing."[1903] (What) Even if Satan was inviting them to the punishment of the Blazing Fire?[1904] [21]

•   •   •

[1895] 2 Timothy 1:3 I am grateful to God—whom I worship with a clear conscience, as my ancestors did—when I remember you constantly in my prayers night and day.

[1896] 1 Chronicles 16:25 For great is the Lord, and greatly to be praised; he is to be revered above all gods.

[1897] Proverbs 23:25 Let your father and mother be glad; let her who bore you rejoice.

[1898] Luke 17:6, And the Lord said, "If you had faith like a mustard seed, you would say to this mulberry tree, 'Be uprooted and be planted in the sea'; and it would obey you.

[1899] What is obviously right or wrong is time, place and culture sensative.

[1900] Psalm 101:5 One who secretly slanders a neighbor I will destroy. A haughty look and an arrogant heart I will not tolerate.

[1901] Philippians 4:5 Let your gentleness be known to everyone. The Lord is near.

[1902] Job 38:2 'Who is this that darkens counsel by words without knowledge?

[1903] Acts 7:51-53 'You stiff-necked people, uncircumcised in heart and ears, you are for ever opposing the Holy Spirit, just as your ancestors used to do. [52] Which of the prophets did your ancestors not persecute? They killed those who foretold the coming of the Righteous One, and now you have become his betrayers and murderers. [53] You are the ones that received the law as ordained by angels, and yet you have not kept it.'

[1904] Matthew 25:41 Then he will say to those at his left hand, "You that are accursed, depart from me into the eternal fire prepared for the devil and his angels;

Whoever turns his face in submission to God[1905] while he is doing good has grasped the most trustworthy handhold. God determines the outcome of (all) matters.[1906] (22) And do not let the denial of those who continue to deny the truth grieve you, (Prophet). They will return to Us, and We will tell them everything that they have done. God knows everything that lies within the heart.[1907] (23) We will grant them some enjoyment for a while, (but) then We will force a massive punishment on them. [1908] (24)

And, if you asked them, "Who created the heavens and earth?" They would say, "God." Say, "(All) praise is (due) to God," but most of them do not understand. (25) Whatever is in the heavens and earth belongs to God, for God is the Rich beyond need, the Praiseworthy. [1909] (26) If all the trees on earth were pens and the sea (were) ink with seven (more) seas to replenish it, God's[1910] words would not be exhausted[1911], for God is almighty[1912] and wise. [1913] (27) Creating and resurrecting all of you is (for God) like creating and resurrecting a single soul. God is All-Hearing and All-Seeing. (28)

Do you not see that God causes the night to merge into the day and causes the day to merge into the night, and has made the sun and the moon subservient (to His laws), each running its course for a specified term, and that God is aware of all you do? (29) Thus it is, because God is the Truth, and whatever they invoke besides Him is falsehood, and because God is the Most High,[1914] the Most Great.[1915] (30) Do you not see that ships sail through the sea by the grace of God, so that He may show you some of His signs? In this are signs for everyone patient and grateful. (31) And when waves come over them like (giant) shadows, they call out to God, sincere in their devotion to Him,[1916] but when He delivers them safely to shore, some of them waver.[1917] Only a treacherous and ungrateful person refuses to acknowledge our signs. (32)

People, be conscious of your Lord and fear a Day when no father will be able to rescue his son, nor will a son be able to rescue his father at all. God's promise

• • •

[1905] James 4:7 Submit yourselves therefore to God. Resist the devil, and he will flee from you.

[1906] Psalm 147:4 He determines the number of the stars; he gives to all of them their names.

[1907] Romans 8:27 And God, who searches the heart, knows what is the mind of the Spirit, because the Spirit intercedes for the saints according to the will of God.

[1908] Isaiah 13:11 I will punish the world for its evil, and the wicked for their iniquity; I will put an end to the pride of the arrogant, and lay low the insolence of tyrants.

[1909] 2 Samuel 22:4 I call upon the Lord, who is worthy to be praised, and I am saved from my enemies

[1910] The words of God are his creation instruments. The whole universe exist base on a word from God and so does the Qur'an and Jesus who was a word of God.

[1911] John 16:12-13 "I have many more things to say to you, but you cannot bear them now. 13"But when He, the Spirit of truth, comes, He will guide you into all the truth;

[1912] Psalm 50:1 The mighty one, God the Lord, speaks and summons the earth from the rising of the sun to its setting.

[1913] Job 9:4 He is wise in heart, and mighty in strength —who has resisted him, and succeeded? —

[1914] Genesis 14:20 and blessed be God Most High, who has delivered your enemies into your hand!' And Abram gave him one-tenth of everything.

[1915] Psalm 70:4 Let all who seek you rejoice and be glad in you. Let those who love your salvation say evermore, 'God is great!'

[1916] Psalm 107:28-29 Then they cried to the Lord in their trouble, and he brought them out from their distress; 29 he made the storm be still, and the waves of the sea were hushed.

[1917] Psalm 78:32 In spite of all this they still sinned; they did not believe in his wonders.

(of resurrection) is the Truth, so do not let this worldly life deceive you,[1918] nor deceptive thoughts about God delude you. (33) God has knowledge of the Hour [1919] and sends down the rain, and knows what is in the wombs,[1920] but no soul knows what it will reap tomorrow,[1921] and no soul knows in what land it will die.[1922] God (alone) is All-knowing and All-Aware.[1923] (34)

• • •

[1918] 1 John 2:15-16 Do not love the world or the things in the world. The love of the Father is not in those who love the world; [16] for all that is in the world—the desire of the flesh, the desire of the eyes, the pride in riches—comes not from the Father but from the world.

[1919] Mark 13:32 'But about that day or hour no one knows, neither the angels in heaven, nor the Son, but only the Father.

[1920] Psalm 139:13 For it was you who formed my inward parts; you knit me together in my mother's womb.

[1921] James 4:13-14 Come now, you who say, 'Today or tomorrow we will go to such and such a town and spend a year there, doing business and making money.' [14] Yet you do not even know what tomorrow will bring. What is your life? For you are a mist that appears for a little while and then vanishes.

[1922] Matthew 6:34 Therefore do not worry about tomorrow, for tomorrow will worry about itself.

[1923] Isaiah 40:28 Have you not known? Have you not heard? The Lord is the everlasting God, the Creator of the ends of the earth. He does not faint or grow weary; his understanding is unsearchable.

CHAPTER THIRTY TWO

AS-SAJDAH
THE PROSTRATION

THE **MECCA** PERIOD

In the name of God, the Merciful-to-all, the Mercy Giver:
Alif Lam Meem.[1924] [01]
There is no doubt that this book has been sent down exactly as it is[1925] from the Lord of the Worlds. [02] Or do they say, "He invented it?" Rather, it is the Truth from your Lord, so that you will warn a people to whom no warner has come before you, and that they may be guided. [03]

It is God who created the heavens and the earth and all that is between them in six days;[1926] then He sat down on the Throne of His majesty. Apart from Him, You have no one to protect you or to intercede for you, so, will you not remember this? [04] He manages everything from heaven to earth; then, it will all ascend to Him on a Day whose measure is a thousand years [1927] as you count them. [05] Such is He, the Knower of the unseen and the witnessed, the Almighty,[1928] the Merciful-to-all[1929] [06] He perfected everything which He created, and began the creation of the human being from clay;[1930] [07] then He made his descendants from the extract of a common fluid; [08] then He formed

• • •

[1924] Here and at the beginning of many chapters there are unvowelled letters of unknown meaning. Numerous theories have been proposed, but there is no agreement on the subject.

[1925] The word "tanzil" means: exactly as it is. In the case of other prophets, the word used was "nazzala" meaning the revelation was sent to a prophet and he had the express what was revealed to him, his own way.

[1926] Genesis 1:1-2 In the beginning when God created the heavens and the earth, 2 the earth was a formless void and darkness covered the face of the deep, while a wind from God swept over the face of the waters.

[1927] 2 Peter 3:8 But do not ignore this one fact, beloved, that with the Lord one day is like a thousand years, and a thousand years are like on day.

[1928] Psalm 50:1 The mighty one, God the Lord, speaks and summons the earth from the rising of the sun to its setting.

[1929] Exodus 34:6 The Lord passed before him, and proclaimed, 'The Lord, the Lord, a God merciful and gracious, slow to anger, and abounding in steadfast love and faithfulness

[1930] Genesis 2:7 then the Lord God formed man from the dust of the ground, and breathed into his nostrils the breath of life; and the man became a living being.

him and breathed into him from His spirit, and made hearing and vision and hearts for you, yet you seldom are grateful. (32:9) And they ask, "When we have decayed into the earth, will we be created anew?" In fact, they are denying that they will meet their Lord. [10] Say, "The angel of death, who has been put in charge of you, will retrieve you. Then you will be brought back to your Lord [11]

If you could only see those who forced others to reject Our messages, bowing their heads before their Lord, (saying), "Our Lord, We have seen and heard, so send us back, and we will do good, we are (now) certain." [12] If it had been Our will, We could have given every soul its guidance, but My word came to be true: "I will surely fill up Hell with jinn and human beings all together. [13] Taste (punishment). Because you ignored the meeting of this Day of your Judgment, We will ignore you, so taste the punishment[1931] of eternity for all you have done."[14]

True believers in Our signs are those who, when they are reminded of them, fall down in prostration[1932], and praise their Lord's limitless glory, and do not think they are too arrogant to do it. [15] They forsake their beds as they call upon their Lord in fear [1933] and hope, and they share with others from what We have provided them. [16] No soul knows what delight[1934] lies in store for them; a reward for what they have done. [17] Is a believer the same as one who was defiantly disobedient? (No), they are not equal. [18] As for those who believed and did good deeds, there will be Gardens of Refuge for them as an accommodation for what they have done. [19] But as for those who defiantly disobeyed, their refuge is the Fire. Every time they want to get out of it, they will be returned to it, while being told, "Taste the punishment of the Fire[1935] which you used to deny." [20] However, We will first let them taste a lesser punishment[1936] (on earth) prior to the greater punishment, so that perhaps they may return (to the right path). [21] Who is more unjust than one who is reminded of the signs of his Lord and then turns away from them? We will make those who force others to reject God's messages to pay a price. [22]

We gave Moses (Musa) the Book, so do not be in doubt that you are receiving the same (revelation). And we made the Book guidance for the Children of Israel. [23] We raised leaders from among them who, as long as they were steadfast and believed firmly in Our messages, guided them according to Our command. [24] Your Lord will judge between them on the Day of Resurrection regarding their differences. [25]

Hasn't it become clear to them yet how many generations We destroyed before them, through whose ruined homes they now walk? In that are signs;

• • •

[1931] Matthew 25:46 And these will go away into eternal punishment, but the righteous into eternal life.'
[1932] Exodus 34:8 'Then Moses quickly went down on his face in worship.' Joshua 5:14 ' . . . Then Joshua, falling down with his face to the earth in worship . . . ' Matthew 26:39 'And he (Jesus) went forward a little and falling down on his face in prayer . . .'
[1933] Psalm 119:62 At midnight I rise to praise you, because of your righteous ordinances.
[1934] 1 Corinthians 2:9 But, as it is written, 'What no eye has seen, nor ear heard, nor the human heart conceived, what God has prepared for those who love him'—
[1935] Matthew 25:41 Then he will say to those at his left hand, "You that are accursed, depart from me into the eternal fire prepared for the devil and his angels;
[1936] Revelation 9:5-6 They were allowed to torture them for five months, but not to kill them, and their torture was like the torture of a scorpion when it stings someone. [6] And in those days people will seek death but will not find it; they will long to die, but death will flee from them.

don't they listen? (26) Have they not seen that We drive rain to barren land and bring forth vegetation from which they and their livestock eat? Do they not see? (27) They say, "When will this judgment be, if you are telling the truth?" (28) Say, "On the Day of Judgment, it will be of no use for the unbelievers to believe, nor will they be given amnesty." (29) So turn away from them and wait. They are waiting. (30)

CHAPTER THIRTY THREE

AL-AHZAB
THE WAR PARTIES

In the name of God, the Merciful-to-all, the Mercy Giver:

Prophet, be mindful of God and do not obey the unbelievers and the hypocrites. God is All-Knowing[1936] and All-Wise.[1937] [(01)] Follow what is revealed to you from your Lord, for God is aware of all you do, [(02)] and put your trust in God, for God is worthy of trust.[1938] [(03)]

God did not place two hearts inside any man's body. Nor has He made your wives whom you equate with your mothers your real mothers, nor has He made your adopted sons your actual sons. These are (merely) words coming out of your mouths. But God speaks the Truth, and He guides to the right path.[1939] [(04)] Call (your adopted sons) after their fathers, this is right in the sight of God, but, if you do not know their fathers, then they are your brothers in faith and entrusted to you. You will not be blamed if you make mistakes (in such matters), but (only for) what your hearts intend. God is most Forgiving and the Mercy giver. [(05)] The Prophet has a higher claim on the believers than (they do on) their own selves, and his wives are their mothers. Blood relations have a higher claim on one another, according to the Book of God, than do other believers and emigrants. Nevertheless, you may act kindly toward your friends. All this is inscribed in the Book.[1940] [(06)]

We took a pledge from the prophets: from you and from Noah, and Abraham, and Moses, and Jesus, the Son of Mary. We took a solemn pledge from them [(07)]

• • •

[1936] 1 John 3:20 whenever our hearts condemn us; for God is greater than our hearts, and he knows everything.

[1937] Proverbs 2:6 For the Lord gives wisdom; from his mouth come knowledge and understanding;

[1938] Psalm 143: Let me hear of your steadfast love in the morning, for in you I put my trust. Teach me the way I should go, for to you I lift up my soul.

[1939] Psalm 23:3 he restores my soul. He leads me in right paths for his name's sake.

[1940] Matthew 7:12 'In everything do to others as you would have them do to you; for this is the law and the prophets.

so that God may question the truthful about their sincerity. And, for the unbelievers He has prepared a painful punishment.[1941] (08)

Believers, remember God's blessings to you when armies came to (attack) you, and We sent a wind and forces that you could not see.[1942] God always sees what you do. (09) When they (the enemy) came at you from above you and from below you, when eyes rolled (in fear), and your hearts rose to your throats, and you had (ill) thoughts of God- (10) there, the believers were tested and severely shaken. (11) The hypocrites and the sick at heart said, "The promise from God and His Messenger is a fantasy," (12) and a faction of them said, "People of Yathrib,[1943] there is nothing for you (here), so return (home)." Yet another group asked permission of the Prophet, saying, "Our houses are exposed," although, in fact they were not. They intended only to flee. (13) Had their town been invaded from every side, and they had been exhorted to revert to idolatry, (the hypocrites) would have done so with very little hesitation, (13) even though they had already pledged before God not to turn back and flee. One is always responsible for a promise made before God.[1944] (15) "Fleeing will not benefit you. If you should flee from death or killing, you will be permitted to enjoy life for only a short while." (16) Say, "Who is it that can prevent God from harming you, if He wishes, or being merciful to you, if He wishes?" They will find no protector or helper other than God.[1945] (17)

God knows those among you who would hold you back, as well as those who would say to their brothers, "Come to us," and hardly go to battle. (18) They do not care about you, and, when fear (of battle) comes, you see them looking at you with their eyes rolling like one overtaken by death. Yet, as soon as the danger has gone, they lash out at you with sharp tongues, resenting any good that comes to you. Such people have no faith, so God has rendered their deeds worthless, that is easy for God. (19) They think the war parties have not (yet) withdrawn, and, if the war parties should come (again), they would wish they were in the desert among the Bedouins, seeking news about you (from a safe distance). Even if they were among you, they would hardly fight at all. (20) The Messenger of God is an excellent model for anyone who puts his hope in God and the Last Day, and remembers God often. (21)

And when the Believers saw the war parties, they said, "This is what God and His Messenger had promised us; God and His Messenger spoke the truth." This only increased their faith and submission. (22) Among the believers are men true to what they promised God. Some died while fulfilling their pledge, and some are still waiting, having never changed in the least. (23) That God may reward the truthful for being true to their pledge and punish the hypocrites, if He wills, or

● ● ●

[1941] 2 Thessalonians 1:9 These will suffer the punishment of eternal destruction, separated from the presence of the Lord and from the glory of his might,

[1942] 2 Kings 6:17 Then Elisha prayed: 'O Lord, please open his eyes that he may see.' So the Lord opened the eyes of the servant, and he saw; the mountain was full of horses and chariots of fire all around Elisha.

[1943] Yathrib is the old name of Medina.

[1944] Ecclesiastes 5:4 When you make a vow to God, do not delay fulfilling it; for he has no pleasure in fools. Fulfil what you vow.

[1945] Judges 10:14 Go and cry to the gods whom you have chosen; let them deliver you in the time of your distress.'

accept their repentance,[1946] for God is the Ever-Forgiving,[1947] the Merciful-to-all.[1948] (24) God drove back the unbelievers in their rage, and they gained no advantage; God spared the believers from fighting, for God is All-Strong [1949] and Almighty.[1950] (25) He brought those People of the Book who supported (the unbelievers) down from their fortresses and threw terror into their hearts. Some of them you killed and others you took captive. (26) He gave you their land, their homes, their property, and a land where you had not set foot before. God is able to do all things. (27)

Prophet, say to your wives, "If your desire is for this worldly life and its finery,[1951] then come, I will provide for you and release you with kindness, (28) but if you desire God, His Messenger, and a home in the Hereafter, then God has prepared a great reward for those among you who do good." (29) Wives of the Prophet, whoever of you should commit a clear immoral act, her punishment would be doubled, and this is easy for God, (30) but the one of you who obeys God and His Messenger and does good deeds, We will give her a double reward, and We have prepared for her a generous provision. (31) Wives of the Prophet, you are not like any of the other woman, provided that you remain mindful of God. Do not, then, be soft spoken, as you do not want the sick at heart to lust after you, but speak in an appropriate manner. (32) Stay at home, and do not display your beauty as you did before, during the time of ignorance. Keep up your prayers, pay alms and obey God and His Messenger. God wishes to remove all impurity from you, people of the household, and to purify you to the utmost degree of purity. (33) And remember all God's messages and Wisdom.[1952] that is recited in your homes, God is Most Subtle and All-Aware (34)

The men and women who have submitted to God, the believing men and women, the obedient men and women, the truthful men and women, the patient men and women, the humble men and women, the charitable men and women, the fasting men and women, the men and women who guard their private parts, and the men and women who remember God often, for them, God has prepared forgiveness and a great reward. (35)

When God and His messenger have decided a matter, it is not for a believing man or a believing woman, to have a choice about it. Anyone who disobeys God and His messenger is clearly misguided. (36)

When you (Muhammad) said to the one whom God has blessed and you have favored, "Keep your wife and be mindful of God," while concealing within yourself that which God was about to disclose. (In doing so) You feared people,

• • •

[1946] Jonah 3:10 When God saw what they did, how they turned from their evil ways, God changed his mind about the calamity that he had said he would bring upon them; and he did not do it.
[1947] Psalm 65:3 When deeds of iniquity overwhelm us, you forgive our transgressions.
[1948] Romans 9:16 So it depends not on human will or exertion, but on God who shows mercy.
[1949] Psalm 18:2 The Lord is my rock, my fortress, and my deliverer, my God, my rock in whom I take refuge, my shield, and the horn of my salvation, my stronghold.
[1950] Psalm 71:16I will come praising the mighty deeds of the Lord God, I will praise your righteousness, yours alone.
[1951] 1 John 2:15-16 Do not love the world or the things in the world. The love of the Father is not in those who love the world; [16] for all that is in the world—the desire of the flesh, the desire of the eyes, the pride in riches—comes not from the Father but from the world.
[1952] Deuteronomy 6:6-7 Keep these words that I am commanding you today in your heart. [7] Recite them to your children and talk about them when you are at home and when you are away, when you lie down and when you rise.

whereas it is God whom you should fear.[1953] So, when Zayd divorced her, We married her to you. We do not want believers to have restrictions concerning their adopted sons' wives after they divorce them, for God's command must be carried out. [37] The Prophet should not have any uneasiness about that which God has ordained for him, since this is God's way with those (prophets) who passed away before. God's will is absolute destiny. [38] (Such is how it is with) those who convey the messages of God, and fear only Him.[1954] God suffices as a reckoner. [39] Muhammad is not the father of (any) one of your men, but (he is) the Messenger of God and last of the prophets. God has knowledge of all things. [40] Believers, remember God often [41] and praise His limitless glory morning and evening. [42] It is He who remembers you, as do His angels, so that He may bring you out of darkness into the enlightenment. He is the Mercy giver to the believers [43] On the Day they meet Him, their greeting will be, "Peace," and He has prepared a generous reward for them. [44]

He it is Who (in return for your remembrance of Him) bestows His special blessings upon you, with His angels (praying and asking His forgiveness for you), that He may lead you out of (all kinds of intellectual, spiritual, social, economic, and political) darkness into light (and keep them firm therein). He is All-Compassionate toward the believers.

Prophet, We have sent you as a witness and a bearer of good news and warning, [45] and as one who calls people to God, with His permission and an illuminated beacon.[1955] [46] Give good news to the believers that they will have great favor from God. [47] Do not follow the call of the unbelievers and the hypocrites; ignore their abuse, but rely on God, for none is as trustworthy as God.[1956] [48] Believers, you have no right to expect a waiting period when you marry believing women and then divorce them before you have touched them, so provide generously for them and give them an honorable release. [49] Prophet, We have made lawful to you your wives to whom you have given their due wedding gifts, and those whom your right hand held in trust, given to you by God, and the daughters of your paternal uncles, the daughters of your paternal aunts, the daughters of your maternal uncles and aunts who migrated with you, and any believing woman who has offered herself to the Prophet if the Prophet wishes to marry her, a privilege (exclusively) for you and not the rest of the believers. We know exactly what We have made obligatory to them concerning their wives and those whom their right hands hold in trust, hence you will not be at fault (if you act according to your privilege), for God is the All-Forgiving, the Mercy giver. [50] You, may make any of them wait, and invite any of them as you wish, but you will not be at fault if you invite one whom you had previously set aside. That is more likely to keep them content and not grieve, and that they should be satisfied with what you have given them. God knows what is in your hearts, for God is All-Knowing and Forbearing. [51] Beyond that, it is not permitted

• • •

[1953] Proverbs 29:25 The fear of others lays a snare, but one who trusts in the Lord is secure.
[1954] Matthew 4:10 Jesus said to him, 'Away with you, Satan! for it is written,
"Worship the Lord your God, and serve only him."
[1955] John 5:35 He was a burning and shining lamp, and you were willing to rejoice for a while in his light.
[1956] 2 Chronicles 14:11 Asa cried to the Lord his God, "O Lord, there is no difference for you between helping the mighty and the weak. Help us, O Lord our God, for we rely on you, and in your name we have come against this multitude. O Lord, you are our God; let no mortal prevail against you.

to you to take any additional women, nor to exchange them for other wives, even if their beauty were to please you, except those from among your own slaves. God is Watchful over all things. (52)

Believers, do not enter the Prophet's houses for a meal except when you are invited, and do not linger, waiting for the food to be ready; but when you are invited, then enter, and, when you have eaten, leave, and do not stay around to chat. That (behavior) troubles the Prophet, and he may be shy about (dismissing) you, but God is not shy about (telling you) the truth. And when you ask (his wives) for something, ask them from behind a partition; that is purer for your hearts and theirs. You are not permitted to offend the Messenger of God or to marry his wives after him, ever; that would be a huge offense in God's sight.(53) Whatever you reveal or conceal, God knows all things. (54) Women are not to blame if they are seen by their fathers, or their sons, or their brothers, or their brothers' sons, or their sisters' sons or their women (servants), or their slaves, if they are mindful of God, for God is the Witness over all things. (55) God and His angels bless the Prophet, so, believers, bless him and give yourselves up in total submission (to his message). (56) Those who insult God and His Messenger, God rejects them in this world and the Hereafter, and has prepared for them a humiliating punishment. (57) And those who unjustifiably harm believing men and women will bear the guilt of slander and clear wrongdoing. (58)

Prophet, tell your wives, your daughters and the believers' women to bring down over themselves (part) of their outer garments[1957]. This will make it more likely that they will be recognized and not abused. God is the All-Forgiving, the Mercy-giver. (59) If the hypocrites and the sick at heart and those who spread bad rumors in Medina do not stop, We will stir you up against them; then they will be living there with you for only a short while. (60) They are cursed, and they should be arrested and put to death wherever they are found. (61) This has been God's way with those who went before, and you will not find any change in the way of God. (62)

People ask you about the Hour (of Judgment). Say," God alone has Knowledge of It.[1958] You never know; the Hour maybe near." (63) The unbelievers have earned God's anger, and He has prepared a Blazing Fire for them. (64) There they will stay forever, where they will find no protector or helper. (65) On the Day, their faces will be turned about in the Fire, and they will say, "How we wish we had obeyed God and obeyed the Messenger." (66) And they will say, "Our Lord, we obeyed our masters and our dignitaries, and they led us down the wrong path. (67) Our Lord, give them double the punishment and curse them in a huge way." (68)

Believers, do not be like those who slandered Moses, but God cleared him of what they said, and that he was distinguished in God's sight. (69) Believers, be mindful of God, and speak in a straightforward way, (70) He will rectify your deeds and forgive you your sins. And whoever obeys God and His Messenger has certainly achieved a great success. (71) We offered the Trust to the heavens, the

• • •

[1957] 1 Corinthians 11:6 'For if a woman is not veiled, let her hair be cut off; but if it is a shame to a woman to have her hair cut off, let her be veiled.'
[1958] Matthew 24:36 "But about that day and hour no one knows, neither the angels of heaven, nor the Son, but only the Father.

earth and the mountains, yet they refused to bear it and feared it, yet man took it on. He has always been unjust and ignorant, [72] (This is in order that) God punishes the hypocrites, men and women, as well as the men and women who associate others with Him, and why God turns mercifully towards the believing men and women, for God is the Ever-Forgiving, the Mercy Giver. [73]

CHAPTER THIRTY FOUR

SABA'

SHEBA

THE **MECCA** PERIOD

In the name of God, the Merciful-to-all, the Mercy Giver:
All) praise is (due) to God, to whom belongs whatever is in the heavens and the earth, and to Him belongs (all) praise in the Hereafter. He is the Wise,[1960] the All-Aware. [(01)] He knows what goes into the earth and what comes out of it, and what comes down from the heaven and what goes up into it.[1961] He is the Mercy-Giver,[1962] the Forgiving.[1963] [(02)] The unbelievers say, "The Hour[1964] of Judgment will never come to us." Say (Prophet), "Yes by God, it will surely come to you. (God is) the Knower of all that is beyond our knowledge."[1965] Not even an atom's weight within the heavens or within the earth escapes His knowledge, nor anything smaller or larger than that. All in a clear record[1966] [(03)] so that He may reward those who believe and do good deeds. They will have forgiveness and generous provision, [(04)] but for those who strive against Our message, trying to undermine it, there will be a painful punishment[1967] of agonizing pain. [(05)]
Those who have been given knowledge see that what is sent down to you from your Lord is the truth, and that it guides to the path of the Almighty, the Praiseworthy. [(06)] The unbelievers say, "Shall we show you a man who will tell you that when you are totally decayed, you will be raised as a new creation? [(07)]

• • •

[1960] Proverbs 2:6 For the Lord gives wisdom; from his mouth come knowledge and understanding;
[1961] Ephesians 4:9-10 (When it says, 'He ascended', what does it mean but that he had also descended into the lower parts of the earth? [10] He who descended is the same one who ascended far above all the heavens, so that he might fill all things.)
[1962] Ephesians 2:4 But God, who is rich in mercy, out of the great love with which he loved us
[1963] Daniel 9:9 To the Lord our God belong mercy and forgiveness, for we have rebelled against him,
[1964] Revelation 14:7 He said in a loud voice, 'Fear God and give him glory, for the hour of his judgment has come; and worship him who made heaven and earth, the sea and the springs of water.'
[1965] Hebrews 11:7 By faith Noah, warned by God about events as yet unseen, respected the warning and built an ark to save his household; by this he condemned the world and became an heir to the righteousness that is in accordance with faith.
[1966] Psalm 139:16 Your eyes beheld my unformed substance. In your book were written all the days that were formed for me, when none of them as yet existed.
[1967] 2 Thessalonians 1:9 These will suffer the punishment of eternal destruction, separated from the presence of the Lord and from the glory of his might,

Has he invented a lie about God or is he mad?" Rather, they who do not believe in the Hereafter will received punishment [1968] and are extremely misguided. [08] Have they not looked at what is before them and what is behind them of the heaven and earth? If We wanted, We could cause the earth to swallow them [1969] or let fragments from the sky fall down on them. [1970] There is a sign in that for every worshiper who turns back to God in repentance. [09]

We gave David great favors from Us: "Mountains, repeat (Our) praises with him, and the birds[1971] (as well)." And We made iron pliable for him, [10] (Instructing him to), "Make full coats of mail, measuring the links carefully. Do good all of you. I am aware of everything you do."[1972] [11] And (We subjected) the wind to Solomon; its morning course (covered) a month's journey, and its evening course (covered) a month's journey. And We made a fountain of molten copper flow for him. And among the jinn were those who worked for him with his Lord's permission, and whoever among them deviated from Our command, We will make him taste of the punishment of the Blazing flame.[1973] [12] They made him whatever he wanted: high arches and statues, bowls like reservoirs, and firmly anchored kettles.[1974] (We said), "Work in gratitude, family of David, for few of My worshipers are grateful." [13] And when We decreed Solomon's death, nothing indicated his death to the jinn except an earthworm eating his staff, but, when he fell down, it became clear to the jinn that, had they known the reality which was beyond their knowledge, they would not have remained in humiliating punishment. [14]

There was a sign (of God's grace) for the people of Sheba in their homeland: two gardens one on the right and one on the left. (They were told), "Eat from the provisions of your Lord, and be grateful to Him for a good land and a forgiving Lord." [15] But they turned away, so We loosed on them the flood from the dam, and We replaced their two gardens with two others of bitter fruit, tamarisks bushes and few thorn trees. [16] This is how We repaid them for their ingratitude. Are any but the ungrateful repaid like this? [17] (Before their demise) We had

• • •

[1968] 2 Peter 2:9 then the Lord knows how to rescue the godly from trial, and to keep the unrighteous under punishment until the day of judgment

[1969] Numbers 16:32-33 The earth opened its mouth and swallowed them up, along with their households—everyone who belonged to Korah and all their goods. 33 So they with all that belonged to them went down alive into Sheol; the earth closed over them, and they perished from the midst of the assembly.

[1970] Genesis 19:24 Then the Lord rained on Sodom and Gomorrah sulphur and fire from the Lord out of heaven;

[1971] Psalm 148:9,10,13 Mountains and all hills, fruit trees and all cedars! 10 Wild animals and all cattle, creeping things and flying birds! 13 Let them praise the name of the LORD, for his name alone is exalted; his glory is above earth and heaven.

[1972] 1 Samuel 2;3 Talk no more so very proudly, let not arrogance come from your mouth; for the Lord is a God of knowledge, and by him actions are weighed.

[1973] Jude 1:7 Likewise, Sodom and Gomorrah and the surrounding cities, which, in the same manner as they, indulged in sexual immorality and pursued unnatural lust, serve as an example by undergoing a punishment of eternal fire.

[1974] 1 Kings 7:40-44 Hiram also made the pots, the shovels, and the basins. So Hiram finished all the work that he did for King Solomon on the house of the Lord: 41 the two pillars, the two bowls of the capitals that were on the tops of the pillars, the two lattice-works to cover the two bowls of the capitals that were on the tops of the pillars; 42 the four hundred pomegranates for the two lattice-works, two rows of pomegranates for each lattice-work, to cover the two bowls of the capitals that were on the pillars; 43 the ten stands, the ten basins on the stands; 44 the one sea, and the twelve oxen underneath the sea.

placed between them and the towns We had blessed other towns within sight of one another to which they could easily have traveled, "Travel safely between them by night or day." [18] But (they complained,) "Our Lord has made the distance between our staging posts so long." (In so doing) they wronged themselves, so We made their fate a tale for all and scattered them in small groups throughout the land. There are certainly signs in this for everyone patient and grateful. [19] What Iblīs thought of them was proven right, since they followed him, except for a group of believers. [20] He had no authority over them[1975] but We wanted to know who believes in the Hereafter and who is in doubt about it. Your Lord is the Preserver over all things. [21]

Say, "Call on those you claim to be gods other than God." They do not have any power over the smallest particle, either in the heavens or on earth,[1976] and they do not have partnership (with Him), nor does He need any assistant from among them. [22] Intercession does not work with Him except when He permits it. (But, on the day of Judgment,) when the terror is removed from their hearts, they will say (to one another), "What has your Lord said?" They will say, "The truth." And He is the Most High, the Most Great. [23] Say, "Who provides for you from the heavens and the earth?"[1977]" Say, "God does. Then either we or you are rightly guided or clearly lost." [24] Say, "You will not be asked about what we have done, and we will not be asked about what you do."[1978] [25] Say, "Our Lord will bring us together; then He will judge between us in truth, for He is the All Knowing,[1979] the Just Decider." [26] Say, "Show me those whom you have joined to Him as partners. No! Rather, He (alone) is God, the Almighty,[1980] the Wise.[1981]" [27] And We have sent you to all people as bearer of good news and to deliver a warning, but most people do not know. [28] And they say, "When is this promise coming,[1982] if you are truthful?" [29] Say, "you have an appointment for a Day[1983] which you can not delay nor bring forward even by a single hour"[1984] [30]

Those who deny the truth say, "We will never believe in this Qur'an or in what came before it." But if only you could only see when the unjust are made to stand

• • •

[1975] 1 John 4:4 Little children, you are from God, and have conquered them; for the one who is in you is greater than the one who is in the world.
[1976] 1 Corinthians 8:4 Hence, as to the eating of food offered to idols, we know that 'no idol in the world really exists', and that 'there is no God but one.'
[1977] Genesis 1:30 And to every beast of the earth, and to every bird of the air, and to everything that creeps on the earth, everything that has the breath of life, I have given every green plant for food.' And it was so.
[1978] Deuteronomy 24:16 Parents shall not be put to death for their children, nor shall children be put to death for their parents; only for their own crimes may persons be put to death.
[1979] 1 John 3:20 whenever our hearts condemn us; for God is greater than our hearts, and he knows everything.
[1980] Psalm 89:8 O Lord God of hosts, who is as mighty as you, O Lord? Your faithfulness surrounds you.
[1981] Psalm 104:24 O Lord, how manifold are your works! In wisdom you have made them all; the earth is full of your creatures.
[1982] 2 Peter 3:4 and saying, 'Where is the promise of his coming? For ever since our ancestors died, all things continue as they were from the beginning of creation!'
[1983] 2 Timothy 4:8 From now on there is reserved for me the crown of righteousness, which the Lord, the righteous judge, will give to me on that day, and not only to me but also to all who have longed for his appearing.
[1984] Matthew 6:27 And can any of you by worrying add a single hour to your span of life?

before their Lord,[1985] blaming each other; those who were thought weak will say to those who had been arrogant, "Had it not been for you, we would have been believers." [31] Those who had been arrogant will say to those who they deemed to be weak, "Did we prevent you from following the right guidance after it had come to you? Rather, you rejected it." [32] Those who had been thought weak will say to those who had been arrogant, "Rather, it was your scheming, night and day, ordering us to deny the truth in God and attribute equals to Him." But when they all see the punishment (that awaits them), they will be unable to express their remorse. We will put shackles around the necks of those who rejected the truth, and they will be repaid only for what they have done.[1986] [33] Never have We sent a warning into a town without those who were corrupted by wealth saying, "We reject the message with which you have been sent." [34] They also say, "We are wealthier and have more children (than you), and We will not be punished."[1987] [35] Say, (Prophet) "My Lord gives abundant provisions to whom He wills, or (likewise) restricts (it), but most people do not know." [36] It is neither your wealth nor your children that will bring you nearer to Us,[1988] but rather (your choice) to believe and to do good deeds. For those there will be double reward for what they did, and they will be safe in the upper chambers (of Paradise). [37] But as for those who rejected Our messages, trying to undermine them, they will be consigned to the punishment. [38] Say, "My Lord gives abundantly to whomever of His worshipers He wills[1989] or (likewise) restricts (it), but whatever you spend (in His cause), He will replace, for[1990] He is the best of providers." [39]

And one Day He will gather them all and say to the angels, "Was it you whom these people worshipped?" [40] They will say, "May You be exalted in Your glory. You are our protector, not them.[1991] Rather, they (the unbelievers) used to worship the jinn; most of them believed in them."[1992] [41] "Today, none of you hold any power to benefit or harm another," and We will say to those who wronged themselves, "Taste the punishment of the Fire, which you used to deny." [42] When our clear verses are recited to them (your people), they say, "This is only a man who wants to turn you away from what your ancestors worshipped."[1993] They (also) say, "This is only a lie that he has invented." When the truth comes to them, the unbelievers say, "This is nothing but sorcery." [43]

• • •

[1985] Romans 14:10 Why do you pass judgment on your brother or sister? Or you, why do you despise your brother or sister? For we will all stand before the judgment seat of God.
[1986] Revelation 22:12 'See, I am coming soon; my reward is with me, to repay according to everyone's work.
[1987] Luke 16:25 But Abraham said, "Child, remember that during your lifetime you received your good things, and Lazarus in like manner evil things; but now he is comforted here, and you are in agony.
[1988] Psalm 49:6-7 those who trust in their wealth and boast of the abundance of their riches?
[7] Truly, no ransom avails for one's life, there is no price one can give to God for it.
[1989] 1 Samuel 2:7 The Lord makes poor and makes rich; he brings low, he also exalts.
[1990] Proverbs 19:17 Whoever is kind to the poor lends to the LORD, and will be repaid in full.
[1991] Samuel 22:47 The Lord lives! Blessed be my rock, and exalted be my God, the rock of my salvation,
[1992] Revelation 9:20 The rest of humankind, who were not killed by these plagues, did not repent of the works of their hands or give up worshipping demons and idols of gold and silver and bronze and stone and wood, which cannot see or hear or walk.
[1993] Judges 2:19 But whenever the judge died, they would relapse and behave worse than their ancestors, following other gods, worshipping them and bowing down to them. They would not drop any of their practices or their stubborn ways.

(Even) though We had not given them any Books to study nor sent any one before you (Prophet) to warn them. [44] Those before them similarly rejected the truth, when they did not received a tenth of what We had given them (your people), yet they (the previous people) rejected My messengers, and how (terrible) was My disapproval. [45]

Say, "The only have one advice for you: Stand up before God, in pairs or individually, and then reflect. Your companion is not crazy. He is here only to warn you of a severe impending punishment."[1994] [46] Say, "The payment for which you think I ask you is yours. My payment comes only from God, and He is the Witness over all things." [47] Say, "My Lord hurls forth the Truth,[1995] for He has the full knowledge of all that is beyond our knowledge." [48] Say, "The truth has come[1996], and falsehood can neither originate anything nor regenerate it." [49] Say, "If I should be misguided, it is only to my own detriment, but if I am guided, it is through what my Lord reveals to me.[1997] He is the All-Hearing, the Near." [50]

If only you could see when they are terrified-but there will be no escape, and they are seized from a place nearby. [51] They will (then) say, "We do believe in it!" But how can they reach it from such a distant place? [52] They had already denied the truth and were prone to guessing from afar about things beyond their perception. [53] A barrier will be placed between them and what they desire, as was done with their kind before, for they too were in hopeless doubt.[1998] [54]

• • •

[1994] Jeremiah 25:29 See, I am beginning to bring disaster on the city that is called by my name, and how can you possibly avoid punishment? You shall not go unpunished, for I am summoning a sword against all the inhabitants of the earth, says the Lord of hosts.

[1995] Jeremiah 5:3 O Lord, do your eyes not look for truth? You have struck them, but they felt no anguish; you have consumed them, but they refused to take correction. They have made their faces harder than rock; they have refused to turn back.

[1996] John 8:32 The truth will set you free.

[1997] Deuteronomy 29:29 The secret things belong to the Lord our God, but the revealed things belong to us and to our children for ever, to observe all the words of this law.

[1998] Romans 1:21 for though they knew God, they did not honor him as God or give thanks to him, but they became futile in their thinking, and their senseless minds were darkened.

CHAPTER **THIRTY FIVE**

FATIR²⁰⁰⁰

THE CREATOR/PROGRAMMER

In the name of God, the Merciful-to-all, the Mercy Giver:
(All) praise is due to God, the Programmer²⁰⁰⁰ of the heavens and the earth.²⁰⁰¹ He made the angels messengers²⁰⁰² with wings, two, three and four (pairs).²⁰⁰³ He adds to His creation anyway He wills, for God has power over all things²⁰⁰⁴ ⁽⁰¹⁾ Whatever mercy God grants to people, no one can prevent, whatever He withholds, no one can release, for He is the Almighty,²⁰⁰⁵ the Wise.²⁰⁰⁶ ⁽⁰²⁾ People, remember the favor of God upon you.²⁰⁰⁷ Is there any creator other than God²⁰⁰⁸ who provides for you from the heaven and earth? There is no God except Him, so what lies are you inventing? ⁽⁰³⁾ And if they deny

• • •

¹⁹⁹⁹ The Arabic word "Fatir" is an attribute of God that means the Creator who separated His creation and gave each a purpose.
²⁰⁰⁰ Fater was traditionally translated as the Creator, the Originator, the Bringer into Being etc. . . But we investigated the meaning, searching dictionaries, classical commentaries, as well as discussions with various scholars, and we discovered that the meaning of Fater should be the Creator who separated and gave purpose to each of His creations
²⁰⁰¹ Genesis 2:1-3 Thus the heavens and the earth were finished, and all their multitude. And on the seventh day God finished the work that he had done, and he rested on the seventh day from all the work that he had done. So God blessed the seventh day and hallowed it, because on it God rested from all the work that he had done in creation.
²⁰⁰² Hebrews 1:14 Are not all angels spirits in the divine service, sent to serve for the sake of those who are to inherit salvation?
²⁰⁰³ Revelation 4:8 And the four living creatures, each of them with six wings, are full of eyes all around and inside. Day and night without ceasing they sing, 'Holy, holy, holy, the Lord God the Almighty, who was and is and is to come.'
²⁰⁰⁴ 1 Chronicles 29:11 Yours, O Lord, are the greatness, the power, the glory, the victory, and the majesty; for all that is in the heavens and on the earth is yours; yours is the kingdom, O Lord, and you are exalted as head above all.
²⁰⁰⁵ Luke 1:49-50 for the Mighty One has done great things for me, and holy is his name. ⁵⁰ His mercy is for those who fear him from generation to generation.
²⁰⁰⁶ 1 Corinthians 1:25 For God's foolishness is wiser than human wisdom, and God's weakness is stronger than human strength.
²⁰⁰⁷ Psalm 105:5 Remember the wonderful works he has done, his miracles, and the judgments he has uttered,
²⁰⁰⁸ Isaiah 44:8 This God—his way is perfect; the promise of the Lord proves true; he is a shield for all who take refuge in him.

you, (Prophet), other messengers were denied before you. To God will all matters be returned. (04)

People, God's promise is true,[2009] so do not let the worldly life delude you, and don't let the deceiver deceive you about God. (05) Satan is your enemy, so treat him as an enemy. His call on his followers (will only lead them) to be among those of the Blazing Fire. (06) The unbelievers will have a severe punishment,[2010] and those who believe and do good deeds will have forgiveness and great reward.[2011] (07) What about the one whose evil deeds were made to look attractive to him so he regards them as good? God lets stray (those) who choose (to be misguided)[2012] and guides (those) who choose (guidance). So don't let your sorrow over them destroy you. God knows what they do. (08)

It is God who sends the winds, which lift the clouds, which We then drive to a dead land and thereby bring the earth to life after its death. Such is the resurrection.[2013] (09) Whoever desires might, (they should know that) all might belongs to God. To Him all good words ascend, and He lifts up righteous deeds. But they who plot evil deeds will have a severe punishment, and their plots will perish.[2014] (10) God created you from dust,[2015] then from a drop of sperm, and then He made you into pairs.[2016] No female conceives nor does she give birth without His knowledge,[2017] and no being grows old or has his life cut short except in accordance with a record. That is easy for God. (11)

The two seas are not alike: one is fresh and sweet, suitable for drinking, and the other is salty and bitter.[2018] Yet from each you eat fresh meat and extract ornaments to wear. You see ships making their way through [2019] (each of them)

• • •

[2009] Psalm 18:30 This God—his way is perfect; the promise of the Lord proves true; he is a shield for all who take refuge in him.
[2010] Ezekiel 5:15 You shall be a mockery and a taunt, a warning and a horror, to the nations around you, when I execute judgments on you in anger and fury, and with furious punishments —I, the Lord, have spoken—
[2011] Luke 6:35 But love your enemies, do good, and lend, expecting nothing in return. Your reward will be great, and you will be children of the Most High; for he is kind to the ungrateful and the wicked.
[2012] Romans 9:18, So then he has mercy on whomsoever he chooses, and he hardens the heart of whomsoever he chooses. 2 Thessalonians 2:11 For this reason God sends them a powerful delusion, leading them to believe what is false,
[2013] 1 Corinthians 15:42 So it is with the resurrection of the dead. What is sown is perishable, what is raised is imperishable.
[2014] Psalm 2:1-6 Why do the nations conspire, and the peoples plot in vain? [2] The kings of the earth set themselves, and the rulers take counsel together, against the Lord and his anointed, saying, [3] 'Let us burst their bonds asunder, and cast their cords from us.' [4] He who sits in the heavens laughs; the Lord has them in derision. [5] Then he will speak to them in his wrath, and terrify them in his fury, saying, [6] 'I have set my king on Zion, my holy hill.'
[2015] Genesis 2:7 then the Lord God formed man from the dust of the ground, and breathed into his nostrils the breath of life; and the man became a living being.
[2016] Genesis 2:22 And the rib that the Lord God had taken from the man he made into a woman and brought her to the man.
[2017] Psalm 139:13-15 For it was you who formed my inward parts; you knit me together in my mother's womb. [14] I praise you, for I am fearfully and wonderfully made. Wonderful are your works; that I know very well. [15] My frame was not hidden from you, when I was being made in secret, intricately woven in the depths of the earth.
[2018] James 3:10-11 From the same mouth come blessing and cursing. My brothers and sisters, this ought not to be so. [11] Does a spring pour forth from the same opening both fresh and brackish water?
[2019] James 3:4 Or look at ships: though they are so large that it takes strong winds to drive them, yet they are guided by a very small rudder wherever the will of the pilot directs.

so that you might seek His bounty and so perhaps you will be thankful.[12] He merges the night into the day and the day into the night, and has made the sun and the moon[2020] subservient (to His laws), each running (its course) for an appointed time. This is God, your Lord. Sovereignty belongs to Him,[2021] while those whom you invoke beside Him do not even control (as much as) the skin of a date seed. [13] If you invoke them, they do not hear you [2022] and even if they could hear, they would not respond to you.[2023] On the Day of Resurrection, they will reject your having associated them with God, and no one can inform you (of the Truth) like the One who is All-Aware.[14]

People, you are in need of God, while God is the Rich Beyond Need, the One Praiseworthy.[2024] [15] If He wishes, He can do away with you and bring forth a new creation, [16] (which) for God is not difficult. [17] No bearer of burdens will bear the burdens of another.[2025] and if a heavily laden soul calls (another) to (carry some of) its load, nothing of it will be carried, even if they were related. You can only warn those who stand in awe of their Lord even though He is beyond the reach of their perception, and those who perform prayer. Whoever purifies himself (does so) for the good of his soul.[2026] God is the (final) destination. [18] The blind and the seeing are not equal, [19] nor are ignorance and enlightenment,[2027] [20] nor shade and heat, [21] nor are the living and the dead alike. God can make anyone He wills hear, but you cannot make those in the grave hear. [22] You are only a warner. [23] We have sent you with the Truth as a bearer of good news and a warner, for there is no community to which a warner has not come. [24] If they reject you, those before them also rejected the truth. Their messengers came to them with clear signs and Psalms and with the enlightening Book.[2028] [25] Then I seized the ones who denied the truth, and how (terrible) was My punishment.[2029] [26]

· · ·

[2020] Genesis 1:16-18 God made the two great lights—the greater light to rule the day and the lesser light to rule the night—and the stars. God set them in the dome of the sky to give light upon the earth, to rule over the day and over the night, and to separate the light from the darkness. And God saw that it was good.

[2021] Daniel 4:3 How great are his signs, how mighty his wonders! His kingdom is an everlasting kingdom, and his sovereignty is from generation to generation.

[2022] Psalm 135:17 they have ears, but they do not hear, and there is no breath in their mouths.

[2023] Isaiah 46:7 They lift it to their shoulders, they carry it, they set it in its place, and it stands there; it cannot move from its place. If one cries out to it, it does not answer or save anyone from trouble.

[2024] Revelation 4:11 'You are worthy, our Lord and God, to receive glory and honor and power, for you created all things, and by your will they existed and were created.'

[2025] Galatians 6:5 "For every one shall bear his own burden".

[2026] 2 Timothy 2:21 All who cleanse themselves of the things I have mentioned will become special utensils, dedicated and useful to the owner of the house, ready for every good work.

[2027] 2 Corinthians 6:14 Do not be mismatched with unbelievers. For what partnership is there between righteousness and lawlessness? Or what fellowship is there between light and darkness?

[2028] Psalm 19:8 the precepts of the Lord are right, rejoicing the heart; the commandment of the Lord is clear, enlightening the eyes;

[2029] Ezekiel 25:17 I will execute great vengeance on them with wrathful punishments. Then they shall know that I am the Lord, when I lay my vengeance on them.

Don't you see that God sends down rain from the sky,[2030] with which produce fruits of varying colors,[2031] (just as) in the mountains there are layers, white and red of varying shades, and some extremely black? [(27)] Similarly, among people, animals, and livestock there are also many hues. Of all of his worshipers, only those with knowledge, are amazed at God. God is Almighty,[2032] most forgiving.[2033] [(28)] Those who recite the Book of God, and perform prayer and spend out (on charity) from what We have provided them, secretly[2034] and openly, may expect a trade that will never perish, [(29)] for He may give them their full rewards and increase for them out of His bounty. He is ever-forgiving [2035] and ever-thankful.[2036] [(30)]

What We revealed to you of the Book, is the very Truth, confirming what is available to you of previous revelations. God is All-Aware of His worshipers, and All-Seeing. [(31)] We then bestowed this Book as an inheritance on those of our worshipers whom We selected; and among them are some who wrong their own souls, some are moderate, and some who, by God's grace, are foremost in good deeds. That is the greatest favor, [(32)] for they will enter Gardens of Eden, where they will be adorned with bracelets of gold and pearls, and where their garments will be silk. [(33)] They will say, "Praise be to God, who has removed all our sorrow from us,[2037] for Our Lord is truly ever-forgiving[2038] and ever-thankful[2039] [(34)] it is He who has settled us in the everlasting Home[2040] out of His favor where no weariness or fatigue will touch us." [(35)] But the unbelievers will be in Hell, where they will neither be finished off and die,[2041] nor will they be relived from Hell's punishment[2042] That is how we reward everyone who is ungrateful. [(36)] They will cry out loud, "Our Lord, let us out; We will do good deeds, different from what we were doing before!" "But didn't We give you sufficient time so that those

• • •

[2030] Zechariah 10:1 Ask rain from the Lord in the season of the spring rain, from the Lord who makes the storm-clouds, who gives showers of rain to you, the vegetation in the field to everyone.
[2031] Leviticus 26:4 I will give you your rains in their season, and the land shall yield its produce, and the trees of the field shall yield their fruit.
[2032] Psalm 93:4 More majestic than the thunders of mighty waters, more majestic than the waves of the sea, majestic on high is the Lord!
[2033] Ephesians 2:4 But God, who is rich in mercy, out of the great love with which he loved us
[2034] Matthew 6:1-4 'Beware of practicing your piety before others in order to be seen by them; for then you have no reward from your Father in heaven. [2] 'So whenever you give alms, do not sound a trumpet before you, as the hypocrites do in the synagogues and in the streets, so that they may be praised by others. Truly I tell you, they have received their reward. [3] But when you give alms, do not let your left hand know what your right hand is doing, [4] so that your alms may be done in secret; and your Father who sees in secret will reward you.
[2035] 1 John 1:9 If we confess our sins, he who is faithful and just will forgive us our sins and cleanse us from all unrighteousness.
[2036] Psalm 107, O give thanks to the Lord, for he is good; for his steadfast love endures for ever.
[2037] Revelation 21:4 he will wipe every tear from their eyes. Death will be no more; mourning and crying and pain will be no more, for the first things have passed away.'
[2038] Daniel 9:9 To the Lord our God belong mercy and forgiveness, for we have rebelled against him,
[2039] Psalm 107, O give thanks to the Lord, for he is good; for his steadfast love endures for ever.
[2040] Revelation 21:3 And I heard a loud voice from the throne saying, 'See, the home of God is among mortals. He will dwell with them; they will be his peoples, and God himself will be with them;
[2041] Matthew 25:46 And these will go away into eternal punishment, but the righteous into eternal life.'
[2042] Revelation 20:10 And the devil who had deceived them was thrown into the lake of fire and sulphur, where the beast and the false prophet were, and they will be tormented day and night for ever and ever.

who would be mindful could be mindful? And we even sent you the warner. Taste, then, (the punishment), for the unjust will have no helper. [37] God knows all the unknown of the heavens and earth;[2043] He Knows what is in the hearts.[2044] [38] It is He who has put you in charge of the earth. Whoever denies the truth will bear the consequences. Their denial will increase their rejection in the sight of their Lord, and their denial will only increase their loss. [39] Say, "Have you considered your 'partners' whom you invoke besides God? Show me what part of earth they have created, or do they have a partnership (with Him) in the heavens? Or have We given them a Book that has clear evidence? (No indeed); Rather, the unjust promise each other nothing but delusion."[2045] [40] God upholds the heavens and the earth lest they fall apart, and, should they fall apart, no one other than He could hold them (in place), for He is forbearing and most forgiving. [41]

They swore by God their most solemn oaths that, if a warning came to them, they would be better guided than any one of the previous communities. But, when a warner did come to them, they only turned further away [42] because of their arrogance on earth and their evil schemes. Yet evil schemes overwhelm only those who plot them.[2046] Do they expect anything different, given what happened to earlier people? You will never find any change in the way of God, and you will never find any deviation in the His way. [43] Have they not traveled through the land and observed the final fate of those who preceded them, who were even greater than they in strength? Nothing in the heavens or earth will prevent God from accomplishing His purpose, for He is All-Knowing, infinite in His power.[2047] [44] Were God to take people to task for what they have earned, He would not leave any creature on the earth, but He defers them for a specified time. Then when their time comes, God sees all that is in (the hearts of) His worshipers. [2048] [45]

• • •

[2043] Psalm 139:1-6 O Lord, you have searched me and known me. [2] You know when I sit down and when I rise up; you discern my thoughts from far away. [3] You search out my path and my lying down, and are acquainted with all my ways. [4] Even before a word is on my tongue, O Lord, you know it completely. [5] You hem me in, behind and before, and lay your hand upon me. [6] Such knowledge is too wonderful for me; it is so high that I cannot attain it.
[2044] 1 Samuel 16:7 But the Lord said to Samuel, 'Do not look on his appearance or on the height of his stature, because I have rejected him; for the LORD does not see as mortals see; they look on the outward appearance, but the Lord looks on the heart.'
[2045] 1 Samuel 12:21 and do not turn aside after useless things that cannot profit or save, for they are useless.
[2046] Proverbs 26:27 Whoever digs a pit will fall into it, and a stone will come back on the one who starts it rolling.
[2047] Job 42:2 'I know that you can do all things, and that no purpose of yours can be thwarted.
[2048] Psalm 34:22 The Lord redeems the life of his servants; none of those who take refuge in him will be condemned.

CHAPTER **THIRTY SIX**

YA SEEN
YASIN

THE **MECCA** PERIOD

In the name of God, the Merciful-to-all, the Mercy Giver:
Ya Seen,[2048] (01) by the wise Qur'an (02) you are one of the messengers, (03) on a straight path. (04) This revelation has been brought down from the Almighty,[2049] the Merciful[2050] (05) to warn a people whose forefathers were not warned, so they are unaware. (06) (However), the word (of God) is bound to come true for most of them, for they will not believe. (07) We have put shackles round their necks, reaching to their chins, so that their heads are forced up, (08) and We have put a barrier before them and behind them, and have blindfolded them, so that they cannot see. (09) It is all the same to them whether you warn them or do not warn them, they won't believe. (10) You can only warn someone who follows the message and stands in awe of the Merciful-to-all[2051] even though He is beyond his perception. So give him good news of forgiveness[2052] and generous reward.[2053] (11) It is We who bring the dead to life, and record what they have done and the results of their deeds. We account for everything in a clear record.[12]
Give them the example of the people whose town was visited by the messengers (13) We sent two to them, but they rejected both, so We reinforced them with a third, and they declared, "We are messengers to you." (14) They replied, "You are only human beings like us, and the Merciful-to-all has not revealed a thing. You are only telling lies." (15) They said, "Our Lord knows that we are messengers to you, (16) and we are responsible only for delivering (the message) clearly." (17) They said, "We feel that you are an evil omen. If you do not stop, We will surely stone you, and cause you to suffer severely." (18) They said, "Your evil omen is upon you. How can it be evil that you were reminded

• • •

2048 Here and at the beginning of many chapters there are letters of unknown meaning called Al Muquatta'at. Numerous theories have been proposed, but there is no agreement on what they signify yet.
2049 Isaiah 28:2 See, the Lord has one who is mighty and strong; like a storm of hail, a destroying tempest, like a storm of mighty, overflowing waters; with his hand he will hurl them down to the earth.
2050 Psalm 130:4 But there is forgiveness with you, so that you may be revered.
2051 Romans 11:32 For God has imprisoned all in disobedience so that he may be Merciful-to-all.
2052 Daniel 9:9 To the Lord our God belong mercy and forgiveness, for we have rebelled against him
2053 Jeremiah 17:10 I the Lord test the mind and search the heart, to give to all according to their ways, according to the fruit of their doings

(about God)? You are rather going too far." [19] Then a man came running from the farthest end of the town, saying, "O, my people, follow the Messengers. [20] Follow those who do not ask you for (any) payment; they are (rightly) guided. [21] Why should I not worship the One who brought me into being and gave me a purpose and to whom you will be returned?[2054] [22] Would I take any gods other than Him? if the Merciful intends me some harm, their intercession will not help me at all, nor can they save me.[2055] [23] I would then be clearly misguided. [24] I have believed in your Lord, so listen to me." [25] It was said (to him), "Enter Paradise." He said, "I wish that my people only knew [26] how my Lord has forgiven me and placed me among the highly honored."[2056] [27] After him, We did not send any host from heaven to his people, nor would We send one down. [28] It was only one shout, and immediately they were extinguished. [29]

Alas for our servants. Whenever a messenger comes to them, they ridicule him.[2057] [30] Have they not considered how many generations We destroyed before them, none of whom will ever come back to them? [31] Yet each and every one of them will be brought before Us. [32] A sign for them is the dead land that We have brought to life; from it We have brought forth grain, from which they eat.[2058] [33] And We have placed gardens of palm trees and grapevines in it, and caused springs of water to burst from it, [34] so that they may eat its fruit. It was not their hands that produced it, will they not be grateful? [35] Exalted in His glory is He who created pairs out of whatever the earth produces,[2059] as well as from themselves and from other things unknown to them. [36] Night is a sign for them. We remove the daylight from it, so they are (left) in darkness, [37] and the sun runs its course toward its destined point. Such is the determination of the Almighty, the All-Knowing.[2060][38] And the moon, We have determined its phases, until it finally appears like the old date-palm stalk. [39] The sun is not allowed to reach the moon, nor does the night overtake the day, but each floats in its' own orbit. [2061] [40]

• • •

[2054] Psalm 57:1-2 1 Be merciful to me, O God, be merciful to me, for in you my soul takes refuge; in the shadow of your wings I will take refuge, until the destroying storms pass by. [2] I cry to God Most High, to God who fulfills his purpose for me.

[2055] Isaiah 45:20 Assemble yourselves and come together, draw near, you survivors of the nations! They have no knowledge—those who carry about their wooden idols, and keep on praying to a god that cannot save.

[2056] Psalm 84:11 For the LORD God is a sun and shield; he bestows favor and honor. No good thing does the Lord withhold from those who walk uprightly.

[2057] Matthew 27:29 and after twisting some thorns into a crown, they put it on his head. They put a reed in his right hand and knelt before him and mocked him, saying, 'Hail, King of the Jews!'

[2058] Job 38:25-27 'Who has cut a channel for the torrents of rain, and a way for the thunderbolt, [26] to bring rain on a land where no one lives, on the desert, which is empty of human life, [27] to satisfy the waste and desolate land, and to make the ground put forth grass?

[2059] Genesis 1:21-22 So God created the great sea monsters and every living creature that moves, of every kind, with which the waters swarm, and every winged bird of every kind. And God saw that it was good. [22] God blessed them, saying, 'Be fruitful and multiply and fill the waters in the seas, and let birds multiply on the earth.'

[2060] 1 John 3:20 whenever our hearts condemn us; for God is greater than our hearts, and he knows everything.

[2061] Ecclesiastes 1:5, The sun rises and the sun goes down, and hurries to the place where it rises. Genesis 1:16 God made the two great lights—the greater light to rule the day and the lesser light to rule the night—and the stars.

Another sign for them is that We carried their offspring in the loaded Ark.[2062] [41] And that We have created for them similar vessels in which to ride. [42] If We wish, We could drown them, with no one to respond to their cry for help, nor would they be saved, [43] except through Our mercy, that they could be given a while to enjoy life. [44] But when they are told, "Beware of what lies before you and what lies behind you; perhaps you will be shown mercy," [45] they turn away from every sign that comes to them from their Lord. [46] And when It is said to them, "Give to others from what God has provided for you,"[2063] the unbelievers say to those who believe, "Should we feed one whom, if God had willed, He would have fed? You are clearly misguided." [47] They say, "When will this promise come about, if you are truthful?" [48] All it takes is one blast that will seize them while they still arguing about it. [49] They will not be able (to give) any testimony, nor will they return to their people. [50]

And then the Horn will be blown,[2064] and at once they will rush out of the graves to their Lord. [51] They will say, "How terrible for us! Who has raised us up from our resting-place?" (They will be told), "This is what the Merciful-to-all had promised, and the Messengers told the Truth." [52] It will be only one blast, and at once they are all brought before Us. [53] "Today no soul will be wronged at all, and you will be repaid[2065] for what you did." [54] The people of Paradise will on that Day be joyfully engaged; [55] they and their spouses will lie in shades, reclining on couches [56] where they will have fruit and whatever they wish, [57] and their Lord, the Mercy giver, will great them with "Peace." [58] (But to the guilty, He will say), "Those who forced others to reject Our messages should stand apart today." [59] Children of Adam, did I not make a covenant with you not to worship Satan, who is clearly your enemy, [60] and that you worship (only) Me? This is a straight path. [61] (Satan) has already led a great many of you astray; why do you not use your reason? [62] This is the Hell that you were promised. [63] Enter it today as a result of your having denied the truth." [64]

Today, We will seal over their mouths, but their hands will speak to Us, and their feet will testify about what they used to do. [65] And if We willed it, We could have taken away their sight, and they would have struggled to (find) the path, but how could they have seen it? [66] And if We had so willed, We could have crippled them where they stood, so that they could move neither forward nor backward. [67] When We grant a person long life, We also cause him to decline in power, so will they not understand? [68]

We did not teach (the Prophet) poetry, nor it is suitable for him. This is simply a reminder and a self-evident Qur'an [69] to warn those whose hearts are alive, and to pass God's verdict against the unbelievers. [70] Can they not see that, by Our own handiwork, We have created livestock,[2066] for them, that they now

• • •

[2062] Genesis 7:17 The flood continued for forty days on the earth; and the waters increased, and bore up the ark, and it rose high above the earth.

[2063] Luke 6:38 give, and it will be given to you. A good measure, pressed down, shaken together, running over, will be put into your lap; for the measure you give will be the measure you get back.'

[2064] 1 Corinthians 15:52 in a moment, in the twinkling of an eye, at the last trumpet. For the trumpet will sound, and the dead will be raised imperishable, and we will be changed.

[2065] Luke 14:14 And you will be blessed, because they cannot repay you, for you will be repaid at the resurrection of the righteous.'

[2066] Genesis 1:24 And God said, 'Let the earth bring forth living creatures of every kind: cattle and creeping things and wild animals of the earth of every kind.' And it was so.

control? [71] We have tamed (those animals) for them, so that they can ride some of them, and some they can eat, [72] and some have other benefits, (such as milk) to drink. Will they not, then, be grateful? [73] Yet they have taken (false) gods besides God, hoping that they will help them, [74] but (their false gods) cannot help them, even if they were soldiers standing by, ready to support them. [75] So do not let what they say grieve you. We know what they conceal [2067] and what they reveal. [76]

Does a human being not consider that We created him from a (mere) drop of sperm, yet he becomes a fierce adversary? [77] Now, he argues about Us while he overlooks how he himself was created. He says, "Who will give life to bones when they are disintegrated?" [2068] [78] Say, "He who made them in the first instance will give them life again [2069] He has full knowledge of all creation, [79] He, who produces fire for you from green trees, so that you use them to light your fires." [80] Is not He who created the heavens and the earth able to create the same again? Yes, indeed, for He is the All-Knowing[2070] the Creator.[2071] [81] When He wills something to be, His simply says, "Be"– and it is.[2072] [82] Exalted in His glory is He who has the Dominion of all things in His hand,[2073] and to Him you will return.[2074] [83]

•   •   •

[2067] Luke 8:17 For nothing is hidden that will not be disclosed, nor is anything secret that will not become known and come to light.

[2068] Ezekiel 37:1-6 The hand of the LORD came upon me, and he brought me out by the spirit of the Lord and set me down in the middle of a valley; it was full of bones. 2 He led me all round them; there were very many lying in the valley, and they were very dry. 3 He said to me, 'Mortal, can these bones live?' I answered, 'O Lord God, you know.' 4 Then he said to me, 'Prophesy to these bones, and say to them: O dry bones, hear the word of the Lord. 5 Thus says the Lord GOD to these bones: I will cause breath to enter you, and you shall live. 6 I will lay sinews on you, and will cause flesh to come upon you, and cover you with skin, and put breath in you, and you shall live; and you shall know that I am the Lord.'

[2069] Romans 4:17 as it is written, 'I have made you the father of many nations')—in the presence of the God in whom he believed, who gives life to the dead and calls into existence the things that do not exist.

[2070] Psalm 44:21 Would not God find this out? For He knows the secrets of the heart

[2071] Isaiah 40:28 Have you not known? Have you not heard? The Lord is the everlasting God, the Creator of the ends of the earth. He does not faint or grow weary; his understanding is unsearchable.

[2072] Psalm 33: 9 For he spoke, and it came to be; he commanded, and it stood firm.

[2073] Psalm 8:1-2 O Lord, our Sovereign, how majestic is your name in all the earth! You have set your glory above the heavens. 2 Out of the mouths of babes and infants you have founded a bulwark because of your foes, to silence the enemy and the avenger.

[2074] Ecclesiastes 12:7 and the dust returns to the earth as it was, and the breath returns to God who gave it.

CHAPTER THIRTY SEVEN

AS-SAFFAT
THE RANKS

THE **MECCA** PERIOD

In the name of God, the Merciful-to-all, the Mercy Giver:
By those lined up in ranks, [01] and those who warn, crying warnings, [02] and those who recite God's word, [03] your God is One, [2075] [04] Lord of the heavens and the earth and everything between them, Lord of every sunrise. [05] We have adorned the nearest heaven with planets [06] and protected them against every rebellious devil, [07] (so that the devils) may not listen to the highest assembly (of angels) but be repelled from every side, [08] driven away. For them there is a continuous punishment, [2076] [09] except for him who snatches a glimpse (of such knowledge), He will be pursued by a piercing flame [10]

Then ask those who persist on denying the truth if they were more difficult to create than those other beings We have created, for We created them from sticky clay. [2077] [11] No wonder you are surprised, to see them ridicule (the message), [12] and when they are reminded (of the Truth), they don't want to remember, [13] and when they see a sign, they ridicule it, [2078] [14] saying, "This is mere magic. [15] When We have died and become dust and bones, are we to be resurrected, [16] and our forefathers too?" [17] Say, "Yes, and (on that Day of Judgment) you will be humiliated." [18] (On that Day,) there will be only a single shout, and at once they will begin to see. [19] They will say, "How terrible for us!

• • •

[2075] 2 Kings 19:15, And Hezekiah prayed before the Lord, and said: 'O Lord the God of Israel, who are enthroned above the cherubim, you are God, you alone, of all the kingdoms of the earth; you have made heaven and earth.
[2076] 2 Thessalonians 1:9 These will suffer the punishment of eternal destruction, separated from the presence of the Lord and from the glory of his might,
[2077] Genesis 2:7 then the Lord God formed man from the dust of the ground, and breathed into his nostrils the breath of life; and the man became a living being.
[2078] 2 Chronicles 36:16 but they kept mocking the messengers of God, despising his words, and scoffing at his prophets, until the wrath of the Lord against his people became so great that there was no remedy.

This is the Day of Judgment," [20] and (They will be told), "This is the Day of separation (between the good and the bad), which you used to deny."[2079] [21]
(The angels will be ordered), "Gather those who were unjust, all those like them, and the idols they used to worship [22] instead of God, and show them to the path of Hell [23] And stop them, for they are to be questioned: [24] "Why do you not help each other now?" [25] No, today they come in absolute submission, [26] and they will turn on one another, questioning each other. [27] (Some) will say, "You used to approach us from a position of power." [28] The others will say, "No, you (yourselves) were not believers, [29] and we had no authority over you, but you were exceedingly arrogant people. [30] Our Lord's Word has been carried out against us, and we will all taste punishment. [31] We misled you, and we were ourselves misled." [32] On that Day, they will share in the punishment,[2080] [33] for that is how We deal with those who forced others to reject Our messages. [34] Whenever they were told, "There is no god but God," they became arrogant, [35] and would say, "Are we to give up our gods for a mad poet?" [36] Rather, the Prophet has come with the Truth and confirmed the (previous) messengers. [37] You (who deny the truth) will taste the painful punishment,[2081] [38] and you will be repaid only for what you used to do [39]
Not so for God's devoted worshipers, [40] they will have recognizable provision, [41] of fruits, and they will be honored [42] in Gardens of delight,[2082][43] (resting) on couches and facing one another. [44] A cup from a flowing spring will be passed among them, [45] white and delicious to the drinkers, [46] which will neither sicken nor intoxicate them. [47] With them are mates of modest gaze with beautiful eyes [48] just like closely guarded pearls. [49] They will turn to one another, inquiring [50] One of them says" I used to have a friend (on earth) [51] who used to say to me, are you of those who believe [52] that, when we have died and become dust and bones, we will be brought for judgment?'" [53] And he will add, "Shall we look for him?" [54] And he looks and sees (his former companion) in the midst of Hell. [55] He says to him, "By God, you almost ruined me. [56] Were It not for the grace of my Lord, I would have been with those taken (to Hell). [57] Then, (he says to those in paradise), "Will we really not die [58] except for our first death, and will we really not be punished?" [59] Truly, this is the ultimate success." [60] This is what everyone should strive to attain. [61]
Is Paradise a better place to be, or the tree of Bitterness? [62] We have made (this tree) a punishment for the unjust. [63] It is a tree that grows in the heart of Hell, [64] Its fruit like devils' heads, [65] and (the people in Hell) will eat from it and fill their bellies with it. [66] On top of that, they will have a boiling brew to drink.

• • •

[2079] Matthew 25:41 Then he will say to those at his left hand, "You that are accursed, depart from me into the eternal fire prepared for the devil and his angels;
[2080] Matthew 25:46 And these will go away into eternal punishment, but the righteous into eternal life.'
[2081] Revelation 20:10 And the devil who had deceived them was thrown into the lake of fire and sulphur, where the beast and the false prophet were, and they will be tormented day and night for ever and ever.
[2082] Revelation 22:1-5 Then the angel showed me the river of the water of life, bright as crystal, flowing from the throne of God and of the Lamb through the middle of the street of the city. On either side of the river is the tree of life with its twelve kinds of fruit, producing its fruit each month; and the leaves of the tree are for the healing of the nations. 4 Nothing accursed will be found there any more. But the throne of God and of the Lamb will be in it, and his servants will worship him; they will see his face, and his name will be on their foreheads. 5 And there will be no more night; they need no light of lamp or sun, for the Lord God will be their light, and they will reign for ever and ever.

(67) Then they will return to Hell, (68) for they found their fathers misguided, (69) so they rushed (to follow) in their footsteps. (70) Most of the earlier peoples went astray before them, (71) though We had already sent them someone to give warning. (72) Look, then, at the final fate of those who were warned, (73) except for the devout worshipers of God. (74)

Noah called Us, and how excellent was Our response.2083 (75) We saved him and his family from the great distress.2084 (76) We made his descendants the survivors,2085 (77) and left for him (favorable mention) among later generations: (78) "Peace upon Noah, among all people." (79) This is how we reward those who do good, (80) for he was among Our believing worshipers.2086 (81) We drowned the rest.2087 (82)

Abraham was like him2088 (83) He came to his Lord with a faultless heart, (84) and said to his father and his people, "What are you worshiping? (85) Are you fooling yourselves by choosing false gods other than God? (86) What do you think about the Lord of the worlds?" (87) Then he took a look at the stars (88) and said, "I am sick (of you worshipping these)," (89) so they turned away from him and left. (90) Then he turned to their gods and said, "Will you not eat? (91) What is wrong with you that you do not speak?" (92) And he turned on them, striking them with his right hand. (93) His people came rushing back to him. (94) He said, "How can you worship that which you (yourselves) carve, (95) while God created you and everything you do?" (96) They said, "Construct a furnace and throw him into the burning fire." (97) They plotted against him, but We humiliated them (98)

(Abraham) said, "I will go away to my Lord, He will guide me. (99) My Lord, grant me a righteous son." (100) So We gave him the good news of a gentle boy.2089 (101) And when (the boy) was old enough to work with him, he said, "My son, I have seen in a dream that I (must) sacrifice you, so see what you think." He said, "My father, do as you are ordered. You will find me, God willing, patient." (102) But as soon as they had both submitted to (what they thought to be) God's will, and (Abraham) had laid (his son) down on the side of his face, (103) We called to him, "Abraham, (104) you have fulfilled the vision."2090 This is how we reward

• • •

2083 Genesis 6:8,13 But Noah found favor in the sight of the Lord. 13 And God said to Noah, 'I have determined to make an end of all flesh, for the earth is filled with violence because of them; now I am going to destroy them along with the earth.
2084 Genesis 8:18 So Noah went out with his sons and his wife and his sons' wives.
2085 Genesis 8:16-17 Go out of the ark, you and your wife, and your sons and your sons' wives with you. 17 Bring out with you every living thing that is with you of all flesh—birds and animals and every creeping thing that creeps on the earth—so that they may abound on the earth, and be fruitful and multiply on the earth.'
2086 Hebrews 11:7 By faith Noah, warned by God about events as yet unseen, respected the warning and built an ark to save his household; by this he condemned the world and became an heir to the righteousness that is in accordance with faith.
2087 Genesis 7:20-21 the waters swelled above the mountains, covering them fifteen cubits deep. 21 And all flesh died that moved on the earth, birds, domestic animals, wild animals, all swarming creatures that swarm on the earth, and all human beings;
2088 Genesis 15:18 On that day the Lord made a covenant with Abram, saying, 'To your descendants I give this land, from the river of Egypt to the great river, the river Euphrates,
2089 Genesis 18:10 Then one said, 'I will surely return to you in due season, and your wife Sarah shall have a son.' And Sarah was listening at the tent entrance behind him.
2090 Genesis 22:11-12 But the angel of the Lord called to him from heaven, and said, 'Abraham, Abraham!' And he said, 'Here I am.' 12 He said, 'Do not lay your hand on the boy or do anything to him; for now I know that you fear God, since you have not withheld your son, your only son, from me.'

those who do good. [105] This was clearly a grave trial, [106] and We ransomed him with a great sacrifice,[2091] [107] and We left the later generations saying of him: [108] "Peace be upon Abraham." [109] This is how we reward those who do good, [110] for (Abraham) was among Our believing worshipers. [111] Then We gave him the good news of Isaac, a prophet from among the righteous, [112] and We blessed him and Isaac. Among their descendants are those who do good, and those who clearly wrong themselves. [113]

We certainly showed great kindness to Moses and Aaron. [114] We saved them and their people from a terrible predicament,[2092] [115] and We supported them so that they prevailed,[2093] [116] and We gave them the clarifying Book,[2094] [117] and We guided them on the straight path, [118] and We left the later generations saying of them: [119] "Peace be upon Moses and Aaron." [120] This is how We reward those who do good, [121] for they were among Our believing worshipers.[122]

Elijah was indeed one of the messengers. [123] When he said to his people, "Will you not remain mindful of God? [124] Do you call upon Baal and leave the best of creators,[2095] [125] God, your Lord and the Lord of your forefathers?"[2096] [126] But they denied him, so they will be brought (for punishment), [127] except for God's devout worshipers. [128] And We left the later generations saying of him: [129] "Peace be upon the House of Elijah." [130] This how we reward those who do good, [131] for he was among Our believing worshipers. [132]

Lot[2097] was indeed one of the messengers. [133] We saved him and all of his family, [134] except an old woman who stayed behind.[2098] [135] Then We destroyed

•   •   •

[2091] Genesis 22:13 And Abraham looked up and saw a ram, caught in a thicket by its horns. Abraham went and took the ram and offered it up as a burnt-offering instead of his son.

[2092] Exodus 14.23-30 The Egyptians pursued, and went into the sea after them, all of Pharaoh's horses, chariots, and chariot drivers. 24 At the morning watch the Lord in the pillar of fire and cloud looked down upon the Egyptian army, and threw the Egyptian army into panic. 25 He clogged their chariot wheels so that they turned with difficulty. The Egyptians said, 'Let us flee from the Israelites, for the Lord is fighting for them against Egypt.' 26 Then the Lord said to Moses, 'Stretch out your hand over the sea, so that the water may come back upon the Egyptians, upon their chariots and chariot drivers.' 27 So Moses stretched out his hand over the sea, and at dawn the sea returned to its normal depth. As the Egyptians fled before it, the Lord tossed the Egyptians into the sea. 28 The waters returned and covered the chariots and the chariot drivers, the entire army of Pharaoh that had followed them into the sea; not one of them remained. 29 But the Israelites walked on dry ground through the sea, the waters forming a wall for them on their right and on their left. 30 Thus the Lord saved Israel that day from the Egyptians; and Israel saw the Egyptians dead on the seashore.

[2093] Exodus 14:31 Israel saw the great work that the LORD did against the Egyptians. So the people feared the LORD and believed in the Lord and in his servant Moses.

[2094] Exodus 31:18 When God finished speaking with Moses on Mount Sinai, he gave him the two tablets of the covenant, tablets of stone, written with the finger of God.

[2095] 1 Kings 18:17-18 When Ahab saw Elijah, Ahab said to him, 'Is it you, you troubler of Israel?' 18 He answered, 'I have not troubled Israel; but you have, and your father's house, because you have forsaken the commandments of the Lord and followed the Baals.

[2096] 1 Kings 18:36 At the time of the offering of the oblation, the prophet Elijah came near and said, 'O Lord, God of Abraham, Isaac, and Israel, let it be known this day that you are God in Israel, that I am your servant, and that I have done all these things at your bidding.

[2097] Lot, nephew of Abraham.

[2098] Genesis 19:26 But Lot's wife, behind him, looked back, and she became a pillar of salt. Genesis 19:29 So it was that, when God destroyed the cities of the Plain, God remembered Abraham, and sent Lot out of the midst of the overthrow, when he overthrew the cities in which Lot had settled.

the others.[2099] [(136)] You pass by them morning [(137)] and night, so will you not use your reason? [(138)] Jonah was one of the messengers.[2100] [(139)] He ran away to an loaded ship,[2101] [(140)] but they cast lots, and he lost,[2102] [(141)] (so they threw him into the sea),[2103] and a great fish swallowed him,[2104] for He was blameworthy (for what he had done). [(142)] And had he not been one of those who glorify God's limitless glory, [(143)] he would have remained inside its belly until the Day they are resurrected.[2105] [(144)] But We cast him,[2106] ill, on an open shore. [(145)] and We made a gourd vine to grow over him,[2107] [(146)] and We sent him to a hundred thousand people or more.[2108] [(147)] They believed, so We let them enjoy their life. [2109(148)]

So (Prophet) inquire (of the idolaters), "Why do they think their Lord has daughters while they have sons"? [(149)] Or, maybe they witnessed the creation of the angels as females?" [(150)] No indeed, It is out of their (invented) falsehood that they say, [(151)] "God has begotten," and they are liars. [(152)] Has He chosen

• • •

[2099] Genesis 19:24 Then the LORD rained on Sodom and Gomorrah sulphur and fire from the Lord out of heaven;
[2100] Jonah 1:1-2 Now the word of the LORD came to Jonah son of Amittai, saying, [2] Go at once to Nineveh, that great city, and cry out against it; for their wickedness has come up before me.'
[2101] Jonah 1:3 But Jonah set out to flee to Tarshish from the presence of the Lord. He went down to Joppa and found a ship going to Tarshish; so he paid his fare and went on board, to go with them to Tarshish, away from the presence of the Lord.
[2102] Jonah 1:7-10 The sailors said to one another, 'Come, let us cast lots, so that we may know on whose account this calamity has come upon us.' So they cast lots, and the lot fell on Jonah. [8] Then they said to him, 'Tell us why this calamity has come upon us. What is your occupation? Where do you come from? What is your country? And of what people are you?' [9] 'I am a Hebrew,' he replied. 'I worship the Lord, the God of heaven, who made the sea and the dry land.' [10] Then the men were even more afraid, and said to him, 'What is this that you have done!' For the men knew that he was fleeing from the presence of the Lord, because he had told them so.
[2103] Jonah 1:11-12, 15 Then they said to him, 'What shall we do to you, that the sea may quieten down for us?' For the sea was growing more and more tempestuous. [12] He said to them, 'Pick me up and throw me into the sea; then the sea will quieten down for you; for I know it is because of me that this great storm has come upon you.' [15] So they picked Jonah up and threw him into the sea; and the sea ceased from its raging.
[2104] Jonah 1:16-17 Then the men feared the Lord even more, and they offered a sacrifice to the Lord and made vows. But the Lord provided a large fish to swallow up Jonah; and Jonah was in the belly of the fish for three days and three nights.
[2105] Jonah 2:9-10 But I with the voice of thanksgiving will sacrifice to you; what I have vowed I will pay.Deliverance belongs to the Lord!' [10] Then the Lord spoke to the fish, and it spewed Jonah out upon the dry land.
[2106] Jonah 2:10 Then the Lord spoke to the fish, and it spewed Jonah out upon the dry land.
[2107] Jonah 4:6 The Lord God appointed a bush, and made it come up over Jonah, to give shade over his head, to save him from his discomfort; so Jonah was very happy about the bush.
[2108] Jonah 3:2, 4:11 'Get up, go to Nineveh, that great city, and proclaim to it the message that I tell you.' 4:11 And should I not be concerned about Nineveh, that great city, in which there are more than a hundred and twenty thousand people who do not know their right hand from their left, and also many animals?'
[2109] Jonah 3:6-10 When the news reached the king of Nineveh, he rose from his throne, removed his robe, covered himself with sackcloth, and sat in ashes. [7] Then he had a proclamation made in Nineveh: 'By the decree of the king and his nobles: No human being or animal, no herd or flock, shall taste anything. They shall not feed, nor shall they drink water. [8] Human beings and animals shall be covered with sackcloth, and they shall cry mightily to God. All shall turn from their evil ways and from the violence that is in their hands. [9] Who knows? God may relent and change his mind; he may turn from his fierce anger, so that we do not perish.' [10] When God saw what they did, how they turned from their evil ways, God changed his mind about the calamity that he had said he would bring upon them; and he did not do it.

daughters over sons? [153] What is (wrong) with you? How do you reach your judgments? [154] Will you not be reminded (of the warning against such thinking)? [155] Or do you have a clear authority (for what you allege)? [156] Then, produce your Book,[2110] if you are truthful. [157]

They also claimed a lineage between Him and the jinn, but the jinn know that they will be brought before Him for (judgment).[2111] [158] May God be exalted in His glory above all they describe,[2112] [159] except for God's devout worshipers (who don't make such claims). [160] So you (who deny the truth) and whatever you worship, [161] cannot tempt (anyone) away from Him [162] except for him who will burn in Hell. [163] (All of God's creations will say), "Among us, too, there is none but has a known place. [164] We are ranged in ranks, [165] and we are those who glorify God." [166]

The unbelievers used to say, [167] "If only we had a message from those who lived before us, [168] we would have been faithful worshipers of God." [169] But they rejected the message, so they will soon realize (the consequences). [170] Our word has already been given to Our worshiping Messengers [171] (that) they would indeed be victorious, [172] and (that) Our soldiers will be those who overcome. [173] So (Prophet), leave them for a time. [174] And watch them, for they will soon see. [175] Do they really want to hasten Our punishment?[2113] [176] When it descends on them, how terrible will that morning be for those who were warned. [177] Leave them for a time, [178] and watch them, for they will soon see. [179] May your Lord, the Lord of Might, be exalted in His glory above all they describe. [180] And Peace be on the Messengers, [181] and praise be to God, Lord of the worlds.[2114] [182]

• • •

[2110] Isaiah 45:21 Declare and present your case; let them take counsel together! Who told this long ago? Who declared it of old? Was it not I, the Lord? There is no other god besides me, a righteous God and a Savior; there is no one besides me.

[2111] James 2:19 You believe that God is one; you do well. Even the demons believe—and shudder.

[2112] Psalm 29:1 Ascribe to the Lord, O heavenly beings, ascribe to the Lord glory and strength.

[2113] Matthew 25:41 Then he will say to those at his left hand, "You that are accursed, depart from me into the eternal fire prepared for the devil and his angels;

[2114] Psalm 47:7 For God is the king of all the earth; sing praises with a psalm.

CHAPTER THIRTY EIGHT

SAAD

THE LETTER SAAD

THE **MECCA** PERIOD

In the name of God, the Merciful-to-all, the Mercy Giver:
Saad,[2115] by the Qur'an, which contains all that one ought to know. [01] The unbelievers are full of arrogance and dissent. [02] How many generations have We destroyed before them (for the same sins)? They called out (to Us), but it was too late to escape.[2116] [03] They are surprised that one of their own has come out to warn them, so those who want to deny the truth are saying, "This is a magician and a liar."[04] How can he claim that the gods are (only) one God? This is a strange thing." [05] Their leaders went off, saying, "Walk away, and be faithful to your gods. This is what you must do. [06] We have not heard of this in the latest religion. This must be an invention. [07] How can the message be revealed to him alone out of all of us?"

In fact, they are in doubt about My message. In fact, They have not yet tasted My punishment.[2117] [08] Or do They have the stores of your Lord's mercy, the Almighty, the Ever-Giving? [09] Or is theirs the dominion of the heavens, and the earth, and what is between them? Then let them ascend through any means of access. [10] (They are only) soldiers (who will be) defeated regardless of what alliance they have. [11] The people of Noah denied (My messages) before them, as did (the tribe of) Aad,[2118] Pharaoh-the owner of (many) tent-poles- [12] (the tribe of) Thamud,[2119] the people of Lot,[2120] the woods-dwellers: those were the parties, [13] each of whom rejected the messengers, so My punishment was justified. [14] And these, too, (who now deny the truth) are only awaiting a single

• • •

[2115] Here and at the beginning of many chapters there are unvowelled letters of unknown meaning. Numerous theories have been proposed, but there is no agreement on the subject.

[2116] 1 Thessalonians 5:3 When they say, 'There is peace and security', then sudden destruction will come upon them, as labor pains come upon a pregnant woman, and there will be no escape!

[2117] 2 Peter 2:9 then the Lord knows how to rescue the godly from trial, and to keep the unrighteous under punishment until the day of judgment

[2118] See Glossary

[2119] Ibid

[2120] Lot, nephew of Abraham.

blast, which will not be stopped. [15] And they say, "Our Lord, hasten for us our share (of the punishment) before the Day of Account"[16] Be patient over what they say, and remember Our servant, David, the possessor of strength;[2121] he was one who repeatedly turned back (to Us).[2122] [17] We subjected the mountains to join him[2123] in praising Our limitless glory in the evening and daybreak, [18] and the birds to assemble, all repeating (praises) with him.[2124] [19] And We strengthened his kingdom, and gave him wisdom[2125] and keen judgment. [20] And has the story come to you of the disputants who climbed over the wall of (his) prayer chamber? [21] When they entered upon David, he was alarmed, (but) they said, "Do not be afraid. (We are) two disputants. One of us has wronged the other, so judge between us with truth, and do not be unjust, and guide us to the right way. [22] This is my brother. He has ninety-nine ewes, and I have one ewe, so he said, 'Entrust it to me,' and got the better of me with his words." [23] (David) said, "He has certainly wronged you in demanding that your ewe be added to his ewes. And many associates oppress one another, except for those who believe and do righteous deeds, and they are few."

David then realized that We had been testing him, and he asked forgiveness of his Lord, and fell down bowing (in prostration), and turned (to God) in repentance, [24] so We forgave him, and, he has nearness to Us, and a good place in the Hereafter. [25] (We said), "David, We have made you a steward over this land, so judge between the people in truth and do not follow (your own) whim,[2126] as it will lead you away from the way of God." Those who wander away from His path will have a severe punishment [2127] for having forgotten the Day of Account. [26]

We have not created the heaven and the earth and all that lies between them without meaning and purpose.[2128] That is the assumption of the unbelievers. How terrible the fire will be for the unbelievers. [27] Would we treat those who believe and do righteous deeds like those who spread corruption on earth? Or would We treat those who are mindful of God like the wicked? [28] This is a blessed Book, which We have revealed to you so that they might reflect upon its verses and that those of understanding would be reminded. [29]

● ● ●

[2121] 1 Samuel 16:18 One of the young men answered, 'I have seen a son of Jesse the Bethlehemite who is skilful in playing, a man of valor, a warrior, prudent in speech, and a man of good presence; and the Lord is with him.'

[2122] Psalm 32:5 Then I acknowledged my sin to you, and I did not hide my iniquity; I said, 'I will confess my transgressions to the Lord', and you forgave the guilt of my sin.

[2123] Psalm 148:9 Mountains and all hills, fruit trees and all cedars! Let them praise the name of the Lord, for his name alone is exalted; his glory is above earth and heaven.

[2124] Psalm 148:10,13 Wild animals and all cattle, creeping things and flying birds! Let them praise the name of the LORD, for his name alone is exalted; his glory is above earth and heaven.

[2125] Matthew 13:45-46 The kingdom of heaven is like a merchant seeking fine pearls, [46] and upon finding one pearl of great value, he went and sold all that he had and bought it.

[2126] 2 Samuel 11:2-12:25 The story of King David's sin with Bathsheba in details

[2127] 2 Thessalonians 1:9 These will suffer the punishment of eternal destruction, separated from the presence of the Lord and from the glory of his might,

[2128] Isaiah 45:18 For thus says the Lord, who created the heavens (he is God!), who formed the earth and made it (he established it; he did not create it a chaos, he formed it to be inhabited!): I am the Lord, and there is no other.

And to David (Dawud) We gave Solomon (Sulayman), an excellent servant[2129], He repeatedly turned back (to Us). [30] When well-bred, swift horses were paraded before him at dusk,[2130] [31] he said, "I love to love good things out of remembrance of my Lord," (and when) the horses disappeared into the distance, [32] he would say, "Bring them back to me," and stroke their legs and necks. [33] But (previously), We had indeed tested Solomon (by) placing a lifeless body on his throne, he then turned toward us [34] and prayed, "My Lord, forgive me, and grant me a kingdom the like of which will not belong to anyone after me.[2131] You are the Ever Giving." [35] So We gave him power over the wind, to direct it to blow gently wherever he wished, [36] and over the devils (shayatin), every kind of builder and diver [37] and over others bound in shackles. [38] (We said), "This is Our gift, (for you to) give or withhold without (rendering any) account." [39] He is closed to Us and (has) a good place in the Hereafter. [40]

And remember Our servant Job, (Ayyub)[2132] when he called to his Lord, "Satan has afflict me with hardship and suffering." [41] (So he was told), "Strike (the ground) with your foot; here is a (spring for) a cool bath and a drink." [42] And We restored his family, and their like with them;[2133] as a mercy from Us and a reminder for those of understanding. [43] (We said), "And take in your hand a bunch of grass and strike with it, and do not break your oath."[2134] We found him patient, an excellent servant, one who repeatedly turning back (to Us). [44]

And remember Our servants Abraham, Isaac and Jacob, men of true strength and vision, [45] for We purified them with a most pure quality-remembrance of the (Hereafter), [46] and (in our sight) they are among the chosen and the outstanding. [47] And remember Ishmael, Elisha (Al-yasa) and Ezekiel (Dhul-Kifl), for they are all among the truly outstanding [48]

• • •

[2129] "Servant" is much more common in English than the word "slave," but both this Arabic word /abd/ and the corresponding words in the Law /abd/ and the Gospel /doulos/ are stronger than this. This word means both slave and worshiper. All the holy books call the believers slaves of God.

[2130] 1 Kings 4:26 Solomon also had forty thousand stalls of horses for his chariots, and twelve thousand horsemen.

[2131] 1 Kings 3:5-14 At Gibeon the Lord appeared to Solomon in a dream by night; and God said, 'Ask what I should give you.' [6] And Solomon said, 'You have shown great and steadfast love to your servant my father David, because he walked before you in faithfulness, in righteousness, and in uprightness of heart towards you; and you have kept for him this great and steadfast love, and have given him a son to sit on his throne today. [7] And now, O Lord my God, you have made your servant king in place of my father David, although I am only a little child; I do not know how to go out or come in. [8] And your servant is in the midst of the people whom you have chosen, a great people, so numerous they cannot be numbered or counted. [9] Give your servant therefore an understanding mind to govern your people, able to discern between good and evil; for who can govern this your great people?' [10] It pleased the Lord that Solomon had asked this. [11] God said to him, 'Because you have asked this, and have not asked for yourself long life or riches, or for the life of your enemies, but have asked for yourself understanding to discern what is right, [12] I now do according to your word. Indeed, I give you a wise and discerning mind; no one like you has been before you and no one like you shall arise after you. [13] I give you also what you have not asked, both riches and honor all your life; no other king shall compare with you. [14] If you will walk in my ways, keeping my statutes and my commandments, as your father David walked, then I will lengthen your life.'

[2132] the prophet known for patience

[2133] Job 42:12-13 The Lord blessed the latter days of Job more than his beginning; and he had fourteen thousand sheep, six thousand camels, a thousand yoke of oxen, and a thousand donkeys. [13] He also had seven sons and three daughters.

[2134] Numbers 30:2 When a man makes a vow to the Lord, or swears an oath to bind himself by a pledge, he shall not break his word; he shall do according to all that proceeds out of his mouth.

This is a reminder, for the mindful of God will have a good place of return, [49] Gardens of Eden, whose gates will open to them, [50] where they will recline, calling for abundant fruit and drink, [51] having beside them well-matched mates of modest gaze. [52] This is what you are promised for the Day of Account. [53] This is Our provision, which will never run out. [54]

But, truly, for the transgressors is an evil place of return- [55] Hell, where they will burn. What an evil resting place! [56] This! So let them taste boiling water and (foul) pus- [57] and other such punishments. [58] (Its inhabitants will say), "This is a crowd (of people) rushing in to where you are. No welcome for them. They will burn in the Fire." [59] They will say, "Nor you! No welcome for you. You, (our leaders), brought this upon us, what an evil place to settle! [60] "They will say, "Our Lord, whoever brought this upon us, double his punishment in the Fire,"[2135] [61] and they will wonder, "Why we do not see men whom we used to count among the worst, [62] whom we used to mock? Did our eyes miss them?" [63] This is how it will really be, the bickering of the people of the Fire. [64]

Say (Prophet), "I am only here to give a warning, and there is no god but God, the One, the All- Conquering, [65] Lord of the heavens and the earth and whatever is between them, the Almighty, the Ever-Forgiving." [66] Say, "It is tremendous news, [67] yet you ignore it. [68] I had no knowledge of what those on high bicker about, [69] had it not been revealed to me. However, I am but a clear warner." [70]

(So mention) when your Lord said to the angels, " I am going to create a human being from clay, [71] and when I have proportioned him and breathed of My spirit into him, then prostrate yourselves to him." [72] The angels prostrated, all of them together [73] except Iblis;[2136] he was arrogant and became a (rebel) who denied the truth. [74] (God) said, "Iblīs, what prevented you from prostrating yourself to what I created with My hands? Is it your arrogance, or do you think that you are so high above all others?" [75] He said, "I am better than him. You created me from fire and created him from clay." [76] (God) said, "Then be gone, you are expelled, [77] and My curse will follow you until the Day of Judgment." [78] (Iblīs) said, "My Lord, reprieve me until the Day they are resurrected." [79] (God) said, "You are reprieved [80] until the Day of the time well-known." [81] (Iblīs) said, "By your might, I will mislead them all, [82] except for Your devoted worshipers among them." [83] (God) said, "This is the Truth, and the Truth do I speak: [84] I will fill Hell with you and those of them that follow you, all of you together." [85]

Say: " I ask from you no reward for this (message), and I am not one of those who claim to be what they are not. [86] This is no less than a reminder to all the worlds, [87] and you will come to grasp its significance in the fullness of time!" [88]

●   ●   ●

[2135] Matthew 25:41 Then he will say to those at his left hand, "You that are accursed, depart from me into the eternal fire prepared for the devil and his angels;
[2136] Devil

CHAPTER THIRTY NINE

AZ-ZUMAR
THE THRONGS

THE **MECCA** PERIOD

In the name of God, the Merciful-to-all, the Mercy Giver:
This Book is sent down to you from God, the Almighty,[2137] the Wise.[2138] (01) We have sent down the Book to you in Truth, so worship God, sincere in your faith in Him alone. (02) Pure faith is owed to God alone. Those who take protectors besides Him (say), "We worship them only so that they may bring us nearer to God." God will judge between them concerning their differences. God does not guide any liar and denier of the truth.[2139] (03) If God had intended to take a son, He could have chosen anyone He willed from whatever He created, may He be exalted in His glory! He is God, the One God, the One who holds absolute sway over all that exists. [2140] (04) He created the heavens and earth in Truth.[2141] He wraps the night over the day and wraps the day over the night,[2142] and has made the sun and the moon subservient (to His laws), each running (its course) for an appointed time.[2143] He is the Almighty,[2144] the Ever-Forgiving.[2145] (05) He created you from a single soul, from which He made its mate,[2146] and He gave you eight kinds of grazing livestock in pairs(male and female). He creates you in your mothers' wombs,[2147] one creation after another, within threefold of darkness.

• • •

[2137] Job 9:4 He is wise in heart, and mighty in strength—who has resisted him, and succeeded? —
[2138] Proverbs 2:6For the Lord gives wisdom; from his mouth come knowledge and understanding;
[2139] 1 John 2:4 Whoever says, 'I have come to know him', but does not obey his commandments, is a liar, and in such a person the truth does not exist;
[2140] Psalm 21:13 Be exalted, O Lord, in your strength! We will sing and praise your power.
[2141] Genesis 1:1 In the beginning when God created the heavens and the earth,
[2142] Psalm 139:12 even the darkness is not dark to you; the night is as bright as the day, for darkness is as light to you.
[2143] Psalm 104:19 You have made the moon to mark the seasons; the sun knows its time for setting.
[2144] Psalm 89:8 O Lord God of hosts, who is as mighty as you, O Lord? Your faithfulness surrounds you.
[2145] Daniel 9:9. To the Lord our God belong mercy and forgiveness, for we have rebelled against him,
[2146] Genesis 2:22 And the rib that the Lord God had taken from the man he made into a woman and brought her to the man.
[2147] Psalm 139:13-14 For it was you who formed my inward parts; you knit me together in my mother's womb. [14] I praise you, for I am fearfully and wonderfully made. Wonderful are your works; that I know very well.

That is God, your Lord;[2148] to Him belongs all Sovereignty. There is no deity except Him, so how can you lose site of the truth?[2149 (06)] If you deny the truth, God has no need of you. Yet He does not approve of ingratitude in His servants.[2150] but, if you do show gratitude, He welcomes it in you. No bearer of burdens will bear the burdens of another.[2151] Then you will return to your Lord,[2152] and He will inform you of what you have done. He knows what is within your hearts.[2153 (07)]

When a human being encounters some hard times, he calls upon his Lord, turning to Him (in repentance), but when He blesses him with His favors, he forgets his Lord whom he called before and he sets up equals to God [2154] in order to mislead others from His way. Say, "Enjoy your unbelief for a little, for you are included among the inhabitants of the Fire." [2155 (08)] Is one who worships devoutly during periods of the night[2156]- bowing down and standing (in prayer), being mindful of the Hereafter, and hoping for his Lord's mercy,[2157] (like one who does not)? Say, "Are those who know equal to those who do not know?" Only those who have understanding will keep this in mind. [(09)]

Say, "O My worshipers who have believed, be ever mindful of your Lord. Good (reward) awaits those who persevere in doing good in this world[2158]. (Remember that) God's earth is spacious.[2159] They who are patient will be given their reward beyond all account."[2160 (10)] Say, "I have been commanded to worship God, dedicating my faith to Him. [(11)] And I have been commanded to be the first (among you) to submit." [2161 (12)] " I fear the punishment of a terrible Day[2162] should I disobey my Lord."[(13)] Say, "God (alone) do I worship, sincere to Him in my faith, [(14)] so worship what you will besides Him." Say, "Truly doomed are the ones who will lose themselves and their families on the Day of Resurrection. Truly, that is a self-evident loss." [(15)] They will have curtains of fire

• • •

[2148] Deuteronomy 6:4 Hear, O Israel: The LORD is our God, the Lord alone
[2149] Lamentations 5:19 But you, O Lord, reign forever; your throne endures to all generations.
[2150] Romans 11:20 That is true. They were broken off because of their unbelief, but you stand only through faith. So do not become proud, but stand in awe.
[2151] Galatians 6:5 "For every one shall bear his own burden.
[2152] Ecclesiastes 12:7 and the dust returns to the earth as it was, and the breath returns to God who gave it.
[2153] Luke 16:15 So he said to them, 'You are those who justify yourselves in the sight of others; but God knows your hearts; for what is prized by human beings is an abomination in the sight of God.
[2154] Isaiah 46:9 remember the former things of old; for I am God, and there is no other; I am God, and there is no one like me,
[2155] Isaiah 50:11 But all of you are kindlers of fire, lighters of firebrands. Walk in the flame of your fire, and among the brands that you have kindled! This is what you shall have from my hand: you shall lie down in torment.
[2156] Psalm 88:1 O Lord, God of my salvation, when, at night, I cry out in your presence,
[2157] Psalm 33:18 Truly the eye of the LORD is on those who fear him, on those who hope in his steadfast love,
[2158] Matthew 5:7 Blessed are the merciful, for they will be shown mercy.
[2159] Job 38:18 Have you comprehended the expanse of the earth? Declare, if you know all this.
[2160] Lamentations 3:25-26 The Lord is good to those who wait for him, to the soul that seeks him
[26] It is good that one should wait quietly for the salvation of the Lord.
[2161] James 4:7 Submit yourselves therefore to God. Resist the devil, and he will flee from you.
[2162] 2 Peter 2:9 then the Lord knows how to rescue the godly from trial, and to keep the unrighteous under punishment until the day of judgment

above them and below them. With this God puts fear into His worshipers. So be ever mindful of Me, My worshipers. [16]

Those who have avoided the worship of false deities and turned toward God will have good news, so give good news to My worshipers [17] who listen to what is said and follow what is best. Those are the ones God has guided, and those are the people endowed with insight. [18] As for one who deserved the decree of punishment, can you (Prophet) save one who is already in the Fire? [19] But those who are mindful of their Lord, for them are dwellings built one above the other, beneath which rivers flow.[2163] (This is) God's promise and God does not fail to deliver (His) promise.[2164] [20] Do you not see that God sends down rain from the sky[2165] and guides it through the earth to flow as springs?[2166] Then with it He produces vegetation[2167] of varying colors, which later withers,[2168] and you see it turning yellow, then He turns it into waste. That is a reminder for those endowed with insight. [21]

Is one whose heart God has open to submit to Him [2169] and who has received enlightenment from his Lord (like one whose heart rejects God)? Misery, then, to those whose hearts are hardened even more by the mention of God. They are clearly lost. [22] God has sent down the best of narrations: a Book that is perfectly consistent within itself, repeating various statements (of the Truth) in forms that causes the skin of those who revere their Lord to shiver (in awe), after which their skin and their hearts soften at the mention of God. Such is God's guidance; He guides with it (the Qur'an) whoever is willing to be guided, but no one can guide those God leaves to stray[2170] [23]

What about someone who shields his face against the worst of punishment [2171] on the Day of Resurrection (is he like one secure from it)? (On that day) it will be said to the unjust, "Taste what you have earned." [24] Those before them also denied the truth, and punishment came upon them before they realize what is happening.[2172] [25] God made them taste disgrace in this worldly life, but the punishment of the Hereafter is greater, if they only knew. [26]

• • •

[2163] Revelation 22:1-2 Then the angel showed me the river of the water of life, bright as crystal, flowing from the throne of God and of the Lamb through the middle of the street of the city. 2 On either side of the river is the tree of life with its twelve kinds of fruit, producing its fruit each month; and the leaves of the tree are for the healing of the nations.

[2164] Joshua 23:14 'And now I am about to go the way of all the earth, and you know in your hearts and souls, all of you, that not one thing has failed of all the good things that the Lord your God promised concerning you; all have come to pass for you, not one of them has failed.

[2165] Jeremiah 14:22 Can any idols of the nations bring rain? Or can the heavens give showers? Is it not you, O Lord our God? We set our hope on you, for it is you who do all this.

[2166] Zechariah 10:1 Ask rain from the Lord in the season of the spring rain, from the Lord who makes the storm-clouds, who gives showers of rain to you, the vegetation in the field to everyone.

[2167] Leviticus 26:4 I will give you your rains in their season, and the land shall yield its produce, and the trees of the field shall yield their fruit.

[2168] Isaiah 40:7, 8 The grass withers, the flower fades, when the breath of the LORD blows upon it; surely the people are grass. 8 The grass withers, the flower fades; but the word of our God will stand for ever.

[2169] James 4:7 Submit yourselves therefore to God. Resist the devil, and he will flee from you.

[2170] 2 Thessalonians 2:11 For this reason God sends them a powerful delusion, leading them to believe what is false,

[2171] 2 Thessalonians 1:9 These will suffer the punishment of eternal destruction, separated from the presence of the Lord and from the glory of his might,

[2172] 1 Thessalonians 5:3 When they say, 'There is peace and security', then sudden destruction will come upon them, as labor pains come upon a pregnant woman, and there will be no escape!

We have cited in this Qur'an every (kind of) example for people, so that they might remember. [27] (It is) an Arabic Qur'an, without any distortion, so that they might become mindful. [28] (To this end), God presents an example: (consider) a man owned by quarreling partners, and another (who is) devoted exclusively to one master, are they considered equal[2173] in status? All praise be to God! But most of them do not know. [29]

You will die, and they will die. [30] Then, on the Day of Resurrection, you will dispute with each other before your Lord. [31] So who is more unjust than one who invents lies about God and denies the Truth when it has come to him? Is there not (enough) room in Hell for the unbelievers?[2174] [32] He who promotes the truth and testifies to it, it is they who are mindful of God. [33] They will have with their Lord whatever they desire. This is the reward for those who do good; [34] that God may remove from them the worst of their deeds and reward them according to the best of what they have done. [35]

Is not God adequately sufficient for His worshiper? (Yet), they threaten you with others beside Him. If God allows someone to be lost, for him there is no guide, [2175] [36] and whomever God guides, no one can mislead him. Is not God Almighty and capable of retribution?[2176] [37] If you asked them, "Who created the heavens and the earth?"[2177] they would say, "God." So say, "Then do you see those you pray to besides God? If God wishes to harm me, can they remove His harm;[2178] or if He wants to show me a blessing, can they withhold His blessing?" Say, "God suffices for me; all those who truly trust put their trust in Him"[2179] [38] Say, "My people, do all you can, and so will I. Eventually you will know [39] who will receive a shameful punishment, and on whom will fall a lasting punishment."[2180] [40]

We sent down to you the Book offering the Truth to humanity. So whoever is guided, it is for his own good; and he who strays only does so to his own detriment. You are not their guardian.[2181] [41] God retrieves people's souls at the time of their death, and the souls of the living during their sleep. He then keeps those for whom He has decreed death and releases the others until an appointed term. There are signs in this for people who reflect. [42] Or have they taken intercessors besides God? Say, "Even though they do not have any power, nor

• • •

[2173] Matthew 6:24 "No one can serve two masters. Either you will hate the one and love the other, or you will be devoted to the one and despise the other. You cannot serve both God and money.

[2174] Matthew 25:41 Then he will say to those at his left hand, "You that are accursed, depart from me into the eternal fire prepared for the devil and his angels;

[2175] 2 Thessalonians 2:11 For this reason God sends them a powerful delusion, leading them to believe what is false,

[2176] Romans 12:19 Beloved, never avenge yourselves, but leave room for the wrath of God; for it is written, 'Vengeance is mine, I will repay, says the Lord.'

[2177] Genesis 1:1 In the beginning when God created the heavens and the earth

[2178] Psalm 115:4-8 Their idols are silver and gold, the work of human hands.⁵ They have mouths, but do not speak; eyes, but do not see. ⁶ They have ears, but do not hear; noses, but do not smell. ⁷ They have hands, but do not feel; feet, but do not walk; they make no sound in their throats. ⁸ Those who make them are like them; so are all who trust in them.

[2179] Proverbs 3:5-6 Trust in the Lord with all your heart, and do not rely on your own insight. ⁶ In all your ways acknowledge him, and he will make straight your paths.

[2180] Habakkuk 1:12 Are you not from of old, O Lord my God, my Holy One? You shall not die. O Lord, you have marked them for judgment; and you, O Rock, have established them for punishment.

[2181] Ezekiel 2:5 Whether they hear or refuse to hear (for they are a rebellious house), they shall know that there has been a prophet among them.

do they reason?" [43] Say, "To God belongs all intercession. To Him belongs the kingdom of the heavens and the earth.[2182] Then to Him you will all return."[2183] [44] The hearts of those who do not believe in the Hereafter shrink with disgust when God alone[2184] is mentioned, but when those other than Him are mentioned, they suddenly rejoice. [45] Say, "Our God, the Programmer of the heavens and the earth, Knower of all that is beyond our ability to witness [2185] and all that we can witness, You will judge between your worshipers concerning their differences."[2186] [46] If the unjust owned everything on earth and the like of it with it, they would gladly offer it to ransom themselves[2187] from the terrible suffering on the Day of Resurrection, but there will appear to them from God what they never expected. [47] The evils of their deeds will become clear to them, and they will be surrounded by what they used to ridicule. [48]

If hard times touch man, he calls on Us. Then, when We favor him with Our blessing, he says, "I have only been given this only because of my knowledge." In fact, it is only a test, though most of them do not know. [49] Those (who lived) before them said (the same thing), but what they had earned did not do them any good, [50] for the evil of their deeds caught up with them. (Similarly,) the evil deeds of those who have wronged themselves among these people will also catch up with them, and they will not be able to evade God. [51] Do they not know that God expands and restricts His provision for whomever He wills? In this are signs for a People who believe. [52]

Say, "My worshipers who have transgressed against themselves, do not despair of God's mercy, for God forgives all sins.[2188] He is the Ever-Forgiving,[2189] the Mercy- Giver."[2190] [53] Turn in repentance to your Lord and submit to Him[2191] before the punishment comes upon you and you cannot be helped. [54] Follow the best teaching sent down to you from your Lord before the punishment comes upon you suddenly, when you are not expecting it, [2192] [55] so that a soul may not say, " How sorry I am for having neglected my duty to God and having been among the mockers;" [56] or say, "Had God guided me, I would have been among those who are mindful of God;" [57] or say, when it sees the punishment,[2193] "If only I had another chance to be among those who do good."

• • •

[2182] Deuteronomy 10:14 Although heaven and the heaven of heavens belong to the Lord your God, the earth with all that is in it,

[2183] Ecclesiastes 12:7 and the dust returns to the earth as it was, and the breath returns to God who gave it.

[2184] Deuteronomy 6:4 Hear, O Israel: The Lord is our God, the Lord alone.

[2185] 2 Corinthians 4:18 because we look not at what can be seen but at what cannot be seen; for what can be seen is temporary, but what cannot be seen is eternal.

[2186] Genesis 18:25 Far be it from you to do such a thing, to slay the righteous with the wicked, so that the righteous fare as the wicked! Far be that from you! Shall not the Judge of all the earth do what is just?'

[2187] Psalm 49:7,8 Truly, no ransom avails for one's life, there is no price one can give to God for it.
[8] For the ransom of life is costly, and can never suffice.

[2188] Jeremiah 33:8 I will cleanse them from all the guilt of their sin against me, and I will forgive all the guilt of their sin and rebellion against me.

[2189] Psalm 130:4 But there is forgiveness with you, so that you may be revered.

[2190] Ephesians 2:4 But God, who is rich in mercy, out of the great love with which he loved us.

[2191] James 4:7 Submit yourselves therefore to God. Resist the devil, and he will flee from you.

[2192] 1 Thessalonians 5:3When they say, 'There is peace and security', then sudden destruction will come upon them, as labor pains come upon a pregnant woman, and there will be no escape!

[2193] 2 Thessalonians 1:9 These will suffer the punishment of eternal destruction, separated from the presence of the Lord and from the glory of his might,

⁽⁵⁸⁾ (But God will reply) "No! My verses did come to you, but you denied them, turned arrogant, and denied the truth. ⁽⁵⁹⁾ On the Day of Resurrection you will see those who lied about God with their faces darkened (by grief and sorrow). Is not Hell the proper place for the arrogant? ⁽⁶⁰⁾ God will save those who were mindful of Him by the virtue of their successful choices; no harm will touch them, nor will they grieve.^{2194 (61)}

God is the Creator of all things,²¹⁹⁵ and He is the Guardian over all things. ⁽⁶²⁾ The keys of the heavens and the earth are His.²¹⁹⁶ Those who reject the verses of God, it is they who are the doomed. ⁽⁶³⁾ Say, "Do you order me to worship something other than God, you ignorant people?" ⁽⁶⁴⁾ Yet, It has already been revealed to you, and to those before you, that "If you should associate (anything) with God, your work will be in vain, and you will surely be among the doomed. ⁽⁶⁵⁾ Then, worship (only) God ²¹⁹⁷ and be among the grateful.^{2198 (66)}

(The unbelievers) have not valued God the way He ought to be valued. The whole earth will lie within His grasp²¹⁹⁹ on the Day of Resurrection, while Heaven will be folded up²²⁰⁰ in His right hand. May He be exalted in His glory, ²²⁰¹ high above anything they associate with Him. ⁽⁶⁷⁾ The Horn will be blown, and whoever is in the heavens and the earth will be stunned, except whom God wills. Then it will be blown again,²²⁰² and they will be stand, looking on. ⁽⁶⁸⁾ And the earth will shine with the light of its Lord.²²⁰³ The Book will be set in place,²²⁰⁴ and the prophets and the witnesses will be brought in. Judgment will be passed among them equitably, and they will not be wronged. ⁽⁶⁹⁾ Every soul will be fully compensated (for) what it has done, for He knows best what they do. ⁽⁷⁰⁾

• • •

²¹⁹⁴ Revelation 21:14 And the wall of the city has twelve foundations, and on them are the twelve names of the twelve apostles of the Lamb.

²¹⁹⁵ Colossians 1:16 for in him all things in heaven and on earth were created, things visible and invisible, whether thrones or dominions or rulers or powers—all things have been created through him and for him.

²¹⁹⁶ Psalm 89:11 Although heaven and the heaven of heavens belong to the LORD your God, the earth with all that is in it,

²¹⁹⁷ Psalm 95:6,7 O come, let us worship and bow down, let us kneel before the LORD, our Maker! 7 For he is our God, and we are the people of his pasture, and the sheep of his hand.

²¹⁹⁸ Psalm 107:1-3 O give thanks to the Lord, for he is good; for his steadfast love endures for ever. Let the redeemed of the Lord say so, those he redeemed from trouble and gathered in from the lands, from the east and from the west, from the north and from the south.

²¹⁹⁹ Isaiah 13:4-6 Listen, a tumult on the mountains as of a great multitude! Listen, an uproar of kingdoms, of nations gathering together! The Lord of hosts is mustering an army for battle. ⁵ They come from a distant land, from the end of the heavens, the Lord and the weapons of his indignation, to destroy the whole earth. ⁶ Wail, for the day of the Lord is near; it will come like destruction from the Almighty!

²²⁰⁰ Hebrews 1:12 like a cloak you will roll them up, and like clothing they will be changed. But you are the same, and your years will never end.'

²²⁰¹ Psalm 47:9, 40:16 The princes of the peoples gather as the people of the God of Abraham. For the shields of the earth belong to God; he is highly exalted. 40:16 But may all who seek you rejoice and be glad in you; may those who love your salvation say continually, 'Great is the Lord!

²²⁰² 1 Corinthians 15:52 in a moment, in the twinkling of an eye, at the last trumpet. For the trumpet will sound, and the dead will be raised imperishable, and we will be changed.

²²⁰³ Isaiah 60:1, 9:2 Arise, shine; for your light has come, and the glory of the Lord has risen upon you. 9:2 The people who walked in darkness have seen a great light; those who lived in a land of deep darkness— on them light has shined.

²²⁰⁴ Daniel 7:10 A stream of fire issued and flowed out from his presence. A thousand thousand served him, and ten thousand times ten thousand stood attending him. The court sat in judgment, and the books were opened.

Those who denied the truth will be driven to Hell in crowds. When they reach it, its gates will open and its custodians will say, "Did not messengers from among you come to you, reciting to you the verses of your Lord, and warning you of the meeting of this Day of yours?" They will say, "Yes, but the decree of punishment is justified against the unbelievers. [71] They will be told, "Enter the gates of Hell and stay there eternally. How evil is the residence of the arrogant." [72]

But those who were mindful of their Lord will be driven to Paradise in crowds. When they reach it, its gates will open, and custodians will say, "Peace be upon you; you have done well, so enter it to reside there eternally." [73] And they will say, "Praise be to God, who has fulfilled His promise to us and made us inherit the land, letting us settle in Paradise wherever we will. How excellent is the reward for those who act on their faith." [74] You will see the angels hovering around the Throne of His majesty, glorifying their Lord with praise.[2205] It will be judged between them equitably, and it will be said, "All praise be to God,[2206] Lord of the worlds." [75]

· · ·

[2205] Revelation 5:11-12 Then I looked, and I heard the voice of many angels surrounding the throne and the living creatures and the elders; they numbered myriads of myriads and thousands of thousands, [12] singing with full voice, 'Worthy is the Lamb that was slaughtered to receive power and wealth and wisdom and might and honor and glory and blessing!'
[2206] Psalm 150:1-6 Praise the Lord! Praise God in his sanctuary; praise him in his mighty firmament! [2] Praise him for his mighty deeds; praise him according to his surpassing greatness! [3] Praise him with trumpet sound; praise him with lute and harp! [4] Praise him with tambourine and dance; praise him with strings and pipe! [5] Praise him with clanging cymbals; praise him with loud clashing cymbals! [6] Let everything that breathes praise the Lord! Praise the Lord!

CHAPTER FORTY

GHAFIR
THE FORGIVER (GOD)

In the name of God, the Merciful-to-all, the Mercy Giver:
Ha Meem,²²⁰⁷ ⁽⁰¹⁾ The gradual revelation of the Book is from God, the Almighty,²²⁰⁸ the All-Knowing.²²⁰⁹ ⁽⁰²⁾ Forgiver of sin,²²¹⁰ Acceptor of repentance,²²¹¹ Severe in punishment²²¹² and Infinite in favor, there is no god except Him;²²¹³ to Him is the ultimate return.²²¹⁴ ⁽⁰³⁾ No one argues about God's signs except the unbelievers, so do not be deceived by their freedom to move around in the land. ⁽⁰⁴⁾ Before them the people of Noah (Nuh) rejected the truth,²²¹⁵ as did the parties after them. Every nation plotted to destroy their messenger and argued to defeat truth with falsehood.²²¹⁶ So, I seized them. What a punishment it was. ⁽⁰⁵⁾ In this way, your Lord's sentence was passed against those who denied the truth, that they would be the inhabitants of the Fire. ⁽⁰⁶⁾

• • •

---

²²⁰⁷ Here and at the beginning of many chapters there are unvowelled letters of unknown meaning. Numerous theories have been proposed, but there is no agreement on the subject.
²²⁰⁸ Job 9:4 He is wise in heart, and mighty in strength—who has resisted him, and succeeded? —
²²⁰⁹ Psalm 44:21 would not God discover this? For he knows the secrets of the heart.
²²¹⁰ Numbers 14:20 Then the Lord said, 'I do forgive, just as you have asked;
²²¹¹ Acts 26:20 but declared first to those in Damascus, then in Jerusalem and throughout the countryside of Judea, and also to the Gentiles, that they should repent and turn to God and do deeds consistent with repentance.
²²¹² Ezekiel 5:15 You shall be a mockery and a taunt, a warning and a horror, to the nations around you, when I execute judgments on you in anger and fury, and with furious punishments —I, the Lord, have spoken—
²²¹³ Mark 12:29 Jesus answered, 'The first is, "Hear, O Israel: the Lord our God, the Lord is one;
²²¹⁴ Ecclesiastes 12:7 and the dust returns to the earth as it was, and the breath returns to God who gave
²²¹⁵ Genesis 6:5 The Lord saw that the wickedness of humankind was great in the earth, and that every inclination of the thoughts of their hearts was only evil continually.
²²¹⁶ 1 Timothy 1:6 Some people have deviated from these and turned to meaningless talk,

Those who carry the Throne of His majesty, and those around it, praise their Lord's limitless glory,[2217] and believe in Him, and ask forgiveness for the Believers, (saying), "Our Lord, Your mercy and knowledge have encompassed all things,[2218] so forgive those who repent and follow Your path, and spare them from the punishment of Hell.[2219] [07] Our Lord, admit them to Gardens of Eden, which You have promised them, together with the righteous among their fathers, their spouses and their offspring. You are the Almighty,[2220] the Wise.[2221] [08] And guide them away (from committing) evil deeds.[2222] You would be Merciful that Day to anyone you have guided away (from committing) evil deeds, and that is the supreme triumph." [09] The unbelievers will be told (on the same Day), "When you were called to believe and rejected it, God's disgust with you was even greater than the self-disgust you now feel." [10] They will say, "Our Lord, twice You caused us to die, and twice You gave us life. We now admit our sins. Is there possibly a way out?" [11] (They will be told) "That is because, when God alone was called upon, you denied Him, but when others were associated with Him, you believed. Judgment belongs to God, the Most High,[2223] the Most Great."[2224] [12]

It is He who shows you His signs, and sends down provisions from the sky to sustain you, but only the one who turns to God will take heed, [13] so call upon God and dedicate your faith sincerely to Him, even though it is resented by unbelievers. [14] He is high above (all) ranks, the Lord of the Throne. He confers the Spirit by His command on whoever He wills of His worshipers to warn of the Day when they will meet Him. [15] The Day they will emerge, when nothing about them is concealed from God. "To whom belongs (all) sovereignty this Day?" "To God, the One,[2225] the All- Conquering."[2226] [16] This Day every soul will be rewarded for what it earned.[2227] There will be no injustice today, for God is swift to settle accounts. [17]

And warn them, of the Imminent Day, when the hearts are at the throats, choking them. The unjust will have no dependable friend and no intercessor (who is) obeyed. [18] God knows the eyes' deceptive glances and what the hearts conceal.[2228] [19] God judges with Truth, while those besides Him whom they

• • •

[2217] Revelation 4:8 And the four living creatures, each of them with six wings, are full of eyes all around and inside. Day and night without ceasing they sing, 'Holy, holy, holy, the Lord God the Almighty, who was and is and is to come.'

[2218] Psalm 145:9 The Lord is good to all, and his compassion is over all that he has made.

[2219] Psalm 119:88 In your steadfast love spare my life, so that I may keep the decrees of your mouth.

[2220] Psalm 106:8 Yet he saved them for his name's sake, so that he might make known his mighty power.

[2221] Proverbs 2:6 For the Lord gives wisdom; from his mouth come knowledge and understanding;

[2222] 1 Corinthians 10:13 No testing has overtaken you that is not common to everyone. God is faithful, and he will not let you be tested beyond your strength, but with the testing he will also provide the way out so that you may be able to endure it.

[2223] Psalm 47:2 For the Lord, the Most High, is awesome, a great king over all the earth.

[2224] Psalm 147:5-6 Great is our Lord, and abundant in power; his understanding is beyond measure.
[6] The Lord lifts up the downtrodden; he casts the wicked to the ground.

[2225] Deuteronomy 6:4 Hear, O Israel: The Lord is our God, the Lord alone.

[2226] 1 Chronicles 29:11 Yours, O Lord, are the greatness, the power, the glory, the victory, and the majesty; for all that is in the heavens and on the earth is yours; yours is the kingdom, O Lord, and you are exalted as head above all.

[2227] Luke 14:14 And you will be blessed, because they cannot repay you, for you will be repaid at the resurrection of the righteous.'

[2228] Psalm 44:21 would not God discover this? For he knows the secrets of the heart.

invoke will not judge with anything at all. It is God who is the All-Hearing, the All-Seeing. [20] Have they not traveled through the land and seen the fate of those (who lived) before them? They were mightier than they are, and they left more impact on the land, but God seized them for their sins, and they had no protector from God. [21] This is because they repeatedly rejected the self-evident signs their messengers brought them, so God seized them. He is All-Strong and severe in punishment [22]

We sent Moses (Musa) with Our signs and a clear authority [23] to Pharaoh, Haman[2229] and Korah (Qarun), but they said, "(He is) a lying magician." [24] Then, when he brought them the Truth from Us, they said, "Kill the sons of those who have believed with him and spare the women."[2230] But the schemes of the unbelievers can only fail. [25] Pharaoh said, "Let me kill[2231] "Let me kill Moses and let him appeal to his Lord. I fear that he may change your religion or spread disorder in the land." [26] But Moses said, "I have sought refuge in my Lord and yours from every arrogant tyrant who does not believe in the Day of Reckoning."[2232(27)]

A believing man from Pharaoh's family, who concealed his faith, said, "Are you going to kill a man (merely) because he says, 'My Lord is God, 'when he has brought you clear signs from your Lord? If he is lying, then the consequence of his lie will be on him, but if he is truthful, then some of what he promises you will happen to you. God does not guide the blatant liars.[2233] [28] My people, you reign today, masters in the land, but who will protect us from God's mighty punishment if it should come to us?" Pharaoh said, "I show you only what I see, and I am guiding you along the right path." [29]

But the believer said, "My people, I fear for you a day as befell the parties (who opposed their messengers), [30] Like what happen to Noah's people, Aad[2234] and Thamud[2235] and those after them. God does not want any injustice for His worshipers. [31] My people, I fear for you the Day of Calling [32] the Day when you will turn away, hoping to flee, with no one to protect you from God. Whomever God allows to stray has no guide.[2236] [33] Joseph had already come to you with clear evidence, but you never stopped doubting what he brought to you until, when he perished, you said, 'God will never send a messenger after him.' This is how God lets those who never cease doubting to stray." [34] Those who argue about God's revelations without having been given an authority are doing something despised by God and by those who believe. This is how God seals up

• • •

[2229] Pharaoh's chief adviser

[2230] Exodus 1:22 Then Pharaoh commanded all his people, 'Every boy that is born to the Hebrews you shall throw into the Nile, but you shall let every girl live.'

[2231] Exodus 2:15 When Pharaoh heard of it, he sought to kill Moses. But Moses fled from Pharaoh. He settled in the land of Midian, and sat down by a well.

[2232] Psalm 91:1-2 You who live in the shelter of the Most High, who abide in the shadow of the Almighty, [2] will say to the Lord, "My refuge and my fortress; my God, in whom I trust."

[2233] Proverbs 6:16-18 There are six things that the Lord hates, seven that are an abomination to him: [17] haughty eyes, a lying tongue, and hands that shed innocent blood, 18 a heart that devises wicked plans, feet that hurry to run to evil,

[2234] See Glossary

[2235] Ibid

[2236] 2 Thessalonians 2:11 For this reason God sends them a powerful delusion, leading them to believe what is false,

the heart of every arrogant tyrant.[2237] [35] (Then) Pharaoh said, "Haman, build me a tower that I may gain means of access, [36] access to the heavens, so that I may have a look at this god of Moses, though I think he is a liar." This is how Pharaoh's evil deeds were made to appear good to him, and he was diverted from the (right) way. Pharaoh's scheming led to nothing but ruin. [37]

But he who believed said, "My people, follow me, I will guide you through the correct path. [38] My people, this worldly life is only temporary enjoyment,[2238] but the Hereafter is the lasting home.[2239] [39] Whoever does a bad deed will be repaid with its like, but whoever does good and is a believer, whether male or female, they will enter Paradise, where they will be provided for without measure. [40] My people, how is it that I call you to salvation while you call me to the Fire? [41] You call me to deny God and to associate with Him something of which I have no knowledge, whereas I call you to the Almighty, the Ever-Forgiving. [42] Without a doubt, that to which you call me has no foundation either in this world or in the Hereafter, (nor is there doubt) that our return is to God, whereas those who overstate (their disbelief) shall inhabit the Fire. [43] You will remember what I say to you, so I entrust myself to God, for God is well aware of (His) worshipers." [44]

So God protected him from the evils they plotted, while a terrible punishment encompassed Pharaoh's clan,[2240] [45] the Fire, to which they will be exposed morning and evening. On the Day the Hour comes (it will be said), "Admit Pharaoh's clan to the most intense punishment." [46] In the Fire, they will bicker, and the meek will say to those who were arrogant, "We were your followers, so can you provide us some relief from the Fire?" [47] But those who were arrogant will say, "We are all in it together. God has judged between the worshipers." [48] Those in the Fire will say to the keepers of Hell, "Pray to your Lord to lighten our punishment[2241] for a day." [49] (The keepers) will say, "Did not your messengers come to you with clear evidence?" They will say, "Yes." (The keepers) will reply, "Then pray (yourselves), but the prayers of the unbelievers will always be in vain." [50]

We will surely support Our Messengers and those who believe during this life; and, on the Day when the witnesses arise- [51] the day when excuses will not benefit the unjust- they will be rejected and they will have the worst of homes.

• • •

[2237] Exodus 9:12 But the Lord hardened the heart of Pharaoh, and he would not listen to them, just as the LORD had spoken to Moses.

[2238] 1 John 2:17 And the world and its desire are passing away, but those who do the will of God live for ever.

[2239] Hebrews 12:28 Therefore, since we are receiving a kingdom that cannot be shaken, let us give thanks, by which we offer to God an acceptable worship with reverence and awe;

[2240] Exodus 6-14 The full story of God's dealing with Pharaoh through Moses

[2241] Matthew 25:41, 46 Then he will say to those at his left hand, "You that are accursed, depart from me into the eternal fire prepared for the devil and his angels; [46] And these will go away into eternal punishment, but the righteous into eternal life.'

[52] We gave Moses guidance, and We made the Children of Israel heirs to the Book[2242] [53] as guidance[2243] and a reminder[2244] for those with understanding. [54] Be patient, for God's promise is true.[2245] And ask forgiveness for your sin,[2246] and glorify your Lord with praise evening and morning.[2247] [55] Those who dispute God's revelations without any authority to do so have nothing within their hearts except arrogance,[2248] which they will never be able to satisfy, so seek refuge in God, for He is the All-Hearing, the All-Seeing.[56]

The creation of the heavens and earth[2249] is far greater than the creation of human beings, but most people do not know. [57] The blind and the seeing are not the same, nor are those who believe and do good deeds equal to the evildoers. How seldom you reflect. [58] The Hour is sure to come,[2250] there is no doubt about it, but most people do not believe. [59] Your Lord says, "Call upon Me, and I will answer you,[2251] but those who are too proud to worship Me will enter Hell, humiliated." [60]

It is God who made the night for you so that you may rest, and the day (so that you may) see. God is truly gracious to people,[2252] but most people are not thankful. [61] Such is God, your Lord, Creator of all things.[2253] There is no God but Him,[2254] so how can you be so misled? [62] Thus it is: those who reject God's signs are misled. [63] It is God who made the earth for you to settle and the heaven as a canopy. He designed you, and perfected [2255] your design, and provided you

• • •

[2242] Exodus 31:18 When God finished speaking with Moses on Mount Sinai, he gave him the two tablets of the covenant, tablets of stone, written with the finger of God.
[2243] Proverbs 1:2-6 For learning about wisdom and instruction, for understanding words of insight, 3 for gaining instruction in wise dealing, righteousness, justice, and equity; 4 to teach shrewdness to the simple, knowledge and prudence to the young— 5 let the wise also hear and gain in learning, and the discerning acquire skill, 6 to understand a proverb and a figure, the words of the wise and their riddles.
[2244] Deuteronomy 8:2 Remember the long way that the LORD your God has led you these forty years in the wilderness, in order to humble you, testing you to know what was in your heart, whether or not you would keep his commandments.
[2245] 2 Corinthians 1:20 For in him every one of God's promises is a 'Yes.' For this reason, it is through him that we say the 'Amen', to the glory of God.,
[2246] Numbers 14:20 Then the LORD said, 'I do forgive, just as you have asked;
[2247] Psalm 66: 1-4 Make a joyful noise to God, all the earth; 2 sing the glory of his name; give to him glorious praise. 3 Say to God, "How awesome are your deeds! Because of your great power, your enemies cringe before you 4 All the earth worships you; they sing praises to you, sing praises to your name."
[2248] James 4:16 As it is, you boast in your arrogance; all such boasting is evil.
[2249] Psalm 19:1 The heavens are telling the glory of God; and the firmament proclaims his handiwork.
[2250] Revelation 14:7 He said in a loud voice, 'Fear God and give him glory, for the hour of his judgment has come; and worship him who made heaven and earth, the sea and the springs of water.'
[2251] Jeremiah 33:3 Call to me and I will answer you, and will tell you great and hidden things that you have not known. Mark 11:24 So I tell you, whatever you ask for in prayer, believe that you have received it, and it will be yours.
[2252] Psalm 41:4 As for me, I said, "O Lord, be gracious to me; heal me, for I have sinned against you."
[2253] Revelation 4:11 'You are worthy, our Lord and God, to receive glory and honor and power, for you created all things, and by your will they existed and were created.'
[2254] Deuteronomy 6:4 Hear, O Israel: The Lord is our God, the Lord alone.
[2255] Psalm 139:13-16 For it was you who formed my inward parts; you knit me together in my mother's womb. 14 I praise you, for I am fearfully and wonderfully made. Wonderful are your works; that I know very well. 15 My frame was not hidden from you, when I was being made in secret, intricately woven in the depths of the earth. 16 Your eyes beheld my unformed substance. In your book were written all the days that were formed for me, when none of them as yet existed.

with wholesome things. Such is God, your Lord,[2256] so blessed be God,[2257] Lord of the worlds.[2258] [(64)] He is the Ever-Living. There is no God except Him,[2259] So call on Him, making your faith sincerely His. Praise be to God, Lord of the worlds. [(65)]

Say, "Now that clear evidence has come to me from my Lord, I have been prohibited from worshiping those you call upon besides God, and I am commanded to submit [2260] to the Lord of the worlds." [2261(66)] It is He who created you from dust,[2262] then from a sperm-drop, then from a clinging clot;[2263] then He brings you out as infants; then He allows you to reach maturity; and then you become elderly- although some of you die sooner-so that you may reach a predetermined age,[2264] and perhaps you may understand. [(67)] It is He who gives life and death;[2265] when He decides on a thing, He simply says, "Be," and It is.[2266(68)]

Do you not see how misled are those who dispute God's signs, [(69)] those who deny the Book and the messages We sent with Our Messengers? They will surely come to know, [(70)] when they have shackles and chains around their necks, and are dragged [(71)] in boiling water, and are then thrown into the Fire, where they will be consumed. [(72)] It will then be said to them, "Where are those (associates) whom you used to consider divine [(73)] other than God?" They will say, "They have departed from us; or, rather, those we used to call upon proved to be nothing. (They will be told,) "This is how God let those who deny the truth stray,[2267] [(74)] all because you used to rejoice on earth in things other than the truth, and you were full of vanity. [(75)] Enter the gates of Hell, to remain there eternally, a terrible home for the arrogant." [(76)]

So be patient, (Prophet,) for God's promise is true.[2268] Whether We show you some of what We have promised them or We cause you to die, It is to Us that

•   •   •

[2256] Deuteronomy 8:6,10 Therefore keep the commandments of the Lord your God, by walking in his ways and by fearing him. 10 You shall eat your fill and bless the Lord your God for the good land that he has given you.

[2257] Psalm 103:1-2 Of David. Bless the LORD, O my soul, and all that is within me, bless his holy name. 2 Bless the Lord, O my soul, and do not forget all his benefits—

[2258] 2 Kings 19:15 And Hezekiah prayed before the LORD, and said: 'O Lord the God of Israel, who are enthroned above the cherubim, you are God, you alone, of all the kingdoms of the earth; you have made heaven and earth.

[2259] Deuteronomy 6:4 Hear, O Israel: The Lord is our God, the Lord alone.

[2260] James 4:7 Submit yourselves therefore to God. Resist the devil, and he will flee from you.

[2261] Nehemiah 9:5-6 Then the Levites, Jeshua, Kadmiel, Bani, Hashabneiah, Sherebiah, Hodiah, Shebaniah, and Pethahiah, said, "Stand up and bless the Lord your God from everlasting to everlasting. Blessed be your glorious name, which is exalted above all blessing and praise." 6 And Ezra said: "You are the Lord, you alone; you have made heaven, the heaven of heavens, with all their host, the earth and all that is on it, the seas and all that is in them. To all of them you give life, and the host of heaven worships you.

[2262] Genesis 2:7 then the Lord God formed man from the dust of the ground, and breathed into his nostrils the breath of life; and the man became a living being.

[2263] Psalm 139:13,16 For it was you who formed my inward parts; you knit me together in my mother's womb. Your eyes beheld my unformed substance. 16 In your book were written all the days that were formed for me, when none of them as yet existed.

[2264] Psalm 39:4 'Lord, let me know my end, and what is the measure of my days; let me know how fleeting my life is.

[2265] 1 Samuel 2:6 The Lord kills and brings to life; he brings down to Sheol and raises up.

[2266] Psalm 33: 9 For he spoke, and it came to be; he commanded, and it stood firm.

[2267] 2 Thessalonians 2:11, For this reason God sends them a powerful delusion, leading them to believe what is false,

[2268] James 5:8 You also must be patient. Strengthen your hearts, for the coming of the Lord is near.

they will be returned. [(77)] We have sent messengers before you. Some We have told you about, and others We did not. No messenger can produce a miracle except with God's permission. Then, when God's command comes, just judgment will be passed, and those who followed falsehood will be lost then and there. [(78)]

It is God who made the domestic animals,[2269] some for you to ride, and some to eat. [(79)] You have other benefits from them as well. You can reach any destination you wish on them, and on them and on ships, you are transported. [(80)] And (thus) He shows you His signs. So, which of God's signs do you deny? [(81)]

Have they not traveled through the land and seen the fate of those who lived before them? They were more numerous than they are, and had greater power, and left more impressive marks on the land. Yet what they achieved was of no use to them. [(82)] When their messengers came to them with self-evident signs, they showed satisfaction with the knowledge they had, and so they were engulfed by the very punishment they had mocked. [(83)] Then, when they saw Our might, they said," We believe in God alone, and we reject what we used to associate with Him." [(84)] But believing after seeing Our might did not help them at all. This has been God's way of dealing with His worshipers, and those who denied the truth were lost, then and there. [(85)]

·   ·   ·

[2269] Genesis 1:24-25 And God said, 'Let the earth bring forth living creatures of every kind: cattle and creeping things and wild animals of the earth of every kind.' And it was so. 25 God made the wild animals of the earth of every kind, and the cattle of every kind, and everything that creeps upon the ground of every kind. And God saw that it was good.

CHAPTER **FORTY ONE**

FUSSILAT
MADE CLEAR

THE **MECCA** PERIOD

In the name of God, the Merciful-to-all, the Mercy Giver:
Ha Meem,[2270] [(01)] revelation have come down to you) from the Merciful-to-all,[2271] the Mercy Giver[2272] [(02)] a Book whose verses have been made clear, an Arabic Qur'an for people who know, [(03)] giving good news and warning. Yet, most of them turn away, so they do not hear, [(04)] and they say, "There is a barrier between our hearts and what you call us to, and there is heaviness in our ears.[2273] There is a curtain between us and you.[2274] So do whatever you want, and so shall we." [(05)] Say, "I am only a human like you. It has been revealed to me that your god is but one God.[2275] So be upright towards Him, and seek His forgiveness." How terrible it is for the idolaters [2276] [(06)] those who do not give the purifying alms, and refuse to believe in the Hereafter. [(07)] Those who believe and do good deeds will have an endless reward.[2277] [(08)]

• • •

[2270] Here and at the beginning of many chapters there are unvowelled letters of unknown meaning. Numerous theories have been proposed, but there is no agreement on the subject.
[2271] Psalm 145:8. The Lord is merciful and gracious, slow to anger and abounding in steadfast love.
[2272] Ephesians 2:4 But God, who is rich in mercy, out of the great love with which he loved us
[2273] Micah 7:16 The nations shall see and be ashamed of all their might; they shall lay their hands on their mouths; their ears shall be deaf;
[2274] 2 Corinthians 3:15-16 Indeed, to this very day whenever Moses is read, a veil lies over their minds; [16] but when one turns to the Lord, the veil is removed.
[2275] Mark 12:29 Jesus answered, 'The first is, "Hear, O Israel: the Lord our God, the Lord is one;
[2276] Ezekiel 23:49 They shall repay you for your lewdness, and you shall bear the penalty for your sinful idolatry; and you shall know that I am the Lord God.
[2277] 2 John 8 Be on your guard, so that you do not lose what we have worked for, but may receive a full reward.

Say, "Do you deny the One who created the earth[2278] in two days and attribute equals to Him? That is the Lord of the worlds."[2279] [(09)] He placed firm mountains over it, and He blessed it and apportioned its provisions to all who would seek them, (all) in four days. [(10)] Then He turned to the Heaven while it was smoke and said to it and to the earth, "Come willingly or unwillingly." They said, "We come willingly." [(11)] He decreed that they are seven heavens in two days, and He revealed to each its mandate. And We decorated the lower heaven with lanterns and protection. Such is the design of the Almighty,[2280] the All-Knowing.[2281][(12)]

If they turn away, say, "I have warned you of a thunderbolt like the one which struck Aad[2282] and Thamud[2283] [(13)] when their messengers came to them from all around them, saying "Do not worship anyone but God." They said, "Had our Lord willed, He would have sent down angels; therefore, we reject the message with which you were sent." [(14)]

As for Aad, they were arrogant in the land, opposed justice and said, "Who could have a power greater than ours?" Did they not see that God who created them is more powerful than they?[2284] But they continued to reject Our signs. [(15)] so We sent a screaming wind upon them for a few miserable days to make them taste the punishment of disgrace in this worldly life; but the punishment[2285] of the Hereafter is more disgracing, and they will not be helped. [(16)] And as for Thamud,[2286] We guided them, but they preferred blindness over guidance, so the thunderbolt of humiliating punishment seized them, just as they deserved. [(17)] And We saved those who believed and were mindful of God. [(18)]

On the Day when God's enemies will be herded to the Fire, driven in rows, [(19)] until, when they have reached it, their hearing, their sight and their skins will testify against them concerning what they were doing. [(20)] They will ask their skins, "Why did you testify against us?" They will say, "God, who gave speech to everything, has given us speech; it is He Who created you the first time, and to Him you will return.[2287] [(21)] You did not even try to conceal yourselves from your hearing or your sights or your skins to prevent them from testifying against you, but you assumed that God did not know much of what you were doing.[2288] [(22)] It is this thought which you assumed about your Lord that led you to ruin, so that

• • •

[2278] Genesis 1:9-10 And God said, 'Let the waters under the sky be gathered together into one place, and let the dry land appear.' And it was so. [10] God called the dry land Earth, and the waters that were gathered together he called Seas. And God saw that it was good.

[2279] 2 Kings 19:15 And Hezekiah prayed before the Lord, and said: 'O Lord the God of Israel, who are enthroned above the cherubim, you are God, you alone, of all the kingdoms of the earth; you have made heaven and earth.

[2280] Job 9:4 He is wise in heart, and mighty in strength —who has resisted him, and succeeded? —

[2281] 1 John 3:20 whenever our hearts condemn us; for God is greater than our hearts, and he knows everything.

[2282] See Glossary

[2283] Ibid

[2284] Psalm 93:4 More majestic than the thunders of mighty waters, more majestic than the waves of the sea, majestic on high is the Lord!

[2285] 2 Thessalonians 1:9 These will suffer the punishment of eternal destruction, separated from the presence of the Lord and from the glory of his might,

[2286] See Glossary

[2287] Ecclesiastes 12:7 and the dust returns to the earth as it was, and the breath returns to God who gave it.

[2288] Psalm 44:21 would not God discover this? For he knows the secrets of the heart.

you became doomed. [23] So (even) if they are patient, the Fire will be their home, and if they plead for a favor, none will be given them, [24] (for) We had assigned them companions, who made what is before them and what was behind them seem alluring. But the sentence has already been passed against them, together with generations of jinn and men before them: they were doomed. [25]

The unbelievers say, "Do not listen to this Qur'an but talk over it, so that you may prevail." [26] But We will surely cause the unbelievers to taste a severe punishment,[2289] and We will reward them according to the worst of their deeds. [27] Such is the repayment of God's enemies, the Fire, where they will have their permanent home as payment for having disregarded Our revelations. [28] The unbelievers will say, "Our Lord, show us those jinn and men who misled us; we will trample them under our feet so that they become the lowest of the low." [29] Those who say, "Our Lord is God"[2290] and then stay on the right course, on them the angels will descend on them and say, "Do not fear or grieve, but (rather) rejoice in the news of Paradise,[2291] which you were promised [2292][30] we are your allies in this life and in the Hereafter, where you will have whatever your souls desire, and you will have whatever you wish [31] as a welcoming gift from the Most Forgiving,[2293] the Mercy Giver." [32]

Who speaks better than someone who calls people to God, does good deeds, and says, "I am among those who submit to God."[2294] [33] Good and evil are never equal. Repel evil with good[2295], and your enemy will become like an intimate friend.[2296] [34] But, none will attain it except those who are steadfast in patience, and none will attain it except the very fortunate. [35] And when a temptation from Satan provokes you, seek refuge in God;[2297] He is the All-Hearing[2298] and the All-Knowing.[2299] [36]

• • •

[2289] Habakkuk 1 :12 Are you not from of old, O Lord my God, my Holy One? You shall not die. O Lord, you have marked them for judgment; and you, O Rock, have established them for punishment
[2290] Revelation 4:11 'You are worthy, our Lord and God, to receive glory and honor and power, for you created all things, and by your will they existed and were created.'
[2291] Psalm 32:11 Be glad in the Lord and rejoice, O righteous, and shout for joy, all you upright in heart.
[2292] Psalm 5:11 But let all who take refuge in you rejoice; let them ever sing for joy. Spread your protection over them, so that those who love your name may exult in you.
[2293] Luke 1:50 His mercy is for those who fear him from generation to generation.
[2294] James 4:7 Submit yourselves therefore to God. Resist the devil, and he will flee from you.
[2295] Romans 12:21, "Do not be overcome by evil, but overcome evil with good."
Matthew 5:44 But I say to you, Love your enemies and pray for those who persecute you.
[2296] Proverbs 16:7 When the ways of people please the Lord, he causes even their enemies to be at peace with them. Matthew 7:12 "In everything do to others as you would have them do to you; for this is the law and the prophets."
[2297] Psalm 46:1 God is our refuge and strength, a very present help in trouble.
[2298] Psalm 34:15 The eyes of the Lord are on the righteous, and his ears are open to their cry.
[2299] 1 John 3:20 whenever our hearts condemn us; for God is greater than our hearts, and he knows everything.

Among His signs are the night, the day, the sun and the moon.[2300] Do not bow down in worship to the sun, nor to the moon,[2301] but bow down to God,[2302] Who created them, if it is Him that you worship. [(37)] But if they respond arrogantly, (it matters not) for those who are near your Lord praise His limitless glory by night and by day, and never grow tired. [(38)] Another of His signs is that you see the earth humbly desolate, but when We send down rain on it, it quivers and swells. He who revived it will revive the dead.[2303] He has power over all things.[2304] [(39)]

Those who distort Our verses are not hidden from Us. Does he who is thrown into the Fire fare better than he who will arrive securely on the Day of Resurrection? Do what you want; He Sees everything you do. [(40)] Those who reject this Reminder after it has come to them (are losers), as it is a mighty Book [(41)] that falsehood cannot approach either openly or secretly, (one) sent down from the All-Wise [2305] and Praiseworthy.[2306] [(42)] Nothing has been said to you (Prophet) that was not said to the messengers before you. Your Lord is a Lord of Forgiveness, but also of painful punishment. [(43)] Had We made it a Qur'an in a foreign language, they would have said, "If only its verses were made clear." What? A (book in a) foreign language to an Arab?" Say, "It is guidance and healing for those who believe, but for those who do not believe, it is heaviness in their ears, and it is blindness for them, as if they were being called from a distant place." [(44)] We gave Moses (Musa) the Book, but there was disagreement about it. And had it not to a prior decree from your Lord, their differences would already have been settled.[2307] But they are still in suspicious and in doubt about it. [(45)]

Whoever does good works, does so for his own soul; and whoever does evil, does so to its detriment[2308]. Your Lord is never unjust to His worshipers. [(46)] Knowledge of the Hour [2309] belongs solely to him; no fruit emerges from its husk nor does a female conceive or give birth without His knowledge. On the Day when He calls out to them, "Where are My associates?" They will then say, "We

• • •

[2300] Genesis 1:14-16 And God said, 'Let there be lights in the dome of the sky to separate the day from the night; and let them be for signs and for seasons and for days and years, [15] and let them be lights in the dome of the sky to give light upon the earth.' And it was so. [16] God made the two great lights—the greater light to rule the day and the lesser light to rule the night—and the stars.

[2301] Deuteronomy 17:3 by going to serve other gods and worshipping them—whether the sun or the moon or any of the host of heaven, which I have forbidden

[2302] Psalm 95:6 O come, let us worship and bow down, let us kneel before the Lord, our Maker!

[2303] Romans 4:16-17 For this reason it depends on faith, in order that the promise may rest on grace and be guaranteed to all his descendants, not only to the adherents of the law but also to those who share the faith of Abraham (for he is the father of all of us, [17] as it is written, 'I have made you the father of many nations')—in the presence of the God in whom he believed, who gives life to the dead and calls into existence the things that do not exist.

[2304] Job 42:2 'I know that you can do all things, and that no purpose of yours can be thwarted.

[2305] Proverbs 2:6 For the Lord gives wisdom; from his mouth come knowledge and understanding;

[2306] 2 Samuel 22:4 I call upon the Lord, who is worthy to be praised, and I am saved from my enemies.

[2307] 1 Corinthians 10:13 No testing has overtaken you that is not common to everyone. God is faithful, and he will not let you be tested beyond your strength, but with the testing he will also provide the way out so that you may be able to endure it.

[2308] John 5:29 and will come forth; those who did the good deeds to a resurrection of life, those who committed the evil deeds to a resurrection of judgment.

[2309] Revelation 14:7 He said in a loud voice, 'Fear God and give him glory, for the hour of his judgment has come; and worship him who made heaven and earth, the sea and the springs of water.'

admit to You, none of us witnessed any."[47] What they used to pray to before will forsake them, and they will realize that they have no escape. [48]

A human being never tires of praying for good things; but when hard times afflict him, he despairs and loses hope. [49] And if We let him taste mercy from Us, after hard times have afflicted him, he will say, "This is my due, and I do not think the Hour [2310] (of Judgment) is going to come; but even if I were to be returned to my Lord, I will (surely) have the very best reward from Him." But We will inform the unbelievers of what they did, and We will make them taste an awful punishment. [50] And whenever We're gracious to a human being, he turns away and distances himself, but when hard times touch him, he starts endless prayers. [51] Say, "What if this revelation is truly from God, and you are rejecting it[2311]? Who is more misguided than he who is cutoff and alienated (from God)?" [52] We will show them Our signs on the horizons[2312] and in themselves, until it is clear to them that this is the Truth. Is it not sufficient that your Lord is a Witness over all things? [2313] [53] Surely they are in doubt about meeting their Lord. Surely He encompasses everything. [54]

• • •

[2310] John 5:28 Do not be astonished at this; for the hour is coming when all who are in their graves will hear his voice
[2311] Deuteronomy 18:19 It shall come about that whoever will not listen to My words which he shall speak in My name, I Myself will require it of him. John 16:13 When the Spirit of truth comes, he will guide you into all the truth, for he will not speak on his own authority, but whatever he hears he will speak, and he will declare to you the things that are to come.
[2312] https://www.youtube.com/watch?v=udAL48P5NJU#t=67
[2313] Job 28:24 For he looks to the ends of the earth, and s everything under the heavens.

CHAPTER FORTY TWO

ASH-SHURA

CONSULTATION

THE **MECCA** PERIOD

Ha Meem.[01] A'yn Seen Qaf,[2314] [02] thus God, the Almighty,[2315] the Wise[2316] reveals to you, as He did to those before you. [03] To Him belongs everything in the heavens and everything on earth.[2317] He is the Most High,[2318] the Most Great.[2319] [04]The heavens above them almost burst apart (from awe of Him), while the angels praise their Lord's limitless glory[2320] and ask forgiveness for those on earth. God is indeed the Ever Forgiving,[2321] the Mercy giver.[2322] [05] As for those who take other than Him as protectors, God is in charge of them and you are not their keeper. [06]

Thus We have revealed to you an Arabic Qur'an that you may warn this main city and all others around it and to give warning of the Day of Gathering,[2323] about which there is no doubt, when some will be in the Garden and some in the Blazing Fire. [07] Had God willed, He could have made them one community, but He admits into His mercy him that wills. As for the unjust, they will have no

• • •

[2314] Here and at the beginning of many chapters there are unvowelled letters of unknown meaning. Numerous theories have been proposed, but there is no agreement on the subject.
[2315] Jeremiah 10:6-7 There is none like you, O Lord; you are great, and your name is great in might. Who would not fear you, O King of the nations? [7] For that is your due; among all the wise ones of the nations and in all their kingdoms there is no one like you.
[2316] Proverbs 2:6 For the Lord gives wisdom; from his mouth come knowledge and understanding;
[2317] Deuteronomy 10:14 Although heaven and the heaven of heavens belong to the Lord your God, the earth with all that is in it,
[2318] Psalm 47:2 For the Lord, the Most High, is awesome, a great king over all the earth.
[2319] Psalm 147:5, Great is our Lord, and abundant in power; his understanding is beyond measure.
[2320] Psalm 29:2 Ascribe to the Lord the glory of his name; worship the LORD in holy splendor.
[2321] Daniel 9:9 To the Lord our God belong mercy and forgiveness, for we have rebelled against him . . .
[2322] Ephesians 2:4 But God, who is rich in mercy, out of the great love with which he loved us
[2323] Matthew 25:32 All the nations will be gathered before him, and he will separate people one from another as a shepherd separates the sheep from the goats,

protector and no helper. [08] Or do they think that they have protectors other than Him? God is the Protector, for He gives life to the dead,[2324] and He is able to do all things.[2325] [09] Whatever matters you differ about, is for God to judge. Such is God, my Lord, in whom I trust, and unto Him I repent, [10] the Creator of the heavens and earth[2326] who separated them and gave each a purpose. He has made mates for you from among yourselves, and gave mates to the animals, so that you may multiply.[2327] There is nothing like Him.[2328] He is the All-Hearing, the All-Seeing. [11] To Him belong the controls of the heavens and the earth.[2329] He provides abundantly or scarcely to whoever He Wills. He is, the All Knowing.[2330][12]

He has ordained for you the same faith He commanded Noah (Nuh), and what We have revealed to you, and what We commanded Abraham (Iberahim) and Moses (Musa) and Jesus (Esa): "You shall uphold the faith and do not break up into factions." Although what you are calling the idolaters to do is too hard for them. (However) God draws to Himself everyone who is willing, and guides unto Himself everyone who turns to Him.[2331] [13] Yet they (the followers) split into factions, out of rivalry between them only after they came to know the truth. Judgment between them would have been pronounced, were it not for a decision from your Lord to postpone it until a set time. Yet those who have inherited the Book after them are in grave doubt about it. [14] Therefore, go on inviting them and stay the course as you have been commanded. Do not follow their whims and desires but say, "I have believed in what God has sent down of the Book, and I have been commanded to judge equitably between you.[2332] God is our Lord and your Lord. We have our deeds, and you have your deeds. Let there be no quarrel between us and you. God will bring us all together, and to Him is the ultimate return."[2333] [15] And those who argue about God after having answered His call, their argument has no basis whatsoever with their Lord. Anger enfolds them, and a severe punishment awaits them.[2334] [16] It is God who has

• • •

[2324] Romans 4:17 as it is written, 'I have made you the father of many nations')—in the presence of the God in whom he believed, who gives life to the dead and calls into existence the things that do not exist.
[2325] Job 42:2 'I know that you can do all things, and that no purpose of yours can be thwarted. Luke 1:37 For nothing will be impossible with God.'
[2326] Revelation 14:7 He said in a loud voice, 'Fear God and give him glory, for the hour of his judgment has come; and worship him who made heaven and earth, the sea and the springs of water.'
[2327] Genesis 1:22 God blessed them, saying, 'Be fruitful and multiply and fill the waters in the seas, and let birds multiply on the earth.'
[2328] Jeremiah 10:6 There is none like you, O Lord; You are great, and your name is great in might. Exodus 15:11 "Who is like you, O Lord, among the gods? Who is like you, majestic in holiness, awesome in splendor, doing wonders?
[2329] Psalm 89:11 The heavens are yours, the earth also is yours; the world and all that is in it—you have founded them
[2330] 1 John 3:20 whenever our hearts condemn us; for God is greater than our hearts, and he knows everything.
[2331] Acts 3:19 Repent therefore, and turn to God so that your sins may be wiped out,
[2332] Micah 6:8 He has told you, O mortal, what is good; and what does the LORD require of you but to do justice, and to love kindness, and to walk humbly with your God?
[2333] Psalm 22:27 All the ends of the earth shall remember and turn to the LORD; and all the families of the nations shall worship before him.
[2334] 2 Peter 2:21-22 For it would have been better for them never to have known the way

sent down the Book with Truth and Balance. For all you know, the Hour[2335] might be near. [17] Those who do not believe in it seek to hasten it; but those who believe are concerned about it, as they know it is the Truth. Unquestionably, those who question the Hour are in extreme error. [18]

God is very gentle with His worshipers; He provides for whomever He wills. He is the All Powerful,[2336] the Almighty.[2337] [19] If anyone desires the harvest of the Hereafter, We will increase for him his harvest. And if he desires the harvest of this world, We will give him a share of it, but He will have no share of the Hereafter[2338]. [20] Or do they have partners who have ordained for them some faith that is not authorized by God? Were it not for (God's) decisive word, Judgment would have been made between them. The unjust will have a painful punishment.[2339] [21] You will see the unjust worried about what they have committed, as they will have to answer for it. While those who have believed and done good deeds are in flowering meadows of the Gardens,[2340] having whatever they wish from their Lord: that is the supreme blessing. [22] This is the good news God gives to His worshipers who believe and do good deeds.

Say, "I do not ask you any wage for it, except affection due to kin."[2341] Whoever does a good deed, We will increase it for him. God is Ever Forgiving[2342] and Most Appreciative. [23] Or do they say, "He falsely claimed lies about God?" If God so willed, He could have sealed your heart, exterminated falsehood and confirmed the Truth with His Words. He has full Knowledge of what is in the hearts[2343] [24] It is He who accepts repentance[2344] from His worshipers and forgives bad deeds, He knows what you do. [25] He answers those who have believed and done good deeds and increases for them out of His grace. But the unbelievers will have a severe punishment. [26] Were God to expand provision to His worshipers, they would have committed tyranny on earth. But He sends down whatever He wills in due measures. He is, well Acquainted and Fully Aware

• • •

of righteousness than, after knowing it, to turn back from the holy commandment that was passed on to them. [22] It has happened to them according to the true proverb, 'The dog turns back to its own vomit', and, 'The sow is washed only to wallow in the mud.'

[2335] John 5:28 Do not be astonished at this; for the hour is coming when all who are in their graves will hear his voice.

[2336] Psalm 62:11 Once God has spoken; twice have I heard this: that power belongs to God,

[2337] Psalm 150:2 Praise him for his mighty deeds; praise him according to his surpassing greatness!

[2338] "Do not store up for yourselves treasures on earth, where moth and rust destroy, and where thieves break in and steal. "But store up for yourselves treasures in heaven, where neither moth nor rust destroys, and where thieves do not break in or steal; for where your treasure is, there your heart will be also.

[2339] Matthew 25:41, 46 Then he will say to those at his left hand, "You that are accursed, depart from me into the eternal fire prepared for the devil and his angels; [46] And these will go away into eternal punishment, but the righteous into eternal life.'

[2340] John 5:29 and will come out—those who have done good, to the resurrection of life, and those who have done evil, to the resurrection of condemnation.

[2341] Romans 13:8 Owe no one anything, except to love one another; for the one who loves another has fulfilled the law.

[2342] Numbers 14:20 Then the Lord said, 'I do forgive, just as you have asked;

[2343] 1 Samuel 16:7But the Lord said to Samuel, 'Do not look on his appearance or on the height of his stature, because I have rejected him; for the LORD does not see as mortals see; they look on the outward appearance, but the Lord looks on the heart.'

[2344] 1 John 1:9 If we confess our sins, he is faithful and just to forgive us our sins and to cleanse us from all unrighteousness.

of His worshipers. [(27)] It is He who sends down the rain[2345] after they have lost hope and unfolds His mercy. He is the Protector, the Praiseworthy.[2346] [(28)]

Among His signs is the creation of the heavens and earth and the creatures He has spread throughout them: He is Able to gather them together if He so wishes. [(29)] Whatever disaster strikes you, It is for what your hands have done[2347]; Yet He forgives much.[2348] [(30)] On earth you will not be beyond God's reach. You do not have any protector or helper besides God.[2349] [(31)] Among His Signs are ships floating like mountains through the sea. [(32)] If He wills, He could have settled down the winds, leaving them motionless on its surface. Surely in that are signs for every patient and grateful person. [(33)] Or He could destroy them for what they have earned; yet He pardons much. [(34)] Those who argue about Our signs know that there is no escape for them. [(35)]

Whatever You have been given is only the provision of this life.[2350] But that which is with God is better and more enduring for those who believe and trust in their Lord;[2351] [(36)] those who avoid major sins and gross indecencies, and even if they became angry, they will forgive;[2352] [(37)] and those who respond to their Lord, pray regularly, conduct their affairs by mutual consultation, and give of what We have provided for them; [(38)] and those who, when tyranny strikes them, they defend themselves. [(39)] The retribution for a bad deed is one like it,[2353] but whoever forgives and makes peace will have his reward with God.[2354] He certainly does not like those who do wrong. [(40)] Yet whoever defends himself after having been wronged, there is no blame on them. [(41)] Blame lies on those who wrong others and transgress in the land without any justification. Those will have a painful punishment.[2355] [(42)] As for him who endures patiently and forgives, that is a sign of real resolve. [(43)]

•   •   •

[2345] Jeremiah 14:22 Can any idols of the nations bring rain? Or can the heavens give showers? Is it not you, O Lord our God? We set our hope on you, for it is you who do all this.
[2346] 2 Samuel 22:4 I call upon the Lord, who is worthy to be praised, and I am saved from my enemies
[2347] Galatians 6:7 Do not be deceived: God is not mocked, for whatever one sows, that will he also reap. Matthew 26:52 All who draw the sword will die by the sword.
[2348] Micah 7:18-20 Who is a God like you, pardoning iniquity and passing over the transgression of the remnant of your possession? He does not retain his anger forever, because he delights in showing clemency. [19] He will again have compassion upon us; he will tread our iniquities under foot. You will cast all our sins into the depths of the sea. [20] You will show faithfulness to Jacob and unswerving loyalty to Abraham, as you have sworn to our ancestors from the days of old.
[2349] Hosea 13:4 Yet I have been the Lord your God ever since the land of Egypt; you know no God but me, and besides me there is no savior.
[2350] Mark 8:36-37 For what will it profit them to gain the whole world and forfeit their life? [37] Indeed, what can they give in return for their life?
[2351] Psalm 37:3-6 Trust in the Lord, and do good; so you will live in the land, and enjoy security. 4 Take delight in the Lord, and he will give you the desires of your heart. 5 Commit your way to the Lord; trust in him, and he will act. 6 He will make your vindication shine like the light, and the justice of your cause like the noonday.
[2352] Mark 11:25 'Whenever you stand praying, forgive, if you have anything against anyone; so that your Father in heaven may also forgive you your trespasses.'
[2353] Mark 4:24 "With the measure you use, it will be measured to you--and even more.
[2354] Luke 6:37 'Do not judge, and you will not be judged; do not condemn, and you will not be condemned. Forgive, and you will be forgiven; Matthew 7:12 "In everything do to others as you would have them do to you; for this is the law and the prophets."
[2355] 2 Thessalonians 1:9 These will suffer the punishment of eternal destruction, separated from the presence of the Lord and from the glory of his might,

Whoever God lets go astray[2356] will have no protector apart from Him. And you will see the transgressors, when they see the punishment, saying, "Is there a way of going back?" [44] As they are exposed to the Fire, you will see them humbled from humiliation, glancing around covertly. While those who believed will say, "The losers are those who lost themselves and their kin on the Day of Resurrection." Verily, the unjust are in an enduring punishment [45] they have no allies to support them apart from God. Anyone God lets go astray will find no way out. [46]

Respond to your Lord before a Day comes from God's judgment that cannot be turned back.[2357] You will have no refuge on that Day and no means of denial. [47] But if they turn away, We did not send you as their guardian. Your only duty is to deliver the message. When We let man taste Our mercy,[2358] he rejoices in it; but if harm afflicts him for what his hands have done, then man turns to denial. [48] The kingdom of the heavens and the earth belongs to God.[2359] He creates what he wills. He gives daughters to whomever He wills, and He gives sons to whom He wills. [49] Or, and He makes whom He wills sterile. He is All Knowing [2360] and Able to do all things.[2361] [50]

God will not speak to any human being except by revelation[2362] or from behind a veil, or by sending a messenger who then reveals, by His permission whatever He wills. He is Most High[2363] and All Wise.[2364] [51] Accordingly We have revealed to you a Spirit of Our command. You did not know what is the Book or what faith is, but We have made it an enlightenment, guiding with it whom We wish of Our worshipers. You indeed guide to a straight path[2365] [52] the path of

· · ·

[2356] 2 Thessalonians 2:11 For this reason God sends them a powerful delusion, leading them to believe what is false,

[2357] Ecclesiastes 12:1-7 Remember your creator in the days of your youth, before the days of trouble come, and the years draw near when you will say, 'I have no pleasure in them'; [2] before the sun and the light and the moon and the stars are darkened and the clouds return with the rain; [3] on the day when the guards of the house tremble, and the strong men are bent, and the women who grind cease working because they are few, and those who look through the windows see dimly; [4] when the doors on the street are shut, and the sound of the grinding is low, and one rises up at the sound of a bird, and all the daughters of song are brought low; [5] when one is afraid of heights, and terrors are in the road; the almond tree blossoms, the grasshopper drags itself along and desire fails; because all must go to their eternal home, and the mourners will go about the streets; [6] before the silver cord is snapped, and the golden bowl is broken, and the pitcher is broken at the fountain, and the wheel broken at the cistern, [7] and the dust returns to the earth as it was, and the breath returns to God who gave it.

[2358] 1 Peter 2:1-3 Rid yourselves, therefore, of all malice, and all guile, insincerity, envy, and all slander. [2] Like newborn infants, long for the pure, spiritual milk, so that by it you may grow into salvation— [3] if indeed you have tasted that the Lord is good.

[2359] Deuteronomy 10:14 Although heaven and the heaven of heavens belong to the Lord your God, the earth with all that is in it,

[2360] Romans 11:33 O the depth of the riches and wisdom and knowledge of God! How unsearchable are his judgments and how inscrutable his ways!

[2361] Job 42:2 'I know that you can do all things, and that no purpose of yours can be thwarted.

[2362] 2 Timothy 3:16-17 All scripture is inspired by God and is useful for teaching, for reproof, for correction, and for training in righteousness, [17] so that everyone who belongs to God may be proficient, equipped for every good work.

[2363] Psalm 93:4 More majestic than the thunders of mighty waters, more majestic than the waves of the sea, majestic on high is the Lord!

[2364] Proverbs 2:6 For the Lord gives wisdom; from his mouth come knowledge and understanding;

[2365] Proverbs 3:6 In all your ways acknowledge him, and he will make straight your paths.

God, to whom belongs everything that is in the heavens and earth.[2366] Truly, all will eventually return to God.[2367] (53)

• • •

[2366] Psalm 89:11 The heavens are yours, the earth also is yours;
the world and all that is in it—you have founded them.
[2367] Ecclesiastes 12:7 and the dust returns to the earth as it was, and the breath returns
to God who gave it.

CHAPTER FORTY THREE

AZ-ZUKHRUF

ORNAMENTS

THE **MECCA** PERIOD

In the name of God, the Merciful-to-all, the Mercy Giver:
Ha Meem,[2368] [01] by the Book that make things clear, [02] We have caused it to be[2369] an Arabic Qur'an that you may understand. [03] It is in the Source of the Book with Us, exalted and full of Wisdom. [04]

Should we then withdraw the Reminder from you, because you are excessive in your rejection? [05] How many prophets We sent among the earlier people [06] and they used to ridicule every one of them.[2370] [07] We destroyed people mightier than these, and their example has gone down in history. [08] And if you ask them, "Who created the heavens and the earth?" they would say, "They were created by the Almighty,[2371] the All-Knowing."[2372] [09] It is He who made the earth a cradle for you and made pathways in it for you, that you might be guided. [10] It is He who sends down rain[2373] from the sky in measured portions; We resurrect with it a dead town back to life. Similarly you will be brought forth [11] It is He who created the pairs, all of them,[2374] and has made it possible for you to ride

• • •

[2368] Here and at the beginning of many chapters there are unvowelled letters of unknown meaning. Numerous theories have been proposed, but there is no agreement on the subject

[2369] The word used in Arabic is Ja'ala meaning the Qur'an existed before in a format known to God, but was transformed into Araic and sent down so it can be gradually understood.

[2370] Matthew 23:33-35 You snakes; you brood of vipers! [34] How can you escape being sentenced to hell? Therefore, I send you prophets, sages, and scribes, some of whom you will kill and crucify, and some you will flog in your synagogues and pursue from town to town, [35] so that upon you may come all the righteous blood shed on earth, from the blood of righteous Abel to the blood of Zechariah son of Barachiah, whom you murdered between the sanctuary and the altar.

[2371] Luke 1:49 for the Mighty One has done great things for me, and holy is his name.

[2372] 1 John 3:20 whenever our hearts condemn us; for God is greater than our hearts, and he knows everything.

[2373] Zechariah 10:1 Ask rain from the Lord in the season of the spring rain, from the Lord who makes the storm-clouds, who gives showers of rain to you, the vegetation in the field to everyone.

[2374] Genesis 1:24-25 And God said, 'Let the earth bring forth living creatures of every kind: cattle and creeping things and wild animals of the earth of every kind.' And it was so. [25] God made the wild animals of the earth of every kind, and the cattle of every kind, and everything that creeps upon the ground of every kind. And God saw that it was good.

ships and animals [12] That you may settle on their backs and remember your Lord's blessings when you have settled and say. "Exalted in His glory[2375] is He who subjected this to us. We on our own would not have been able to have it. [13] We will surely return to our Lord."[2376] [14]

Yet they attribute to Him only some of what He has created. Man is clearly ungrateful. [15] Or has He taken daughters for himself and favored you with sons? [16] Yet when any of them is given the good news of what he himself attributes to the Merciful,[2377] his face darkens, and he suppresses grief; [17] what (am I to have a daughter), someone to be brought up in ornaments but cannot help in a fight? [18] Yet, they designated the angels, [2378] who are created to worship the Merciful,[2379] as females. Have they witnessed their creation? Their claim will be recorded,[2380] and they will be questioned about it. [19]

They say, "If the Merciful willed it, we would not have worshipped them." But they do not know that. They are merely guessing. [20] Or have We given them a Book prior to this one, to which they are adhering? [21] No they say, but "We found our fathers following this path, and we are guided by their footsteps." [22] Similarly, every time We sent someone before you to a town to warn them, those corrupted by abundance would say, "We found our fathers following this path, and we are following in their footsteps."[2381] [23] Say, even if I bring you better guidance than what you found your fathers following?" They reply, "We reject, what You have been sent with." [2382][24] So we punish them; reflect then on the end of those who rejected the truth. [25] And when Abraham said to his father and his people, "I have nothing to do with what you worship [26] I worship only the One who created me[2383] and gave me purpose, He will guide me."[2384] [27] He made this as an enduring word remaining among Abraham's descendants that they might return (to it).[2385] [28]

•   •   •

[2375] Psalm 19:1 The heavens are telling the glory of God; and the firmament proclaims his handiwork.

[2376] Ecclesiastes 12:7 and the dust returns to the earth as it was, and the breath returns to God who gave it.

[2377] Matthew 5:7 'Blessed are the merciful, for they will receive mercy.

[2378] Psalm 103:20 Bless the Lord, O you his angels, you mighty ones who do his bidding, obedient to his spoken word.

[2379] Psalm 116:5 Gracious is the Lord, and righteous; our God is merciful.

[2380] Revelation 20:12 And I saw the dead, great and small, standing before the throne, and books were opened. Also another book was opened, the book of life. And the dead were judged according to their works, as recorded in the books

[2381] Numbers 32:13-15 And the Lord's anger was kindled against Israel, and he made them wander in the wilderness for forty years, until all the generation that had done evil in the sight of the Lord had disappeared. 14 And now you, a brood of sinners, have risen in place of your fathers, to increase the LORD's fierce anger against Israel! 15 If you turn away from following him, he will again abandon them in the wilderness; and you will destroy all this people.'

[2382] 2 Timothy 4:3-4 For the time is coming when people will not put up with sound doctrine, but having itching ears, they will accumulate for themselves teachers to suit their own desires, 4 and will turn away from listening to the truth and wander away to myths.

[2383] Psalm 139:13 For it was you who formed my inward parts; you knit me together in my mother's womb.

[2384] Isaiah 58:11 The Lord will guide you continually, and satisfy your needs in parched places, and make your bones strong; and you shall be like a watered garden, like a spring of water, whose waters never fail.

[2385] Isaiah 30:8 Go now, write it before them on a tablet, and inscribe it in a book, so that it may be for the time to come as a witness for ever.

Now, I let these people of yours (Prophet) and their forefathers have some enjoyment, until the Truth and a messenger who made things clear came to them. (29) But when the Truth came to them, they said, "This is magic and we refuse to believe it." (30) They also said, "If only this Qur'an was sent down to a great man from the two cities." (31) Is it they who distribute your Lord's blessing? It is We who have allocated their livelihood among them in this life. We have raised some of them in rank, so that some would hire others for service. But your Lord's mercy is better than whatever they accumulate.[2386] (32) Were it not that people might become a single community, We would have provided those who deny the Merciful-to-all,[2387] silver roofs for their houses and silver stairways to ascend (33) and silver doors to their houses and furnishings on which to recline, (34) and gold ornaments. But all that is merely the possessions of this life, while the Hereafter with your Lord is for those who are mindful of Him. (35) Whoever overlooks the remembrance of the Merciful, We assign him a devil (shayatin), for a companion. (36) They hinder them from the path, though they think they are guided. (37) Then, when such a person comes to Us, he says (to his companion) "I wish you had been as far away from me as east is from west. What an evil companion." (38) Since you were both unjust, It will not benefit you today to know, that you are partners in the punishment.[2388] (39)

Can you make the deaf hear, or guide the blind and whoever is clearly misguided? (40) Whether We take you away, We will afflict retribution on them. (41) Or, We show you what We have promised them; for We have perfect ability to control them. (42) So adhere to what is revealed to you. You are on a straight path.[2389] (43) It is a remembrance for you and your people, and you are all going to be questioned. (44) Ask those of Our messengers We sent before you; did We ever appoint any deities besides the Merciful[2390] to be worshipped? (45)

We send Moses (Musa) with Our signs to Pharaoh and his inner circle. He said, "I am the Messenger of the Lord of the worlds." (46) But when he came to them with Our signs, they laughed at them.[2391] (47) Each sign We showed them was more marvelous than the previous one. So We afflicted them with punishment, so that they might return. (48) They said "Magician, pray to your Lord for us, as He has a covenant with you, and We will be guided."[2392] (49) But when

• • •

[2386] Luke 12:16-21 Then he told them a parable: 'The land of a rich man produced abundantly. [17] And he thought to himself, "What should I do, for I have no place to store my crops?" [18] Then he said, "I will do this: I will pull down my barns and build larger ones, and there I will store all my grain and my goods. [19] And I will say to my soul, Soul, you have ample goods laid up for many years; relax, eat, drink, be merry." [20] But God said to him, "You fool! This very night your life is being demanded of you. And the things you have prepared, whose will they be?" [21] So it is with those who store up treasures for themselves but are not rich towards God.'

[2387] Exodus 34:6 The Lord passed before him, and proclaimed, 'The Lord, the Lord, a God merciful and gracious, slow to anger, and abounding in steadfast love and faithfulness,

[2388] Ezekiel 25:17 I will execute great vengeance on them with wrathful punishments. Then they shall know that I am the LORD, when I lay my vengeance on them.

[2389] Proverbs 4:26-27 Keep straight the path of your feet, and all your ways will be sure. [27] Do not swerve to the right or to the left; turn your foot away from evil.

[2390] Exodus 34:6 The Lord passed before him, and proclaimed, 'The Lord, the Lord, a God merciful and gracious, slow to anger, and abounding in steadfast love and faithfulness,

[2391] Exodus 7:13 Still Pharaoh's heart was hardened, and he would not listen to them, as the Lord had said.

[2392] Exodus 12:32 Take your flocks and your herds, as you said, and be gone. And bring a blessing on me too!'

We lifted the punishment from them, they broke their word.[2393] [50] Then Pharaoh called out among his people; he said, "My people, does not the kingdom of Egypt belong to me, and these rivers that flow under my feet? Do not you see? [51] Am I not better than this insignificant person who can barely make himself understood?[2394] [52] Why then are not golden bracelets placed on him, or the angels are accompanying him?" [53] He (Pharaoh) easily swayed his people, and they obeyed him. (To Us) they were disobedient people [54] but when they continued to challenge Us, We inflicted Our punishment on them, and drowned them all:[2395] [55] We made them a precedent and an example for the others.[2396][56]

And when the son of Mary[2397] was given as an example, immediately your people (prophet) loudly objected[2398] [57] and they said, "who is better, our gods or him?" They cited him only for argument sake. In fact, they are a confrontational people. [58] (Jesus) was a servant whom We blessed, and We made him an example for the Children of Israel. [59] Had We so willed, We could have made you into angels succeeding one another on earth. [60]

He (Jesus) is a (sign for) knowledge of the Hour,[2399] so have no doubt about it, and follow Me. This is a straight path.[2400] [61] Never let Satan divert you.[2401] He is a clear enemy to you all. [62]When Jesus came with clear evidence, he said, "I have brought you Wisdom[2402] and to clarify for you some of what you differ about.[2403] Be always mindful of God and obey me. [63] God is my Lord and your Lord,[2404] so worship Him.[2405] This is a straight path."[2406] [64] But the factions

• • •

[2393] Exodus 9:34 But when Pharaoh saw that the rain and the hail and the thunder had ceased, he sinned once more and hardened his heart, he and his officials.

[2394] Exodus 4:10 But Moses said to the Lord, 'O my Lord, I have never been eloquent, neither in the past nor even now that you have spoken to your servant; but I am slow of speech and slow of tongue.'

[2395] Exodus 14:28 The waters returned and covered the chariots and the chariot drivers, the entire army of Pharaoh that had followed them into the sea; not one of them remained.

[2396] Psalm 136:15 but overthrew Pharaoh and his army in the Red Sea, for his steadfast love endures for ever;

[2397] Mary, mother of Jesus.

[2398] Mark 6:3 Is not this the carpenter, the son of Mary and brother of James and Joses and Judas and Simon, and are not his sisters here with us?' And they took offence at him.

[2399] Revelation 14:7 He said in a loud voice, 'Fear God and give him glory, for the hour of his judgment has come; and worship him who made heaven and earth, the sea and the springs of water.'

[2400] Proverbs 3:6 In all your ways acknowledge him, and he will make straight your paths.

[2401] Matthew 4:10 Jesus said to him, 'Away with you, Satan! for it is written, "Worship the Lord your God, and serve only him."'

[2402] Mark 6:2 On the Sabbath he began to teach in the synagogue, and many who heard him were astounded. They said, 'Where did this man get all this? What is this wisdom that has been given to him? What deeds of power are being done by his hands!

[2403] Matthew 19:3-9 Some Pharisees came to him, and to test him they asked, 'Is it lawful for a man to divorce his wife for any cause?' [4] He answered, 'Have you not read that the one who made them at the beginning "made them male and female", [5] and said, "For this reason a man shall leave his father and mother and be joined to his wife, and the two shall become one flesh"? [6] So they are no longer two, but one flesh. Therefore, what God has joined together, let no one separate.' [7] They said to him, 'Why then did Moses command us to give a certificate of dismissal and to divorce her?' [8] He said to them, 'It was because you were so hard-hearted that Moses allowed you to divorce your wives, but at the beginning it was not so. [9] And I say to you, whoever divorces his wife, except for unchastity, and marries another commits adultery.'

[2404] Mark 12:29 Jesus answered, 'The first is, "Hear, O Israel: the Lord our God, the Lord is one;

[2405] Deuteronomy 10:20 To him shay our God; him alone you shall worship Lord You shall fear the hold fast and by his name shall you swear.

[2406] Proverbs 3:6 In all your ways acknowledge him, and he will make straight your paths.

differed among themselves. How terrible is the punishment of a painful Day to the unjust. [65] What are they waiting for except for the Hour to come suddenly upon them when they are not expecting it?[2407] [66] On that Day, close friends will be enemies to each other, except for those who are mindful of God [67] "My worshipers, you have nothing to fear on that Day, nor will you grieve, [68] those who believed in Our revelations and were submissive. [2408] [69] Enter the Garden, you and your spouses, filled with Joy." [70] Passed among them will be plates and cups of gold. They will have whatever their soul desire and whatever delights their eyes. There you will remain forever.[2409] [71] That is the Garden[2410] which you are made to inherit because of what you have done. [72] There will be much fruit for you to eat. [73]Those who force others to reject Our messages will be in the punishment of Hell forever.[2411] [74] It will not be allowed to be eased for them. In it, they will be crushed by despair. [75] We did not wrong them, but it was they who were the unjust. [76] They will call, "Malik[2412], let your Lord finish us off!" He will say, "You are staying." [77] We have given you the Truth, but most of you, hate the Truth.[2413] [78]

Or have they thought up some scheme? We too have been scheming [79] Or do they think that We cannot hear their secrets and their private talk? Yes, We can, and Our messengers are with them writing it down.[2414] [80]

Say, "If the Merciful-to-all had a son, then I would be the first to worship him." [81] Exalted is the Lord of the heavens and the earth[2415] in His glory, Lord of the Throne, totally above what they ascribe to Him .[2416] [82] So let them indulge in idle talk and play until they face that Day of theirs which they have been promised: [83] It is He who is God in heaven, and God on earth [2417] He is the All-Wise, the All-Knowing. [84] And blessed is He Who has sovereignty over the heavens and the earth and everything between them. He alone has knowledge of the Hour. You will all be returned to Him. [85] Those deities they invoke besides Him have no power of intercession; only those who testify to the Truth and have full knowledge. [86] And if you asked them who created them, they would say, "God." Why do they mislead? [87] As for his saying, "My Lord, these are people

• • •

[2407] 1 Thessalonians 5:3 When they say, 'There is peace and security', then sudden destruction will come upon them, as labor pains come upon a pregnant woman, and there will be no escape!
[2408] James 4:7 Submit yourselves therefore to God. Resist the devil, and he will flee from you.
[2409] Matthew 19:29 And everyone who has left houses or brothers or sisters or father or mother or children or fields, for my name's sake, will receive a hundredfold, and will inherit eternal life.
[2410] Revelation 22:2 through the middle of the street of the city. On either side of the river is the tree of life with its twelve kinds of fruit, producing its fruit each month; and the leaves of the tree are for the healing of the nations.
[2411] Matthew 23:33 You snakes, you brood of vipers! How can you escape being sentenced to hell?
[2412] An angel in charge of Hell
[2413] John 8:39-40 They answered him, 'Abraham is our father.' Jesus said to them, 'If you were Abraham's children, you would be doing what Abraham did, [40] but now you are trying to kill me, a man who has told you the truth that I heard from God. This is not what Abraham did.
[2414] Revelation 20:12 And I saw the dead, great and small, standing before the throne, and books were opened. Also another book was opened, the book of life. And the dead were judged according to their works, as recorded in the books.
[2415] Psalm 89:11 The heavens are yours, the earth also is yours; the world and all that is in it—you have founded them.
[2416] Psalm 147:5 Great is our Lord, and abundant in power; his understanding is beyond measure.
[2417] Jeremiah 32:17 Ah Lord God! It is you who made the heavens and the earth by your great power and by your outstretched arm! Nothing is too hard for you.

who do not believe." [88] So forgive them and talk peace. Eventually they will come to know. [89]

CHAPTER FORTY FOUR

AD-DUKHAN

SMOKE

THE **MECCA** PERIOD

In the name of God, the Merciful-to -all, the Mercy Giver:
Ha Meem,[2418] [(01)] by the Book that makes things clear, [(02)] We have revealed it on a Blessed Night; We have been warning. [(03)] On that night every matter of wisdom is made distinct. [(04)] A decree from Us. We have been sending messages [(05)] as mercy from your Lord. He is the All-Hearing, the All-Knowing. [(06)] The Sustainer of the heavens and the earth [2419] and everything between them, if you only can grasp this with certainty. [(07)] There is no god but Him;[2420] He gives life and causes death.[2421] (He is) your Sustainer and the Sustainer of your forefathers [2422] from the beginning. [(08)] Yet they who lack certainty just keep toying with their doubts. [(09)]
So watch out for the Day when the sky will bring visible smoke[2423] [(10)] enveloping all people; "This is a painful punishment." [(11)] (Then they will say), "Our Lord, lift the punishment from us, we now believe." [(12)] But how can this sudden remembrance benefit them? When a messenger explaining things clearly has already come to them, [(13)] and they turned away from him saying, "He is tutored but possessed." [(14)] We will postpone the punishment for a while. But

•   •   •

[2418] Here and at the beginning of many chapters there are unvowelled letters of unknown meaning. Numerous theories have been proposed, but there is no agreement on the subject.
[2419] Psalm 55:22 Cast your burden on the Lord, and he will sustain you; he will never permit the righteous to be moved.
[2420] Exodus 20:2-3 I am the Lord your God, who brought you out of the land of Egypt, out of the house of slavery; 3 you shall have no other gods before me.
[2421] Deuteronomy 32:39 See now that I, even I, am he; there is no god besides me. I kill and I make alive; I wound and I heal; and no one can deliver from my hand.
[2422] Deuteronomy 6:3 Hear therefore, O Israel, and observe them diligently, so that it may go well with you, and so that you may multiply greatly in a land flowing with milk and honey, as the Lord, the God of your ancestors, has promised you.
[2423] Revelation 9:2 he opened the shaft of the bottomless pit, and from the shaft rose smoke like the smoke of a great furnace, and the sun and the air were darkened with the smoke from the shaft.

you will eventually return to us. [15] The Day when We will strike with the greatest assault, We will take retribution. [16]

We had already tested Pharaoh's people before them, when a noble messenger came to them,[2424] [17] (saying), "Hand over to me the servants of God. I am a trustworthy messenger to you,"[2425] [18] "Never be arrogant with God. I come to you with clear authority. [19] I have sought refuge with my Lord and your Lord,[2426] against your condemnation. [20] If you do not believe me, then (at least) leave me alone." [21]

He then called out to his Lord that these were evil people. [22] (God said), "Then set out with My servants by night.[2427] You will be pursued.[2428] [23] Cross the sea quickly and leave it as is.[2429] They are an army to be drowned."[2430] [24] How many gardens and fountains did they leave behind? [25] And crops and noble residences (44:26) and that life of ease that they used to enjoy? [27] So it was; Yet We passed it on to other people to inherit.[2431] [28] Neither heaven nor earth wept for them, nor were they given a reprieve. [29] And We saved the Children of Israel from the humiliating persecution [2432] [30] from Pharaoh. He was an arrogant transgressor. [2433] [31] And We chose them knowingly over all people[2434] [32] We gave them many revelations,[2435] that were an obvious trial.[2436] [33]

Yet these people say, [34] "There is nothing but our one death, and we will not be resurrected. [35] Bring back our forefathers, if you are telling the truth." [36] Are

• • •

[2424] Acts 7:35 'It was this Moses whom they rejected when they said, "Who made you a ruler and a judge?" and whom God now sent as both ruler and liberator through the angel who appeared to him in the bush.

[2425] Exodus 5:1 Afterwards Moses and Aaron went to Pharaoh and said, 'Thus says the Lord, the God of Israel, "Let my people go, so that they may celebrate a festival to me in the wilderness."'

[2426] Psalm 18:2 The Lord is my rock, my fortress, and my deliverer, my God, my rock in whom I take refuge, my shield, and the horn of my salvation, my stronghold.

[2427] Exodus 12:31,42 Then he summoned Moses and Aaron in the night, and said, 'Rise up, go away from my people, both you and the Israelites! Go, worship the Lord, as you said. [42] That was for the Lord a night of vigil, to bring them out of the land of Egypt. That same night is a vigil to be kept for the Lord by all the Israelites throughout their generations.

[2428] Exodus 14:6-8 So he had his chariot made ready, and took his army with him; [7] he took six hundred picked chariots and all the other chariots of Egypt with officers over all of them. [8] The Lord hardened the heart of Pharaoh king of Egypt and he pursued the Israelites, who were going out boldly.

[2429] Exodus 14:29 But the Israelites walked on dry ground through the sea, the waters forming a wall for them on their right and on their left.

[2430] Exodus 14:28 The waters returned and covered the chariots and the chariot drivers, the entire army of Pharaoh that had followed them into the sea; not one of them remained.

[2431] Psalm 136:21 and gave their land as a heritage, for his steadfast love endures for ever;

[2432] Exodus 14.30-31 Thus the Lord saved Israel that day from the Egyptians; and Israel saw the Egyptians dead on the seashore. [31] Israel saw the great work that the Lord did against the Egyptians. So the people feared the Lord and believed in the Lord and in his servant Moses.

[2433] Exodus 5:2 But Pharaoh said, 'Who is the Lord, that I should heed him and let Israel go? I do not know the Lord, and I will not let Israel go.'

[2434] Deuteronomy 7:7-8 It was not because you were more numerous than any other people that the Lord set his heart on you and chose you—for you were the fewest of all peoples. [8] It was because the Lord loved you and kept the oath that he swore to your ancestors, that the Lord has brought you out with a mighty hand, and redeemed you from the house of slavery, from the hand of Pharaoh king of Egypt.

[2435] Numbers 14:11 And the Lord said to Moses, 'How long will this people despise me? And how long will they refuse to believe in me, in spite of all the signs that I have done among them?

[2436] Deuteronomy 13:3 you must not heed the words of those prophets or those who divine by dreams; for the Lord your God is testing you, to know whether you indeed love the Lord your God with all your heart and soul.

they better than the people of Tubba' and those before them? We destroyed them, (for) they were among those who rejected our messages and have severed all relations to God, [37] And We did not create the heavens and earth and everything between them to play a game.[2437] [38] We created them with the Truth,[2438] (for a meaningful purpose), but most of them do not know.[39]

The Day of Distinction is the appointed time for all of them.[2439] [40] The Day when a friend will not be of any use to his friend, nor will they are helped[2440] [41] except those on whom God has mercy. He is the Almighty,[2441] the Merciful-to -all.[2442] [42] The tree of Zaqqum [43] is food for the sinner. [44] It boils inside bellies like boiling oil, [45] like the boiling of seething water. [46] "Seize him and drag him into the midst of Hell,[47] then pour scalding water over his head as punishment!'" [48] "Taste it, you are the mighty one, the noble, [49] this is what you used to dispute." [50] But those who were mindful of God will be in a safe place; [51] in the midst of Gardens and springs[2443] [52] wearing fine silk and brocade, facing each other. [53] So it will be. And We shall pair them with Hoor Ein.[2444] [54] Safe and secure, they will call there for every kind of fruit. [55] Except the first death, they will not taste death there. [2445] He will protect them from the punishment of Hell, [56] a grace from your Lord. That is the supreme triumph. [57]

We have made this Qur'an easy to understand in your own language that they might remember. [58] So wait and watch; they are also on their watch. [59]

• • •

[2437] Isaiah 45:18 For thus says the Lord, who created the heavens (he is God!), who formed the earth and made it (he established it; he did not create it a chaos, he formed it to be inhabited!): I am the Lord, and there is no other.

[2438] Isaiah 45:12 I made the earth, and created humankind upon it; it was my hands that stretched out the heavens, and I commanded all their host.

[2439] Matthew 25:32 All the nations will be gathered before him, and he will separate people one from another as a shepherd separates the sheep from the goats,

[2440] Isaiah 10:3 What will you do on the day of punishment, in the calamity that will come from far away? To whom will you flee for help, and where will you leave your wealth

[2441] Psalm 24:8 Who is the King of glory? The Lord, strong and mighty, the Lord, mighty in battle.

[2442] Psalm 103:8 The Lord is merciful and gracious, slow to anger and abounding in steadfast love.

[2443] Revelation 22:2 through the middle of the street of the city. On either side of the river is the tree of life with its twelve kinds of fruit, producing its fruit each month; and the leaves of the tree are for the healing of the nations.

[2444] see Glossary

[2445] Revelation 2:11 Let anyone who has an ear listen to what the Spirit is saying to the churches. Whoever conquers will not be harmed by the second death.

CHAPTER FORTY FIVE

AL-JATHIYAH
KNEELING

THE **MECCA** PERIOD

In the name of God, the Merciful-to -all, the Mercy Giver:

Ha Meem,[2446] [01] the gradual revelations of the Book are from God, the Almighty,[2447] the Wise.[2448] [02] In the heavens and earth are Signs for the believers. [03] And in your creation and in the creatures He scattered are Signs for people gifted with inner certainty. [04] The alternation of night and day,[2449] the sustenance God sends down from the sky, using it to revive the earth after its death,[2450] and in the circulation of the winds,[2451] are all signs for people who use their reason. [05] These are God's verses, We convey them to you, setting forth the truth.

If they deny God and His verses, what message will they then believe? [06] How terrible it is to every sinful liar [07] who hears God's revelations being recited to him, yet he persists arrogantly, as if he did not hear them. So give him the news of a painful punishment awaiting him.[2452] [08] And when he does learn some of Our verses, he ridicules them.[2453] Such people will have a humiliating

●   ●   ●

[2446] Here and at the beginning of many chapters there are unvowelled letters of unknown meaning. Numerous theories have been proposed, but there is no agreement on the subject.
[2447] Psalm 24:8 Who is the King of glory? The Lord, strong and mighty, the Lord, mighty in battle.
[2448] Job 9:4, He is wise in heart, and mighty in strength—who has resisted him, and succeeded?—
[2449] Genesis 1:16 God made the two great lights—the greater light to rule the day and the lesser light to rule the night—and the stars.
[2450] Isaiah 55:10 For as the rain and the snow come down from heaven, and do not return there until they have watered the earth, making it bring forth and sprout, giving seed to the sower and bread to the eater,
[2451] Job 37:9 From its chamber comes the whirlwind, and cold from the scattering winds.
[2452] Matthew 25:41 Then he will say to those at his left hand, 'You that are accursed, depart from me into the eternal fire prepared for the devil and his angels;
[2453] 2 Kings 19:22-23 "Whom have you mocked and reviled? Against whom have you raised your voice and haughtily lifted your eyes? [23] Against the Holy One of Israel! By your messengers you have mocked the Lord,"

punishment.[2454] [(09)] Hell awaits them. Nothing they have earned will be of any use to them, nor will those they have adopted as protectors instead of God. They will have a great punishment. [(10)] This is true guidance. Those who have rejected the truth of their Lord's revelations will have a punishment of grievous pain. [(11)]

It is God who subjected the sea for you so that ships may sail with His approval[2455] and that you may seek of His favor, and that you may give Him thanks.[2456] [(12)] And He has subjected to you all that is in the heavens and on the earth;[2457] a blessing from Him. There are signs in this for people who reflect. [(13)]

Tell the Believers that they should forgive[2458] those who do not anticipate the Days of God as it is He alone who will hold people accountable for what they have earned. [(14)] Whoever does good, benefits his own soul; and whoever does evil, harms his soul;[2459] Then you will all be returned to your Lord.[2460] [(15)]

We gave the Children of Israel the Book, Wisdom and prophecy. We provided them with good things and preferred them over all people.[2461] [(16)] We gave them clear details of the matter (faith). Yet, they differed out of rivalry between them, only after knowledge came to them. Your Lord will judge between them on the Day of Resurrection regarding their differences. [(17)] Then We put you on a pathway of the matter, so follow it, and do not follow the whims and desires of those who do not know. [(18)] They will not help you in any way if you decide to defy God. The unjust protect each other, while God is the Protector of those who are mindful of Him. [(19)] This is clear insight for mankind and guidance and mercy for people gifted with inner certainty. [(20)]

Or do those who indulge in evil deeds assume that We will regard them the same as those who believe and do good deeds, that they will be alike whether in life or in death? How bad is their judgment? [(21)] God created the heavens and earth in Truth, so that every soul may be rewarded according to its deeds. They will not be wronged. [(22)] Have you considered him who has taken his whims and desires for his god? [2462] Then God knowingly allows him to stray,[2463] sealing his

• • •

[2454] 2 Kings 19:28 Because you have raged against me and your arrogance has come to my ears, I will put my hook in your nose and my bit in your mouth; I will turn you back on the way by which you came.
[2455] Psalm 107:23 Some went down to the sea in ships, doing business on the mighty waters;
[2456] 1 Chronicles 16:8 O give thanks to the Lord, call on his name, make known his deeds among the peoples
[2457] Genesis 1:28 God blessed them, and God said to them, "Be fruitful and multiply, and fill the earth and subdue it; and have dominion over the fish of the sea and over the birds of the air and over every living thing that moves upon the earth."
[2458] Colossians 3:13 Bear with one another and, if anyone has a complaint against another, forgive each other; just as the Lord has forgiven you, so you also must forgive.
[2459] Romans 2:6-10 For he will repay according to each one's deeds: [7] to those who by patiently doing good seek for glory and honor and immortality, he will give eternal life; [8] while for those who are self-seeking and who obey not the truth but wickedness, there will be wrath and fury. [9] There will be anguish and distress for everyone who does evil, the Jew first and also the Greek, [10] but glory and honor and peace for everyone who does good, the Jew first and also the Greek.
[2460] Ecclesiastes 12:7 and the dust returns to the earth as it was, and the breath returns to God who gave it.
[2461] Deuteronomy 7:7 It was not because you were more numerous than any other people that the Lord set his heart on you and chose you—for you were the fewest of all peoples.
[2462] Philippians 3:19 Their end is destruction; their god is the belly; and their glory is in their shame; their minds are set on earthly things.
[2463] 2 Thessalonians 2:11 For this reason God sends them a powerful delusion, leading them to believe what is false,

hearing and his heart,[2464] and has placed a veil over his vision.[2465] So who can guide him after God? Will you not reflect? [(23)]

They say, "There is nothing but our life in this world; we die, we live, and nothing but time destroys us." But they have no knowledge of this; they are only guessing. [(24)] And when Our clear verses are recited to them, their only argument is to say, "Bring back our forefathers, if you are telling the truth." [(25)] Say, "It is God who gives you life, then causes you to die,[2466] and then He gathers you for the Day of Resurrection,[2467] about which there is no doubt. But most people do not know." [(26)]

To God belongs the kingdom of the heavens and the earth.[2468] On the Day when the Hour takes place,[2469] on that Day those who dealt in falsehood will lose. [(27)] You will see every nation on its knees; every nation summoned [2470] to its Book, "Today you are being repaid for what you did. [(28)] This is Our record; it speaks about you in Truth. We were recording what You have been doing." [(29)] As for those who believed and did good deeds, their Lord will admit them into His mercy. That is the clear triumph. [(30)] But for the unbelievers, "Were My verses not recited to you? But you were an arrogant and dissenting people. [(31)]

And when you were told, 'God's promise is true [2471] and there is no doubt about the Hour,' you said, 'We do not know what is the Hour. We're assuming that these are only speculations, and we're by no means certain.' "[(32)] The evil consequences of what they did will become evident to them, and the very thing they used to ridicule will haunt them. [(33)] They were told, "Today We will ignore you as you ignored the encounter of this Day. The Fire will be your refuge,[2472] and you will have no helpers.[2473] [(34)] That is because you took the verses of God

• • •

[2464] Exodus 8:15 But when Pharaoh saw that there was a respite, he hardened his heart, and would not listen to them, just as the Lord had said.

[2465] 1 John 2:11But whoever hates another believer is in the darkness, walks in the darkness, and does not know the way to go, because the darkness has brought on blindness.

[2466] Deuteronomy 30:19 I call heaven and earth to witness against you today that I have set before you life and death, blessings and curses. Choose life so that you and your descendants may live,

[2467] Matthew 12:36 I tell you, on the day of judgment you will have to give an account for every careless word you utter;

[2468] Psalm 89:11, The heavens are yours, the earth also is yours; the world and all that is in it—you have founded them. Deuteronomy 10:14 Although heaven and the heaven of heavens belong to the Lord your God, the earth with all that is in it,

[2469] John 5:28 Do not be astonished at this; for the hour is coming when all who are in their graves will hear his voice. Revelation 14:7 He said in a loud voice, "Fear God and give him glory, for the hour of his judgment has come; and worship him who made heaven and earth, the sea and the springs of water."

[2470] Matthew 25:32 All the nations will be gathered before him, and he will separate people one from another as a shepherd separates the sheep from the goats Isaiah 45:22-23 22 Turn to me and be saved, all the ends of the earth! For I am God, and there is no other. 23 By myself I have sworn, from my mouth has gone forth in righteousness a word that shall not return: "To me every knee shall bow, every tongue shall swear."

[2471] 2 Samuel 22:31 This God—his way is perfect; the promise of the Lord proves true; he is a shield for all who take refuge in him.

[2472] Revelation 14:11 And the smoke of their torment goes up forever and ever. There is no rest day or night for those who worship the beast and its image and for anyone who receives the mark of its name."

[2473] Hosea 13:4 Yet I have been the Lord your God ever since the land of Egypt; you know no God but me, and besides me there is no savior.

in ridicule, and the worldly life enticed you."[2474] Therefore, today they will not get out of it and they will no longer have the opportunity to repent. [(35)]

All praise be to God,[2475] Lord of the heavens and Lord of the earth,[2476] Lord of the worlds.[2477] [(36)] His alone is all majestic greatness within the heavens and the earth.[2478] He is the Almighty, the Wise. [(37)]

• • •

[2474] 1 John 2:15-17 Do not love the world or the things in the world. The love of the Father is not in those who love the world; [16] for all that is in the world—the desire of the flesh, the desire of the eyes, the pride in riches—comes not from the Father but from the world. [17] And the world and its desire are passing away, but those who do the will of God live forever.

[2475] Psalm 106:48 Blessed be the Lord, the God of Israel, from everlasting to everlasting. And let all the people say, "Amen." Praise the Lord!

[2476] Joshua 2:11 As soon as we heard it, our hearts melted, and there was no courage left in any of us because of you. The Lord your God is indeed God in heaven above and on earth below.

[2477] Hebrews 11:3 By faith we understand that the worlds were prepared by the word of God, so that what is seen was made from things that are not visible.

[2478] Psalm 148:13 Let them praise the name of the Lord, for his name alone is exalted; his glory is above earth and heaven.

CHAPTER **FORTY SIX**

AL-AHQAT
THE SAND DUNES

THE **MECCA** PERIOD

In the name of God, the Merciful-to -all, the Mercy Giver:
Ha Meem,[2479] [01] The gradual revelations of the Book are from God, the Almighty,[2480] the Wise.[2481] [02] We did not create the heavens and earth and everything in between them except in Truth and for a specified term.[2482] Yet the unbelievers continue to ignore what they have been warned about. [03] Say, "Do you see those you pray to other than God? Show me what part of earth they have; or do they own a share in the heavens? [2483] Bring me a Book preceding this one, or a shred of knowledge, if you are truthful." [04] Who can be more misguided than he who calls on others beside God that do not respond to him even till the Day of Resurrection?[2484] and are not even aware that callers are calling on them. [05] And when people are gathered (that Day), they will be enemies to those who worshiped them, and they will renounce their worship.[06]

But when our clear verses are recited to them, the unbelievers say to the Truth when it comes to them: "This is obvious magic." [07] Or do they say, "He has invented it?" Say, "If I have invented it, there is nothing at all you can do to protect me from God. He knows well what you are engaged in.

• • •

[2479] Here and at the beginning of many chapters there are unvowelled letters of unknown meaning. Numerous theories have been proposed, but there is no agreement on the subject.
[2480] Psalm 93:4 More majestic than the thunders of mighty waters, more majestic than the waves of the sea, majestic on high is the Lord!
[2481] Job 9:4 He is wise in heart, and mighty in strength—who has resisted him, and succeeded?
[2482] Isaiah 45:18 For thus says the Lord, who created the heavens (he is God!), who formed the earth and made it (he established it; he did not create it a chaos, he formed it to be inhabited!): I am the Lord, and there is no other.
[2483] Jeremiah 10:11 Thus shall you say to them: The gods who did not make the heavens and the earth shall perish from the earth and from under the heavens.
[2484] Psalm 115:4-7 Their idols are silver and gold, the work of human hands. [5] They have mouths, but do not speak; eyes, but do not see. [6] They have ears, but do not hear; noses, but do not smell. [7] They have hands, but do not feel; feet, but do not walk; they make no sound in their throats.

345

He is sufficient Witness between me and you. He is the Most-Forgiving[2485] the Merciful-to-all."[2486] [(08)] Say, "I am not different from the other messengers, and I do not know what will be done with me, or with you. I only follow what has been revealed to me. I only warn plainly." [(09)] Say, "Have you considered: what if the Qur'an is really from God, and you are rejecting it? When a witness from the Children of Israel[2487] has already testified to its similarity (to earlier scripture) and believed in it, and yet you are too proud to do the same? God does not guide the unjust people." [(10)]

The unbelievers say about the believers, "If it were anything good, they would not have preceded us to it." And since they were not guided by it, they will say, "This is an ancient lie." [(11)] Yet before it, was the Book revealed to Moses, as a guide and a mercy.[2488] And this is a Book confirming it in the Arabic tongue to warn those who are unjust and to bring good news to those who do good. [(12)] Those who say, "Our Lord is God,"[2489] and then remained on a straight path, they will have nothing to fear, nor shall they grieve.[2490] [(13)] Those are destined for Paradise, where they will dwell forever, a reward for what they used to do.[2491(14)]

We have instructed man to be kind to his parents.[2492] His mother carried him with difficulty and gave birth to him with difficulty.[2493] His bearing and weaning period is thirty months. Until, when he reaches his full strength, and is forty years of age, he says, "My Lord, help me to be grateful for the blessings You have bestowed on me and on my parents; help me to do the right deeds that are pleasing to you. Make my children good.[2494] I have sincerely repented, and I am of those who submit to You."[2495] [(15)] Those are the ones whose best deeds will be accepted and whose bad deeds will be overlooked.[2496] They will be among the dwellers of Paradise. This is the promise of truth which they had been promised.[(16)]

As for him who says to his parents, "Enough of you; Are you warning me that I will be resurrected when generations have passed and gone before me?" While they both cry for God's help, "Please believe! The promise of God is true." But he says, "These are only ancient tales" [(17)] Those are the ones upon whom the

• • •

[2485] Daniel 9:9 To the Lord our God belong mercy and forgiveness, for we have rebelled against him.
[2486] Psalm 116:5 Gracious is the Lord, and righteous; our God is merciful.
[2487] Could be Abdullah Bin Salaam who was a Rabbi and accepted Islam. See Commentary by Tafseer Al Tabari. https://islaambooks.wordpress.com/2012/05/28/the-commentary-on-the-quran-volume-i-tafsir-al-tabari/
[2488] Psalm 119:77 Let your mercy come to me, that I may live; for your law is my delight.
[2489] Revelation 4:11 'You are worthy, our Lord and God, to receive glory and honor and power, for you created all things, and by your will they existed and were created.'
[2490] Psalm 139:23-24 Search me, O God, and know my heart; test me and know my thoughts. 24 See if there is any wicked way in me, and lead me in the way everlasting.
[2491] Luke 6:35 But love your enemies, do good, and lend, expecting nothing in return. Your reward will be great, and you will be children of the Most High; for he is kind to the ungrateful and the wicked.
[2492] Exodus 20:12 Honor your father and your mother, so that your days may be long in the land that the Lord your God is giving you.
[2493] Genesis 3:16 To the woman he said, 'I will greatly increase your pangs in childbearing; in pain you shall bring forth children, yet your desire shall be for your husband, and he shall rule over you.'
[2494] Proverbs 23:24 The father of the righteous will greatly rejoice; he who begets a wise son will be glad in him.
[2495] James 4:7 Submit yourselves therefore to God. Resist the devil, and he will flee from you.
[2496] Acts 17:30 While God has overlooked the times of human ignorance, now he commands all people everywhere to repent,

verdict is justified, among nations that went before them of jinn and humans. They are truly doomed. [18] Everyone will be ranked according to what they have done. He will pay them in full for their deeds, and they will not be wronged. [19] On the Day when the unbelievers are exposed to the Fire: "You have squandered the good things you had in your worldly life, and you took your portion of pleasure there. So today you are being repaid with a punishment of humiliation,[2497] because of your unjustifiable arrogance on earth, and for transgressing all bounds."[2498] [20]

And mention, the brother of Aad, as he warned his people at the sand dunes. Others, delivering warnings, have come and gone before him and after him: "Worship only God,[2499] they said. I fear for you the punishment of a terrible Day." [21] They replied, "Did you come to turn us away from our gods? Then bring us the punishment you promise us, if you are telling the truth." [22] He said, "Its knowledge is only with God, I only convey to you the message that I was sent with. But I see you are insolent people." [23] When they saw a cloud approaching their valleys they said, "This is a cloud that will bring us rain." No, it is rather what you wanted to speed up : a wind, in which there is a painful punishment,[2500] [24] it will destroy everything by the command of its Lord. That morning, there was nothing to be seen except their ruined dwellings. This is how We repay those who force others to reject Our messages [25]

We had empowered them far better than We empowered you, and We gave them hearing, vision and hearts. But their hearing, vision and hearts were of no use to them[2501] as they were rejecting the signs of God; and so they became surrounded by the very punishment they used to ridicule. [26] We have destroyed other towns around you, after We have diversified Our signs to them that perhaps they will return to the right path. [27] Why then did those idols, whom they worshiped to bring them nearer to God, not help them? In fact, they abandoned them. It was all falsehood of their own making. [28]

We sent a group of jinn to you (Prophet) to listen to the Qur'an. When they heard it, they said "Listen quietly." Then when it was concluded, they went back to their people to warn them.[2502] [29] They said, "our people, We have heard a Book revealed after Moses confirming what is available of it, guiding to the Truth and to a straight path.[2503] [30] Our people, respond to the Caller to God. Believe in Him; He will forgive you your sins and will protect you from a painful punishment. [31] But he who does not respond to God's call can never escape

• • •

[2497] Isaiah 10:3 What will you do on the day of punishment, in the calamity that will come from far away? To whom will you flee for help, and where will you leave your wealth,

[2498] Luke 16:25 But Abraham said, "Child, remember that during your lifetime you received your good things, and Lazarus in like manner evil things; but now he is comforted here, and you are in agony.

[2499] Matthew 4:10 Jesus said to him, 'Away with you, Satan! for it is written, "Worship the Lord your God, and serve only him."'

[2500] Ezekiel 13:13-14 Therefore thus says the Lord God: In my wrath I will make a stormy wind break out, and in my anger there shall be a deluge of rain, and hailstones in wrath to destroy it. [14] I will break down the wall that you have smeared with whitewash, and bring it to the ground, so that its foundation will be laid bare; when it falls, you shall perish within it; and you shall know that I am the Lord.

[2501] Romans 11:8 as it is written, 'God gave them a sluggish spirit, eyes that would not see and ears that would not hear, down to this very day.'

[2502] James 2:19 You believe that God is one; you do well. Even the demons believe—and shudder.

[2503] Proverbs 4:26-27 Keep straight the path of your feet, and all your ways will be sure. [27] Do not swerve to the right or to the left; turn your foot away from evil.

God's reach on earth, and have no protectors besides Him. Those are clearly misguided." [32]

Do they not see that God, who created the heavens and earth[2504] and was never tired in doing so, is He Able to bring the dead back to life? Yes, indeed. He is Able to do all things.[2505] [33] On the Day when the unbelievers are exposed to the Fire "Is this not the truth?" They will say, "Yes, by our Lord." He will say, "Then taste the punishment for having rejected the Truth." [34]

Be patient, as were those messengers of firm resolve.[2506] And do not seek to hasten punishment for them. On the Day when they see what they are promised, it will seem as they had only stayed for an hour of a single day (on earth).[2507] An announcement: will any be destroyed except the defiantly rebellious people? [35]

• • •

[2504] Genesis 1:1 In the beginning when God created the heavens and the earth,
[2505] Job 42:2 'I know that you can do all things, and that no purpose of yours can be thwarted., Matthew 19:26 But Jesus looked at them and said, 'For mortals it is impossible, but for God all things are possible.'
[2506] James 5:10 As an example of suffering and patience, beloved, take the prophets who spoke in the name of the Lord.
[2507] James 4:14 Yet you do not even know what tomorrow will bring. What is your life? For you are a mist that appears for a little while and then vanishes.

CHAPTER FORTY SEVEN

MUHAMMAD

THE PROPHET MOHAMMAD

THE **MEDINA** PERIOD

In the name of God, the Merciful-to -all, the Mercy Giver:

Those who reject the truth and turn others away from the path of God,[2508] He will let their deeds go to waste. [01] While those who believe, and do good deeds and believe in what has been sent down to Muhammad as the Truth from their Lord, He will remove their bad deeds and relieve their concerns. [02] That is because those who deny the truth follow falsehood, while those who believe follow the Truth from their Lord. In this way God shows to mankind their examples. [03]

So, when you encounter the unbelievers (in battle), strike at their necks[2509]. Then, once they are defeated, bind them firmly. Then either release them by grace, or by ransom, until the war is over. God could have defeated them Himself if He had willed, but He wants to test some of you by means of others. As for those who are killed in the cause of God, He will not let their deeds go to waste. [04] He will guide them and will put their mind at ease [05] And He will admit them to Paradise,[2510] which He has already made known to them. [06] Believers, if you help God, He will help you and make you stand firm. [07]

As for the unbelievers, how miserable will they be? God brought their deeds to nothing. [08] They hated what God revealed, so He rendered their deeds worthless. [09] Have they not journeyed through the land and seen the fate of those before them? God destroyed them, and a similar fate awaits all those who

• • •

[2508] Matthew 23:13,15 "But woe to you, scribes and Pharisees, hypocrites! For you lock people out of the kingdom of heaven. For you do not go in yourselves, and when others are going in, you stop them. 15 Woe to you, scribes and Pharisees, hypocrites! For you cross sea and land to make a single convert, and you make the new convert twice as much a child of hell as yourselves."

[2509] This verse is specifically discussing mutual battle with those idol worshippers engaged in warfare as noted by Ibn Jareer al-Tabari. This is clear from the opening line of the chapter which states, "Those who disbelieve and prevent people from the path of God", which as Ibn Abbas has stated, is in reference to the idol worshipers of Quraysh, who oppressed the believers by denying them the freedom to practice their faith and then went to war with them to exterminate their community.

[2510] Acts 14:22 There they strengthened the souls of the disciples and encouraged them to continue in the faith, saying, "It is through many persecutions that we must enter the kingdom of God."

persist on denying the truth. ⁽¹⁰⁾ That is because God is the protector of those who believe while those who deny the truth have no protector. ⁽¹¹⁾ God will admit those who have believed and done good deeds to Gardens with rivers flowing through them.[2511] While those who disbelieved, who enjoyed themselves, and eat like cattle eat, the Fire will be their final dwelling. ⁽¹²⁾ And how many towns We have destroyed who were greater in power than your town which drove you out? There was no helper for them ⁽¹³⁾

Is the one who has clear evidence from his Lord like someone whose evil deeds have been made to look attractive to him? So they follow their (own) whims and desires. ⁽¹⁴⁾ The example of the Paradise promised to those who are mindful of God is that of a place that has rivers of pure water, and rivers of milk forever fresh, and rivers of wine delightful to all who drink it, and rivers of strained honey. They will have in it all kinds of fruits[2512] and forgiveness[2513] from their Lord. Is this like those who will abide eternally in the Fire and are given to drink boiling water that will cut through their bowels? ⁽¹⁵⁾

Among them are those who listen to you, but when they leave you, they say to those given knowledge, "What was that he just said?" Those are the ones whose hearts God has sealed. They follow their own whims and desires. ⁽¹⁶⁾ While those who were (willing to be) guided, God increases them in guidance and causes them to grow in God-consciousness.[2514] ⁽¹⁷⁾ What are the unbelievers waiting for, other than the Hour to come upon them suddenly?[2515] Its Signs have already come. But what good will it be to remind them once the Hour[2516] has actually arrived? ⁽¹⁸⁾ Know then that there is no god but God[2517] and ask forgiveness for your sins[2518] and for the believing men and women. God knows when you get up and when you lie down. ⁽¹⁹⁾

Those who believe ask "why no chapter has been sent down (about fighting)." Yet when a decisive chapter is sent down, and fighting is mentioned in it,[2519] you see those with sickness in their hearts[2520] looking at you like someone about to

•   •   •

[2511] Genesis 2:10 A river flows out of Eden to water the garden, and from there it divides and becomes four branches.
[2512] Revelation 22:2 through the middle of the street of the city. On either side of the river is the tree of life with its twelve kinds of fruit, producing its fruit each month; and the leaves of the tree are for the healing of the nations.
[2513] Romans 4:7 "Blessed are those whose iniquities are forgiven, and whose sins are covered;
[2514] 1 Peter 5:2 to tend the flock of God that is in your charge, exercising the oversight, not under compulsion but willingly, as God would have you do it—not for sordid gain but eagerly
[2515] 1 Thessalonians 5:3 When they say, "There is peace and security," then sudden destruction will come upon them, as labor pains come upon a pregnant woman, and there will be no escape!
[2516] Revelation 14:7, He said in a loud voice, "Fear God and give him glory, for the hour of his judgment has come; and worship him who made heaven and earth, the sea and the springs of water."
[2517] 2 Kings 19:15 And Hezekiah prayed before the Lord, and said: "O Lord the God of Israel, who are enthroned above the cherubim, you are God, you alone, of all the kingdoms of the earth; you have made heaven and earth. Exodus 20: 3: Thou shalt have no other gods before me.
[2518] 1 John 1:9 If we confess our sins, he who is faithful and just will forgive us our sins and cleanse us from all unrighteousness.
[2519] Joshua 1:14 Your wives, your little ones, and your livestock shall remain in the land that Moses gave you beyond the Jordan. But all the warriors among you shall cross over armed before your kindred and shall help them,
[2520] Jeremiah 17:9-10 The heart is devious above all else; it is perverse—who can understand it?
[10] I the Lord test the mind and search the heart, to give to all according to their ways, according to the fruit of their doings.

faint from fear of death. It is more appropriate [20] To show Obedience and good words. Then, when the decision to fight has been made, being true to God would have been better for them. [21] Would you prefer to turn away and go spreading corruption on earth and sever your ties of kinship? [22] Those are the ones that God has rejected,[2521] so He deafened them and blinded their vision. [23] Will they not ponder the Qur'an? Or are there locks upon their hearts? [24] Those who turned back in their tracks after guidance became clear to them, Satan enticed them and has given them false hope. [25] That is because they said to those who hate what God has sent down, "We will obey you in certain matters." But God knows their secrets. [26]

How will it be when the angels gather them in death, beating their faces and their backs? [27] That is because they pursued what displeases God and hated what pleases Him. So He rendered their deeds worthless. [28]

Or do those with sickness in their hearts think that God will not expose their malice? [29] Had We willed, We could have show them to you, and you would have recognized them by their features; Yet you will surely know them by the tone of their speech. God knows all you do. [30] We will test you[2522], until We know those who strive among you, and those who are patient, and We will test the sincerity of your assertions.[2523] [31] The unbelievers who turn others away from the path of God and oppose the Messenger after guidance has become clear to them, will not hurt God in the least, but He will render their deeds worthless. [32] Believers, obey God and obey the Messenger and do not let your deeds go to waste. [33] The unbelievers who turn others away from the path of God[2524] and then die while they were unbelievers, God will not forgive them. [34]

So do not waiver and call for peace[2525] while you have the upper hand. God is with you.[2526] He will not waste your deeds. [35] This worldly life is only amusement and pastime. But if you believe and become mindful of God, He will give you your rewards and not ask you for your properties. [36] Were He to ask you for them and put you under pressure, you would become tightfisted, and He would expose your unwillingness. [37] Here you are, called upon to spend in the cause of God. Among you are those who are tightfisted; but whoever withholds only withholds from his own soul. God is the Rich Beyond Need, while you are the needy. And if you turn away, He will replace you with another people, and they will not be the likes of you. [38]

• • •

[2521] Galatians 3:10 For all who rely on the works of the law are under a curse; for it is written, "Cursed is everyone who does not observe and obey all the things written in the book of the law."
[2522] Luke 9:62 But Jesus said to him, "No one, after putting his hand to the plow and looking back, is fit for the kingdom of God."
[2523] Revelation 2:2 "I know your works, your toil and your patient endurance. I know that you cannot tolerate evildoers; you have tested those who claim to be apostles but are not, and have found them to be false.
[2524] Matthew 23:13 "But woe to you, scribes and Pharisees, hypocrites! For you lock people out of the kingdom of heaven. For you do not go in yourselves, and when others are going in, you stop them.
[2525] Joshua 1:7 Only be strong and very courageous, being careful to act in accordance with all the law that my servant Moses commanded you; do not turn from it to the right hand or to the left, so that you may be successful wherever you go.
[2526] Exodus 14:14 The Lord will fight for you, and you have only to keep still."

CHAPTER **FORTY EIGHT**

AL-FATH
THE VICTORY

THE **MEDINA** PERIOD

In the name of God, the Merciful-to-all, the Mercy Giver:

We have opened the way for you to a clear victory [01] That God may forgive you your previous and later sins, complete His grace upon you and guide you on a straight path[2527] [02] That God may help you to a mighty victory. [03] It is He who sent down tranquility into the hearts of the believers that they would add faith to their faith. To God belong the forces of the heavens and earth. God is All-Knowing[2528] and All Wise. [2529] [04] He will admit the believing men and the believing women to Gardens with rivers flowing[2530] through them to remain there eternally and to remove their offenses. That, with God, is a great triumph [05] And He will punish[2531] the hypocrite men and hypocrite women, and the idolater men and idolater women, those who harbor evil thoughts about God. They will suffer an evil turn of fate; God is angry with them, has rejected them, and has prepared Hell[2532] for them. What a miserable destination. [06] And to God belong the forces of heavens and earth. God is Almighty[2533] and All-Wise.[2534] [07] We have sent you as a witness, a bearer of good news and a giver of warning. [08]

. . .

[2527] Psalm 25:4-6 Make me to know your ways, O Lord; teach your paths. [5] Lead me in your truth, and teach me, for you are the God of my salvation; for you I wait all day long. [6] Be mindful of your mercy, O Lord, and of your steadfast love, for they have been from of old.

[2528] 1 John 3:20 Whenever our hearts condemn us God is greater than our hearts and he knows everything

[2529] Proverbs 2:6 For the Lord gives wisdom; from his mouth come knowledge and understanding;

[2530] Revelation 22:1-2 Then the angel showed me the river of the water of life, bright as crystal, flowing from the throne of God and of the Lamb through the middle of the street of the city. [2] On either side of the river is the tree of life with its twelve kinds of fruit, producing its fruit each month; and the leaves of the tree are for the healing of the nations.

[2531] Jeremiah 10:15 They are worthless, a work of delusion; at the time of their punishment they shall perish.

[2532] The Arabic word is jahannam, which is related to gehenna

[2533] Psalm 77:12 I will meditate on all your work, and muse on your mighty deeds.

[2534] 1 Corinthians 1:25 For God's foolishness is wiser than human wisdom, and God's weakness is stronger than human strength.

352

That you may believe in God and His Messenger, and honor Him, revere Him and to praise His limitless glory morning and evening. [09] Those who pledge allegiance to you (Prophet), are actually pledging allegiance to God. God's hand is placed over theirs. Whoever breaks his pledge breaks it to his own detriment. And whoever fulfills his pledge with God, He will give him a great reward. [10] The Dessert-Arabs who stayed behind (when you went to battle) will say to you, "We were preoccupied with our properties and our families, so ask forgiveness for us." They say with their tongues what is not in their hearts. Say, "If God intended harm for you or intended benefit, who can intervene for you? God is fully aware of what you do. [11] But you thought that the Messenger and the believers will never return to their families, ever, and this seemed fine to your hearts. You harbored evil thoughts, and were corrupt people." [12] For those who do not believe in God and His Messenger, We have prepared a blazing Fire [13] To God belongs the kingdom of the heavens and the earth.[2535] He forgives whom He wills and punishes whom He wills.[2536] And ever is God Ever Forgiving,[2537] the Mercy Giver.[2538] [14]

As soon as you are about to depart on a war that promises gains, those who (previously) stayed behind will say, "Allow us to go with you". They wish to alter the Words of God. Say: "You may not go with us: God has said so before." They will say, "You envy us". How little they understand. [15]

Say to those Dessert-Arabs who stayed behind, "Eventually, you will be called to face people of great military might; you will either have to fight them, or they will submit to God's will. If you obey, God will give you a good reward; but if you turn away as you turned away before, He will punish you with a painful punishment." [16] There is no blame on the blind, the lame or the ill. God will admit anyone who obeys Him and His Messenger to Gardens (Jannah) with rivers flowing through them;[2539] But He will painfully punish anyone who turns away. [17]

God was pleased with the believers when they pledged allegiance to you under the tree. He knew what was in their hearts, so He sent down tranquility to them, and rewarded them with an imminent victory [18] and abundant gains to capture. God is the Almighty and All-Wise. [19] God has promised you abundant future gains. He has expedited this for you (victory), and has held hostile people's hands back from you; that it may be a sign for the believers, and that He may guide you to a straight path.[2540] [20] And there are yet other gains to come. God has already covered for you. God is Able to do all things. [21]

• • •

[2535] Psalm 89:11 The heavens are yours, the earth also is yours; the world and all that is in it—you have founded them. Deuteronomy 10:14 Although heaven and the heaven of heavens belong to the Lord your God, the earth with all that is in it,

[2536] Romans 9:15, 18 For he says to Moses, "I will have mercy on whom I have mercy, and I will have compassion on whom I have compassion." [18] So then he has mercy on whomever he chooses, and he hardens the heart of whomever he chooses.

[2537] Daniel 9:9. To the Lord our God belong mercy and forgiveness, for we have rebelled against him,

[2538] Ephesians 2:4 But God, who is rich in mercy, out of the great love with which he loved us

[2539] Revelation 22:1-2 Then the angel showed me the river of the water of life, bright as crystal, flowing from the throne of God and of the Lamb through the middle of the street of the city. [2] On either side of the river is the tree of life with its twelve kinds of fruit, producing its fruit each month; and the leaves of the tree are for the healing of the nations.

[2540] Jeremiah 31:9 With weeping they shall come, and with consolations I will lead them back, I will let them walk by brooks of water, in a straight path in which they shall not stumble;

If the unbelievers had fought you, they would have turned back and fled. Then they will find neither a protector nor a helper. [22] Such is God's way which is ongoing. You will never find any change in God's way. [23] It is He who held their hands from you and your hands from them, in the Makah valley, after He gave you the upper hand over them. God is ever seeing of what you do. [24] It is they who denied the truth, and barred you from the Sacred House, and prevented the offering from reaching its destination. Were it not for some believing men and believing women, whom you did not know, you were about to hurt them, and become unknowingly guilty. Thus God admits into His mercy whomever He wills.[2541] Had the unbelievers been clearly distinguishable, We would have inflicted on them a painful punishment. [25] The unbelievers had filled their hearts with fury, the fury of ignorance. But God sent down His tranquility on His Messenger and the believers, and made binding on them the word of God consciousness, to which they were most entitled and most deserving. God is Knowing of all things.[2542] [26]

God has fulfilled His Messenger's vision in Truth: "You will enter the Sacred House, God willing, in safety, with your heads shaved or hair shortened, with no fear. He knew what you did not know, and has granted you besides this, a victory soon to come. [27] It is He who sent His Messenger with guidance and the religion of Truth, to prevail over all religions. God suffices as a Witness. [28] Muhammad is the messenger of God.

Those with him are tough on the unbelievers, yet compassionate to one another. You see them kneeling and bowing down, seeking God's blessings and His approval. Their faces bear the mark of their prostrations. Such is their example in the Torah. And their description in the Gospel is like a plant that sprouts, becoming strong, grows thick, and rises on its stem to the delight of the farmer[2543]. Through them God infuriates the unbelievers. God has promised forgiveness and a great reward to those among them, who believe and do good deeds. [29]

• • •

[2541] Romans 9:15, 18 For he says to Moses, "I will have mercy on whom I have mercy, and I will have compassion on whom I have compassion." 18 So then he has mercy on whomever he chooses, and he hardens the heart of whomever he chooses.

[2542] 1 John 3:20 whenever our hearts condemn us; for God is greater than our hearts, and he knows everything.

[2543] Mark 4:26-29 And He was saying, "The kingdom of God is like a man who casts seed upon the soil; 27 and he goes to bed at night and gets up by day, and the seed sprouts and grows—how, he himself does not know. 28 "The soil produces crops by itself; first the blade, then the head, then the mature grain in the head. 29 "But when the crop permits, he immediately puts in the sickle, because the harvest has come."

CHAPTER **FORTY NINE**

AL-HUJURAT
THE PRIVATE ROOMS

THE **MEDINA** PERIOD

In the name of God, the Merciful-to-all, the Mercy Giver:
Believers, do not put your opinions ahead of that of God and His Messenger, but remain mindful of God. God is All-Hearing and All-Knowing.[2544] [(01)] Believers, do not raise your voices above the voice of the Prophet or be as loud when you are speaking to him like you do to one another, unless you want your deeds to become worthless without you realizing. [(02)] Those who lower their voices before the Messenger of God, they are the ones whose hearts God has tested for being fully aware of Him. For them, there is forgiveness and great reward. [(03)] But those who call you from outside your private chambers, most of them do not understand. [(04)] Had they been patient until you came out to them, it would have been better for them. But God is Ever Forgiving[2545] and Merciful-to-all.[2546] [(05)]

Believers, if a known wicked person brings you news, investigate, to avoid harming people out of ignorance and later regret what you have done. [(06)] Be aware that God's Messenger is among you. Had he obeyed you in many things, you would suffer hardship. But God has endeared your faith to you and made it pleasing to your hearts and made disbelief, mischief, and rebellion hateful to you. These are the rightly guided [(07)] a favor and a blessing from God. God is All-knowing and All-Wise.[2547] [(08)]

If two groups of believers should fight each other, then try to reconcile them.[2548] But if one of them oppresses the other, then fight the oppressing group until it complies with God's command. Once it has complied, make peace between them with justice and be equitable. God loves those who are equitable.

• • •

[2544] Psalm 44:21Would not God find this out? For He knows the secrets of the heart
[2545] Isaiah 43:25 I, I am He who blots out your transgressions for my own sake, and I will not remember your sins.
[2546] Psalm 86:15 But you, O Lord, are a God merciful and gracious, slow to anger and abounding in steadfast love and faithfulness.
[2547] Proverbs 2:6, For the Lord gives wisdom; from his mouth come knowledge and understanding;
[2548] Matthew 5:24 leave your gift there before the altar and go; first be reconciled to your brother or sister, and then come and offer your gift.

355

(09) The Believers are brothers[2549] so make peace between your brothers and remain mindful of God that you may receive mercy. (10) Believers, no men shall ridicule others, for they may be better than them. Nor shall any women ridicule other women, for they may be better than them. Nor shall you slander one another, nor shall you call each other names.[2550] How bad it is to be called disobedient after accepting faith! Those who do not repent of this behavior are unjust. (11) Believers, avoid being suspicious. Some suspicions are sinful. And don't spy or backbite[2551] one another. Would any of you like to eat the flesh of his dead brother? No, you would hate it. So remain mindful of God. God is the Acceptor of repentance, the Mercy giver.[2552] (12) People, We created you from a male and a female, and made you nations and tribes so that you may know one another. The best among you in the sight of God is the one who is most mindful of God[2553]. God is All-knowing and All-Aware. (13) The Desert-Arabs say, "We have believed." Say, "You have not believed yet; but say (instead), 'We have submitted,'[2554] for faith has not yet entered your hearts.[2555] But if you obey God and His messenger, He will not diminish any of your deeds. God is Ever Forgiving[2556] and Merciful-to-all.[2557]" (14) The believers are those who believe in God and His Messenger, leave all doubt behind, and strive with their wealth and their persons for God's cause. Those are the ones who are true to their word[2558]. (15) Say, "Do you presume to inform God about your religion, when God knows everything in the heavens and earth, and God has full Knowledge of all things?" (16) They consider it a favor to you that they have submitted[2559]. Say, "Do not consider your submission[2560] a favor to me; it is God who has done you a favor, by guiding you to faith, if you are truly sincere." (17) God knows all that is beyond our senses of the heavens and the earth.[2561] God sees everything you do. (18)

• • •

[2549] Matthew 5:9 Blessed are the peacemakers, for they will be called children of God. Romans 12:18 If it is possible, so far as it depends on you, live peaceably with all.
[2550] Matthew 7:1-5 "Judge not, that you be not judged. ² For with the judgment you pronounce you will be judged, and with the measure you use it will be measured to you. ³ Why do you see the speck that is in your brother's eye, but do not notice the log that is in your own eye? ⁴ Or how can you say to your brother, 'Let me take the speck out of your eye,' when there is the log in your own eye? ⁵ You hypocrite, first take the log out of your own eye, and then you will see clearly to take the speck out of your brother's eye.
[2551] Galatians 5:14-15 For the whole law is summed up in a single commandment, "You shall love your neighbor as yourself." ¹⁵ If, however, you bite and devour one another, take care that you are not consumed by one another.
[2552] Ephesians 2:4 But God, who is rich in mercy, out of the great love with which he loved us
[2553] Psalm 19:14 Let the words of my mouth and the meditation of my heart be acceptable in your sight, O Lord, my rock and my redeemer.
[2554] James 4:7 Submit yourselves therefore to God. Resist the devil, and he will flee from you.
[2555] Acts 15:9 and in cleansing their hearts by faith he has made no distinction between them and us.
[2556] Daniel 9:9. To the Lord our God belong mercy and forgiveness, for we have rebelled against him,
[2557] Psalm 111:4 He has gained renown by his wonderful deeds; the Lord is gracious and merciful.
[2558] Psalm 119:1-5 Blessed are those whose way is blameless, who walk in the law of the Lord! ² Blessed are those who keep his testimonies, who seek him with their whole heart, ³ who also do no wrong, but walk in his ways! ⁴ You have commanded your precepts to be kept diligently. ⁵ Oh that my ways may be steadfast in keeping your statutes!
[2559] See Glossary for Submission or Islam.
[2560] Ibid.
[2561] 2 Corinthians 4:18 because we look not at what can be seen but at what cannot be seen; for what can be seen is temporary, but what cannot be seen is eternal.

CHAPTER **FIFTY**

OAF

THE LETTER OAF

THE **MECCA** PERIOD

In the name of God, the Merciful-to-all, the Mercy Giver:

Qaf[2562] and the Glorious Qur'an. [01] They marveled that someone from among their midst has come to them with a warning. The unbelievers say, "This is an amazing thing. [02] Once We have died and become dust? That is a most unlikely return." [03] We know how many of them the earth consumes, and We keep a comprehensive record (about each one of them). [04] But when the Truth came to them, they denied it; they are in a state of confusion. [05] Have they not looked at the sky above them, how We structured it, and beautified it with all its gateways? [06] And the earth, how We spread it out [2563] and placed on it firm mountains, and made every beautiful pair of plants grow in it [07] This is an insight and a reminder to every worshiper who willingly turns to God. [08] And We sent down blessed rain from the sky[2564] and grew gardens and grain to harvest [09] And soaring palm trees, with clustered dates [10] as provision for the worshipers. By it (the rain) We gave life to a dead town. This is how the emergence (from the graves) will take place. [11] Before them the people of Noah denied the truth,[2565] and so did the dwellers of Rass,[2566] Thamud[2567] [12] Aad,[2568] Pharaoh[2569] and the

. . .

[2562] Here and at the beginning of many chapters there are letters of unknown meaning called Al Muquatta'at. Numerous theories have been proposed, but there is no agreement on what they signify yet.

[2563] Isaiah 44:24, Thus says the Lord, your Redeemer, who formed you in the womb: I am the Lord, who made all things, who alone stretched out the heavens, who by myself spread out the earth;

[2564] Jeremiah 5:24, James 5:18, Zechariah 10:1 Ask rain from the Lord in the season of the spring rain, from the Lord who makes the storm clouds, who gives showers of rain to you, the vegetation in the field to everyone.

[2565] The story of Noah and the Flood is detailed in Genesis 6-8

[2566] The companions of the Rass, known alternatively as the People of the Well were an ancient community listed with other communities who were punished for their sins.

[2567] See Ref. 617

[2568] See Ref. 615

[2569] The story of Moses and Pharaoh and the exodus from Egypt is detailed in Exodus 4-12

brothers[2570] of Lot,[2571] (13) the woods-dwellers[2572] and the people of Tubba'.[2573] All of these people rejected their messengers, so My threat was justly fulfilled.[(14)]

Were We exhausted by the first creation? But they are dubious of a new creation. [(15)] We have created man and We know what his inner soul is whispering. We are closer to him than his jugular vein [(16)] as he receives the two recording agents,[2574] seated one on the right and one on the left. [(17)] He does not utter any word, without a vigilant observer present with him. [(18)] Eventually, the trance of death will come with the Truth. This is what you were trying to evade.[(19)]

The Horn will be blown.[2575] This is the Promised Day. [(20)] Every soul will come, with it a driver and a witness. [(21)] "You did not pay much attention to this day, but as We lifted your veil from you, your vision today is keen." [(22)] His inseparable companion, will say, "This is what I have recorded." [(23)] (God will say), "Cast into Hell everyone who stubbornly denied the truth, [(24)] everyone who prevented good from reaching others, aggressor, who caused others to doubt, [(25)] who made other gods as equal with God;[2576] then cast him into severe punishment." [(26)] His (evil) companion will say, "Our Lord, I did not make him transgress, but he (himself), was extremely lost." [(27)] (God) will say, "Do not feud in My presence, when I had warned you in advance. [(28)] My judgment, once given, is not subject to change and I do not wrong My servants." [(29)] On the Day We will say to Hell, "Are you full?" And it will say, "Are there some more?"[2577] [(30)] And Paradise will be brought near to those who were ever mindful of God, it will not be far [(31)] (It will be said), "This is what you were promised. for every repentant, keeper of his covenant with God [(32)] who feared the Merciful although He was beyond his perception and came with a repenting heart. [(33)] Enter it in peace. This is the Day of Eternity." [(34)] Whatever they want there, they will have and with Us is still more. [(35)]

How many a generation We destroyed before them, who were more powerful and had searched every land. Was there any escape? [(36)] There is a reminder in this for whoever has a heart or cared to listen and witness. [(37)] And We did create the heavens and earth and everything between them in six

• • •

[2570] The story of Lot and the destruction of Gomorrah and Sodom is detailed in Genesis 18-19

[2571] Lot, nephew of Abraham.

[2572] The woods dwellers were among the Midianites, a people mentioned in the Torah and the Qur'an. Scholars generally consider Midian to have been located in the northwest Arabian Peninsula on the east shore of the gulf of Aqaba on the Red Sea and have long associated it with the region of Modiana, reported in the same area by Ptolemy.

[2573] Tubba were Arab discendants of Qahtan, just as Quraysh were discendants of Adnan. Among the people of Himyar- also known as Saba'-when a man became their king, the called him Tubba', just as the title Caesar was given to the king of the Romans, Pharoah to the disbelieving ruler of Egypt, Negus to the king of Ethiopia, etc. Taken from Tafsir ibn Kathir.

[2574] Angels.

[2575] 1 Corinthians 15:52 in a moment, in the twinkling of an eye, at the last trumpet. For the trumpet will sound, and the dead will be raised imperishable, and we will be changed.

[2576] Revelation 21:8 But as for the cowardly, the faithless, the polluted, the murderers, the fornicators, the sorcerers, the idolaters, and all liars, their place will be in the lake that burns with fire and sulfur, which is the second death."

[2577] Proverbs 30:16 Sheol, the barren womb, the earth ever thirsty for water, and the fire that never says, "Enough."

days,[2578] and We were not the least weary.[2579] (38) So (Prophet) endure what they say and praise your Lord's limitless glory before the rising of the sun and before its setting, (39) and glorify Him part of the night and after prostration. (40) Listen for the Day when the Caller will call out from a place that is near. (41) The Day they will hear the blast in all Truth, that is the Day of Emergence (from the graves). (42) It is We who give life and cause death, and to Us is their final destination (43) The Day when the earth cracks as they emerge rapidly;[2580] That is an easy gathering for Us. (44) We know best what they say, and you are not there to force them. So remind with the Quran those who fear My warning. (45)

. . .

[2578] Genesis 2:1-3 Thus the heavens and the earth were finished, and all their multitude. [2] And on the seventh day God finished the work that he had done, and he rested on the seventh day from all the work that he had done. [3] So God blessed the seventh day and hallowed it, because on it God rested from all the work that he had done in creation. Exodus 31:17 for in six days the Lord made heaven and earth, and on the seventh day he rested, and was refreshed.

[2579] Isaiah 40:28 Have you not known? Have you not heard? The Lord is the everlasting God, the Creator of the ends of the earth. He does not faint or grow weary; his understanding is unsearchable.

[2580] Revelation 16:19 The great city was split into three parts, and the cities of the nations fell. God remembered great Babylon and gave her the wine-cup of the fury of his wrath.

CHAPTER **FIFTY ONE**

ATH-THARIYAT
THE SCATTERING WIND

THE **MECCA** PERIOD

In the name of God, the Merciful-to-all, the Mercy Giver:

By those (winds) scattering dust, ⁽⁰¹⁾ and those heavily laden (with water) and those sailing with ease ⁽⁰³⁾ and those distributing (rain) as ordained, ⁽⁰⁴⁾ what you are promised is true. ⁽⁰⁵⁾ The judgment will come^{2581 (06)} By the sky that is woven, ⁽⁰⁷⁾ you differ in what you say (about this message). ⁽⁰⁸⁾ He who deceives himself is misled away from it. ⁽⁰⁹⁾ The speculators destroy themselves ⁽¹⁰⁾ they are unaware that they are lost in ignorance. ⁽¹¹⁾ They ask, "When is the Day of Judgment?"^{2582 (12)} The Day they will be tested when they see the Fire ⁽¹³⁾ (And will be told), "Taste your scheme. This is what you were rushing toward." ⁽¹⁴⁾ While those who were mindful of God will be among Gardens and springs, ⁽¹⁵⁾ accepting what their Lord has given them. Verily, they were those who do good.^{2583 (16)} They used to sleep a little at night,^{2584 (17)} And at dawn they would pray for forgiveness,^{2585 (18)} And assign a share of their wealth to the needy and the deprived.^{2586 (19)} For the certain (in faith), they are signs on earth ⁽²⁰⁾ and in yourselves, will you not see?^{2587 (21)} And in the heaven is your provision and whatever you are promised.^{2588 (22)} By the Lord of the heaven and earth, it is as true as the fact that you speak. ⁽²³⁾

Has the story of Abraham's honored guests reached you?^{2589 (24)} When they entered to see him,²⁵⁹⁰ they said, "Peace." He answered, "Peace to you

• • •

²⁵⁸¹ Joel 2:1 Blow the trumpet in Zion; sound the alarm on my holy mountain! Let all the inhabitants of the land tremble, for the day of the Lord is coming, it is near—
²⁵⁸² Mark 13:4 'Tell us, when will this be, and what will be the sign that all these things are about to be accomplished?'
²⁵⁸³ 1 Timothy 6:18 They are to do good, to be rich in good works, generous, and ready to share,
²⁵⁸⁴ Psalm 119:62 At midnight I rise to praise you, because of your righteous ordinances.
²⁵⁸⁵ Psalm 5:3 O Lord, in the morning you hear my voice; in the morning I plead my case to you, and watch.
²⁵⁸⁶ Isaiah 58:7 Is it not to share your bread with the hungry, and bring the homeless poor into your house; when you see the naked, to cover them, and not to hide yourself from your own kin?
²⁵⁸⁷ Romans 1:19-20 For what can be known about God is plain to them, because God has shown it to them. Ever since the creation of the world his eternal power and divine nature, invisible though they are, have been understood and seen through the things he has made. So they are without excuse;
²⁵⁸⁸ 1 Peter 1:4 and into an inheritance that is imperishable, undefiled, and unfading, kept in heaven for you,
²⁵⁸⁹ Genesis 18 A Son Promised to Abraham and Sarah
²⁵⁹⁰ Genesis 18:2 He looked up and saw three men standing near him. When he saw them, he ran from the tent entrance to meet them, and bowed down to the ground.

strangers."[2591] [(25)] Then he went off to his family[2592] and came with a fat (roasted) calf[2593] [(26)] and placed it near them; he said, "Will you not eat?" [(27)] He then began to feel apprehensive. They said, "Do not fear," and gave him good news of a boy who would be gifted with knowledge.[2594] [(28)] His wife approached with a scream, struck her face and protested, "A barren old woman (like me)!"[2595] [(29)] They said, "Thus said your Lord;[2596] He is the All Wise,[2597] the All Knowing."[2598] [(30)] (Abraham) then enquired, "What is your business, messengers?" [(31)] They said, " We have been sent to a dissenting people [(32)] to send down on them rocks of clay,[2599] [(33)] marked by your Lord for those who rejected His messages and have severed all relations with God [(34)] So We brought out the believers that were in town..[2600] [(35)] But found only one household of people who submitted to God.[2601] [(36)] And We left in town a sign[2602] for those who fear the painful punishment.[2603(37)]

There is another sign in Moses, when We sent him to Pharaoh with clear authority. [(38)] But Pharaoh turned away with his supporters and said, "A magician[2604] or a madman." [(39)] So We seized him and his soldiers and threw them into the sea.[2605] Pharaoh was to blame. [(40)] And a sign in Aad,[2606] when We unleashed against them the devastating wind. [(41)] It spared nothing it came upon, and left it like decayed ruins. [(42)] And a sign in Thamud,[2607] it was said to them, "Enjoy yourselves for a while." [(43)] But they defied their Lord's command, so the thunderbolt struck them as they looked. [(44)] They were unable to rise, nor could they find help. [(45)] And before that the people of Noah. They were wicked

• • •

[2591] Genesis 18:3 He said, 'My Lord, if I find favor with you, do not pass by your servant.

[2592] Genesis 18:6 And Abraham hastened into the tent to Sarah, and said, 'Make ready quickly three measures of choice flour, knead it, and make cakes.'

[2593] Genesis 18:7 Abraham ran to the herd, and took a calf, tender and good, and gave it to the servant, who hastened to prepare it.

[2594] Genesis 18:10 Then one said, 'I will surely return to you in due season, and your wife Sarah shall have a son.' And Sarah was listening at the tent entrance behind him.

[2595] Genesis 18:12 So Sarah laughed to herself, saying, 'After I have grown old, and my husband is old, shall I have pleasure?'

[2596] Genesis 18:14 Is anything too wonderful for the Lord? At the set time I will return to you, in due season, and Sarah shall have a son.'

[2597] Job 9:4, He is wise in heart, and mighty in strength—who has resisted him, and succeeded?

[2598] 1 John 3:20 whenever our hearts condemn us; for God is greater than our hearts, and he knows everything.

[2599] Genesis 18:20 Then the Lord said, 'How great is the outcry against Sodom and Gomorrah and how very grave their sin!

[2600] Genesis 19:16 But he lingered; so the men seized him and his wife and his two daughters by the hand, the Lord being merciful to him, and they brought him out and left him outside the city.

[2601] James 4:7 Submit yourselves therefore to God. Resist the devil, and he will flee from you.

[2602] Genesis 19:25, 28 and he overthrew those cities, and all the Plain, and all the inhabitants of the cities, and what grew on the ground. [28] and he looked down towards Sodom and Gomorrah and towards all the land of the Plain, and saw the smoke of the land going up like the smoke of a furnace.

[2603] Matthew 25:41, 46 Then he will say to those at his left hand, "You that are accursed, depart from me into the eternal fire prepared for the devil and his angels; [46] And these will go away into eternal punishment, but the righteous into eternal life.'

[2604] Exodus 7:11 Then Pharaoh summoned the wise men and the sorcerers; and they also, the magicians of Egypt, did the same by their secret arts.

[2605] Exodus 15:4 'Pharaoh's chariots and his army he cast into the sea; his picked officers were sunk in the Red Sea.

[2606] See Glossary

[2607] See Glossary

people.[2608] (46) We built the universe with power, and We are steadily expanding it.[2609] (47) And the earth We spread it out, How well We smooth it out.[2610] (48) And of all things We created two mates;[2611] perhaps you will reflect. (49)

So flee towards God.[2612] I am from Him a clear warning for you. (50) and do not set up any other god with God.[2613] I come to you with a clear warning from Him. (51) Similarly, every time a messenger came to those before them, they said, "A magician or a madman." (52) Did they recommend it to one another? Rather, they are people full of tyranny. (53) So turn away from them, you are not to blame. (54) And go on reminding them. It is good for the believers to be reminded.[2614] (55)

I only created Jinn and Human beings to worship Me.[2615] (56) I do not require any provision from them,[2616] nor do I require them to feed Me.[2617] (57) It is God who is the Provider to all,[2618] the Possessor of Power,[2619] the Strong.[2620] (58) Those who were unjust have their share of bad deeds just like their predecessors,[2621] so let them not rush My punishment. (59) How terrible for the unbelievers their Day which they are promised. (60)

. . .

[2608] Genesis 6:5 The Lord saw that the wickedness of humankind was great in the earth, and that every inclination of the thoughts of their hearts was only evil continually.

[2609] Genesis 1:7-8 So God made the dome and separated the waters that were under the dome from the waters that were above the dome. And it was so. ⁸ God called the dome Sky. And there was evening and there was morning, the second day.

[2610] Psalm 104:5, You set the earth on its foundations, so that it shall never be shaken.

[2611] Isaiah 34:16 Seek and read from the book of the Lord: Not one of these shall be missing; none shall be without its mate. For the mouth of the Lord has commanded, and his spirit has gathered them.

[2612] Psalm 7:1 O Lord my God, in you I take refuge; save me from all my pursuers, and deliver me,

[2613] Exodus 20:3-4 you shall have no other gods before me. ⁴ You shall not make for yourself an idol, whether in the form of anything that is in heaven above, or that is on the earth beneath, or that is in the water under the earth.

[2614] Deuteronomy 8:2 Remember the long way that the Lord your God has led you these forty years in the wilderness, in order to humble you, testing you to know what was in your heart, whether or not you would keep his commandments.

[2615] Isaiah 43:7 everyone who is called by my name, whom I created for my glory, whom I formed and made.'

[2616] Isaiah 66:1-2 Thus says the Lord: Heaven is my throne and the earth is my footstool; what is the house that you would build for me, and what is my resting-place? All these things my hand has made, and so all these things are mine, says the Lord. But this is the one to whom I will look, to the humble and contrite in spirit, who trembles at my word.

[2617] Psalm 50:12-13 'If I were hungry, I would not tell you, for the world and all that is in it is mine. ¹³ Do I eat the flesh of bulls, or drink the blood of goats?

[2618] Psalm 136:25 who gives food to all flesh, for his steadfast love endures for ever.

[2619] 1 Chronicles 29:11, Yours, O Lord, are the greatness, the power, the glory, the victory, and the majesty; for all that is in the heavens and on the earth is yours; yours is the kingdom, O Lord, and you are exalted as head above all.

[2620] Psalm 136:12 with a strong hand and an outstretched arm, for his steadfast love endures for ever;

[2621] Romans 2:1 Therefore you have no excuse, whoever you are, when you judge others; for in passing judgment on another you condemn yourself, because you, the judge, are doing the very same things.

CHAPTER FIFTY TWO

AT-TUR
THE MOUNTAIN

In the name of God, the Merciful-to-all, the Mercy Giver:
By the mountain called Al Tur, [01] and (by) a Book inscribed [02] In a wide open parchment, [03] and (by) the frequented House, [04] and (by) the canopy raised high, [05] and (by) the surf-swollen sea,[2622] [06] the punishment[2623] of your Lord will occur.[2624] [07] nothing can prevent it. (52:8) On the Day the heaven sways with agitation[2625] [09] and the mountains shift about,[2626] [10] how terrible it is that Day, for the unbelievers, [11] who are chatting carelessly to amuse themselves. [12] The Day they are forcefully shoved into the fire of Hell [2627] [13] "This is the Fire which you didn't believe in. [14] Is this magic, or do you still not see? [15] Burn in it. Then be patient or impatient, it is all the same for you. You are only being repaid for what you have done."[2628] [16]

Those who were mindful of God will be in Gardens and bliss, [17] rejoicing in what their Lord has given them.[2629] For their Lord has spared them the suffering of Hell. [18] "Eat and drink enjoyably, a reward for what You have done." [19] Reclining on luxurious furniture, beautifully arranged laced, We will pair them with Hoor Ein.[2630] [20] Those who believed and whose offspring followed them in

• • •

[2622] Habakkuk 2:14 But the earth will be filled with the knowledge of the glory of the Lord, as the waters cover the sea.
[2623] 2 Peter 2:9 then the Lord knows how to rescue the godly from trial, and to keep the unrighteous under punishment until the day of judgment
[2624] Romans 2:5 But by your hard and impenitent heart you are storing up wrath for yourself on the day of wrath, when God's righteous judgment will be revealed.
[2625] 2 Peter 3:12 waiting for and hastening the coming of the day of God, because of which the heavens will be set ablaze and dissolved, and the elements will melt with fire?
[2626] Revelation 16:20 And every island fled away, and no mountains were to be found;
[2627] Matthew 25:46 And these will go away into eternal punishment, but the righteous into eternal life.'
[2628] Matthew 12:36 I tell you, on the day of judgment you will have to give an account for every careless word you utter;
[2629] Romans 8:18 I consider that the sufferings of this present time are not worth comparing with the glory about to be revealed to us.
[2630] See Glossary.

faith, We will unite them with their offspring without depriving anybody of their reward for their deeds. Each one according to what he has earned [21] And We will provide them with any fruit and meat they desire.[2631] [22] They pass around a cup which does not lead to either idle talk, or sin. [23] Circulating among them to serve them, will be youths like hidden pearls [24] They will approach one another, wondering, [25] they will say "When we were previously among our families we used to live in fear. [26] But God blessed us, and spared us the suffering of the Scorching Fire. [27] Before this, we used to pray to Him. It is He who is the Most Kind, the Merciful-to-all."[2632] [28] So go on reminding.

By the grace of your Lord, you are neither an oracle nor a madman. [29] Or do they say (of you), "He's only a poet let's wait to see what time will do to him?" [30] Say, "Go on waiting, I will be waiting with you." [31] Or is it their dreams compelling them to say this? Or are they people full of tyranny? [32] Or do they say, "He has simply made it up?" Rather, they do not want to believe. [33] Then let them produce something like it, if they are truthful. [34] Or were they created out of nothing? Or are they the creators? [35] Or did they create the heavens and the earth?[2633] In truth, they are not certain of anything. [36] Or do they possess your Lord's treasuries? Or do they have control over them? [37] Or do they have a stairway[2634] (into the heaven) to climb and eavesdrop? Then let their eavesdropper produce clear proof.[2635] [38] Or does He have daughters while you have sons? [39] Or do you demand a wage from them that would burden them with debt? [40] Or if they know the future, so they write (it) down? [41] Or are they plotting against you? The plot will fall back on the unbelievers [42] Or do they have a god other than God? May He be exalted in His glory,[2636] God is far above, anything they associate with Him. [43]

Even if they were to see a piece the sky falling, they would say, "Just a heap of clouds." [44] So leave them until they meet their Day in which they will be stunned, [45] the Day when their plotting will not do them any good, nor will they be helped. [46] Another punishment [2637] awaits the unjust, but most of them are unaware of it. [47] So wait patiently for your Lord's judgment, for you are before Our eyes. And praise your Lord of limitless glory when you arise.[2638] [48] And glorify Him at night, and at time when the stars retreat.[2639] [49]

· · ·

[2631] Luke 22:30 so that you may eat and drink at my table in my kingdom, and you will sit on thrones judging the twelve tribes of Israel.

[2632] Psalm 116:5, Gracious is the Lord, and righteous; our God is merciful.

[2633] Psalm 89:11 The heavens are yours, the earth also is yours; the world and all that is in it—you have founded them.

[2634] Genesis 28:12 And he dreamed that there was a ladder set up on the earth, the top of it reaching to heaven; and the angels of God were ascending and descending on it.

[2635] Isaiah 45:21 Declare and present your case; let them take counsel together! Who told this long ago? Who declared it of old? Was it not I, the Lord? There is no other god besides me, a righteous God and a Savior; there is no one besides me.

[2636] Isaiah 2:17 The haughtiness of people shall be humbled, and the pride of everyone shall be brought low; and the Lord alone will be exalted on that day

[2637] Matthew 25:41,46; Then he will say to those at his left hand, "You that are accursed, depart from me into the eternal fire prepared for the devil and his angels; And these will go away into eternal punishment, but the righteous into eternal life.'

[2638] Psalm 35:28 Then my tongue shall tell of your righteousness and of your praise all day long.

[2639] Psalm 7:17 I will give to the Lord the thanks due to his righteousness, and sing praise to the name of the Lord, the Most High.

CHAPTER FIFTY THREE

AN-NAJM

THE STAR

By the falling star,[2640] [(01)] your friend has not strayed, nor has he erred, [(02)] Nor does he speak from his own whims. [(03)] It is a revealed revelation, [(04)] taught to him by one with mighty powers [(05)] and splendor who stood still [(06)] while he was at the highest horizon. [(07)] Then he drew near coming down [(08)] to within two bows' length or closer. [(09)] Then God (through that angel) revealed to His servant what He revealed. [(10)] The heart did not doubt what it saw. [(11)] Do you dispute with him what he saw? [(12)] Indeed, he saw him in another descent, [(13)] at the Lotus Tree of the Utmost Boundary, [(14)] near the Garden of Refuge [(15)] where the Lotus Tree was shrouded (in mystery) with what shrouded it. [(16)] The eye did not waver, nor did it exceed its limit. [(17)] He saw some of the greatest signs of his Lord. [(18)]

So have you considered al-Lat and al-'Uzza? [(19)] and Manat,[2641] the third, the other one? [(20)] Why do you chose for yourself male offspring and assign to God the female? [(21)] That, then, is an unfair distribution. [(22)] These (allegedly divine beings) are nothing but names, which you (who worship them) and your forefathers have invented. God sent no authority for them.[2642] They (who worship them) follow nothing but guesswork and their egotistical whims,[2643] although guidance has come to them (your people) from their Lord.[2644] [(23)] Should man have whatever he wishes for, [(24)] when this life and the life to come belong only to God? [2645] [(25)] There are many angels in the heavens whose

• • •

[2640] See life cycles of stars
http://www.bbc.co.uk/schools/gcsebitesize/science/add_aqa/stars/lifecyclestarsrev2.shtml.
[2641] Idol names. These idols were worshiped by the Arabs and were placed in or around the Ka'ba.
[2642] 1 Corinthians 8:4 Hence, as to the eating of food offered to idols, we know that 'no idol in the world really exists', and that 'there is no God but one.'
[2643] Leviticus 19:4 Do not turn to idols or make cast images for yourselves: I am the Lord your God.
[2644] Isaiah 58:11 The Lord will guide you continually, and satisfy your needs in parched places, and make your bones strong; and you shall be like a watered garden, like a spring of water, whose waters never fail.
[2645] Deuteronomy 3:24 "O Lord God, you have only begun to show your servant your greatness and your might; what god in heaven or on earth can perform deeds and mighty acts like yours!

intercession is of no benefit at all until God gives permission to whomever He wills, and approves. [26] Those who do not believe in the Hereafter give the angels female names, [27] they have no knowledge of this. They only follow guesswork. Guesswork is no substitute at all for the Truth. [28] So pay no attention to whoever turns away from Our message and desires only this worldly life. [29] That is the extent of their knowledge. Your Lord knows best who strayed from His path, and He knows best who is guided. [30] To God belongs everything in the heavens and on earth.[2646] He will repay those who do evil according to their deeds, and reward those who do good with the best[2647] [31] those who avoid major sins and indecencies, except for minor lapses[2648] expected; your Lord's forgiveness is vast. He knows you well, ever since He created you[2649] from the earth and ever since you were embryos in your mothers' wombs.[2650] So do not attest your own virtues;[2651] He knows best those who are mindful of Him.[2652] [32]

Have you seen the one who turned away [33] And gave a little and then held back?[2653] [34] Does he have knowledge of all that beyond, enabling him to see the future? [35] Or has he not been told of what was in the scrolls of Moses [36] and (of) Abraham, who fulfilled his duty [37] that no bearer of burdens will bear the burdens of another[2654] [38] that a human being attains only what he strives for,[2655] [39] and that his striving will be seen. [2656] [40] Then he will receive for it the fullest reward[2657] [41] that the ultimate end is to your Lord [42] that It is He who causes

• • •

[2646] Psalm 89:11, The heavens are yours, the earth also is yours; the world and all that is in it—you have founded them

[2647] Psalm 31:23 Love the Lord, all you his saints. The Lord preserves the faithful, but abundantly repays the one who acts haughtily.

[2648] Psalm 19:12,13 But who can detect their errors? Clear me from hidden faults. Keep back your servant also from the insolent; do not let them have dominion over me. Then I shall be blameless, and innocent of great transgression.

[2649] Psalm 103:12-14 as far as the east is from the west, so far he removes our transgressions from us. As a father has compassion for his children, so the Lord has compassion for those who fear him. For he knows how we were made; he remembers that we are dust.

[2650] Psalm 139:13-16 For it was you who formed my inward parts; you knit me together in my mother's womb. [14] I praise you, for I am fearfully and wonderfully made. Wonderful are your works; that I know very well. [15] My frame was not hidden from you, when I was being made in secret, intricately woven in the depths of the earth. [16] Your eyes beheld my unformed substance. In your book were written all the days that were formed for me, when none of them as yet existed.

[2651] Romans 3:28 For we hold that a person is justified by faith apart from works prescribed by the law.

[2652] 2 Timothy 2:19 But God's firm foundation stands, bearing this inscription: 'The Lord knows those who are his', and, 'Let everyone who calls on the name of the Lord turn away from wickedness.'

[2653] Proverbs 28:22 The miser is in a hurry to get rich and does not know that loss is sure to come.

[2654] Galatians 6:5 "For every one shall bear his own burden.

[2655] Matthew 12: 36 "But I tell you that every careless word that people speak, they shall give an accounting for it in the day of judgment.'

[2656] 1 Peter 2:12 Conduct yourselves honorably among the Gentiles, so that, though they malign you as evildoers, they may see your honorable deeds and glorify God when he comes to judge.

[2657] 2 John 8 Be on your guard, so that you do not lose what we have worked for, but may receive a full reward.

(one) laugh[2658] and weep[2659] (43) that It is He who causes death and gives life[2660] (44) that He creates the two mates - the male and female (45) from a sperm-drop when It is emitted (46) that the next creation is incumbent upon Him[2661] (47) that It is He who enriches[2662] and impoverishes (48) that It is He who is the Lord of Sirius,[2663] (49) that it is He who destroyed the first people of Aad[2664] (50) And Thamud.[2665] He spared no one (51) And before that the people of Noah (Nuh) who were most unjust and most oppressive.[2666] (52) That it is He who brought down the ruined cities[2667] (53) And covered them by that whatever He covered them. (54) Which then of your Lord's blessings do you doubt? (55) This is a warning just like the earlier warnings. (56) The inevitable Day draws near. (57) No one, besides God, can disclose it. (58) Do you marvel at this discourse? (59) And you laugh and do not weep (50) While you are lost in your playfulness? (61) So bow down before God and worship (Him).[2668] (62)

. . .

[2658] Luke 6:21 'Blessed are you who are hungry now, for you will be filled. 'Blessed are you who weep now, for you will laugh.
[2659] Luke 6:25 'Woe to you who are full now, for you will be hungry. 'Woe to you who are laughing now, for you will mourn and weep.
[2660] 1 Samuel 2:6 The Lord kills and brings to life; he brings down to Sheol and raises up. Deuteronomy 32:39, See now that I, even I, am he; there is no god besides me. I kill and I make alive; I wound and I heal; and no one can deliver from my hand.
[2661] 1 Corinthians 3:7 So neither the one who plants nor the one who waters is anything, but only God who gives the growth.
[2662] 1 Timothy 6:17 As for those who in the present age are rich, command them not to be haughty, or to set their hopes on the uncertainty of riches, but rather on God who richly provides us with everything for our enjoyment.
[2663] Ash-Shi'ra, a star that was worshiped before Islam
[2664] See Glossary
[2665] Ibid
[2666] Genesis 6:5 The LORD saw that the wickedness of humankind was great in the earth, and that every inclination of the thoughts of their hearts was only evil continually.
[2667] Genesis 19:24-25, Then the Lord rained on Sodom and Gomorrah sulphur and fire from the Lord out of heaven; and he overthrew those cities, 25 and all the Plain, and all the inhabitants of the cities, and what grew on the ground.
[2668] Psalm 95:6, O come, let us worship and bow down, let us kneel before the Lord, our Maker!

CHAPTER FIFTY FOUR

AL-QAMAR
THE MOON

In the name of God, the Merciful-to-all, the Mercy Giver:

The Hour has come near, and the moon has split. [01] If they see a sign, they turn away and say, "same old magic." [02] They rejected the truth and followed their desires. But everything has its time. [03] Stories to warn them have already come, that should have restrained them. [04] Profound Wisdom, yet these warnings had no effect. [05] So, turn away from them. The Day the Caller calls to something terrible, [06] with their eyes humbled, they will emerge from the graves as if they were swarming locusts,[2671] [07] scrambling towards the Caller. The unbelievers will cry, "This is a disastrous Day." [08]

Before them the people of Noah rejected the truth, they rejected Our servant saying, "A madman," and he was rebuked. [09] So he called upon his Lord, "I am overwhelmed, (please) help me." [10] So We opened the floodgates of heaven with torrential rain,[2672] [11] made the earth burst with gushing springs, and the waters met[2673] for an already destined purpose. [12] And We carried him on a craft of planks and nails,[2674] [13] sailing before our watchful eyes,[2675] a reward for him who was rejected. [14] We left it as a sign,[2676] who then is willing to take it to

• • •

[2671] John 5:28 Do not be astonished at this; for the hour is coming when all who are in their graves will hear his voice

[2672] Genesis 7:11-12 In the six-hundredth year of Noah's life, in the second month, on the seventeenth day of the month, on that day all the fountains of the great deep burst forth, and the windows of the heavens were opened. 12 The rain fell on the earth for forty days and forty nights.

[2673] Genesis 7:17-19 The flood continued for forty days on the earth; and the waters increased, and bore up the ark, and it rose high above the earth. The waters swelled and increased greatly on the earth; and the ark floated on the face of the waters. The waters swelled so mightily on the earth that all the high mountains under the whole heaven were covered;

[2674] Genesis 6:14 Make yourself an ark of cypress wood; make rooms in the ark, and cover it inside and out with pitch.

[2675] Genesis 8:1 But God remembered Noah and all the wild animals and all the domestic animals that were with him in the ark. And God made a wind blow over the earth, and the waters subsided;

[2676] Genesis 9:12 God said, 'This is the sign of the covenant that I make between me and you and every living creature that is with you, for all future generations:

heart? [15] How terrible was My punishment and My warning. [16] Hence, We made it easy to bear this Qur'an in mind. Who, then, is willing to keep it in mind?[17]

The people of Aad[2677] rejected the truth. How then was My punishment and My warning? [18] We unleashed upon them a screaming wind, on a day of continuous catastrophe, [19] plucking people away, as if they were trunks of uprooted palm trees. [20] How terrible was My punishment and My warning. [21] Hence, We made it easy to bear this Qur'an in mind. Who, then, is willing to keep it in mind? [22]

The people of Thamud[2678] rejected the warnings [23] They said, "Are we to follow a human being, one of us? We would then be misguided and quite insane. [24] Why should he alone from among all of us be chosen to receive the message? He is nothing but a wicked liar." [25] They will know tomorrow who the wicked liar is. [26] We are sending the she-camel as a test for them. Just watch them and be patient. [27] Tell them that the water is to be shared between them, with each share equitably apportioned. [28] But they called their friend, who dared to slaughter (her). [29] How then was My punishment and My warning. [30] We released against them a single blast, and they became like crumbling twigs. [31] Hence, We made it easy to bear this Qur'an in mind. Who, then, is willing to keep it in mind? [32]

The people of Lot[2679] rejected the warnings. [33] We unleashed upon them a shower of stones, except for the family of Lot; We rescued them before dawn [34] as a blessing from us. Thus We reward those who are thankful. [2680][35] Lot had already warned them of Our assault, but they dismissed the warning.[2681] [36] They even lusted for his guest, so We blinded their eyes.[2682] "Taste My punishment and (the fulfillment of) My warnings." [37] Early morning brought them enduring punishment.[2683] [38] So taste My punishment (which is the fulfillment of) My warning [39] Hence, We made it easy to bear this Qur'an in mind. Who, then, is willing to keep it in mind? [40]

The people of Pharaoh also received warnings. [41] They rejected all Our signs, so We seized them as only the Almighty, the Dominant will [42]

Are those among you who deny the truth any better than these others, or do you have immunity in the Books? [43] Or do they say, "We are united and bound to win"? [44] They will all be defeated, and they will turn their backs and flee. [45] Rather the Hour is their appointed time and the Hour is more disastrous and bitter. [46] Those who force others to reject God's messages are misguided and insane. [47] The Day when they are dragged on their faces into the fire: "Taste the

• • •

2677 See Glossary

2678 See Glossary

2679 Lot, nephew of Abraham

2680 Psalm 75:1 We give thanks to you, O God; we give thanks; your name is near. People tell of your wondrous deeds.

2681 Genesis 19:14 So Lot went out and said to his sons-in-law, who were to marry his daughters, 'Up, get out of this place; for the Lord is about to destroy the city.' But he seemed to his sons-in-law to be jesting.

2682 Genesis 19:5,11 and they called to Lot, 'Where are the men who came to you tonight? Bring them out to us, so that we may know them.' 11 And they struck with blindness the men who were at the door of the house, both small and great, so that they were unable to find the door.

2683 Genesis 19:23-24 The sun had risen on the earth when Lot came to Zoar. 24 Then the Lord rained on Sodom and Gomorrah sulphur and fire from the Lord out of heaven;

scorching touch of Saqar."[2684] (48) We have created all things in precise measure. (49) Our command is but one word, like a twinkling of an eye.[2685] (50) And We have already destroyed the likes of you. Who, then, is willing to take heed? (51)

Everything They have done is noted in their records. (52) Every action small or big is written down.[2686] (53) Those who are mindful of God will be among Gardens and rivers,[2687] (54) In a seat of honor in the presence of a Sovereign who determines all things. (55)

. . .

[2684] A place in Hell

[2685] 1 Corinthians 15:52 in a moment, in the twinkling of an eye, at the last trumpet. For the trumpet will sound, and the dead will be raised imperishable, and we will be changed.

[2686] Ecclesiastes 12:14 For God will bring every deed into judgment, including every secret thing, whether good or evil.

[2687] Revelation 22:2 through the middle of the street of the city. On either side of the river is the tree of life with its twelve kinds of fruit, producing its fruit each month; and the leaves of the tree are for the healing of the nations.

CHAPTER FIFTY FIVE

AR-RAHMAN
THE MERCIFUL-TO-ALL

THE **MEDINA** PERIOD

In the name of God, the Merciful-to-all, the Mercy Giver:
The Merciful-to-all [01] taught the Qur'an, [02] created man, [03] taught him articulate speech. [04] The sun and the moon run on precise calculations. [2686] [05] The stars [2687] and the trees [2688] submit to Him. [06] The skies, He raised high [2689] and has established the balance [2690] [07] That you may not transgress in the balance. [2691] [08] but weight with justice, and do not violate the balance. [2692] [09] The earth, He laid out for all living creatures. [2693] [10] In it are fruits, and date-palms in clusters. [11] And grains on flourishing stems and fragrant plants. [2694] [12] So which of your Lord's blessings do you both deny? [13]

• • •

[2686] Genesis 1:16-17 God made the two great lights—the greater light to rule the day and the lesser light to rule the night—and the stars. [17] God set them in the dome of the sky to give light upon the earth,
[2687] Psalm 8:3 When I look at your heavens, the work of your fingers, the moon and the stars that you have established;
[2688] Genesis 1:12 The earth brought forth vegetation: plants yielding seed of every kind, and trees of every kind bearing fruit with the seed in it. And God saw that it was good.
[2689] Genesis 1:6-8 And God said, 'Let there be a dome in the midst of the waters, and let it separate the waters from the waters.' [7] So God made the dome and separated the waters that were under the dome from the waters that were above the dome. [8] And it was so. God called the dome Sky. And there was evening and there was morning, the second day.
[2690] Isaiah 40:12 Who has measured the waters in the hollow of his hand and marked off the heavens with a span, enclosed the dust of the earth in a measure, and weighed the mountains in scales and the hills in a balance?
[2691] Proverbs 16:11 Honest balances and scales are the Lord's; all the weights in the bag are his work
[2692] Leviticus 19:36 You shall have honest balances, honest weights, an honest ephah, and an honest hin: I am the LORD your God, who brought you out of the land of Egypt.
[2693] Genesis 2:8,19 And the Lord God planted a garden in Eden, in the east; and there he put the man whom he had formed. [19] So out of the ground the Lord God formed every animal of the field and every bird of the air, and brought them to the man to see what he would call them; and whatever the man called each living creature, that was its name.
[2694] Genesis 2:16 And the Lord God commanded the man, 'You may freely eat of every tree of the garden;

He created human beings from dry clay,[2695] ringing like pottery. (14) And He created the jinn from a fusion of fire. (15) So which of your Lord's blessings will you deny? (16) He is Lord of the two sunrises and Lord of the two sunsets. (17) So which of your Lord's blessings will you deny? (18)

He merged the two seas, converging together,[2696] (19) with a barrier (so that) they do not over run between them. (20) So which of your Lord's blessings will you deny? (21) From out of both comes pearl and coral. (22) So which of your Lord's blessings will you deny? (23) His are all floating objects,[2697] raised above the sea like mountain peaks. (24) So which of your Lord's blessings will you deny? (25)

Everyone on it is perishing; (26) but forever will remain the Face of your Lord, full of Majesty and Glory.[2698] (27) So which of your Lord's blessings will you deny?(28) To Him turn everyone in the heavens and on earth for their needs;[2699] and every day He manifests Himself in yet another way.[2700] (29) So which of your Lord's blessings will you deny? (30) We will soon attend to your judgment, you burdensome two. (31) So which of your Lord's blessings will you deny? (32)

Jinn and Human beings, if you are able to break through the confines of the heavens and earth, then break through them. You will not break through except with authority. (33) So which of your Lord's blessings will you deny? (34) A flash of fire and brass will be sent against you, and you will not be helped. (35) So which of your Lord's blessings will you deny? (36)

And when the heaven is split open and becomes rose-colored like oil (37) So which of your Lord's blessings will you deny? (38) On that Day, no human and no jinn will be asked about his sins. (39) So which of your Lord's blessings will you deny? (40) Those who forced others to reject Our messages will be known by their marks,[2701] and they will be seized by the foreheads and the feet. (41) So which of your Lord's blessings will you deny? (42)

This is Hell, which those who forced others to reject Our messages denied. (43) They will circulate them between fire and scalding water. (44) So which of your Lord's blessings will you deny?(45) But for he who feared to be one day in the Presence of his Lord[2702] are two Gardens (46) So which of your Lord's blessings will you deny? (47) With shading branches. (48) So which of your Lord's blessings will you deny?(49)

• • •

[2695] Genesis 2:7 then the Lord God formed man from the dust of the ground, and breathed into his nostrils the breath of life; and the man became a living being.

[2696] Psalm 104:9 You set a boundary that they may not pass, so that they might not again cover the earth.

[2697] Tall ships, iceburgs, etc.

[2698] 1Timothy 1:17, To the King of the ages, immortal, invisible, the only God, be honor and glory for ever and ever. Amen.

[2699] Psalm 65:2-3 O you who answer prayer! To you all flesh shall come. ³ When deeds of iniquity overwhelm us, you forgive our transgressions

[2700] Psalm 7:10-11, God is my shield, who saves the upright in heart. ¹¹ God is a righteous judge, and a God who has indignation every day.

[2701] Revelation 14:9-11 Then another angel, a third, followed them, crying with a loud voice, "Those who worship the beast and its image, and receive a mark on their foreheads or on their hands, ¹⁰ they will also drink the wine of God's wrath, poured unmixed into the cup of his anger, and they will be tormented with fire and sulfur in the presence of the holy angels and in the presence of the Lamb. ¹¹ And the smoke of their torment goes up forever and ever. There is no rest day or night for those who worship the beast and its image and for anyone who receives the mark of its name."

[2702] Revelation 15:4 Lord, who will not fear and glorify your name? For you alone are holy. All nations will come and worship before you, for your judgments have been revealed.'

In them are two flowing springs.[2703] [50] So which of your Lord's blessings will you deny? [51] and they have pairs of every kind of fruits.[2704] [52] So which of your Lord's blessings will you deny?[53] They will be reclining on couches lined with silk brocade, and the fruit of the two Gardens are near at hand. [54] So which of your Lord's blessings will you deny? [55]

In them are creatures of modest gaze, untouched before them by man or jinn.[2705] [56] So which of your Lord's blessings will you deny?[57] As though they were rubies and coral. [58] So which of your Lord's blessings will you deny? [59] Will the reward for goodness be anything but goodness?[2706] [60] So which of your Lord's blessings will you deny? [61] And beneath them are two other Gardens [62] So which of your Lord's blessings will you deny? [63] Dark green. [64] So which of your Lord's blessings will you deny?? [65]

With two gushing springs. [66] So which of your Lord's blessings will you deny?[67] In them are fruits, dates palms and pomegranates. [68] So which of your Lord's blessings will you deny? [69] In them are sweet and lovely creatures [70] So which of your Lord's blessings will you deny? [71]

Hoor, kept close in their pavilions [72] So which of your Lord's blessings will you deny? [73] Untouched before them by man or jinn [74] So which of your Lord's blessings will you deny? [75]

Reclining on green cushions and beautiful fine carpets. [76] So which of your Lord's blessings will you deny? [77] Blessed be the name of your Lord, full of Majesty and Glory.[2707] [78]

•   •   •

[2703] Revelation 7:17 for the Lamb at the center of the throne will be their shepherd, and he will guide them to springs of the water of life, and God will wipe away every tear from their eyes.'

[2704] Revelation 22:2 through the middle of the street of the city. On either side of the river is the tree of life with its twelve kinds of fruit, producing its fruit each month; and the leaves of the tree are for the healing of the nations.

[2705] Demons

[2706] Romans 2:7 to those who by patiently doing good seek for glory and honor and immortality, he will give eternal life;

[2707] Revelation 4:9 And whenever the living creatures give glory and honor and thanks to the one who is seated on the throne, who lives for ever and ever,

CHAPTER FIFTY SIX

AL-WAQL'AH
THE INEVITABLE CALAMITY

THE **MECCA** PERIOD

In the name of God, the Merciful-to-all, the Mercy Giver:
When the Inevitable Event occurs, [01] no one will deny its occurrence. [02] Lowering some and raising others.[2708] [03] When the earth is shaken violently[2709] [04] And the mountains are crushed and crumbles[2710] [05] and become scattered dust, [06] then you (human beings) will be divided into three separate groups: [07] Those on the right. What of those on the right? [2711] [08] And those on the left. What of those on the left?[2712] [09] And those who are ahead upfront [10] they are the ones brought near [11] in the Gardens of Bliss, [12] They are a large group of the earlier generations [13] and a few of later generations, [14] They recline on luxurious woven couches. [15] Reclining on them, facing each other [16] circulating among them will be ever youthful beings [17] with vessels, pitchers and a cup of a pure drink [18] causing no headache and no intoxication. [19] There will be a selection of fruits [20] and any bird meat they desire [21] and Hoor Ein [22] like well-protected pearls, [23] a reward for what they used to do. [24] They will hear no idle or sinful talk there, [25] only the greeting: "Peace, peace." [26]

Those on the right, what of those on the right? [27] (They will be) among thorns free lotus trees [28] and fruit-laden acacias [29] and extended shade, [30] outpouring water [31] abundant fruits [32] neither withheld nor forbidden, [33] on elevated daybeds [34] We have specially created them [35] originals, [36] perfectly

• • •

[2708] Psalm 75:7 but it is God who executes judgment, putting down one and lifting up another.

[2709] Revelation 16:18 And there came flashes of lightning, rumblings, peals of thunder, and a violent earthquake, such as had not occurred since people were upon the earth, so violent was that earthquake.

[2710] Revelation 16:20 And every island fled away, and no mountains were to be found; And every island fled away, and no mountains were to be found;

[2711] Matthew 25:34 Then the king will say to those at his right hand, "Come, you that are blessed by my Father, inherit the kingdom prepared for you from the foundation of the world;

[2712] Matthew 25:41 Then he will say to those at his left hand, "You that are accursed, depart from me into the eternal fire prepared for the devil and his angels;

created and perfectly matching. [37] For those of the right[2713] [38] a group of the earlier generation [39] and a group of the later generation. [40] Those of the left,[2714] what of those on the left? [41] (They will be) amidst scorching fire and scalding water [42] and a shade of black smoke, [43] neither cool nor refreshing. [44] They used to live luxuriously, [45] but they persisted in the greatest offenses against God,[2715] [46] And they used to say, "When we are dead and turned to dust[2716] shall we then be resurrected, [47] and our forefathers too?" [48] Say, "The former and the later people [49] will all be gathered on a predetermined Day." [50] Then you, you who are misguided and reject the truth, [51] will be eating from trees of Zaqqum.[2717] [52] You will be filling your bellies with it, [53] drinking boiling water on top of it, [54] drinking it like thirsty camels. [55] That will be their welcome on Judgment Day. [56]

We created you, so why you do not believe? [57] Have you seen the semen which you ejaculate? [58] Is it you who creates it, or are We the Creator? [59] We have decreed death among you, and nothing can stop Us [60] if We want to replace you [2718] and to recreate you in a way that you know nothing about. [61] You have already known the first creation, so will you not remember? [62] Have you seen what you cultivate? [63] Is it you who makes it grow, or are We the grower? [64] If We wish, We can turn it into ruins, and you would be left to wonder, [65] (Saying), "we are now in debt; [66] Rather, We have been deprived." [67] And have you seen the water that you drink? [68] Is it you who sent it down from the clouds, or are We the Sender?[2719] [69] If We wish, We can make it bitter, why then you are not grateful?[2720] [70] And have you seen the fire that you kindle? [71] Is it you who produced its tree, or are We the Producer? [72] We have made it a reminder and provision for all who kindle it, [73] exalt, then, the glory of your Lord's Name; the Magnificent.[2721] [74]

• • •

[2713] Matthew 25:34 Then the king will say to those at his right hand, "Come, you that are blessed by my Father, inherit the kingdom prepared for you from the foundation of the world;
[2714] Matthew 25:41 Then he will say to those at his left hand, "You that are accursed, depart from me into the eternal fire prepared for the devil and his angels;
[2715] Revelation 18:2-3 He called out with a mighty voice, 'Fallen, fallen is Babylon the great! It has become a dwelling-place of demons, a haunt of every foul spirit, a haunt of every foul bird, a haunt of every foul and hateful beast. ³ For all the nations have drunk of the wine of the wrath of her fornication, and the kings of the earth have committed fornication with her, and the merchants of the earth have grown rich from the power of her luxury.'
[2716] Job 10:9 Remember that you fashioned me like clay; and will you turn me to dust again?
[2717] The name of a tree in Hell
[2718] Matthew 21:43 Therefore I tell you, the kingdom of God will be taken away from you and given to a people that produces the fruits of the kingdom.
[2719] Job 5:10 He gives rain on the earth and sends waters on the fields;
[2720] Romans 1:21 for though they knew God, they did not honor him as God or give thanks to him, but they became futile in their thinking, and their senseless minds were darkened.
[2721] 2 Samuel 7:22 Therefore you are great, O Lord God; for there is no one like you, and there is no God besides you, according to all that we have heard with our ears.

I swear by the positioning of the stars,[2722] [(75)] a tremendous oath, if you only knew, [(76)] it is a noble Qur'an[2723] [(77)] kept in a well-protected record;[2724] [(78)] where none will be allowed to touch it except the purified[2725], [(79)] revealed gradually by the Lord of the worlds. [(80)] Is it then this statement that you are ridiculing [(81)] and you deny it as if your livelihood depends on it? [(82)] Why then, when the soul at death reaches the throat, [(83)] and you are at that time looking on, [(84)] when we're closer to him than you are,[2726] but you do not see. [(85)] Why then, if you are not dependent on Us, [(86)] don't you restore his soul back to him, if your claim is true? [(87)] If the deceased was of those brought near to God, [(88)] he will then have eternal harmony, eternal delight and a Garden of Bliss. [(89)] And if he was from those on the Right,[2727] [(90)] then "Peace be to you, from your companions on the Right." [(91)] But if he was from those who called the truth a lie and were misguided, [(92)] he will be welcomed with boiling water [(93)] and will burn in Hell. [2728] [(94)] This is the certain Truth, [(95)] exalt, then, the glory of your Lord's name; the Magnificent. [2729] [(96)]

· · ·

[2722] It can also mean according to some scholars the partial delivery of the Qur'an to the Prophet after it was brought down in its entirety to our lower heaven in Ramadan. See Kitab Alfara' (192/ﺏ) and Tafsir Jamea Al Bayan by Al Tabari (cf. Tabari and Ibn Kathir). "The interpreters had a disagreement over its meaning, Ibn 'Abbas, 'Ikrimah and As-Suddi were definitely of the opinion, strongly supported by The subsequent verses, that this phrase refers to the gradual revelation or "coming-down in parts (nujum)" - of the Qur'an.
[2723] The original document kept with God.
[2724] In a very protected place of God's choosing in Heaven.
[2725] Angels in charge of its protection.
[2726] Jeremiah 23:23-24 Am I a God near by, says the Lord, and not a God far off? 24 Who can hide in secret places so that I cannot see them? says the Lord. Do I not fill heaven and earth? says the Lord.
[2727] Matthew 25:34 Then the king will say to those at his right hand, "Come, you that are blessed by my Father, inherit the kingdom prepared for you from the foundation of the world;
[2728] Revelation 21:8 But as for the cowardly, the faithless, the polluted, the murderers, the fornicators, the sorcerers, the idolaters, and all liars, their place will be in the lake that burns with fire and sulphur, which is the second death.'
[2729] 2 Samuel 7:22 Therefore you are great, O Lord God; for there is no one like you, and there is no God besides you, according to all that we have heard with our ears.

CHAPTER FIFTY SEVEN

AL-HADEED

THE IRON

THE **MEDINA** PERIOD

In the name of God, the Merciful-to-all, the Mercy Giver:

Everything in the heavens and earth exalts God's limitless glory. He is the Almighty,[2730] the Wise.[2731] (01) The Kingdom of the heavens and earth belongs to Him.[2732] He gives life and causes death,[2733] and He is Able to do all things.[2734] (02) He is the First and the Last,[2735] the Outer and the Inner, and He has knowledge of all things.[2736] (03) It is He who created the heavens and the earth in six days,[2737] then established Himself above the Throne of His majesty. He knows what penetrates into the earth and what comes out of it, and what descends from the heaven and what ascends to it. He is with you wherever you may be.[2738] God sees everything you do.[2739] (04) The Kingdom of the heavens and the earth belongs to

. . .

[2730] Job 9:4 He is wise in heart, and mighty in strength —who has resisted him, and succeeded?

[2731] Proverbs 2:6, For the Lord gives wisdom; from his mouth come knowledge and understanding;

[2732] Psalm 89:11 The heavens are yours, the earth also is yours; the world and all that is in it—you have founded them.

[2733] Deuteronomy 30:19 I call heaven and earth to witness against you today that I have set before you life and death, blessings and curses. Choose life so that you and your descendants may live,

[2734] Job 42:2 'I know that you can do all things, and that no purpose of yours can be thwarted.

[2735] Revelation 22:13 I am the Alpha and the Omega, the first and the last, the beginning and the end."

[2736] 1 John 3:20 whenever our hearts condemn us; for God is greater than our hearts, and he knows everything.

[2737] Exodus 31:17 it is a sign forever between me and the people of Israel that in six days the Lord made heaven and earth, and on the seventh day he rested, and was refreshed."

[2738] Deuteronomy 2:7 Surely the Lord your God has blessed you in all your undertakings; he knows your going through this great wilderness. These forty years the Lord your God has been with you; you have lacked nothing.

[2739] Psalm 94: 7-11 and they say, "The Lord does not see; the God of Jacob does not perceive." [8] Understand, O dullest of the people; fools, when will you be wise? [9] He who planted the ear, does he not hear? He who formed the eye, does he not see? [10] He who disciplines the nations, he who teaches knowledge to humankind, does he not chastise? [11] The Lord knows our thoughts, that they are but an empty breath.

Him. All matters are referred back to God. (05) He merges the night into the day and merges the day into the night.2740 He knows what is in your hearts.2741 (06) Believe in God and His Messenger and give out from that with which He has entrusted you. Those among the believers who give will have a great reward.2742 (07) Why would you not believe in God, when the Messenger is inviting you to believe in your Lord and He has received a pledge from you, if you are believers? (08) It is He who sends down clear revelations to His servant, that He may bring you out from the darkness of ignorance into enlightenment.2743 God is kind to you and Merciful-to-all.2744 (09) And why shouldn't you spend in the cause of God, when the inheritance of the heavens and the earth belongs to God?2745 Those of you who contributed before the conquest, and fought, are not equal to those who contributed and fought afterwards. They are higher in rank. But God promises both a good reward. God is All-Aware of what you do. (10)

Who will make a loan of goodness to God, so that He may multiply it for him and reward him generously?2746 (11) On the Day when you see the believing men and believing women, their light proceeding ahead of them and to their right, "Good news for you today: Gardens with rivers flowing through them,2747 where you will remain eternally. That is the great victory". (12) On the Day, the hypocritical men and hypocritical women will say to the believers, "Wait for us. Let us have some of your light."2748 They will be told, "Go back and look for light."2749 And a wall will be raised between them with a gate in it; inside it there is mercy, but outside lies punishment 2750 (13) The hypocrites will call to the believers, "Were we not with you?" They will say, "Yes, but you allowed yourselves to be tempted, and waited and doubted, deceived by wishful thinking until God's command came and the Deceiver deceived you about God." (14) Today

• • •

2740 Genesis 8:22 As long as the earth endures, seedtime and harvest, cold and heat, summer and winter, day and night, shall not cease.'
2741 Luke 16:15 So he said to them, "You are those who justify yourselves in the sight of others; but God knows your hearts;
2742 Luke 6:38 give, and it will be given to you. A good measure, pressed down, shaken together, running over, will be put into your lap; for the measure you give will be the measure you get back."
2743 1 Peter 2:9 But you are a chosen race, a royal priesthood, a holy nation, God's own people, in order that you may proclaim the mighty acts of him who called you out of darkness into his marvelous light.
2744 Psalm 116:5, Gracious is the Lord, and righteous; our God is merciful
2745 1 Chronicles 29:11-13 Yours, O Lord, are the greatness, the power, the glory, the victory, and the majesty; for all that is in the heavens and on the earth is yours; yours is the kingdom, O Lord, and you are exalted as head above all. 12 Riches and honor come from you, and you rule over all. In your hand are power and might; and it is in your hand to make great and to give strength to all. 13 And now, our God, we give thanks to you and praise your glorious name.
2746 Proverbs 19:17 Whoever is kind to the poor lends to the Lord, and will be repaid in full.
2747 Revelation 22:1-2 Then the angel showed me the river of the water of life, bright as crystal, flowing from the throne of God and of the Lamb through the middle of the street of the city. 2 On either side of the river is the tree of life with its twelve kinds of fruit, producing its fruit each month; and the leaves of the tree are for the healing of the nations.
2748 Matthew 25:8 The foolish said to the wise, "Give us some of your oil, for our lamps are going out."
2749 Matthew 25:9 But the wise replied, "No! there will not be enough for you and for us; you had better go to the dealers and buy some for yourselves."
2750 Matthew 25:10-12 And while they went to buy it, the bridegroom came, and those who were ready went with him into the wedding banquet; and the door was shut. 11 Later the other bridesmaids came also, saying, "Lord, Lord, open to us." 12 But he replied, "Truly I tell you, I do not know you."

no ransom will be accepted from you,[2751] nor from those who rejected the truth. Your home is the Fire. It is most worthy of you. What a miserable destination. [15]

Is it not time for those believers' hearts to become humbly submissive to the remembrance of God and to the Truth He has sent down? So they are not like those who were given the Book before them, whose time was extended but whose hearts hardened, and many of them are wicked. [16]

Know that God revives the earth after it dies.[2752] We made clear to you the signs; that you may comprehend. [17] For charitable men and women who have loaned God a loan of goodness, it will be multiplied for them, and they will have a generous reward.[2753] [18] Those who believed in God and His Messengers are the truthful ones who will bear witness before their Lord. They will have their reward and their light[2754]. But the unbelievers and those who reject Our revelations will be the inhabitants of Hell. [19] Know that the life of this world is just a game; recreation, glitter, boasting to one another and rivalry in wealth and children. It is like a rain that helps plants grow, pleasing the growers, but then it dries up and you see it turn yellow, then it becomes stubble. There is severe punishment[2755] in the Hereafter, as well as forgiveness from God and (His) approval. The life of this world is only an illusion.[2756] [20] So pursue forgiveness from your Lord and a Garden as vast as the heavens and the earth is prepared for (or 'awaits') those who believed in God and His Messengers. That is the blessing of God which He gives to whom He wills. God is limitless in His blessings.[21]

No misfortune occurs, either on earth or in your souls but it is recorded in a Book even before We make it happen. That is easy for God [22] So you will not grieve for what you missed or rejoice over what He has given you. For God does not like the vain and the arrogant,[2757] [23] those who are stingy and direct others to be stingy. Whoever turns away, (remember) God is rich beyond need, worthy of all praise.[2758] [24] We sent Our Messengers with clear evidence and We sent down with them the Book and the Balance, that people may establish justice.[2759] And We sent down iron, which can be used for military might and to benefit

· · ·

[2751] Psalm 49:8 For the ransom of life is costly, and can never suffice,
[2752] Leviticus 26:4 4 I will give you your rains in their season, and the land shall yield its produce, and the trees of the field shall yield their fruit.
[2753] Luke 6:38 give, and it will be given to you. A good measure, pressed down, shaken together, running over, will be put into your lap; for the measure you give will be the measure you get back."
[2754] Matthew 5:14 "You are the light of the world. A city set on a hill cannot be hidden.
[2755] Ezekiel 25:17 I will execute great vengeance on them with wrathful punishments. Then they shall know that I am the Lord, when I lay my vengeance on them.
[2756] James 4: 14 - 16 What is your life? For you are a mist that appears for a little while and then vanishes. 15 Instead you ought to say, "If the Lord wishes, we will live and do this or that." 16 As it is, you boast in your arrogance; all such boasting is evil.
[2757] Luke 14:8-11"When you are invited by someone to a wedding feast, do not take the place of honor, for someone more distinguished than you may have been invited by him, 9 and he who invited you both will come and say to you, 'Give your place to this man,' and then in disgrace you proceed to occupy the last place. 10 "But when you are invited, go and recline at the last place, so that when the one who has invited you comes, he may say to you, 'Friend, move up higher'; then you will have honor in the sight of all who are at the table with you. 11 "For everyone who exalts himself will be humbled, and he who humbles himself will be exalted."
[2758] 2 Samuel 22:4 I call upon the Lord, who is worthy to be praised, and I am saved from my enemies
[2759] Deuteronomy 32:4 The Rock, his work is perfect, and all his ways are just. A faithful God, without deceit, just and upright is he;

people in many different ways. So that God may know those who uplifted Him and His Messengers though He is beyond their senses. God is All-Powerful,[2760] Almighty.[2761] (25)

We sent Noah (Nuh) and Abraham (Ibrahim) and placed prophethood and the Book among some of their descendants. Some of them were guided, but many were wicked. (26) Then We sent Our messengers to follow in their footsteps and followed up with Jesus (Esa), the son of Mary,[2762] and gave him the Gospel. We placed compassion[2763] and mercy[2764] in the hearts of those who followed him. As for monasticism, which they invented to seek God's pleasure,[2765] We did not ordain it for them, and they did not observe it properly. So We gave those who believed among them their reward, but many of them are wicked. (27) Believers, be ever mindful of God and believe in His Messenger; He will give you a double share of His mercy, provide you a light to guide you and forgive you; God is Ever Forgiving[2766] and Merciful-to-all. (28) That the people of the Book may know that they have no power whatsoever over God's blessings, and that all blessings are in God's Hand; He gives it to whomever He wills.[2767] God is limitless with his blessings. (29)

．　．　．

[2760] Psalm 147:5, Great is our Lord, and abundant in power; his understanding is beyond measure.

[2761] Luke 1:49 for the Mighty One has done great things for me, and holy is his name.

[2762] Arabic / Mariam / Mother of Jesus

[2763] Colossians 3:12 As God's chosen ones, holy and beloved, clothe yourselves with compassion, kindness, humility, meekness, and patience.

[2764] Matthew 5:7 'Blessed are the merciful, for they will receive mercy.

[2765] Matthew 6:33 But strive first for the kingdom of God and his righteousness, and all these things will be given to you as well.

[2766] Daniel 9:9 To the Lord our God belong mercy and forgiveness, for we have rebelled against him,

[2767] Romans 9:18 So then he has mercy on whomsoever he chooses, and he hardens the heart of whomsoever he chooses.

CHAPTER FIFTY EIGHT

AL-MUJADILAH
THE DISPUTE

THE **MEDINA** PERIOD

In the name of God, the Merciful-to-all, the Mercy Giver:

God has heard the words of the woman who argued with you concerning her husband, while complaining to God. God heard your conversation. God is All-Hearing,[2768] All-Seeing.[2769] (01) There are those of you who divorce their wives by equating them with their mothers, they are not their mothers. Their mothers are those who gave birth to them. What they said is wrong and a blatant lie. But God is All-Pardoning and All-Forgiving.[2770] (02) Those of you who divorce your wives by equating them with your mothers, then wish to go back on what you said, must set free a slave before they touch one another. This is what you are instructed to do, and God is well aware of what you do. (03) But he who does not find the means, must fast for two months consecutively before touching one another. And if he is unable, then he should feed sixty needy people. This is to affirm your faith in God and His Messenger. These are the limits set by God. And the unbelievers will have a painful punishment.[2771] (04) Those who oppose God and His Messenger will be restrained, like those before them. We have sent down self-evident messages. The unbelievers will have a painful punishment (05) on the Day when God will resurrect them all, and tells them what they did. God has kept accounts of it all, while they have forgotten it; God is Witness over all things. (06)

• • •

[2768] Psalm 5:3, O Lord, in the morning you hear my voice; in the morning I plead my case to you, and watch.

[2769] Jeremiah 23:24 Who can hide in secret places so that I cannot see them? says the Lord. Do I not fill heaven and earth? says the Lord.

[2770] 1 John 1:9 If we confess our sins, he who is faithful and just will forgive us our sins and cleanse us from all unrighteousness.

[2771] Matthew 25:41, 46 Then he will say to those at his left hand, "You that are accursed, depart from me into the eternal fire prepared for the devil and his angels; 46 And these will go away into eternal punishment, but the righteous into eternal life."

Do you not realize that God knows everything in the heavens and on earth?[2772] There is no secret conversation between three people, but He is their fourth; nor between five, but He is their sixth; nor between less than that, nor more, but He is with them wherever they are.[2773] Then, on the Day of Resurrection, He will inform them of what they did. God is All-knowing of everything. (07) Have you not noticed that those who were prohibited from conspiring secretly, have returned to what they were prohibited from doing? They conspire to commit wrongdoing, aggression, and defiance of the Messenger. And when they come to you, they greet you with a greeting that God never greeted you with. And they say to themselves, "Why does not God punish us for what we say?" Hell will be enough for them. They will burn there. What a miserable destiny. (08)

Believers, when you converse privately, do not converse about committing wrongdoing, aggression and defiance of the Messenger, but converse about righteousness [2774] and being mindful of God. Be ever mindful of God,[2775] to whom you will be gathered.[2776] (09) Conversing in secret to conspire is from Satan, to dishearten the believers, though it will not harm them at all, unless God permits it. So let the believers put their trust in God.[2777] (10)

Believers, when you are told to make room in your gathering, then do so; God will make room for you. And when you are told, "Get up," then get up; God will elevate in rank those who believed among you and those who were given knowledge. God is well aware of what you do. (11) Believers, when you privately converse with the Messenger, proceed by offering something in charity. That is better for you and purer. But if you do not find the means to do so, then God is Ever-Forgiving and Merciful-to-all. (12)

Do you regret not offering charity before your conversation with the Prophet? If you did not give, and God pardoned you, then perform prayers, and give charitable gifts, and obey God and His Messenger. God is well Aware of what you do. (13)

Do you not see that those who befriend a people with whom God is angry,[2778] are neither with you nor with them, and knowingly swear to lies. (14) God has prepared a severe punishment[2779] for them. What they were doing is evil. (15) They took their oaths as a cover-up, and turned others away from the way of

• • •

[2772] 1 John 3:20 whenever our hearts condemn us; for God is greater than our hearts, and he knows everything.

[2773] Matthew 18:20 'For where two or three are gathered in my name, I am there among them.'

[2774] Colossians 4:6 Let your speech always be gracious, seasoned with salt, so that you may know how you ought to answer everyone.

[2775] Proverbs 1:7 The fear of the Lord is the beginning of knowledge; fools despise wisdom and instruction.

[2776] Matthew 25:32 All the nations will be gathered before him, and he will separate people one from another as a shepherd separates the sheep from the goats,

[2777] Psalm 118:5-8 Out of my distress I called on the LORD; the LORD answered me and set me in a broad place. ⁶With the Lord on my side I do not fear. What can mortals do to me? ⁷ The Lord is on my side to help me; I shall look in triumph on those who hate me. ⁸ It is better to take refuge in the Lord than to put confidence in mortals.

[2778] 1 Corinthians 15:33 Do not be deceived: 'Bad company ruins good morals.'

[2779] 2 Thessalonians 1:9 These will suffer the punishment of eternal destruction, separated from the presence of the Lord and from the glory of his might,

God. They will have a humiliating punishment. (16) Neither their wealth [2780] nor their children will be of any use to them against God. They will be the inhabitants of the Fire, where they will remain (17) On the Day when God will resurrect them [2781] altogether, they will swear to Him as they swear to you, thinking that this will help them. What liars they are. (18) Satan has overcome them and made them forget [2782] the remembrance of God. Those are the party of Satan. Unquestionably, the party of Satan will be the doomed. (19) Those who oppose God and His Messenger are among the most humiliated. (20) God has written, "I will surely prevail, I and My Messengers." God is All- Powerful,[2783] Almighty.[2784](21)

You will not find a people who believe in God and the Last Day, loyal to those who oppose God and His Messenger, even if they were their parents or their children, or their brothers or their close relatives.[2785] God has written faith into the hearts of these people, and has strengthened them with His spirit.[2786] He will admit them to Gardens graced with flowing streams, where they will dwell forever. God is pleased with them, and they are pleased with Him. These are of the party of God.[2787] Unquestionably, the party of God will be the successful. (22)

• • •

[2780] Psalm 49:7-9 Truly, no ransom avails for one's life, there is no price one can give to God for it. [8] For the ransom of life is costly, and can never suffice, [9] that one should live on for ever and never see the grave.

[2781] John 5:28-29 Do not be astonished at this; for the hour is coming when all who are in their graves will hear his voice [29] and will come out—those who have done good, to the resurrection of life, and those who have done evil, to the resurrection of condemnation.

[2782] Mark 4:15 These are the ones on the path where the word is sown: when they hear, Satan immediately comes and takes away the word that is sown in them.

[2783] Psalm 147:5 Great is our Lord, and abundant in power; his understanding is beyond measure.

[2784] Jeremiah 32:18,19 O great and mighty God whose name is the Lord of hosts, [19] great in counsel and mighty in deed; whose eyes are open to all the ways of mortals, rewarding all according to their ways and according to the fruit of their doings.

[2785] Matthew 10:37 Whoever loves father or mother more than me is not worthy of me; and whoever loves son or daughter more than me is not worthy of me;

[2786] Ephesians 1:13-14 In him you also, when you had heard the word of truth, the gospel of your salvation, and had believed in him, were marked with the seal of the promised Holy Spirit; [14] this is the pledge of our inheritance towards redemption as God's own people, to the praise of his glory.

[2787] Arabic / Hezbollah.

CHAPTER FIFTY NINE

AL-HASHR

THE GATHERING

THE **MEDINA** PERIOD

In the name of God, the Merciful-to-all, the Mercy Giver:
All that exists in the heavens and the earth is praising God's limitless glory.[2788] He is the Almighty,[2789] the Most Wise.[2790] [01] It is He who evicted those who broke faith among the people of the Book from their homes at the first mobilization. You did not think they would leave, and they thought their fortresses would protect them from God. But God came at them from where they least expected it, and He put panic into their hearts.[2791] They wrecked their homes with their own hands, and by the hands of the believers. Therefore, take a lesson, all of you with insight. [02] Had God not decreed evacuation for them, He would have punished them in this world, and in the Hereafter they will have the punishment[2792] of the Fire. [03] That is because they opposed God and His messenger. God is severe in punishment toward anyone opposing God. [04]

Whatever you have cut down of their palm trees or left standing on its roots, it is by permission of God. So that He might disgrace the defiantly disobedient. [05] Whatever God has given to His Messenger from them; you did not have to spur your horses or camels for them, but God gives authority to His Messengers over whomever He will. God is able to do all things.[2793] [06] Whatever gains God has restored to His Messenger from the villages' inhabitants belongs to God, the Messenger, the relatives, the orphans, the needy, and to the wayfarer; so that it may not circulate mainly between the wealthy among you. So accept whatever

• • •

[2788] Psalm 150:6 Let everything that breathes praise the Lord! Praise the Lord!

[2789] Psalm 24:8 Who is the King of glory? The Lord, strong and mighty, the Lord, mighty in battle.

[2790] Proverbs 2:6 For the Lord gives wisdom; from his mouth come knowledge and understanding;

[2791] Deuteronomy 28:20 The Lord will send upon you disaster, panic, and frustration in everything you attempt to do, until you are destroyed and perish quickly, on account of the evil of your deeds, because you have forsaken me.

[2792] Deuteronomy 32:34-36 Is not this laid up in store with me, sealed up in my treasuries? [34] Vengeance is mine, and recompense, for the time when their foot shall slip; [36] because the day of their calamity is at hand, their doom comes swiftly.

[2793] Job 42:2 'I know that you can do all things, and that no purpose of yours can be thwarted.'

the Messenger gives you, and abstain from whatever he forbids you. And be mindful of God. God is severe in punishment. [07]

It is also for the poor emigrants who were driven out of their homes and their possessions, who seek God's blessings and His approval, and support God and His Messenger. Those are the truly sincere. [08] And (also for) those who before them, were already established in their homes (in Medina), and have accepted faith. They love those who migrated to them, and find no hesitation in their hearts in helping them. They give them preference over themselves, even if they themselves are needy. Whoever is spared his own soul's greed is truly successful. [09] Those who came after them, say, "Our Lord, forgive us and our brothers who preceded us in faith, and leave no malice in our hearts toward those who believe. Our Lord, You are Most Compassionate,[2794] Merciful-to-all."[2795] [10]

Have you noticed those who act hypocritically? They say to their brothers, the faithless among the people of the Book, "If you are driven out, we will surely leave with you, and we will not obey anyone who wants to harm you; and should anyone fight you, we will certainly support you." But God bears witness that they are truly liars. [11] If they are driven out, they will not leave with them, and if they are fought, they will not support them. Even if they should support them, they will surely turn their backs and flee; then they will not be helped. [12] Indeed, you (believers) strike more terror in their hearts than their fear of God. That is because they are a people who do not understand. [13] Even united they will not fight you except within fortified strongholds, or from behind walls. There is much hostility between them. You think they are united, but their hearts are diverse. That is because they are a people without reason. [14] Like those who went shortly before them. They experience the evil consequences of their decisions. A painful punishment awaits them.[2796] [15] They are like Satan who says to a human being, "Do not believe."[2797] But when he denies the truth, he says, "I disown you; I fear God, the Lord of the worlds."[2798] [16]The ultimate end of both is the Fire, where they will dwell forever. That is the reward of the unjust. [17]

Believers, be mindful of God. And let every soul consider what it has put forth for tomorrow, and be mindful of God, for God is well aware of what you do. [18] And do not be like those who forgot God, so He made them forget themselves. These are the defiantly disobedient. [19] The inhabitants of the Fire and the

• • •

[2794] James 5:11 Indeed we call blessed those who showed endurance. You have heard of the endurance of Job, and you have seen the purpose of the Lord, how the Lord is compassionate and merciful.
[2795] Psalm 116:5, Gracious is the Lord, and righteous; our God is merciful.
[2796] Matthew 25:41, 46 Then he will say to those at his left hand, "You that are accursed, depart from me into the eternal fire prepared for the devil and his angels; [46] And these will go away into eternal punishment, but the righteous into eternal life."
[2797] Genesis 3:1-6 Now the serpent was more crafty than any other wild animal that the Lord God had made. He said to the woman, 'Did God say, "You shall not eat from any tree in the garden"?' [2]The woman said to the serpent, 'We may eat of the fruit of the trees in the garden; [3] but God said, "You shall not eat of the fruit of the tree that is in the middle of the garden, nor shall you touch it, or you shall die." ' [4] But the serpent said to the woman, 'You will not die; [5] for God knows that when you eat of it your eyes will be opened, and you will be like God, knowing good and evil.[6] So when the woman saw that the tree was good for food, and that it was a delight to the eyes, and that the tree was to be desired to make one wise, she took of its fruit and ate; and she also gave some to her husband, who was with her, and he ate.
[2798] 2 Kings 19:15 And Hezekiah prayed before the Lord, and said: "O Lord the God of Israel, who are enthroned above the cherubim, you are God, you alone, of all the kingdoms of the earth; you have made heaven and earth.

inhabitants of Paradise are not equal. It is the inhabitants of Paradise who are the winners. [20] Had We sent down this Qur'an on a mountain, you would have seen it humbling itself and crumbling in awe of God. These examples We mention for the people, that they may reflect.[2799] [21]

He is God, there is no god but Him,[2800] the Knower of all that is beyond our senses and all that we can witness.[2801] He is the Mercy giver,[2802] the Merciful-to-all. [22] He is God, there is no god but Him,[2803] the Sovereign,[2804] the Holy,[2805] the Peace Giver, the Faith Giver, the Overseer, the Almighty,[2806] the Powerful,[2807] the Supremely Great.[2808] May God be exalted in His glory, above all they associate with Him. [23] He is God, the Creator,[2809] the Maker,[2810] the Fashioner; to Him belongs the Most Beautiful Names.[2811] Whatever is in the heavens and earth glorifies Him.[2812] He is the Almighty, [2813] the Wise.[2814] [24]

• • •

[2799] Proverbs 1:1-7 The proverbs of Solomon son of David, King of Israel. 2 For learning about wisdom and instruction, for understanding words of insight, 3 for gaining instruction in wise dealing, righteousness, justice, and equity; 4 to teach shrewdness to the simple, knowledge and prudence to the young— 5 let the wise also hear and gain in learning, and the discerning acquire skill, 6 to understand a proverb and a figure, the words of the wise and their riddles. 7 The fear of the Lord is the beginning of knowledge; fools despise wisdom and instruction.

[2800] Exodus 20:3 you shall have no other gods before me.

[2801] 1 Samuel 2:3 Talk no more so very proudly, let not arrogance come from your mouth; for the Lord is a God of knowledge, and by him actions are weighed.

[2802] Psalm 111:4 He has gained renown by his wonderful deeds; the Lord is gracious and merciful.

[2803] Nehemiah 9:6 And Ezra said: "You are the Lord, you alone; you have made heaven, the heaven of heavens, with all their host, the earth and all that is on it, the seas and all that is in them. To all of them you give life, and the host of heaven worships you.

[2804] Acts 4:24 When they heard it, they raised their voices together to God and said, 'Sovereign Lord, who made the heaven and the earth, the sea, and everything in them,

[2805] Isaiah 6:3 And one called to another and said: 'Holy, holy, holy is the Lord of hosts; the whole earth is full of his glory.

[2806] Psalm 91:1 You who live in the shelter of the Most High, who abide in the shadow of the Almighty,

[2807] Psalm 62:11 Once God has spoken; twice have I heard this: that power belongs to God,

[2808] Job 36:26 Surely God is great, and we do not know him; the number of his years is unsearchable.

[2809] Isaiah 40:28 Have you not known? Have you not heard? The Lord is the everlasting God, the Creator of the ends of the earth. He does not faint or grow weary; his understanding is unsearchable.

[2810] Hebrews 11:10, For he looked forward to the city that has foundations, whose architect and builder is God.

[2811] Deuteronomy 28:58, If you do not diligently observe all the words of this law that are written in this book, fearing this glorious and awesome name, the Lord your God, Exodus 3:14 God said to Moses, "I am who I am." He said further, "Thus you shall say to the Israelites, 'I am has sent me to you.'"

[2812] Psalm 150:6 Let everything that breathes praise the Lord! Praise the Lord!

[2813] Psalm 24:8 Who is the King of glory? The Lord, strong and mighty, the Lord, mighty in battle.

[2814] Job 12:13 "With God are wisdom and strength; he has counsel and understanding.

CHAPTER SIXTY

AL-MUMTAHINAH

THE WOMEN TESTED

THE **MEDINA** PERIOD

In the name of God, the Merciful-to-all, the Mercy Giver:
Believers do not take My enemies and yours as allies,[2815] offering them affection, when They have rejected the Truth[2816] that has come to you. They have driven you and the Messenger out, because you believe in God, your Lord. If you have decided to struggle in My way, seeking My approval, how can you secretly love them? I know what you concealed[2817] and what you reveal. Whoever among you does that is straying from the right path.[2818] [01] If they ever gain dominance over you, they will treat you as enemies, and they will stretch out their hands and tongues to hurt you. They would dearly wish that you renounce your faith.[02]

Never will your blood lines or your children be of any use to you. God will separate you on the Day of Resurrection. God is All-Seeing of what you do. [03] There has already been a good example for you in Abraham (Ibrahim) and those with him, when they said to their people, "we disown you and what you worship besides God. We reject you, and there will be animosity and hatred forever between us and you until you believe in God alone." Except for Abraham's words to his father, "I will ask forgiveness for you, though I cannot protect you from God". "Our Lord, in You we trust, and to You we repent. To You is the ultimate destination. [2819] [04] Our Lord, do not make us a target for the unbelievers, and

• • •

[2815] 2 Corinthians 6:14-17 Do not be mismatched with unbelievers. For what partnership is there between righteousness and lawlessness? Or what fellowship is there between light and darkness? 15 What agreement does Christ have with Beliar? Or what does a believer share with an unbeliever? 16 What agreement has the temple of God with idols? For we are the temple of the living God; as God said, 'I will live in them and walk among them, and I will be their God, and they shall be my people. 17 Therefore, come out from them, and be separate from them, says the Lord, and touch nothing unclean; then I will welcome you,

[2816] 1 Corinthians 15:33 Do not be deceived: 'Bad company ruins good morals.'

[2817] Psalm 44:21 would not God discover this? For he knows the secrets of the heart.

[2818] Proverbs 3:6 In all your ways acknowledge him, and he will make straight your paths.

[2819] Psalm 143:8 Let me hear of your steadfast love in the morning, for in you I put my trust. Teach me the way I should go, for to you I lift up my soul.

forgive us. Our Lord, You are the Almighty,[2820] the Wise."[2821] (05) There is a good example in them for you, for anyone who seeks God and the Last Day.[2822] But if anyone turns away, God is the Rich Beyond Need, the Praiseworthy.[2823] (06)

Perhaps God will restore affection between you and your present enemies.[2824] God is able to do all things.[2825] God is Ever Forgiving[2826] and Merciful-to-all. (07) God does not forbid you from dealing kindly and equitably with those who did not fight you because of your faith and did not drive you out of your homes. God loves those who are equitable. (08) But God forbids you from befriending those who fought against you over your faith and drove you from your homes and helped others to drive you out. Any who takes them for friends are the wrongdoers. (09)

Believers, when believing women come to you as emigrants, test them. God knows best about their faith. And if you find them to be faithful, then do not return them [2827] to the unbelievers. They are not lawful wives for them, nor are they their lawful husbands. But give the unbelievers what they have spent. You are not to blame if you marry them later provided you give them their dues. And do not hold to marriage bonds with unbelieving women, but ask for what you have spent and let them ask for what they have spent. This is God's judgment; He judges between you. God is All-knowing[2828] and Wise.[2829] (10) If any of your wives rejoin the unbelievers, and you decide to penalize them, then give those whose wives have gone the equivalent of what they had spent (out of what you owe the unbelievers). And be mindful of God, in whom you are believers. (11)

Prophet, when believing women come to you, pledging that they will not associate anything with God, nor steal, nor commit adultery, nor will they kill their children, nor lie about who has fathered their children, nor disobey you in what is right, then accept their pledge of allegiance and ask God's forgiveness for them. God is Forgiving and Merciful-to-all.[2830] (12)

Believers do not take as allies those with whom God is angry.[2831] They have despaired of the Hereafter, as unbelievers despair of those buried in their graves.[13]

· · ·

[2820] Psalm 62:7 On God rests my deliverance and my honor; my mighty rock, my refuge is in God.
[2821] 1 Corinthians 1:25 For God's foolishness is wiser than human wisdom, and God's weakness is stronger than human strength.
[2822] Hebrews 13:7 Remember your leaders, those who spoke the word of God to you; consider the outcome of their way of life, and imitate their faith.
[2823] 2 Samuel 22:4 I call upon the Lord, who is worthy to be praised, and I am saved from my enemies
[2824] Matthew 5:9 'Blessed are the peacemakers, for they will be called children of God.'
[2825] Job 42:2 'I know that you can do all things, and that no purpose of yours can be thwarted.'
[2826] 1 John 1:9 If we confess our sins, he who is faithful and just will forgive us our sins and cleanse us from all unrighteousness.
[2827] Deuteronomy 23:15 Slaves who have escaped to you from their owners shall not be given back to them.
[2828] 1 John 3:20 whenever our hearts condemn us; for God is greater than our hearts, and he knows everything.
[2829] Proverbs 2:6 For the Lord gives wisdom; from his mouth come knowledge and understanding.
[2830] Psalm 116:5 Gracious is the Lord, and righteous; our God is merciful.
[2831] 1 Corinthians 15:33 Do not be deceived: 'Bad company ruins good morals.'

CHAPTER SIXTY ONE

AS SAAF

SOLID LINES

THE **MEDINA** PERIOD

In the name of God, the Merciful-to-all, the Mercy Giver:

Everything in the heavens and the earth declare the praises of God's limitless glory.[2832] He is the Almighty,[2833] the Wise.[2834] [(01)] Believers, why do you say what you do not do? [(02)] it is most despicable in God's sight that you say what you do not do[2835]. [(03)] God loves those who fight in solid lines for His cause, as though they were a well-built structure. [(04)]

And mention when Moses (Musa) said to his people, "My people, why do you hurt me when you know that I am God's Messenger to you?" And when they turned away, God caused their hearts to turn away. God does not guide the defiantly disobedient people. [(05)] And when Jesus son of Mary said, "O children of Israel, I am God's Messenger to you, confirming what is available of the Torah,[2836] and bringing good news of a messenger who will come after me,[2837] whose name is Ahmad."[2838] But when he came to them with clear evidence, they said, "This is obvious magic." [(06)]

• • •

[2832] Psalm 150:6 Let everything that breathes praise the Lord! Praise the Lord! Psalm 19:1 The heavens declare the glory of God, and the sky above proclaims his handiwork. Psalm 147:1 Praise the Lord! For it is good to sing praises to our God; for it is pleasant, and a song of praise is fitting.

[2833] Job 9:4 He is wise in heart, and mighty in strength —who has resisted him, and succeeded?

[2834] Proverbs 2:6 For the Lord gives wisdom; from his mouth come knowledge and understanding;

[2835] Matthew 23:2-4 "The scribes and the Pharisees have seated themselves in the chair of Moses; [3] therefore all that they tell you, do and observe, but do not do according to their deeds; [4] for they say things and do not do them.

[2836] The Law. Matthew 5:17-18 'Do not think that I have come to abolish the law or the prophets; I have come not to abolish but to fulfill. [18] For truly I tell you, until heaven and earth pass away, not one letter, not one stroke of a letter, will pass from the law until all is accomplished.

[2837] John 14:16-17 And I will ask the Father, and he will give you another Advocate, to be with you for ever. [17] This is the Spirit of truth, whom the world cannot receive, because it neither sees him nor knows him. You know him, because he abides with you, and he will be in you.

[2838] The Prophet's name before he was born.

And who is more unjust than one who invents lies and attributes them to God when invited to submit?[2839] God does not guide the unjust people. [07] They wish to extinguish God's enlightenment[2840] with their mouths, but God will perfect His light, even though the unbelievers dislike it. [08] It is He who sent His Messenger with guidance and the religion of Truth, that he may proclaim it over all religions, even though those who associate others with God will dislike it. [09]

Believers, will I guide you to a transaction that will save you from a painful punishment?[2841] [10] That you believe in God and His Messenger, and strive in the cause of God with your wealth and yourselves. That is best for you, if you only knew. [11] He will forgive you your sins; and will admit you to Gardens with rivers flowing[2842] through them and pleasant dwellings in the Gardens of Eden. That is the great success. [12] And another thing you love: support from God and imminent victory; Give good news to the believers. [13] Believers, be supporters of God, as Jesus (Esa), the son of Mary (Mariam), said to the disciples (hawariyyoona), "Who are my supporters to God?" The disciples said, "We are God's supporters." A faction of the Children of Israel believed, and another faction disbelieved. So We supported those who believed against their foe, and they became dominant. [14]

• • •

[2839] See Glossary for Submission or Islam.
[2840] 1 John 1:5 This is the message we have heard from him and proclaim to you, that God is light and in him there is no darkness at all.
[2841] Matthew 25:41, 46 Then he will say to those at his left hand, "You that are accursed, depart from me into the eternal fire prepared for the devil and his angels; [46] And these will go away into eternal punishment, but the righteous into eternal life."
[2842] Revelation 22:1-2 Then the angel showed me the river of the water of life, bright as crystal, flowing from the throne of God and of the Lamb through the middle of the street of the city. On either side of the river is the tree of life with its twelve kinds of fruit, producing its fruit each month; and the leaves of the tree are for the healing of the nations.

CHAPTER SIXTY TWO

AL-JUMUA

FRIDAY

Everything in the heavens and the earth declare the praises of God's limitless glory,[2843] the Sovereign, the Holy,[2844] the Almighty,[2845] the Wise.[2846] (01) It is He who raised a messenger from among the Gentiles;[2847] reciting His revelations to them, purifying them, and teaching them the Book and Wisdom; although before that they were clearly misguided (02) and (he is sent) to others of them who have not yet joined them. God is the Almighty, the Wise. (03) Such is God's favor, which He gives to whom He wills; God is the possessor of great favors. (04) The example of those who were entrusted to uphold the Torah,[2848] but then failed to uphold it, is that of a donkey carrying volumes of knowledge. Terrible is the example of the people who reject the signs of God.[2849] God does not guide the unjust People. (05)

Say, " you who follow Judaism, if you claim that out of all people you alone are friends of God, then wish for death if you are truthful." (06) But they will not wish for it, ever, because of what their hands have done. God knows the unjust well. (07) Say, "The death from which you are fleeing will catch up with you. Then you will be returned to the Knower of the unknown and the known, and He will inform you about what you used to do." (08)

• • •

[2843] Psalm 150:6 Let everything that breathes praise the Lord! Praise the Lord!

[2844] Isaiah 43:15 I am the LORD, your Holy One, the Creator of Israel, your King.

[2845] Job 9:4 He is wise in heart, and mighty in strength—who has resisted him, and succeeded?

[2846] Proverbs 2:6 For the Lord gives wisdom; from his mouth come knowledge and understanding;

[2847] 1Timothy 2:7 For this I was appointed a herald and an apostle (I am telling the truth, I am not lying), a teacher of the Gentiles in faith and truth.

[2848] Deuteronomy 27:26 "Cursed be anyone who does not uphold the words of this law by observing them." All the people shall say, "Amen!"

[2849] Isaiah 30:12-13 Therefore thus says the Holy One of Israel: Because you reject this word, and put your trust in oppression and deceit, and rely on them; [13] therefore, this iniquity shall become for you like a break in a high wall, bulging out, and about to collapse, whose crash comes suddenly, in an instant;

Believers, when the call is made for prayer on Friday, drop all business[2850] and rush to the remembrance of God. That is better for you, if you only knew. [09] Then when the prayer is concluded, disperse through the land, and seek God's favor, and remember to call on God without ceasing, so that you may prosper.[2851] [10] Yet whenever they come across some business, or some entertainment, they scramble towards it, and leave you standing there. Say, "That which is with God is better than entertainment and business; God is the Best of providers."[2852] [11]

. . .

[2850] Nehemiah 13:15-18 In those days I saw in Judah people treading wine presses on the Sabbath, and bringing in heaps of grain and loading them on donkeys; and also wine, grapes, figs, and all kinds of burdens, which they brought into Jerusalem on the Sabbath day; and I warned them at that time against selling food. [16] Tyrians also, who lived in the city, brought in fish and all kinds of merchandise and sold them on the Sabbath to the people of Judah, and in Jerusalem. [17] Then I remonstrated with the nobles of Judah and said to them, 'What is this evil thing that you are doing, profaning the Sabbath day? [18] Did not your ancestors act in this way, and did not our God bring all this disaster on us and on this city? Yet you bring more wrath on Israel by profaning the Sabbath.'

[2851] Joshua 1:8, This book of the law shall not depart out of your mouth; you shall meditate on it day and night, so that you may be careful to act in accordance with all that is written in it. For then you shall make your way prosperous, and then you shall be successful.

[2852] Matthew 6:25-26 'Therefore I tell you, do not worry about your life, what you will eat or what you will drink, or about your body, what you will wear. Is not life more than food, and the body more than clothing? Look at the birds of the air; they neither sow nor reap nor gather into barns, and yet your heavenly Father feeds them. Are you not of more value than they?'

CHAPTER SIXTY THREE

AL-MUNAFIQUN
THE HYPOCRITES

THE **MEDINA** PERIOD

In the name of God, the Merciful-to-all, the Mercy Giver:

When the hypocrites come to you, they say, "We bear witness that you are indeed God's Messenger." God knows that you are indeed His Messenger and God bears witness that the hypocrites are indeed liars. (01) They have taken their oaths as a cover, to divert people from the way of God.[2853] Evil is what they do. (02) That is because they believed, and then rejected the truth; so their hearts have been sealed, and they cannot understand. (03) When you see them, their appearance appeals to you. And when they speak, you listen to what they say. They are like propped up timber. They think every shout is aimed at them.[2854] They are the enemy,[2855] so beware of them. May God destroy them; how devious they are. (04)

And when It is said to them, "Come, the Messenger of God will ask forgiveness for you," they turn their heads aside in contempt and you see them turning away arrogantly.[2856] (05) It is all the same for them whether you ask forgiveness for them or do not ask forgiveness for them; God will not forgive

• • •

[2853] Matthew 23:13 'But woe to you, scribes and Pharisees, hypocrites! For you lock people out of the kingdom of heaven. For you do not go in yourselves, and when others are going in, you stop them.'
[2854] Proverbs 28:1 The wicked flee when no one pursues, but the righteous are as bold as a lion. Psalm 75:4 To the arrogant I say, 'Boast no more,'to the wicked, 'Do not lift up your horns.'
[2855] Acts 13:10 "You are a child of the devil and an enemy of everything that is right! You are full of all kinds of deceit and trickery. Will you never stop perverting the right ways of the Lord?"
[2856] Luke 18:9-14 He also told this parable to some who trusted in themselves that they were righteous and regarded others with contempt: 10 "Two men went up to the temple to pray, one a Pharisee and the other a tax collector. 11 The Pharisee, standing by himself, was praying thus, 'God, I thank you that I am not like other people: thieves, rogues, adulterers, or even like this tax collector. 12 I fast twice a week; I give a tenth of all my income.' 13 But the tax collector, standing far off, would not even look up to heaven, but was beating his breast and saying, 'God, be merciful to me, a sinner!' 14 I tell you, this man went down to his home justified rather than the other; for all who exalt themselves will be humbled, but all who humble themselves will be exalted."

them. God does not guide such defiantly disobedient people. (06) It is they who say, "Give nothing to those who follow God's Messenger, until they dispersed from around him." To God belongs the treasuries of the heavens and the earth,[2857] but the hypocrites do not understand. (07) They say, "If we return to Medina, the more worthy will drive out the disgraced." But all worth belongs to God, His Messenger, and the believers; though the hypocrites do not know it. (08)

Believers, let neither your wealth nor your children distract you from remembering to call upon God.[2858] Whoever does that are the doomed. (09) Give from what We have provided for you, before death comes to one of you,[2859] and he says, "My Lord, if You would only delay me for a little while, so that I may be charitable, and be among the righteous." (10) But God will never delay a soul when its time has come. God is well aware of what you do. (11)

. . .

[2857] Psalm 50:9-12 I have no need of a bull from your stall or of goats from your pens, [10] for every animal of the forest is mine, and the cattle on a thousand hills. [11] I know every bird in the mountains, and the insects in the fields are mine. [12] If I were hungry I would not tell you, for the world is mine, and all that is in it.

[2858] Job 31:24-28 "If I have made gold my trust, or called fine gold my confidence; [25] if I have rejoiced because my wealth was great, or because my hand had gotten much; [26] if I have looked at the sun when it shone, or the moon moving in splendor, [27] and my heart has been secretly enticed, and my mouth has kissed my hand; [28] this also would be an iniquity to be punished by the judges, for I should have been false to God above.

[2859] James 5:1-3 Come now, you rich people, weep and wail for the miseries that are coming to you. [2] Your riches have rotted, and your clothes are moth-eaten. [3] Your gold and silver have rusted, and their rust will be evidence against you, and it will eat your flesh like fire. You have laid up treasure for the last days.

CHAPTER SIXTY FOUR

AT-TAGHABUN

MUTUAL NEGLECT

THE **MEDINA** PERIOD

In the name of God, the Merciful-to-all, the Mercy Giver:

Everything in the heavens and the earth declare the praises of God's limitless glory.[2860] To Him belongs the Kingdom,[2861] and to Him all praise is due.[2862] He is able to do all things.[2863] (01) It is He who created you. Yet some of you deny the truth, and some believe it. God sees everything you do. (02) He created the heavens and earth in Truth,[2864] and shaped you[2865] and perfected your shapes;[2866] and to Him is the ultimate destination.[2867] (03) He knows everything in the heavens and the earth,[2868] and He knows what you conceal and what you reveal. God knows very well the secrets of every heart.[2869] (04)

Has the news not reached you, of those who rejected the truth before you? They tasted the ill consequences of their conduct, and they will have a painful punishment.[2870] (05) That is because their messengers came to them with clear

. . .

[2860] Psalm 150:6 Let everything that breathes praise the Lord! Praise the Lord!

[2861] 1 Chronicles 29:11 Yours, O Lord, are the greatness, the power, the glory, the victory, and the majesty; for all that is in the heavens and on the earth is yours; yours is the kingdom, O Lord, and you are exalted as head above all.

[2862] 2 Samuel 22:4 I call upon the Lord, who is worthy to be praised, and I am saved from my enemies

[2863] Job 42:2 'I know that you can do all things, and that no purpose of yours can be thwarted.

[2864] Genesis 1:1 In the beginning when God created the heavens and the earth,

[2865] Genesis 2:7 then the Lord God formed man from the dust of the ground, and breathed into his nostrils the breath of life; and the man became a living being.

[2866] Genesis 1:31 God saw everything that he had made, and indeed, it was very good. And there was evening and there was morning, the sixth day.

[2867] Ecclesiastes 12:7 and the dust returns to the earth as it was, and the breath returns to God who gave it.

[2868] 1 John 3:20 whenever our hearts condemn us; for God is greater than our hearts, and he knows everything.

[2869] Psalm 44:21 would not God have discovered it, since he knows the secrets of the heart?

[2870] Matthew 25:41,46 Then he will say to those at his left hand, "You that are accursed, depart from me into the eternal fire prepared for the devil and his angels; [46] And these will go away into eternal punishment, but the righteous into eternal life.'

evidence, but they said, "Are human beings going to guide us?" So they denied their messengers and turned away. God had no need for them;[2871] God is rich beyond need[2872] and praiseworthy.[2873] (06)

The unbelievers claim that they will never be resurrected. Say, "Yes indeed, by my Lord, you will be resurrected;[2874] then you will be informed of everything you did; that is easy for God." (07)

So believe in God and His messenger and the enlightenment[2875] We have sent down. God is well aware of what you do.[2876] (08) When He gathers you for the Day of Gathering,[2877] the Day of mutual neglect. Whoever believes in God and does good deeds, He will forgive him his misdeeds and admit him to Gardens with rivers flowing[2878] through them, where they will remain forever. That is the great success. (09) But for those who disbelieve and denied Our revelations - these are the companions of the Fire, remaining there forever; and what a miserable destination. (10)

No disaster occurs except by permission of God. Whoever believes in God, He will guide his heart. God has full knowledge of everything. (11) Obey God and obey the Messenger. But if you turn away, it is only incumbent on Our messenger to deliver the clear message. (12) God, there is no god but Him.[2879] So let the believers put their trust in Him. (13) Believers, there are enemies to you among your wives and your children,[2880] so beware of them. But if you pardon, overlook, and forgive[2881], God is forgiving[2882] and Merciful-to-all.[2883] (14)

Your possessions and your children are a test for you,[2884] but with God there is a great reward.[2885] (15) So be mindful of God as much as you can; hear and obey

• • •

[2871] Job 35:7 If you are righteous, what do you give to him; or what does he receive from your hand?
[2872] Acts 7:48-50 However, the Most High does not live in houses made by human hands. As the prophet says: 49 'Heaven is my throne, and the earth is my footstool. What kind of house will you build for me? says the Lord. Or where will my resting place be? [50] Has not my hand made all these things?'
[2875] 1 Chronicles 16:25 For great is the Lord, and greatly to be praised; he is to be revered above all gods.
[2874] John 5:29 and will come out—those who have done good, to the resurrection of life, and those who have done evil, to the resurrection of condemnation.
[2875] John 1:8-9 He himself was not the light, but he came to testify to the light. The true light, which enlightens everyone, was coming into the world.
[2876] Luke 12:2 Nothing is covered up that will not be uncovered, and nothing secret that will not become known.
[2877] Matthew 25:32 All the nations will be gathered before him, and he will separate people one from another as a shepherd separates the sheep from the goats,
[2878] Revelation 22:2 through the middle of the street of the city. On either side of the river is the tree of life with its twelve kinds of fruit, producing its fruit each month; and the leaves of the tree are for the healing of the nations.
[2879] Exodus 20:3 you shall have no other gods before me.
[2880] Matthew 24:10, 10:21,35,36 Then many will fall away, and they will betray one another and hate one another. 10:21 Brother will betray brother to death, and a father his child, and children will rise against parents and have them put to death; [35] For I have come to set a man against his father, and a daughter against her mother, and a daughter-in-law against her mother-in-law; [36] and one's foes will be members of one's own household.
[2882] Matthew 6:14 "If you forgive those who sin against you, your heavenly Father will forgive you.
[2882] Daniel 9:9. To the Lord our God belong mercy and forgiveness, for we have rebelled against him,
[2883] Psalm 116:5, Gracious is the Lord, and righteous; our God is merciful.
[2884] 1 Timothy 6:10, For the love of money is a root of all kinds of evil, and in their eagerness to be rich some have wandered away from the faith and pierced themselves with many pains.
[2885] Matthew 5:12 Rejoice and be glad, for your reward is great in heaven, for in the same way they persecuted the prophets who were before you.

and be charitable, it is for your own good. He who is safe-guarded from his own greed, those are the successful ones. [16] If you loan God a loan of goodness, He will multiply it for you, and forgive you. God is appreciative and forbearing.[2886] [17] He's the Knower of all that is beyond our senses and all that we can witness, the Almighty, the Wise. [18]

• • •

[2886] Psalm 145:17 The Lord is just in all his ways, and kind in all his doings.
Proverbs 19:17 Whoever is kind to the poor lends to the Lord, and will be repaid in full.

CHAPTER SIXTY FIVE

AT-TALAQ
THE DIVORCE

THE **MEDINA** PERIOD

In the name of God, the Merciful-to-all, the Mercy Giver:
Prophet, when any of you intend to divorce wives, do so at the beginning of their prescribed waiting period.[2887] Calculate the period's term carefully and be mindful of God, your Lord. Do not drive them out of their homes, nor should they leave during that period, unless they have committed a proven adultery. These are the limits of God and whoever oversteps God's limits wrongs his own soul. You never know what new situation God may bring about. [01]

When They have fulfilled their term, either retain them honorably, or part with them honorably. And call from among your just witnesses,[2888] to give testimony for God's sake. Anyone who believes in God and the Last day should heed this. God will find a way out for whoever is mindful of Him [2889] [02] and will provide for him from unexpected source.[2890] God will suffice for those who put their trust in Him. God will achieve His purpose. God has set a due measure for everything.[2891] [03]

• • •

[2887] Period, Arabic "Iddah" a woman's post marital waiting period, is the period in which a woman waits before she may remarry to verify that she is not pregnant, or out of mourning for her deceased husband. 'Iddah is obligatory upon every woman who leaves her husband, or whose husband leaves her, whether the cause is divorce (talaaq), annulment of the marriage or the death of the husband, except when the divorce occurs before the marriage has been consummated, in which case the woman does not have to observe 'iddah. Iddah starts right after the menstrual cycle and it generally ends after the completed third cycle.

[2888] Generally two men

[2889] 1 Corinthians 10:13 No testing has overtaken you that is not common to everyone. God is faithful, and he will not let you be tested beyond your strength, but with the testing he will also provide the way out so that you may be able to endure it.

[2890] Genesis 22:8,14 Abraham said, 'God himself will provide the lamb for a burnt-offering, my son.' So the two of them walked on together. [14] So Abraham called that place 'The LORD will provide'; as it is said to this day, 'On the mount of the Lord it shall be provided.'

[2891] Psalm 138:8 The Lord will fulfill his purpose for me; your steadfast love, O Lord, endures forever. Do not forsake the work of your hands.

If you have any doubts, regarding a wife who has ceased menstruating and for one who have not yet menstruated, the period of waiting shall be three months. And for those who are pregnant, their term shall be until they have delivered. God makes things easy for those who are mindful of Him.[2892] [04] This is God's command which He sent down to you. God will forgive the misdeeds[2893] and increase the rewards of anyone who is mindful of Him. [05]

Allow the wives you are divorcing to reside where you reside, according to your means. Do not harass them in order to make things difficult for them. If they are pregnant, maintain them until they give birth. And if they nurse your infant, compensate them fairly. Maintain your relationship in a friendly and honorable way. But if you disagree, then let another woman nurse him. [06] Let the wealthy spend according to his wealth, and he whose resources are restricted shall spend according to what God has given him.[2894] God does not burden a soul beyond what He has given it.[2895] After hardship, God will bring ease[07]

Many a town defied the command of its Lord and His Messengers, so We held them strictly accountable, and We punished them with a horrifying punishment[2896] [08] to experience the consequence of its decisions, and the outcome of its decisions was total loss. [09] God has prepared a severe punishment for them.

So you who are endowed with insight and have faith, be conscious of God. He has sent down a Reminder to you, [10] a Messenger who recites God's verses that make things clear to you, that he may bring those who believe and do good deeds from the darkness of ignorance into enlightenment.[2897] God will admit those who believe in Him and do good deeds into Gardens (Jannah) with rivers flowing through[2898] them, to dwell there forever and ever.[2899] God has provided excellently for them. [11]

It is God who created seven heavens, and a similar number of earths. His command descends through them, so that you may know that God is able to do all things,[2900] and that God's knowledge has encompassed all things. [12]

· · ·

[2892] 1 John 5:3 For the love of God is this, that we obey his commandments. And his commandments are not burdensome,
[2893] 1 John 1:9 If we confess our sins, he who is faithful and just will forgive us our sins and cleanse us from all unrighteousness.
[2894] 2 Corinthians 8:12 For if the eagerness is there, the gift is acceptable according to what one has—not according to what one does not have.
[2895] 1 Corinthians 10:13 No testing has overtaken you that is not common to everyone. God is faithful, and he will not let you be tested beyond your strength, but with the testing he will also provide the way out so that you may be able to endure it.
[2896] Matthew 25:41, Then he will say to those at his left hand, "You that are accursed, depart from me into the eternal fire prepared for the devil and his angels; [46] And these will go away into eternal punishment, but the righteous into eternal life.'
[2897] Isaiah 9:2 The people who walked in darkness have seen a great light; those who lived in a land of deep darkness—on them light has shined.
[2898] Revelation 22:2 through the middle of the street of the city. On either side of the river is the tree of life with its twelve kinds of fruit, producing its fruit each month; and the leaves of the tree are for the healing of the nations.
[2899] Matthew 25:34, Then the king will say to those at his right hand, "Come, you that are blessed by my Father, inherit the kingdom prepared for you from the foundation of the world;
[2900] Job 42:2 'I know that you can do all things, and that no purpose of yours can be thwarted.

CHAPTER SIXTY SIX

AT-TEHREEM
PROHIBITION

THE **MEDINA** PERIOD

In the name of God, the Merciful-to-all, the Mercy Giver:

Prophet, why do you prohibit what God has made lawful to you, seeking to please your wives?[2903] God is forgiving[2904] and Merciful-to-all.[2905] [01] God has already ordained for you (believers) to release you from such oaths. God is your protector and He is the All-Knowing,[2906] the All-Wise.[2907] [02]

The Prophet told something in confidence to one of his wives. But when she disclosed it (to another wife), God made it known to him; he confirmed part of it, and ignored another part. Then when he confronted her with it, she asked, "Who told you this?" He said, "I was informed by the All-knowing, the All-Aware." [03] You two (wives) need to repent to God, for your hearts have clearly deviated. But if you band together against him, then God is his protector, as is Gabriel and the righteous believers. In addition, the angels will come to his support. [04] Perhaps if he divorced you, his Lord will give him wives better than you: submissive to God, believing, obedient, repentant, worshipping, who fast much; previously married as well as virgins. [05]

Believers, safeguard yourselves and your families from a Fire fueled by people and stones. fierce and powerful angels stand over it. They never disobey God's commands to them, but do as they are commanded. [06] Unbelievers make no excuses today. You are only being repaid for what you used to do. [07]

• • •

[2903] 1 Corinthians 7:33 but the married man is anxious about the affairs of the world, how to please his wife,

[2904] Ephesians 2:4 But God, who is rich in mercy, out of great love with which he loved us.

[2905] Psalm 116:5 Gracious is the Lord, and righteous; our God is merciful.,

[2906] 1 John 3:20 whenever our hearts condemn us; for God is greater than our hearts, and he knows everything.

[2907] Proverbs 2:6 For the Lord gives wisdom; from his mouth come knowledge and understanding;

Believers, turn to God in sincere repentance[2908]. Your Lord may remove your sins[2909], and admit you into Gardens with rivers flowing through them, on the Day when God will not disgrace the Prophet and those who believed with him. Their light will proceed before them[2910], and to their right, they will say, "Our Lord, perfect our light for us and forgive us. You are able to do all things."[2911 (08)]

Prophet, strive against the unbelievers and the hypocrites and be harsh with them. Hell will be their dwelling. What a miserable destination. (66:9) God has given an example to those who reject the truth: the wife of Noah and the wife of Lot.[2912] They were married to two of Our righteous worshipers but they betrayed them. They were not able to help them at all with God, and it was said, "Enter the Fire with those who are entering." [(10)] And God has given an example to those who believed: Pharaoh's wife, when she said, "My Lord, build for me near You, a house in Paradise, and rescue me from Pharaoh and his works and save me from the unjust people." [(11)] And the example of Mary,[2913] Imran's daughter, who guarded her chastity.[2914] So We breathed into her from Our Spirit;[2915] and she believed in her Lord's Words and His Books,[2916] and was of the devoutly obedient.[2917 (12)]

● ● ●

[2908] Matthew 4:17 From that time Jesus began to preach, saying, "Repent, for the kingdom of heaven is at hand."
[2909] Jeremiah 33:8 I will cleanse them from all the guilt of their sin against me, and I will forgive all the guilt of their sin and rebellion against me.
[2910] John 8:12 "I am the light of the world. Whoever follows me will never walk in darkness, but will have the light of life."
[2911] Job 42:2 'I know that you can do all things, and that no purpose of yours can be thwarted.
[2912] Lot, nephew of Abraham
[2913] Arabic /Mariam/Mother of Jesus
[2914] Luke 1:34 Mary said to the angel, 'How can this be, since I am a virgin?'
[2915] Luke 1:35 The angel said to her, 'The Holy Spirit will come upon you, and the power of the Most High will overshadow you; therefore, the child to be born will be holy.
[2916] Luke 1:45 And blessed is she who believed that there would be a fulfilment of what was spoken to her by the Lord.'
[2917] Luke 1:38, 46-7, 49-50 Then Mary said, 'Here am I, the servant of the Lord; let it be with me according to your word.' Then the angel departed from her. [46] And Mary said, "My soul magnifies the Lord, [47] and my spirit rejoices in God my Savior, [49] for the Mighty One has done great things for me, and holy is his name. [50] His mercy is for those who fear him from generation to generation

CHAPTER SIXTY SEVEN

AL-MULK

THE SOVEREIGNTY

In The name of God, the Merciful-to-all, The Mercy Giver:

Exalted is He who has all Sovereignty[2918] in His Hand, who has power over all things[2919] [01] He who created death and life[2920] to test you as to which of you is best in deed. He is the Almighty,[2921] the Forgiving[2922] [02] It is He who created seven heavens in total harmony with one another. You will not see any discrepancy in the creation of the Merciful-to-all.[2923] Look again; do you see any gaps? [03] Then look again, and again, and your sight will return to you dazzled and exhausted. [04]

We have beautified the lowest heaven with lit objects [2924] and use them as tools to stone devils (shayatin) and have prepared for them the punishment[2925] of the Blazing fire. [05] For those who reject their Lord, there is the punishment of Hell, a miserable destination.[2926] [06] When they are thrown into it, they will hear it roaring, as it seethes. [07] It almost bursts with rage. Every time a group is thrown into it, its keepers ask them, "Did no one come to warn you?" [08] They will say, "Yes, someone came to warn us, but we did not believe in him and said, 'God has not sent down anything. You are in greatly misguided.' " [09] They will

· · ·

[2918] 1 Chronicles 29:11Yours, O Lord, are the greatness, the power, the glory, the victory, and the majesty; for all that is in the heavens and on the earth is yours; yours is the kingdom, O Lord, and you are exalted as head above all.

[2919] Job 42:2 'I know that you can do all things, and that no purpose of yours can be thwarted.

[2920] 1 Samuel 2:6 The Lord kills and brings to life; he brings down to Sheol and raises up.

[2921] Job 9:4 He is wise in heart, and mighty in strength—who has resisted him, and succeeded

[2922] Daniel 9:9. To the Lord our God belong mercy and forgiveness, for we have rebelled against him,

[2923] Psalm 116:5, Gracious is the Lord, and righteous; our God is merciful

[2924] Genesis 1:16 God made the two great lights—the greater light to rule the day and the lesser light to rule the night—and the stars.

[2925] Matthew 25:41 Then he will say to those at his left hand, "You that are accursed, depart from me into the eternal fire prepared for the devil and his angels; And these will go away into eternal punishment, but the righteous into eternal life.

[2926] Revelation 20:10 And the devil who had deceived them was thrown into the lake of fire and sulphur, where the beast and the false prophet were, and they will be tormented day and night for ever and ever.

say, "Had we listened or reasoned, we would not have been included among the inhabitants of the Blazing fire." [10] So they will come to realize and admit their sin. Away with the inhabitants of the Blazing fire. [11] Forgiveness and great reward await those who stand in awe of their Lord [2927] although He is beyond the reach of their perception. [12]

Whether you keep your thoughts to yourself, or state them openly, He knows what is within the hearts. [2928] [13] Would He who created[2929] not know, when He is the Most Subtle, the Totally Aware?[2930] [14] It is He who tamed the earth for you, so travel its regions, and eat of His provision. To Him you will be resurrected. [15] Do you feel confident that He who is in the heaven would not cause the earth to swallow [2931] you as it spins? [16] Or are you confident that He who is in heaven would not unleash a violent storm of stones against you?

Then you will know how true My warning was. [17] Those before them had already denied my warnings, and how terrible was My condemnation. [18] Have they not seen the birds above them, with wings outspread or folded in? None holds them except the Merciful-to-all. [2932] He is, The Ever Insightful. [19] Or who can be a force to protect you other than the Merciful-to-all?[2933] The unbelievers are really living in delusion. [20] Or who can provide for you if He withhold His provision?[2934] Yet they persist in their disrespect and evasion. [21] Is he who walks, stumbles and falls on his face better guided or he who walks upright on a straight path? [22]

Say, "It is He who brought you into being; and gave you hearing and vision and understanding. But you are rarely grateful." [23] Say, "It is He who scattered you on earth,[2935] and to Him you will be gathered."[2936] [24] And they say, "When will this promise will be fulfilled, if what you say is true?" [25] Say, "God alone has

• • •

[2927] Psalm 108:1-5 My heart is steadfast, O God, my heart is steadfast; I will sing and make melody. Awake, my soul 2 Awake, O harp and lyre! I will awake the dawn. 3 I will give thanks to you, O Lord, among the peoples, and I will sing praises to you among the nations. 4 For your steadfast love is higher than the heavens, and your faithfulness reaches to the clouds. 5 Be exalted, O God, above the heavens, and let your glory be over all the earth.

[2928] John 2:25, and needed no one to testify about anyone; for he himself knew what was in everyone.

[2929] Isaiah 43:7 everyone who is called by my name, whom I created for my glory, whom I formed and made.'

[2930] Romans 11:33 O the depth of the riches and wisdom and knowledge of God! How unsearchable are his judgments and how inscrutable his ways!

[2931] Numbers 16:30-32 But if the Lord creates something new, and the ground opens its mouth and swallows them up, with all that belongs to them, and they go down alive into Sheol, then you shall know that these men have despised the Lord.' 31 As soon as he finished speaking all these words, the ground under them was split apart. 32 The earth opened its mouth and swallowed them up, along with their households—everyone who belonged to Korah and all their goods.

[2932] Matthew 6:26, Look at the birds of the air; they neither sow nor reap nor gather into barns, and yet your heavenly Father feeds them. Are you not of more value than they? 10:29 Are not two sparrows sold for a penny? Yet not one of them will fall to the ground unperceived by your Father.

[2933] Deuteronomy 23:14 For the Lord your God moves about in your camp to protect you and to deliver your enemies to you. Your camp must be holy, so that he will not see among you anything indecent and turn away from you.

[2934] 2 Peter 2:9 if this is so, then the Lord knows how to rescue the godly from trials and to hold the unrighteous for punishment on the day of judgment.

[2935] Genesis 9:7 As for you, be fruitful and increase in number; multiply on the earth and increase upon it."

[2936] Matthew 25:32 All the nations will be gathered before him, and he will separate people one from another as a shepherd separates the sheep from the goats,

knowledge of this,[2937] and I am only delivering a clear warning." [26] But when they see it approaching, the unbelievers' faces will turn gloomy, and it will be said, "This is what you were calling for." [27] Say, "Just think: should God destroy me and those with me, or if He decides to have mercy on us, who will protect the unbelievers from a painful punishment?"[2938] [28] Say, "He is the Merciful-to-all; We have believed in Him, and in Him We trust.[2939] You will come to know who It is in evident error." [29] Say, "Just think: if your water drains away, who will bring you pure flowing water?" [30]

. . .

[2937] Matthew 24:36, 'But about that day and hour no one knows, neither the angels of heaven, nor the Son, but only the Father.

[2938] 2 Thessalonians 1:9 These will suffer the punishment of eternal destruction, separated from the presence of the Lord and from the glory of his might,

[2939] Psalm 143: Let me hear of your steadfast love in the morning, for in you I put my trust. Teach me the way I should go, for to you I lift up my soul.

CHAPTER SIXTY EIGHT

AL-QALAM
THE PEN

THE **MECCA** PERIOD

In the name of God, the Merciful-to-all, the Mercy Giver:

Nun.[2940] By the pen and all they write, [01] you are not, by the grace of your Lord, a madman. [02] And you will have a never ending reward. [03] And you are a man of great moral character. [04] You will see and they will see [05] which of you is afflicted by madness. [06] Your Lord knows best who has strayed from His path, and He knows.[2941] Then do not obey the unbelievers. [08] They wish that you compromise, so they too can compromise. [09] And do not obey any worthless contemptible swearer [10] or any backbiter and slander-monger, [11] preventer of good, aggressor and one who is sinner, [12] cruel, moreover, and furthermore one who is despicable.[2942] [13] Just because he has money and children, [14] when Our verses are recited to him, he says, "Myth of former people." [15] We will brand him on the snout. [16]

We have tested them, as We tested the owners of a certain garden, when they vowed to harvest it in the morning [17] and made no allowance (for the Will of God).[2943] [18] But a disaster from your Lord came upon it while they slept. [19] By morning it became barren and bleak. [20] At day break they called to one another, [21] saying, "Go early to your crop if you want to harvest the fruit." [22] So they set out, whispering, [23] "Make sure no poor person enters the garden

• • •

[2940] Here and at the beginning of many chapters there are unvowelled letters of unknown meaning. Numerous theories have been proposed, but there is no agreement on the subject.

[2941] 1 John 3:20 whenever our hearts condemn us; for God is greater than our hearts, and he knows everything.

[2942] Romans 1:29-31 They were filled with every kind of wickedness, evil, covetousness, malice. Full of envy, murder, strife, deceit, craftiness, they are gossips, [30] slanderers, God-haters, insolent, haughty, boastful, inventors of evil, rebellious towards parents, [31] foolish, faithless, heartless, ruthless.

[2943] James 4:13-16 Come now, you who say, 'Today or tomorrow we will go to such and such a town and spend a year there, doing business and making money.' [14] Yet you do not even know what tomorrow will bring. What is your life? For you are a mist that appears for a little while and then vanishes. [15] Instead you ought to say, 'If the Lord wishes, we will live and do this or that.' [16] As it is, you boast in your arrogance; all such boasting is evil.

today." (24) And early they went bent on their purpose. (25) But when they saw it, they said, " We are lost; (26) Rather, we have been ruined. (27) The most moderate of them said, "Did I not say to you, that you should praise your Lord's glory? (28) They said, "May our Lord be exalted in His glory, we were unjust." (29) Then they turned to one another, each blaming the other. (30) They said, "How terrible for us; we were aggressors. (31) Perhaps our Lord will give us a better substitute for it. We are turning to our Lord in hope."2944 (32) Such is the punishment. And the punishment2945 of the Hereafter is greater, if they only knew. (33)

There will be Gardens of delight2946 for those who are mindful of God. (34) Would We treat those who submit2947 to us like those who forced others to reject Our messages. (35) What is the matter with you? How do you judge? (36) Or do you have a Book which you study? (37) And in it do you find all that you wish for? (38) Or do you have oaths from Us, that are binding until the Day of Resurrection, allowing you to have whatever you want? (39) Ask them which of them, will be responsible for that claim. (40)

Or do they have partners? Then let them bring their partners, if they are telling the truth. (41) On the Day when legs are bared, they will be called to bow down, but will not be able. (42) Their eyes humbled, humiliation will cover them. They were invited to bow down while they were healthy. (43)

So leave those who deny this revelation to Me. We will proceed against them gradually, from whence they do not know. (44) And I will give them time. My plan is firm. (45) Or do you ask them for a wage, so they are burdened with debt? (46) Or do they know the future, and they write what is going to happen? (47) So be patient for your Lord's judgment, and do not be like the fellow of the whale2948 who called out in despair.2949 (48) Had a blessing from his Lord not reached him,2950 he would have been abandoned and disgraced on a naked shore. (49) But his Lord chose him2951 and made him among the righteous. (50) Those unbelievers all but kill you with their evil looks when they hear the message, and they say, "He must be mad." (51) But it is only a reminder to all people. (52)

• • •

2944 Psalm 37:34 Hope in the Lord and keep his way. He will exalt you to inherit the land; when the wicked are destroyed, you will see it.
2945 Matthew 25:41,46 Then he will say to those at his left hand, "You that are accursed, depart from me into the eternal fire prepared for the devil and his angels; 46 And these will go away into eternal punishment, but the righteous into eternal life.'
2946 Psalm 16:11 You show me the path of life. In your presence there is fullness of joy; in your right hand are pleasures for evermore
2947 James 4:7 Submit yourselves therefore to God. Resist the devil, and he will flee from you.
2948 Jonah 1:17 But the Lord provided a large fish to swallow up Jonah; and Jonah was in the belly of the fish for three days and three nights.
2949 Jonah 2:1-9 Then Jonah prayed to the Lord his God from the belly of the fish, saying, 'I called to the Lord out of my distress, and he answered me; out of the belly of Sheol I cried, and you heard my voice
2950 Jonah 2:10 Then the Lord spoke to the fish, and it spewed Jonah out upon the dry land.
2951 Jonah 3:2 'Get up, go to Nineveh, that great city, and proclaim to it the message that I tell you.'

CHAPTER SIXTY NINE

AL-HAAQAH

THE HOUR OF TRUTH

THE **MECCA** PERIOD

In the name of God, the Merciful-to-all, the Mercy Giver:

The Hour of Truth [01] What is the Hour of Truth? [02] And how would you know what is the Hour of Truth? [03]

The people of Thamud[2952] and 'Aad[2953] denied (that there would be a) sudden calamity. [04] So as for Thamud, they were destroyed by the overpowering blast. [05] And as for Aad, they were destroyed by a furious, roaring wind [06] which He unleashed against them for seven nights and eight days, nonstop. You could have seen its people lying dead as if they were hollow palm tree trunks. [07] Do you see anything left of them? [08] Then came Pharaoh [2954] and those before him, and the destroyed towns[2955] that indulged in sin. [09] They disobeyed their Lord's Messenger, so He seized them with an overpowering grip. [10] When the water overflowed, We carried your ancestors in the sailing ship[2956] [11] To make it a lesson for you to remember, so listening ears may recall it. [12]

Then when the Horn is blown with a single blast,[2957] [13] and the earth and the mountains are lifted up and crushed with one blow,[2958] [14] on that Day, the Hour of Truth will occur. [15] The heaven will split open on that Day, since it will be so

• • •

[2952] See Glossary

[2953] Ibid

[2954] Romans 9:16-18 It does not, therefore, depend on human desire or effort, but on God's mercy. [17] For Scripture says to Pharaoh: "I raised you up for this very purpose, that I might display my power in you and that my name might be proclaimed in all the earth." [18] Therefore, God has mercy on whom he wants to have mercy, and he hardens whom he wants to harden.

[2955] Genesis 19:29 So when God destroyed the cities of the plain, he remembered Abraham, and he brought Lot out of the catastrophe that overthrew the cities where Lot had lived.

[2956] Genesis 7: 17-18 For forty days the flood kept coming on the earth, and as the waters increased they lifted the ark high above the earth. [18] The waters rose and increased greatly on the earth, and the ark floated on the surface of the water.

[2957] 1 Corinthians 15:52 in a moment, in the twinkling of an eye, at the last trumpet. For the trumpet will sound, and the dead will be raised imperishable, and we will be changed.

[2958] Hebrews 1:10-12 And, 'In the beginning, Lord, you founded the earth, and the heavens are the work of your hands; [11] they will perish, but you remain; they will all wear out like clothing; [12] like a cloak you will roll them up, and like clothing they will be changed. But you are the same, and your years will never end.'

frail.[2959] [16] And the angels will be round its edges. On that Day, eight of them will bear your Lord's Throne of His majesty above them. [17] On that Day you will be exposed, and no secret of yours will remain hidden.[2960] [18] As for him who is given his record in his right hand,[2961] he will say, "Here, take my record and read it, [19] I expected that I would be held accountable." [20] So, he will have a pleasant life [21] in an elevated Garden, [22] its pickings are within easy reach. [23] "Eat and drink merrily for what you have done in days gone by." [24] As for him who is given his record in his left hand, he will say, "I wish I was never given my record [25] and never knew what my account was. [26] If only death had really been the end. [27] My wealth has been of no use to me [28] and my power has vanished." [29] (God will say), "Seize him and shackle him. [30] Then drive him into Hell.[2962] [31] Then tie him with a chain whose length is seventy cubits." [32] For he would not believe in God, the Magnificent [2963] [33] nor would he encourage feeding of the poor.[2964] [34] So he has no friend here this Day, [35] nor any food except scum, [36] that only sinners eat. [37]

So I swear by what you see [38] and what you do not see [39] that this is the word of a noble Messenger. [40] And It is not the word of a poet; how little you believe, [41] nor the word of a soothsayer; how little you remember, [42] The gradual revelations of the Book, is from the Lord of the worlds. [43] Had he (the Messenger) falsely attributed some statements to Us, [44] We would have seized him by the right arm. [45] Then We would have slashed his lifeline, [46] and none of you could have protected him. [47] It (The Qur'an) is a reminder for the those who are mindful of God. [48] And We know that some of you will deny it. [49] It is a cause of great distress to the unbelievers. [50] And it is the Truth of certainty. [51] Exalt, then, the limitless glory of your Lord's magnificent name.[2965] [52]

• • •

[2959] Revelation 6:14 The sky vanished like a scroll rolling itself up, and every mountain and island was removed from its place.
[2960] Luke 12:3, Therefore whatever you have said in the dark will be heard in the light, and what you have whispered behind closed doors will be proclaimed from the housetops.
[2961] Matthew 25:34 Then the king will say to those at his right hand, "Come, you that are blessed by my Father, inherit the kingdom prepared for you from the foundation of the world;
[2962] Matthew 25:41 "Then he will say to those on his left, 'Depart from me, you who are cursed, into the eternal fire prepared for the devil and his angels
[2963] Psalm 145:3 Great is the Lord, and greatly to be praised; his greatness is unsearchable. Romans 11:33 O the depth of the riches and wisdom and knowledge of God! How unsearchable are his judgments and how inscrutable his ways!
[2964] Luke 14:13 But when you give a banquet, invite the poor, the crippled, the lame, and the blind. 19:8 Zacchaeus stood there and said to the Lord, 'Look, half of my possessions, Lord, I will give to the poor; and if I have defrauded anyone of anything, I will pay back four times as much.'
[2965] Psalm 145:3 Great is the Lord, and greatly to be praised; his greatness is unsearchable.

CHAPTER SEVENTY

AL-MA'ARIJ
THE GATES OF ASCENT

THE **MECCA** PERIOD

In the name of God, the Merciful-to-all, the Mercy Giver:
An inquirer asked about an impending punishment[2966] [01] to the unbelievers that cannot be prevented[2967] [02] from God, the Lord of the Gates of Ascent. [03] Unto Him the angels and the Spirit will ascend[2968] in a Day whose length is fifty thousand years. [04] So be patient with gracious patience. [05] They (the unbelievers) see it as something distant, [06] but We see it near. [07] On the Day the sky will be like molten brass,[2969] [08] and the mountains will be like tufted wool. [09] No good friend will ask about his friend, [10] even though they can see each other. The one who forced others to reject Our messages will wish he could ransom himself from the punishment of that Day, by sacrificing his children [11] and his wife and his brother [12] and his family who shelter him [13] and everyone on earth, if that could save him. [14] Not today! But a raging blaze [15] that strips away the skin [16] and claims everyone who turned his back to the truth and went away [17] and accumulated and hoarded (wealth). [18]

The Human being was created full of anxiety: [19] desperate when bad things happen, [20] but tight-fisted when good fortune comes his way, [21] The exception are those who pray, [22] those who are steady in their prayer [23] and those who have set aside a known rightful share within their wealth [24] for the poor and the deprived [25] and those who believe in the Day of Judgment,[2970] [26] and those who dread their Lord's punishment. [27] They know not to take their Lord's

• • •

[2966] Matthew 25:41,46 Then he will say to those at his left hand, "You that are accursed, depart from me into the eternal fire prepared for the devil and his angels; [46] And these will go away into eternal punishment, but the righteous into eternal life.'

[2967] 1 Thessalonians 5:3 When they say, 'There is peace and security', then sudden destruction will come upon them, as labor pains come upon a pregnant woman, and there will be no escape!

[2968] John 1:51 And he said to him, 'Very truly, I tell you, you will see heaven opened and the angels of God ascending and descending upon the Son of Man.'

[2969] Deuteronomy 28:23 The sky over your head shall be bronze, and the earth under you iron.

[2970] 1 John 4:17 This is how love is made complete among us so that we will have confidence on the day of judgment: in the world we are like Jesus.

punishment for granted. ⁽²⁸⁾ Those who guard their chastity, ⁽²⁹⁾ except from their spouses and from those whom their right hands hold in trust, are free of blame. ⁽³⁰⁾ But whoever seeks beyond that, they are transgressors²⁹⁷¹ ⁽³¹⁾ Those who honor their trusts and pledges ⁽³²⁾ and those who stand by their testimonies ²⁹⁷² ⁽³³⁾ and those who maintain their prayer with dedication: ⁽³⁴⁾ those will be honored in Gardens. ⁽³⁵⁾

So what is (the matter) with the unbelievers? They run about in front of you in groups, with outstretched necks and staring eyes, ⁽³⁶⁾ from the right, and from the left. ⁽³⁷⁾ Does each one of them aspire to enter the Garden of Delight? ⁽³⁸⁾ Never! We have created them from that which they well know. ⁽³⁹⁾ So I swear by the Lord of all risings and settings²⁹⁷³ that We are able ⁽⁴⁰⁾ to replace them with better than they;²⁹⁷⁴ and nothing can prevent Us from doing this. ⁽⁴¹⁾ So leave them to blunder and play around, until they meet their Day which they are promised, ⁽⁴²⁾ The Day when they will emerge from the graves rushing²⁹⁷⁵ as if rallying to a flag, ⁽⁴³⁾ their eyes humbled, overwhelmed by humiliation. This is the Day which they were promised. ⁽⁴⁴⁾

• • •

²⁹⁷¹ 1 Thessalonians 4:3-6 For this is the will of God, your sanctification: ⁴ that you abstain from fornication; ⁵ that each one of you knows how to control your own body in holiness and honor, ⁶ not with lustful passion, like the Gentiles who do not know God;
²⁹⁷² John 19:35 The man who saw it has given testimony, and his testimony is true. He knows that he tells the truth, and he testifies so that you also may believe.
²⁹⁷³ Or Easts and Wests. Luke 13:29 Then people will come from east and west, from north and south, and will eat in the kingdom of God.
²⁹⁷⁴ Matthew 21:43 Therefore I tell you, the kingdom of God will be taken away from you and given to a people that produces the fruits of the kingdom.
²⁹⁷⁵ John 5:28, 29 Do not be astonished at this; for the hour is coming when all who are in their graves will hear his voice ²⁹ and will come out—those who have done good, to the resurrection of life, and those who have done evil, to the resurrection of condemnation.

CHAPTER SEVENTY ONE

NUH

NOAH

THE **MECCA** PERIOD

We sent Noah to his people, (saying), "Warn your People[2974] before a painful punishment comes to them." [01] He said, "My people, I am coming to you with clear warnings, [02] 'Worship God, be mindful of Him and obey me. [03] God will forgive you of your sins,[2975] and reprieve you until an appointed time. When God's appointed time arrives it cannot be postponed, if you only knew'" [04]

He said, "My Lord, I invited my people night and day. [05] but the more I called them, the further they ran away: [06] Every time I called them to Your forgiveness, they put their fingers into their ears, wrapped themselves in their garments, and insisted, and became increasingly more arrogant. [07] I invited them openly. [08] Then I appealed to them publicly, and I spoke to them privately, [09] and said, 'Ask forgiveness of your Lord. He is ever forgiving.[2976] [10] He will send down abundant rain from the sky for you [2977] [11] and will provide you with wealth and children and He will give you gardens and rivers. [12] What is the matter with you? Why can't you appreciate God's majesty?[2978] [13] when He has created you stage by stage? [14] Do you not see how God created seven superimposed[2979] heavens [15] and placed the moon in them as a enlightenment[2980] and He made the sun a

• • •

[2974] Genesis 6:13 And God said to Noah, 'I have determined to make an end of all flesh, for the earth is filled with violence because of them; now I am going to destroy them along with the earth.

[2975] Luke 11:4, And forgive us our sins, for we ourselves forgive everyone indebted to us. And do not bring us to the time of trial.'

[2976] Daniel 9:9 To the Lord our God belong mercy and forgiveness, for we have rebelled against him,

[2977] Jeremiah 14:22 Can any idols of the nations bring rain? Or can the heavens give showers? Is it not you, O Lord our God? We set our hope on you, for it is you who do all this.

[2978] Romans 2:4 Or do you despise the riches of his kindness and forbearance and patience? Do you not realize that God's kindness is meant to lead you to repentance?

[2979] "Tabak طبق" is a noun meaning "a layer". The adjective "Tibak طباق" as mentioned in this verse, means "superimposed" and is used in describing the seven heavens "سبع سموات طباق". The superimposed heavens in the Quran are the extra spatial dimensions in modern physics.

[2980] The Moon is mentioned here as enlightenment because the Qur'an instructs people to calculate the month and the year based on the moon. In that sense, the moon is a source of enlightenment and knowledge.

source of light? [2981] [(16)] God germinated you from the earth like plants.[2982] [(17)] Then He will return you into it, and will bring you out again. [(18)] And God has spread the earth out for you [(19)] that you may travel its valleys as roadways.' " [(20)]

Noah (Nuh) said, "My Lord, they have defied me, and followed those whose wealth and children lead them increasingly into loss. [(21)] And they schemed outrageously. [(22)] And said, 'Do not abandon your gods. Never leave Wadd or Suwa'or Yaghuth and Ya'uq and Nasr. [(23)] They have already misled many. My Lord, increase these transgressors only in misguidance." [(24)]

Because of their sins they were drowned and sent to Hell. They could not find any one to help them against God. [(25)] And Noah said, "My Lord, do not leave a single unbeliever on the face of the earth. [(26)] if You leave them, they will mislead Your worshipers and breed only wicked unbelievers. [(27)] My Lord, forgive me and my parents[2983] and whoever enters my house as a believer. Forgive all the believing men and women, but bring nothing but ruin down on the transgressors."[2984] [(28)]

• • •

[2981] Genesis 1:16-18 God made the two great lights—the greater light to rule the day and the lesser light to rule the night—and the stars. [17] God set them in the dome of the sky to give light upon the earth, [18] to rule over the day and over the night, and to separate the light from the darkness. And God saw that it was good.
[2982] Genesis 1:11 Then God said, 'Let the earth put forth vegetation: plants yielding seed, and fruit trees of every kind on earth that bear fruit with the seed in it.' And it was so.
[2983] Genesis 6:8,9 But Noah found favor in the sight of the Lord. These are the descendants of Noah. Noah was a righteous man, blameless in his generation; Noah walked with God.
[2984] Genesis 6:13 And God said to Noah, 'I have determined to make an end of all flesh, for the earth is filled with violence because of them; now I am going to destroy them along with the earth.

CHAPTER SEVENTY TWO

AL-JINN
THE JINN

THE **MECCA** PERIOD

In the name of God, the Merciful-to-all, the Mercy Giver:

Say, "It has been revealed to me that a group of jinn listened in and said, 'We have heard an amazing Recitation. [01] It guides to righteousness, and we have believed it: We will never assign divinity to anyone except our Lord. [02] And exalted be the glory of our Lord! He never had a spouse nor a child. [03] But the fools among us had been saying outrageous things about God[2987] [04] although we had thought that no human or jinn would dare tell a lie about God. [05] Some individual humans used to seek power through some individual jinn,[2988] but they (the jinn) only increased their confusion. [06] And they thought, as you thought, that God would not send anyone[2989] (as a messenger).[2990] [07] We as usual probed heaven (in search of news), and found it filled with fierce guards and projectiles. [08] We used to take up certain positions to listen in; but anyone trying to listen now finds a projectile in wait for him. [09] We do not know therefore whether ill is intended for those on earth, or whether their Lord intends to guide them. [10] Some of us are righteous, but others are less so; we follow different paths. [11] And we have come to realize that we can never evade God living on earth, nor can we evade Him by escaping (from life). [12] So when we heard this call to guidance, we believed in it[2991] Whoever believes in his Lord will no longer fear

• • •

[2987] John 8:44 You are from your father the devil, and you choose to do your father's desires. He was a murderer from the beginning and does not stand in the truth, because there is no truth in him. When he lies, he speaks according to his own nature, for he is a liar and the father of lies.
[2988] 1 Corinthians 10:20 No, I imply that what pagans sacrifice, they sacrifice to demons and not to God. I do not want you to be partners with demons.
[2989] See Tafsir Al Tabari http://en.wikipedia.org/wiki/Tafsir_al http://islaambooks.wordpress.com/2012/05/28/the
[2990] 2 Peter 3:4 and saying, 'Where is the promise of his coming? For ever since our ancestors died, all things continue as they were from the beginning of creation!'
[2991] Isaiah 50:5, The Lord God has opened my ear, and I was not rebellious, I did not turn backwards. 30:20-21 Though the Lord may give you the bread of adversity and the water of affliction, yet your Teacher will not hide himself any more, but your eyes shall see your Teacher. [21] And when you turn to the right or when you turn to the left, your ears shall hear a word behind you, saying, 'This is the way; walk in it.'

the burden of life or injustice. ⁽¹³⁾ Some of us submitted to God, while others are transgressors. Those who submitted have sought out right guidance.^{2992 (14)} As for the transgressors, they will be, firewood for Hell.'²⁹⁹³⁽¹⁵⁾

Had (your people) kept true to the path, We would have given them abundant drinking water supply, ⁽¹⁶⁾ a test for them. Whoever turns away from remembering to call on his Lord will be put into an arduous punishment.^{2994 (17)} Places of worship are for God. So do not call on anyone else besides God.^{2995 (18)} Yet when God's servant²⁹⁹⁶ stood up calling on Him, they (the unbelievers) overwhelmed him with their crowds." ⁽¹⁹⁾ Say, "I only call on my Lord and I never associate anyone with Him." ⁽²⁰⁾ Say, "It is not in my power to harm you, nor to guide you rightly." ⁽²¹⁾ Say, "No one can protect me from God,²⁹⁹⁷ and I will never find any refuge except in Him."^{2998 (22)} I only deliver what I receive from God and His messages.

He who disobeys God and His messenger, will have the fire of Hell where they will be forever.^{2999 (23)} until they see that which they were promised and they will know who has less support and are fewer in number. ⁽²⁴⁾ Say, "I do not know whether what you are promised will happen soon or whether it will be delayed by my Lord for a period." ⁽²⁵⁾ He alone knows what is beyond our perception,³⁰⁰⁰ and He doesn't disclose His knowledge of the unseen to anyone, ⁽²⁶⁾ except to a Messenger of His choosing. He then dispatches guards before him and behind him. ⁽²⁷⁾ That he may know that they have conveyed the messages of their Lord. He encompasses what they have, and has counted everything by number. ⁽²⁸⁾

• • •

²⁹⁹² Proverbs 3:6, In all your ways acknowledge him, and he will make straight your paths.
²⁹⁹³ Revelation 20:14-15 Then Death and Hades were thrown into the lake of fire. This is the second death, the lake of fire; ¹⁵ and anyone whose name was not found written in the book of life was thrown into the lake of fire.
²⁹⁹⁴ Matthew 25:41, Then he will say to those at his left hand, "You that are accursed, depart from me into the eternal fire prepared for the devil and his angels; And these will go away into eternal punishment, but the righteous into eternal life."
²⁹⁹⁵ Exodus 20:3 you shall have no other gods before me. Repeated in Kings 19:15, Nehemiah 9:6, Isaiah 37:20, Isaiah 46:9, Zechariah 14:9, John 5:44
²⁹⁹⁶ The Messenger.
²⁹⁹⁷ 1 Samuel 4:8 Woe to us! Who can deliver us from the power of these mighty gods? These are the gods who struck the Egyptians with every sort of plague in the wilderness.
²⁹⁹⁸ 2 Samuel 22:3 my God, my rock, in whom I take refuge, my shield and the horn of my salvation, my stronghold and my refuge, my savior; you save me from violence.
²⁹⁹⁹ Matthew 25:46 'And these will go away into eternal punishment, but the righteous into eternal life.'
³⁰⁰⁰ Romans 11:33-34 O the depth of the riches and wisdom and knowledge of God! How unsearchable are his judgments and how inscrutable his ways! ³⁴ "For who has known the mind of the Lord? Or who has been his counselor?"

CHAPTER SEVENTY THREE

AL-MUZZAMMIL
THE ENWRAPPED

THE **MECCA** PERIOD
THE **MEDINA** PERIOD VERSE 20

In the name of God, the Merciful-to-all, the Mercy Giver:
You who wraps himself (in his clothing), [01] stay up during the night,[3001] except for a little, [02] for half of it, or a little less, [03] or a little more, and recite the Qur'an slowly and distinctly. [04] We will send a weighty message to you. [05] Rising at night has a stronger effect and is more conducive to concentration. [06] In the daytime, you are kept busy for long periods. [07] So remember to call upon the name of your Lord and devote yourself to Him wholeheartedly.[3002] [08] The Lord of the East and the West; there is no god[3003] but Him. assign to Him alone the power to determine your fate. [09] And patiently endure what they say, and withdraw from them politely [10] and leave those who deny the truth and live in luxury to Me Just bear with them a little longer; [11] We have shackles and Hell [12] And food that chokes and a painful punishment reserved for them,[3004] [13] on the Day when the earth and the mountains tremble,[3005] and the mountains become heaps of sand.[3006] [14]

We have sent to you a messenger, a witness over you just as We sent to Pharaoh[3007] a messenger. [15] But Pharaoh disobeyed the messenger,[3008] so We

• • •

[3001] 1 Thessalonians 5:6 So then, let us not fall asleep as others do, but let us keep awake and be sober;
[3002] Psalm 37:5 Commit your way to the Lord; trust in him, and he will act.
[3003] Exodus 20:3 you shall have no other gods before me.
[3004] Matthew 25:41, Then he will say to those at his left hand, "You that are accursed, depart from me into the eternal fire prepared for the devil and his angels; And these will go away into eternal punishment, but the righteous into eternal life."
[3005] Revelation 16:18 And there came flashes of lightning, rumblings, peals of thunder, and a violent earthquake, such as had not occurred since people were upon the earth, so violent was that earthquake.
[3006] Revelation 16:20 And every island fled away, and no mountains were to be found;
[3007] Acts 7:35 'It was this Moses whom they rejected when they said, "Who made you a ruler and a judge?" and whom God now sent as both ruler and liberator through the angel who appeared to him in the bush.
[3008] Exodus 8:15 But when Pharaoh saw that there was a respite, he hardened his heart, and would not listen to them, just as the Lord had said.

seized him with a crushing grip. [16] How, then, if you refuse to acknowledge the truth, will you protect yourself from a Day which will turn the children gray-haired? [17] A Day when the heavens will shatter. God's promise is always fulfilled. [18] This is a reminder, so let anyone who wills set a path towards his Lord. [19]

Your Lord knows that you stay up praying nearly two-thirds of the night, or half of it, or one-third of it, along with a group of those with you. God justly evaluates the night and the day. He knows that you will not be able to sustain it, so He will not require it of you. Read from the Qur'an what you can. He knows that some of you may be ill; and others travelling through the land, seeking God's bounty; yet others will be fighting in God's cause. So read from it what is easy for you, and observe the prayers, and pay The purifying alms, and lend God a loan[3009] of goodness. Whatever good you advance for yourselves,[3010] you will find it with God, improved and increased for you.[3011] Ask God's forgiveness, for God is Forgiving and Merciful. [20]

• • •

[3009] Proverbs 19:17 Whoever is kind to the poor lends to the LORD, and will be repaid in full.
[3010] Proverbs 16:20 Those who are attentive to a matter will prosper, and happy are those who trust in the Lord.
[3011] 2 Timothy 1:12 and for this reason I suffer as I do. But I am not ashamed, for I know the one in whom I have put my trust, and I am sure that he is able to guard until that day what I have entrusted to him.

CHAPTER SEVENTY FOUR

AL-MUDDAThThIR

THE ENROBED

THE **MECCA** PERIOD

In the name of God, the Merciful-to-all, the Mercy Giver:

You, wrapped in your shroud, [01] arise and give warning, [02] glorify your Lord's greatness [3012] [03] purify your clothing and [04] avoid all filth [3013] [05] Do not give out of a desire for gain. [3014] [06] But be steadfast for your Lord's cause. [3015] [07]

When the trumpet is blown, [3016] [08] that Day will be a difficult day, [09] not easy for the unbelievers. [10] Leave Me alone with the one I created [11] to whom I gave great wealth, [12] sons around him, [13] and for whom I smoothed all things. [3017] [14] Then he desires that I should add more. [15] No! He was stubbornly hostile to Our revelation. [16] I will increasingly exhaust him. [17] He reflected and plotted. [18] So, may he perish how he plotted. [19] Then may he perish how he plotted. [20] Then he looked, [21] then he frowned and glared; [22] Then he turned back to his old

• • •

[3012] Psalm 40:16 But may all who seek you rejoice and be glad in you; may those who love your salvation say continually, 'Great is the Lord!'

[3013] Colossians 3:5, Put to death, therefore, whatever in you is earthly: fornication, impurity, passion, evil desire, and greed (which is idolatry).

[3014] 1 Timothy 6:5 and wrangling among those who are depraved in mind and bereft of the truth, imagining that godliness is a means of gain.

[3015] 1 Corinthians 15:58 Therefore, my beloved, be steadfast, immovable, always excelling in the work of the Lord, because you know that in the Lord your labor is not in vain.

[3016] Revelation 8:7, The first angel blew his trumpet, and there came hail and fire, mixed with blood, and they were hurled to the earth; and a third of the earth was burned up, and a third of the trees were burned up, and all green grass was burned up. Revelation 11:15 Then the seventh angel blew his trumpet, and there were loud voices in heaven, saying, "The kingdom of the world has become the kingdom of our Lord and of his Messiah, and he will reign forever and ever."

[3017] Job 21:7-13 Why do the wicked live on, reach old age, and grow mighty in power? [8] Their children are established in their presence, and their offspring before their eyes. [9] Their houses are safe from fear, and no rod of God is upon them. [10] Their bull breeds without fail; their cow calves and never miscarries. [11] They send out their little ones like a flock, and their children dance around. [12] They sing to the tambourine and the lyre, and rejoice to the sound of the pipe. [13] They spend their days in prosperity, and in peace they go down to Sheol.

arrogance [23] and said, "This is nothing but magic handed down from the past. [24] This is not but the word of a human being." [25]

I will roast him into Saqar. [3018] [26] And how would you know what is Saqar? [27] It neither leaves, nor spares, [28] scorching the flesh. [29] There are nineteen in charge of it. [30] We have appointed only angels to be wardens of the Fire, and caused their number to be a stumbling block for those who disbelieve; so that those given the Book may attain certainty; and those who believe may increase in faith; and those given the Book and the believers may not doubt; and those in whose hearts is sickness [3019] and the unbelievers may say, "What did God ever mean by this example?" In this way God lets go astray the one who wishes to go astray, [3020] and guides him who wish to be guided. [3021] None knows your Lord's forces but Him. [3022] This is nothing but a reminder to all human beings. [31] No! By the moon [32] and the night when it departs [33] and the morning as it brightens, [34] it is one of those great things [35] as a warning to human beings, [36] to whomever among you wishes to advance or regress. [37]

Every soul, is held in pledge for its own deeds [38] Except for those on the right, [3023] [39] in Gardens (Jannah), inquiring [40] about those who forced others to reject Our messages, [41] "What caused you to be in Saqar?" [42] They will say, "We were not among those who prayed, [43] nor did we feed the poor. [3024] [44] And we used to indulge in vain discussions with those who indulged (in mocking the believers) [45] And we used to deny the Day of Judgment [3025] [46] until the Certain End came upon us." [47] The intercession of intercessors will not help them. [3026][48]

Why then are they turning away from this reminder [49] as if they were panicked donkeys [50] fleeing from a lion? [51] Yet, every one of them wishes to be given scriptures unrolled before their very eyes. [52] No! But they do not fear the Hereafter. [53] No! This is but a reminder [54] and whoever wills may take it to heart. [55] But they will not remember, unless God so wills. He is the Source of all righteousness, and the source of all forgiveness. [3027] [56]

• • •

[3018] A place in Hell.

[3019] Jeremiah 8:18, My joy is gone, grief is upon me, my heart is sick. Jeremiah 17:9-10 The heart is devious above all else; it is perverse— who can understand it? I the Lord test the mind and search the heart, to give to all according to their ways, according to the fruit of their doings.

[3020] 2 Thessalonians 2:11 For this reason God sends them a powerful delusion, leading them to believe what is false,

[3021] Romans 9:18 So then he has mercy on whomsoever he chooses, and he hardens the heart of whomsoever he chooses.

[3022] Psalm 24:10 Who is this King of glory? The Lord of hosts, he is the King of glory. *Selah*

[3023] Matthew 25:34 Then the king will say to those at his right hand, "Come, you that are blessed by my Father, inherit the kingdom prepared for you from the foundation of the world;"

[3024] Matthew 25:42 for I was hungry and you gave me no food, I was thirsty and you gave me nothing to drink,

[3025] Matthew 12:36 I tell you, on the day of judgment you will have to give an account for every careless word you utter;

[3026] 1 Samuel 2:25, If one person sins against another, someone can intercede for the sinner with the Lord; but if someone sins against the Lord, who can make intercession?' But they would not listen to the voice of their father; for it was the will of the Lord to kill them.

[3027] Daniel 9:9 To the Lord our God belong mercy and forgiveness, for we have rebelled against him,

CHAPTER SEVENTY FIVE

AL-QIYAMAH
THE RESURRECTION

In the name of God, the Merciful-to-all, the Mercy Giver:

I swear by the Day of Resurrection[3026] (01) And I swear by the self-reproaching soul. (02) Does man think that We will not reassemble his bones?[3027] (03) Yes indeed. We are able even to reshape his fingertips. (04) Yet human beings want to deny what lies ahead of them. (05) He asks, "When is this Day of Resurrection?"[3028] (06)

When vision is dazzled, (07) the moon is eclipsed [3029] (08) and the sun and the moon are joined together,[3030] (09) on that Day, man will say, "Where is the escape?"[3031] (10) No indeed! There is no refuge. (11) Your Lord is the final destination on that Day. (12) On that Day the Human being will be informed of all deeds he put forward for this day and everything that should have been left behind [3032] (13) Rather, the human being, will give evidence against himself, (14) in spite of any excuses he presents. (15)

• • •

[3026] Hebrews 9:27, And just as it is appointed for mortals to die once, and after that the judgment,

[3027] Ezekiel 37:1-6 The hand of the Lord came upon me, and he brought me out by the spirit of the Lord and set me down in the middle of a valley; it was full of bones. 2 He led me all round them; there were very many lying in the valley, and they were very dry. 3 He said to me, 'Mortal, can these bones live?' I answered, 'O Lord God, you know.' 4 Then he said to me, 'Prophesy to these bones, and say to them: O dry bones, hear the word of the Lord. 5 Thus says the Lord God to these bones: I will cause breath to enter you, and you shall live. 6 I will lay sinews on you, and will cause flesh to come upon you, and cover you with skin, and put breath in you, and you shall live; and you shall know that I am the Lord.'

[3028] 2 Peter 3:4 and saying, 'Where is the promise of his coming? For ever since our ancestors died, all things continue as they were from the beginning of creation!'

[3029] Revelation 6:12 When he opened the sixth seal, I looked, and there came a great earthquake; the sun became black as sackcloth, the full moon became like blood,

[3030] Isaiah 13:10, For the stars of the heavens and their constellations will not give their light; the sun will be dark at its rising, and the moon will not shed its light.

[3031] Hebrews 2:3 how can we escape if we neglect so great a salvation? It was declared at first through the Lord, and it was attested to us by those who heard him,

[3032] Romans 14:12 So then, each of us will be accountable to God.

(Prophet), do not move your tongue attempting to rush your memorization of the Revelation. [16] Its collection and recitation are up to us. [17] So, when We recite it, follow its recitation, [18] it is then up to Us, to make it all clear [19]

But you love this brief life [20] and disregard the Hereafter.[3033] [21] There are faces on that Day that will be bright, [22] looking toward their Lord.[3034] [23] While other faces on that Day, will be gloomy with despair, [24] realizing that a backbreaking blow has befallen them. [25]

But when the last breath has reached the throat [26] and It is said, "Who will heal him now?" [27] And he realizes that it is parting time, [28] when one leg is entwined with the other, [29] that Day the journey is to your Lord. [30] He neither believed, nor prayed, [31] but he denied (the truth) and turned away. [32] Then he went to his people, full of himself and false pride. [33]

Your demise is getting closer to you and closer, [34] yet closer and closer still. [35] Does a person think that he (was created) to be forgotten? [36] Was he not a drop of ejaculated semen? [37] Then he became a clot. And (God) created and proportioned,[3035] [38] and made of him the two sexes, the male and the female. [39] Is not that (Creator) able to bring the dead to life?[3036] [40]

• • •

[3033] Isaiah 47:8 Now therefore hear this, you lover of pleasures, who sit securely, who say in your heart, "I am, and there is no one besides me; Isaiah 47:10-11 You felt secure in your wickedness; you said, "No one sees me." Your wisdom and your knowledge led you astray, and you said in your heart, "I am, and there is no one besides me. "But evil shall come upon you, which you cannot charm away; disaster shall fall upon you, which you will not be able to ward off; and ruin shall come on you suddenly, of which you know nothing."

[3034] 2 Corinthians 3:18, And all of us, with unveiled faces, seeing the glory of the Lord as though reflected in a mirror, are being transformed into the same image from one degree of glory to another; for this comes from the Lord, the Spirit.

[3035] Psalm 139:13-14 For it was you who formed my inward parts; you knit me together in my mother's womb. 14 I praise you, for I am fearfully and wonderfully made. Wonderful are your works; that I know very well.

[3036] Hebrews 11:19 He considered the fact that God is able even to raise someone from the dead—and figuratively speaking, he did receive him back.

CHAPTER SEVENTY SIX

AL-INSAN

HUMAN BEING

THE **MECCA** PERIOD

In the name of God, the Merciful-to-all, the Mercy Giver:

Has there come upon the human being a span of time when he was nothing to be mentioned? [01] We created the human being from a drop of mingled fluid to test him; and We gave him hearing and sight. [02] Then We guided him to the right path, whether he is grateful or not.[3039] [03] We have prepared chains, shackles and a Searing Fire for the unbelievers. [04] But the righteous will drink from a cup whose mixture is Kafour, [05] a spring from which God's worshipers shall drink, making it gush abundantly at will. [06] They are the ones who fulfill their vows and fear a Day whose evil will be widespread. [07] They feed the needy, the orphan, and the prisoner, for the love of Him.[3040] [08] (Saying), "We feed you for the sake of God. We want neither compensation, nor gratitude from you. [09] We simply dread an austere and stressful Day promised by our Lord." [10] So God will spare them the evil of that Day[3041] and will give them radiance and joy. [11] and will reward them for what they patiently endured with a Garden and silk, [12] reclining there on couches. They will not experience there either burning sun or bitter cold. [13] Shade covers them, and its fruit hanging close ready to be picked. [14] Circulated among them are vessels of silver, and cups of pure crystal [15] clear glasses made from silver according to their own measure. [16] They will be given a drink mixed with ginger [17] from a spring there named Salsabeel. [18] Passing among them are immortal youths. If you see them, you would think they were like sprinkled pearls. [19] If you were to look around, you would see a heavenly and vast kingdom. [20] They will wear green garments of fine silk and brocade. And they will be adorned with silver bracelets. Their

• • •

[3039] Matthew 5:45 He causes his sun to rise on the evil and the good, and sends rain on the righteous and the unrighteous.

[3040] James 1:27 Religion that is pure and undefiled before God, the Father, is this: to care for orphans and widows in their distress, and to keep oneself unstained by the world.

[3041] Deuteronomy 7:9 Know therefore that the Lord your God is God, the faithful God who maintains covenant loyalty with those who love him and keep his commandments, to a thousand generations,

Lord will give them a purified drink. (21) "This is a reward for you. Your efforts are well appreciated." (22)

It is We who have sent down the Qur'an to you in gradual revelations. (23) So await your Lord's Judgment with patience;[3042] and do not obey a sinner or a denier of the truth from among them. (24) Remember to call on the name of your Lord morning and evening (25) And during the night bow down to Him and exalt His limitless glory long into the night.[3043] (26)

These people love the present life, and leave behind a Heavy Day. (27) We have created them, and strengthened their frame; and if We wish, We can replace them with others like them. (28)

This is a reminder. Let whoever wills, take a path to his Lord. (29) Yet you cannot will, unless God wills. God is Knowing[3044] and Wise.[3045] (30) He admits whom He wills into His mercy. But He has prepared a painful punishment[3046] for the unjust. (31)

. . .

[3042] Lamentations 3:25-26 The Lord is good to those who wait for him, to the soul that seeks him 26 It is good that one should wait quietly for the salvation of the Lord.
[3043] Psalm 119:62,160 At midnight I rise to praise you, because of your righteous ordinances. 160 The sum of your word is truth; and every one of your righteous ordinances endures for ever.
[3044] 1 John 3:20 whenever our hearts condemn us; for God is greater than our hearts, and he knows everything.
[3045] Job 9:4, He is wise in heart, and mighty in strength —who has resisted him, and succeeded?
[3046] Matthew 25:41, Then he will say to those at his left hand, "You that are accursed, depart from me into the eternal fire prepared for the devil and his angels; And these will go away into eternal punishment, but the righteous into eternal life."

CHAPTER SEVENTY SEVEN

AL-MURSALAT

THOSE SENT FORTH

THE **MECCA** PERIOD

In the name of God, the Merciful-to-all, the Mercy Giver:

By those (winds)[3045] and those violently storming, (02) consider these (messages) that spread (the Truth) far and wide, (03) thus separating (right and wrong) with all clarity, (04) and then delivering a reminder, (05) (promising) freedom from blame or (offering) a warning, (06) what you are promised will surely happen. (07) So when the stars are extinguished, (08) the heaven is split open, (09) the mountains are blown away,[3046] (10) And when the messengers are called together to an appointed time, (11) for what Day was it postponed? (12) For the Day of Decision. (13) And what do you know about the Day of Decision? (14) How horrible is that Day for those who deny the truth. (15) Did We not destroy the earlier people? (16) And We shall make the latter follow them. (17) This is how We deal with those who forced others to reject Our messages (18) How horrible is that Day for those who reject the truth. (19)

Did We not create you from an insignificant liquid?[3047] (20) Then lodged it in a secure place,[3048] (21) And when the messengers are called together to an appointed time, (22) for what Day was it postponed? (23) For the Day of Decision. (13) And what do you know about the Day of Decision? (24) How horrible is that Day for those who deny the truth. (25) Did We not destroy the earlier people? (26) And We shall make the latter follow them. (27) This is how We deal with those

• • •

[3045] Psalm 104:4 you make the winds your messengers, fire and flame your ministers
[3046] Isaiah 54:10 For the mountains may depart and the hills be removed, but my steadfast love shall not depart from you, and my covenant of peace shall not be removed, says the Lord, who has compassion on you.
[3047] i.e. semen
[3048] i.e. the womb. Psalm 139:13-14 For it was you who formed my inward parts; you knit me together in my mother's womb. [12] I praise you, for I am fearfully and wonderfully made. Wonderful are your works; that I know very well.

who forced others to reject Our messages [(28)] How horrible is that Day for those who reject the truth. [(29)]

"Proceed to what you used to deny. [(30)] "Proceed to a shadow with three columns, [(31)] that has no shade and will not prevent you from the flame." [(32)] It shoots sparks (as huge) as a fortress, [(33)] like giant fiery ropes. [(34)] How terrible is that Day for those who deny the truth. [(35)] On that Day they will be speechless, [(36)] and they not be given permission to offer any excuses. [(37)] How terrible is that Day for those who deny the truth. [(38)] This is the Day of Decision; We will have gathered you together with the earlier people.[3049] [(39)] So if you have a ploy, then use it against my plan now. [(40)] How terrible is that Day for those who deny the truth. [(41)] The God-conscious will be amidst shades and springs, [(42)] and any fruits they desire, [(43)] "Eat and drink and enjoy it as a reward for your deeds."[3050] [(44)] This is how We reward those who do good. [(45)] How terrible is that Day for those who deny the truth. [(46)]

You are but dissenters. So eat and enjoy yourselves a little (while you can).[3051] [(47)] How terrible is that Day for those who deny the truth. [(48)] And when It is said to them, "Bow down (in prayer)," they do not bow. [(49)] How terrible is that Day for those who denied the truth. [(50)] In what message beyond this will they believe?[3052] [(51)]

. . .

[3049] Matthew 25:32 All the nations will be gathered before him, and he will separate people one from another as a shepherd separates the sheep from the goats,

[3050] Matthew 25:34 Then the king will say to those at his right hand, "Come, you that are blessed by my Father, inherit the kingdom prepared for you from the foundation of the world;

[3051] Luke 12:19 And I will say to my soul, Soul, you have ample goods laid up for many years; relax, eat, drink, be merry."

[3052] Luke 16:30-31 He said, "No, father Abraham; but if someone goes to them from the dead, they will repent." [31] He said to him, "If they do not listen to Moses and the prophets, neither will they be convinced even if someone rises from the dead."'

CHAPTER SEVENTY EIGHT

AN-NABA'

THE ANNOUNCEMENT

THE **MECCA** PERIOD

In the name of God, the Merciful-to-all, the Mercy Giver:

What are they wondering about? [01] About the huge announcement [02] over which they are in disagreement. [03] They will know. [04] For sure they will know. [05] Have We not made the earth a cradle? [06] And the mountains as pegs? [07] And We created you in pairs? [3055] [08] And made your sleep to rest? [3056] [09] And made the night a cover? [3057] [10] And made the day for livelihood? [11] And constructed above you seven strong (heavens)? [12] And made (the sun) a glowing lamp? [13] And sent down from the clouds pouring water [14] to produce with it grain, vegetation [15] and luxuriant gardens? [16] The Day of Decision has been appointed. [17] The Day the Horn is blown[3058] and you will come forth in droves. [3059] [18] And the heaven are opened and becomes gateways. [19] And the mountains are set in motion[3060] and will become a mirage. [20] Hell has been lying in wait, [21] to be a home for the oppressors, [22] to stay in for a long, long time, [3061] [23] They will not taste any coolness there or drink, [24] except for boiling water and sizzling pus. [25] An appropriate reward. [26] They were not expecting to be held accountable. [27] And utterly rejected Our verses. [28] We have recorded

. . .

[3055] Genesis 1:27 So God created humankind in his image, in the image of God he created them; male and female he created them.

[3056] Psalm 127:2 It is in vain that you rise up early and go late to rest, eating the bread of anxious toil; for he gives sleep to his beloved.

[3057] Psalm 104:23 People go out to their work and to their labor until the evening.

[3058] Revelation 11:15 Then the seventh angel blew his trumpet, and there were loud voices in heaven, saying, 'The kingdom of the world has become the kingdom of our Lord and of his Messiah, and he will reign for ever and ever.'

[3059] Matthew 25:32 All the nations will be gathered before him, and he will separate people one from another as a shepherd separates the sheep from the goats,

[3060] Revelation 16:20 And every island fled away, and no mountains were to be found;

[3061] Matthew 25:46 And these will go away into eternal punishment, but the righteous into eternal life.

everything in writing.[3062] (29) "So feel it, We will only increase your punishment."[3063] (30)

For those who were mindful of God there is a great achievement, (31) gardens and grapevines, (32) splendid, well matched spouses, (33) and a full cup. (34) There, they will hear no gossip or lies. (35) A reward from your Lord, a fitting gift, (36) The Lord of the heavens and the earth and everything between them,[3064] the Merciful-to-all.[3065]

They will have no authority from Him to speak. (37) On the Day when the Spirit and the angels will stand in rows.[3066] They will not speak except for those to whom the Merciful gives permission, and he will say what is right. (38) That is the True Day; so whoever wills, may take now a way back to his Lord. (39) We have warned you of an eminent punishment on the Day when a person will see what he has done, and the unbeliever will say, "I wish that I were dust!" (40)

• • •

[3062] Revelation 20:12 And I saw the dead, great and small, standing before the throne, and books were opened. Also another book was opened, the book of life. And the dead were judged according to their works, as recorded in the books.

[3063] Matthew 25:41,46 Then he will say to those at his left hand, "You that are accursed, depart from me into the eternal fire prepared for the devil and his angels; [46] And these will go away into eternal punishment, but the righteous into eternal life.'

[3064] Psalm 89:11 The heavens are yours, the earth also is yours; the world and all that is in it—you have founded them.

[3065] Psalm 116:5, Gracious is the Lord, and righteous; our God is merciful.

[3066] Revelation 5:11 Then I looked, and I heard the voice of many angels surrounding the throne and the living creatures and the elders; they numbered myriads of myriads and thousands of thousands,

CHAPTER SEVENTY NINE

AN-NAZI'AT

THE FORCEFUL CHARGERS

THE **MECCA** PERIOD

In the name of God, the Merciful-to-all, the Mercy Giver:

By those (stars) who rise only to sit. [01] And move (in their orbits) steadily. [02] And float (through space) smoothly. [03] And yet some overtake (others) swiftly. [04] Thus they fulfill the (Creator's) purpose. [05] On the Day when the world shudders.[3067] [06] followed by a tremor. [07] Hearts, that Day, will shiver, [08] and eyes are humbled.[3068] [09] They say, "Are we to be restored to the original condition? [10] After we have turned into decayed bones?"[3069] [11] They say, "This will be a losing come back." [12] But all it will take is a single blast, [13] and they will be awake and above ground. [14]

Has there the story of Moses (Musa) reached you? [15] When his Lord called out to him in the sacred valley of Tuwa, [16] "Go to Pharaoh.[3070] For he has transgressed. [17] and ask him, "Would you be willing to purify yourself? [18] And I will guide you to your Lord so you would be in awe of Him. [19] And he showed him the greatest sign,[3071] [20] but Pharaoh rejected the offer and disobeyed.[3072] [21] Then he hastily turned away, [22] and gathered (his people) and proclaimed, [23] "I am your lord, the most high." [24] So God seized him with punishment[3073] as

• • •

[3067] Joel 2:1 Blow the trumpet in Zion; sound the alarm on my holy mountain! Let all the inhabitants of the land tremble, for the day of the Lord is coming, it is near.

[3068] Isaiah 2:17 The haughtiness of people shall be humbled, and the pride of everyone shall be brought low; and the Lord alone will be exalted on that day.

[3069] Ezekiel 37:3 He said to me, "Mortal, can these bones live?" I answered, "O Lord God, you know."

[3070] Exodus 3:10 So come, I will send you to Pharaoh to bring my people, the Israelites, out of Egypt."

[3071] The complete story of Moses and Pharaoh is detailed in Exodus 7-12

[3072] Exodus 14:5 When the king of Egypt was told that the people had fled, the minds of Pharaoh and his officials were changed toward the people, and they said, "What have we done, letting Israel leave our service?"

[3073] Exodus 14:26-28 Then the Lord said to Moses, "Stretch out your hand over the sea, so that the water may come back upon the Egyptians, upon their chariots and chariot drivers." 27 So Moses stretched out his hand over the sea, and at dawn the sea returned to its normal depth. As the Egyptians fled before it, the Lord tossed the Egyptians into the sea. 28 The waters returned and covered the chariots and the chariot drivers, the entire army of Pharaoh that had followed them into the sea; not one of them remained.

an example, in the life to come as well as in this life: [25] In this, there is a warning for whomever would fear (God). [26]

Are you more difficult to create or is the heaven that He built?[3074] [27] He raised it high and proportioned it. [28] He darkened its night and brought out its morning light.[3075] [29] After that He spread out the earth,[3076] [30] From it, He produced its water and its pasture,[3077] [31] And He set the mountains firmly in place [3078] [32] for you and for your animals to enjoy. [33] But when the Great Calamity arrives, [34] a Day when the human being will remember what he has done, [35] and Hell will be there for all to see, [36] for him who transgressed [37] and preferred the life of this world, [38] Hell will be his home. [39] But as for him who feared to stand one day in front of his Lord and therefore restrained himself from following his whims and desires, [40] then Heaven will be home. [41]

They ask you about the Hour, "when will it take place?" [42] How can you possibly know that? [43] Its time is only known to your Lord. [44] You are only to warn those who dread it. [45] On the Day they see it, it will seem as though they only stayed an evening or a morning. [46]

• • •

[3074] Genesis 1:7-8 So God made the dome and separated the waters that were under the dome from the waters that were above the dome. And it was so. [8] God called the dome Sky. And there was evening and there was morning, the second day.

[3075] Genesis 1:4-5 And God saw that the light was good; and God separated the light from the darkness. [5] God called the light Day, and the darkness he called Night. And there was evening and there was morning, the first day.

[3076] Isaiah 37:16 "O Lord of hosts, God of Israel, who are enthroned above the cherubim, you are God, you alone, of all the kingdoms of the earth; you have made heaven and earth.

[3077] Isaiah 30:23 He will give rain for the seed with which you sow the ground, and grain, the produce of the ground, which will be rich and plenteous. On that day your cattle will graze in broad pastures;

[3078] Psalm 65:6 By your strength you established the mountains; you are girded with might.

CHAPTER EIGHTY

ABASA

HE FROWNED

THE **MECCA** PERIOD

In the name of God, the Merciful-to-all, the Mercy Giver:

He frowned and turned away [01] when the blind man approached him. [02] For all you know, he might be seeking to purify himself? [03] or to be reminded and be helped by being reminded? [04] As for him who was indifferent, [05] you (Prophet) gave him your attention. [06] Though it is not up to you whether or not he is purified. [07] As for him who came to you eagerly [08] with God's fear in his heart [09] from him you are distracted. [10] Indeed this is a reminder; [11] So, whoever wills may remember it. [12] it is (written) on honored sheets, [13] Exalted and purified, [14] by the hands of scribes, [15] honorable and virtuous. [16]

How regretful it is for human beings to have so much self-destructive ingratitude. [17] From what did He create him? [18] From a sperm-drop He created him and proportioned him; [19] Then He eased the way for him; [20] Then He causes him to die and to be buried. [21] Then when He wills, He will resurrect him. [22] No! He did not fulfill what He has commanded him. [23] A human being has only to consider the food he eats. [24] We poured down water in abundance, [25] and caused the soil to break open, [26] and grew grains in it, [27] and grapes and legumes [28] olive and dates, [29] and luxurious gardens [30] and fruits and vegetable, [31] for you and your livestock to enjoy. [32]

But when the Deafening Blast comes, [33] on the Day when a human being will flee from his brother, [34] his mother, his father, [35] his wife and his children, [36] every one of them, on that Day, will have enough to preoccupy him. [37] Faces on that Day will be beaming, [38] laughing and rejoicing. [39] And (other) faces, on that Day, will be covered with dust, [40] overwhelmed by sorrow. [41] These are the unbelievers, the wicked ones. [42]

CHAPTER EIGHTY ONE

AT-TAKWEER
THE FOLDING

In the name of God, the Merciful-to-all, the Mercy Giver:

When the sun folds[3079] [(01)] And the planets are dispersed,[3080] [(02)] when the mountains are shifting[3081] [(03)] And when full-term she-camels are neglected [(04)] And when the wild beasts are gathered, [(05)] when the seas are set aflame[3082] [(06)] when the souls are paired [(07)] when the female baby who was buried alive is asked,[(08)] 'For what sin she was killed?' [(09)] When the records are made public[3083] [(10)] when the sky is stripped away[3084] [(11)] when Hell is set ablaze[3085] [(12)] when Paradise is brought into view, [(13)] every soul will then know what it has brought with it.[3086] [(14)]

I swear by the planets, [(15)] the runners and sweepers, [(16)] and by the night as it recedes [(17)] and the dawn when it breathes, [(18)] this revelation is indeed the word of an honorable Messenger, [(19)] endowed with strength, secure with the Lord of the Throne, [(20)] obeyed and trustworthy. [(21)] This fellow of yours is not

• • •

[3079] This might be referring to the period when the Red Giant start folding to become a Red Dwarf. See life cycles of stars
http://www.bbc.co.uk/schools/gcsebitesize/science/add_aqa/stars/lifecyclestarsrev2.shtml.
[3080] Matthew 24:29 "Immediately after the suffering of those days the sun will be darkened, and the moon will not give its light; the stars will fall from heaven, and the powers of heaven will be shaken."
[3081] Revelation 16:20 And every island fled away, and no mountains were to be found;
[3082] Luke 21:25 "There will be signs in the sun, the moon, and the stars, and on the earth distress among nations confused by the roaring of the sea and the waves."
[3083] Revelation 20:12 And I saw the dead, great and small, standing before the throne, and books were opened. Also another book was opened, the book of life. And the dead were judged according to their works, as recorded in the books.
[3084] Hebrews 1:12 "like a cloak you will roll them up, and like clothing they will be changed. But you are the same, and your years will never end."
[3085] Revelation 21:8 "But as for the cowardly, the faithless, the polluted, the murderers, the fornicators, the sorcerers, the idolaters, and all liars, their place will be in the lake that burns with fire and sulfur, which is the second death."
[3086] Luke 14:14 "And you will be blessed, because they cannot repay you, for you will be repaid at the resurrection of the righteous."

mad, [22] he has already seen him (Gabriel) in the clear horizon. [23] He does not withhold what is revealed to him from beyond. [24] And it (the Qur'an) is not the word of a devil, expelled from Heaven. [25]

So where, then, will you go? [26] It is only a reminder to all human beings [27] For whoever wills among you to go straight. [28] But you cannot will, unless God, the Lord of the worlds, so wills. [29]

CHAPTER EIGHTY TWO

AL-INFITAR
TORN APART

THE **MECCA** PERIOD

In the name of God, the Merciful-to-all, the Mercy Giver:

When the heavens are torn apart, [01] when the planets are sprinkled, [02] when the oceans are exploded, [03] when the graves are scattered,[3087] [04] each soul will then know what it has sent ahead and what it left behind. [05] People, what has lured you away from your Lord, the Most Generous, [06] Who created you, formed you,[3088] and proportioned you? [07] In whatever shape He willed, He assembled you.[3089] [08] Yet you still deny the Judgment. [09] When guardians are standing over you, [10] honorable recorders; [11] They know everything you do. [12] Indeed, the truly good will be in bliss, [13] while the wicked will be in Hell. [14] They will roast in it on the Day of Judgment, [15] and will never get away from it. [16] And how would you know what is the Day of Judgment? [17] Truly, how would you know what is the Day of Judgment? [18] It is the Day when no soul will be able to do anything for another soul; and the decision on that Day is God's alone. [19]

• • •

[3087] Matthew 27:52 The tombs also were opened, and many bodies of the saints who had fallen asleep were raised.

[3088] Genesis 2:7 then the Lord God formed man from the dust of the ground, and breathed into his nostrils the breath of life; and the man became a living being.

[3089] Psalm 139:13 For it was you who formed my inward parts; you knit me together in my mother's womb.

CHAPTER EIGHTY THREE

AL-MUTAFFIFEEN
THE CHEATERS

THE **MECCA** PERIOD

In the name of God, the Merciful-to-all, the Mercy Giver:
How terrible it is to those who give short measures, $^{(01)}$ who, when they take a measure from people, take in full. $^{(02)}$ But when they measure or weigh for others, they cheat. $^{(03)}$ Don't such people realize that they will be resurrected $^{(04)}$ for a grievous Day, $^{(05)}$ the Day when human beings will stand before the Lord of the worlds? $^{(06)}$ Indeed, the record of the wicked is in *Sijjeen*. $^{(07)}$ And how would you know what *Sijjeen* is? $^{(08)}$ It is a locked-in digital data^{3090} record. $^{(09)}$ How terrible it is that Day for the deniers, $^{(10)}$ who deny the Day of Judgment, $^{(11)}$ when only sinful aggressors deny it. $^{(12)}$ When Our verses are recited to him, he says, "Legends of ancient people." $^{(13)}$ Not at all! Rather, their hearts have become encrusted by what they were earning. $^{(14)}$ They will be separated from their Lord, that Day. $^{(15)}$ Then, they will be rekindling Hell. $^{(16)}$ They will be then told, "This is what you used to deny." $^{(17)}$

No indeed! The righteous' record is in *'Illiyyun*. $^{(18)}$ And how would you know what is *Illiyyun*? $^{(19)}$ It is a digital data record, $^{(20)}$ open to be witnessed by those brought near (to God). $^{(21)}$ Indeed, the righteous will be in perfect bliss $^{(22)}$ seated on couches, looking around. $^{(23)}$ You will recognize the radiance of bliss on their faces. $^{(24)}$ They will be given pure virgin nectar to drink $^{(25)}$ leaving a great taste in the mouth. Let people with aspirations, aspire to that. $^{(26)}$ It is mixed with the water from Tasneem, $^{(27)}$ a spring from which those near (to God) drink. $^{(28)}$ Those who rejected the faith and severed their relation with God used to laugh at those who believed. $^{(29)}$ They would wink at one another when the believers passed by them, $^{(30)}$ joking about them when they returned to their people. $^{(31)}$ And if they saw them, they would say, "Indeed, those are truly lost." $^{(32)}$ Yet, they were not sent as guardians over them. $^{(33)}$ So today those who believed will laugh at the unbelievers, $^{(34)}$ while seated on luxurious furnishings, looking around. $^{(35)}$ Have the unbelievers been rewarded for their deeds? $^{(36)}$

• • •

---

^{3090} Data here is not like our digital data but it is a form of God's digital data.

CHAPTER EIGHTY FOUR

AL-INSHIQAQ
THE RUPTURE

In the name of God, the Merciful-to-all, the Mercy Giver:
When the sky is ruptured, [01] obeying its Lord, as it is bound to do. [02] When the earth is leveled out [03] and has cast out what is in it, and becomes empty, [04] obeying its Lord as it is bound to do, [05] People, you are laboring toward your Lord[3091] and you will meet Him. [06] Then, as for him who is given his record in his right hand, [07] he will have an easy settlement, [08] and will return to his family delighted. [09] But, as for him who is given his record behind his back, [10] he will cry out for destruction, [11] and will rekindle the Blaze. [12] He used to be happy among his family. [13] He thought he would never return (to His Lord). [14] Yes he will! His Lord was always watching him. [15] So I swear by the twilight glow, [16] and the night and all it gathers, [17] and the moon when it is full, [18] you will move onward from stage to stage. [19]

So what is the matter with them that they do not believe, [20] and when the Qur'an is recited to them, they do not bow down (to God)? [21] But the unbelievers say it is lies, [22] but God knows best what they comprehend. [23] So give them the news of a painful punishment,[3092] [24] except for those who believe and do good deeds. They will have a never ending reward. [25]

．　．　．

[3091] 1 Corinthians 15:58 Therefore, my beloved, be steadfast, immovable, always excelling in the work of the Lord, because you know that in the Lord your labor is not in vain.
[3092] Jeremiah 10:15 They are worthless, a work of delusion; at the time of their punishment they shall perish.

CHAPTER EIGHTY FIVE

AL-BURUJ
THE TOWERING CONSTELLATIONS

In the name of God, the Merciful-to-all, the Mercy Giver:

By the heavens full of great constellations, (01) by the promised Day, (02) and by the witness and the witnessed, (03) how terrible were the people of the trench (04) (using) fire supplied with fuel, (05) while they sat around it, (06) to watch what they were doing to the believers. (07) The only reason they punish them was because they believed in God, the Almighty,³⁰⁹³ the Praiseworthy,³⁰⁹⁴ (08) to whom belongs the Kingdom of the heavens and the earth.³⁰⁹⁵ God, is Witness over all things. (09)

Those who persecute believing men and women, and have not repented³⁰⁹⁶ afterwards, will have the punishment of Hell, and they will have the punishment of Burning. (10) Indeed, those who believe and do good deeds will have Gardens with rivers flowing³⁰⁹⁷ through them. That is the great victory. (11) Your Lord's punishment is truly severe. (12) It is He who begins (creation) and repeats it. (13) He alone is Truly-Forgiving,³⁰⁹⁸ All-Embracing in His love. (14) The Glorious Lord of the Throne of His majesty, (15) Doer of whatever He wills.³⁰⁹⁹ (16)

· · ·

---

³⁰⁹³ Psalm 24:8 Who is the King of glory? The Lord, strong and mighty, the Lord, mighty in battle.
³⁰⁹⁴ 2 Samuel 22:4 I call upon the Lord, who is worthy to be praised, and I am saved from my enemies
³⁰⁹⁵ Psalm 89:11, The heavens are yours, the earth also is yours; the world and all that is in it—you have founded them.
³⁰⁹⁶ Psalm 7:12-13 If one does not repent, God will whet his sword; he has bent and strung his bow; ¹³ he has prepared his deadly weapons, making his arrows fiery shafts.
³⁰⁹⁷ Revelation 22:1-2 Then the angel showed me the river of the water of life, bright as crystal, flowing from the throne of God and of the Lamb through the middle of the street of the city. ² On either side of the river is the tree of life with its twelve kinds of fruit, producing its fruit each month; and the leaves of the tree are for the healing of the nations.
³⁰⁹⁸ 1 John 1:9 If we confess our sins, he who is faithful and just will forgive us our sins and cleanse us from all unrighteousness.
³⁰⁹⁹ Psalm 135:6 Whatever the Lord pleases he does, in heaven and on earth, in the seas and all deeps.

Has the story of the legions reached you [17] (those of) Pharaoh[3100] and Thamud?[3101] [18] Yet those who deny the truth are persistent in denial, [19] while God will encircle them from behind.[3102] [20]

This is indeed a Glorious Qur'an [21] in a Preserved Tablet.[3103] [22]

. . .

[3100] The story of Moses and Pharaoh is detailed in Exodus 6-14

[3101] See Glossary

[3102] Psalm 89:31-32 if they violate my statutes and do not keep my commandments, [32] then I will punish their transgression with the rod and their iniquity with scourges;

[3103] Name of a place where God keeps the original Qur'anic text in Heaven.

CHAPTER EIGHTY SIX

AT-TARIQ

THE KNOCKING STAR

THE **MECCA** PERIOD

In the name of God, the Merciful-to-all, the Mercy Giver:

By the sky and the knocking star, [01] what do you know about the knocking star?[3104] [02] It is the Piercing Star, [03] there is no soul without a protector over it.[04]

So let the human being consider what he was created from. [05] He was created from ejected fluid, [06] emerging from the vicinity of the backbone and the ribs.[3105] [07] Indeed, God is able to bring him (the human being) back to life. [08] On a Day when secrets are disclosed, [09] a human being will have no power or anyone to help him. [10]

By the sky and its cyclical system [11] and the earth which cracks open, [12] indeed, this is a decisive statement, [13] not to be taken lightly. [14] They plot and scheme, [15] but I am planning too. [16] So bear with the unbelievers. Let them be for a while. [17]

. . .

[3104] A Pulsating star. Listen to a pulsating star
http://www.parkes.atnf.csiro.au/people/sar049/eternal_life/supernova/pulsars.html
[3105] Psalm 139:13, For it was you who formed my inward parts; you knit me together in my mother's womb.

CHAPTER **EIGHTY SEVEN**

AL-A'LA
THE MOST HIGH

THE **MECCA** PERIOD

In the name of God, the Merciful-to-all, the Mercy Giver:
Praise the limitless glory of your Lord's name, the Most High, [01] Who created and proportioned, [02] Who destined and (then) guided. [03] He who brought out the green pasture [04] and then made it black stubble. [05] We will make you recite, and you will not forget, [06] except what God wills. He knows what is open to one's perception and what is hidden. [07] And We will ease you toward the easy way. [08] So, remind, if reminding helps. [09] He who fears God will remember. [10] But the most wicked will ignore it. [11] He will kindle the greatest fire, [12] where he will remain, neither dying nor living. [13] Successful is he who purifies himself,[3106] [14] and remembers to call on his Lord and pray. [15] But you prefer this worldly life, [16] whereas the Hereafter is better and more enduring.[3107] [17] All this is can be found in the earlier Scriptures, [18] the Scriptures of Abraham and Moses. [19]

• • •

[3106] Joshua 1:8 This book of the law shall not depart out of your mouth; you shall meditate on it day and night, so that you may be careful to act in accordance with all that is written in it. For then you shall make your way prosperous, and then you shall be successful.
[3107] 1 John 2:15-17 Do not love the world or the things in the world. The love of the Father is not in those who love the world; [16] for all that is in the world—the desire of the flesh, the desire of the eyes, the pride in riches—comes not from the Father but from the world. [17] And the world and its desire are passing away, but those who do the will of God live forever.

438

CHAPTER EIGHTY EIGHT

AL-GHASHIYAH
THE OVERWHELMING EVENT

THE **MECCA** PERIOD

In the name of God, the Merciful-to-all, the Mercy Giver:
Have you heard about the Overwhelming Event? [01] Some faces, that Day, will be humbled, [02] working hard and exhausted. [03] They will kindle an intensely hot Fire [04] and will be given drinks from a boiling spring. [05] They will have no food except from a thorny plant, [06] that neither nourishes nor satisfies hunger. [07] Other faces, that day, will be peaceful. [08] Well pleased with their endeavor,[3108] [09] in an elevated Garden, [10] where they will hear no idle talk. [11] A flowing spring runs through it. [12] Raised couches are placed there, [13] cups put in place [14] cushions lined up [15] and carpets spread around. [16] Don't they look at how the camels are created,[3109] [17] at how the sky is raised[3110] [18] And at how the mountains are erected[3111] [19] And at how the earth is spread out?[3112] [20] So remind them, you are but a reminder. [21] You are not in control of them. [22] But whoever turns away and rejects the truth, [23] God will inflict him with the greatest punishment.[3113] [24] To Us is their return.[3114] [25] Then it is for Us to call them to account.[3115] [26]

• • •

[3108] Ephesians 6:8 knowing that whatever good we do, we will receive the same again from the Lord, whether we are slaves or free.
[3109] Genesis 1:24-25 And God said, "Let the earth bring forth living creatures of every kind: cattle and creeping things and wild animals of the earth of every kind." And it was so. 25 God made the wild animals of the earth of every kind, and the cattle of every kind, and everything that creeps upon the ground of every kind. And God saw that it was good.
[3110] Isaiah 40:22, It is he who sits above the circle of the earth, and its inhabitants are like grasshoppers; who stretches out the heavens like a curtain, and spreads them like a tent to live in;
[3111] Psalm 65:6 By your strength you established the mountains; you are girded with might.
[3112] Psalm 136:6 who spread out the earth on the waters, for his steadfast love endures forever;
[3113] Isaiah 10:3 What will you do on the day of punishment, in the calamity that will come from far away? To whom will you flee for help, and where will you leave your wealth,
[3114] Ecclesiastes 12:7 and the dust returns to the earth as it was, and the breath returns to God who gave it.
[3115] Hebrews 9:27 And just as it is appointed for mortals to die once, and after that the judgment,

439

CHAPTER **EIGHTY NINE**

AL-FAJR
DAYBREAK

THE **MECCA** PERIOD

In the name of God, the Merciful-to-all, the Mercy Giver:
By the daybreak $^{(01)}$ and by ten nights $^{(02)}$ by the even and the odd $^{(03)}$ and by the night as it recedes, $^{(04)}$ is there not in (all) that an oath for a rational person? $^{(05)}$ Have you not considered how your Lord dealt with Aad,$^{3116(06)}$ With Iram of the pillars, $^{(07)}$ whose like was never created in any land, $^{(08)}$ with Thamud,^{3117} those who carved the rocks in the valley $^{(09)}$ And with Pharaoh, of the stakes? $^{3118 (10)}$ All of them committed excesses in the lands, $^{(11)}$ and spread much corruption there. $^{(12)}$ So your Lord poured on them a scourge of punishment. $^{(13)}$ Your Lord is always watchful. $^{(14)}$

As for human beings, whenever his Lord tests him, by honoring him, and blessing him, he says, "My Lord has honored me."$^{3119 (15)}$ But when He tries him, and restricts his provision for him, he says, "My Lord has humiliated me." $^{(16)}$ Not at all! It is you who are not generous with the orphans,,$^{3120 (17)}$ you who devour the inheritance (of others) with obvious greed, $^{(19)}$ and you who passionately love wealth.$^{3121 (20)}$ No indeed! When the earth is crushed, pounded and crushed $^{(21)}$

• • •

---

^{3116} See Glossary
^{3117} Ibid
^{3118} 'of the stakes' might be a term signifying power and prestige. "In classical Arabic, this ancient bedouin term is used idiomatically as a metonym for "mighty dominion" or "firmness of power" (Zamakhsharī).
^{3119} Deuteronomy 26:19 for him to set you high above all nations that he has made, in praise and in fame and in honor; and for you to be a people holy to the Lord your God, as he promised.
^{3120} James 1:27 Religion that is pure and undefiled before God, the Father, is this: to care for orphans and widows in their distress, and to keep oneself unstained by the world.
^{3121} Luke 16:10-13, 12:5 "Whoever is faithful in a very little is faithful also in much; and whoever is dishonest in a very little is dishonest also in much. ^{11} If then you have not been faithful with the dishonest wealth, who will entrust to you the true riches? ^{12} And if you have not been faithful with what belongs to another, who will give you what is your own? ^{13} No slave can serve two masters; for a slave will either hate the one and love the other, or be devoted to the one and despise the other. You cannot serve God and wealth." 12:15 And he said to them, "Take care! Be on your guard against all kinds of greed; for one's life does not consist in the abundance of possessions."

and your Lord comes with the angels, row after row,[3122] (22) on that Day, Hell will be brought near. On that Day, the human being will remember, but what good will that be to him then? (23) He will say, "I wish I had provided for this life to come." (24) On that Day, none will punish as He punishes. (25) And none will shackle as severely as He shackles. (26) (To the righteous it will be said), "Tranquil soul, (27) Return to your Lord,[3123] well-pleased and pleasing (to Him), (28) go in among My worshipers, (29) and into My Garden." (30)

• • •

[3122] Mark 13:27 Then he will send out the angels, and gather his elect from the four winds, from the ends of the earth to the ends of heaven.
[3123] Psalm 116:7 Return, O my soul, to your rest, for the Lord has dealt bountifully with you.

CHAPTER NINETY

AL-BALAD

THE TOWN

THE **MECCA** PERIOD

In the name of God, the Merciful-to-all, the Mercy Giver:
I swear by this town, [01] and you (Prophet) are free to dwell in this town, [02] And (I swear by) a father and his offspring, [03] We have created human being for a life of hardship. [04] Does he think that no one will have power over him? [05] "I have wasted much money," he says, [06] Does he think that no one sees him? [07] Have We not given him two eyes? [08] And a tongue and two lips [09] and have shown him the two ways (of good and evil)? [10] But he did not take the difficult path. [11] And how would you know what is the difficult path? [12] It is to free a slave, [13] or to feed on a day of hunger [14] an orphaned relative [15] or a needy person in distress. [16] Then (it is) to become one of those who believe and urge one another to endure and to urge each other to be compassionate. [17] Those are the people of righteousness. [18] But those who defy Our revelations are the people of despair. [19] With the fire closing in above them [20]

CHAPTER NINETY ONE

ASH-SHAMS

THE SUN

THE **MECCA** PERIOD

In the name of God, the Merciful-to-all, the Mercy Giver:

By the sun and its morning light, [01] and the moon as it follows it, [02] and the day when it reveals it, [03] and the night when it conceals it, [04] and the sky and He who built it, [05] and the earth and He who spread it, [06] and by the soul and He who proportioned it, [07] and inspired it (with knowledge to distinguish) its wickedness and its righteousness. [08] Successful is he who purifies it, [09] and failing is he who corrupts it. [10] In their overwhelming arrogance, the people of Thamud called the Messenger a liar, [11] and allowed their most wicked to lead them. [12] The Messenger of God said to them, "This is the she-camel of God, so let her drink." [13] But they called him a liar, and hamstrung her. So their Lord destroyed them for their crime, and leveled it.[3124] [14] He doesn't fear the consequence. [15]

. . .

[3124] Leveled their town

CHAPTER NINETY TWO

AL-LAYL

THE NIGHT

THE **MECCA** PERIOD

In the name of God, the Merciful-to-all, the Mercy Giver:

By the night as it conceals, [01] and the day when it reveals, [02] and He who created the male and the female, [03] your striving is indeed diverse. [04] As for he who gives and is mindful of God, [05] and believes in goodness, [3125] [06] We will smooth his way toward all that is easy. [07] But as for he who is stingy and considers himself self-sufficient, [3126] [08] and denies goodness, [09] We will ease him toward hardship. [3127] [10] His wealth will not help him the least when he falls. [3128][11]

Indeed, it is upon Us to guide you. [12] And indeed, to Us belong the last life and this first life [13] so, I have warned you of a Blazing Fire. [14] None will burn in it except the most wicked [15] who had rejected and turned away. [3129] [16] But the one who was most mindful of God will be spared, [17] who gives his wealth away to purify himself, [18] not as payment for received favors, [19] but only seeking the pleasure of his Lord, the Most High. [20] He will be well pleased. [21]

• • •

[3125] Psalm 27:13 I believe that I shall see the goodness of the Lord in the land of the living.

[3126] 1 Timothy 6:10 For the love of money is a root of all kinds of evil, and in their eagerness to be rich some have wandered away from the faith and pierced themselves with many pains.

[3127] Luke 16:24-26 He called out, 'Father Abraham, have mercy on me, and send Lazarus to dip the tip of his finger in water and cool my tongue; for I am in agony in these flames.' [25] But Abraham said, 'Child, remember that during your lifetime you received your good things, and Lazarus in like manner evil things; but now he is comforted here, and you are in agony. [26] Besides all this, between you and us a great chasm has been fixed, so that those who might want to pass from here to you cannot do so, and no one can cross from there to us.'

[3128] Psalm 49:6-8 those who trust in their wealth and boast of the abundance of their riches? [7] Truly, no ransom avails for one's life, there is no price one can give to God for it. [8] For the ransom of life is costly, and can never suffice,

[3129] Revelation 21:8 But as for the cowardly, the faithless, the polluted, the murderers, the fornicators, the sorcerers, the idolaters, and all liars, their place will be in the lake that burns with fire and sulfur, which is the second death."

CHAPTER NINETY THREE

AD-DUHA
THE MORNING LIGHT

THE **MECCA** PERIOD

In the name of God, the Merciful-to-all, the Mercy Giver:

By the morning light [01] and the night as it settles, [02] your Lord did not abandon you, nor is He displeased. [03] The life to come is better for you than this first life. [04] And your Lord is sure to give you (so much), and you will be satisfied. [05] Did He not find you orphaned, and shelter you? [06] Did He not find you lost and guide you? [07] Did He not find you impoverished and enrich you? [08]

So do not mistreat the orphan, [09] and do not snub the one who asks for help;[3130] [10] Instead proclaim the blessings of your Lord. [11]

• • •

[3130] Matthew 5:42 Give to everyone who begs from you, and do not refuse anyone who wants to borrow from you.

CHAPTER NINETY FOUR

ASH-SHARH

THE RELIEF

THE **MECCA** PERIOD

In the name of God, the Merciful-to-all, the Mercy Giver:
Did We not relieve the tightness in your chest [01] and lift your burden, [02] that weighed heavily on your back [03] and raised high your reputation? [04] For truly, with hardship comes ease. [05] Indeed, with hardship comes ease. [06] So, when you are done, get ready for serious devotion, [07] and focus all your attention on your Lord. [3131] [08]

• • •

[3131] Psalm 63:1-2 O God, you are my God, I seek you, my soul thirsts for you; my flesh faints for you, as in a dry and weary land where there is no water. [2] So I have looked upon you in the sanctuary, beholding your power and glory.

CHAPTER **NINETY FIVE**

AT-TEEN

THE FIG

THE **MECCA** PERIOD

In the Name of God, the Merciful-to-all, the Mercy Giver:

By the fig and the olive [01] and (by) Mount Sinai [02] and (by) this secure city (Mecca), [03] We have certainly created the human being in the best of stature; [04] Then We return him to the lowest of the low, [05] except for those who believe and do righteous deeds, for they will have an uninterrupted reward. [06] So, do you still deny this faith? [07] Isn't God the most Just of Judges? [08]

CHAPTER NINETY SIX

AL-'ALAQL
THE CLOT

THE **MECCA** PERIOD

In the name of God, the Merciful-to-all, the Mercy Giver:

Recite in the name of your Lord who created, [01] created the human being from a clinging substance. [02] Recite, and your Lord is the most generous, [03] Who taught by the pen. [04] He taught the human being that which he knew not. [05]

No! (But) indeed, the human being transgresses [06] because he sees himself self-sufficient. [07] Indeed, to your Lord is the return. [08] Have you seen the one who forbids [09] a servant from praying? [10] Have you seen if he is on (the road of) guidance? [11] Or enjoins righteousness? [12] Have you seen if he rejects and turns away? [13] Does he not know that God sees? [14] No! If he doesn't stop, We will surely drag him by the forelock, [15] a lying, sinning forelock. [16] Then let him call his associates; [17] We will call the angels of Hell. [18] No! Do not obey him. But prostrate yourselves and draw near (to God). [19]

CHAPTER NINETY SEVEN

AL-QADR
THE NIGHT OF DECREE

THE **MECCA** PERIOD

In the name of God, the Merciful-to-all, the Mercy Giver:

We sent this (Qur'an) down during the Night of Decree. [01] But how would you know what is the Night of Decree? [02] The Night of Decree is better than a thousand months. [03] During that Night, the angels and the Spirit descend by their Lord's authority for a variety of matters. [04] There is peace that night until the coming of dawn. [05]

CHAPTER NINETY EIGHT

AL-BAYYINAH
THE CLEAR EVIDENCE

THE **MEDINA** PERIOD

In the name of God, the Merciful-to-all, the Mercy Giver:

The unbelievers from among the people of the Book and the idolaters will continue to deny the truth until clear evidence is sent to them, [01] a Messenger from God, reciting purified texts, [02] containing valuable books. [03] Those who were given the Scripture did not become divided until after they were given clear evidence. [04] They were only asked to worship God alone, [3132] making their faith sincerely His, to keep up with prayer, [3133] and to pay the Purifying alms, for that is the true religion. [3134] [05] Those who reject the truth among the People of the Book and the idolaters —will have the Fire of Hell, [3135] to remain there eternally, forever. They are the worst of creatures, [06] while those who believe and do good deeds are the best of creatures. [07] Their reward is with their Lord: Gardens of Eden, graced with flowing streams, [3136] remaining in them timelessly, forever and ever. God is well pleased with them and they are pleased with Him. All this is for whoever stands in awe of his Lord. [08]

• • •

[3132] Matthew 4:10 Jesus said to him, "Away with you, Satan! for it is written, 'Worship the Lord your God, and serve only him.'"

[3133] Matthew 6:7-8 "When you are praying, do not heap up empty phrases as the Gentiles do; for they think that they will be heard because of their many words. [8] Do not be like them, for your Father knows what you need before you ask him.

[3134] James 1:27 Religion that is pure and undefiled before God, the Father, is this: to care for orphans and widows in their distress, and to keep oneself unstained by the world.

[3135] Matthew 25:41 Then he will say to those at his left hand, 'You that are accursed, depart from me into the eternal fire prepared for the devil and his angels;

[3136] Revelation 22:1-2 then the angel showed me the river of the water of life, bright as crystal, flowing from the throne of God and of the Lamb [2] through the middle of the street of the city. On either side of the river is the tree of life with its twelve kinds of fruit, producing its fruit each month; and the leaves of the tree are for the healing of the nations.

CHAPTER NINETY NINE

AZ-ZALZAIAH

THE EARTHQUAKE

THE **MEDINA** PERIOD

In the Name of God, the Merciful-to-all, the Mercy Giver:
When the Earth is shaken by its (last) earthquake [01] and the Earth throws out its burdens [02] and the human being says: 'What is wrong with it?' [03] On that Day, it will impart its news [04] because your Lord has inspired it. [05] On that Day, people will come forward, separated from one another, to be shown their deeds. [06] So, whoever has done an atom's weight of good deeds will see it [3137] [07] and whoever has done an atom's weight of evil will see it[3138] [08]

. . .

[3137] Hebrews 6:10 For God is not unjust; he will not overlook your work and the love that you showed for his sake in serving the saints, as you still do.
[3138] John 5:29 and will come out—those who have done good, to the resurrection of life, and those who have done evil, to the resurrection of condemnation.

AL-AADIYAT

THE CHARGING WARHORSE

THE **MECCA** PERIOD

In the name of God, the Merciful-to-all, the Mercy Giver:

(I swear) by the charging breathless warhorses, [01] striking sparks with their hooves, [02] raiding at early dawn, [03] raising a cloud of dust [04] and storming into the center collectively, [05] the human being is ungrateful to his Lord, [06] even though he is a witness to that. [07] And he is fiercely in love with wealth [08]

But does he not know that when what are in the graves are scattered [09] and the hearts contents are retrieved[3139] [10] On that Day, their Lord is fully knowledgeable? [11]

• • •

[3139] 1 Corinthians 14:25 After the secrets of the unbeliever's heart are disclosed, that person will bow down before God and worship him, declaring, "God is really among you."

AL-QARI'AH
THE STRIKING CALAMITY

THE **MECCA** PERIOD

In the name of God, the Merciful-to-all, the Mercy Giver:

The striking calamity: [01] What is the striking calamity? [02] And how would you know what is the striking calamity? [03] It is the Day when human beings will be like dispersed moths [04] and the mountains will be like fluffed up wool [05] and then, the one whose scales are heavy (with good deeds) [06] will have a pleasant life, [07] but the one whose scales are light, [08] his refuge will be an abyss. [09] And what will convey to you what that is? [10] a Raging Fire [11]

CHAPTER **ONE HUNDRED TWO**

AT-TAKATHUR

GREED FOR MORE

THE **MECCA** PERIOD

In the name of God, the Merciful-to-all, the Mercy Giver:
Your greed for more has distracted you³¹⁴⁰ ⁽⁰¹⁾ until you go down to your graves. ⁽⁰²⁾ No, indeed you will soon know. ⁽⁰³⁾ Certainly you will soon know. ⁽⁰⁴⁾ Indeed, If you knew the knowledge of certainty ⁽⁰⁵⁾ you would see Hell, ⁽⁰⁶⁾ then you would surely see it with the eye of certainty. ⁽⁰⁷⁾ And on that Day you will be asked about the pleasures you enjoyed. ⁽⁰⁸⁾

• • •

---

³¹⁴⁰ Luke 12:16-21 Then he told them a parable: "The land of a rich man produced abundantly. ¹⁷ And he thought to himself, 'What should I do, for I have no place to store my crops?' ¹⁸ Then he said, 'I will do this: I will pull down my barns and build larger ones, and there I will store all my grain and my goods. ¹⁹ And I will say to my soul, Soul, you have ample goods laid up for many years; relax, eat, drink, be merry.' ²⁰ But God said to him, 'You fool! This very night your life is being demanded of you. And the things you have prepared, whose will they be?' ²¹ So it is with those who store up treasures for themselves but are not rich toward God."

454

AL-'ASR

THE LATE AFTERNOON

THE **MECCA** PERIOD

In the name of God, the Merciful-to-all, the Mercy Giver:

[01] I swear by the Late Afternoon, the human being is surely, in a state of loss. [02] Except for those who have believed and done good deeds [3141] and urged one another to Truth[3142] and urged one another to patience[3143] [03]

· · ·

[3141] James 2:15-17 What good is it, my brothers and sisters, if you say you have faith but do not have works? [16] Can faith save you? If a brother or sister is naked and lacks daily food, and one of you says to them, "Go in peace; keep warm and eat your fill," and yet you do not supply their bodily needs, what is the good of that? [17] So faith by itself, if it has no works, is dead.

[3142] Hebrews 10:24-25 And let us consider how to provoke one another to love and good deeds, [25] not neglecting to meet together, as is the habit of some, but encouraging one another, and all the more as you see the Day approaching.

[3143] James 5:7-8 Be patient, therefore, beloved, until the coming of the Lord. The farmer waits for the precious crop from the earth, being patient with it until it receives the early and the late rains. [8] You also must be patient. Strengthen your hearts, for the coming of the Lord is near.

AL-HUMAZAH

THE BACKBITER

THE **MECCA** PERIOD

In the name of God, the Merciful-to-all, the Mercy Giver:

Woe to every scorning backbiter[3144] [(01)] who has amassed wealth and diversified it[3145] [(02)] thinking that his wealth will make him immortal[3146] [(03)] No! He will surely be thrown into the Crusher. [(04)] And what will convey to you what is the Crusher? [(05)] It is the kindled Fire of God [(06)] reaching right into the hearts. [(07)] it will engulf them [(08)] in extended columns. [(09)]

. . .

[3144] Proverbs 10:18 Lying lips conceal hatred, and whoever utters slander is a fool.
[3145] James 5:3 Your gold and silver have rusted, and their rust will be evidence against you, and it will eat your flesh like fire. You have laid up treasure for the last days.
[3146] Ecclesiastes 5:10 The lover of money will not be satisfied with money; nor the lover of wealth, with gain. This also is vanity.

AL-FIL
THE ELEPHANT

THE **MECCA** PERIOD

In the name of God, the Merciful-to-all, the Mercy Giver:

Have you not seen how your Lord dealt with the army who had Elephants? [01] Did He not utterly bring their perfect planning to nothing? [02] And He sent birds in flocks against them [03] striking them with stones of hard clay, [04] He made them like eaten straw. [05]

CHAPTER **ONE HUNDRED SIX**

QURAYSH

THE **MECCA** PERIOD

In the name of God, the Merciful-to-all, the Mercy Giver:

So that Quraysh[3147] remains secure, [01] secure in their Winter and Summer journeys [02] Let them worship the Lord of this House[3148] [03] who has fed them after hunger,[3149] and made then safe after fear[3150] [04]

· · ·

[3147] The main tribe in Mecca.
[3148] Ka'ba at the Holy Sanctuary in Mecca.
[3149] Psalm 145:16 You open your hand, satisfying the desire of every living thing.
[3150] Psalm 46:1-2 God is our refuge and strength, a very present help in trouble. [2] Therefore, we will not fear, though the earth should change, though the mountains shake in the heart of the sea;

458

CHAPTER **ONE HUNDRED SEVEN**

AL-MA'UN
ASSISTANCE

THE **MECCA** PERIOD

In the name of God, the Merciful-to-all, the Mercy Giver:

Have you seen the one who denies this faith? [01] For that is the one who drives the orphan away [02] and does not encourage the feeding of the poor.[3151] [03] So woe to those who pray [04] but, who do not pay attention to their prayer.[3152] [05] Those who make a show (of their deeds)[3153] [06] And withhold help to others. [07]

• • •

[3151] James 1:27 Religion that is pure and undefiled before God, the Father, is this: to care for orphans and widows in their distress, and to keep oneself unstained by the world.

[3152] Matthew 6:5-7 "And whenever you pray, do not be like the hypocrites; for they love to stand and pray in the synagogues and at the street corners, so that they may be seen by others. Truly I tell you, they have received their reward. [6] But whenever you pray, go into your room and shut the door and pray to your Father who is in secret; and your Father who sees in secret will reward you. [7] "When you are praying, do not heap up empty phrases as the Gentiles do; for they think that they will be heard because of their many words.

[3153] Matthew 23:27-28 "Woe to you, scribes and Pharisees, hypocrites! For you are like whitewashed tombs, which on the outside look beautiful, but inside they are full of the bones of the dead and of all kinds of filth. [28] So you also on the outside look righteous to others, but inside you are full of hypocrisy and lawlessness.

459

AL-KAWTHAR

A RIVER IN PARADISE

THE **MECCA** PERIOD

In the name of God, the Merciful-to-all, the Mercy Giver:
We have given you all that is good in abundance[3154] (01) So pray to your Lord and sacrifice for Him. (02) Your enemy is the one who is cut off. (03)

. . .

[3154] 2 Corinthians 9:10-11 He who supplies seed to the sower and bread for food will supply and multiply your seed for sowing and increase the harvest of your righteousness. You will be enriched in every way for your great generosity, which will produce thanksgiving to God through us;

AL-KAFIRUN
THOSE WHO DENY THE TRUTH

THE **MECCA** PERIOD

In the Name of God, the Merciful-to-all, the Mercy Giver:
Say: "You who deny the truth, (01) I do not worship what you worship (02) and you do not worship what I worship, (03) and I will never worship what you worship. (04) Neither will you worship what I worship. (05) You have your own religion, and I have mine." (06)

AN-NASR
THE HELP

THE **MEDINA** PERIOD

In the name of God, the Merciful-to-all, the Mercy Giver:

When God's victory has come, together with His conquest [01] and you see people embracing God's religion in multitudes [02] exult your Lord's glory, and praise Him, and ask for His forgiveness;[3155] for He is ever-accepting of repentance[3156] [03]

• • •

AL-MASAD

THE PALM FIBER

THE **MECCA** PERIOD

In the name of God, the Merciful-to-all, the Mercy Giver:

Doomed are the hands of Abu Lahab, and he is doomed too.[3157] [01] His wealth and all that he gained would not help him [02] He will burn in a fire strongly glowing [03] and his wife as well, the carrier of firewood. [04] Around her neck is a rope of Palm Fiber [05]

. . .

[3157] Proverbs 14:11 The house of the wicked is destroyed, but the tent of the upright flourishes.

CHAPTER **ONE HUNDRED TWELVE**

AL-IKHLAS

THE PURITY OF FAITH

THE **MECCA** PERIOD

In the name of God, the Merciful-to-all, the Mercy Giver:

Say: He is God who is Uniquely Singular[3158] (01) Who is Eternal, (the uncaused cause of all that exists) (02) Who has not given birth nor is He born (03) and there is no equivalent to Him[3159] (04)

• • •

[3158] Isaiah 46:9 remember the former things of old; For I am God, and there is no other; I am God, and there is no one like me.
[3159] Deuteronomy 6:4 Hear, O Israel: The Lord is our God, the Lord alone.

AL-FALAQ

THE DAYBREAK

THE **MECCA** PERIOD

In the name of God, the Merciful-to-all, the Mercy Giver:

Say: "I seek refuge with the lord of the Daybreak[3160] (01) From the evil in that which He has created (02) and from the evil of the darkness when it settles (03) and from women who blow on knots (04) and from the evil of the envious when he envies (05)

• • •

[3160] Job 38:12 "Have you commanded the morning since your days began, and caused the dawn to know it's place."

AN-NAS
HUMAN BEINGS

THE **MECCA** PERIOD

In the name of God, the Merciful-to-all, the Mercy Giver:

Say: "I seek refuge[3161] with the lord of human beings,[3162] (01) the King of human beings,[3163] (02) the God of human beings, [3164] (03) from the evil of the insidious whisperer (04) who whispers (evil) into the hearts of humans (05) from among the Jinn or humans."[3165] (06)

• • •

[3161] Psalm 59:16 But I will sing of your might; I will sing aloud of your steadfast love in the morning. For you have been a fortress for me and a refuge in the day of my distress.
[3162] Romans 10:12 For there is no distinction between Jew and Greek; the same Lord is Lord of all and is generous to all who call on him.
[3163] Psalm 47:7 For God is the king of all the earth; sing praises with a psalm.
[3164] Jeremiah 32:27 See, I am the Lord, the God of all flesh; is anything to hard for me?
Timothy 4:18 The Lord will rescue me from every evil attack and save me for his heavenly kingdom.
[3165] To him be glory forever.

GLOSSARY
TERMS & CONCEPTS

Introduction

This glossary is organized to serve two audiences. The first audience is the English- speaking people who are reading the translation to simply learn more about the Qur'an. Our glossary offers this audience the term in English and then our understanding based on our knowledge and research.

The second audience is defined as those who are multilingual who want to determine how a certain Arabic word is translated. For this audience the word is transliterated in Arabic along with its English definition.

This translation started with the assumption that each word in the Qur'an has a specific meaning. So, "Creator" and "Originator" referring to God are not the same, because "Originator" in this translation means to create something original that did not pre-exist. Many creators can exist with the permission of God, but there is only one Originator. This assumption led the translator to avoid the use of synonyms as much as possible, and to search for the specific meaning of each word, in particular, those words that hold deeper meaning today than in the past because of advances in knowledge. This category covers all words and sentences related to the universe and celestial objects.

A second assumption is that this is a dynamic translation. We realize that in Arabic the meaning of the same word will be defined by the context. So when the word zalemoon (ظالمون) is used, it can mean either those who are unjust or oppressors. The same applies for many other words defined by the use and the context of the word in the sentence.

468

Terms and Concepts

Abraham: In Arabic it is pronounced *"Ibrahim"* (ميهاربإ) originally "Abram." This prophet's name appears as Abram in Surat Al Bakara and in the Old Testament book of Genesis, chapter 12. However, when Muslims read the Qur'an, it is pronounced "Ibrahim" throughout the Qur'an as all pronunciation was unified during the time of the Caliph (*Uthmān ibn 'Affān*) (577 – 20 June 656).

Abraham is the same patriarch mentioned in the Bible. He is considered the first prophet to reestablish modern monotheism after Adam. Abraham is a prominent figure in the Old Testament, New Testament and the Qur'an. He is mentioned 69 times in the Qur'an, and he is the only prophet called the "Friend of God" in all three Abrahamic holy books. Both Jews and Arabs (including the Prophet Mohammad ﷺ) are considered descendants from Abraham; the Jews through his son Isaac and the Arabs through his son Ishmael. Abraham, according to the Qur'an, was the first to call the believers "submitters" or as they are called in Arabic, *Muslims*.

'Ad: The community to which The Prophet Hud was sent.

Angels: Described in the Qur'an as creatures from a noble species created by God to perform certain tasks. A single angel in Arabic is called كلم *malak*, a name that indicates strength and superiority. The Qur'an describes angels as:

- They are obedient to God their Creator in every way.

- They are neither male nor female.

- They are intelligent and able to understand specifically what God is communicating to them.

- They are mentioned as messengers to certain people on Earth, such as Abraham, Zachariah and Mary.

- They are bearers of good news (Fussilat 30)

- They are described in Fatir:1 that they have multiple wings. Two, three or four pairs.

- They move throughout the universe and beyond (Al Maarij 4)

- They are without fear. They live without the need to obtain their energy from an outside source, so they don't need to eat, drink, or sleep. They constantly sing the praises of their Lord and never tire. Some of them are in charge of carrying

469

their Lord's throne. They ask forgiveness for the believers. Others are in charge of Hell and its gates, being strict and harsh.

Ansaar: "Supporters," "helpers," as were Jesus' disciples.

Aya: "A sign from God" or "a miracle." Another common meaning is a verse of the Qur'an.

Al Furquan: The general meaning of this word is the tool used to help a person distinguish between good and evil. The proper noun *Al Furquan* is usually translated as "The Criterion" and is thought to refer to the Qur'an itself as the a guide or compass in discerning good and evil. "Discernment" may best express the meaning of "Al Furquan," for English readers.

Modern interpretation/understanding claims that *Al Furquan* refers specifically to the Ten Commandments given to Moses and to the verses 151, 152 and 153 of chapter 6, Al An'aam in the Qur'an.

Al Ghayb: Translated as what is beyond our senses and/or human perception or knowledge such as the laws of creation, phases in the life of a star or the day of resurrection or even the existence of God Himself. The term "ghayb" is relative to time and human knowledge. What is today common knowledge about the solar system and its location within the galaxy was *ghayb* for our grandparents. *Ghayb* has also to do with all the providential events of one's life (e.g. birth, marriage, death, or future earthly events).

Blazing fire: (*al jahim*) This word for hell is used 26 times in the Qur'an.

Believers: (*al mu'minun*) singular (*mu'min*). Refers to those who believe in God as the One Creator. It can also refer to those who become followers of Mohammad's message.

Bottomless pit: (هيواه *haawiya*). This word for hell occurs once, in Qur'an 101:9 and is related to falling into an abyss.

Burning fire: (رسعير *as sa'ir*) This word for hell is used 16 times in the Qur'an.

Christians: Arabic مسيحيين *Masihiyeen*. According to the New Testament, the term "Christian" was first used in Antioch to describe Paul and his followers, possibly ten to twenty years after Jesus. Later, it became the term used to describe all those who follow Pauline Christianity.

The word *Masihiyeen* or Christians is never mentioned in the Qur'an. Instead, the Qur'an refers to the followers of Jesus as "Nasara" (نصارى) which might be related to the term Nazarene. We are specifically told in Acts, that this was the name of the group (See Acts 24:5).

Many authors have argued that "Nazarene" was not simply one of many terms that were used before "Christian" came into use, but it was the dominant term. The original Greek forms of all four gospels call Jesus, in places, "*Iesou Nazarene*" (e.g. Matthew 26:71; Mark 1:24, 10:47, 14:67; Luke 4:34; John 17:5; Acts 2:22) .[1]

In this translation, and most existing translations that I have read (more than 60), we translate the Arabic نصارى *Nasara* as "Christians," however, even those who translate it as "Nazarenes" follow the word by "(Christians)." Hence, we opted to translate it as "Christians." See Nazarenes.

Criminals: Arabic مجرمون *mujrimun*. This is a term referring to those who decide to sever all relations to God and to reject Him and His messages, while forcing others to reject the revelations and the Message of the Prophet. Forcing others and plotting to keep them from believing made them criminals in the eyes of God.

Crushing fire: (*al Hutama*) This word for Hell occurs only in 104:4, 5. It is from the word "crushing."

Day of Resurrection: (يوم القيامة *yawm al qiyamah*). The Qur'an uses several ways to refer to this very important Day: the Day of Resurrection *yawm al qiyamah* Qur'an 10:59, the Day of Judgment *yawm al din* 15:35 et al, the Last Day *al-yawm al-akhir* 2:8 et al., that Day *yawma 'idhin* 11:66 et al., a Great Day yawmun azim 10:15, et al., a Painful Day *yawm alim* 11:26, 43:65, a Great Day *yawmun kabir* 11:4, a Grievous Day *yawmun 'asib* 11:77, a day that Surrounds *yawm muhit* 11:84, a Day that will be witnessed *yawmun mashhud* 11:103, or simply, that Day. All these refer to the same event, but focuses on different aspects of it.

Deen: Generally accepted by Muslims to mean "a way of life as prescribed by God." It is understood to be "religion" in the broadest sense, but it is not a precise translation. It is a basic creed, faith, dogma, system, way of life and/or religion.

In the Qur'an it equates to the simple acceptance of God as the one and only Creator (Qur'an 39: 11 & 14, 40:14 & 65). It is also defined as

• • •

1 - http://www.wordiq.com/definition/Nazarene40:

submission. (Qur'an 3:19, 3:83, 3:85). There is no compulsion to accept it, (Qur'an2:256). In this same verse, it is defined as rejecting false gods and accepting the one true God.

Waging war against Muslims to force them to change this basic belief is just cause to defend one's faith (Qur'an 60:9).

There are many religions, whereas there is only one *Deen*, defined in the Qur'an as submission to God's will. The Qur'an tells us that *deen* started with Adam, was gradually completed by many prophets, most notably Noah, Abraham, Moses, Jesus Christ and Mohammad and was finally given to humanity by God, in the form of Islam (Qur'an 42:13).

The word *Deen* is mentioned in the Qur'an often, but there is no mention of its plural form,'*adyan*, which goes to confirm that there is only one message (Deen).

Du'a': "Supplication," a "humble prayer."

Demon: Is a word used to describe any human or *jinn* who are committing transgression against God. References to demons in the Old Testament are scarce. The Old Testament focus is not on demons and their schemes but on God and his sovereignty. Demons are not depicted as free, independent agents, but operate under God's direct control. Though they are not revealed as the malicious beings seen in the New Testament. There, one is instructed to avoid them, to flee from them[2]. The Qur'an actually presents a different understanding of demons, describing some human beings or *jinn* to be demons, while the New Testament assumes the existence of separate demonic beings created to war against humans and God and His creation.

The Devil: (*Iblis*) This name or title is derived from the Greek *diábolos* and means "he who causes trouble between people."

Devils/a devil: (shaytan/shayateen) This name is thought to be the same word as "Satan" but without the definite article. This name is used in the Qur'an six times in the singular (devil) and 18 times in the plural (devils). See also "demon" and "Satan." In this translation we use *Iblis* as a proper name any time it is used as a proper name in the original Arabic text.

Unbelief: (*kufr*). This is the primary meaning of the word, though the root meaning is also connected with ungratefulness and covering of the truth. The unbelievers mentioned in the Qur'an in this sense were

• • •

2 - http://www.biblestudytools.com/dictionary/demon/

the idolaters during and before the time the Qur'an was revealed. Later on, it referred to anyone who had heard the Message given to Prophet Mohammadﷺ yet decided to reject it.

Endure: (yasber) This word can also mean "to be patient." Since the Qur'an usually uses this in the context of enduring trials and difficulties, and since "patience" today usually implies waiting, but not suffering, we have translated it as "to endure, endurance."

Esa, Essa, Isa et al: See "Jesus." Greek: Iησους *Iesous*. Arabic: عيسى is the name of Jesus as mentioned in the Qur'an. Hence, Muslims believe that the name Esa in Arabic or Esu in Hebrew, is the name Jesus was called throughout his life.

However, Christians believe that Jesus is a translation from the Hebrew Yeshua. This could possibly be because *Yeshua was a translation of the name to Hebrew after it was Hellenized.* In other words, Esu became Jesus to become later Yeshua.

False gods: (*al taghut*) This word is used in the Qur'an 8 times, and can be either singular or plural. It refers to worshiping or submitting one's devotion to anything other than God.

Fater: This word is traditionally translated as the Creator, the Originator, the Bringer into Being etc. . . . But as we investigated the meaning, searching dictionaries, classical commentaries, as well as discussions with various scholars, we discovered that the meaning of *Fater* should be the Creator who separated and gave purpose to each of His creations. So we translated it "Creator/Programmer."

Ferdous: One of many names given to heaven and perhaps a particular place in Heaven. It is mentioned twice in Qur'an 18:107 and 23:11.

Fetna: Sedition, trial, temptation, civil disturbance. It is mentioned in the Qur'an in different contexts 33 times.

Gabriel: *Jibril* or *Jibra'il*, is an archangel who typically serves as an emissary sent by God to certain people. In Islam, it is believed that he is the angel who brought down the Qur'an from God to our world and then delivered it in portions as ordered by God to Prophet Mohammad over a period of 23 years. The first verse given by Gabriel to Prophet Mohammad was 96:1. Gabriel is mentioned several times in the Qur'an.

In the Gospel of Luke, as in the Qur'an, Gabriel appeared to Zechariah, and to the Virgin Mary, giving the good news of the births of John the Baptist and Jesus, respectively (Luke 1:11–38) and)Qur'an 3:39-45).

Gabriel is also mentioned in the Old Testament. He appeared to the prophet Daniel, delivering the Book of Daniel to the prophet (Daniel 8:15–26, 9:21–27).

The Qur'an also mentioned that Gabriel provided strength to Jesus throughout his life.

God: Arabic: الله *Allāh*, is the Arabic word for **God**. It is used mainly by Muslims to refer to the Creator. Arab Christians, Maltese Christians, Mizrahi Jews, Indonesian Christians and Sikhs in Malaysia also use the word to refer to God.

Cognates of the name *"Allāh"* exist in other Semitic languages, including Hebrew and Aramaic[3]. The corresponding Aramaic form is *'Ĕlāhā* and *'Alâhâ* in Syriac as used by the Assyrian Church, both meaning simply 'God'.[4] Biblical Hebrew mostly uses the plural form (but functional singular) *Elohim*.

The name was previously used by pagans in Mecca as a reference to the supreme deity in pre-Islamic Arabia. It is supposed that they originally learned it from Ishmael who learned it from his father Abraham.[5]

According to Islamic belief, Allah refers to the only God, the One (*wāhid*), who is uniquely singular (*Ahad*), the Merciful to All and the Mercy Giver. He is the Almighty, Creator and Sustainer of the universe, who is similar to nothing and nothing is comparable to Him. He has no beginning and no end. Everything other than Him is created by Him and all will perish one day, but He will be there to resurrect all human beings and to reign over the Day of Judgment.

The Qur'an sheds light on the various attributes of God as He chose to reveal them to us so we could better understand who He is.

In the Qur'an, Allah has two main aspects that He chose for Himself. He is *Rubb*, Arabic رب, English "God". It means that He is the Sovereign, the Creator and the Sustainer of what He created, including the entire universe, which has no choice about this relationship. His creation functions according to universal laws created by Him. God is Sovereign over all creations, including living creatures. He provides them with the right environment to sustain them according to the needs He created for them. Within this relationship with their Creator, human beings must

3 - Columbia Encyclopaedia says: Derived from an old Semitic root referring to the Divine and used in the Canaanite *El*, the Mesopotamian *ilu*, and the biblical *Elohim* and *Eloah*, the word Allah is used by all Arabic-speaking Muslims, Christians, Jews, and other monotheists.
4 - The Comprehensive Aramaic Lexicon – Entry for *'lh*
5 - L. Gardet, "Allah", *Encyclopedia of Islam*

do nothing to earn the right to breathe the air or to enjoy the sunlight. In addition to basic instincts He created within all living creatures, He provided consciousness to human beings. So, while the human race enjoys the consciousness God gave them, they are required to make choices. If they choose to believe and to submit to Him, He will become their Lord. This will enable them to enter into a special and personal relationship with Him. As a result, their Lord promises them, out of His mercy and grace, to enlighten them through His prophets. If they submit (by faith) to Him, willingly following His guidance, they will have eternal life with Him in Heaven.

So while He is the God of everyone, He is the Lord for those who choose to submit to His will for them.

All the holy books of the Abrahamic religions agree there is only one God, and that submission by faith to God is necessary.

god: The word god (ilah) is used 147 times in the Qur'an. It can be singular, dual, or plural, masculine or feminine. It refers to anything other than God that people worship.

Hadith: A record of the sayings of Prophet Mohammad, published over two centuries after his death. For a saying to be accepted as "authentic" it has to be quoted by a chain of reliable sources starting with an original witness to what the Prophet said. This process was followed by Mohammad Ibn Ismā'īl Al Bukhārī (19 July 810 – September 870), commonly referred to as Imam Al Bukhari, who authored the Hadith collection known as Sahih Al Bukhari, regarded by Sunni Muslims as one of the most sahih (authentic) of all Hadith compilations[6].

This process is called in Arabic "Sanad". A complete reputable linkage is necessary for an authentic Hadith, which is called "Sanad Mutawater".

Each Hadith is composed of two parts, a chain of authorities reporting the Hadith (isnad), and the text itself (matn). A new trend among some Muslim scholars today, requires not only reliance on the reputable linkage of the narrators of a certain hadith, but also consideration of the substance "matn" of the hadith in relation to the Qur'an. A Hadith should be accepted only if it does not contradict the Qur'an.

Hajj: The Hajj (Arabic: حج "pilgrimage") is the pilgrimage to Mecca, the largest gathering of Muslim people, occurring annually. It is one of the Five Pillars of Islam, and an obligation on every able-bodied Muslim

• • •

6 - http://en.wikipedia.org/wiki/Hadith

who can afford physically and financially to perform it at least once in their lifetime. The Hajj is a demonstration of the solidarity of the Muslim people and their submission to God. The word *hajj* means "to intend a journey" which connotes both the inward act of intentions and the outward act of a journey.

Halal: "Lawful" or "permissible," according to the Shari'a, is everything that God created or made available to human beings, except 26 specific things that are mentioned in the Qur'an to be unlawful or *haraam*. They are generally forbidden to keep one from harming himself, physically or spiritually.

Haraam: "Unlawful." The only authority to forbid anything or to make it unlawful in Islam is God. He specifically mentioned all that is forbidden in the following verses: 3:3, 6:151 to 153, 5:90 to 92. In total I was able to count 26 specific items considered unlawful. No human being has the authority to declare unlawful what God has declared lawful.

Hell: Arabic: *Jahannam* جَهَنَّم. This is the usual word for hell, and is related to the Hebrew word *Gehenna* for Hell. It is used 77 times in the Qur'an. *Jahannam* is also known under different Arabic names cited in the Qur'an: *Hawia, Jahim, Saqar, Hutama, Naar*, etc.

Hellfire: Arabic *al naar*. This word literally means "the fire" and is used 104 times in the Qur'an to mean the fire of Hell. When this is not the meaning, it is translated "fire" (41 times).

Hijra: This word signifies migration for the sake of God. In Islamic history, all events are referred to in relation to the *hijra*; the migration of Prophet Mohammad from Mecca to Medina, in 621 CE, which initiated the Islamic calendar.

Holy Spirit: (*Al Rūh Al Quddus*) The Archangel Gabriel is believed by Muslims to be the Holy Spirit. He is also called in the Qur'an the Trustworthy Spirit or simply the Spirit. He is generally interpreted by Muslims as being the same Holy Spirit referred to in both the Old and the New Testaments of the Bible. However, the Qur'an emphatically states that neither God nor the Holy Spirit are part of an equal union or trinity.

Hoor Ein: The word *hoor* is mentioned in the Qur'an in no less than four different places:

1. In chapter Dukhan: " **And We shall pair them with Hoor Ein.**"(44:54)
2. In chapter Al Tur: **"We will pair them with Hoor Ein."**(52:20)

do nothing to earn the right to breathe the air or to enjoy the sunlight. In addition to basic instincts He created within all living creatures, He provided consciousness to human beings. So, while the human race enjoys the consciousness God gave them, they are required to make choices. If they choose to believe and to submit to Him, He will become their Lord. This will enable them to enter into a special and personal relationship with Him. As a result, their Lord promises them, out of His mercy and grace, to enlighten them through His prophets. If they submit (by faith) to Him, willingly following His guidance, they will have eternal life with Him in Heaven.

So while He is the God of everyone, He is the Lord for those who choose to submit to His will for them.

All the holy books of the Abrahamic religions agree there is only one God, and that submission by faith to God is necessary.

god: The word god (*ilah*) is used 147 times in the Qur'an. It can be singular, dual, or plural, masculine or feminine. It refers to anything other than God that people worship.

Hadith: A record of the sayings of Prophet Mohammad, published over two centuries after his death. For a saying to be accepted as "authentic" it has to be quoted by a chain of reliable sources starting with an original witness to what the Prophet said. This process was followed by Mohammad Ibn Ismāʿīl Al Bukhārī (19 July 810 – September 870), commonly referred to as Imam Al Bukhari, who authored the Hadith collection known as *Sahih Al Bukhari*, regarded by Sunni Muslims as one of the most *sahih* (authentic) of all Hadith compilations[6].

This process is called in Arabic *"Sanad"*. A complete reputable linkage is necessary for an authentic Hadith, which is called *"Sanad Mutawater"*.

Each Hadith is composed of two parts, a chain of authorities reporting the *Hadith (isnad)*, and the text itself *(matn)*. A new trend among some Muslim scholars today, requires not only reliance on the reputable linkage of the narrators of a certain hadith, but also consideration of the substance *"matn"* of the hadith in relation to the Qur'an. A Hadith should be accepted only if it does not contradict the Qur'an.

Hajj: The *Hajj* (Arabic: حج "pilgrimage") is the pilgrimage to Mecca, the largest gathering of Muslim people, occurring annually. It is one of the Five Pillars of Islam, and an obligation on every able-bodied Muslim

• • •

6 - http://en.wikipedia.org/wiki/Hadith

who can afford physically and financially to perform it at least once in their lifetime. The Hajj is a demonstration of the solidarity of the Muslim people and their submission to God. The word *hajj* means "to intend a journey" which connotes both the inward act of intentions and the outward act of a journey.

Halal: "Lawful" or "permissible," according to the Shari'a, is everything that God created or made available to human beings, except 26 specific things that are mentioned in the Qur'an to be unlawful or *haraam*. They are generally forbidden to keep one from harming himself, physically or spiritually.

Haraam: "Unlawful." The only authority to forbid anything or to make it unlawful in Islam is God. He specifically mentioned all that is forbidden in the following verses: 3:3, 6:151 to 153, 5:90 to 92. In total I was able to count 26 specific items considered unlawful. No human being has the authority to declare unlawful what God has declared lawful.

Hell: Arabic: *Jahannam* جهنم. This is the usual word for hell, and is related to the Hebrew word *Gehenna* for Hell. It is used 77 times in the Qur'an. *Jahannam* is also known under different Arabic names cited in the Qur'an: *Hawia, Jahim, Saqar, Hutama, Naar*, etc.

Hellfire: Arabic *al naar*. This word literally means "the fire" and is used 104 times in the Qur'an to mean the fire of Hell. When this is not the meaning, it is translated "fire" (41 times).

Hijra: This word signifies migration for the sake of God. In Islamic history, all events are referred to in relation to the *hijra*; the migration of Prophet Mohammad from Mecca to Medina, in 621 CE, which initiated the Islamic calendar.

Holy Spirit: (*Al Rūh Al Quddus*) The Archangel Gabriel is believed by Muslims to be the Holy Spirit. He is also called in the Qur'an the Trustworthy Spirit or simply the Spirit. He is generally interpreted by Muslims as being the same Holy Spirit referred to in both the Old and the New Testaments of the Bible. However, the Qur'an emphatically states that neither God nor the Holy Spirit are part of an equal union or trinity.

Hoor Ein: The word *hoor* is mentioned in the Qur'an in no less than four different places:

1. In chapter Dukhan: " **And We shall pair them with Hoor Ein.**"[44:54]
2. In chapter Al Tur: **"We will pair them with Hoor Ein."**[52:20]

3. In chapter Al Rahman: **"Hoor, kept close in their pavilions"**(55:72)

4. In chapter Al Waqiah: **"and Hoor Ein**(56:22) **like well-protected pearls,"**(56:23)

Many translators of the Qur'an have translated the word *hoor* as 'beautiful maidens'.

The word *hoor* in Arabic is actually the plural of *ahwar* (applicable to man) and of *haura* (applicable to woman) and signifies a person having eyes characterized by *hauar*, a special quality bestowed upon a good soul, male or female in paradise and it denotes the intense whiteness of the white part of the spiritual eye.

The Qur'an describes in several other verses that in Paradise you will have *azwaj* which means a "pair" or "spouse" or "companion" which means you will have spouses or companions pure and holy (*mutaharratun* means "pure," "holy").

> **"As for those who believe and do righteous deeds, We will bring them into gardens with flowing rivers and they will live there eternally. They will have pure spouses there, and We will give them abundant shade."**(Qur'an 4:57)

Therefore the word *hoor* has no specific gender. According to some scholars all believers will be paired with *Hoor Ein* regardless of gender.

In a Hadith Kudsi the Prophet (P) had explained that what is in Heaven is not like what we are accustomed to see or hear or even what our hearts ever desired. Hence, I considered throughout the translation that all descriptions of Heaven or Paradise are relative to our ability to understand rather than what they really are.

Iblīs: The Devil in Islam is known as *Iblīs* or Satan or Arabic: *Shaytān* شيطان. In the Qur'an, *Iblis* is the jinn who refused to bow to Adam. The concept of Satan is a commonly shared belief of Muslims, Christians and Jews. According to the Qur'an, when God ordered the angels to bow down to the newly created man, Adam, *Iblis*, perhaps as the leader of the *jinns*, refused to do so, because he, being made of fire, thought himself superior to a creature made of clay. He became the sworn enemy of the human race, tempting humans, especially through the whisper (*waswas*, "he whispered") and false suggestion.

"Shaytan", is often simply translated as "the Devil," but the term can refer to any of the *jinn* who disobeyed God and followed *Iblīs*. Some scholars are of the view that *Iblīs* is the father of all of the *jinn*, as mentioned in the Qur'an *"Do you (seriously consider to) choose him (Iblīs) and his descendants as allies instead of Me (God), when they are your enemies? How despicable a bargain this is for the unjust?* "(18:50)

Injil: *Injīl*, is the Arabic name for what Muslims believe to be the Gospel of Jesus Christ, however, it is generally understood to refer to the New Testament.

Injil is similar to the Greek word *euangelion*, which means "gospel" or "good news." Christian belief holds that it refers to the four canonized Gospels, though Muslims believe it means every word uttered by Jesus. The Qur'an states that God gave Jesus the "good news."(5:46) It also tells us that God gave Jesus all evidence of the truth and strengthened him with the Holy Spirit.(2:87) As such, every word Jesus spoke was *injil.*

Ihram: This is a state of holiness one enters into if he intends to perform *Hajj* or *Umra*. It starts with the intention of obtaining. During *Ihram* it is prohibited to practice certain deeds that are lawful at other times.

Islam: Originally, when the word was revealed for the first time, people understood it to mean an act of submission to God that one should strive to achieve every moment of life. Hence, submission to God is the translation we have chosen to use for the word *islam*. It was originally an action-oriented verb and not a noun. In the present day, Islam is used as a proper noun referring to a particular faith. As such, the Qur'an calls all the prophets and their followers *muslims*, or those who submitted (by faith) to God's will for their lives. However, once the word Islam began being used as a proper name of the faith, it immediately separated the followers of Prophet Mohammad from other believers who had submitted (by faith) to God but were followers of other prophets.

Jesus: Greek: Ιησους *Iesous*. Arabic عيسى Esa for Muslims and يسوع Yashua for *Arab Christians*. The Qur'an teaches that Jesus was born of the Virgin Mary through the Immaculate Conception. He had a miraculous birth, a miraculous life and a miraculous death and resurrection. He is "a Word and a Spirit from God." The Qur'an tells us that he was born "full of the spirit" and that he was strengthen by the Holy Spirit throughout his life. Hence, he spoke the moment he was born, and he was born knowing the Book, the Wisdom, the Torah and the Gospel. He performed many miracles. To make certain points, some miracles were mentioned in the Qur'an as in the following verses of *Al Umran*: "I have come to you with a sign from your Lord: I will create a bird for you out of clay, then breathe into it and, with God's permission, it will become a bird;

I will heal the blind and the leper, and bring the dead back to life with God's permission... I have come to confirm the truth of the Torah which preceded me, and to make some things lawful to you which used to be forbidden. I have come to you as a sign and with a sign from your Lord. Be mindful of God and obey me". (Qur'an 3:50)

"God is my Lord and your Lord - so serve Him: that is a straight path". (Qur'an 3:51)

Such is Jesus "The statement of truth" as the Qur'an calls him in 19:34.

Jinn: The Arabic word *jinn* refers to another type of creature, created by God from fire, as we are told in the Qur'an, while humans are created from clay. Like humans, some *jinn* are believers and some are unbelievers.

Some translations translate *jinn* as demons while others object to this translation, saying that *jinn* in the Qur'an have believers among them (see 27:17,39, 34:12, 72:11), while in the Torah and the Gospel demons are always considered evil.

The word *jinn* appears 32 times in 30 verses in Quran. (See also The Devil and Satan.)

Kaaba: The cubic structure, located at the center of the Mecca Sanctuary. It is thought to be the oldest house of worship built specifically for the purpose of worshipping God. Islamic traditions hold that it was first built by Adam. But it is certain that its construction goes back at least to the time of Abraham and his son Ishmael. The same traditions tells us, after the reestablishment of monotheism and the worship of the true Creator by the Prophet Abraham, gradually, through the centuries, people returned to idol worship until Prophet Mohammad was called to worship the One, uniquely singular God. At that time the Kaaba was cleared of idols, and the worship of the One True God was reestablished.

Muslims worldwide, turn toward the Kaaba when praying. The Kaaba is also a focal point for the unity of Muslims when they gather together during the pilgrimage.

Kafir: Arabic رفاك One who rejects God and the Message sent through various Messengers. We translated *kafir* as "unbeliever."

Madyan: Madianites. The Prophet Jethro was commissioned by God for guidance of this community.

Mohammad: The Prophet of Islam. Abū al-Qāsim Mohammad ibn 'Abd Allāh ibn 'Abd al-Muttalib ibn Hāshim, also transliterated as

Mohammadﷺ. He was a man from Mecca who unified Arabia into a single religious polity under Islam. See: http://www.youtube.com/watch?v=D0qqxRRBdAA

At age 40, Mohammed was called by God to be both a Prophet (*Nabiy*) and a Messenger *(Rasoul)*. His miracle is the Qur'an.

Mujrimun: This is a term referring to those who decide to severe all relations to God and to reject Him, while forcing others to stay away from accepting the revelations and the message of the Prophet. Forcing others and plotting to keep them from believing made them criminals in the eyes of God.

Mubeen: According to A. Yusuf Ali, the renowned translator of the Glorious Qur'an, *mubeen* means "beautifully plain, clear, unambiguous, self-evident, not involved in mysteries of origin, history, or meaning, one which everyone can understand as to the essentials necessary for him (or her)." *Mubeen* occurs in the Qur'an many times.

Mushrik: Arabic مشرك One who worships others along with God or ascribes to others attributes which in fact belong to God alone.

Messiah: (المسيح *Al Masih*) The Arabic word Masih is the same as the Hebrew word *Mashíah*. The word Christ, comes from the Greek word *Khristós* and was a title equivalent to Messiah. Messiah is used 11 times in the Qur'an. Jesus, Esa as he is called in the Qur'an, is the only one the Qur'an calls Messiah.

Minor pilgrimage: see Umra. This is a pilgrimage that is done at any time of the year.

The Merciful to all, The Mercy Giver: (Al Rahman Al Rahim) These two words are from the same root "mercy," Arabic رحم *rahmah*, which implies "mercy, "compassion", "loving kindness" and more comprehensively, "grace". According to Mohammad Asad, "From the very earliest times, Islamic scholars have endeavored to define the exact shades of meaning which differentiate the two terms. The best and simplest of these explanations is undoubtedly the one advanced by Ibn al-Qayyim (as quoted in Manar I:48) The term *rahman* encompasses the quality of abounding grace inherent in, and inseparable from, the concept of God's being, whereas *rahim* expresses the manifestation of that grace in, and its effect upon His creation--in other words, an aspect of His activity." Hence Rahman is who He is " The Merciful to All". It implies that God, out of His love, allows all human beings, regardless of whether they believe in Him, follow His guidance or are in opposition to Him, to enjoy life on earth. Out of His mercy, He gives endless opportunities to every human being to choose to recognize Him as the Creator and to follow the guidance He sent us out of His love for all of us. While the proper name "Mercy Giver" explains what He does. He manifests His mercy and grace in one's daily life, but more importantly, on the Day of Judgment, where one's deeds alone will not suffice to allow us to enter His Heaven, one will enter God's Heaven only by His mercy and grace.

Every chapter of the Qur'an starts with the invocation "In the Name of God, the Merciful to All, the Mercy Giver" except one, number 9, *At Tawbah* (Repentance).

Naskh: Arabic (خسن) translated as "abrogation." It generally refers to the qura'nic verses said to be abrogated or nullified by later verses. However, in time, new theological and philosophical theories emerged denying that any verses in the Qur'an abrogate others. The abrogation mentioned in 2:107 refers to the Qur'an abrogating previous messages.

Nazarenes: Arabic *Nasara* ىراصن meaning "helpers" or "supporters." It might be related to the term Nazarene by which Jesus (referred to as "Jesus the Nazarene" in a few places in the Greek texts of the New Testament) and his Jewish followers were known in the early years after his death[7].

"Nazarene" is also the name by which the Jerusalem church was known. In Acts, we are specifically told this was the name of the followers of Jesus. In Paul's trial before Felix in Caesarea, the lawyer for the prosecution, Tertullus made this remark: "For we have found this man a real pest and a fellow who stirs up dissension among all the Jews throughout the world, and a ringleader of the sect of the Nazarenes." (Acts 24:5).

It is also the name used by certain Church Fathers to refer to several, possibly distinct, factions of Jewish Christians, continuity up to the fourth century.

Nur and Daow': In Arabic ءوض و رون, these two words should have a very distinct meaning, except most of the time they are translated as light. Daow' is light in its physical presence, light, lighted (lit), reflection of a luminous body or light bulb. Light has a measurable speed and can be manipulated, while *nur* as used in the Qur'an indicates "enlightenment".

• • •

7 - http://www.wordiq.com/definition/Nazarene

Its source is always God. Example: "God is the Light of the heavens and the earth"(Qur'an 24:35) What we mean is that God is the source of energy that keeps the universe going.

Perform prayers: (*yusalli*) This word is used for performing ritual prayers. *Yad'u* is used for supplication, private petitions and is translated "pray".

Purity: *Tahara* طهارة It is a state that a Muslim seeks to achieve by making the intention for purity, and then by immersing or covering oneself with water. This rite is called *ghusol* غسل.

Qur'an: Refers to the book in the Arabic language containing all revelations given to Prophet Mohammad, from around 610–632 CE. It is the central text of Islam and is divided into 114 chapters known as *suras*. These *suras*, in turn, are divided into numbered verses (ayas), of which there are nearly 6,000 in all. Chronologically, some of these *suras* and ayas were revealed in Mecca while others were revealed in Medina after the migration (*hijra*) of Prophet Mohammad to that city. There is widespread agreement among both Muslim and modern Euro-American scholars that the basic text emerged in sections during the lifetime of the Prophet Mohammad.

The word Qur'an literally means "reading" or "reciting." Muslims believe the Qur'an to be the book of divine guidance to all human beings. They also consider the text, in its original Arabic, to be the literal word of God delivered, as the Qur'an itself tells us, by the Archangel Gabriel (*Jibreel*) to Prophet Mohammad over a period of twenty-three years. Muslims view the Qur'an as God's final revelation.

The Qur'an refers to itself as The Book, the Wise Reminder(3:58), the Wise Book(10:1, 31:2), the Noble Qur'an(56:77), the Great Qur'an(15:87) and the Wise Qur'an(36:2).

Textually, the Qur'an has been very stable from the time of Khalif Usman until today. Various complete original texts from the first and the second century of Hijra still exist today. There are variant readings found in different manuscripts with largely minor differences in pronunciation or the numbering of verses such as the differences between the reading of Hafs (or the Eastern reading) used by 80% of Muslims from Egypt Eastward, versus the reading of Warsh (or the Maghrib reading). Both of these readings and many other have been well documented to be authorized by the Prophet himself during his lifetime.

Rasul: Messenger

Risalah: Message. The mission given by God to a Messenger.

Reminder: (*thikr*) This word, which means "mention" or "remembrance," is assumed by many to refer to the Qur'an exclusively. Parts of the Qur'an are also considered "reminders", and certain verses of the Qur'an are also "reminders." However, *thikr* is also used in reference to other revealed Abrahamic books. Muslims follow the sunna of repeating attributes of God after each prayer and they call that *thikr*.

Revelation: According to the Qur'an, revelations from God to various prophets were not sent down the same way. The Qur'an mentions two means of revelations, *inzal* and *tanzil*. Both of these Arabic words are indicative of sending something down from a higher to a lower place, although it might be figurative. *Inzal* is sending down an entire revelation such as in the case of Moses and the tablets of the Ten Commandments. Generally the prophets received the revelation, not as dictation but wrote in their own style. In the case of the Qur'an, this happened in two stages. The entire Qur'an was brought down to the lower heaven in relation to earth and that is *inzal*. Later it was revealed to the Prophet in gradual revelations dictated to him during a 23-year period. This is called *tanzil*. Muslim scholars are all in agreement that the wording of the Qur'an is from God. Prophet Mohammed's role, they explain, was to simply deliver what God put in his mouth. See Al Umran 3:3 and Al Nisaa 4:136 where the two methods are mentioned.

Salat: The ritually subscribed, obligatory five daily prayers. This is one of the five pillars of Islam.

Satan: in Arabic الشيطان Al Shaytan. It is similar to both the Hebrew !j'Þf' or !j'ÞF'h; and the Greek o` satana/j). This name in the original language meant "adversary." It is used in the Qur'an 64 times. /Al-Taghut/ is also translated Satan 3 times[4:51,60,76] See also Demon and Devil.

Scorching fire: (*saqar*) This word for hell is used 4 times in the Qur'an.

Servant: (*abd*). Although "slave" is closer to the meaning of the Arabic word, "servant" is much more common in English. Both this Arabic word abd and the corresponding words in the Torah abd and the Gospel *doulos* are similar. The plural of servant is "عبيد abeed" yet the Qur'an when referring to believers calls them "عباد ebad" meaning worshipers. This lead us to explain that in the Qur'an, a human being versus his Creator is always considered a worshiper, as he has a choice and a free will, except once during the Day of Judgment where one has no will or choice and he is then a slave.

Shari'a: The canon of norms given to various Prophets/Messengers. Judaism has its own *shari'a*. Some modern commentators assert that certain aspects of Shari'a are time and place sensitive. Some also assert that in the interest of equitability, *shari'a* laws should have upper limits and lower limits.

Sign: Arabic آية *ayah*. This word can also refer to a "miracle" or a verse from the Qur'an. For consistency, we have translated it as "sign," or when the context requires it "verse." (See "miracle.") The Qur'an has harsh words to say about those who deny, reject, or disbelieve in God's signs.

Most of the signs in the Qur'an have to do with observable creation and life: the creation of the heavens and the earth, the difference of night and day, ships sailing the sea, the rain God sends down, etc.

Sijjeen: A kind of a lock-in digital data record where God keeps in heaven the list of فجّار *fujjar*. It includes all those who rejected God's message and are open about their rebellion. This is the opposite of *illliyyin* علّيون which is an open source data base where God keeps somewhere in heaven the digital list of those who were true to their faith. These lists are mentioned in Qur'an 83:7 to 21 and appear to have the meaning described above. However, the digital information here is not like our digital information. It is God's digital system.

Straight path: Arabic Assirat Al Mustaqueem الصراط المستقيم. The straight path is defined in *Surat Al An'aam*, verse 6:151 to 153. They encompass the Ten Commandments given to Moses. The straight path is mentioned often in the Qur'an.

Submission to God: (*islam*). An action-oriented verb, that describes someone who is sumitting his life to God's will. However, it evolved to become a noun referring to the followers of Prophet Mohammad ﷺ. Hence, some translators choose not to translate this word, but just transliterate it as *Islam*, referring to all followers of Prophet Mohammad ﷺ as Muslims.

Sunnah: This is the way of life prescribed as normative for Muslims on the basis of the teachings and practices of Prophet Mohammad and interpretations of the Qur'an. *Sunnah* meaning "the path," denotes the practices of Prophet Mohammad that he taught and instituted as a teacher of the faith.

According to Muslim belief, this practice is to be adhered to in fulfilling the divine injunctions, carrying out religious rites, and molding life in accordance with the will of God. Instituting these practices was, as the Qur'an states, a part of Mohammad's responsibility as a messenger of God.(Qur'an 3:164, 33:21)

The *sunnah* of Prophet Mohammad includes his specific words, habits, practices, and silent approvals. It is significant because it addresses ways of life dealing with friends, family and government.

Sura: A chapter in the Qur'an. Total chapters are 114.

Tafsir: "Exegesis", "commentary", "explanation", "interpretation."

Thamud: Thamud is the community to which God sent the Prophet Salih.

Taqwa: From *Ittaqua,* an Arabic word meaning "sheltered from." But its use in the Qur'an refers to seeking shelter in God by being ever conscious of Him. As such it becomes a concept. I chose to translate it as "being mindful of God" or "being ever conscious of Him."

Tayammum: Purification for prayer with dust, earth or stone in case there is no water or if it is deemed that water should not be used for medical reasons.

Torah: (The Law). In the Qur'an, the Arabic word *Tawrah* is always presented as the Book God revealed to the people of Israel.

Thinkers: (ulu al-albab) Literally, possessors of minds (or hearts). This phrase is used in the Qur'an 16 times.

Umrah: The *umrah* is an Arabic term meaning minor pilgrimage to Mecca. It can be undertaken by Muslims at any time of the year. In the Sharia, *umrah* means to perform *tawaf* round the Kaaba and *sa'i* between the hills of Al Safa and Al Marwah. The *umrah* is not compulsory but highly recommended.

Unjust: Arabic *zalem* ظالم. Usually it refers to one who is unjust to himself by rejecting the Message sent from God to the Prophet. If this person is trying to pressure others to leave the faith, then we translate the word as "oppressor". If one uses force on others causing him to leave the faith then he/she is called a "criminal" or *mujrim* مجرم.

The Wise Revelation: Arabic *At Tanzeel Al Hakeem* (التنزيل الحكيم). This comprises all revealed topics which the *Book* contains from the first to its last page. Muslims believe that it is today the way it was given to Prophet Mohammad. It is not just divinely inspired knowledge, but it is composed by God and revealed verbatim to Mohammad.

Zakah: The general use of the term in the Qur'an is for charitable giving. However, for Muslims, it means specifically "purification of wealth." It is basically 2.5% calculated on one's idle wealth and is obligatory for all Muslims. It is given either directly or through an institution to seven categories of needy people. The practice is one of the Five Pillars of Islam.

Zalem: Arabic ملاظ. Translated to unjust. Usually it refers to one who is unjust to himself by rejecting the message sent from God to the Prophet. If this person is trying to pressure others to leave the faith, then we translate the word as "oppressor". If one forces others to leave the faith then he/she is called "criminal" or *mujrim* مجرم.

Zaqqum: A tree in Hell

Available worldwide at

acontemporary**understanding**.org

\+

Amazon
Barnes & Noble
and all major online outlets

Library, University & Bulk Orders
please contact
sales@acontemporaryunderstanding.com

Author / Media
info@acontemporaryunderstanding.com

CPSIA information can be obtained at www.ICGtesting.com
Printed in the USA
BVOW08s1154270216

437896BV00010B/74/P